STUDIES IN CLASSICAL AND BYZANTINE MANUSCRIPT ILLUMINATION

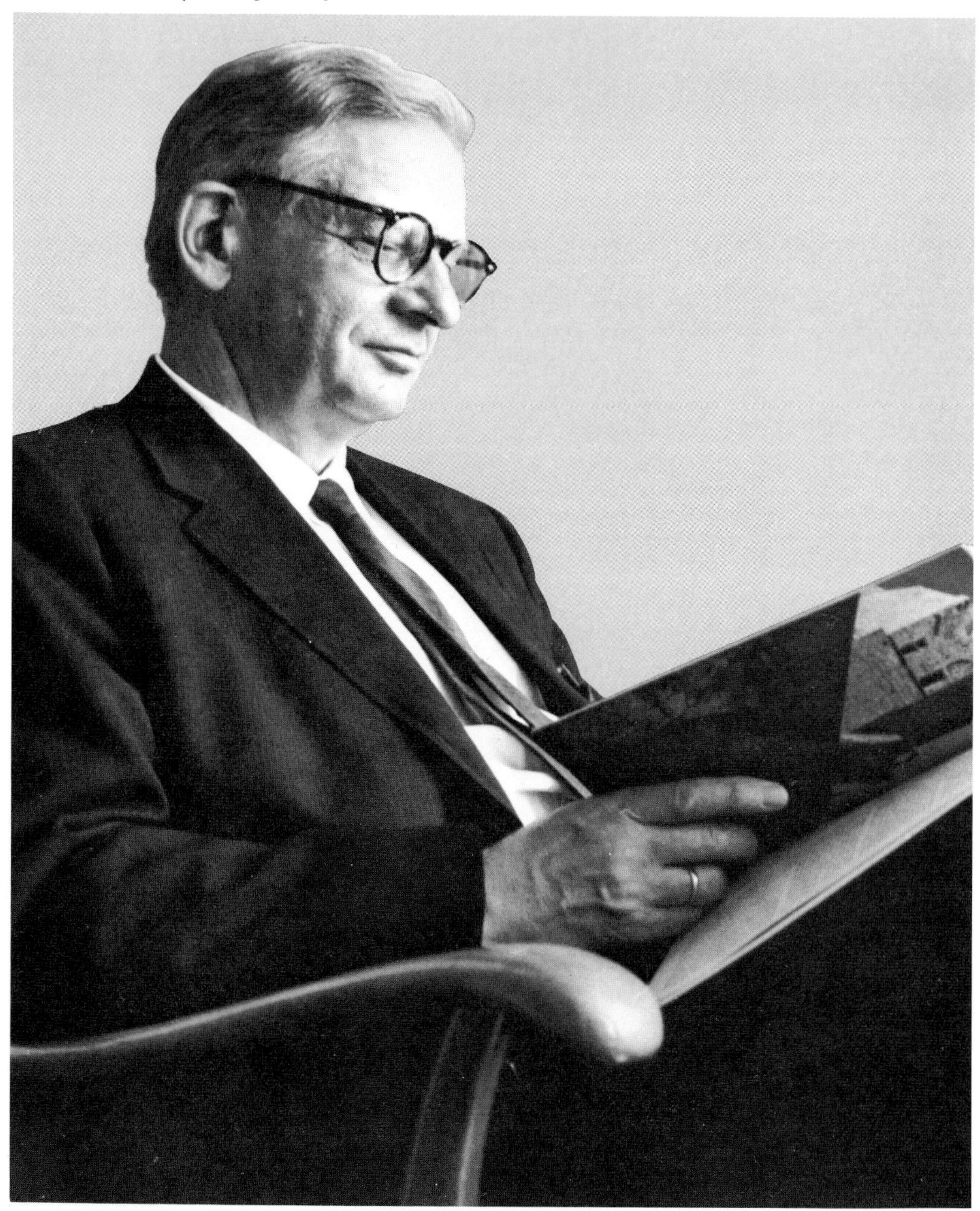

Kurt Weitzmann (Photo: J. Galey, Basel)

Kurt Weitzmann

STUDIES IN CLASSICAL AND BYZANTINE MANUSCRIPT ILLUMINATION

Edited by
Herbert L. Kessler

With an Introduction by
Hugo Buchthal

THE UNIVERSITY OF CHICAGO PRESS
CHICAGO AND LONDON

International Standard Book Number:
226-89246-8
Library of Congress Catalog Card Number:
71-116381
The University of Chicago Press, Chicago 60637
The University of Chicago Press, Ltd., London

© 1971 by The University of Chicago
All rights reserved
Published 1971
Printed in the United States of America

Contents

List of Illustrations

OF Kurt Weitzmann's extensive contributions to our understanding of ancient and medieval art—his analysis of the classical heritage in Christian imagery, his studies of ivory carving in Byzantium and the West, and his productive investigations of mosaics, frescoes, and icon painting—the most significant is his systematic and detailed examination of manuscript illustration. The twelve essays collected in this volume present various aspects of this contribution. Each contains ideas that have had a decisive impact on scholarship and each treats a problem that has been central in Weitzmann's research—the reconstruction of ancient and Jewish manuscript illustration from reflections of it in other media and from Christian and Islamic copies, the effect of the pagan tradition on the style and iconography of Byzantine art, or the characteristic innovations of manuscript illumination during the fourth century, the Macedonian Renaissance, the eleventh century, and the period of the Latin Conquest. Although the volume covers a considerable span of time and a vast range of ideas, it is of one piece—its unity deriving from the consistent methodological principles Weitzmann applies to the several questions he considers. It is appropriate, therefore, that this collection of essays should be published in the same year that Weitzmann's fundamental methodological exposition, *Illustrations in Roll and Codex*, is to be re-issued in revised form by the Princeton University Press. As statements of principle and application the two will stand as companion volumes.

Four articles were translated from the German by Dr. Judith Binder, to whom I am most grateful for her diligence and interest. Minor alterations were introduced into the other essays, primarily for stylistic reasons; but the substance, argumentation, and significant details of all twelve remain essentially unchanged. Editorial remarks, generally references to subsequent publications, are inserted within brackets. The footnotes have been standardized and, in several essays, the addition of editor's notes or changes of order in the translation have necessitated renumbering. Many new photographs were obtained for this publication, and a small number of supplementary illustrations has been introduced.

The suggestion for this volume came initially from Rensselaer Lee. Ernst Kitzinger advised me on the selection of articles and made other valuable suggestions. I am particularly indebted to Hugo Buchthal for his continual assistance and for preparing the Introduction. The Publication Committee of the Department of Art and Archaeology of Princeton University generously subsidized the cost of illustrations; the Samuel H. Kress Foundation provided a grant for the translations; and the Division of the Humanities and the College of the University of Chicago allowed me time to work on the publication. Photographs of the mosaics, icons, and manuscripts of Saint Catherine's Monastery at Mount Sinai were provided by the Alexandria-Michigan-Princeton Archaeological Expeditions. Lawrence P. Nees, Peter Parshall, and Laura Brimm ably assisted me in the tasks of proofreading and indexing. I deeply appreciate the support of these organizations and the counsel of these individuals.

Kurt Weitzmann graciously opened to me the excellent facilities of the Manuscript Room in Marquand Library of Princeton University, supplied the photographs and diagrams that are reproduced herewith, and approved the several translations. More important, his dedicated research and devoted teaching were the motivation for this undertaking.

Weitzmann's scholarly achievement stands as a highest honor to him; to his colleagues and students it remains a continuing source of enlightenment and inspiration.

HERBERT L. KESSLER

N 1929 two papers in the field of Byzantine illumination were published which were of outstanding interest and had a lasting influence on art-historical writing: C. R. Morey's "Notes on East Christian Miniatures" in the March number of the *Art Bulletin*, and Kurt Weitzmann's "Der Pariser Psalter MS grec 139 und die mittelbyzantinische Renaissance" in Vol. 6 of the *Jahrbuch für Kunstwissenschaft*. The first, in spite of its modest title, was a programmatic work, a balanced and considered summary of the theories and results obtained by Professor Morey and his pupils over many years of common endeavor, a mature statement of the methods and beliefs on which his teaching at Princeton was founded. The second was the first venture into print of a young man of 25, and it contained in a nutshell many of the ideas which Weitzmann was to elaborate in his later work. Most of the ideas of the younger man were, in due course, to supersede those of the older scholar who in characteristic generosity was instrumental in bringing Weitzmann to this country. Morey dated the miniatures of the Paris Psalter in the seventh or early eighth century, and attached them to the Alexandrian tradition. To him their outstanding feature was the continuity which linked them with their supposed early Christian prototypes. Weitzmann, on the other hand, considered the famous miniatures to be tenth-century works from Constantinople, and characterized them as artificial and not quite successful ad hoc compilations from heterogeneous sources: a nucleus of traditional Byzantine motifs had been expanded and enriched by a number of additions taken at random from genuinely classical, i.e., pagan, models. A greater contrast between the approach of these two scholars can hardly be imagined, and the implications of both theories for the entire history of Byzantine art are obvious. Weitzmann's was a first attempt to define with precision the character of the "Renaissance" of the arts in Byzantium under the Macedonian emperors, a subject to which he was to return frequently in the course of his subsequent work. He elaborated his main theories with only slight modifications in his "definitive" study of the Macedonian Renaissance published almost 35 years later and reprinted in this volume.

It was ultimately his pre-occupation with the problems of the origin and transmission of Byzantine Psalter imagery which eventually led Weitzmann to a systematic study of the relation between text and illustration in illuminated manuscripts. The results of this work are contained in what is perhaps his most important and most impressive single contribution to scholarship: *Illustrations in Roll and Codex*. He showed that in the period before the invention of the codex, book rolls were not illustrated by continuous friezes, as had hitherto been almost generally assumed, but by small, self-contained pictures inserted into the single writing columns. This type of book illustration was, according to Weitzmann, not only used for scientific treatises but also for literary texts, such as Homer and Euripides. The evidence can still be pieced together. In one paper included in this volume he traces scientific illustrations in Arabic manuscripts to their classical Greek origins, and in another he identifies part of a lost illustration of the Odyssey which is reflected in a few unpretentious narrative scenes on an Iliac Tablet. Thus he was able to reconstruct a whole missing chapter in the history of classical art, namely, ancient book illumination; classical archeologists now increasingly acknowledge his significant contribution to their own field. Still, he has not been blind to the fact that in antiquity the art of the book, even if practiced on a considerable scale, was of a rather modest scope artistically. The transformation of a humble handicraft into an ambitious major art form coincides with the definite disappearance of the book roll and its substitution by the codex with its separate pages in the fourth century of our era. The interaction of the various new elements which raised miniature painting to the level of an aristocratic activity is graphically described in Weitzmann's most recent paper included in the present volume, on tradition and innovation in book illustration during that period of transition.

Another outstanding feature of the book on "Roll and Codex" is the systematic demonstration of the migration of pictures from the "basic" text for which they had been created, i.e., in the case of biblical subjects, the Old and New Testaments, into "secondary" texts, such as patristic and hagiographical works, and also into Psalter illustration itself. The argument also works the other way: many miniatures which survive only in secondary contexts may be used to reconstruct Byzantine illustrations of biblical books of which no narrative cycles survive, such as Proph-

ets or Acts. What this fertile and imaginative method means in concrete terms for the study of Byzantine Old Testament illustration was brilliantly demonstrated in the paper on "Die Illustration der Septuaginta," which is also reprinted in this volume.

On one of his visits to Mount Athos Weitzmann discovered the beautiful miniatures of the "Phocas" lectionary, and this discovery may perhaps be said to stand at the beginning of his interest in the illustration of liturgical manuscripts. The grandiose project of a corpus of Byzantine lectionary illustration has not yet materialized, but he has devoted several important papers to a study of the interrelation between narrative and liturgical Gospel illustration, one of which, up to now not easily accessible, is included in this volume. The miniatures found in Byzantine lectionaries vary considerably from one manuscript to the other, and a careful analysis of an individual cycle may sometimes point to the manuscript's place of origin or destination. Moreover, the difference between comprehensive illustrative cycles, for instance in the two eleventh-century Gospel manuscripts in Paris and Florence, is not so much one of separate iconographical traditions as that between, on the one hand, a straightforward narrative based only on the Gospel text, and, on the other, an illustration reflecting liturgical considerations. A comprehensive treatment of these problems is found in Weitzmann's report on eleventh-century miniature and icon painting presented to the International Congress of Byzantine Studies at Oxford, where the development from purely narrative and descriptive miniature cycles toward an illustration inspired by liturgical and monastic ideals is recognized as one of the principal achievements of eleventh-century Byzantine art. This gradual change has its counterpart in the development of style, away from "Macedonian" classicism toward a more restrained and spiritualized art which is a perfect vehicle for the ascetic tendencies of that great century of monasticism and monastic foundations.

In fact, Weitzmann has never been unmindful of problems of style. His lecture on the deeper significance of the classical component of Byzantine style, delivered before an illustrious audience on the occasion of the exhibition of Byzantine art at Athens, will be found in this volume. Moreover, in a paper which has made little impact because the periodical in which it appeared never had a wide circulation and soon stopped publication altogether, he traced the classical current in the art of Constantinople, mainly during the sixth and seventh centuries, and this at a time when the pre-iconoclastic icons of Sinai were still virtually unknown. His supreme chance in this field came when he joined the Michigan-Alexandria-Princeton Expedition to Sinai, and then started work on the definitive publications of the great apse mosaic and of the icons. Those early icons which are now generally attributed to the Byzantine capital fully vindicate the thesis which he had put forward some years before. More recently he has given us a steady output of papers on single icons and groups of icons, most of which break entirely new ground. Special mention must be made of the article on the *Mandylion*, the holy image of Edessa: an inspired masterpiece of historical, art-historical and theological interpretation, which reads almost like a detective story. King Abgarus assumes the features of the Emperor Constantine Porphyrogennetos, the *spiritus rector* of the Macedonian Renaissance, who here claims the credit for the transfer of the famous relic to Constantinople. There is more to come, and the final publication of the volumes of the corpus of icons will be a major event in the history of Byzantine studies.

Finally, Weitzmann has repeatedly turned his attention to Byzantine art of the thirteenth century. His first venture in the field was the article on Constantinopolitan book illumination. It had generally been taken for granted that Constantinople during the period of the Latin Empire was artistically barren. By attributing an important school of illumination in the Byzantine capital to the period of the Latin occupation, Weitzmann filled this vacuum, and for the first time traced the various stages of the gradual transition from late Comnenian to Palaeologan illumination. Two other articles are closely related to this subject: an evaluation of the Byzantine sources of the famous *Musterbuch* of Wolfenbüttel, which again mostly belong to the same period; and a discussion of the various thirteenth-century copies of the Paris Psalter, which demonstrates more clearly than any other group of manuscripts the dependence of what is called the "Palaeologan Renaissance" on Macedonian models.

This brief survey is hardly adequate to do justice to the wide range of subjects and problems covered by Weitzmann's *œuvre* to date. Thus, his pioneer work on Byzantine ivories has not even been mentioned. Still, his principal contribution remains in the field of illuminated manuscripts. His various books and papers, seen as a whole, constitute an imposing edifice, of remarkable homogeneity and consistency; they may be said to have completely transformed the current ideas on the origin and development of Byzantine illumination, and will form the indispensable basis for any future research in the field for a long time to come. Room for argument and disagreement inevitably remains. Weitzmann would be the first to acknowledge the need for continued critical discussion, and it is only fair to admit that I myself have not always been convinced by his reasoning. I am all the more grateful for this opportunity to pay tribute to his scholarship, and to welcome the publication of this representative selection of his papers which will make his principal ideas and achievements more easily accessible.

HUGO BUCHTHAL
Institute of Fine Arts
New York University
October, 1969

N 1873 Otto Jahn published a series of small relief tablets, with illustrations of various epic poems of the Trojan War as well as other subjects, in his *Griechische Bilderchroniken*.[1] Very few new pieces of this sort have since become known. One in the British Museum, said to have been found at Taranto with an illustration of the Iliad, two in the Museo Capitolino, with representations of the Shield of Achilles, and one in the collection of M. Thierry, with scenes chiefly from the Aethiopis, are the only additions given in the introductory paragraph of a new treatise by Umberto Mancuso[2] on the great tabula of the Museo Capitolino. The more recent list of the *Tabulae Iliacae* by Lippold[3] does not add a single new piece, although it might have called attention to a fragment of a tablet in the Metropolitan Museum in New York.[4] This latter work consists of part of a central panel with the Iliupersis and small scenes from the Iliad, Books XIX to XXIV, surrounding it.

Not very long after Jahn's publication one more piece—unrecorded in Mancuso's list and Lippold's list for the obvious reason that neither editor[5] was able to explain the picture-cycle surrounding the central panel—was published in the *Monumenti inediti* by Stornaiuolo (Fig. 1).[6] At the time Stornaiuolo published this tablet, it was in the possession of Professor Tommassetti, and since this first notice, it was not heard of again until, after the present study was written and the interpretations had been made on the basis of the drawing in the *Monumenti inediti*, Professor Morey, to the greatest surprise of the writer, produced the photograph of the original, now in the Museo Sacro in the Vatican. Thanks to the generosity of Morey, to whom the writer feels deeply obliged, we are not only permitted to reproduce a photograph of the original (Fig. 2) but also to use the notes he made of the piece preparatory to writing the catalogue of the Museo Sacro. The following remarks are taken from Morey's description:

Material: white marble. No. 0066.
Dimensions H. 20.4, W. (max.) 17.2.

Reprinted with permission from the *American Journal of Archaeology*, XLV (1941), pp. 166–81.

[1] O. Jahn, *Griechische Bilderchroniken*, ed. posth. A. Michaelis (Bonn, 1873).

[2] U. Manusco, *La "Tabula Iliaca" del Museo Capitolino* ("Atti della R. Accademia nazionale dei Lincei, Memoria della classe di scienze morali," ser. V, 14 [Rome, 1909]), 662 ff.

[3] G. Lippold, "Tabula Iliaca," in Paulys, *Real-Encyclopädie der classischen Altertumswissenschaft*, 2d series, 4² (Stuttgart, 1932), cols. 1886 ff.

[4] M. E. Prinney, "Miscellaneous Greek and Roman Sculptures," *Bulletin of the Metropolitan Museum of Art*, 19 (1924), 239 ff. and fig. 2.

[5] C. Stornaiuolo, "Adunanze dell Instituto 30," *Bulletino dell'instituto di corrispondenza archeologica*, 54 (1882), 33. [The comprehensive study by Anna Sadurska, *Les Tables Iliaques* (Warsaw, 1964) presents the earlier literature on nineteen tables but omits a twentieth in the Cabinet des Medailles de la Bibliothèque Nationale in Paris which had already been presented by K. Weitzmann in *Greek Mythology in Byzantine Art* (Princeton, 1951), pp. 100 ff. and pl. XXX, fig. 106. Sadurska rectifies this oversight in "La vingtième table iliaque," in *Mélanges Offerts à Kazimierz Michalowski* (Warsaw, 1966), pp. 653 ff.]

[6] C. Stornaiuolo, *Monumenti inediti dell'instituto di corrispondenza archeologica*, Supplemento (1910), pl. XXXI.

Fig. 1 *Vatican, Museo Sacro. Tabula Odysseaca. Scenes from the Iliad (after Stornaiuolo)*

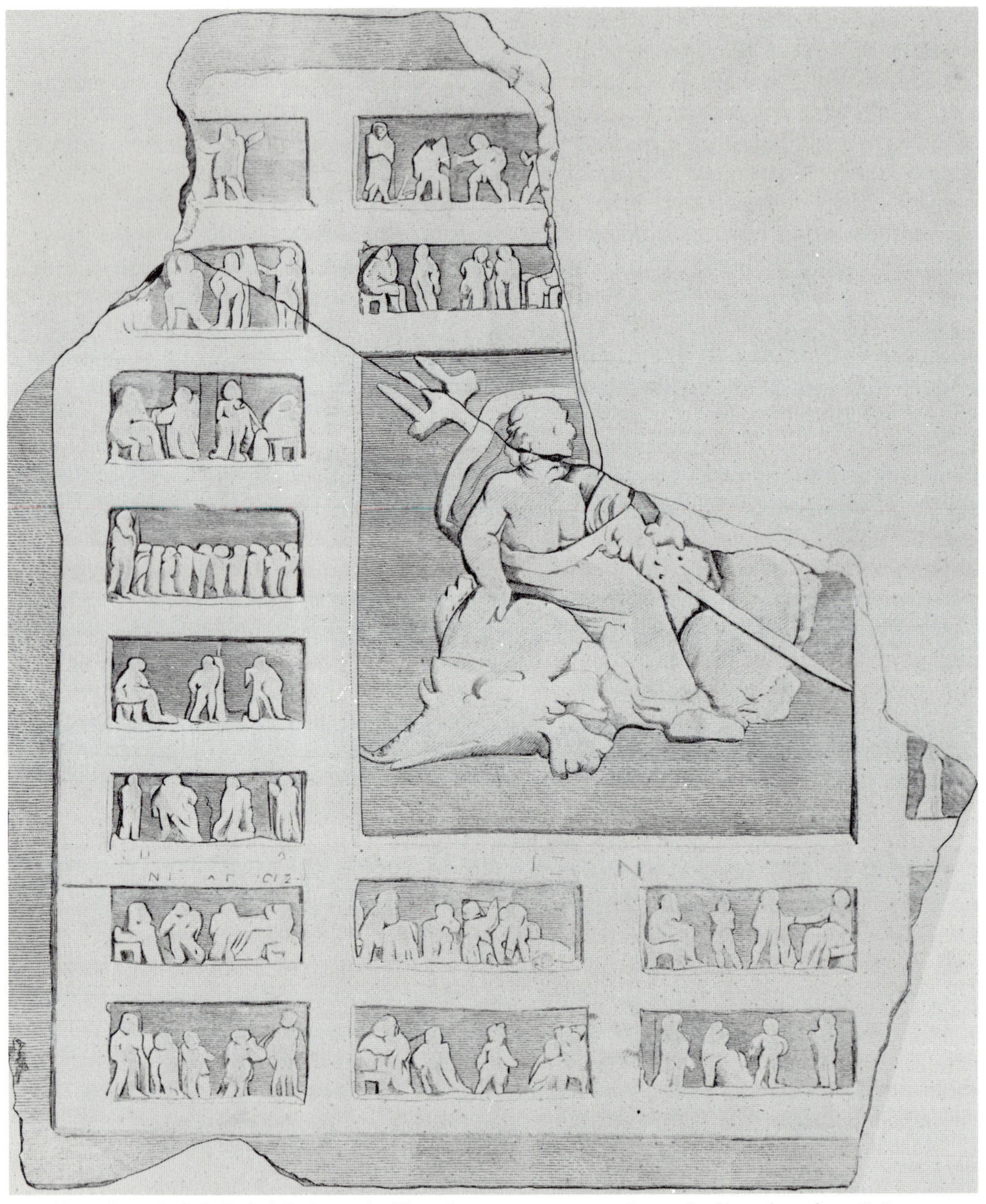

Panels to left 3.7–3.9 in length. Panels over and below center 4.1. (these dimensions include border). Central panel, excluding border, 9.0 square. Condition: broken off in upper left corner and whole of right side. Up-

Fig. 2 *Vatican, Museo Sacro. Tabula Odysseaca. Scenes from the Iliad*

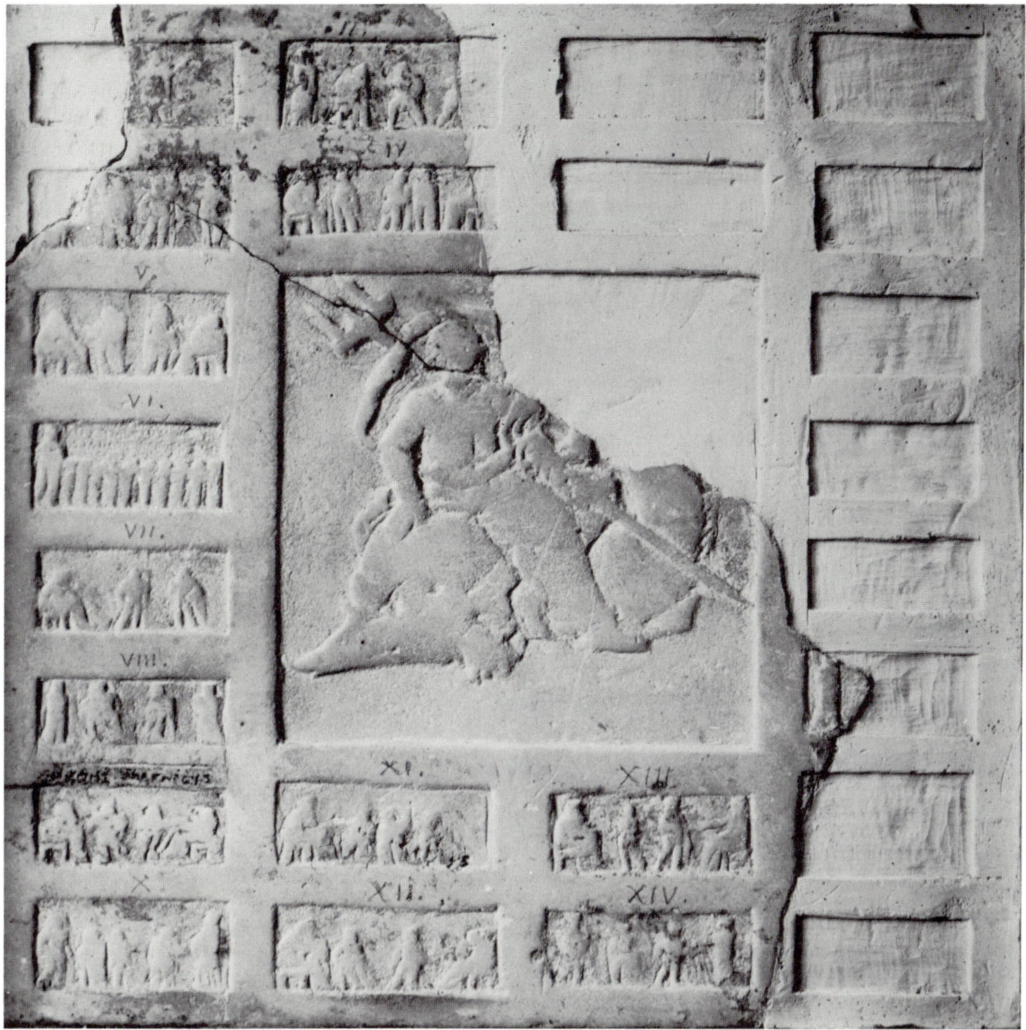

per portion broken from main piece by diagonal crack running from top of second panel down on left side, to and through Neptune's neck. Discoloration of surface on smaller piece, less so on larger.

There seems to be no record of when the piece entered the Vatican or of where it had been in the meantime. Now having the original, we have a means of evaluating the abilities of the mid-nineteenth century draftsman and can judge his faithfulness. He neither omitted any-thing essential nor was guilty of the op-posite fault, namely of trying to *interpret* in cases where the original was not suf-ficiently clear in the outlines of the fig-ures. Accordingly, after the photograph of the original came into our hands, the first description of the relief, made on the basis of the drawing, had to be changed in only a few details.

According to Stornaiuolo this piece, like most of the Iliac tablets, was found in the neighborhood of Rome. Not much more than half of it remained at the time of its discovery. The central panel, with only the right upper corner missing, is fairly complete, and fourteen small scenes of equal size, with only the upper four sections damaged, still surround it. It is obvious from the general arrange-ment that the center originally was sur-rounded by twenty-four scenes, the eight at the top and the eight at the bottom being organized in each case in two strips of four scenes. Of the eight scenes at the top, four remain, and of the bottom strips, six. Of the four scenes along each side of the center only those at the left are preserved.

On the frame below Poseidon and its prolongation toward the left outer frame remain a few letters of inscriptions, which are not sufficient to reconstruct any complete words. The original does not reveal any more than the few strokes be-longing to letters that the draftsman has indicated. By analogy with other tablets, however, we can assume that the divid-ing bands of the original were covered with inscriptions, which, not deeply enough incised, are almost completely rubbed off. Thus we are deprived of valuable epigraphical assistance in iden-tifying the scenes and are forced to inter-pret the scenes exclusively on the basis of actions and gestures expressed in the outlines of the small figures. But even in these carelessly modeled reliefs the figures speak a vivid language.

Easily recognizable at first glance is the figure in the central panel: it is Po-seidon, characterized by the trident and riding on a dolphinlike sea-monster. His mantle is blown out over his head like a veil to indicate the speed of his move-ment. This figure is a rare type since Poseidon, as a maritime god, is usually represented either standing in a chariot drawn by hippocamps or riding on the back of a hippocamp. Overbeck[7] cites as the only example of Poseidon riding on a dolphin a gold plaque in Leningrad and quotes at the same time a passage of Lucian, who mentions the dolphin as the animal on which Poseidon rides.[8]

Any attempt to interpret the small scenes of our tablet must also explain the meaning of Poseidon in relationship to the whole cycle of which he is the center. Furthermore, it is obvious that the actual number of small panels, orig-inally twenty-four, must have some mean-ing. Also, our choice of subjects is rather limited by what we know of the whole group of this category of the so-called *Tabulae Iliacae*. We must stay in the realm of the famous epic poems which comprise the program of the *Bilderchroni-ken*.[9] If we glance over the small panels,

---

[7] J. Overbeck, *Griechische Kunstmythologie*, 3 (Leipzig, 1871–89), 219 and fig. 7.
[8] *Dialogi deorum*, vi. 2.
[9] [For a detailed discussion of the illustration of epic poetry in antiquity consult K. Weitz-mann, *Ancient Book Illumination* (Cambridge,

we observe at once the complete absence of fighting scenes. Hence the Iliad and all the other epic poems treating the Trojan War, such as the Little Iliad of Leschis, the Aethiopis of Arktinos, the Iliupersis of Stesichoris, and so on, must be excluded. Next in order, then, is the Odyssey, and it is our belief that the tablet depicts scenes from this poem.

The fact that the *Tabulae Iliacae* included a cycle of the Odyssey is not only proved by the rather unusual tablet, formerly in the Rondanini collection, which represents three scenes of the Circe adventure,[10] but also by the inscription on another tablet of which only the drawing by Sarti is left to us.[11] This fragmentary inscription reads:

Ἰλιάδα καὶ ’Ο]δυσσείαν ῥαψωδιῶν
μη′. Ἰλιουπέρσ[ιν . . . .

From this we can assume that this tablet, of which a small part of the central Iliupersis is preserved, together with scenes of Iliad I–IX, originally possessed not only scenes of all twenty-four books of the Iliad but also of the twenty-four books of the Odyssey. The only possible place for the latter must have been at the bottom of the tablet, just where the great *Tabula* in the Museo Capitolino (Jahn A)[12] has the scenes of the Little Iliad and the Aethiopis, but with the probable difference that in the Sarti tablet (Jahn B) the Odyssey scenes extended on both sides to the outer frame of

Fig. 3 *Scheme of the Sarti Tablet*

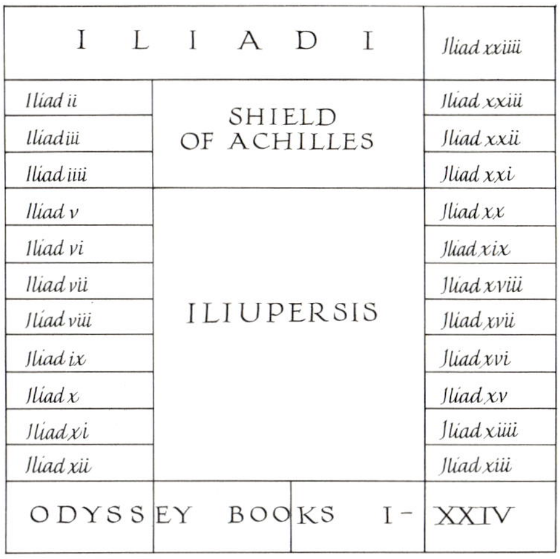

I L I A D I		Iliad xxiiii
Iliad ii	SHIELD OF ACHILLES	Iliad xxiii
Iliad iii		Iliad xxii
Iliad iiii		Iliad xxi
Iliad v	ILIUPERSIS	Iliad xx
Iliad vi		Iliad xix
Iliad vii		Iliad xviii
Iliad viii		Iliad xvii
Iliad ix		Iliad xvi
Iliad x		Iliad xv
Iliad xi		Iliad xiiii
Iliad xii		Iliad xiii
ODYSSEY BOOKS I –		XXIV

the whole tablet. The reason for this supposition is that the central panel of B was *higher* than that of A, since it inserts the representation of the shield of Achilles between the top frieze with illustrations of Iliad I and those of the Iliupersis. Because of this enlargement the twelve strips of Iliad scenes at either side of the central panel did not fill the whole space down to the bottom, thus allowing for the extension of the Odyssey scenes. We can assume, therefore, strips at the bottom of tablet B long enough to give at least one scene from each book of the Odyssey (Fig. 3). Since this part of the tablet B is entirely lost, and since no other Odyssey cycle is as yet known in this group of monuments, the Tommassetti tablet, if our proposed identification is correct, might fill this important gap in the representations of epic poems.

It is not difficult to find an explanation for the appearance of Poseidon in the middle of this cycle since in the Odyssey the wrath of Poseidon causes the wanderings of Odysseus, just as in the

---

Mass., 1959), pp. 31 ff. and *passim*; here also the older literature. See also R. Bianchi-Bandinelli, *Hellenistic-Byzantine Miniatures of the Iliad* (Olten, 1955) and Weitzmann's review of this book in *Gnomon*, XXIX (1957), 606 ff.]
[10] Jahn, *Bilderchroniken*, no. H.
[11] Ibid., no. B.
[12] Ibid., no. A.

Iliad the wrath of Apollo determines the action and keeps it going. It is Poseidon who destroys the ships and raft of Odysseus,[13] and Poseidon who keeps Odysseus away from his native land.[14]

Naturally, each of the twenty-four scenes that surrounded Poseidon when the tablet was still intact represented one book of the Odyssey, just as in the Iliac tablets the scenes of each book inclose a central panel. In order to find the beginning of the cycle in the Tommassetti tablet we must look for the comparatively surest identification of one of the scenes and then work backward and forward from it. In the left lower corner is a scene in which two human beings flank three small figures decidedly not human. With some imagination one can identify the latter as the three sirens. The right-hand one, the most easily recognizable, holds a lyre. A small wing, a short tail, and birdlike legs are clearly indicated. The figure next to her holds the double flute, marked in the silhouette. The third is not so readily determinable from her attributes. Three sirens, one playing the lyre and one the flute, correspond to well-known Hellenistic and Roman iconography.[15] For the moment, let us consider this scene a representation of Book XII of the Odyssey and use it as a point of departure to work out the sequence of the panels. Only if in the system thus reconstructed we find a suitable explanation for each scene following and preceding it can we be certain that our first identification is correct.

[13] *Od.* v. 291; vii. 271; ix. 283; xi. 399; xxiii. 234.
[14] *Od.* i. 20; v. 286; xi. 101.
[15] F. Müller, *Die antiken Odyssee-Illustrationen in ihrer kunsthistorischen Entwicklung* (Berlin, 1913), p. 44.

Starting from this point we look up five panels to the one at the left of the trident. This, then, may be an illustration of Book VII (Fig. 4). In the upper two friezes, therefore, which together originally contained eight panels, six of them must have been devoted to the first six books of the Odyssey. There remains only the question of whether the cycle starts in the upper left corner, obliging us to read from left to right, or whether it starts above the tail of the dolphin and runs from right to left. The second panel, toward which the trident points and through which the crack runs, gives the clue: we see a person holding up a garment toward another individual who seems to be grasping it. Who can fail to recall at once the episode in which one of Nausicaa's maidens gives a garment to Odysseus? This scene, then, is from the sixth book. Above this panel we must assume an illustration of Book V and, therefore, on the right the panels for Books I–IV. Figure 4 gives the whole scheme, showing the arrangement of the panels book by book and the direction we must follow. Starting, then, above the lost tail of the dolphin, we look to the left and then down the left margin. Afterward we look to the right around the central plaque and then upward until we end with what must be an illustration of Book XXIV in the upper right hand corner. This arrangement corresponds to that of the great *Tabula* of the Museo Capitolino (Jahn A), where the illustrations of the first and the last book meet exactly at the same place. Now we can be sure about the surviving and the lost illustrations. The scenes of Books I and II are lost entirely; those of III–VI are slightly damaged. The series is com-

Fig. 4 *Scheme of the Vatican Tablet*

V	III	I	XXIV
VI	IV	II	XXIII
VII			XXII
VIII			XXI
IX			XX
X			XIX
XI	XIV	XV	XVIII
XII	XIII	XVI	XVII

plete from Books VII to XVI, while from
XVII to XXIV only one figure, a representation from Book XIX, is left. For
the following description of each single
panel Fig. 4 indicates the location.
The Roman numbers written in pencil
upon the dividing frames (Fig. 2) are
of recent date, made by someone who
wished to enumerate the panels, not knowing their content. Except for the letters
III and IV—and this only by accident
—no other penciled number agrees with
our numbering, which follows the books
of the Odyssey.

Book III. The figure most clearly recognizable is that of a youth in a short
tunic who steps quickly toward the left
and stretches out his right arm in order
to greet a youth advancing toward him.
The second youth is not so easily made
out: one leg is back, indicating that he
is striding toward the right. His head,
as the original seems to indicate, inclines
slightly forward and is covered with a
helmet or a *pilos.* From the front of the
head to the ground runs a straight line,
the meaning of which is not quite clear.

Does it belong to a support, upon which
the figure is leaning? The draftsman
apparently did not understand the structure of this figure. It looks as if the head
were lacking entirely and as if he were
holding a shieldlike object, thus allowing a misinterpretation of the *pilos* and
the part below it. At the left is a female
figure who seems to be dressed in a peplos which in the drawing is opened to
expose the right leg. But this is apparently inaccurate. The original indicates
fine folds of a garment that falls to the
feet. And if in the drawing this figure
seems to look toward the spectator, this
again is an interpretation that cannot be
confirmed by the original. All this seems
to resemble the situation described at
the beginning of the third book, in which
Telemachos arrives in Pylos at the court
of Nestor. It is not Nestor who greets
him first, however, but Peisistratos, his
son, whom we identify with the first figure described. It is in accordance with
III, 36–39: "First Peisistratos, son of
Nestor, drew nigh, and took the hands
of each, and made them to sit down at
the feast on soft fleeces upon the sea sand,
beside his brother Thrasymedes and his
father."[16] Here Peisistratos stretches out
his arm in order to take the hand of the
newcomer, Telemachos. The classical
artist would not have been so literal as
to depict Peisistratos grasping Telemachos' hand and at the same time Athena's;
but he could not have omitted in this
scene the goddess who accompanies the
young Telemachos as his mentor. There-

---

[16] πρῶτος Νεστορίδης Πεισίστρατος ἐγγύθεν
  ἐλθὼν
  ἀμφοτέρων ἕλε χεῖρα καὶ ἵδρυσεν παρὰ δαιτὶ
  κώεσιν ἐν μαλακοῖσιν, ἐπὶ ψαμάθοις ἁλίῃσι,
  πάρ τε κασιγνήτῳ Θρασυμήδεϊ καὶ πατέρι ᾧ.

fore, we assume the person in the peplos to be Athena, standing aside and merely looking at the action rather than taking part in it herself. There is still a fourth person—only half-preserved at the right —obviously a youth. He moves away from Peisistratos and therefore hardly can be related immediately to the scene of welcome. There was no space for a second figure, with whom he could have constituted a second scene. This is most likely Peisistratos' brother, Thrasymedes, who is mentioned in the text quoted above. He raises his arms in surprise and does not accompany his brother to the welcome. It seems surprising to omit Nestor from this episode. The artist was obviously forced to reduce the number of figures in the small panel at his disposal; but he had a good reason to choose Peisistratos as the central figure, since Nestor's son is the first to greet Telemachos and as the future companion of Odysseus' son in the search for his father he is also the more important person. This preference for Peisistratos makes it quite certain that the very beginning of the third book is illustrated in our scene, because once he is introduced as speaker (lines 69 ff.) Nestor could not have been absent in any later scene of this book.

Book IV. This panel is clearly divided into two scenes. The left one represents a conversation between a seated figure leaning his head upon his arm and a youth standing before him. The right half of the panel shows a similar composition: two youths are standing before a seated figure, which is partly broken off. The youth in the middle seems to be raising one arm in a vivid speaking gesture. Again the beginning of the

book provides an easy explanation. After Telemachos and Peisistratos come to Lacedaemon, their arrival is announced to Menelaos by Eteoneus: "And the Lord Eteoneus came forth and saw them, the ready squire of renowned Menelaos; and he went through the palace to bear the tidings to the shepherd of the people, and standing near spake to him winged words" (IV, 22).[17] The man at the left seated on a throne is Menelaos. The outline of the relief clearly indicates an old man bent forward. "Standing near" is Eteoneus. In the second scene the enthroned figure again may be taken as Menelaos, and the two youths standing before him can only be Telemachos and Peisistratos. The artist seems to have taken some liberty in the representation of this second scene. After Telemachos and Peisistratos enter the palace of Menelaos, they are first taken to the bath, and then after the maidens have bathed them and cast upon them thick cloaks, "they sat on chairs by Menelaos, son of Atreus" (IV, 51).[18] This passage would require that Telemachos and Peisistratos be seated opposite Menelaos. But it seems to be not mere carelessness on the part of the illustrator to represent them standing. Rather it was his desire to express in a visual way the distinction between an old man, whose dignity is indicated by a seated attitude, and a standing youth. This distinction is used as a formula wherever a similar distinction between an old man and a youth is intended. No later passage in the fourth

[17] . . . . ὁ δὲ προμολὼν ἴδετο κρείων Ἐτεωνεύς,
ὀτρηρὸς θεράπων Μενελάου κυδαλίμοιο,
βῆ δ'ἴμεν ἀγγελέων διὰ δώματα ποιμένι λαῶν,
ἀγχοῦ δ' ἱστάμενος ἔπεα πτερόεντα προσηύδα·
[18] ἔς ῥα θρόνους ἔζοντο παρ' Ἀτρείδην Μενέλαον.

book seems to fit so well with this sequence of events. Later in the book Peisistratos is kept in the background; and the long tale of Menelaos' adventure the next morning, which he had heard from Proteus, is told only to Telemachos. After this, at the end of the book the scene changes to Ithaca.

Book V. This panel shows only one figure in a short tunic moving toward the right and raising his right arm in a speaking gesture. A second figure, to whom he is talking, is entirely broken away and nothing indicates whether this figure was sitting or standing. A strange object protrudes from the shoulder of the man. At the beginning of the fifth book Hermes is sent down to the earth by Zeus, with the command that Calypso let Odysseus go. The preserved figure of our scene, then, could be Hermes receiving the message from Zeus (V, 52 ff.). The strange object behind his neck is probably the *kerykeion*, although in the drawing it is somewhat shorter and thicker and thus resembles the *petasos*, which appears attached to the shoulder of Hermes in the Orpheus relief of the Villa Albani or on the column of Ephesus. But it seems a contradiction that Hermes raises his arm as if he were speaking himself, whereas in the council of the gods it is Zeus who speaks to Hermes, and the latter silently receives the message. It seems likely, therefore, that this is a representation of a later episode (V. 95) where Hermes speaks to Calypso: "Now after he had supped and comforted his soul with food, at the last he answered, and spake to her on this wise."[19] So the lost figure at the left would be Cal-

ypso, supposedly in a seated position. The only other dialogue of the fifth book is that between Calypso and Odysseus sitting by the seashore; but this episode does not seem to fit in with the standing figure of the relief.

Book VI. Since the two figures in the middle of this panel are not related to each other in pose, we must assume two different scenes. The left half, partly destroyed, contains a seated figure, turning to the left and holding some object in his raised arm. Opposite him is another figure, of which the upper part is broken off. The space available is not wide enough to allow for a seated person as the drawing might suggest. In the original, rather, it looks like the lower part of a standing woman in a long garment that falls to her feet. The first figure described seemingly has the very characteristic outline of a woman spinning, holding the spindle upright and letting the yarn float down behind her to the floor. At the beginning of the sixth book, after Athena had appeared to her in the night, Nausicaa enters the hall of the palace to see her parents, as is related in VI, 51–53: "And she found them within, her mother sitting by the hearth with the women her handmaids, spinning yarn of sea-purple stain. . . ."[20] So the spinning woman is Arete, and Nausicaa must have been shown standing before her.

In the scene on the right the action is quite intelligible. One figure is holding up what seems to be a garment and the second figure is grasping it. Can there be a more natural explanation than that

[19] αὐτὰρ ἐπεὶ δείπνησε καὶ ἤραρε θυμὸν ἐδωδῇ,
  καὶ τότε δή μιν ἔπεσσιν ἀμειβόμενος προσέειπεν·

[20] . . . . κιχήσατο δ᾽ἔνδον ἐόντας·
  ἡ μὲν ἐπ᾽ ἐσχάρῃ ἧστο σὺν ἀμφιπόλοισι
    γυναιξίν,
  ἠλάκατα στρωφῶσ᾽ ἁλιπόρφυρα·

of Odysseus' arrival in the country of the Phaeacians, where he meets the Princess Nausicaa and where one of her maidens gives him a raiment to cover his nakedness, according to VI, 214: "Beside him they laid a mantle, and a doublet for raiment. . . ."[21] But which of the two persons composing the scene is Odysseus and which is the maid? Is the right-hand figure the maid, who offers the garment with one hand, and is the left-hand one Odysseus, who has already taken the garment? Or is the left-hand figure the maid, who still holds the raiment in her hand toward which Odysseus is reaching? The first assumption seems to be more likely, since the left figure looks like a strong male person and resembles the central figure of the panels to the Books VII and IX, which surely represents Odysseus. As to the figure at the right, the drawing and the original differ in one detail: what in the former appears to be a fully rounded hip is actually a bent knee, as the sharp design of the original makes clear. The figure is seen from the back and the bent knee indicates a movement toward the right, i.e., away from Odysseus, toward whom she turns her head. Though she is quite graceful, it is not perfectly clear in the relief that she is wearing a long garment as one would expect in a female figure, and in this instance it can only be inferred from the text that she must be one of Nausicaa's maidens, who modestly turns away when she gives the raiment to Odysseus. The scene seems to be an abbreviation of a fuller model in which Nausicaa could hardly have been missing. In cases where the sculptor of

the relief tries to press two episodes into the very small panel at his disposal, he is forced to make abbreviations of this sort.

Book VII contains two scenes which are of a similar character. In each of them one person is standing before a seated figure, so again we have to deal with two conversation scenes, not unlike the one in Book IV and those we shall see in Books XIII and XV. In both scenes of Book VII the standing figure seems to be male because of the treatment of the legs which show no covering with a peplos, as a female would be dressed. Upon the chairs sit the most dignified persons, but neither in the original nor in the drawing is their sex clearly recognizable. The main content of Book VII is the reception of Odysseus in the palace of the king of the Phaeacians. When he entered the palace, as Athena had prophesied to him, he first meets Arete, the wife of Alcinous, as described in VII, 139–142: "Now the steadfast goodly Odysseus went through the hall, clad in a thick mist, which Athene shed around him, till he came to Arete and the king Alcinous. And Odysseus cast his hands about the knees of Arete. . . ."[22] And later on, after Alcinous has announced to his captains and counselors that he is going to entertain the stranger on the morrow (VII, 186 ff.), Odysseus answers him saying (VII, 208–210): "Alcinous, that thought be far from thee! for I bear no likeness either in form or fashion to the deathless gods, who keep wide heaven,

---

[21] πὰρ δ᾽ ἄρα οἱ φᾶρός τε χιτῶνά τε εἵματ᾽ ἔθηκαν

[22] αὐτὰρ ὁ βῆ διὰ δῶμα πολύτλας δῖος
  Ὀδυσσεύς
  πολλὴν ἠέρ᾽ ἔχων, ἥν οἱ περίχευεν Ἀθήνη,
  ὄφρ᾽ ἵκετ᾽ Ἀρήτην τε καὶ Ἀλκίνοον βασιλῆα.
  ἀμφὶ δ᾽ ἄρ᾽ Ἀρήτης βάλε γούνασι χεῖρας
  Ὀδυσσεύς

but to men that die. . . ."[23] If we are right in relating the relief to these two text passages, then the two standing figures would twice represent Odysseus as he addresses the rulers of the Phaeacians. Assuming that the sculptor follows the text very closely, then the figure at the left would be Arete and that at the right Alcinous, both of whom seem to be resting their heads upon their arms. Behind each Odysseus figure two straight lines run up to the frame. These lines may indicate in each case the palace door. It should not be overlooked, however, that both scenes deviate slightly from the text in some details. According to the text, "Odysseus first cast his hands about the knees" of Arete. But this does not seem to be represented here. It is rather the moment afterward, when Odysseus is addressing Arete and stands before her with a gesture of speaking. And furthermore, it is not in accordance with the text to show Odysseus standing when he speaks with Alcinous, since lines 167 ff. explicitly state that the king made him sit down on a shining chair. But apparently, as we noticed in Book IV, a conventional scheme was adopted for a conversation scene with a ruling king, paying honor to him by representing him seated while the guest is characterized as standing.

Book VIII. Nearly the whole panel is filled with a crowd of ten people, who seem to be treated as equals. There is little distinction among them, except that those on the left appear to turn to the right and those on the right to the left. This concentrates the figures and connects them with each other in one scene. Their attitudes are not defined. For standing figures they are too small, yet it is not clear from the relief that they are seated. Especially huge in size is the figure at the left who confronts the crowd. The eighth book brings Odysseus to the assembly of the Phaeacians, who had met at the assembly place, "which they had established hard by the ships." Here the captains and counselors of the Phaeacians "sat down on the polished stone close by each other." Just this "sitting close together" may have prevented the artist from showing clearly the stones on which they were placed. And then the text continues, VIII, 17: "yea, and many an one marveled at the sight of the wise son of Laertes, for wondrous was the grace Athene poured upon his head and shoulders, and she made him greater and more mighty to behold."[24] These lines may account for the emphasis on the huge size of Odysseus in our relief panel.

Book IX. The three figures of this panel seemingly belong to one scene. At the left a man is represented sitting in a chair, leaning his arm upon his knee in a gesture similar to that of Menelaos in the illustration to Book IV and to Alcinous of Book VII, thus marking the type of an older or at least an honorable man. Two men are standing before him, obviously seeking his attention. The one in the middle of the scene is represented *en face* leaning upon a long staff. The drawing creates the impression of a mantle

---

[23] "'Ἀλκίνο᾽, ἄλλο τί τοι μελέτω φρεσίν· οὐ γὰρ ἐγώ γε
ἀθανάτοισιν ἔοικα, τοὶ οὐρανὸν εὐρὺν ἔχουσιν,
οὐ δέμας οὐδὲ φυήν, ἀλλὰ θνητοῖσι βροτοῖσιν·

[24] . . . . πολλοὶ δ᾽ἄρα θηήσαντο ἰδόντες
υἱὸν Λαέρταο δαΐφρονα. τῷ δ᾽ἄρ᾽ Ἀθήνη
θεσπεσίην κατέχευε χάριν κεφαλῇ τε καὶ ὤμοις,
καί μιν μακρότερον καὶ πάσσονα θῆκεν ἰδέσθαι

over the raised arm, partly concealing the staff, but in the original the staff is fully visible. The unclothed legs suggest that the figure at the right, like the preceding one, is either nude or clad in a short tunic. Seen in profile, he raises his right arm in a gesture of speech, while his left arm either rests on what looks like a pedestal or has the end of a mantle thrown over it. This figure is somewhat misunderstood in the drawing, in which he seems to be clad in a long garment with long wide sleeves and appears to move with a theatrical attitude. The ninth book, to which this panel must be related, at the beginning describes the intense dramatic moment when Odysseus reveals his identity to Alcinous, reciting the famous words (IX, 19): "I am Odysseus, son of Laertes, who am in men's minds for all manner of wiles, and my fame reaches unto heaven."[25] If the identification of our scene with this episode is correct, then the seated man would undoubtedly be Alcinous, "most notable of all the people." But which of the two standing figures is Odysseus? We are inclined to identify the man standing in the middle and leaning upon his staff as Odysseus. Thus he would be in the very center of the scene. The first words of the tale of Odysseus are in praise of the famous minstrel who had just finished his recital of the Trojan War at the end of the preceding book and who, therefore, is still in the palace when Odysseus makes his confession. So the figure at the right is to be interpreted as the minstrel Demodocus, who with his minstrelsy had just melted the heart of Odysseus.

Book X. Here again we have two scenes in one panel. The scene at the left shows a man standing in repose. Another figure, with visible effort, is dragging toward him an object that is the size of a sack and seems to be open. At the beginning of the tenth book we meet Odysseus in the country of Aeolus, the god of the winds. Aeolus is helpful to Odysseus and gives him a wallet containing the winds, as related in X, 19–20: "He gave me a wallet, made of the hide of an ox of nine seasons old, which he let flay, and therein he bound the ways of all the noisy winds."[26] Thus, the man dragging the sack is Aeolus, who fills the wallet and seems to need his entire strength to bind the winds and tie them up. The person standing before him must be Odysseus, who is about to receive this sack.

The second scene is very much like the first one in composition and therefore it might be another moment of the same episode. The figures are now reversed: at the right of the frame we see the person standing in repose and before him is the man who holds the sack-like object. This scene is, in all probability, related to the moment described in X, 47 where the companions of Odysseus open the sack: "they loosed the wallet, and all the winds brake forth."[27] The man who opens the sack is turned to the right and holds the wallet before him. It is impossible to tell whether the escaping of the winds was visualized by a head coming out of the wallet, as on a gem in the Cabinet des Médailles in

[25] εἴμ' Ὀδυσεὺς Λαερτιάδης, ὃς πᾶσι δόλοισιν
  ἀνθρώποισι μέλω, καί μευ κλέος οὐρανὸν ἵκει.

[26] δῶκε δέ μ'ἐκδείρας ἀσκὸν βοὸς ἐννεώροιο,
  ἔνθα δὲ βυκτάων ἀνέμων κατέδησε κέλευθα·
[27] ἀσκὸν μὲν λῦσαν, ἄνεμοι δ'ἐκ πάντες ὄρουσαν

Paris.[28] The best suggestion for the figure confronting the person in repose would again be Odysseus, as he describes himself in X, 49–52: "But as for me, I awoke and communed with my great heart, whether I should cast myself from the ship and perish in the deep, or endure in silence and abide yet among the living." His attitude is not clear in the relief. Does he raise his arm in anger or dread, or mournfulness over the deed of his companion?

Book XI. This panel is similar to the compositions in the panels of Books IV and VII. Here we see two scenes of conversation, with seated figures in the corners and standing figures in the middle of the panel, turning their backs upon each other. In the left scene a figure is seated on a throne rather than on a simple chair. The rich bolsters of the throne, marked out with such emphasis, indicate a splendor which we do not find elsewhere on this relief. The eleventh book begins with the farewell of Odysseus to Circe. According to the text, this happened near the ships at the shore. If our identification of the seated figure with Circe is correct, it is not in agreement with the text to have Circe enthroned at that moment. But our sculptor seems to use certain conventional formulae to represent greeting and farewell scenes and expresses the dignity of gods or honorable people by having them seated on a throne. The common use of such formulae in Hellenistic-Roman times may be shown by the decorations on a terracotta lamp, where Odysseus is standing in a similar way before Circe, who is represented as an enthroned goddess.[29] The relief on the lamp also shows an elaborate throne. Twice in the tenth book the splendid chairs in the house of Circe are described as "with studs of silver and goodly carven" (X, 314 and 366); and how common the conception of Circe seated on a richly decorated throne must have been may be inferred from another monument, an Etruscan urn in Volterra.[30] If our identification with Circe is correct, the figure standing before her naturally would be Odysseus. His attitude and gestures, however, are not distinct enough to allow a more precise analysis.

In the second scene of the panel, it looks as if a seated figure raises one arm to his head. This gesture seems to give the clue for the identification. After Odysseus left the island of Circe and at her command has gone to the dwelling of Hades, the first person he meets is Elpenor, his companion who had fallen from the roof of Circe's palace. This meeting is told of in XI, 51–52: "and first came the soul of Elpenor, my companion, that had not yet been buried beneath the wide-wayed earth."[31] In the fresco from the Esquiline[32] we see him sitting on a rock, his face mournfully covered with his hands. This gesture might call Elpenor to our minds and justify the identification of the seated figure as the companion with whom Odysseus had the first dialogue in Hades.

[28] A. Furtwängler, *Die antiken Gemmen* (Berlin and Leipzig, 1900), pl. XX, no. 20.

[29] O. Jahn, "Kirke," *Archäologische Zeitung*, 23 (1865), 20 and pl. 194, no. 4.

[30] E. Brunn, *I relievi delle urne etrusche*, 1 (Ravenna, 1870), 118 and pl. LXXXIX, no. 3.

[31] Πρώτη δὲ ψυχὴ Ἐλπήνορος ἦλθεν ἑταίρου· οὐ γάρ πω ἐτέθαπτο ὑπὸ χθονὸς εὐρυοδείης·

[32] B. Nogara, *Le Nozze Aldobrandine, i paesaggi con scene dell'Odissea e le altre pitture murali antiche* (Milan, 1907), pls. 23–24.

Again there may be a deviation from the text so far as Odysseus is standing before Elpenor, because verse XI, 81, "Even so we twain were sitting holding sad discourse,"[33] makes it clear that both were seated during the conversation. But the fact that at least Elpenor is represented seated is important enough, since in no other instance in the Nekyia is a phantom mentioned as sitting. As a whole, this scene is so rough and indistinct that our identification must remain in question.

Book XII. The middle of this panel contains the three sirens, as we said above. The one on the right is playing the lyre, the middle one, as one might guess rather than actually recognize, the double flute, and the one on the left, who is not quite clear either in the original or in the drawing, by analogy with other representations of the subject, is supposed to be singing. At the right the man who seems to hold his arms behind his back is obviously Odysseus, bound to the mast of the ship when passing the island of the sirens. His head, covered with the *pilos*, turns backward, as the original makes clear, thus indicating that the danger has passed. For lack of space the ship is not represented, except for the mast which is visible between the legs of the fettered Odysseus. But who is the man at the left? We would suppose that again Odysseus is shown at the moment before he reached the island of the sirens and is about to be bound to the mast by one of his companions. We would then have two episodes in the adventure of Odysseus and the sirens, in which the latter are represented only once, in the middle of the

scene, and are related to both the Odysseus figures. This kind of contamination is not at all unusual in cases of limited space. We find it on the well-known omphalos plate of Canoleius[34] where, in the same manner, one set of sirens is related first to the ship which is approaching the rocks during the binding of Odysseus, and at the same time to another ship, on which Odysseus is tied to the mast, as it passes the rocks. The adventure of the sirens is told twice in the twelfth book: in the instruction by Circe on how to behave when Odysseus arrives at the island (XII, 37 ff.) and, second, during the actual event (XII, 165 ff.). The panel could be related to either passage.

Book XIII. Here again we find the scheme, already seen in several instances, of two seated figures at the corners of the panel. The seated figure at the left seems to hold some object in its lap, but both the drawing and the original are indistinct in details. The thirteenth book opens with a speech of Alcinous asking the counselors of the Phaeacians to bring tripods and cauldrons as gifts for Odysseus (XIII, 13 ff.). The seated figure seems to be Alcinous, occupying the same place as in the panel of Book IX. Is it possible that he holds a tripod, a cauldron, or something of the sort in his lap, in order to make visible the gift he is going to make to Odysseus? In front of him we expect Odysseus, who asks Alcinous to send him safely upon his way (XIII, 38 ff.): "My lord Alcinous, most notable of all the people, pour ye the drink offering, and send me safe upon

---

[33] Νῶϊ μὲν ὣς ἐπέεσσιν ἀμειβομένω στυγεροῖσιν ἥμεθ'. . . .

[34] R. Pagenstecher, *Die calenische Reliefkeramik* (Berlin, 1909), p. 81 and fig. 36.

my way, and as for you, fare ye well. . . ."[35] Though the figure in the drawing resembles a person draped in a long garment, the original does not give this impression. Here we see the legs fully drawn, suggesting a nude figure or one in a short tunic, and the head seems to be covered with a *pilos*. Both points favor the interpretation of this figure as Odysseus.

The figure next to him, belonging to the second scene, is very similar, and since he likewise seems to wear a *pilos*, we can be quite sure that Odysseus is again represented. The seated figure to whom Odysseus is turning is, in all probability, Arete, according to XIII, 56: "Then goodly Odysseus uprose, and placed in Arete's hand the two-handled cup."[36] She too seems to hold something in her lap. Is it the two-handled cup which Odysseus had placed in Arete's hand, as the quoted lines indicate? Immediately after his address to the queen, Odysseus leaves the hospitable palace, so no later episode of this book is to be considered in connection with the panel. Thus we have a panel nearly analogous to that of Book VII, in which, in a similar way, Odysseus separately faces the king and queen of the Phaeacians, except that in the former instance Alcinous and Arete, in accord with the text, are in reverse order.

Book XIV. At the left of this panel a man is sitting, not on a chair as in other instances, but on a bench. To judge from the drawing and the original as well, he may be bearded. He is busy with some large object which lies in his lap and falls to the ground. The middle of the panel is rather hard to describe, but it is certain that three persons are busy with something which covers the ground. When Odysseus, at the opening of Book XIV, makes his way through familiar Ithaca, the first person he meets is the goodly swineherd Eumaeus. After describing the building and the courtyard for the swine, the poet says of Eumaeus himself: "Now he was fitting sandals to his feet, cutting a good brown oxhide while the rest of his fellows, three in all, were abroad this way and that, with the droves of swine" (XIV, 23).[37] This passage is illustrated precisely in our panel. At the left Eumaeus is sitting and holding in his lap the good brown oxhide from which he is cutting sandals. Before him are his three fellows (the fourth he has sent to the city to take a boar to the proud wooers: XIV, 26). On the ground we expect to see the swine. One swine might be between the legs of the fellow in the middle. Is he raising his arm in order to slaughter one with an ax, as in XIV, 74 where the sacrificing of two swine in honor of Odysseus is told? The original is badly damaged in the lower right corner of the panel, and it was wise of the draftsman not to fill in any suggestions of his own. It is not possible to go beyond the identification of the subject in general, but this is very clear indeed.

Book XV. Once more we find the well-known compositional scheme of two stand-

---

[35] "'Ἀλκίνοε κρεῖον, πάντων ἀριδείκετε λαῶν,
πέμπετέ με σπείσαντες ἀπήμονα, χαίρετε
δ'αὐτοί·

[36]   . . . . ἀνὰ δ'ἵστατο δῖος 'Οδυσσεύς,
'Ἀρήτῃ δ'ἐν χειρὶ τίθει δέπας ἀμφικύπελλον

[37] αὐτὸς δ'ἀμφὶ πόδεσσιν ἑοῖς ἀράρισκε πέδιλα,
τάμνων δέρμα βόειον ἐΰχροές· οἱ δὲ δὴ ἄλλοι
οἴχοντ' ἄλλυδις ἄλλος ἄμ' ἀγρομένοισι σύεσσιν,
οἱ τρεῖς· . . . .

ing figures between two seated ones. The figure sitting at the left is that of an old man slightly bent forward and obviously bearded. Before him stands a youth. The beginning of Book XIV leads us again into the palace of Menelaos, and we can easily identify the seated old man as the son of Atreus. Before him stands Telemachos, probably as he addresses Menelaos, according to XV, 64: "Menelaos, son of Atreus, fosterling of Zeus, leader of the people, even now do thou speed me hence, to mine own dear country."[38] Since the dialogue between Menelaos and Telemachos continues for quite a while, this scene just as easily may be an illustration of some subsequent passage.

More precisely related to a special passage in the text is the scene on the right. The seated figure is a woman dressed in a girdled peplos. She stretches her right arm out toward a standing youth before her, as if she has just given him something which he is now holding over his arm. The woman is Helen, who gives Telemachos a robe as a memorial of her hands for his future bride, as told in XV, 123: "And Helen came up, beautiful Helen, with the robe in her hands, and spake and hailed him: 'Lo, I too give thee this gift, dear child, a memorial of the hands of Helen, against the day of thy desire, even of thy bridal, for thy bride to wear it. . . ."[39] Helen is sitting

with great dignity, and Telemachos, standing before her, has already taken the robe and put it over his arm.

Book XVI. Reading this panel from the left, the first figure, turned to the right in the drawing, looks like a woman in a long garment, but the original does not confirm this impression. Two legs, fairly well recognizable, the one at the left being free, would speak rather in favor of a male person who had just entered from the left and now approaches the figure before him. This second figure is even more doubtful, since the lines are so roughly cut that no more can be suggested than a possible sitting position though not even this much is certain. From reading the sixteenth book one might expect a scene in which Telemachos has crossed the threshold of Eumaeus' hut, according to XVI, 42–44: "As he came near, his father Odysseus arose from his seat to give him place; but Telemachos, on his part, stayed him and spake saying: 'Be seated, stranger . . . ."[40] So the person approaching from the left would be Telemachos, and the figure seated before him would be Odysseus, though the latter's attitude, as already mentioned, cannot be clearly made out.

The second scene is somewhat clearer. Here the figure near the frame is decidedly a woman, to judge from the original as well as from the drawing, as revealed by the long garment that conceals any indication of legs. She addresses the man before her, who is probably nude or perhaps dressed in a short tunic. The first woman to appear in Book XVI is Athena who, after Eumaeus the swine-

38 "'Ἀτρεΐδη Μενέλαε διοτρεφές, ὄρχαμε λαῶν,
   ἤδη νῦν μ'ἀπόπεμπε φίλην ἐς πατρίδα γαῖαν·
39 . . . . Ἑλένη δὲ παρίστατο καλλιπάρηος
   πέπλον ἔχουσ' ἐν χερσίν, ἔπος τ'ἔφατ' ἔκ τ'
      ὀνόμαζε·
   "δῶρόν τοι καὶ ἐγώ, τέκνον φίλε, τοῦτο
      δίδωμι,
   μνῆμ' Ἑλένης χειρῶν, πολυηράτου ἐς γάμου
      ὤρην,
   σῇ ἀλόχῳ φορέειν·. . . .

40 τῷ δ'ἕδρης ἐπιόντι πατὴρ ὑπόειξεν Ὀδυσσεύς·
   Τηλέμαχος δ'ἑτέρωθεν ἐρήτυε φώνησέν τε·
   "ἧσο, ξεῖν'·. . . ."

herd departed for the city, entered his hut, as told in XVI, 157–160: ". . . and she drew nigh in the semblance of a woman fair and tall, and skilled in splendid handiwork. And she stood in presence manifest to Odysseus over against the doorway of the hut; but it was so that Telemachos saw her not before him and marked her not. . . ."[41] The woman standing at the right would be Athena and the man before her again Odysseus. With this panel the cycle breaks off.

Book XIX. Only a small part of one of the panels at the right side is preserved, which must have contained a scene from the nineteenth book. A woman, turned to the right and with head broken off, is visible. Most probably she is Eurykleia and before her we can assume, perhaps, Telemachos, who according to XIX, 22 commands her to shut the women in their chambers.

In only a few of the representations in the cycle can parallels be found among classical monuments.[42] The beginning of Book III is illustrated on an Apulian amphora,[43] but here Telemachos is faced with Nestor and not, as in the relief, with Peisistratos. No illustration to Book IV seems to exist at all. Numerous are the monuments which depict

Odysseus on Ortygia and his shipwreck of Book V, but as far as we know no parallel exists to the message of Hermes. Of the two scenes of Book VI in the relief, only the right-hand one with Odysseus and Nausicaa occurs as a subject on red-figured vases,[44] but the iconography is so different that this illustration cannot be derived from it. The scene of Odysseus before Arete in the left half of the panel to Book VII occurs on a Phlyax vase,[45] but here we do not even expect a similarity of types. The second scene of Book VII, as well as those of the following panels of Books VIII and IX, seem to be unique. Of Book VIII no representation seems to be known at all, and all we know of Book IX concerns Odysseus' adventure among the Cyclopes. The correspondence of the right-hand scene of Book X, in which a companion of Odysseus opens the wallet of Aeolus, with the representation on a gem has already been mentioned, as has the comparison of the mourning Elpenor of Book XI with the frescoes from the Esquiline. Furthermore, the sirens of Book XII have been treated in their relationship to other monuments. Illustrations to Books XIII, XIV and XVI seem to be lacking entirely. The farewell of Telemachos to Menelaos and Helen of Book XV is depicted a second time on a Homeric cup, but here Helen is standing and the attitudes of Menelaos and Telemachos also differ from

---

[41] ἀλλ' ἥ γε σχεδὸν ἦλθε· δέμας δ' ἤϊκτο γυναικὶ
καλῇ τε μεγάλῃ τε καὶ ἀγλαὰ ἔργα ἰδυίῃ.
στῆ δὲ κατ' ἀντίθυρον κλισίης Ὀδυσῆϊ
    φανεῖσα·
οὐδ' ἄρα Τηλέμαχος ἴδεν ἀντίον οὐδ' ἐνόησεν

[42] The most recent comprehensive publication on illustrations of the Odyssey is that of Müller, *Odyssee-Illustrationen,* where the older literature is cited.

[43] W. H. Roscher, *Lexikon der griechischen und römischen Mythologie,* 3 (Leipzig, 1897–1902), 298, fig. 7; Müller, *Odyssee-Illustrationen,* p. 136.

[44] A. Furtwängler and K. Reichhold (eds.), *Griechische Vasenmalerei,* 3 (Munich, 1904–32), 101 and fig. 47. Müller, *Odyssee-Illustrationen,* p. 107.

[45] *Monumenti dell'instituto di corrispondenza archeologica,* 6, pl. XXXV, no. 2; Müller, *Odyssee-Illustrationen,* p. 109.

those on the relief.[46]

If we sum up this search for parallels, we see with astonishment how few are the comparisons which we can establish with preserved monuments. But these few, especially the Aeolus scene and the sirens, are enough to relate the iconography of the Tommassetti tablet to other monuments of the Hellenistic-Roman period which depict Odyssey illustrations.

By far the majority of the scenes are unique and considerably increase, therefore, the repertory of scenes of the Odyssey. But there must be some reason why we find so few parallels with other monuments. It can hardly be explained only by the loss of the material. If we go through the various categories of monuments which have scenes from the Odyssey, we observe that the artists, especially in the archaic and developed Greek periods, preferred the most adventurous and characteristic episodes. The stay in Ortygia, the shipwreck, the Polyphemus story, the adventure with Circe, the Nekyia, the temptation by the sirens, the dangers of Scylla, and finally all the episodes of Odysseus' return home, together with the slaying of the wooers, make up the repertory. All these scenes have an iconographical distinctness which makes them easily recognizable even though they may be isolated and often without inscriptions. In the tablet, on the other hand, we observe that it was not always the most characteristic scene which was chosen.

[46] A. Arvanitoupoulos, "Μεγαρικοι σκυφοι φθιωτιδων θηβων," *Ephemeris archaeologike* (1910), 86 and pl. II, 2. C. Robert, *Archaeologische Hermeneutik* (Berlin, 1919), p. 368 and fig. 280; Müller, *Odyssee-Illustrationen*, p. 141.

We see a widespread use of conventional formulae, especially the scenes of conversation between persons sitting and standing. Such scenes lack a specific significance and would hardly be understandable if one found them isolated. Only their place in the sequence in the books of the Odyssey and the inscriptions, which are much needed and which actually do occur frequently as we know from other *Tabulae Iliacae*, help to identify the scenes. In such conventional compositions we miss the dramatic elements in which Odyssey illustrations in other monuments are so rich. Rather they are narrative and help to keep the story going. Furthermore, we can observe that in nearly all the panels of the tablet the very beginning of each book is represented, sometimes with one and sometimes with two scenes. This gives the impression that a larger cycle stands behind the tablet, a monument which had each book fully illustrated and from which the relief sculptor nearly always chose the beginning scenes. This assumption receives support if we look at the Tabula Rondanini (Jahn H). Here the Circe adventure is depicted in three consecutive scenes, which clearly follow each other and illustrate a passage of about one hundred lines in Book X (278–388). If we assume that the whole book was illustrated with a similar richness of scenes, then we can expect about five or six times as many scenes for this book, as well as for all the others, the average length of which is between 500–600 lines each. Obviously, such an extensive cycle could never have originated in the *Tabulae Iliacae*. These look rather like abbreviated derivations. But in what medium *can* we assume such an extensive illustration of the Odyssey, in which each book had about 15–20 scenes, i.e., 400–500 scenes for the whole poem? In our opinion only one medium could comprise so many scenes: the illustrated papyrus roll. Here we may hark back to an idea originated by Otto Jahn and reiterated in various works by Carl Robert,[47] that the Hellenistic-Roman period possessed illustrated rolls with mythological subjects of which the *Tabulae Iliacae* are only abbreviated copies. But of all *Tabulae Iliacae* the Tommassetti tablet, with its conventional conversation scenes, brings out the narrative character of book illustration in a particularly clear manner.

It is true that classical Greek art does not entirely lack cyclic representations of the Odyssey, and it is the merit of G. W. Elderkin to have identified a series of six scenes of the various books of the Odyssey on an Etruscan stele at Bologna from the fifth century B.C.[48]

The comparison between this early cycle and that of the tablet in each case shows an entirely different relationship between the pictorial representation on the one hand and the epic text on the other. The stele depicts single figures with attributes which are characterized in such a way that each panel, reduced to a nearly symbolic representation, stands for a whole episode or even a whole book. The Tommassetti tablet, on the other hand, shows narrative scenes precisely illustrating certain lines with a much closer dependence on the text. Therefore we are inclined to attribute this new conception to a direct influence of illuminated rolls on this monument.

An exception on the tablet—it hardly needs to be pointed out—is the central panel with Poseidon. Such a decorative Poseidon on a dolphin-like sea monster could have existed in practically any medium and does not need to be connected with an illustrated roll. The present study, concerned as it is with the interpretation of the Tommassetti tablet, cannot, however, go any further into the more general problems of the illustrated roll in classical antiquity. The discussion of the physical structure of illustrated books must be reserved for a later study in which it can be more fully developed. Here it is sufficient to point out the unique importance of the Tommassetti tablet as the only surviving *Tabula* with an extensive cycle of the Odyssey.

---

[47] C. Robert, "Maskengruppen," *Archaeologische Zeitung*, 36 (1878), 24; alluded to in idem, *Homerische Becher* ("50. Berliner Winkelmannsprogramm" [Berlin, 1890]), and clearly discussed in idem, "Homerische Becher mit Illustrationen zu Euripides' 'Phoinissen'," *Jahrbuch des kaiserliche deutschen archäologischen Instituts*, 23 (1908), 193. Furthermore idem, *Oidipus* (Berlin, 1915), p. 451, and at various places in idem, *Die antiken Sarkophag-Reliefs* (Berlin, 1890–1919), e.g., 3, Part III, p. 500, and in other publications by the same author [cf. footnote 9 and K. Weitzmann, *Illustrations in Roll and Codex* (2d ed.; Princeton, 1970), pp. 36 ff., 40 ff., and *passim*].

[48] G. W. Elderkin, "Archaeological Studies, Scenes from the Odyssey on an Etruscan Grave Stele," *American Journal of Archaeology*, 21 (1917), 400 and fig. 2.

The Greek Sources of Islamic Scientific Illustrations

MANY years ago, while studying the Greek sources of the iconography of some Bactrian silver vessels,[1] I had the pleasure of frequently discussing with Professor Ernst Herzfeld the relation between Hellenic and oriental art, and at that time I was deeply impressed not only by his profound knowledge of Greek archeology but also by his sympathetic approach to the various problems of the contribution of the Greek to the oriental world from the Hellenistic period on. Thus, I feel that to honor the memory of the great scholar I can do no better than to choose for the present volume a subject which once more deals with the influence of the Greek tradition upon the Orient. This time the material is chosen from Byzantine and Islamic book illumination.

Quite a few of the earliest preserved Islamic manuscripts with illustrations consist of scientific treatises, of which three are, for various reasons, particularly well known: (1) the *Automata* of al-Jazari in the library of Hagia Sophia in Istanbul, (2) the *Materia Medica* in the Top Kapu Saray in Istanbul (both badly mutilated, their best miniatures having been cut out and dispersed), and (3) the *Theriaca* manuscript in Vienna, attributed to Galen. Generally it has been assumed that not only the text of these three treatises but also their pictures are in various degrees dependent on

Reprinted with permission from *Archaeologica Orientalia in Memoriam Ernst Herzfeld* (Locust Valley, New York: J. Augustin, 1952), pp. 244–66.
[1] K. Weitzmann, "Three 'Bactrian' Silver Vessels with Illustrations from Euripides," *Art Bulletin*, 25 (1943), 289 ff.

Greek sources. But while a great deal has been written about the miniatures of these three manuscripts and their position in Islamic art, little has been said so far about the nature of the Greek sources from which they stem, although it must be obvious that the degree of inventiveness of the Islamic artists and their ability to transform a Greek model can be properly evaluated only if we have as clear as possible a picture of the character of the illustrated Greek texts. In the present study we have refrained from touching on any of the problems of Islamic miniature painting proper, such as questions of style or locality. Instead we shall focus our attention on defining more precisely than has been attempted hitherto the impact of Greek manuscripts on Islamic book painting, looking at this problem primarily from the point of view of a Byzantinist.

HERON AND AL-JAZARI

From the time of their origin to the present day mathematical texts as well as treatises on applied mathematics have always required diagrammatic drawings for the sake of greater clarity. With the beginning of Hellenism, and particularly in the learned atmosphere of Ptolemaic Alexandria, when the natural sciences became more specialized, the variety and intricacy of the explanatory drawings must have increased proportionally. In the library of the Museion which—if we may believe the ancient sources—had about half a million volumes in the third century B.C. at the time of the famous librarian Callimachus, a fair percentage of these papyrus scrolls must have consisted of illustrated scientific treatises. Although this library was destroyed in Caesar's time and perhaps even more material was lost through the natural decay of the perishable papyrus, a few such treatises have survived, primarily owing to the fact that they were copied in parchment codices.[2]

Thus, what is left to us of scientific treatises from Byzantine times is obviously only a fraction of the classical heritage, and while certain types of technical treatises are lost altogether, others fared better. The need to keep alive the science of war engines was perhaps responsible for the preservation of a whole body of poliorcetic treatises by such ancient writers as Philon of Byzantium, Biton, Heron of Alexandria, Athenaeus, Apollodorus of Damascus, the famous architect of Trajan's forum, Aelianus, and Asclepiodotus.[3] Among these, the most prolific and seemingly also the most popular writer was Heron of Alexandria; more illustrated technical treatises by Heron have survived than by any other writer.[4] From his two poliorcetic texts, the Βελοποιϊκά and the Χειροβαλίστρα, an illustration of the former from the eleventh-century manuscript in the Vatican (cod. gr. 1164 [=V]) may be

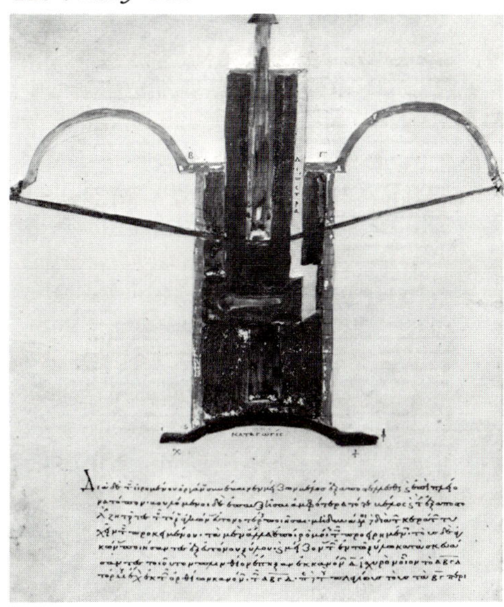

Fig. 5 *Vatican, Biblioteca. Cod. gr. 1164, fol. 110ᵛ. Belly Gun*

chosen as a typical example (Fig. 5).[5] It represents one of the comparatively simple war engines which the Greeks called γαστραφέτης, i.e., belly-gun, a strengthened crossbow pressed against the belly. The illustrator chose the most effective view, in this case a bird's-eye view, to demonstrate the details of the machinery. Moreover, the main part of the weapon is vastly broadened in the design in obvious disregard of natural proportions in order to show the details of the mechanism more clearly.[6] At the

---

[2] [Weitzmann returned to the consideration of illustrated technical treatises in the first chapter of *Ancient Book Illumination* (Cambridge, Mass., 1959); here also the older literature.]

[3] C. Wescher, *Poliorcétique des grecs* (Paris, 1867).

[4] There is a great deal of writing concerning when Heron lived; and the dates postulated vary between the third century B.C. and the second century A.D. Consult K. Tittel, "Heron" in *Paulys Real-Encyclopädie der classischen Altertumswissenschaft*, 8, cols. 992 ff.

[5] For Heron's *Belopoiika* in general consult Wescher, *Poliorcétique*, pp. 71 ff.; H. Diels and E. Schramm, "Herons Belopoiika," *Abhandlungen der Preussischen Akademie der Wissenshaften*, 1918. Here the parallel miniature in Paris (Bibliothèque Nationale, cod. gr. 2442 [=P] is reproduced, p. 9 and fig. 3.)

[6] Cf. the modernized drawing and the reconstructed weapon in Diels and Schramm, "Belopoiika," figs. 4 and 5a–b; see also R. Schneider, *Die antiken Geschütze der Saalburg* (Berlin, 1913), p. 24 and fig. 9.

same time the object is reduced to a two-dimensional plane typical of similar construction drawings in all poliorcetic treatises. Although our earliest examples do not go back beyond the eleventh century, there is no reason to believe that in these points the drawings deviate from the classical archetype.

Among the many treatises of Heron there was also one on *Mechanics* which, save for a few fragments, is lost in the original Greek but has come down to us in an Arabic translation made by a certain Costa ben Luca between A.D. 862 and 866. The title of this translation "About the Lifting of Heavy Objects," signifies the content of the treatise, which in three books deals with apparatus for the lifting of heavy weights.[7] As might be expected, the text is accompanied by much-needed drawings; of these we reproduce two from the manuscript in the University Library of Leiden (cod. 51 Fig. 6).[8] The upper one shows a tackle for lifting heavy stones, consisting of two supports with a crossbeam

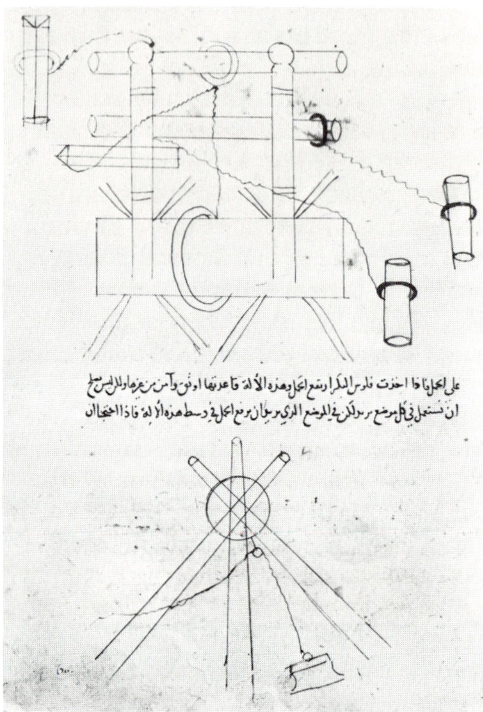

Fig. 6 *Leiden, Bibliotheek der Rijksuniversiteit. Cod. or. 51, p. 61. A Tackle and a Pulley*

to which is fastened a pulley; in order to anchor the two supports more firmly, ropes are pegged into the ground. It is interesting to see that the illustrator who made the drawings for Carra de Vaux's edition[9] redesigned the apparatus in modern perspective. This must have seemed perfectly justified in view of Carra de Vaux's judgment (shared also by Nix and Schmidt) that the drawings are very degenerate and lack perspective. It is, of course, true that the drawings

---

[7] First translated into French by Baron Carra de Vaux, "Les mécaniques ou l'élévateur de Héron d'Alexandrie," *Journal Asiatique*, 9th series, 1 (1893), 386–472; 2 (1893), 152–269, 420–514. Translated into German by L. Nix and edited together with W. Schmidt, *Herons von Alexandria Mechanik und Katoptrik* (Leipzig, 1900).

[8] P. de Jong and M. J. de Goeje, *Catalogus codicum orientalium Bibliothecae Academiae Lugduno Batavae*, 3 (Leiden, 1851–77), 46, where no date is suggested. Carra de Vaux, "Les mécaniques," I, 394 gives A.D. 1445 as the *terminus ante quem* on the basis of an entry from that year in the cover. Professor P. K. Hitti, who kindly gave me his opinion on the date based on paleographical grounds, proposed about the thirteenth century. [*Ancient Book Illumination*, pp. 8 ff.]

[9] "Les mécaniques," 2: 487–88 and figs. 50–51 correspond to those of our photographs. With few exceptions the same drawings were also used for the edition of Nix and Schmidt, *Mechanik und Katoptrik*, pp. xxxiii ff. and figs. 48–49.

of the Leiden codex, far removed as they are from the archetype, are quite crude and full of misunderstandings, but this is not to be confused with the issue of their total lack of perspective. We have observed above that the technically more accomplished poliorcetic drawings in the Greek Heron manuscript also lack perspective and that maximum clarity in every detail, even at the expense of foreshortening, is a consistent principle. Thus we have good reason to believe that the drawings in the Leiden manuscript—and this applies also to the lower apparatus on the page, where a pulley is hung up on three converging supports—basically reflect the Greek method of technical drawings.

It therefore seems to us quite certain that in the ninth-century translation by Costa ben Luca the drawings of a Greek model were copied with no change in the character of the design, and that all later Arabic copies are derived from them including, of course, those of the Leiden manuscript itself. Typical, moreover, of all classical drawings in technical treatises—and this too is reflected in the Byzantine copies of the *Belopoiika* and in the Arabic copy of the *Mechanics*—is the limitation to the absolutely necessary data, with no concession whatsoever to artistic embellishment.

In the tenth century the poliorcetic treatises of Heron were not only copied anew for the great encyclopedic enterprise of the emperor Constantine Porphyrogenitus but were also paraphrased by an anonymous writer who has usually been called Heron of Byzantium.[10] It is interesting to observe that the miniatures of this text, of which the eleventh-century Vatican codex gr. 1605 is the earliest example,[11] show in addition to the war engines themselves the warriors who manipulate them. Such "explanatory" figures are inventions of the Middle Byzantine period[12] and may have been inspired by Chronicle illustrations, where they are familiar types connected with representations of the siege of a city. Significantly, they do not occur in any of the text illustrations to the older Heron of Alexandria, which in this respect preserve the classical tradition in its purity, as is also the case in the Arabic manuscript of the *Mechanics* in Leiden.

By far the most popular and most frequently copied treatises of Heron are the Πνευματικά and the Αὐτοματοποιητική, which deal with the invention of ingenious contrivances in which the love of gadgetry, spreading since the Hellenistic period, found satisfaction.[13] In part they contain the same type of simple construction as that found in the manuscripts of the *Poliorcetica* and the *Mechanics*. For instance, there is the earliest copy of the *Pneumatica*, the codex gr. 516 in the Marciana in Venice, from

---

[10] R. Schneider, "Griechische Poliorketiker, II, Παραγγέλματα πολιορκητικά," *Abhandlungen der Akademie der Wissenschaften zu Göttingen*, N.F. 11 (1908–09), no. 1.

[11] C. Giannelli, *Codices Vaticani graeci, Codices 1485–1683* (Vatican, 1950), pp. 260 ff. [Weitzmann, *Ancient Book Illumination*, pp. 10 ff.]

[12] K. Weitzmann, *Illustrations in Roll and Codex: A Study of the Origin and Method of Text Illustration* (2d ed., Princeton, 1970), p. 167 and fig. 163.

[13] W. Schmidt, *Herons von Alexandria Druckwerke und Automatentheater. Heronis Alex. opera quae supersunt omnia*, 1 (Leipzig, 1899–1903).

about the thirteenth century,[14] a drawing of an automatically emptying siphon (Fig. 7, lower sketch), where within one schematically rendered vessel two different devices are drawn side by side. It seems only natural that the modern illustrator of Schmidt's edition would place each device in a vessel of its own and draw the latter more realistically,[15] but to the Byzantine draftsman, who in this point quite surely follows the classical model, the clear rendering of the mechanical device was more important than the shape of the vessel.

But where compressed air or water power is used for moving automatic human figures or for making them act with mechanical motions, the introduction of the human figure is, of course, a necessity. The same page of the Venetian manuscript shows a contrivance in which two figures pour water on a burning altar, the point being that with the expansion of heated air, pressure is put on a water tank and water driven through a pipe within the representation of the human figure performing the ritual. While the modern reconstruction drawing in Schmidt's edition[16] uses conventional types of a warrior and a woman of the fifth century B.C., i.e., of a period in which this type of automaton did not yet exist, the two figures of the Venetian codex, crude as they are, reflect the types

Fig. 7 *Venice, Marciana. Cod. gr. 516, fol. 171ʳ. Two Automata*

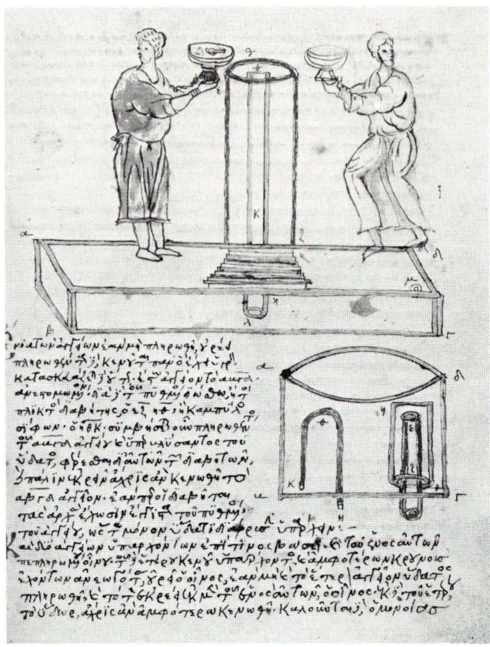

that must have existed in the archetype of Heron.

When al-Jazari wrote his "Book that Combines Theory and Practice Useful in the Craft of Ingenious Contrivances," in the very first year of the thirteenth century, each of the fifty constructions dealt with in six books had its own drawing. Some of the best of those preserved today come from a manuscript in the library of Hagia Sophia in Istanbul (cod. 3606), from which they were cut out and dispersed to many museums and collections.[17] One of the loose leaves of

---

[14] Ibid., suppl. to Vol. 1, 3 ff.; St. J. Gasiorowski, *Malarstwo Minjaturowe Grecko-Rzymskie* (Krakow, 1928), p. 173 and figs. 88–89. The manuscript has variously been dated between the twelfth and fifteenth centuries. In our opinion the thirteenth century is the earliest possible date.

[15] Schmidt, *Druckwerke und Automatentheater*, 1: 83 and figs. 14a–b.

[16] Ibid., pp. 80 ff. and fig. 13.

[17] The bibliography for this manuscript is conveniently gathered by K. Holter, *Die Islamischen Miniaturhandschriften vor 1350* (Leipzig, 1937), pp. 6 ff., no. 13, and supplemented by H. Buchthal, O. Kurz, and R. Ettinghausen, "Supplementary Notes to K. Holter's Check List of Illuminated Islamic Manuscripts before A.D. 1350," *Ars Islamica*, 7

Fig. 8 *Boston, Museum of Fine Arts. Detached leaf from Hagia Sophia Museum, cod. 3606. Automaton*

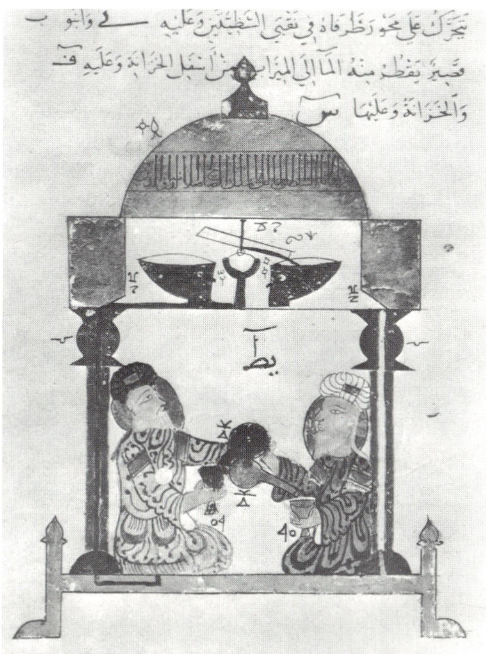

this manuscript, which Riefstahl proved is dated A.D. 1354,[18] is now in the Boston Museum of Fine Arts (Fig. 8)[19] and

represents two crouching men under a domed building; each pours a drink into the other's cup, which is then raised to the lips and emptied. The main mechanism is hidden under the cupola, and the water runs down through the columns and up again through the figures into flasks they hold.

That al-Jazari wrote his treatise under the inspiration of Greek models has generally been recognized, though there is some debate as to the precise texts he used. It has been argued that his source was not Heron of Alexandria or Philon of Byzantium, who certainly were not the only writers on automata although they were undoubtedly the most popular ones in the Middle Ages. Heron is a compiler rather than an inventor, and he himself used Archimedes, Ctesibius, and other writers whose treatises must have included similar types of illustrations. Whatever al-Jazari had before his eyes must have contained drawings like those of the Venetian manuscript of Heron (if it was not actually a Heron manuscript), i.e., illustrations of contrivances in which the automatic human figure played an important role. Of course, the two crouching figures in the Boston miniature are thoroughly Islamic in character. The point is that the Islamic illustrator did not have to invent this type of automata but was in a position to transform into his own style similar contrivances of Greek models and was perfectly capable of designing seated figures where the Greek model may have had standing ones.

DIOSCURIDES

About the time that Costa ben Luca translated Heron's *Mechanics* into Arabic,

---

(1940), 148 ff. In addition, consult the more recent remarks by E. Schroeder, *Persian Miniatures in the Fogg Museum of Art* (Cambridge, 1942), pp. 21 ff. and pl. I. [E. Grube, *Muslim Miniature Paintings* (catalogue of an exhibition, Asia House Gallery, New York [Venice, 1962]), pp. 10 ff. and pl. 9.]

[18] R. M. Riefstahl, "The Date and Provenance of the Automata Miniatures," *Art Bulletin*, XI (1929), 206 ff.

[19] Repeatedly reproduced: E. Blochet, "Peintures de manuscrits arabes à types byzantins," *Revue Archéologique*, 4th ser., 9 (1907), 211 and fig. 9; F. R. Martin (ed.), *Meisterwerke Muhammedanischer Kunst in München* (Munich, 1910), I, pl. 3; G. Marteau and H. Vever, *Miniatures persanes* (Paris, 1913), pl. XXXIX; A. K. Coomaraswamy, "The Treatise of al-Jazari on Automata," *Communications to the Trustees of the Boston Museum of Fine Arts*, 6 (1924), p. 14 and pl. IV.

that is about the middle of the ninth century, one of the several translations into Arabic of the *Materia Medica* of Dioscurides, the main source of pharmaceutical knowledge during the Middle Ages, was made by Stephanos, son of Basilios, a Christian from Baghdad. Fortunately, we still possess two illustrated Greek codices of Dioscurides from the pre-iconoclastic period which are close enough to the classical archetype to reflect its original character. These are the so-called Anicia codex in Vienna (Nationalbibliothek, cod. med. gr. I) from the sixth century,[20] and another which formerly was also in Vienna but is now in Naples (Biblioteca Nazionale cod. olim Vienna suppl. gr. 28) of the seventh century.[21] Particularly in the former there is to be noticed the exclusive concern of the illustrator with the veracity of the outer appearance of the plants. In the Naples manuscript of the seventh century, however, and even more so in a Paris manuscript (Bibliothèque Nationale, cod. gr. 2179) from the ninth

century (Fig. 11),[22] the realistic element has been sacrificed in part in favor of a more simplifying and at the same time a more ornamentalizing tendency. But in the tenth century, as can be seen in an imperial manuscript now in the Morgan Library in New York (cod. 652) which most likely was made for Constantine Porphyrogenitus,[23] a serious and largely successful attempt was made to copy faithfully a good model of the quality of the Anicia codex. From a comparison of the picture of the caraway plant, the Greek καρώ[24] in the Anicia codex,[25] with the corresponding one in the Morgan codex (Fig. 9), we learn that in the latter manuscript the plant is reduced in size and instead of filling a full page has to share the surface area with a second

<hr>

[20] A. v. Premerstein, K. Wessely, and J. Mantuani, *Dioscurides, Codex Aniciae Julianae, picturis illustratis, nunc Vindobonensis Med. gr. 1, photopice editus* (Leiden, 1906); P. Buberl, *Die byzantinischen Handschriften*, 1 ("Beschreibendes Verzeichnis der illuminierten Handschriften in Österreich," Vol. VIII, Part IV [Leipzig, 1937]). [Weitzmann, *Ancient Book Illumination*, 12 ff., 15 ff., and *passim; Der Wiene Dioscurides* (Codex Vindobonensis Med. gr. 1) Introduction by H. Gerstinger (Graz, 1965)].

[21] Palaeographical Society (London), *Facsimiles of Manuscripts and Inscriptions*, 2d ser., 1 (London, 1884–94), pl. 45; Ch. Singer, "The Herbal in Antiquity," *Journal of Hellenic Studies*, 47 (1927), 24 and fig. 16.

[22] Ed. Bonnet, "Essai d'identification des plantes médicinales mentionnées par Dioscoride, d'après les peintures d'un manuscrit de la Bibliothèque Nationale de Paris (Ms. grec. 2179)," *Janus*, 8 (1903), 169 ff., 225 ff., 281 ff.; H. Omont, *Facsimilés des manuscrits grecs, latins et Français du Ve au XIVe siècle exposés dans le Galerie Mazarine* (Paris, [n.d.]), pl. VI; Singer, "Herbal in Antiquity," p. 27 and figs. 23 and 25–26; K. Weitzmann, *Die byzantinsche Buchmalerei des 9. und 10. Jahrhunderts* (Berlin, 1935), p. 82 (here further bibliography) and pl. LXXXVIII, no. 555–56; idem, *Roll and Codex*, p. 71 and fig. 57.

[23] Cf. facsimile of this manuscript: *Pedanii Dioscurides Anazarbaei de Materia Medica* (Paris, 1935); B. da Costa Greene and M. Harrsen, *The Pierpont Morgan Library. Exhibition of Illuminated Manuscripts held at the New York Public Library* (New York, 1933–34), p. 7, no. 12 and pl. XI; Weitzmann, *Byzantinische Buchmalerei*, p. 34 and pl. XLI, 231–33.

[24] M. Wellmann, *Pedanii Dioscuridis Anazarbei de Materia Medica*, 2 (Berlin, 1906), 70 (= Lib. iii, 57).

[25] Premerstein *et al.*, *Dioscurides*, pl. fol. 188[v].

plant and with a few lines of writing in between. Nevertheless, in his realistic approach the painter of the Morgan codex is much akin to his early predecessor, though his plants are slightly less refined in execution.

In many ways related to the Morgan Dioscurides is one of the finest Arabic copies we have today, the codex arab. 4947 in the Bibliothèque Nationale in Paris, which has been variously dated between the ninth and thirteenth century.[26] It is a codex consisting of thick leaves of parchment, a material which at some time must have been considered so precious that most of the margins are cut away save at those spots where the

plant pictures protrude into them (Fig. 10). The organization of the page, in which widely spaced text lines written in monumental script alternate with large plant pictures filling more or less the width of the writing column, is indeed very similar to that of the Morgan manuscript.[27] On the page here reproduced the upper plant is again the caraway. Though deviating somewhat more from the classical archetype than the corresponding miniature in the Morgan manuscript, it still retains the essential features, in spite of the fact that the Dioscurides text, as is repeatedly the case, has no detailed description of the plant's characteristics. There is a tendency to enlarge the umbels, from which the drug is procured, as being the most important part of the plant, even to the point of reducing the foliage. Moreover, a tendency toward stronger symmetry may be observed. These abstractions are only in their initial stages, however, and the illustrator of the Paris manuscript is, in good classical fashion, still primarily concerned with the scientific problem of achieving an effect as close as possible to nature, though he did not succeed to the same degree as his Greek colleague.

Of course, the Morgan manuscript cannot have been the direct model, if for no other reason than that both belong to different recensions, the Morgan manuscript to the alphabetical group, in which the plant following the caraway is the *cyperus*, and the Parisian to the non-alphabetical, according to which

---

[26] Ed. Bonnet, "Étude sur les figures de plantes et d'animaux peintes dans une version arabe, manuscrit de la matière médicale de Dioscuride," *Janus*, 14 (1909), 294 ff.; E. Blochet, *Les peintures des manuscrits orientaux de la Bibliothèque Nationale* (Paris, 1914–20), p. 5, n. I; idem, *Catalogue des manuscrits arabes des nouvelles acquisitions, Bibliothèque Nationale* (Paris, 1925), p. 44. Professor P. K. Hitti, who kindly gave me his opinion, dates the manuscript in the twelfth century at the earliest but more likely even in the thirteenth century on account of the profuse use of diacritical marks. The thirteenth-century date is shared by Bonnet, "Études sur les figures," whereas Blochet proposes the ninth/eleventh century. [More recently, B. Farés, "Un herbier arabe illustré du XIVe siécle," *Archaeologia Orientalia in Memoriam Ernst Herzfeld* (Locust Valley, N.Y., 1952), p. 87, dates it between the twelfth and thirteenth century. See also the study of the Arabic Dioscurides manuscripts by E. Grube, "Materialen zum Dioskurides Arabicus," *Aus der Welt der Islamischen Kunst* (Berlin, 1959), pp. 163 ff. and C. Dubler, *La "Materia Médica" de Dioscórides* (Barcelona, 1953–59), 2, "La version arabe."]

[27] The Arabic manuscript, measuring about 40 × 30 cm., even slightly surpasses in size the Greek one in the Morgan Library; both are quite monumental.

Fig. 9 *New York, Morgan Library. Cod. 652, fol. 77ᵛ. Caraway and Cyperus*

Fig. 10 *Paris, Bibliothèque Nationale. Cod. arab. 4947, fol. 63ᵛ. Caraway and Dill*

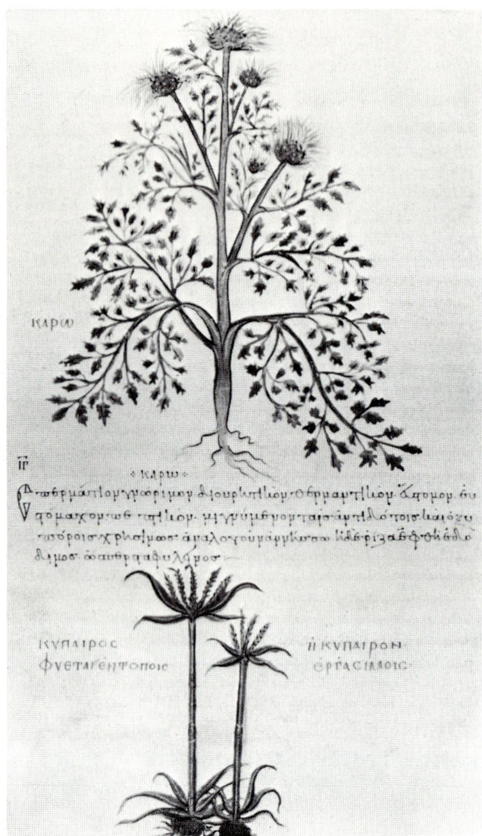

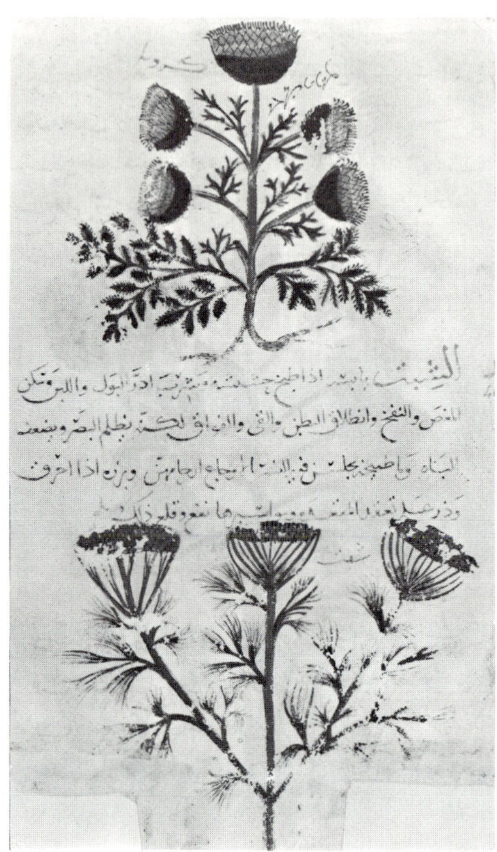

the next plant is the dill, the Greek ἄνηθον. In the former manuscript the drawing of this plant is lost, but it is preserved in the Anicia codex,[28] and compared with it the relationship in size between the umbel and the feathery leaves is even more unbalanced in the Arabic copy, where the netlike ramifications of the leaves are replaced by a simplified type of bundle-like leaves which have lost their resemblance to nature. Even so, among the illustrated Arabic Dioscurides manuscripts that we

are acquainted with this Parisian copy is the closest to a good Greek model.

A desire to enrich the plant pictures artistically beyond the pure scientific requirements led to the addition of human figures who in one way or another busy themselves with a plant. As far as we know, from surveying Arabic Dioscurides manuscripts, the earliest one with a human figure is a manuscript in the University Library of Leiden (cod. or. 289) dated February, A.D. 1083.[29] In the first book Dioscurides

[28] Premerstein *et al.*, *Dioscurides*, pl. fol. 27ᵛ.

[29] De Jong and de Goeje, *Catalogus codicum*

describes, among others, the plant μαλάβαθρον[30] as a leaf floating on the surface of water and being without a root. It is collected, dried, and lined up on a linen thread, and its usefulness is manifold, including the power of healing an inflammation of the eye. The miniature which accompanies this passage (Fig. 11) depicts a pond with leaflike plants floating on its surface, while a man seated at the shore with his legs dangling in the water holds a specimen up close to his eyes. Probably the painter in this manner wanted to indicate that the plant is good, as the text says, for inflammation of the eyes. It must be noticed that this picture is the only one in the manuscript (at least in its present state of preservation) to contain a human figure, a fact which seems to point to an experimental stage in the development of a new type of scientific illustration. Was this a fancy of the illustrator of the Leiden codex or, perhaps, of its Arabic model, or was there a precedent for it in earlier Greek Dioscurides manuscripts? Intrinsic probability as well as the fragmentary, extant material supports the latter alternative.

The first appearance of such complementary human figures associated with plants is, as far as our knowledge goes, in the above-mentioned Greek Dioscurides in Paris (cod. gr. 2179) which on

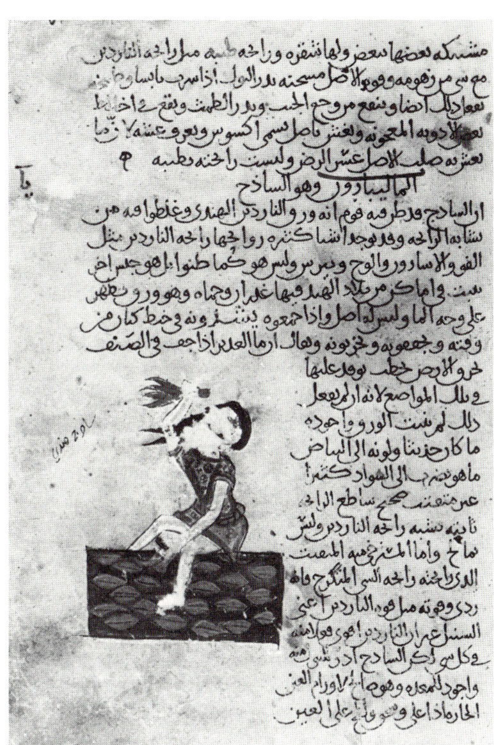

Fig. 11 *Leiden, Bibliotheek der Rijksuniversiteit. Cod. or. 289, fol. 8ʳ. Malabathrum*

paleographical grounds has always been dated in the ninth century.[31] Only a relatively small section of this manuscript, the first seven folios to be precise, has six plants with human figures added to them, but this does not give a true picture of the manuscript in its original state, since at the beginning alone 121 folios are missing which quite possibly

orientalium, 3, 227; M. Meyerhof, "Die Materia Medica des Dioskurides bei den Arabern," *Quellen und Studien zur Geschichte der Naturwissenschaft und der Medizin*, 3 (1933), 81 [289]. The colophon adds that the manuscript was copied from an older one of the year A.D. 900. [Grube, *Dioskuridis*, p. 169 and *passim*.]

[30] Wellmann, *Dioscuridis de Materia Medica*, 16 (= Lib. i. 12).

[31] Cf. n. 22. B. de Montfaucon, *Palaeographia Graeca* (Paris, 1708), pp. 256 ff., proposed an Egyptian origin, an opinion which has been accepted by many scholars either as proof or at least as a working hypothesis. Indeed Egypt seems more likely than the localization to southern Italy which we once proposed (*Byzantinische Buchmalerei*, p. 82) but no longer maintain.

contained representations of other plants with human figures. There is, for example, the plant μυὸς ὦτα (Fig. 12), the root of which is described as having healing power against αἰγίλωψ, i.e., an ulcer in the eye.[32] In order to demonstrate this property, a youth clad in a golden tunic is represented in a reclining attitude, holding one hand in a protective gesture before his eye. Though the type is somewhat different from the one in the Arabic miniature in Leiden, both have a very similar function in explaining the pharmaceutical usefulness of the plant. Significantly, the Anicia codex in Vienna and the Neapolitanus are both devoid of any such human figures, and the fact that in the Greek miniature discussed above the scale of the human figure is incongruous to that of the plant serves, on the formalistic side, to strengthen our thesis that human figures like these were added later. In all likelihood we are dealing with a phenomenon not older than the post-iconoclastic period.

In another Greek Dioscurides manuscript in the Lavra monastery on Mount Athos (cod. Ω75), from about the twelfth century,[33] there are about 25 plant pictures with human figures which are distributed over the whole text. Here we find a new category of supplementary human figure: instead of demonstrating

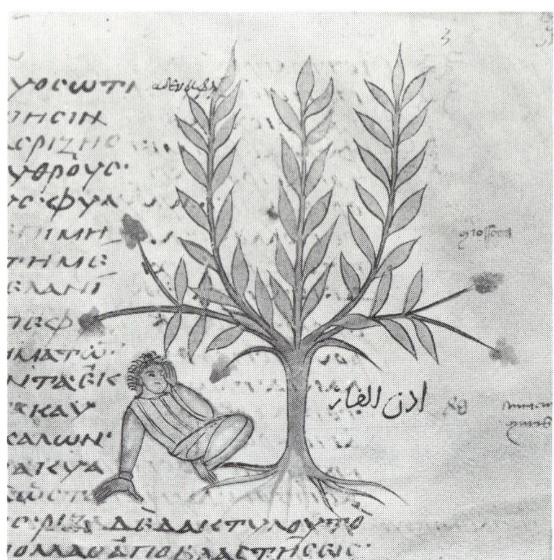

Fig. 12 *Paris, Bibliothèque Nationale. Cod. gr. 2179, fol.5ʳ. Mouse-ear*

by an indicative gesture his affliction, for which the plant provides a cure, he is concerned with collecting those parts of the plants from which the drugs are prepared. There is, for instance, the plant βούνιον[34] of which Dioscurides says that the seeds, both moist and dry, as as well as the juice gained from the roots, stalks, and leaves, are used for healing purposes. The picture, in which this plant takes a central place between two others (Fig. 13), shows in a kneeling position, a bearded man wearing a pointed hat who holds one stalk with his left hand and with the right either cuts the stalk or draws sap from the plant. To the third plant of the same interstice, called βούφθαλμος, is added a youth clad only in a loincloth who swings an ax in order to cut a stalk. In both instances the text does not explicitly say that branches have to be cut, but it is obvious that the painter used this motif in several instances in order to demonstrate how the

---

[32] Wellmann, *Dioscurides de Materia Medica,* 1: 253 (= Lib. ii, 183).
[33] H. Brockhaus, *Die Kunst in den Athosklöstern* (Leipzig, 1891), pp. 168 and 232, n. 1; Spyridon and S. Eustratiades, *Catalogue of the Greek Manuscripts in the Library of the Laura on Mount Athos* (Cambridge, Mass., 1925), p. 343; Weitzmann, *Roll and Codex,* p. 86 and fig. 68.

[34] Wellmann, *Dioscurides de Materia Medica,* 2: 271 (= Lib. iv. 123).

Fig. 13 *Mount Athos, Lavra. Cod. Ω75, fol. 35ᵛ. Bunium and Ox-eye*

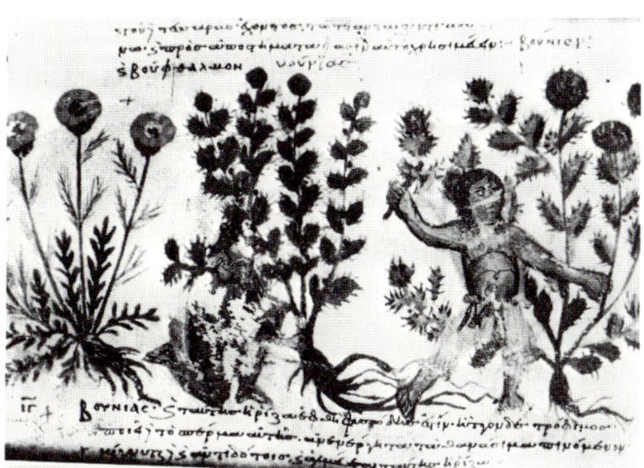

Fig. 14 *Mashhad, Shrine Museum. Dioscurides Manuscript. Balsam Tree*

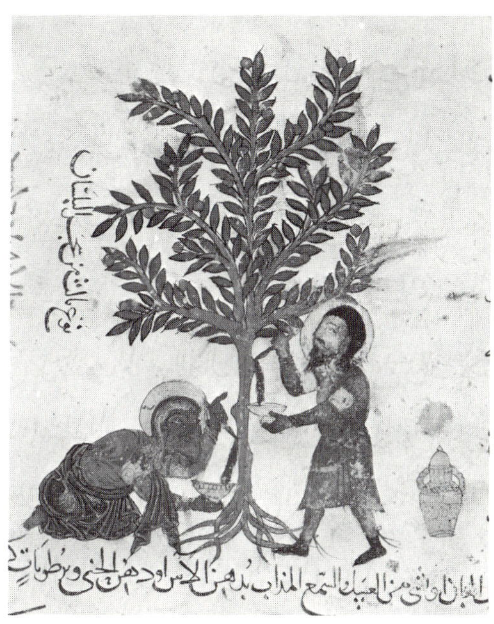

useful parts of the plant are gathered. There is still another type of figure, most often female, who is busy picking flowers or fruit and collecting them in baskets.[35]

Human figures similarly occupied with a plant can also be found in Arabic Dioscurides manuscripts. A Mesopotamian manuscript of the end of the twelfth century in the Shrine Museum of Mashhad[36] includes four with human figures, among its almost 700 plant pictures, one of which represents a balsam tree (Fig. 14). According to the text, this tree is to be tapped by iron nails, and in agreement with this statement the illustrator depicts two men extracting the health-giving sap in the prescribed manner. The kneeling man at the left, who is dressed, as Florence Day rightly

observed, in the conventional costume of classical antiquity, may well be compared with the kneeling man in the Lavra miniature. Once more the Byzantine parallel suggests that the Arab illustrator was inspired by a Greek model, though at the same time he showed himself capable of recasting it in his own outspoken style.

It is in the light of the Greek and Arabic Dioscurides manuscripts mentioned so far that we have to re-evaluate the historical position of those dispersed miniatures which were cut from the manuscript in the Top Kapu Saray in Istanbul (cod. 3703. olim Saraglio Ahmed III, 2147). The manuscript contains Books IV and V of the *Materia Medica* and is dated in the year 1224.[37] Nearly

---

[35] Weitzmann, *Roll and Codex*, fig. 68.

[36] L. Binyon, J. V. S. Wilkinson, and B. Gray, *Persian Miniature Painting* (London, 1933), p. 25, no. 6 and pl. V A–B; M. Bahrami, *Iranian Art* (catalogue of an exhibition in the Metropolitan Museum [New York, 1949]), p. 22, no. 51. The best writing on this manuscript so far is by F. E. Day, "Mesopotamian Manuscripts of Dioscurides," *Bulletin of the Metropolitan Museum of Art*, N.S. 8 (1949–50), 274 ff. with four figures from this manuscript.

[37] The very extensive bibliography on this manuscript and its cut-out miniatures up to 1940 is conveniently gathered in Holter,

all the dispersed miniatures have been traced to the present owners and at least are reassembled photographically in Buchthal's very useful article,[38] which provides a new basis for future studies of this manuscript so important for the history of early Arabic book illumination. In these miniatures we observe the use of the human figure in connection with plants on a much vaster scale than in any previously discussed herbal. At the same time, it must have become obvious, after our acquaintance with the Leiden and Mashhad manuscripts (Figs. 11 and 14), that we are not dealing in the Dioscurides of 1224 with a new phenomenon, as many of the previous writers on this subject would have us believe.[39] No doubt these famous cut-out miniatures surpass their predecessors, in Byzantine and Arabic manuscripts alike, in ornamental splendor and richness of narrative detail. Even so, the figurative compositions here employed are limited to a rather few schemes nearly all of which can be traced to Greek sources, although it should not be over-

looked that the Arabic illustrator has considerable artistic power in transforming whatever the Greek model may have suggested to him into a thoroughly oriental style.

First of all, it must be pointed out that nearly all miniatures with human figures were cut out of the Istanbul manuscript and that in the original codex such miniatures formed the minority among the traditional simple plant pictures.[40] Where a deer biting a snake is introduced[41] without reference to the text as a foil for the plant called *cytisus*, we may recognize a group going back to a Greek *Physiologus* where the story of the deer's fight against the snake is told in detail and illustrated, as we know from the lost Smyrna *Physiologus*.[42] Actually, this very picture existed in classical animal treatises preceding the *Physiologus* and persisted long after in the medieval *Bestiaria*.[43] Moreover, there is a plant with a bull alongside it in the Lavra Dioscurides

---

Islamischen Miniaturhandschriften, pp. 11–12, no. 27, and in the supplement by Buchthal *et al.*, "Supplementary Notes," pp. 151–52, no. 27 [Grube, *Dioskurides*, pp. 171 ff.].

[38] H. Buchthal, "Early Islamic Miniatures from Baghdād," *Journal of the Walters Art Gallery*, 5 (1942), 19 ff. [Grube, *Dioskurides*, pp. 172 ff.; idem, *Miniature Paintings*, pp. 2 ff. and pls. 1–3; and R. Ettinghausen, *Arab Painting* (Geneva, 1962), pp. 87 ff. and color plates.]

[39] Buchthal, "Early Islamic Miniatures." p. 32. Buchthal is not unaware of the earlier Greek parallels but, not having had available the full evidence from the Greek as well as the earlier Arabic Dioscurides manuscripts, he was not yet in a position to establish as close a connection as we believe did exist.

[40] Ibid., figs. 5, 6, 9.

[41] Ibid., fig. 7. This miniature now belongs to the W. R. Nelson Gallery of Art in Kansas City. Cf. *Islamic Art. Selected Examples from the Loan Exhibition of Islamic Art at the Cleveland Museum of Art.* ([Cleveland], 1944), p. 5.

[42] J. Strzygowski, *Der Bilderkreis des griechischen Physiologus* ("Byzantinisches Archiv," 2 [Leipzig, 1899]), 37. [For a detailed study of this motif see R. Ettinghausen, "The Snake-Eating Stag in the East," *Late Classical and Mediaeval Studies in Honor of Albert Mathias Friend, Jr.* (Princeton, 1955), pp. 272 ff.]

[43] Weitzmann, *Roll and Codex*, p. 138 and figs. 120 and 122.

(fol. 8[v])[44] which shows that Greek Dioscurides manuscripts also possessed animals in addition to plants.

The picture of the man bitten by a mad dog,[45] demonstrates the affliction against which a certain herb is a useful remedy and belongs in the same category with those in the Greek and Arabic manuscripts (Figs. 11–12) which show a sick man afflicted by an inflammation of the eye. The doctor who cuts the stalk of the plant *helioscopius*[46] is involved in the same kind of occupation as those who cut stalks and draw the sap in the Lavra and Mashhad manuscripts (Figs. 13–14). Most numerous are the miniatures which demonstrate the preparation of the medicine by a physician, who is usually assisted by one or even two helpers or fellow physicians.[47] The most common procedure is the preparation of the ingredients in a vessel and the subsequent boiling of the mixed fluid in a kettle over a fire. Basically the same manipulations, though in a simpler form, are represented in the Dioscurides of the Morgan Library, which depicts the preparation of white oil (Fig. 126).[48]

The physician advising or treating a patient[49] so far has not been found in any Greek Dioscurides manuscript. But in the Middle Byzantine period, as exemplified by the tenth-century treatise on the dislocation of bones by Apollonius of Citium, now in Florence (Laurentian Library cod. Plut. LXXIV, 7), there still existed copies of ancient medical treatises where the treatment of a patient by a physician is depicted in a great variety of actions as required by the kind of illness.[50] From a medical treatise of this kind an illustrator of the Dioscurides could easily have taken over some such compositional scheme and adjusted it to the special needs of the botanical text. It remains a question whether this adaptation had already taken place, as seems possible, in a Greek Dioscurides now lost or as yet unknown, or whether it was an Arab illustrator who took this step for the first time.

A final group of pictures shows physicians assembled in a learned discussion.[51] One is immediately reminded of two frontispiece miniatures in the Anicia codex in Vienna (Fig. 137)[52] in each of which seven physicians are arranged in horseshoe form, not unlike the representations of the seven wise men one finds in Roman mosaics. The physicians in the Arabic miniatures who crouch on the ground and raise their hands in

[44] The meaning of this bull, however, is not quite clear since the animal is placed alongside plants which are not inscribed, and there is no text on this page.

[45] Buchthal, "Early Islamic Miniatures," fig. 30.

[46] Ibid., fig. 8.

[47] Ibid., figs. 1, 11–14, 16–21, 31.

[48] Morgan Library cod. 652, fol. 225[v]; Weitzmann, *Byzantinische Buchmalerei*, p. 34 and pl. XLI, no. 233 (here wrongly designated as fol. 235[v]).

[49] Buchthal, "Early Islamic Miniatures," figs. 4, 10, 15, 24, 26.

[50] H. Schöne, *Apollonius von Kitium* (Leipzig, 1896).

[51] Buchthal, "Early Islamic Miniatures," figs. 23, 27–29.

[52] Premerstein *et al.*, *Dioscurides*, pls. fols. 2[v] and 3[v]; Buberl, *Byzantinischen Handschriften*, 1, 14 ff. and pls. I–II.

gestures of dispute are comparable to some of the assembled physicians in the Ancia codex who sit on very low pieces of rock which give the impression of the bare ground rather than a bench or chair. It needed no great imagination on the part of the Arab artist to transform this posture into the cross-legged position typical in the Orient.

On the other hand, that an Arabic illustrator of a Dioscurides herbal, in certain instances, may have been able either to invent a new scene or to take over a compositional scheme from other Arabic manuscripts like the *Maqāmāt* of Harīri, as has repeatedly been suggested, by no means should be excluded as a possibility. It is even quite probable in the depiction of the boat on the river Gagos,[53] though less likely in that of the scene representing the slaughtering of a bull.[54] We have not been able to trace the latter motif in a Greek herbal or related scientific text, yet it is a motif so common in classical art that we should be surprised if it were invented by an Arabic artist rather than adapted from some Greek model. We must bear in mind the extremely fragmentary preservation of illustrated manuscripts, Greek and Arabic alike, in those centuries, and we have to realize that the chance of finding a Greek model for every single type of scientific Arabic miniature, even when such may have existed, is not great. On the other hand, we should like to reiterate that Greek scientific manuscripts, which formed the basis for Arabic ones, were enriched

in the Middle Byzantine period by figural representations on a scale much larger and with a much greater variety of motifs than has hitherto been realized and, therefore, the connection between Arabic and Middle Byzantine manuscripts is much closer than once was assumed. The next paragraph, we hope, will lend support to this contention.

Pseudo-Galen

The National Library of Vienna possesses an illustrated thirteenth-century manuscript which bears the signature A.F. 10 and deals with anti-dotes against poisonous snake bites.[55] This treatise on *Theriaca*, which is commonly quoted as being by Galen, is supposedly a commentary on Galen's *De Antidotis Lib. I* by the learned sixth-century Alexandrian scholar John the Grammarian, or Joannes Philoponos, as he is also called. Max Meyerhof has pointed out, however, that the text contains next to none of Galen's recipes and is in fact a more popular pseudo-scientific piece of writing unworthy of a great scholar like John the Grammarian.[56]

---

[53] Buchthal, "Early Islamic Miniatures," fig. 22.
[54] Ibid., fig. 25.

[55] For bibliography consult Holter, *Islamischen Miniaturhandschriften*, pp. 15–16, no. 37, and the supplement by Buchthal *et al.*, "Supplementary Notes," p. 154, no. 37. [See also O. Grabar, "Islamic Art and Byzantium," *Dumbarton Oaks Papers*, 18 (1964), 85 ff. and Ettinghausen, *Arab Painting*, p. 92 and plate on p. 91.]
[56] M. Meyerhof, "Joannes Grammatikos (Philoponos) von Alexandrien und die arabische Medizin," *Mitteilungen des deutschen Institut für ägyptische Altertumskunde in Kairo*, 2 (1931), 16 ff. Meyerhof analyzes the text of a sixteenth-century manuscript in Cairo rather than that of the Vienna Codex.

The Vienna codex was written, it has been generally assumed, around 1240 in Mosul or Aleppo and contains a number of miniatures[57] which resemble in more than one respect those of the Dioscurides manuscript of 1224.

Comparable in character to the pictures of the pure plants in herbals are four pages of the Vienna Galen which depict in strictly scientific fashion various types of poisonous snakes (Fig. 16).[58] The names of the snakes are sometimes corrupted and their coloring becomes rather abstract, so that identification from nature no longer is possible, and yet the artist's method of confining himself to a factual, full-length representation of the serpent without groundline or background still reveals the very essence of classical scientific illustration. A similar treatise on antidotes against snake bites by Nicander of Colophon, who in the second century B.C. wrote his Θηρίακα and Ἀλεξιφάρμακα, is preserved in a beautifully illustrated tenth-century manuscript in Paris (cod. suppl. gr. 247).[59] Individual snakes,

scorpions, and lizards whose bites are poisonous are depicted in quite the same manner as in the Pseudo-Galen, along with numerous pictures of plants which have a healing power against these bites. Moreover, the famous Vienna Dioscurides contains at the end a paraphrase of Nicander by a certain Eutecnius,[60] as does the Morgan Dioscurides (Fig. 15).[61] Both of these include the same simple serpent pictures (cf. Fig. 167) which surely must have existed in the Nicander archetype. Thus, as far as the serpent illustrations are concerned, the Vienna Pseudo-Galen stands in the direct line of the tradition of ancient scientific illustration.

Two miniatures[62] depict serpents attacking, in one case a youth and in another a decoy. In both cases the serpents themselves are killed. In the former instance (Fig. 18) the bitten youth kills the snake with a staff, and the episode takes place in a setting of laurel trees, the berries of which are used as a drug against snakebite. Such a scene has a function similar to those in the Dioscurides manuscripts where men cut branches, draw sap, and collect fruit. In both cases the human figures demonstrate the usefulness of the plant and in this sense can be termed "explanatory" figures. And just as the explanatory figures in the Dioscurides manuscripts turned out to be later additions, first

---

[57] Except for the three pages with snake pictures on folios 12ᵛ, 13ᵛ, and 14ʳ, the miniatures have been completely published by Holter, "Die Galen-Handschrift und die Makamen des Hariri der Wiener National-bibliothek," *Jahrbuch der Kunsthistorischen Sammlungen in Wien*, N.F. 11 (1937), 1 ff.

[58] Gasiorowski, *Malarstwo Minjaturowe*, p. 152 and pl. 70; Holter, "Galen-Handschrift," fig. 6. [A late twelfth-century Arabic *Theriaca* (Bibliothèque Nationale Cod. arabe 2964) was published shortly after Weitzmann's study appeared by B. Farés, *Le livre de la Thériaque* ("Art Islamique," 2, Cairo, 1953).]

[59] The illustrations of this codex are completely published in H. Omont, *Miniatures des plus anciens manuscrits grecs de la Bibliothèque Nationale* (2d ed.; Paris, 1929), p. 34

and plates LXV–LXXII. Cf. also Weitzmann, *Byzantinische Buchmalerei*, p. 33 (here fuller bibliography) and pl. XLI, no. 228.

[60] Premerstein *et al.*, *Dioscurides*, pls. fols. 393ʳ–437ᵛ.

[61] *De Materia Medica* (facsimile), fols. 338ʳ–360ᵛ and 375ʳ–384ᵛ.

[62] Holter, "Galen-Handschrift," figs. 1 and 7.

Fig. 15 *New York, Morgan Library. Cod. 652, fol. 346^v. Serpents*

Fig. 16 *Vienna, Nationalbibliothek. Cod. A.F. 10, fol. 13^v. Serpents*

Fig. 17 *Paris, Bibliothèque Nationale. Cod. suppl. gr. 247, fol. 6^r. Attacking Serpent*

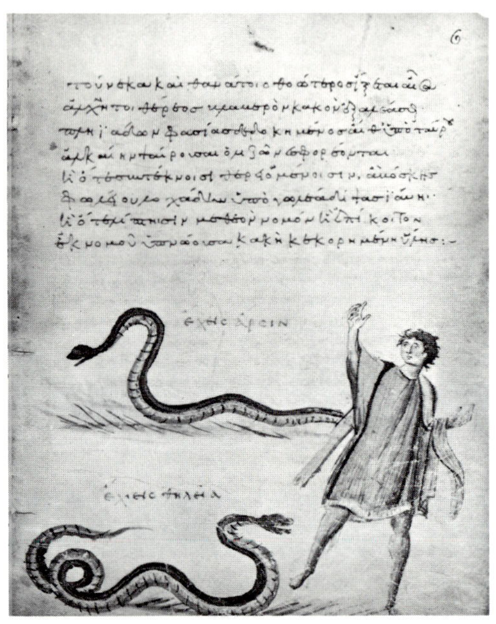

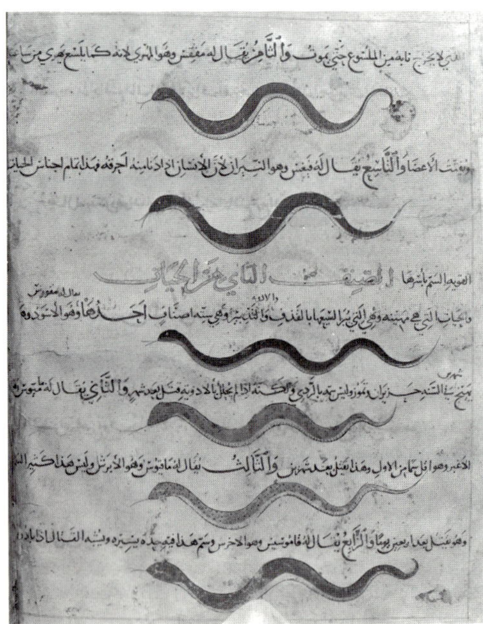

added in post-iconoclastic Greek and then in Arabic manuscripts, so can the same be demonstrated in the case of the *Theriaca* texts.

The Nicander manuscript in Paris, in addition to the illustrations of the serpents as such, possesses a few more elaborate pictures. In one of these a serpent is attacking a boy (Fig. 17)[63] who, unlike the one in the Pseudo-Galen miniature, is not counterattacking but fleeing. There are two reasons for our belief that the fleeing boy and others like him were later additions, most likely of the tenth century when the Paris copy was made. First, there are no human figures in the Nicander paraphrase of the Anicia codex of the sixth century and the Morgan manuscript of the tenth century. We do not know exactly when Eutecnius

---

[63] Omont, *Manuscrits grecs*, pl. LXV, no. 4.

Fig. 18 *Vienna, Nationalbibliothek. Cod. A.F. 10. fol. 2ᵛ. Killing of the Attacking Serpent*

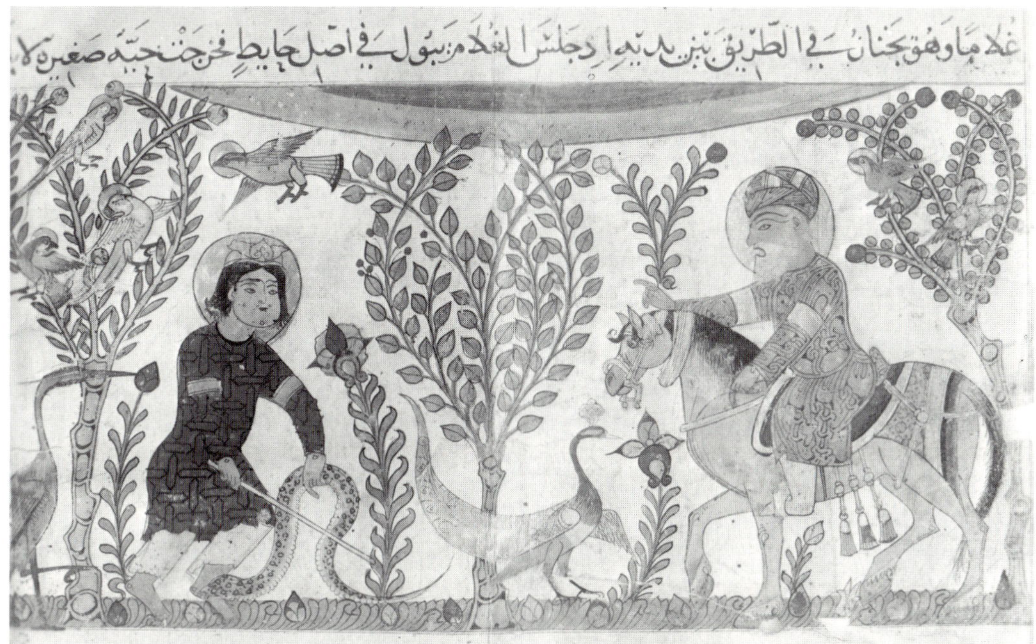

lived, but since he used Aelian's *Natura Animalium*[64] in another paraphrase we must conclude that he lived after the third century A.D. And since the first illustrator of this paraphrase surely used an illustrated Nicander as model, we can be quite sure that at that time, at least, no human figures were represented in the treatise. This is not surprising; indeed, it is in complete agreement with our concept of pure scientific illustrations in the classical period. Second, from the formalistic point of view it is quite apparent in the Nicander miniature described above that the attacking serpent has been moved toward the inner margin in order to provide space for the

human figure.[65]

The fact that in the Paris Nicander men are represented as fleeing but not as fighting back does not mean that the latter type could not have existed in Greek *Theriaca* manuscripts. We must bear in mind that the Paris manuscript is only an accidental survivor of what once was a widespread recension. The Vienna National Library possesses a richly illustrated thirteenth-century Latin compendium of medical treatises including the Pseudo-Apuleius herbal (cod. 93), where, for instance, above the plant *viperina* a youth is represented piercing an

---

[64] W. Schmid and O. Stählin, *Geschichte der griechischen Literatur*, 7, Part II, (7th ed.; Munich, 1929), 788.

[65] Weitzmann, *Roll and Codex*, p. 167 and fig. 162 where to insert the man stricken by a poisonous drink, two lizards had to be pushed aside and their tails turned up.

attacking serpent.[66] Neither the seventh-century Pseudo-Apuleius herbal in Leiden (University Library cod. Voss lat. qu. 9) with its excellent plant pictures,[67] nor any of the copies in the centuries immediately following have any such "explanatory" figure. In the Leiden manuscript (fol. 29[r]) we find, in the true classical tradition, the carefully designed plant *viperina* and underneath, as a separate item so to speak, the venomous serpent, but with no storytelling device connecting the two. Thus in Latin manuscripts we see quite clearly that figures of this kind are medieval additions dating from approximately the same period as that in which they became familiar in the East. The style of the miniatures in Vienna codex 93 is strongly Byzantinizing, and this suggests, as did the Arabic manuscripts we have discussed, that Greek manuscripts of the post-iconoclastic period were the source for the figures.

A third category of miniatures in the Pseudo-Galen depicts the physician and an assistant or fellow physician preparing the medicine, usually in a cauldron over a fire.[68] As in the Arabic Dioscurides

miniatures of the year 1224, where we have had occasion to point out Greek parallels, this is understandably the most popular subject among the scenic representations.

Of special interest are those illustrations of an episodic character which come closest to being, and in some cases quite surely are, ad hoc inventions. One of them[69] illustrates in vivid fashion the story of how the favorite slave of a king was poisoned with opium out of envy and locked up, only to be revived by the bite of a viper and rescued by country laborers. Another[70] depicts the physician Andromachos, who finds a serpent in a jar during a luncheon with his laborers, and a third (Fig. 20)[71] shows Tulunus, the brother of the physician Andromachos, bitten by a snake while peacefully sleeping in the shadow of a tree. Furthermore, the physician Andromachos on horseback advising the above-mentioned snake-killer (Fig. 18) is a narrative expansion of the scene beyond the mere explanatory figure of the victim. Precise parallels to these episodic miniatures can hardly be expected in Greek manuscripts, and here more than in any of the miniatures seen so far one can appreciate the individual capacity, perhaps not of the illustrator of the Vienna codex but of the one who first devised the pictures for these *Theriaca* stories.

Even so, the idea of enriching a *Theriaca* text with scenic illustrations, as in the case of all the other figurative additions, is basically not an Arabic but a Byzantine invention. There is, for instance, a passage which speaks about the African

[66] H. J. Hermann, *Die frühmittelalterlichen Handschriften des Abendlandes*, ("Beschreibendes Verzeichnis der illuminierten Handschriften in Österreich," 8, Part I [Leipzig, 1923]), 15 and fig. 8.

[67] Singer, "Herbal in Antiquity," pp. 43 ff. and figs. 28, 30, 44, 46; Gasiorowski, *Malarstwo Minjaturowe*, p. 68 and figs. 19–22; A. W. Byvanck, "Les principaux manuscrits à peintures . . . du Royaume des Pays-Bas," *Bulletin de la société Française de reproductions de manuscrits à peintures*, 15 (1931), p. 58 and pl. XVII (here further bibliography).

[68] Holter, "Galen-Handschrift," pl. II, no. 2 and figs. 2, 8, 9.

[69] Ibid., fig. 5.
[70] Ibid., fig. 3.
[71] Ibid., fig. 4.

Fig. 19 *Paris, Bibliothèque Nationale. Cod. suppl. gr. 247, fol. 12ʳ. Serpent Biting Canopus*
Fig. 20 *Vienna, Nationalbibliothek. Cod. A.F. 10, fol. 29ᵛ. Serpent Biting Tulunus*

serpent αἱμορροίς and how it once killed Canopus, the pilot of Menelaus, after his return from Troy. Helen in her wrath broke the neck of the serpent, yet Canopus died from the fatal bite. This passage is illustrated in a miniature (Fig. 19)[72] where the deadly serpent is depicted in the foreground attacking Canopus, who lies, seemingly already wounded, at the seashore, while Helen rushes toward him to help and an agitated warrior, probably Menelaus, stands in the center. Once more, it is characteristic that the previously mentioned paraphrase of of Eutecnius, in accordance with classical scientific illustration, has only a representation of the αἱμορροίς without the mythological episode,[73] although the text of the paraphrase likewise refers to the Canopus story. We have every reason to believe, therefore, that this and a few other scenes like it were inserted in the Middle Byzantine period like all the other figurative additions.

Of course, there is this difference: the Canopus miniature illustrates a myth and was surely not invented for the Nicander text, but made up originally for a mythographical text in which the story was told in more detail. This text may have been the handbook of the first-century writer Conon whom we know from the excerpt in the Μυριόβιβλον of Photios, the learned patriarch.[74] Yet a certain similarity in form and content between Canopus lying at the seashore

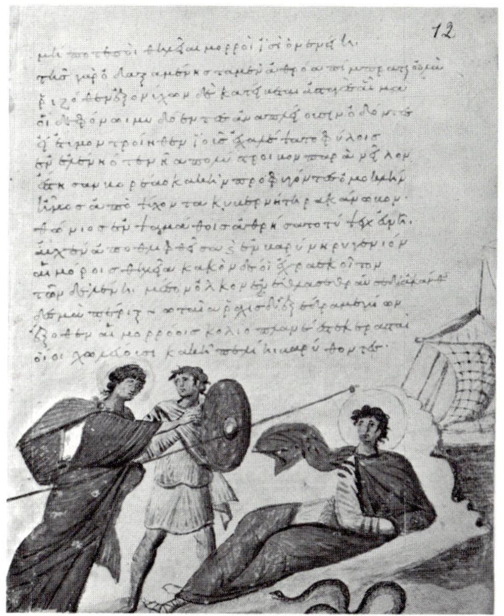

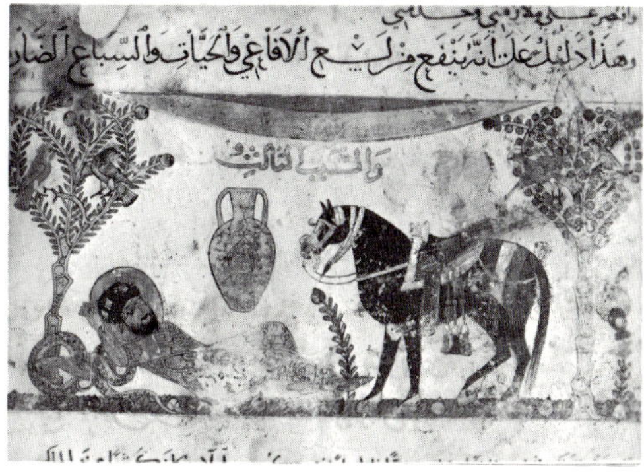

after having been bitten by a serpent and Tulunus lying in the shadow of the tree and meeting the same fate may not be entirely accidental, and although it was apparently not the former miniature itself which served as model but another like it, some such compositional theme of a Greek miniature may well have given the stimulus to the Arabic illustrator to enrich his *Theriaca* with storytelling pictures.

[72] Omont, *Manuscrits grecs*, pl. LXVI, no. 1.
[73] Premerstein *et al.*, *Dioscurides*, pl. fol. 404ʳ (only fragmentarily preserved). Morgan Library, cod. 652, fol. 348ʳ.
[74] K. Weitzmann, *Greek Mythology in Byzantine Art* (Princeton, 1951), pp. 195 ff.

The sumptuous dedication miniature, which depicts the prince for whom the present copy was made,[75] is of no concern to us in the present context, but the back of the page, which is decorated with a series of nine portraits of famous physicians who wrote about theriacs (Fig. 22),[76] has to be investigated for possible classical prototypes. These portraits are arranged three by three, beginning in the upper row with Andromachos, Herakleides, Philagrios, followed in the middle row by Proclos, Pythagoras, Marinos, and at the bottom by Andromachos the Younger, Magnos, and Galenos. Placed in medallions, they are represented as sages sitting in oriental fashion with crossed legs, each holding a book, some opened and some closed. The arrangement is in what must have seemed to the author to be a chronological sequence, ending with Galen, while in reality it is a pseudo-chronological order.[77] It is instructive to compare this miniature with the two assemblies of physicians in the Anicia codex (Fig. 137).[78] Galen appears in both sets, though in the latter he takes a more prominent position, being placed in the center on an easy chair. Buberl quite plausibly concluded from this fact that this picture of the Anicia codex was originally invented as a title miniature for some work of Galen rather than Dioscurides. But in spite of the fact that Galen appears in both sets, we do not

think the Arabic miniature is based on the same pictorial tradition as the Anicia codex. The latter, as has been pointed out repeatedly, is related in concept and composition to the ancient mosaics of the seven wise men, who are represented as a discussion group in a spatial setting. It is true that all spatial elements have been omitted in the Anicia miniature, but even so it is still apparent that the seven physicians have maintained a connection among themselves and thus still form an assembly. In the Arabic miniature, however, we have to do with medallion portraits which are arranged in a decorative system, and although the figures in the outer medallions are turning slightly inward, the miniature is conceived basically as a set of individual portraits and not as a group composition.

The medallion portrait has a long history not only in classical art in general but in classical book illumination in particular. This, of course, is not the place to survey the full evidence and it may suffice to quote two of the best-known examples. The early Virgil manuscript in the Vatican Library (cod. lat. 3225), to judge from an offset opposite the beginning of Book VII,[79] originally had a portrait of Virgil in medallion form in front of every book, and a Carolingian copy of a classical Agrimensores text in the Vatican (cod. Palat. lat. 1564 Fig. 88) has two emperor medallions on one page[80]

---

[75] Holter, "Galen-Handschrift," pl. I.
[76] Ibid., pl. IIA. Cf. also F. R. Martin, *The Miniature Painting and Painters of Persia, India, and Turkey* (London, 1912), p. 9 and pl. 14a; T. W. Arnold and A. Grohmann, *The Islamic Book* ([London], 1929), pl. 32.
[77] Meyerhof, "Joannes Grammatikos," p. 17.
[78] Cf. pp. 33–34 and note 52.

[79] *Fragmenta et picturae Vergiliana codicis Vaticani Latini* 3225 ("Codices e Vaticanis selecti," 1 [2d ed.; Rome, 1930]), pl. fol. 57ᵛ.
[80] E. H. Zimmermann, "Die Fuldaer Buchmalerei in Karolingischer und Ottonischer Zeit," *Kunstgeschichtliches Jahrbuch der K.k. Zentral-Kommission,* 4 (1910), 90 and pl. XIIa; A. Goldschmidt, *German Illumination,*

which look very much like an excerpt from a series. The best evidence, however, introduced here for the first time, is to be gathered from a Late Byzantine manuscript now in the Ambrosian Library in Milan (cod. E. 37. sup.) in which more than 60 medallion portraits of famous physicians are inserted in a text which in the catalogue[81] is described as: *Opus medicum regum philosophorum aliorumque illustrium virorum iconibus parum accurate depictus ornatum.*[82] Among these portraits, as is more or less to be expected, there is also one of Galen (Fig. 21) as a bearded man wearing fashionable robes and headdress. In spite of this contemporary costume, which may be attributed to the copyist's desire to modernize his model, there is good reason to believe that the whole series of portraits of famous physicians goes back, like the medical text itself, to a classical source, and that a classical manuscript of this type inspired the Arabic artist who first added to the Pseudo-Galen treatise a series of medallion portraits but placed them all together in front of the text instead of interspersing them throughout.

1 (Florence, 1928), pl. 16a; Gasiorowski, *Malarstwo Minjaturowe,* p. 76 and fig. 24.
[81] A. Martini and D. Bassi, *Catalogus codicum Graecorum Bibliothecae Ambrosianae,* 1 (Milan, 1906), 313 ff., no. 282. Here the manuscript is dated in the sixteenth century. [Weitzmann considers the question of the author portrait more fully in "Book Illustration of the Fourth Century: Tradition and Innovation," *Akten des VII. Internationalen Kongresses für Christliche Archäologie, Trier, 1965,* (Rome, 1969) pp. 271 ff., reprinted herewith, pp. 113 ff.]
[82] There is no printed edition of this text quoted in the catalogue.

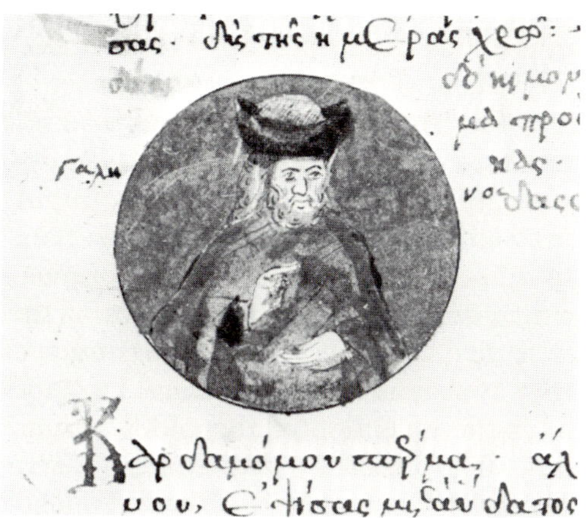

Fig. 21 *Milan, Ambrosiana. Cod. E. 37 suppl., fol. 82^r. Galen*
Fig. 22 *Vienna, Nationalbibliothek. Cod. A.F. 10, fol. 1^v. Portraits of Physicians*

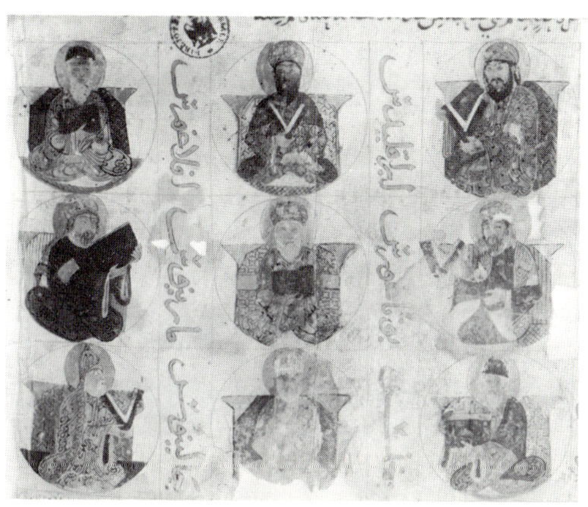

One cannot speak about a series of portraits of famous men in a classical text without touching upon the much-disputed problem of the original system of illustration in Varro's *Hebdomades,* which as we know were illustrated with 700 portraits of famous men, Greek and Latin. Many scholars have argued[83] that

[83] Most recently: A. von Salis, "Imagines Illustrium," in *Eumusia: Festschrift für Ernst Howald* (Zurich, 1947), pp. 11 ff.

the system of illustration of the Varro is reflected in the two pictures of assembled physicians in the Anicia codex, not so much for formal reasons as for the simple fact that in both instances the portraits were grouped by sevens. Yet the grouping in assembly fashion, in our opinion, seems to reflect rather a monumental composition, comparable to the mosaics of the wise men mentioned earlier, inasmuch as they appear as full-page miniatures only after the invention of the codex around A.D. 100,[84] i.e., after the lifetime of Varro. From the formal point of view the medallion portrait seems to us particularly well suited to such an enormous enterprise as the depiction of 700 portraits, in which the facial features must have been the most important element, and where the association of an individual portrait with an explanatory text underneath within the limits of normal writing columns is in agreement with what we know of the picture arrangement in papyrus rolls.[85] Thus we come to the conclusion that the medallion portraits in the Arabic Pseudo-Galen not only reflect an ancient type of serial portrait, but that it is worth considering whether they might not descend ultimately from Varro's *Hebdomades* or one of the similar collections of *Imagines Illustrium* which began to be popular in the sphere of Hellenistic poetry of Alexandria.

SUMMARY

In this brief sketch, of course, it could not be our aim to present a comprehensive picture of the Greek influence upon early Arabic miniature painting. There are other Arabic scientific treatises whose connection with the Greek sources has already been pointed out, while in other cases further investigation, we feel sure, would throw more light on this problem. Buchthal, for example,[86] has demonstrated the close relation between the illustrations of a *Kitāb al-Baiṭarah* manuscript in the Egyptian Library in Cairo, which dates from A.D. 1209 and deals with the *Healing of Sick Horses*, and those of a fourteenth-century Greek manuscript in Paris (Bibliothèque Nationale, cod. gr. 2244), which contains Hierocles' treatise on the *Care of Horses*. Moreover, no detailed study has been made, so far as our knowledge goes, of the Greek sources of the constellation pictures in Al-Sūfi's treatise on this subject,[87] and it still remains to be investigated whether, and if so to what degree, the illustrations of the Fables of Bidpai rest on Byzantine animal treatises such as the Physiologus and others. Yet, we hope that a sufficient number of instances has been discussed in this sketch in order to permit a few generalizing conclusions.[88]

[84] Weitzmann, *Roll and Codex*, p. 70.
[85] Ibid., pp. 69 ff. and especially fig. 60.

[86] Buchthal, "Early Islamic Miniatures," pp. 19 ff. and figs. 2 and 3. [Cf. Weitzmann, *Ancient Book Illumination*, pp. 116 ff.]
[87] [Such a study was published subsequently: E. Wellesz, "An Early Al-Ṣūfī Manuscript in the Bodleian Library in Oxford: A Study in Islamic Constellation Images," *Ars Orientalis*, 3 (1959), 1 ff., and idem, "Islamic Astronomical Imagery: Classical and Bedouin Tradition," *Oriental Art*, 10 (1964), 84 ff.]
[88] [For recent evaluations of Byzantine influence in Islamic art see Ettinghausen, *Arab Painting*, especially "Byzantine Art in Islamic Garb," and O. Grabar, "Islamic Art and Byzantium."]

Most essential has seemed to us the realization that even in Greek illuminations we have to distinguish between two types of scientific illustrations: (1) the pure type which confines itself as closely as possible to a diagrammatic image, and (2) the expanded type which came into being by adding human figures of different kinds for various purposes. The first category corresponds to the classical concept of science, while the second is a later creation and does not become discernible to us before the ninth century. This second type, however, never completely replaces the first and older one, and both exist side by side during the later Middle Ages.

Within the Arabic scientific treatises we find the same two categories. Manuscripts like the *Mechanics* of Heron in Leiden (Fig. 6), the *Automata* of al-Jazari (Fig. 8), and the Dioscurides in Paris (Bibliothèque Nationale, cod. arab. 4947, Fig. 10) belong to the first, whereas the Dioscurides miniatures of 1224 and those of the Pseudo-Galen manuscript in Vienna (Figs. 18, 20 and 22) are the most outspoken representatives of the second. Moreover, it could be demonstrated that the addition of figurative elements is not due to the caprice of some Arabic illustrators of the early thirteenth century, but that in Greek as well as in Arabic manuscripts it is the result of a lengthy process in which manuscripts like the Dioscurides in Leiden (Fig. 11) and the one in Mashhad (Fig. 14) form intermediary steps. It is thus apparent that Arab illustrators were exposed to Byzantine influences not only in the stage of the first reception from the Greek but long thereafter, since they adapt step by step the innovations which in the Greek

manuscripts developed only gradually.

As time goes on we can observe, as is only natural, that the Arabic illustrator becomes increasingly independent of his Greek models, first in the realm of style and later, and no less evidently, in the realm of iconography. Perhaps the lack of a long tradition in figure painting is one of the reasons that the Arabic illustrator is less inhibited in inventing new figures and compositions alongside those he copied from Greek models. The Middle Byzantine artist, on the other hand, depends not only on contemporary Byzantine manuscripts as inspiration for his figurative additions but still has available as a second source, classical literary texts. A case in point is the Nicander miniature (Fig. 19) in which a mythological scene is added to the depiction of a specific poisonous serpent, and elsewhere[89] we have shown the incorporation of a whole series of mythological scenes into the manuscript of the *Cynegetica* of Pseudo-Oppian (cod. Marcianus gr. 479 in Venice), a didactic poem on the various techniques of hunting. In the Nicander as well as in the Pseudo-Oppian the source for these additions was a mythographical handbook, a source which was available to Byzantine artists of the tenth century but which, as far as our knowledge goes, seems nowhere reflected in the early Arabic manuscripts known today.

A similar development in the illustration of scientific treatises can also be observed in western Europe. A Latin Dioscurides in Munich (State Library cod. lat. 337) of the tenth century[90]

---

[89] Weitzmann, *Greek Mythology*, pp. 93 ff.
[90] Idem., *Roll and Codex*, p. 135 and fig. 116.

depicts, together with some plants, animals and human figures which did not exist in earlier Greek Dioscurides manuscripts on which this Latin copy rests. Moreover, these explanatory figures are so placed in the margins that on the basis of formal considerations it becomes quite clear that they are attached to plants which originally were conceived without them. Later the additional elements in Latin manuscripts likewise increase in scope and variety as they did in Greek and Arabic ones. The thirteenth century medical compendium in Vienna (cod. 93), whose pseudo-Apuleius herbal and similar treatises are prolifically illustrated with human figures and whole scenes, is one of the most striking examples.[91]

It must have become obvious by now, as far as the insertion of human figures and scenes into scientific illustrations is concerned, that we are dealing with a general medieval principle. The basic difference, to state this once more with emphasis, is not between Greek and Arabic manuscripts but between classical on the one hand and medieval on the other, no matter what the language. It is in agreement with the highly developed concept of pure science in the Greek world that the illustrations of scientific texts should also be restricted to the clearest and most economical depiction of a given object. It is also well known that, after the great writers of the second century, such as Galen and Ptolemy, had summed up the scientific knowledge of the classical world in handbook fashion, for centuries to come the Middle Ages was content to draw from the classical heritage with hardly any new observations from nature. A more popular type of writing began to develop in which anecdotes, fables, superstitions, moralizing precepts, and so on, penetrated into and often obscured the scientific nucleus. In this process the strict division between scientific and literary writing which had prevailed in the classical world was abandoned more and more. The addition of explanatory and episodic scenes expresses in visual form a similar desire, namely, to enrich strictly scientific pictures by elements which also signify either a didactic purpose or a mere tale-telling intention. Whatever the urge may have been, the result is always the same: to draw scientific images into a more humanizing realm.

---

[91] For a treatment of similar problems in Western scientific treatises of the subsequent centuries we refer to the excellent study by Otto Pächt, "Early Italian Nature Studies and the Early Calendar Landscape," *Journal of the Warburg and Courtauld Institutes*, 13 (1950), 13 ff.

A LECTURE, first delivered in the spring of 1947 on the occasion of the bicentennial anniversary of the founding of Princeton University and given again at the second congress of German art historians at Munich in 1949, with only a few changes and additions, forms the substance of this survey. The purpose of the lecture was to acquaint a wider audience with a research project launched twenty years earlier by the Department of Art and Archaeology of Princeton University: a corpus of the illustrated Greek manuscripts of the Old Testament, the so-called Septuagint.[1] Concerned with a project which is under way, this paper naturally places more emphasis on questions of method and guiding principles than on final results. Consequently, I have limited myself to making clear, by means of a few selected examples, what the specific problems of Septuagint illustrations are and which methods of dealing with these problems lead to answers.

Translated and reprinted, with permission, from "Die Illustration der Septuaginta," *Münchner Jahrbuch der bildenden Kunst*, 3/4 (1952/53), 96–120.

[1] *The Illustrations in the Manuscripts of the Septuagint*, E. T. De Wald, A. M. Friend, Jr., and K. Weitzmann (eds.). It is estimated that the corpus will comprise six volumes: 1, *Octateuch;* 2, *Historical Books;* 3, *Psalms and Odes;* 4, *The Book of Job and the Wisdom Books;* 5, *Prophets;* 6, *History of the Illustration of the Old Testament*. Two volumes have appeared: E. T. De Wald, *Vaticanus graecus 1927* (3, part 1 [Princeton, 1941]) and E. T. De Wald, *Vaticanus graecus 752* (3, part 2 [Princeton, 1942]). Both manuscripts are unique among the Psalters. The next volume to appear will be the Octateuchs.

THE NARRATIVE METHOD

Early Christian art has essentially two methods of expressing content in pictorial form: the *symbolic,* which we know primarily through catacomb frescoes and reliefs of sarcophagi, and the *narrative,* found chiefly in extensive cycles of book illustrations. All indications suggest that the narrative method, which is by nature the most literal pictorial rendering of any given text, was invented for the illustration of books. Of the various branches of art, it is in the illustrated book that picture and text are most closely associated. In creating the illustrations, the artist has the written word constantly before his eyes and can check the iconographic precision of his representation against it. Also, during the writing of a column of text, the transcription could easily be interrupted for the intercalation of a picture. A number of richly illustrated texts exist in which almost every column of writing has one or even several scenes, so that at times the total number of miniatures runs up into the hundreds. No other art form compares to the illustrated book in the extent and richness of of its pictorial content.[2]

The earliest illustrated Septuagint manuscript which we have today is a fifth or sixth century Book of Genesis in London (British Museum, Cotton, Otho B. VI), once owned by Sir Robert Cotton and generally known today as the Cotton Genesis. Unfortunately this manuscript was burned in 1731, and all that we have today are the half-charred

[2] For the nature and origin of the "cyclic method" see Weitzmann, *Illustrations in Roll and Codex: A Study of the Origin and Method of Text Illustration* (2d ed. Princeton, 1970), pp. 17 ff. and *passim*.

parchment remains;[3] but these fragments are numerous enough to permit a reconstruction, in its essential features, of the entire picture cycle. Three of the remaining fragments represent Noah's ark (Fig. 23–25); and an engraving made shortly after the manuscript was destroyed records a fourth fragment, now lost, which contained two additional scenes of Noah's adventure (Fig. 26).[4] Furthermore, a collation of the manuscript[5] made before the fire proves that

[3] Here, as in the following notes, only a selected bibliography is given. *Vetusta Monumenta Rerum Britannicarum*, 1 (London, 1747), pls. LXVII–LXVIII; C. Tischendorf, *Monumenta sacra inedita*, 2 (nova collectio; Leipzig, 1857), 92 ff; R. Garrucci, *Storia dell'arte cristiana*, 3 (Prato, 1876), pls. 124–25; F. W. Gotch, *A Supplement to Tischendorf's Reliquiae ex incendio ereptae codicis celeberrimi Cottoniani* (London, 1881); J. J. Tikkanen, "Die Genesismosaiken von S. Marco in Venedig und ihr Verhältnis zu den Miniaturen der Cottonbibel," *Acta Societatis Scientiarum Fennicae*, 17 (1889), 99 ff.; O. M. Dalton, *Byzantine Art and Archaeology* (Oxford, 1911), p. 446 and figs. 263–64; W. R. Lethaby, "The Painted Book of Genesis in the British Museum," *Archaeological Journal*, 69 (1912), 88 ff. and pls. I–II; ibid., 70 (1913), 162; A. Rahlfs, *Verzeichnis der griechischen Handschriften des Alten Testamentes* (Berlin, 1914), p. 107. [Weitzmann, "Observations on the Cotton Genesis Fragments," *Late Classical and Mediaeval Studies in Honor of Albert Mathias Friend, Jr.* (Princeton, 1955), pp. 112 ff.; idem, "The Mosaics of San Marco and the Cotton Genesis," in *Venezia e l'Europa. Atti del XVIII Congresso internazionale di storia dell'arte* (Venice, 1956), pp. 152 ff.]

[4] *Vetusta Monumenta*, pl. LXVII, no. X.

[5] This collation was made by J. E. Grabe and later was published by H. Owen: *Collatio codicis Cottoniani Geneseos cum editione Romana, a viro clarissimo Joanne Ernesto Grabe jam olim facta, nunc demum summa cura edita ab Henrico Owen* (London, 1778).

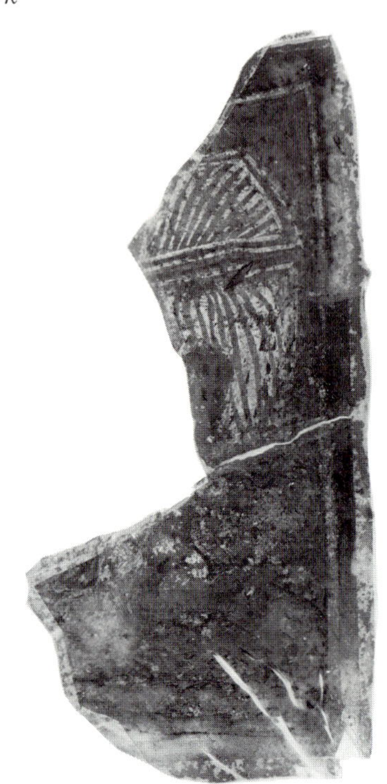

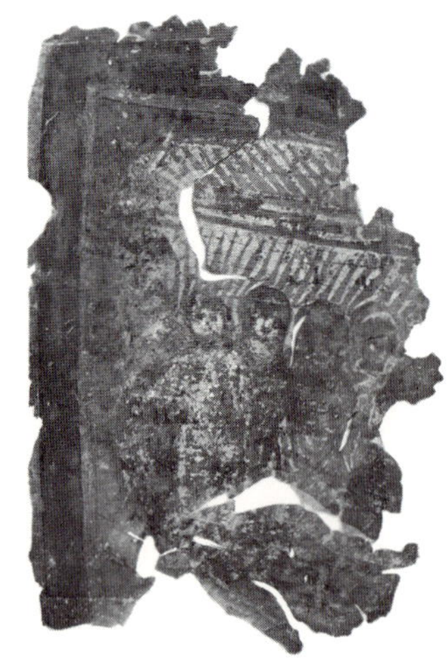

even prior to the destruction of the Cotton Genesis four folios which dealt with the history of Noah's ark were missing.

Fig. 25 *London, British Museum. Cod. Cotton Otho B.VI, fol. 12ᵛ. Noah Sends Forth Raven and Dove*

Fig. 26 *Engraving of lost miniature of the Cotton Genesis [After* Vetusta Monumenta Rerum Britannicarum]. *Noah Sends Forth Second Dove and Noah Sends Forth Third Dove.*

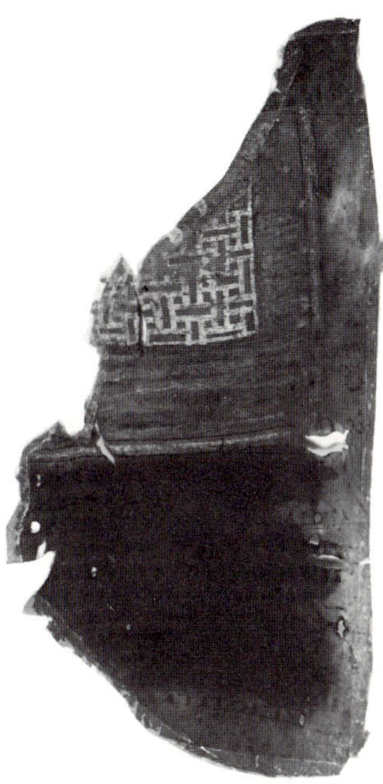

These missing leaves doubtlessly contained other miniatures of the episode of the ark. As Tikkanen has plainly proven, the Cotton manuscript itself, or a contemporary copy made directly from it, served as a model for the thirteenth-century mosaics in the narthex of San Marco in Venice. These mosaics include eight scenes of which only three agree with those preserved among the fragments of the manuscript; the other five must have been on the leaves cut out of the manuscript before the fire. Therefore, an idea even of the scenes lost at an early date may be regained. With the aid of the ivory antependium in Salerno, which belongs to the same recension and which contributes yet another scene to the cycle, we learn that, originally, eleven scenes distributed on eight leaves of the Cotton Genesis had as their subject the story of Noah's ark.[6]

[6] (a) The building of the ark. On a missing leaf with the verses Gen. 6:16–22, but preserved in San Marco. For illustrations of the mosaics consult F. Ongania, *La basilica di S. Marco in Venezia* (Venice, 1880–93), pl. XVII, and S. Bettini, *Mosaici antichi di San Marco a Venezia* (Bergamo, 1944), pls. LVI–LVIII, LX–LXI. (b) God commands Noah to bring his family and the animals into the ark. Fol. 10ᵛ (Fig. 23). (c) Noah brings the birds into the ark. Recto of a missing leaf, but preserved in San Marco. (d) Noah brings the quadrupeds into the ark. Verso of the same leaf. (e) Noah brings his family into the ark. Fol. 11ʳ (Fig. 24) and also a mosaic in San Marco which agrees with the preserved portion of the miniature. (f) God closes the ark. Recto of a missing leaf, but preserved on the Salerno Antependium. Cf. A. Goldschmidt, *Die Elfenbeinskulpturen aus der Zeit der Karolingischen und Sächsischen Kaiser*, 4

The close succession of different phases of this Noah episode in the Cotton Genesis gives us an insight into the mentality of an early Christian illustrator who obviously intended not to omit a single detail of the story when he translated it into pictorial form. Such a dense picture cycle, registering every change in the situation with a separate picture, could be understood without turning to the text for further information about the subject. In this manner the illustration aimed at an effect comparable to that of filmstrip.

In subsequent centuries Christian art never again attempted to illustrate the Noah story in such detail. All later medieval manuscripts which include pictures of this episode present a drastically abbreviated form of the cycle. Naturally, this process of condensing holds true not only for the story of Noah but also for many other episodes in the Book of Genesis. Only one conclusion may be drawn from these facts: narrative illustration of the Bible did not begin with cycles of a limited number of scenes that later were gradually expanded; on the contrary, picture cycles of astounding wealth form the point of departure and these, in turn, were excerpted and shortened during the Middle Ages.

Nevertheless, miniature painting had one serious shortcoming. An illustrated book was not widely circulated, and hence few people had access to it. Because the Church realized the didactic value of Bible illustration and wanted to make it available to the broader masses of the faithful, illustrated Bible manuscripts were used as models for wall paintings and mosaics adorning the interiors of churches. We have already mentioned one example of this practice, namely the mosaics of the narthex of San Marco in Venice for which either the Cotton Genesis or a close contemporary copy was the model. Distributed over five domes and the contiguous lunettes and arches of the San Marco narthex are more than one hundred scenes from Genesis, one of the most extensive picture cycles ever executed in monumental painting. Nevertheless, this mosaic program, by comparison with the manuscript cycle on which it is based, is greatly condensed. The Cotton Genesis originally had about 330 miniatures,[7] which means that the mosaicist selected less than a third of the available scenes for the decoration of the narthex. Therefore, one should always be aware, when analyzing a monumental picture cycle of narrative character, that in most cases one is dealing with an epitome of an extensive miniature cycle. This holds true not only for monumental painting but also for the countless other forms of art which depend iconographically on miniature cycles, such as

---

(Berlin, 1914–26), 38 and pl. XLIII, no. 126, 11. (g) The flood. On the verso of the same leaf, but preserved in San Marco. (h) Noah sends forth a raven and the first dove. Fol. 12^v (Fig. 25) and preserved in San Marco. (i) Noah sends forth the second dove. The upper scene on one of the leaves copied in the *Vetusta Monumenta* (Fig. 26) and also preserved in San Marco. (j) Noah sends forth the third dove. Lower scene of the same folio (Fig. 26). (k) Noah leaves the ark. On a missing leaf and certainly a full-page miniature, also preserved in San Marco.

[7] When Grabe made his pre-fire collation, the manuscript had 250 miniatures; and at that time a whole series of leaves, which according to our calculations would have contained about 80 pictures, was already missing. Cf. Owen, *Collatio codicis Cottoniani.*

certain groups of frieze sarcophagi, silver plates, ivory plaques, and even textiles. Book illustration was the storehouse of iconography. Artists in all fields consulted and copied illustrated manuscripts whenever they sought an exact illustration of a given text; and it is scarcely an exaggeration to assert that, in the last analysis, each "narrative" cycle may be traced to an illustrated book. It is evident then, that the richly illustrated early Christian and medieval manuscript was a major if not, in fact, the principal form of narrative art.

THE BOOKS OF THE SEPTUAGINT

Considered from the literary point of view the Septuagint is not *one* book; rather it is a compendium or series of books, which, in turn, comprises groups. Consequently the first problem to be solved is this: did the illustration of the Greek Old Testament begin with a miniature cycle for the complete Septuagint, or were single books (or groups of texts belonging together) first illustrated as separate units? To answer this question we turn first to the sole preserved example of an illustrated Septuagint, the tenth-century Regina Bible (Vatican, cod. Reg. gr. 1) which once belonged to Queen Christina of Sweden. Although it is no longer a complete copy, since it contains only the books from Genesis through Psalms, certainly it originally included in a second volume the other books of the Septuagint and the New Testament in a third.[8] The lack

of any kind of compositional homogeneity is immediately noticeable in the illustrations of this manuscript. A picture such as the Anointment of David (Fig. 27) is a monumental composition with large-scale figures that move before a landscape background filled with antique architectural elements, whereas the Judith miniature (Fig. 28) reproduces several episodes arranged in narrow strips.

The principle of creating miniatures with large figures is not characteristic of illustrated copies of the four Books of Kings, so far as a generalization may be made from the one preserved example, Vatican codex gr. 333 (to be discussed below, p. 55 and Figs. 34 and 40). It is consistently applied, however, in the group of manuscripts identified by Tikkanen as the "Aristocratic Psalters."[9] All the details of the composition of the Anointment of David in the Regina codex, including the personification of *Metanoia* and the architectural background, agree with the corresponding miniature of the well-known Psalter in Paris (Bibliothèque Nationale, cod. gr. 139)[10] where, in con-

---

[8] *Miniature della Bibbia cod. Vat. Regina Gr. 1 e del Salterio cod. Vat. Palat. Gr. 381. Collez. Paleogr. Vat. Fasc. I* (Milan, 1905). Here the older literature. Weitzmann, *Die byzantinische Buchmalerei des IX. und X. Jahrhunderts*

(Berlin, 1935), pp. 40 ff. and pls. XLVI–XLVII. The author no longer maintains the view that the pictures in this manuscript come from western Asia Minor but accepts the generally held assumption that they were produced in Constantinople.

[9] J. J. Tikkanen, "Die Psalterillustration im Mittelalter," *Acta Societatis Scientiarum Fennicae*, 31, no. 5 (1903).

[10] H. Omont, *Miniatures des plus anciens manuscrits grecs de la Bibliothèque Nationale* (2d ed.; Paris, 1929), pl. III; H. Buchthal, *The Miniatures of the Paris Psalter* (London, 1938), pl. III. [Weitzmann, *Geistige Grundlagen und Wesen der Makedonischen Renaissance* (Cologne and Opladen, 1963), pp. 7 ff. and *passim*. Translated and reprinted herewith, pp. 176 ff. and *passim*.]

Fig. 27 *Vatican, Biblioteca. Cod. Reg. gr. 1, fol. 263ʳ. Anointment of David*

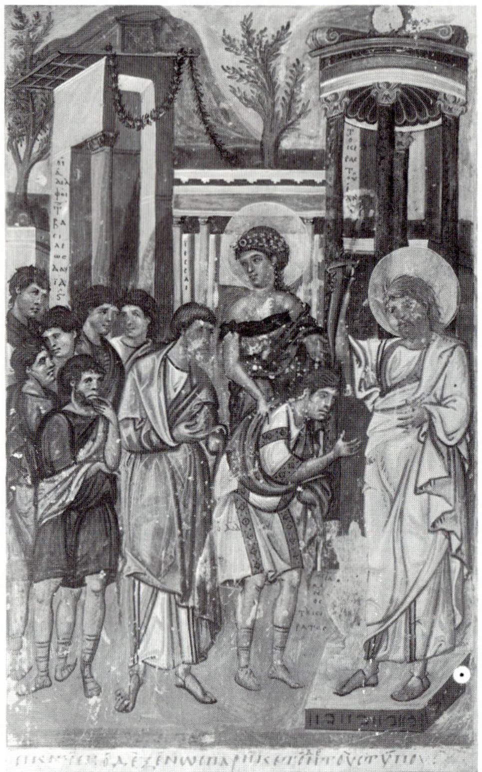

Fig. 28 *Vatican, Biblioteca. Cod. Reg. gr. 1, fol. 383ʳ. Judith and Holophernes*

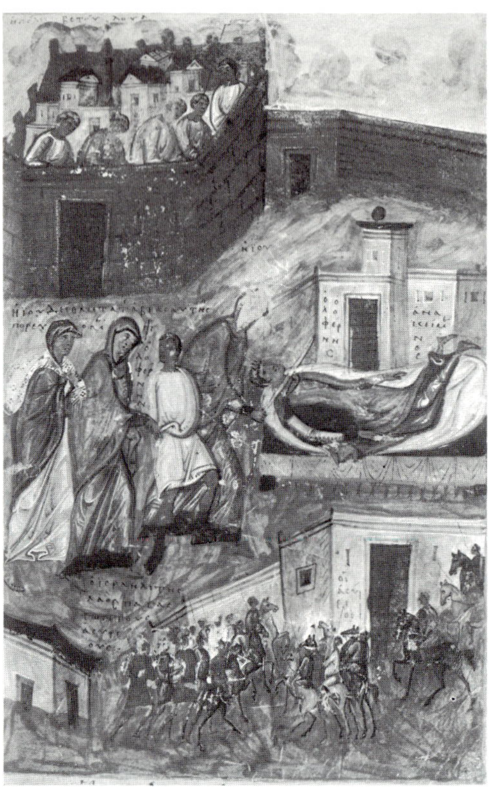

trast to the Book of Kings manuscript, large figures and accumulations of classical elements prevail. Furthermore, the scene of the Anointment of David is misplaced in the text of the Regina Bible; it appears before the Second Book of Kings even though the event is reported in the sixteenth chapter of the First Book. In the Vatican Book of Kings, on the other hand, it is properly placed.[11] In contrast to the Anointment of David, the Judith picture is an epitome of a narrative cycle. The artist of the Regina

[11] J. Lassus, "Les miniatures byzantines du Livre des Rois," *Mélanges d'archéologie et d'histoire*, 45 (1928), 57 and pl. II, no. 4.

codex selected and arranged in strips as many scenes from an extensive cycle as he could fit conveniently onto a full page. Thus, in these two pages we are dealing with the application of two very different principles of composition. Moreover, a fresh examination of the original manuscript has shown that initially it was not intended to have pictures, and that not until several decades after the completion of the text were the full-page pictures inserted as frontispieces for some, but not all, of the books. All this indicates that the Regina Bible is a compilation of the ninth/tenth century and that its heterogeneous manner of illustration does not depend on an earlier tradition of fully and consistently illustrated Septuagint manuscripts.

The Cotton manuscript in London, with its approximately 330 miniatures, had never included more than the text of Genesis; and it is self-evident that a complete Bible or even a complete Old Testament could never have been illustrated on this scale in a single volume. One of the most important conclusions to be drawn from a study of Old Testament miniatures is that in early Christian times extensive picture cycles were created only for single books of the Septuagint, and that consequently, in the search for origins, each cycle must be investigated separately. Therefore, to understand the structure and composition of the illustrated Septuaginta we must first identify the units that received separate illustration. Clearly, as in the Cotton manuscript, the Book of Genesis was one such unit. In it the miniatures are rather evenly distributed throughout the fifty chapters of text so that not only the more momentous events but also the less important ones are illustrated. For example, two birth scenes depicting the geneology recorded in the eleventh chapter are found on both recto and verso of folio 16 (Fig. 29);[12] and other such scenes preceded and followed these on leaves now lost. From the artistic point of view, this repetition of birth scenes permitted little variation in composition and resulted in a certain monotony; and thus, they provide a clear

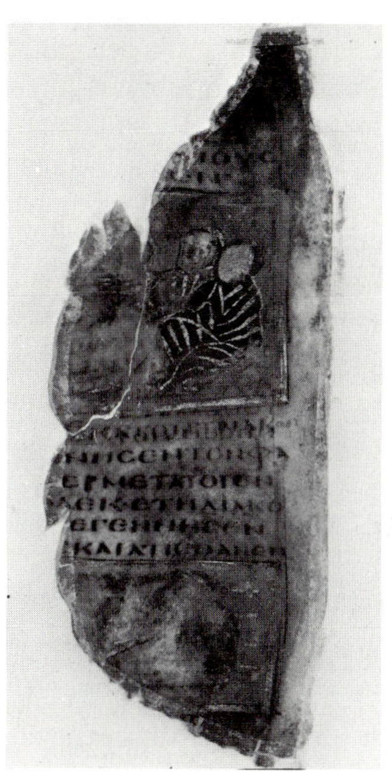

Fig. 29 *London, British Museum. Cod. Cotton Otho B.VI, fol. 16ᵛ Birth Scenes*

insight into the effort of the illustrator to be completely faithful to the text and not to omit any biblical event. It is not surprising that the mosaicists of San Marco omitted this entire series of birth scenes, which must have seemed to them of minor significance.

The well-known sixth-century Vienna Genesis (Nationalbibliothek, cod. theol. gr. 31) derives from an archetype which was illustrated perhaps even more sumptuously than the Cotton Genesis. Twenty-four purple leaves with 48 miniatures are preserved;[13] but it has been estimated

---

[12] Folio 16 has the births of Cainan and Shelah in two separate pictures on the recto and the births of Eber and Peleg on the verso. It is likely that the birth scenes shown on the following leaves, which are now missing, were similarly arranged.

[13] W. Ritter von Hartel and Fr. Wickhoff, *Die Wiener Genesis* (Vienna, 1895); H. Gerstinger, *Die Wiener Genesis* (Vienna, 1931); P. Buberl, *Die byzantinischen Handschriften* ("Beschreibendes Verzeichnis der illuminierten Handschriften in Österreich," 8, Part IV [Leipzig, 1937]), I, 67 ff. [For the recent views of

Fig. 30 *Reconstruction of the Model of the Vienna Genesis*

that the text originally had 96 leaves which, since a miniature per page is the rule throughout, must have contained 192 miniatures. Furthermore, each miniature, occupying the lower half of the page, usually contains several scenes. For instance, the following three scenes appear below the text of Genesis 22:15–19 on the recto of folio 6:[14]

1. The angel making a promise to Abraham after the sacrifice of Isaac.
2. Abraham returning to the young men waiting for him.
3. The servant at the well of Beersheba bringing Abraham the news of the offspring of his brother Nahor.

Dividing the page equally between the text and pictures necessitated a shortening of the text. In the present case the shortened text in the Vienna manuscript explains only the first two scenes; the text to the third scene has been omitted. Without doubt the miniature cycle originally must have been associated with a complete Septuagint text which explained each scene.

To furnish the idea of the appearance of the illustrated manuscript which served as a model for the Vienna Genesis, we have sketched a reconstruction in which each scene is placed as close as possible to the verse it illustrates

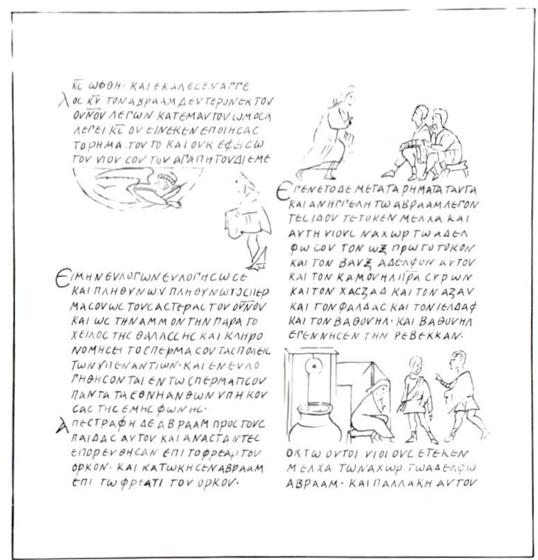

(Fig. 30).[15] This is the system of illustration found in the best manuscripts dependent on ancient models, such as the numerous Aratus manuscripts, the medieval copies of the comedies of Terence, and a great number of scholarly treatises.[16] Considering that, on the average, two or three scenes occupy the lower half of each page of the Vienna Genesis, the number of scenes in the archetype must have run up to four or five hundred. Once again it becomes evident that a complete Septuagint could never have been illustrated on this scale within the compass of a single volume or even of two or three volumes. In fact, in the case of the Vienna Genesis no one has ever contended that the original manuscript contained more than the Book of Genesis.

A Genesis cycle on the scale of the Cotton or of the Vienna manuscripts was

Weitzmann and other scholars on the Vienna Genesis consult H. Fillitz, "Die Wiener Genesis: Résumé der Diskussion," in *Akten zum VII. Internationalen Kongress für Frühmittelalterforschung* (Graz and Cologne, 1962), pp. 44 ff.]
[14] Hartel and Wickhoff, *Wiener Genesis*, p. 149 and pl. XI; Gerstinger, *Wiener Genesis*, p. 84 and pl. XI; Buberl, *Handschriften*, p. 94 and pl. XXVI, no. 11.

[15] Weitzmann, *Roll and Codex*, p. 89, fig. 73 and fig. D.
[16] Ibid., figs. 58–61. [Also, Weitzmann, *Ancient Book Illumination* (Cambridge, Mass., 1959).]

never repeated in the Middle Byzantine period, and it is altogether questionable that after Iconoclasm the Book of Genesis was again illustrated as a separate unit. A new text unit that arose in early Christian times but that seems to have become popular not before the Middle Byzantine period is the Octateuch, comprising the Five Books of Moses, the Book of Joshua, the Book of Judges, and the Book of Ruth.[17] Six illustrated copies of the Octateuch dating from the eleventh to the thirteenth centuries have come down to us.[18]

A typical miniature from one of these Octateuchs (Vatican, cod. gr. 746) is the portrayal of Joseph interpreting the dreams of the butler and the baker (Fig. 31). Joseph sits between the two men and is watched by the captain of the guard who remains outside the cellarlike, vaulted prison. The artist has shown the essential features of the story in the tersest manner; and in order to save

space, he has crowded-in the preceding scene of the accusation of Joseph by including Potiphar and his wife on the walls flanking the prison. This Vatican Octateuch—and the same holds true for the others, so far as their cycles are fully preserved—contains about 400 miniatures of which about 150 belong to the Book of Genesis. Although Genesis is the most richly illustrated book in the Octateuch, it contains fewer than half the number of the miniatures that once embellished the Cotton Genesis and the the archetype of the Vienna Genesis. Thus, we gain the impression that, when several books of the Septuagint were brought together to form a larger unit, the picture cycles of the separate books were abbreviated and condensed proportionately.

It is still too early to make final suggestions about the place of origin for the archetypes of the various Genesis recensions. The Octateuchs are all either in a Constantinopolitan style or in that of a center dependent on the eastern capital. Nevertheless, it would be premature to assume that Constantinople was the place of origin for the Octateuch recension. Excavations by Princeton University in a martyrium at Antioch-on-the-Orontes have unearthed incised marble plaques which date from about the fifth century. The iconography of one of these plaques, showing Joseph in prison (Fig. 32),[19] is so like that of the Octateuchs that a common source must be assumed. One need only compare the way in which the figures are grouped, especially the captain

[17] Fragments of a manuscript dating from the fourth/fifth century in Leiden, Paris, and Leningrad appear to be component parts of a very early Octateuch even though the preserved leaves contain not a single line of the Book of Ruth, a circumstance accounted for by the highly fragmentary state of the manuscript. Rahlfs, *Verzeichnis*, pp. 94–95.

[18] (a) Florence, Laurenziana, cod. Plut. V, 38 (eleventh century). (b) Vatican, cod. gr. 747 (eleventh century). (c) Istanbul, Seraglio, cod. 8 (twelfth century). Cf. T. Ouspensky, *L'octateuque de la Bibliothèque du Sérail à Constantinople* (Sofia, 1907). (d) Smyrna, Evangelical School, cod. A. I (twelfth century). This manuscript was destroyed in 1923 in the course of the Turkish–Greek war. Cf. D. C. Hesseling, *Miniatures de l'octateuque grec de Smyrne* ("Codices Graeci e Latini photographice depicti," suppl. VI [Leiden, 1909]). (e) Vatican, cod. gr. 746 (twelfth century). (f) Athos, Vatopedi, cod. 602 (thirteenth century).

[19] Weitzmann, "The Iconography of the Reliefs from the Martyrion," in *Antioch-on-the-Orontes*, 3, *The Excavations 1937–1939* (Princeton, 1941), p. 138 and pl. 20, no. 390.

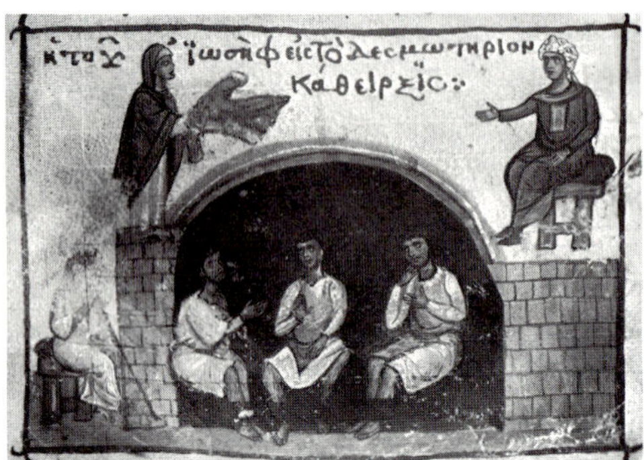

Fig. 31 *Vatican, Biblioteca. Cod. gr. 746, fol. 122[v]. Joseph in Prison*

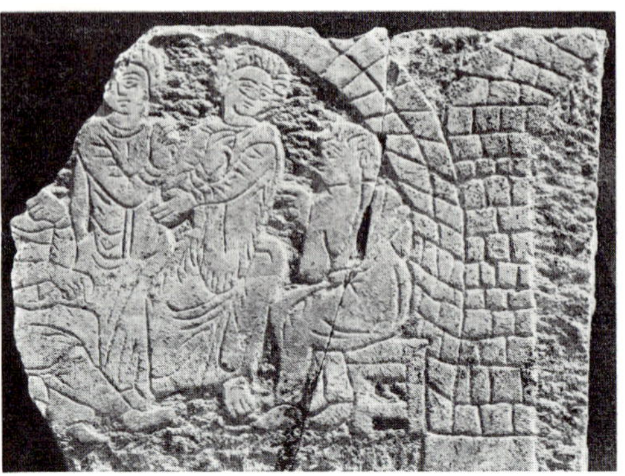

Fig. 32 *Princeton, University Art Museum. Relief from the Martyrium at Antioch. Joseph in Prison*

sitting in the foreground to the left, or note the cellarlike construction of the prison in each case. The plaque suggests Antioch as a possible center of origin for the illustration of the Octateuch, although admittedly it does not constitute definite proof, for the sculptor in Antioch may have used a model which originated elsewhere.[20]

The marble plaque from Antioch makes us conscious, once more, of how important it is, in connection with Septuagint illustration, to take into consideration material in other media derived from manuscripts. At the same time, copies of the Septuagint miniatures in nonbiblical manuscripts have an even more direct bearing on the problem. We must reckon with considerable migration of miniatures from one text to the other, so that, in the last analysis, the study of illustrated Septuagint manuscripts demands an examination of the entire Byzantine manuscript material.[21]

For example, the well-known ninth-century manuscript of the *Christian Topography* of Cosmas Indicopleustes (Vatican, cod. gr. 699)[22] has a whole series of Old Testament scenes which were certainly not created for the Cosmas text but derive instead from an Octateuch. One full-page miniature, fol. 59[r] (Fig. 33), depicts the Sacrifice of Isaac in three phases.[23] The first two have been conflated so that in one we see the two young men with the ass who accompany Abraham but not Abraham himself, and in the other Isaac is shown bringing the wood for the burnt offering, and again Abraham, who places the wood on his son's shoulders in the original version, has been omitted. Only the third and most important scene, the sacrifice, has been copied fully. The Octateuch in Istanbul (Seraglio, cod. 8) has the same three scenes as separate units,[24] each with the figure of Abraham,

[20] [Additional evidence in support of this hypothesis is presented by Weitzmann in "The Jephthah Panel in the Bema of the Church of St. Catherine's Monastery on Mount Sinai," *Dumbarton Oaks Papers*, 18 (1964), 350.]

[21] For a fuller discussion of the migration of miniatures see Weitzmann, *Roll and Codex*, pp. 130 ff.

[22] C. Stornajolo, *Le miniature della Topografia cristiana di Cosma Indicopleuste; codice vaticano greco 699* ("Codices e Vaticanis selecti," 10 [Milan, 1908]).

[23] Ibid., pl. 22. Weitzmann, *Roll and Codex*, p. 141 and fig. 129.

[24] Ouspensky, *Octateuque du Sérail*, p. 132 and pl. XIV, no. 47; Weitzmann, *Roll and Codex*, figs. 126–28.

Fig. 33 *Vatican, Biblioteca. Cod. gr. 699, fol. 59ʳ. Sacrifice of Isaac*

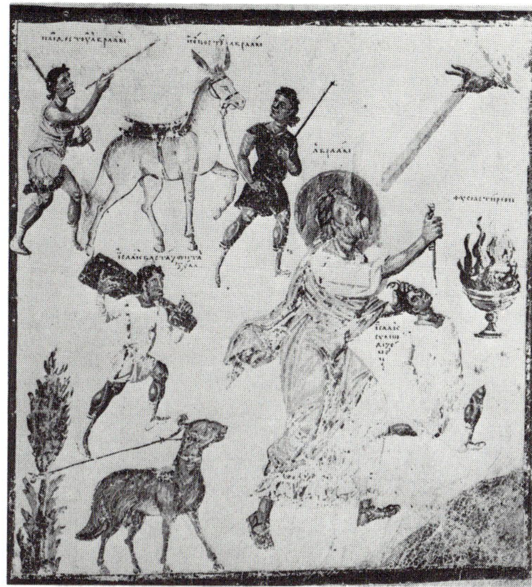

and the iconography is so similar that there can be no doubt that a manuscript of this recension, but of an earlier date (the Seraglio codex dates from the twelfth century), served as model for the Vatican Cosmas miniature.

This knowledge is of fundamental significance in judging the Cosmas miniatures. Since we know that Cosmas wrote his *Topography* in Alexandria,[25] most art historians have assumed that the miniatures in the Vatican manuscript are of Alexandrian origin. When one realizes that the Old Testament scenes in the Cosmas derive from an Octateuch, their Alexandrian origin becomes quite uncertain, for it is possible either that an Octateuch was imported to Alexandria or that the Old Testament scenes were added later, not necessarily in Alexandria. We have already given our reasons for

suggesting Antioch as a possible place of origin for the Octateuch recension.

The full significance of the principle of the migration of pictures from one text to another becomes still clearer when we study the next unit of text to have come down to us with a rich cycle of pictures: the four Books of Kings. Although the most important of the historical books of the Septuagint, only a single illustrated copy of Kings is preserved, the twelfth-century manuscript in the Vatican (cod. gr. 333).[26] Like that of the Octateuch, its picture cycle goes back to an early Christian archetype. The miniatures are distributed very unevenly: Book I by itself has more than 100 scenes, and Book II has about 40 scenes, among which are the three successive scenes of the sixth chapter shown here (Fig. 34):

1. David with the Ark of the Lord at the house of Obed-edom the Gittite.
2. David dancing in front of the ark (which is borne on an oxcart).
3. Michal scolding David because of his dance.

Book III has only nine miniatures, and Book IV finishes the volume with a single miniature of one of the most important events, the Ascension of Elijah. The manuscript obviously suggests that the illustrator began with a fully illustrated model, which he copied more or less picture for picture in Book I, but which he excerpted more and more in

[25] M. V. Anastos, "The Alexandrian Origin of the Christian Topography of Cosmas Indicopleustes," *Dumbarton Oaks Papers*, 3 (1946), 73 ff.

[26] Lassus, "Livre des Rois." See further Weitzmann "The Psalter Vatopedi 761—Its Place in the Aristocratic Psalter Recession," *The Journal of the Walters Art Gallery*, 10 (1947), 38 ff.

Fig. 34 *Vatican, Biblioteca. Cod. gr. 333, fol. 46ᵣ. David and the Ark of the Covenant*

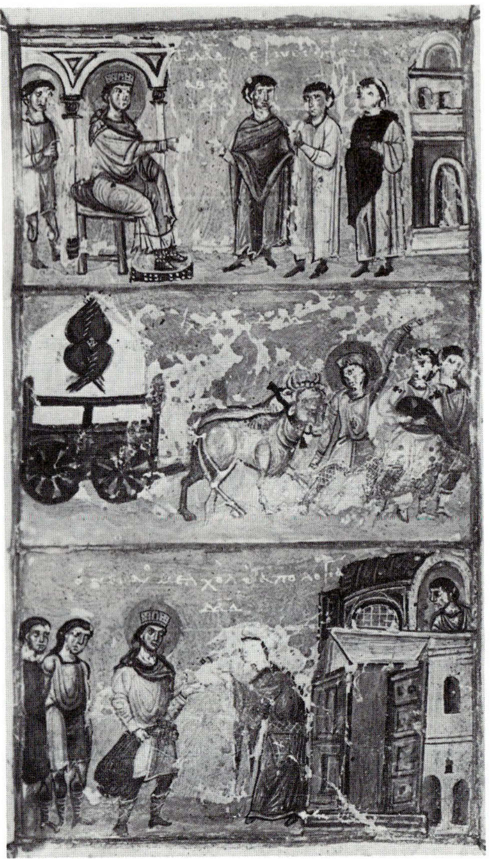

quotations from the Bible and patristic literature. Many of these quotations are illustrated in the margin, making the Paris codex one of the most prolifically illustrated manuscripts of the Middle Ages. Among the illustrations are quite a number of scenes from the four Books of Kings which, so far as they can be compared with the scenes of the Vatican codex, belong to the same picture recension.[28] No parallels exist, however, for other scenes such as Elisha healing the leper Naaman (IV Kings 5:9–14) shown in several phases according to the typical narrative technique (Fig. 35):

1. Elisha sending a messenger to Naaman, the leprous captain of the King of Syria.
2. The messenger bidding Naaman, who approaches in a quadriga, to wash in the Jordan seven times.
3. Naaman taking the healing bath.
4. Naaman climbing out of the Jordan healed.

Such a dense sequence of several phases of one episode is typical of a section from a very extensive picture cycle. An anthology, the florilegium of John of Damascus could not have included more than a limited number of quotations from the Books of Kings and, accordingly, the illustrations would have been correspondingly incomplete. This means that even together the miniatures of the

the last three books for reasons we do not know, perhaps simply because he got tired. Indeed, it can be proven that the original was much more lavishly illustrated in Book II and especially in Books III and IV than the Vatican manuscript witnesses.

The ninth-century manuscript of the *Sacra Parallela* of John of Damascus in Paris (Bibliothèque Nationale, cod. gr. 923), which probably originated in Palestine,[27] is a florilegium containing

---

27 J. Rendel Harris, *Fragments of Philo Judaeus* (Cambridge, 1886); Weitzmann,

Byzantinische Buchmalerei, p. 80 and pl. LXXXVI. Here the author maintained that this codex originated in Italy under Palestinian influence; Palestine itself is now considered by him to be a more likely place of origin.

28 Weitzmann, "Psalter Vatopedi," p. 38 and *passim*.

Fig. 35 *Paris, Bibliothèque Nationale. Cod. gr. 923, fol. 210ᵛ. Story of Naaman*

Fig. 36 *Paris, Bibliothèque Nationale. Cod. gr. 923, fol. 323ᵛ. David Commanding Joab*

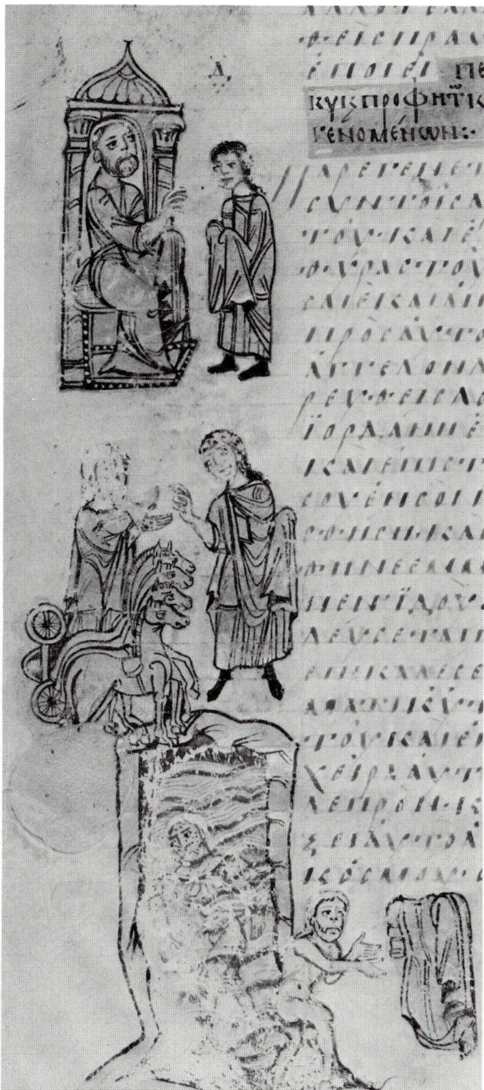

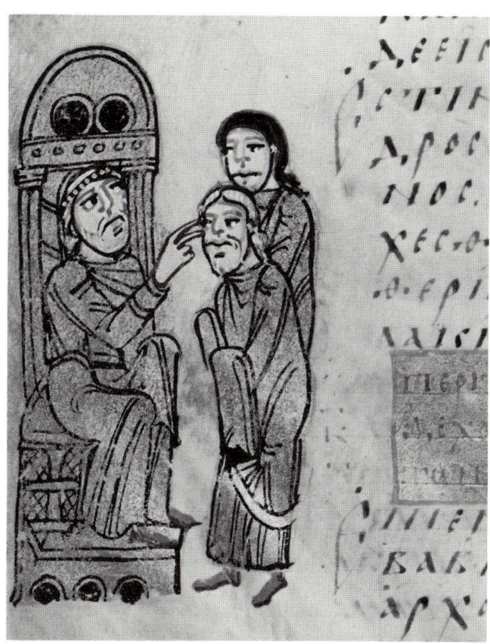

Parallela are several scenes from the two Books of Chronicles. These include one of David, in front of his palace, commanding Joab and the rulers of the people to take a census (I Chronicles 21: 2–3) (Fig. 36).[29] Both the texts and the illustrations from the Books of Chronicles in the *Sacra Parallela* appear to have been chosen very selectively; yet the presence of less eventful as well as of major episodes indicates that the model must have contained an extensive picture cycle, and even though no illustrated copy of the Book of Chronicles has come down to us, we may deduce from the *Sacra Parallela* that such a copy existed.

Consequently, in other cases where no illustrated copy of a given book of the

Vatican and Paris manuscripts by no means give the full extent of the original picture cycle for the Books of Kings, which we estimate to have been four to five hundred single scenes.

Placed beside relevant text passages in the same Paris manuscript of the *Sacra*

[29] For another scene from the same book see Weitzmann, *Roll and Codex*, p. 133 and fig. 114.

Septuagint is extant, we must allow for the possibility that such a copy may have existed. We do not possess illustrated copies of the two Books of Esdras or of the Book of Esther, and we know of no single miniatures that have migrated from these texts to others. Although it is most likely that illustrated copies of these books did exist, it is not possible to determine whether they were illustrated as separate books or whether, for example, the two Books of Esdras formed a unit with Chronicles with which they had long been closely associated. The preserved manuscripts of the unillustrated historical books of the Bible do not yield a consistent picture of how the separate parts were combined.[30]

The Book of Judith demonstrates that the transmission of illustrations has been largely a matter of chance. The miniature in the Regina Bible mentioned above (Fig. 28) is the sole preserved witness in a Greek manuscript for an illustration of this text. Several events are depicted on this page:

> 1. The inhabitants of Bethulia watching Judith leave the town (the figure of Judith was left out or, rather, to avoid repetition it was conflated with the Judith in the following scene).
> 2. A youth leading Judith and her servant girl to the tent of Holofernes (which was not shown for lack of space).
> 3. Judith beheading Holofernes.
> 4. Israelites battling the Assyrians.

These scenes, obviously reduced, condensed, and conflated, are taken from chapters 10 through 14. It is safe to

assume that in the archetype the illustrations were separate units within the columns of text as was usual in early times, that they were spread throughout the whole book, and that the illustrator of the Regina Bible felt obliged to select from this great number of scenes as many as would fit on a full page.

The available manuscript material does not furnish proof of the existence of an illustrated Book of Tobias, but knowledge of an illustrated text of the four Books of the Maccabees again stems from a miniature of the Regina Bible[31] in which the seven Maccabees with their mother Salomona and the scribe Eleazar are shown before King Antiochus. Although the event is recounted in the sixth chapter of the second book, the miniature in the Vatican codex serves as the frontispiece for the fourth book, a discrepancy in accord with the uneven distribution of miniatures in this manuscript already noted above. It would seem, therefore, that this miniature is a *disiectum membrum* from a cycle which originally illustrated all four books.

The character and capabilities of the Greek illustrators are clearly revealed in the illustrations we have examined so far. Their whole activity was directed toward representing in pictures real or imaginary historical events, and they tried to follow the description in the text as faithfully as possible. Symbolism played no great role in the narrative picture cycles, and clearly there was no special inclination to depict the metaphysical. In this respect the Greek illustrator was more rational than his Latin counterpart, who tended more

---

[30] Cf. Rahlfs, *Verzeichnis*, p. 382 ff.

[31] *Miniature della Bibbia cod. Vat. Reg. gr. 1*, pl. 16.

toward the fantastic. It suffices to recall how profoundly the vision of Saint John's Apocalypse affected the artists of the medieval Western world and the wealth of imagination with which they realized it in various original pictures. Characteristically, illustrations of the Apocalypse did not appear in Byzantine art before the sixteenth century, and then only under the impact of Western influence.

The qualities and limitations of the Greek artist are revealed in the way he copes with the poetical books of the Septuagint, which are not well suited to narrative illustration. Among the texts of the Old Testament, the Orthodox Church prized most highly the Book of Job, not only because of its poetical beauty, but above all for its contemplative spirit, for its theme of the unshakable strength of the faith of a great sufferer, and for its divine wisdom. A measure of its popularity is the fact that, with the exception of the Psalter, no other book of the Septuagint is preserved in so many and in such lavishly illustrated copies as the Book of Job. One of the fourteen extant Job manuscripts with extensive picture cycles, Codex Patmos 171 (with at least a considerable portion of its miniatures) apparently goes back as far as the pre-iconoclastic period.[32]

[32] G. Jacopi, "Le miniature dei codici di Patmo," *Clara Rhodos*, 6/7 (1932/33), p. 584, figs. 91–128, and pls. XV–XXII; Weitzmann, *Byzantinische Buchmalerei*, p. 49 and pls. LV–LVI. [*Byzantine Art—An European Art* (catalogue of the Ninth Exhibition of the Council of Europe. Athens, 1964), p. 303. Weitzmann, *Roll and Codex*, 2d ed., addenda to p. 120, now believes that the Patmos codex may have been written and illustrated *during* the period of Iconoclasm.]

The Book of Job is constructed like a Platonic dialogue. The conversations between Job and his friends that form the nucleus of the book are framed by a prologue which treats Satan's dispute with God and Job's trials and sufferings and an epilogue which describes the restoration of Job's prosperity. The illustrators, typically enough, devoted their attention to the chapters that frame the story, picturing in every detail the events that follow each other in quick succession. For the main account, on the other hand, they chiefly repeat again and again a representation of the dispute between Job and his friends, a composition offering only limited possibilities for variation; and therefore, in this sequence, a certain monotony results. A striking miniature from the Patmos manuscript (Fig. 37), belonging to the prologue miniatures, depicts Satan in a dramatic pose as he argues with God in the presence of the angels (Job 1:6)—vividly recalling Mephistopheles' demeanor in the prologue to Goethe's *Faust!*

Of all the books of the Septuagint, Psalms was most often read in church and, with the addition of the Odes, the Psalter had a part in the liturgy surpassed only by the Gospels themselves. Therefore, in spite of the extraordinary problems presented to the artist, it is not surprising that the number of illustrated Psalters far exceeds that of any other of the illustrated books of the Septuagint. The poetic imagery of the Psalms, rich in metaphor and virtually devoid of narrative description, demanded a special kind of ingenuity and imagination from an artist who sought to depict literally the poetic phraseology. In the famous Utrecht Psalter, from the Latin West, a

Fig. 37 *Patmos, Monastery of St. John the Theologian. Cod. 171, page 25. Satan Argues with God*

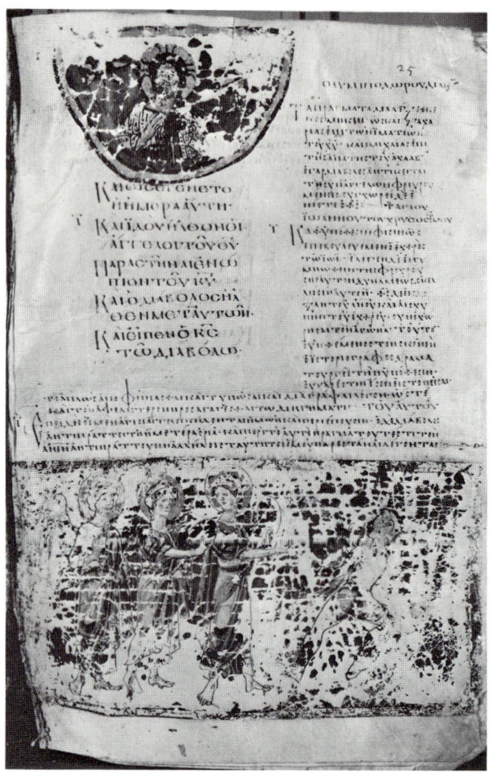

gifted draftsman displayed his talent for this sort of illustration.[33] This approach, however, did not appeal to the same extent to the more rational Byzantine artists.

Literal illustration of the Psalter text does occur in the Greek Psalters, particularly in the manuscripts grouped by Tikkanen into the so-called monastic recension.[34] Until recently seven were known; and now an eighth, which turned up a short time ago in the Philipps Collection in Cheltenham, is in Balti-

more.[35] A miniature from the Moscow Chloudov Psalter may serve as an example of this kind of illustration (Fig. 38). It shows the two ungodly men about whom Psalm 72 says: "They set their

[33] E. T. De Wald, *The Illustrations of the Utrecht Psalter* (Princeton, 1931). For the older literature see p. 73.

[34] Cf. Tikkanen, "Psalterillustration."

[35] (a) Paris, Bibliothèque Nationale, cod. gr. 20 (ninth/tenth century). Cf. Omont, *Manuscrits grecs*, p. 40 and pls. 73–78; Weitzmann, *Byzantinische Buchmalerei*, p. 53 and pl. LIX. (b) Athos, Pantokratoros, cod. 61 (ninth/tenth century). Cf. Weitzmann, *Byzantinische Buchmalerei*, p. 54 and pls. LX–LXI. (c) Moscow, Historical Museum, cod. 129 (ninth/tenth century), the so-called Chloudov Psalter. Cf. N. P. Kondakov, *Miniatures du manuscrit grec du Psautier du IXe siècle de la Collection A. I. Chloudow à Moscou* (Moscow, 1878); Weitzmann, *Byzantinische Buchmalerei*, p. 55 and pls. LXI–LXII. (d) London, British Museum, cod. Add. 40731 (eleventh century), the so-called Bristol Psalter. Cf. M. Ph. Perry, "An Unnoticed Byzantine Psalter," *Burlington Magazine*, 38 (1921), 119 ff. and 282 ff. (e) London, British Museum, cod. Add. 19352 (1066), the so-called Theodore Psalter. Cf. Tikkanen, "Psalterillustration," p. 12. (f) Vatican, cod. Barb. gr. 372 (eleventh century), the so-called Barberini Psalter. Cf. Tikkanen, "Psalterillustration," p. 12; E. T. De Wald, "The Comnenian Portraits in the Barberini Psalter," *Hesperia*, XIII (1944), 78 ff. (g) Berlin, Kupferstichkabinett, cod. 78.A.9 (thirteenth century), the so-called Hamilton Psalter. Cf. P. Wescher, *Beschreibendes Verzeichnis der Miniaturen-Handschriften und Einzelblätter des Kupferstichkabinetts* (Leipzig, 1931), pp. 25 ff. (h) Baltimore, Walters Art Gallery, cod. suppl. 14 (eleventh century). Cf. *Catalogue of the Exhibition of Early Christian and Byzantine Art* (Baltimore, 1947), p. 137, no. 698 and pl. XCIV. [The vast literature on the monastic Psalters is increasing. See A. Grabar, "Quelques notes sur les Psautiers illustrés byzantins du IXe siècle," *Cahiers Archéologiques*, 15 (1965), 61 ff.; S. Dufrenne, *L'illustration des Psautiers grecs du moyen âge* ("Bibliothèque des Cahiers Archéologiques," 1 [Paris, 1966] and idem, "Deux chefs-d'oeuvre de la miniatures de XIe siècle," *Cahiers Archéologiques*, 17 (1967), 177 ff.].

Fig. 38 *Moscow, Historical Museum. Cod. 129, fol. 70ᵛ. Two Ungodly Men*

Fig. 39 *Mount Athos, Pantocrator. Cod. 61, fol. 151ᵛ. Psalm CIV, Journey in the Desert*

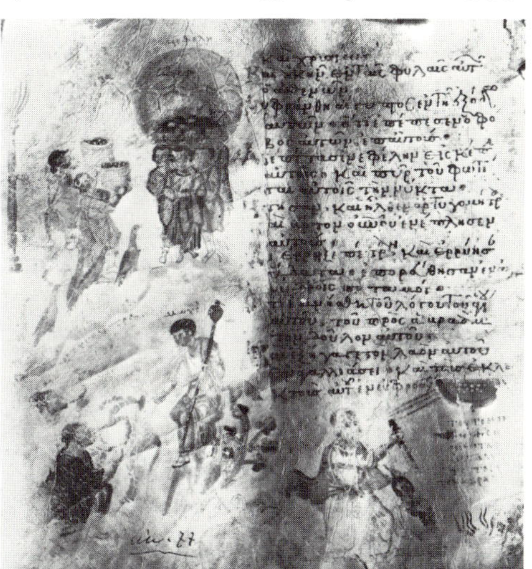

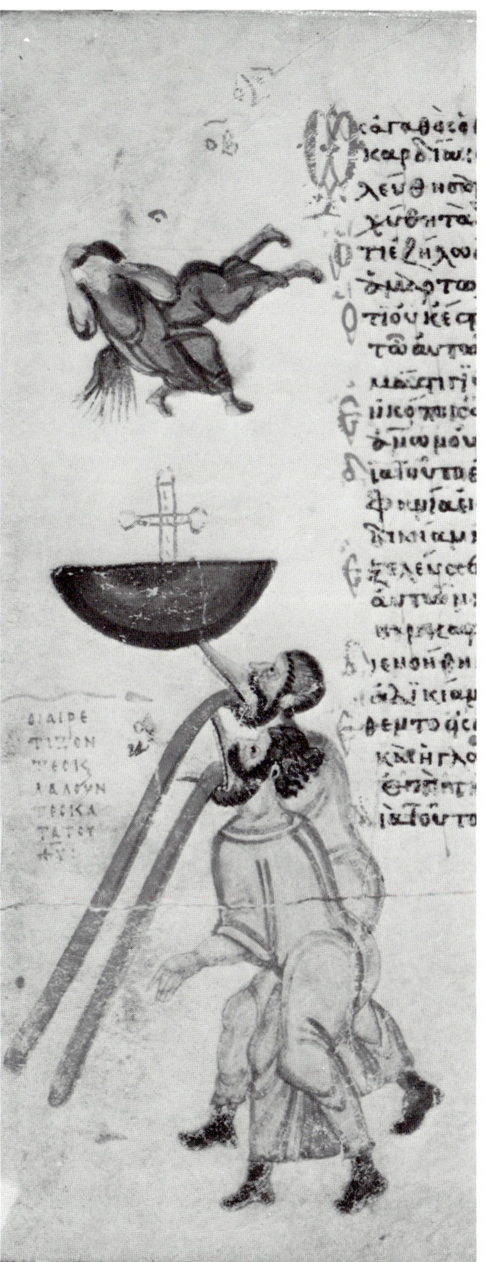

mouth against the heavens and their tongue walketh through the earth." The artist has pictured this verse in a manner bordering on the grotesque, making the mouths of the ungodly men literally reach to the sky and their tongues extend to the earth. In looking through the extensive picture cycle of this as well as others of the so-called monastic manuscripts, however, one soon discovers that this type of literal illustration is relatively rare and that the majority of miniatures can be shown to have migrated from other texts. When, for example, Moses and Abraham are mentioned in Psalm 104, the illustrator of the Pantocrator Psalter (Fig. 39) consulted a Pentateuch or an Octateuch, taking from it three scenes of the Book of Exodus, namely, the exodus of the Israelites under the protection of the cloud, the rain of manna, and Moses smiting the rock, and a fourth scene of the sacrifice of Isaac from the Book of Genesis. Iconographically, then, these scenes should be treated not as Psalter illustra-

tions but rather considered as illustrations for a Pentateuch or Octateuch. It
is worth noting, however, that the
iconography of these scenes does not
agree with that of the Middle Byzantine
Octateuchs discussed above, and thus
we must reckon with the existence of
another recension of illustrated Books of
Moses which has not come down to us
in its original state. In a like manner,
the illustrator of the Psalter excerpted
elements from various other illustrated
manuscripts, thereby making the monastic Psalter one of the most striking
examples of polycyclic illustration.[36]
In addition to the Pentateuch or Octateuch already mentioned, the sources
include: the four Books of Kings, a
manuscript of the Prophets, a Gospel,
an Acts of the Apostles, even nonbiblical
books, namely a menologion, a *Physiologus*, and others. Thus the Psalter
occupies a special position in the history
of the illustrated Septuagint since, in
contrast to the other books where the
pictures were created for the text with
which they are associated, its picture
cycle is essentially derivative.

The second group of Psalters, which
Tikkanen called "aristocratic" because
they are decorated with splendid full-
page pictures, has been preserved in a
great number of examples. Illustration
of the aristocratic Psalters, in comparison
to the monastic group, consists even
more completely of migrated miniatures.
A picture such as the Repentance of
David in the well-known Paris Psalter
(Bibilothèque Nationale, cod. gr. 139)
is not sufficiently explained by the text

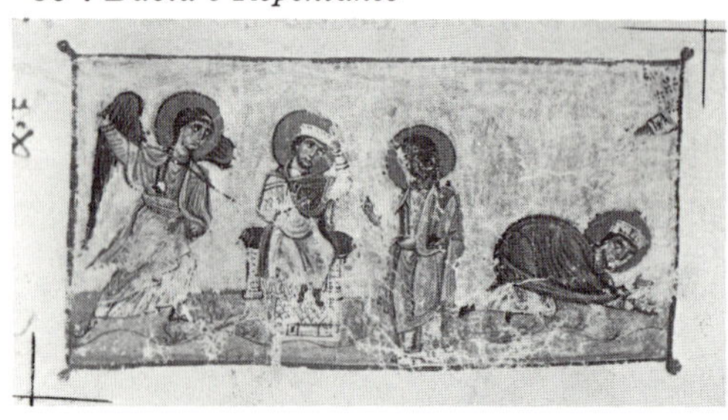

Fig. 40 *Vatican, Biblioteca. Cod. gr. 333, fol. 50ᵛ. David's Repentance*

of Psalm 50 which it precedes.[37] This
miniature was created for the twelfth
chapter of the Second Book of Kings
and, in fact, it is in that section of text
that the same scene appears in the
previously discussed Vatican codex
(Fig. 40).[38] The iconography of the two
miniatures is so similar that a common
source must be assumed; and this source
was certainly a Book of Kings, not a
Psalter. The extensive miniature cycle
of the Book of Kings seems to have
been copied much less frequently than
that of the Psalter, with its limited
number of pictures. In addition, a Book
of Kings was less in demand for liturgical
purposes. Consequently, certain features
of the archetype are better preserved
in the Vatican Kings manuscript, despite
its later date, than in the Paris Psalter,
where, for example, the hand of God
before which David bows in *proskynesis*
is missing.

The Book of Job and the Psalter were
not the only poetical books of the Septuagint to be illustrated in a narrative
manner. The *Sacra Parallela*, so valuable
for the reconstruction of Septuagint

---

[36] Consult the chapter, "Monocyclic and
Polycyclic Manuscripts," in Weitzmann, *Roll
and Codex*, pp. 193 ff.

[37] Omont, *Manuscrits grecs*, pl. VIII; Buchthal,
Paris Psalter, pl. VIII, no. 51.
[38] Lassus, "Livre des Rois," p. 60 and pl. V,
nos. 8–9; Buchthal, *Paris Psalter*, pl. VIII,
no. 51.

Fig. 41 *Paris, Bibliothèque Nationale. Cod. gr. 923, fol. 206ᵛ. Solomon Orders the Building of a Ship*

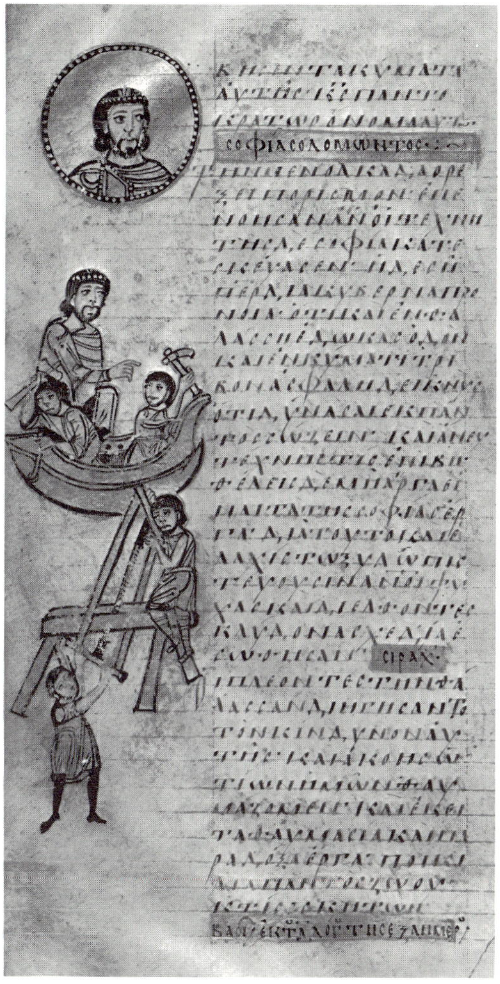

illustration, has several scattered miniatures which can be shown to have derived from at least three other books: the Proverbs of Solomon, the Wisdom of Solomon, and the Wisdom of Sirach (Ecclesiasticus). An example is the illustration for the verse in the Wisdom of Solomon, "For that ship was devised for the hunger for grain and an artificer built it by his wisdom" (14:2. Fig. 41). In the *Sacra Parallela* Solomon, wearing

royal apparel, gives the order to build a ship. Unmistakably, the illustrator has relied on a representation of the building of Noah's ark and simply has substituted Solomon for the figure of Noah supervising the work. We may conclude that in illustrating this poetical text, the artist drew less on his own imagination than on previously existing compositions which were easy to find in the historical books of the Bible. We do not know whether or not the other poetical books, Ecclesiastes, the Song of Songs, and the Psalms of Solomon, also received picture cycles. This is entirely possible, however, since the preservation of manuscript material is due merely to chance.

A number of illustrated examples has survived of the fourth and last group of books in the Septuagint, the Prophets, several of them especially splendid and monumental. The Vatican library possesses a tenth-century manuscript (cod. Chis. R. VIII.54)[39] of a stately format containing the major and minor prophets and adorned with striking figures of standing prophets. Among them is the figure of Jonah (Fig. 42) whose classical drapery treatment suggests a very early model. All of the preserved prophetical manuscripts have only this type of author portrait, which poses the question of whether this was the sole way of illustrating these books or whether there were some with narrative picture cycles of which none are preserved today.

That, in fact, there were books of the Prophets with narrative picture cycles can be inferred once more from the

[39] A. Muñoz, *I codici greci miniati delle minori bibliotheche di Roma* (Florence, 1906), p. 13 and pls. 1–5; Weitzmann, *Byzantinische Buchmalerei*, p. 12 and pl. XII, no. 61.

Fig. 42 *Vatican, Biblioteca. Cod. Chis. gr. R.VIII. 54, fol. 36ᵛ. Jonah*

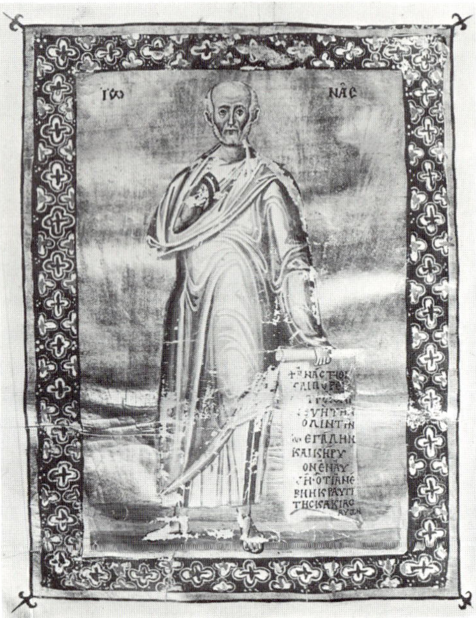

Paris manuscript of the *Sacra Parallela* which has scenes from several of the minor prophets and from all four books of the major prophets. Among the minor prophets the Book of Jonah was a great favorite in early Christian times, as is witnessed by the frequency of Jonah scenes in catacomb painting and on sarcophagus reliefs; and so it is no wonder that this book is our main proof that there were manuscripts of the minor prophets with narrative illustration. Two successive illustrations in the *Sacra Parallela* (Fig. 43) accompany the verses from Jonah 3:3–8. The first shows Jonah preaching before the city gate of Nineveh; the second depicts the inhabitants of Nineveh, covered in sackcloth as a sign of repentance, and the animals within a two-storied architectural setting. From this method of illustration we may conclude that we are dealing

with an excerpt from a cycle originally far more comprehensive than that of catacomb painting, which is confined to the adventure with the whale and the episode of the gourd.

Elsewhere, in connection with two scenes from Jeremiah 52 (the slaying of Zedikiah's sons and the blinding of Zedikiah), we have drawn attention to the existence of an illustrated Book of Jeremiah.[40] We now adduce two scenes from the Book of Daniel (Fig. 44) showing, respectively, King Nebuchadnezzar in front of the palace at Babylon at the moment the prophesy of the ruin of his kingdom was issued from heaven (Daniel 4:26) and the fulfillment of this prophesy, "and he did eat grass as oxen, and his body was wet with the dew of heaven, till his hairs were grown like eagles' feathers, and his nails like birds' claws" (Daniel 4:30). Neither the scenes from Jeremiah nor those from Daniel illustrate the most important or well-known verses in these books, and we may assume, therefore, that other episodes from these prophetical works were also illustrated with dense sequences of phases. Accordingly, we may conclude as in the case of the other books of the Septuagint, that the books of the major and minor prophets were likewise provided with extensive picture cycles of which only *disiecta membra* have come down to us in the form of migrated miniatures.

METHODOLOGICAL CONSIDERATIONS

This brief survey of the illustrated Septuagint manuscripts plainly shows

---

[40] Weitzmann, *Roll and Codex*, p. 133 and fig. 114.

Fig. 43 *Paris, Bibliothèque Nationale. Cod. gr. 923, fol. 15ʳ. Story of Jonah*

Fig. 44 *Paris, Bibliothèque Nationale. Cod. gr. 923, fol. 259ʳ. Nebuchadnezzar*

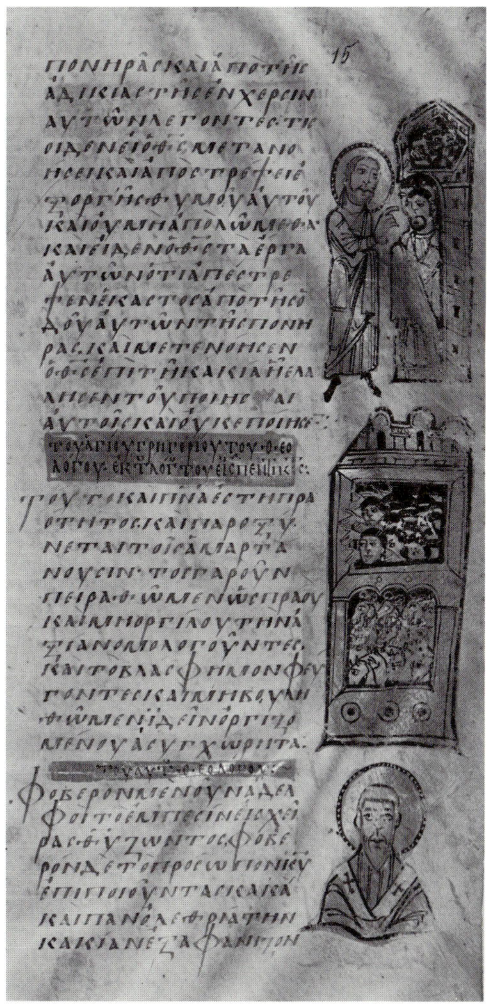

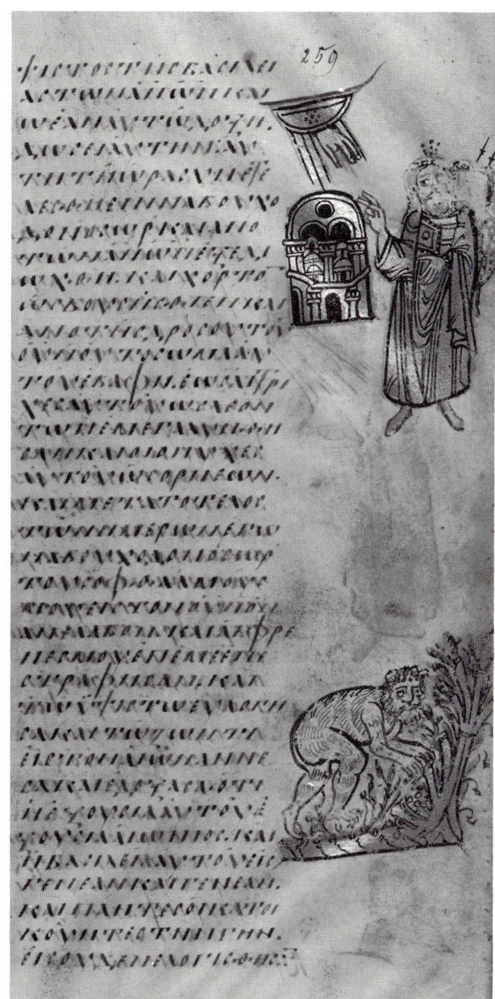

the need for investigating the problem of the archetype separately for each of the various, and not always easily definable, units of this great compilation. When the time comes to write a comprehensive history of Septuagint illustration one or more genealogies will have to be worked out separately for each one of these units. These genealogies or

stemmata will have to be drawn according to principles similar to those used by text critics who are accustomed to working out stemmata of interrelated texts.[41] Here the picture critic is less

[41] For the following discussion consult the chapter, "The Relation between Text Criticism and Picture Criticism," in Weitzmann, *Roll and Codex*, pp. 182 ff.

fortunate than the text critic, who can utilize a long tradition of methodical treatment of manuscripts. Generations of philologists have worked on classifying and grouping the manuscript material of the most important classical and biblical texts, and they have refined the technique so that today the philologist is faced more often with the problems of revising and supplementing an already existing stemma than with establishing one for the first time. In the field of manuscript illustration only a few such attempts have been made so far, as, for example, the stemma for the manuscripts of the *Psychomachia* of Prudentius[42] or that for the medieval Terence manuscripts.[43] Moreover, these two groups of manuscripts contain only limited groups of pictures that exerted little influence on early Christian and medieval book illumination; whereas only a start has been made on working out stemmata for the largest and most informative illustrated texts, the Old and New Testaments.[44]

Naturally the picture critic must use the stemmata worked out by the text critics and must carefully compare them with the results yielded by a study of the pictures. The picture critic should not adapt a text stemma mechanically, however, as has been done so often; but he must work out his own stemma. The fact which will emerge then, that text and picture stemmata are not invariably identical, may be accounted for in several ways. First of all, the archetype of an illustrated manuscript is, as a rule, not as old as the archetype of the text, since it must have been an extremely rare event for the autograph exemplar to have received illustrations; and often some time, occasionally several generations, elapsed before the text became sufficiently popular to lead to the production of an illustrated luxury edition. This, in turn, may have happened far from the place of origin of the text. Second, there are cases where two members of the same textual family were illustrated independently of each other in different localities, so that two stemmata are needed for the illustrations whereas one stemma suffices for the text transmission. Conversely, it is possible for a picture cycle to be taken over without iconographical changes into a new version of the text, a translation, or a paraphrase, so that a single stemma suffices for the pictures, while the text involves different stemmata.

This is not the place to set forth in detail the method of picture criticism for illustrated manuscripts. Like that of text criticism, but to a greater degree, the method of picture criticism is essentially comparative. Whereas a well-established text like the Gospels shows no substantial variations for long periods of time,[45] two copies of a picture are never identical because, in a picture, iconography and form interact more powerfully than meaning and style of handwriting do in a text. There are

[42] R. Stettiner, *Die illustrierten Prudentius-handschriften* (Berlin, 1895), p. 201.
[43] L. W. Jones and C. R. Morey, *The Miniatures of the Manuscripts of Terence* (Princeton, 1931), p. 24.
[44] For example, the Book of Joshua in the Octateuchs. Cf. Weitzmann, *The Joshua Roll, A Work of the Macedonian Renaissance* (Princeton, 1948), p. 38.

[45] B. F. Westcott and F. J. A. Hort, *The New Testament in the Original Greek* (New York, 1882), pp. 2 ff.

various criteria for determining which of two versions of a picture is nearer to the archetype. The main argument concerns which of the two scenes is better explained by the text that served as the basis for the construction of the picture. We assume, a priori, that the first illustrator sought to render the text as closely as possible and that later copyists, either because of carelessness or for other reasons, lost touch with it to a variable degree. Furthermore, the earlier copy is not necessarily the better version; and here, too, text critic and picture critic share the same fundamental attitude. A later copy may well be the better one; for notwithstanding the lapse of time, the fewer the number of links intervening between the archetype and the copy, the closer their relation to each other.

An example from the Book of Joshua may demonstrate this latter point. A miniature of the Vatican Octateuch gr. 747 depicts the emissaries of the Gibeonites before the enthroned Joshua feigning a long voyage and displaying their "wine bottles, old and rent, and bound up; and old shoes and clouted upon their feet, and old garments upon them; and all their bread of their provision . . . dry and mouldy" (Joshua 9:4–5).[46] In the corresponding miniature of the Vatican rotulus,[47] the number of emissaries is reduced to two, and their covered hands, thrust out toward Joshua, are bare of any attributes. There can be no doubt that the miniature in the Octateuch is more precise and that,

therefore, in spite of the later date, it is closer to the archetype.

At the same time the Octateuch miniature is of poorer artistic quality than that of the rotulus, and this proves that iconographical excellence and quality do not necessarily coincide. In other words: artistic quality should be left out of consideration when dealing with genealogical problems which have to be solved on the basis of iconography alone. One can assume by no means that a better artist copies his model more faithfully than a copyist of average competence. The former will surely make fewer gross errors but at the same time he will take the liberty more often to make conscious changes. In the present case, the omission of the attributes in the hands of the Gibeonites is surely not the result of mere negligence, but an intentional alteration in accord with the basic idea of the rotulus.[48]

THE ORIGINS OF SEPTUAGINT ILLUSTRATION

After this digression into method we must touch briefly on a historical problem not so easily answered: when was the Septuagint first provided with large cycles? This problem is linked to another: namely, did the first illustrators of the Septuagint invent the technique of narrative illustration, or had this technique been developed in classical times? In the event that we can prove that classical book illustration had existed, we must ask whether it exerted a lasting influence on the earliest Bible illustration.

Evidence, which we have presented

[46] Weitzmann, *Joshua Roll*, p. 25 and pl. XI, no. 40.
[47] Ibid., pl. XI, no. 37.

[48] Ibid., p. 109.

elsewhere,[49] gives us reason to think that the most famous classics, in particular the scholarly editions of the Homeric epics and the plays of Euripides which first appeared in Hellenistic Alexandria, had been provided with rich picture cycles before the earliest Bible illustration. These illustrations, on papyrus rolls that have been lost save for a few scraps, must have had a far-reaching and almost immediate influence on other branches of art, for we can see their direct effect on Hellenistic terra-cotta bowls, the so-called Homeric bowls, first published by Carl Robert.[50]

Three phases of the Eumaeus episode from the twenty-second book of the Odyssey on a Homeric bowl in Berlin (Fig. 45)[51] show the unfaithful goatherd Melanthius captured and then hanged, and Athena spurring on Odysseus to fight against the suitors. The fact that whole lines of the Odyssey appear on the bowl—which is extremely unusual for this type of relief representation— justifies the assumption that the potter had used for a model an illustrated manuscript in which this association between picture and text column was natural and taken for granted. A recon-struction (Fig. 46) shows what an illus-trated papyrus roll would have looked like in Hellenistic times. Each of the

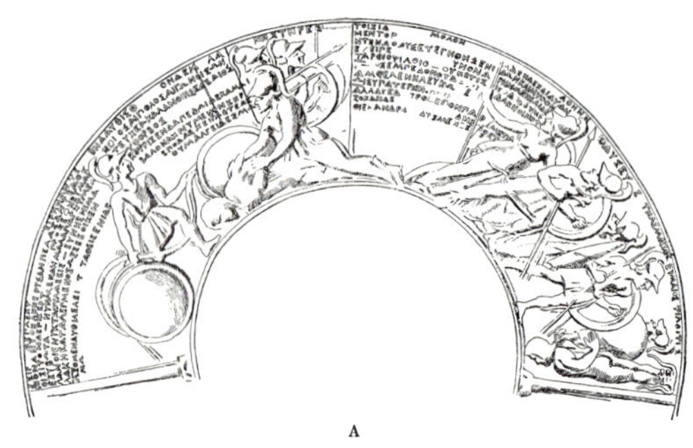

Fig. 45 *Sketch of a cup in Berlin, Staatliche Museen. Scenes from Book XXII of the Odyssey*

three scenes on the Berlin bowl is placed in the column of text nearest the relevant lines. As we mentioned in discussion of the Vienna Genesis (Fig. 30), we encounter the same principle of illustration throughout the entire Middle Ages in those manuscripts which most clearly mirror classical models.

A complete Odyssey, written on twenty-four rolls, with a sequence of illustrations as dense as this excerpt indicates, must have had hundreds of scenes. This would hold true also for the Iliad and for the more than seventy dramas of Euripides, as well as for other literary, didactic, and scholarly texts of classical antiquity. Thus we have every reason to assume that by the time the Old Testament was first provided with pictures, book illustration had been fully developed and there was no need to devise a new branch of art for the illustration of the Holy Scriptures.

But even if we can establish the existence of an ancient book illustration, the question of its direct influence on the illustration of the Old Testament remains. It is still too early to answer this question exhaustively and to gauge the full extent of classical influence. The following example, however, demon-strates that this influence did, indeed,

[49] Weitzmann, *Roll and Codex*, pp. 37 ff. and *passim*. [Most fully: Weitzmann, *Ancient Book Illumination* ("Martin Classical Lec-tures," 16 [Cambridge, Mass., 1959]).]

[50] C. Robert, *Homerische Becher* ("50. Berliner Winckelmannsprogramm" [Berlin, 1890]). [U. Hausmann, *Hellenistische Reliefbecher aus attischen und boötischen Werkstätten* (Stutt-gart, 1959).]

[51] Weitzmann, *Roll and Codex*, p. 77 and figs. 6 and A.

Fig. 46 *Reconstruction of an illustrated Odyssey rotulus from the third century* B.C.

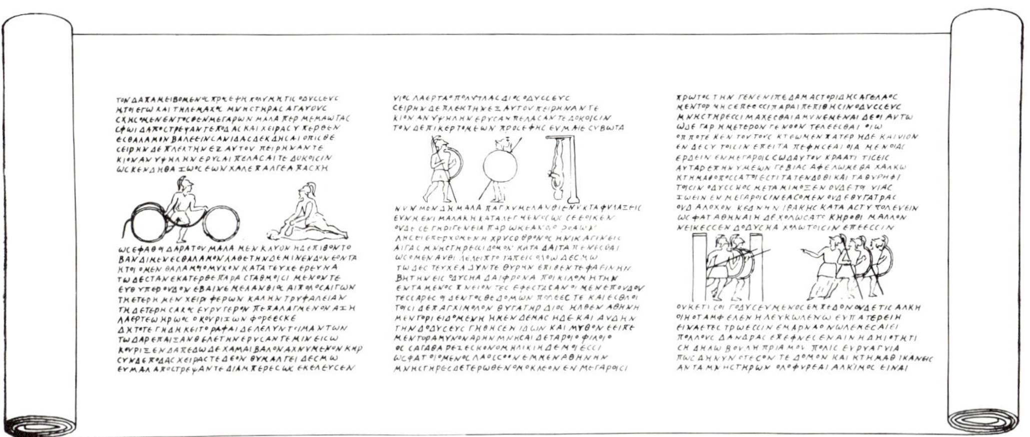

exist.[52] The Creation of Adam was pictured in no fewer than three phases in the Cotton Genesis, to return to the manuscript first discussed. These three scenes can no longer be found among the half-charred fragments, but two are preserved in the mosaics of San Marco and the third in the Grandval Bible from Tours (London, British Museum, Add. 10546) which, as Wilhelm Köhler has shown, has Genesis scenes going back to the Cotton Genesis recension.[53] The

three phases of the Creation of Adam are:

1. Modeling a man from a clod of earth (Fig. 47).
2. Animating the first man by touching his head (Fig. 48).
3. Inducing a soul, the small winged Psyche (Fig. 49).

These same three phases, in very similar compositions, are found on Roman sarcophagi representing the creation of man by Prometheus. The seated Prometheus shapes the clay model of a man (Fig. 50); with a touch of his hand he imparts life to the model lying stiffly on the ground, whereby the spark of life flashes across (Fig. 51); and finally Athena holds a butterfly, a symbol of the living soul, over the head of the newly created man, in much the same

---

[52] Ibid., pp. 176 ff. and figs. 177–82. [The question of the iconographic influence of classical depictions on Christian representations has been discussed in a number of Weitzmann's subsequent studies, most notably: "The Survival of Mythological Representations in Early Christian and Byzantine Art and their Impact on Christian Iconography," *Dumbarton Oaks Papers*, 14 (1960), 45 ff.; and "The Origin of the Threnos," *De Artibus Opuscula LX. Essays in Honor of Erwin Panofsky* (New York, 1961), pp. 487 ff.]
[53] W. Köhler, *Die Schule von Tours* ("Die Karolingischen Miniaturen," 1, Part II [Berlin, 1933]), 186 ff. and pl. 50. [The derivation of the Genesis scenes from the Prometheus

myth has recently been contested in part by H. Schade, "Das Paradies und die Imago Dei," *Probleme der Kunstwissenschaft*, 2 (1966), 79 ff. For a reply to these objections see, Weitzmann, *Roll and Codex*, 2d ed., addendum to p. 176.]

Fig. 47 *Venice, San Marco. Atrium Mosaic. Forming of Adam*

Fig. 48 *London, British Museum. Cod. Add. 10546, fol. 5ᵛ. Enlivenment of Adam*

Fig. 49 *Venice, San Marco. Atrium Mosaic. Animation of Adam*

Fig. 50 *Vatican Museum. Sarcophagus. Prometheus Forming Man*

Fig. 51 *Naples, Museo Nazionale. Sarcophagus. Enlivenment of Man*

Fig. 52 *Rome, Museo Capitolino. Sarcophagus. Animation of Man*

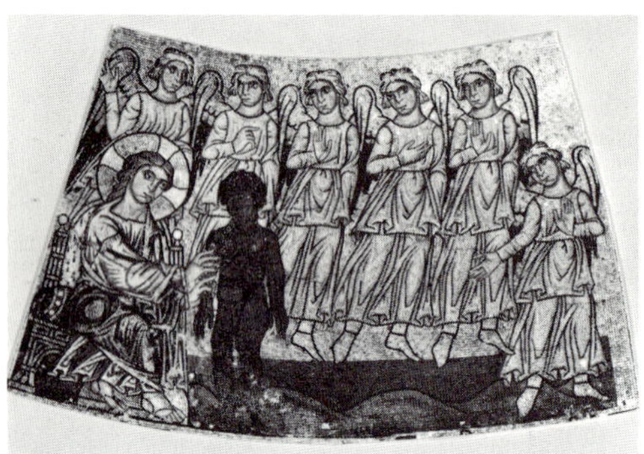

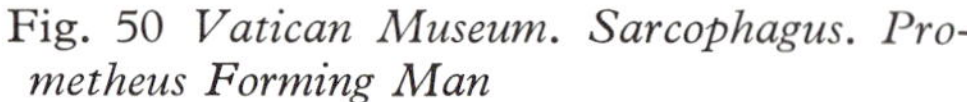

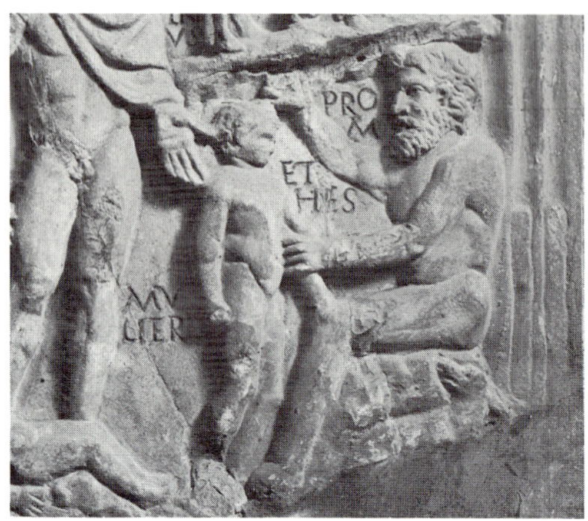

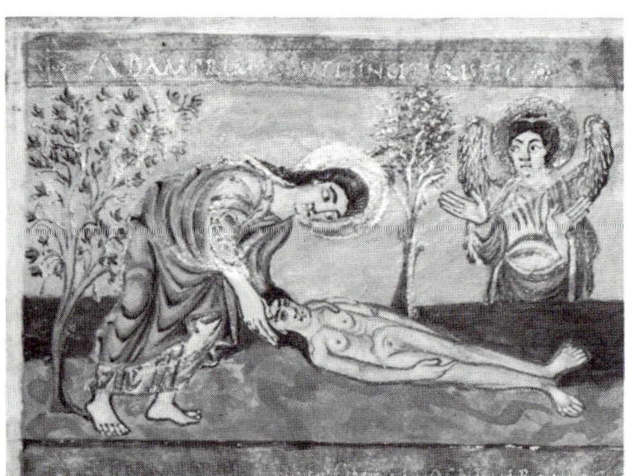

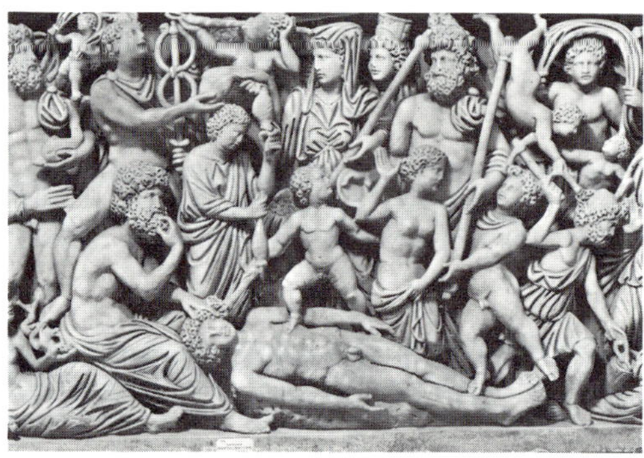

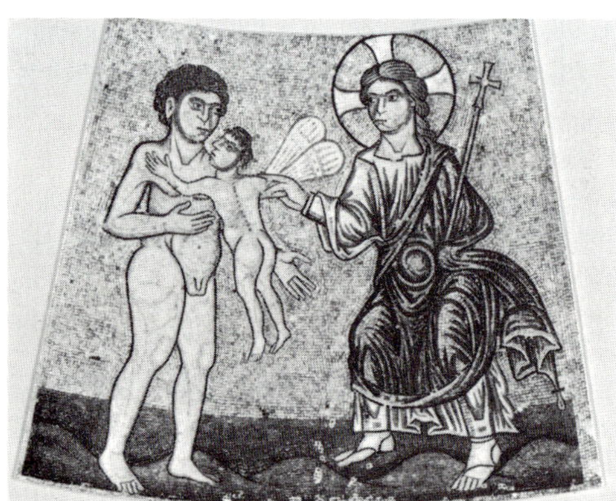

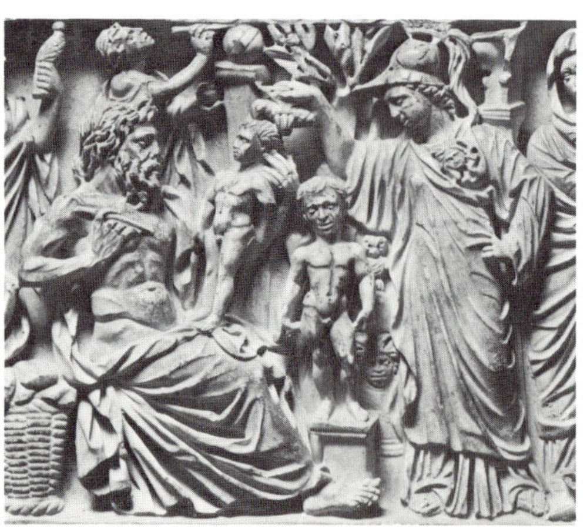

way that God the Father holds Psyche in his raised right hand (Fig. 52).

The close agreement in form and content between the Genesis and Prometheus scenes is explained most easily by the assumption that the first illustrator of the Cotton Genesis recension used as his model an ancient text which had pictures of the Prometheus myth. We do not know exactly which classical text this was, but presumably it was a mythological handbook resembling the *Bibliotheke* of Apollodorus, though apparently not this very text because in it the Prometheus story (Lib. I.VII.I) is treated too summarily.

This example shows clearly not only that Christian illustrators availed themselves of classical compositions for artistic reasons but also must have been fully aware of the original meaning of the models they used. The fascinating process which transformed classical art into Christian art cannot be grasped solely as the migration of a repertory of pictorial types; research must aim at scrutinizing the content of the classical models and, wherever possible, must suggest the reasons that led the Christian illustrator to choose a certain classical theme for his pattern.

But were Christian artists really the first to furnish the Septuagint with large picture cycles? Twenty years ago this was still more or less an academic question. Since the early thirties, however, when the Yale University expedition discovered the synagogue at Dura-Europos on the Euphrates and uncovered its astoundingly rich fresco decoration,[54]

we have had to consider the possibility that manuscripts illustrated by Jews of the Diaspora were directly or indirectly used as models by the fresco painters, in somewhat the same manner in which at a later time the mosaicists of San Marco used the Cotton Genesis. Even though the synagogue frescoes date as late as the middle of the third century of the Christian era, the range and variety of their themes and their provincial Mesopotamian style mingled with elements of Hellenistic origin suggest that we encounter in them an art with a tradition of considerable length behind it, an art whose origin is to be sought in one of the great metropolitan centers of the Greek East. Not only is it possible, indeed, it is highly probable that this Greco-Jewish art came into being even before the Christian era.

The scenes on the walls of the synagogue illustrate events from the Pentateuch, the Books of Kings, the Prophets, and the Book of Esther. A number of the striplike pictures, for example, the finding of Moses in the Nile (Figs. 53–54), have a distinctly narrative character. The manner in which the fresco painter condensed, abbreviated, and fused in order to pack several phases of the episode into one frame leads to the

---

[54] The bibliography on this important monument has proliferated to a virtually incalculable extent. I refer here only to Carl Kraeling's first report in *The Excavations at Dura-Europos, Preliminary Report of the Sixth Season 1932–1933* (New Haven, 1936), pp. 337 ff. and pls. XLVII–LIII, and to Comte Du Mesnil du Buisson, *Les peintures de la Synagogue de Doura-Europos* (Rome, 1939),

which present the material fairly completely. For a profitable discussion of the manifold problems connected with the synagogue frescoes, we must await Carl Kraeling's comprehensive publication. [C. Kraeling, *The Synagogue* ("The Excavations at Dura Europos. Final Report," 8, Part I [New Haven, 1956]). For more recent literature consult L. Mayer, *A Bibliography of Jewish Art* (Jerusalem, 1967).]

Fig. 53 *Dura-Europos, Synagogue. Fresco.*
Finding of Moses

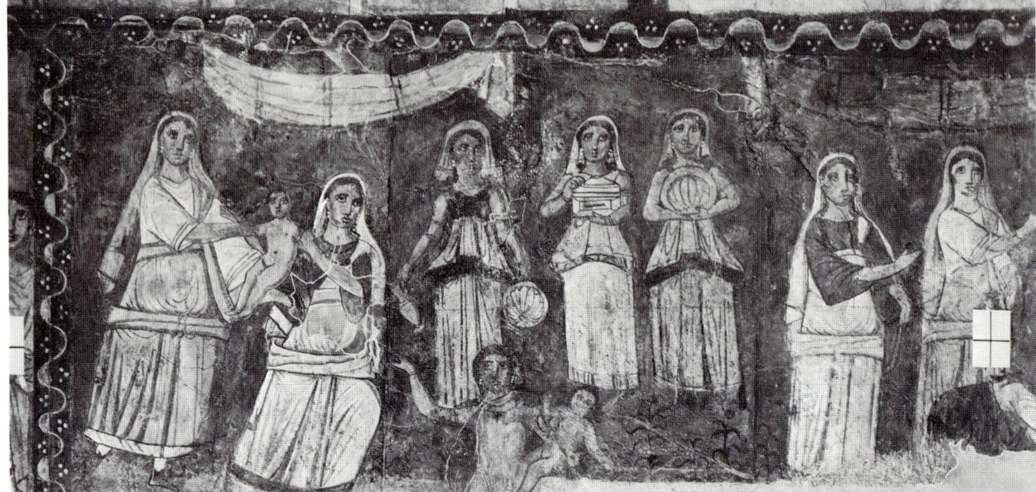

conclusion that, as in the similar case of
the mosaics of San Marco, an extensive
miniature cycle served as the model.
The events assembled in one panel of
the frescoes were most probably pictured in no less than five separate scenes
in the model:

1. Pharaoh commanding the Hebrew
midwives Shiphrah and Puah to
kill the male children of the Jews
(Ex. 1:15 ff).
2. Jochebed exposing Moses in the
ark of bulrushes (destroyed in the
badly damaged lower part of the
fresco) (Ex. 2:3).
3. Pharaoh's daughter wading into
the Nile to save the child, whom she
holds on her left arm. (At this point

the fresco painter has not followed
the Septuagint narrative, where
Pharaoh's daughter sends a maid-
servant into the Nile.)
4. Pharaoh's daughter telling Moses'
sister Miriam to call a nurse for the
child (Ex. 2:7–8). In the fresco this
scene is so shortened and conflated
that Pharaoh's daughter is left out
and, as a result, Miriam talks to
Pharaoh's daughter who stands in the
water and belongs to the preceding
scene.
5. Pharaoh's daughter giving the
child Moses to Jochebed to raise
(Ex. 2:9). Again Pharaoh's daughter
has been left out in the fresco, and
as a result of the fusion of scenes
Miriam, instead of Pharaoh's

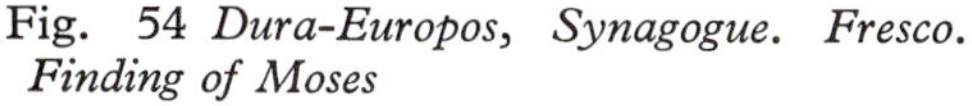

Fig. 54 *Dura-Europos, Synagogue. Fresco.*
Finding of Moses

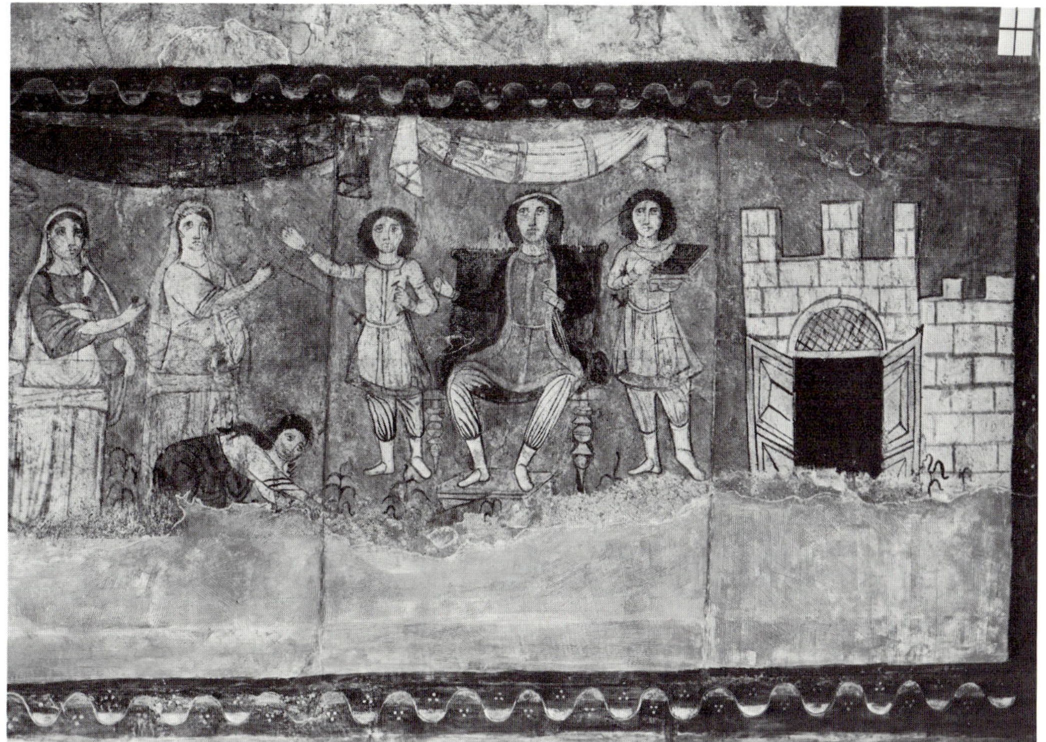

daughter, hands the child over to Jochebed.

It is a striking fact that the first scene, Pharaoh's extirpation order, appears in similar fashion in the Vatican Octateuch (cod. gr. 747. Fig. 55); in the miniature, however, the court officials, who in the fresco stand on either side of Pharaoh, have been moved to the left side. This manuscript is the only one of the Octateuchs to have this scene; at the same place in the other Octateuchs the birth of Moses is shown, a scene obviously patterned after a birth scene in the New Testament, either the birth of Mary or of John the Baptist.[55] Since

in other cases where the Octateuchs vary among each other the Vatican cod. gr. 747 almost always retains the better version,[56] we may safely assume that the composition in Vatican cod. gr. 747 reflects the archetype and that the birth scene was substituted for it at a later time. This correspondence naturally poses the question of whether, by any chance, the Dura frescoes and the Octateuch derive from the same archetype. Naturally a single case is not sufficiently conclusive, but in fact we do believe that such a connection exists and we hope to furnish proof on the

[55] For example, in the Smyrna Octateuch. Cf. Hesseling, *Octateuque de Smyrne*, pl. 50, no. 152.

[56] On the interrelations of the Octateuchs with regard to the Joshua scenes consult Weitzmann, *Joshua Roll*, pp. 30 ff.

Fig. 55 *Vatican, Biblioteca. Cod. 747, fol. 72ʳ.*
Pharaoh's Order

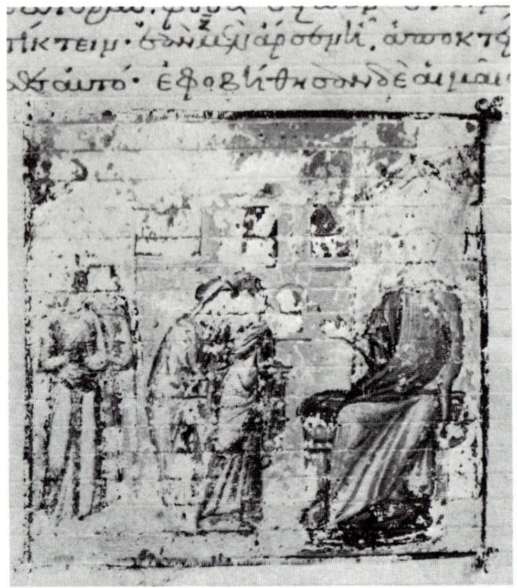

basis of more material in a study to appear shortly.[57]

In his first report Carl Kraeling recognized that a whole series of scenes in the synagogue frescoes are not pure illustrations of the Septuagint text but have divergences which can be accounted for only by reference to Jewish legend. For example, the fact that Pharaoh's daughter herself, and not one of her maidservants, has gone into the Nile is at variance with the Exodus text; apparently it is based on a Jewish apocryphon. If we examine the Byzantine Octateuchs more minutely from this point of view, we become aware of the fact that they,

too, contain miniatures which cannot be explained on the basis of the Septuagint text alone and which seem to depend on Jewish legendary sources.[58]

A typical example is the Temptation of Eve in the Seraglio Octateuch (Fig. 56). Particularly noteworthy is the depiction of the snake on the back of a camel. In the *Pirkê Rabbi Eliezer* the snake of the temptation is described in the following way:[59] "'Now the serpent was more subtil than any beast of the field' (Gen. 3:1). Its appearance was something like that of the camel, and he [Satan] mounted and rode upon it." The illustrator who created this scene must surely have been familiar with the Haggadic literature and apparently this source accounts for the appearance of the snake.

The most immediate explanation for traces of Jewish iconography in a Christian manuscript is, in our view, that the picture cycles of the Octateuchs ultimately go back to an archetype produced for the Jews of the Diaspora. We

---

[57] In 1945 the author delivered a series of lectures on this topic at the Dumbarton Oaks Center for Byzantine Studies, Washington, D.C. [Weitzmann, "The Octateuch of the Seraglio and the History of its Picture Recension," *Actes du Xᵉ Congrés Internationale d'études Byzantines* (Istanbul, 1957), pp. 185 ff.]

[58] [The influence of Jewish legendary sources on the representations in Dura Europos and in other monuments discussed in this article is treated by Weitzmann in "Zur Frage des Einflusses jüdischer Bilderquellen auf die Illustration des Alten Testamentes," *Mullus: Festschrift Theodor Klauser* ("Jahrbuch für Antike und Christentum" Ergänzungsband I, 1964), pp. 401 ff., translated and reprinted herewith, pp. 76 ff.]

[59] *Pirkê de Rabbi Eliezer*, trans. Gerald Friedlander (London, 1916), p. 92. [Although the Pirkê is not earlier than the ninth or tenth century, Friedlander has argued that especially the creation story contains material which goes back to as early as the first century. Consequently, not the Pirkê proper but only its model could have formed the basis for an early illustration.]

Fig. 56 *Istanbul, Seraglio. Cod. 8, fol. 43ᵛ.*
Temptation of Eve

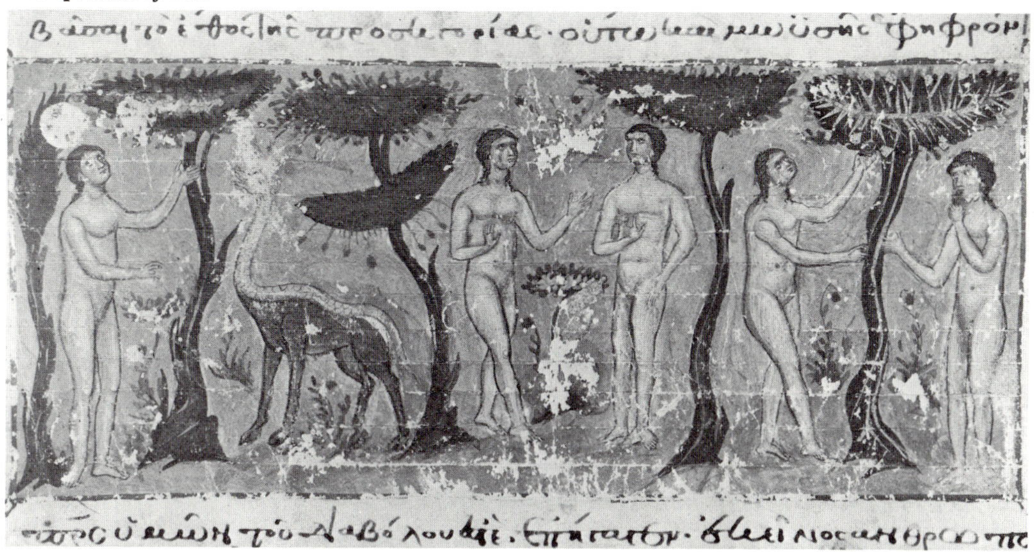

believe that such a Greco-Jewish book illumination, the existence of which can be inferred independently from the Dura frescoes and, as the last example shows, also from the miniatures of the Octateuch, was the connecting link between the illustrated papyrus rolls of the Greek classical authors such as Homer and Euripides and illustrated Christian Bibles. Therefore, we must consider the possibility that the illustration of the Septuagint was undertaken fairly soon after its translation from Hebrew into Greek, which we know was begun in Alexandria in the third century before the Christian era. Thus, when early Christian artists turned their attention to illustrating the Holy Scriptures they apparently found the Old Testament already provided with pictures and needed only to make copies of them.

If the illustration of the Septuagint really began as early as now appears to be the case, it follows that the general question of the origin of Christian art must be seen in a new light. In the beginning we spoke of two ways of expressing the content of Christian texts in picture form, the symbolic and the narrative. Until now the prevailing opinion has been that early Christian art began with symbolic representations, mainly in catacomb painting, and that the narrative style gradually developed through the elaborating of these individual scenes and by increasing their number. If, however, the Hellenized Jews already had a Septuagint with an extensive miniature cycle which the Christians could take over ready-made, one is forced to conclude that narrative painting is as old as the symbolic tradition and that, from the beginning, both modes of expression existed side by side in Christian art.

4

The Question of the Influence of Jewish Pictorial Sources on Old Testament Illustration

AT the congress in Ravenna in 1962 Theodor Klauser closed his profound exegesis of the origin of Early Christian art by urging Early Christian archeologists to pay greater attention to the Jewish sources of Christian art as well as to the classical. In the belief that a response to his exhortation is the most fitting way to honor Klauser, to whom these lines are dedicated, we offer here a few observations on Jewish pictorial art.

Not only the very existence of this Jewish tradition, but also its wide diffusion may be inferred from its influence on Christian art, which was more extensive than has been assumed hitherto. In Part IV of his "Studien zur Enstehungsgeschichte der christlichen Kunst," (*Jahrbuch für Antike und Christentum*, 4 [1961], 128 ff.) Klauser himself demonstrated the probability that shorthand representations of Old Testament subjects on Jewish seal rings influenced Christian intaglios; and he noted that, in turn, these Christian objects affected catacomb painting. In so doing, he placed the controversial question of the origins of Christian art on an entirely new basis.

Klauser's observations find parallels in investigations by a growing number of scholars who have proven Jewish influence on Christian book illustration; and Klauser, thoroughly acquainted with these concurrent studies, collected the relevant bibliography at the end of the work cited above. At this point we would like to introduce a general observation on method. None of the illustrated manuscripts in question is earlier than the sixth century and most of them belong to a considerably later period. Nevertheless, there is no doubt that they derive from archetypes of the Early Christian period; and the probabilities inherent in this situation permit the assumption that Jewish elements identified in the later manuscripts were absorbed in the earlier archetypes and are not later additions. Admittedly the miniatures are to be regarded as secondary evidence; as sources they are not as precise as contemporary Early Christian artifacts such as Klauser's seal rings. But we must draw on these secondary sources for the solution to the problem of the origins of Early Christian art, just as classical archeologists, for a long time, have filled in the gaps in our knowledge of Greek monumental sculpture with copies from the Roman imperial period.

THE DURA SYNAGOGUE

The discovery during the 1930s of the frescoes in the synagogue at Dura Europos[1] did not provide the first proof of the existence of a Jewish figural art. Single scenes on mosaic floors, sarcophagus reliefs, and the like were already

Translated and reprinted with permission from "Zur Frage des Einflusses jüdischer Bilderquellen auf die Illustration des Alten Testamentes," *Mullus: Festschrift Theodor Klauser* (*Jahrbuch für Antike und Christentum Ergänzungsband*, 1, 1964), 401–15.

[1] From the bibliography for the Dura synagogue, which has already grown beyond all bounds, I cite only the most comprehensive and thorough treatment of the frescoes by C. H. Kraeling, *The Synagogue* ("The Excavations at Dura Europos. Final Report," 8, Part I [New Haven, 1956]). [For the constantly increasing literature on the Dura synagogue frescoes consult L. A. Mayer, *Bibliography of Jewish Art* (Jerusalem, 1967).]

known. The frescoes are important for a different reason: they attest to the existence of an extensive narrative Bible illustration, certainly based on rich cyclic originals; and since only the book permits the full development of narrative pictorial cycles of the sort excerpted by the Dura artists, the frescoes lead to the assumption that Jewish manuscript illustration existed.

Very soon after the first publication of the frescoes, the obvious question of the relationship between the iconography of the synagogue frescoes and the Christian pictorial tradition was posed. In the first detailed publication of the frescoes, Du Mesnil du Buisson pointed out several striking similarities between the representation of the Crossing of the Red Sea and the corresponding scene in the Carolingian Bible of S. Paolo fuori le mura;[2] but he did not delve more deeply into the problem of how such a connection could be explained historically. Other comparisons with miniatures are less convincing and so, inevitably, other scholars such as Morey denied any connection with Christian iconography.[3] It seems advisable, therefore, to refrain from offering a conclusive answer to a question so fundamental to the history of Old Testament illustration until a detailed comparison of every scene is available.[4] For the time being, we prefer

to limit ourselves to a few observations which we hope will contribute to a solution of the problem.

We have already adduced two examples of iconographical connections between the Dura frescoes and the miniatures of the Octateuchs, one from the Book of Genesis and the other from Exodus. In the first, the scene of Jacob's Blessing (Fig. 57),[5] the patriarch, apparently beardless, reclines on a couch; Ephraim and Manasse stand frontally instead of turning toward their grandfather who blesses them by placing his hands on their heads; and from the right Joseph, clad in Persian costume, approaches with outstretched hands. Each of these particular details is paralleled in a twelfth-century Octateuch miniature (Istanbul, Seraglio, cod. 8, fol. 141ᵛ, Fig. 58).[6] The fact that so many details of the two representations correspond can be explained only in terms of a common archetype,[7] presumably an early illustrated text of the Septuagint. Whether this Septuagint text was first illustrated for Jews or for Christians had best remain an open question for the time being. The second

---

[2] R. Du Mesnil du Buisson, *Les peintures de la synagogue de Doura-Europos 245–256 après J.-C.* (Rome, 1939), p. 124 and pl. 1a.

[3] C. R. Morey, *Early Christian Art* (2d ed.; Princeton, 1953), pp. 65, 77.

[4] The author made such a comparison in a series of three unpublished lectures delivered at the Fourth Symposium held at the Dumbarton Oaks Center for Byzantine Studies in 1945.

[5] Kraeling, *Synagogue*, p. 221 and pl. 34.

[6] Weitzmann, "The Octateuch of the Seraglio and the History of its Picture Recension," *Actes du Xᵉ Congrès International d'Études Byzantines* (Istanbul, 1957), p. 183 and pl. 40, 1–2.

[7] The correspondences are all the more striking because the Vienna Genesis, which belongs to another recension, has a completely different composition for the same subject (Fig. 138): Jacob sits upright, his grandsons turn to him; and Joseph is accompanied by his Egyptian wife Asenneth. Cf. H. Gerstinger, *Die Wiener Genesis* (Vienna, 1931), p. 109 and folio 23.

Fig. 57 *Dura-Europos, Synagogue. Fresco. Jacob's Blessing*

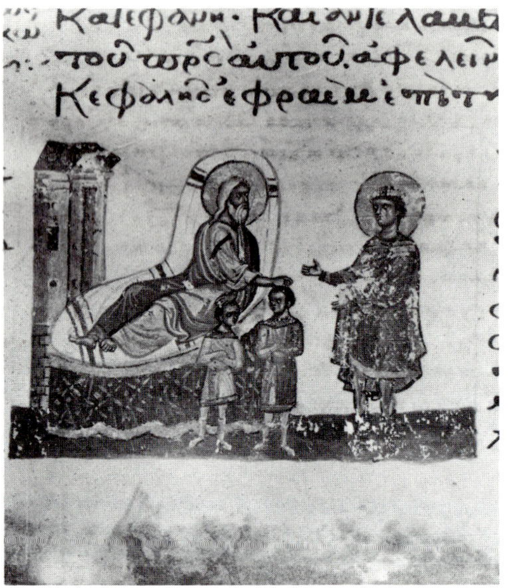

Fig. 58 *Istanbul, Seraglio. Cod. 8, fol. 141ᵛ. Jacob's Blessing*

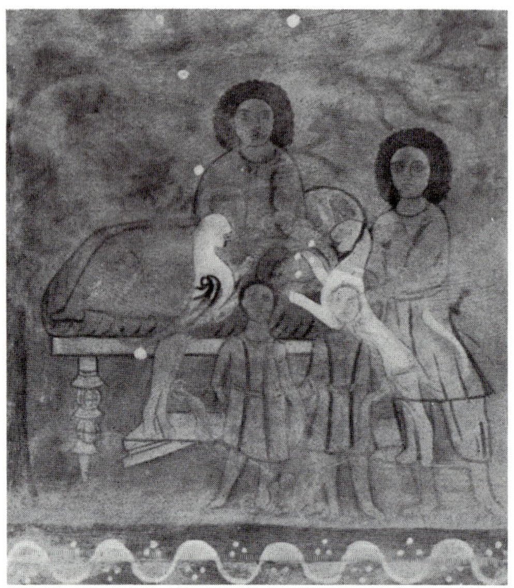

example, a scene from Exodus, pictures Pharaoh ordering the Jewish midwives Shiphrah and Puah to kill the male offspring of the Jews (Fig. 54).[8] The same scene in one of the Octateuchs (Fig. 55)[9] differs compositionally only in that the two court officials are placed behind the midwives, whereas in the Dura fresco they stand on either side of Pharaoh, certainly their original position. Of singular importance for the history of Bible illustration is the fact that this scene occurs only in the earliest extant manuscript of the Octateuch recension, Vatican codex gr. 747, which dates from the eleventh century, and is missing in the other copies. In a considerable number of other cases where the Octateuchs vary among one another, it is Vatican 747 that reproduces most faithfully the oldest and most literal version of the miniature.[10]

Elsewhere, we have attempted to show[11] that the illustration of the Septuagint did not begin with the entire text but rather with separate books or groups of books belonging together. The earliest illustrated Bible manuscripts, themselves, for example the Vienna Genesis (Nationalbibliothek, cod. theol. gr. 31) and the Cotton Genesis (London, British Museum, Cotton Otho B.VI), limited as they are to short textual units, provide evidence for this conclusion; and in view of the vast number of individual scenes in these Genesis manuscripts or in the Books of Kings, an entire Septuagint

[8] Kraeling, *Synagogue*, pp. 169 ff. and pl. 68.
[9] Weitzmann, "Die Illustration der Septuaginta," *Münchener Jahrbuch der bildenden Kunst*, 3/4 (1952/53), p. 118 and fig. 25. Translated and reprinted herewith, p. 73.

[10] Weitzmann, *The Joshua Roll* (Princeton, 1948), pp. 31 ff.
[11] Weitzmann, "Illustration der Septuaginta," p. 100 [herewith reprinted, p. 48].

text illustrated on the same scale would have been a practical impossibility. Therefore, should a connection between the Genesis and Exodus scenes in Dura and those in illustrated Greek books in fact be demonstrable (a hypothesis which cannot be fully proven before further comparisons between fresco and book illustration are published), these results could not be applied immediately to the entire fresco cycle. Proof of an ultimate connection with the Jewish pictorial tradition will have to be established individually for each unit of text that existed as a separate illustrated book.

The four Books of Kings comprise such a unit which, as is evidenced by the Quedlinburger Itala (Berlin, Staatsbibliothek, cod. theol. lat. fol. 485. Fig. 78), already possessed an extensive picture cycle in early Christian times.[12] It is not surprising that the Books of Kings were strong favorites with the artists of the Dura synagogue; and because the largest group of Dura frescoes is based on the Books of Kings, we have selected a characteristic scene from this cycle in order to investigate the connection with Christian book illustration. As Kraeling has observed, the scene of the destruction of the temple of Dagon (1 Kings 5 ff.) represents two successive phases amalgamated in a single composition (Fig. 59).[13] The open cella of the temple at the right presents the curious feature

of the pedestal, duplicated to correspond to the repeated overturning of the idol of Dagon. In accord with the principles of the simultaneous method,[14] the successive falls of the one statue (1 Kings 5:1–5) are rendered pictorially by juxtaposing the two events. At the left, the ark of the covenant, which brought ruin to the Philistines when it was displayed in the temple of Dagon, is being removed on a wagon drawn by a team of oxen (in the text it is "two milch kine") led by two priests and diviners and followed by three lords of the Philistines standing in a row in the background. The ark, presented here but omitted in the first scene, refers to both narrative moments depicted in the fresco.

In the eleventh-century Book of Kings in the Vatican (cod. gr. 333), which has an extensive cycle of miniatures deriving from a very early archetype,[15] the same two phases shown in

---

[12] [Cf. Weitzmann, "Book Illustration of the Fourth Century: Tradition and Innovation," *Akten des VII. Internationalen Kongresses für Christliche Archäologie, Trier, 1965* (Rome, 1969), pp. 263 ff.; reprinted herewith, p. 104.]

[13] Kraeling, *Synagogue*, pp. 99 ff. and pl. 56, here the older bibliography.

[14] Cf. Weitzmann, *Roll and Codex: A Study of the Origin and Method of Text Illustration* (2d ed. Princeton, 1970), pp. 13 ff.

[15] J. Lassus, "Les miniatures byzantines du Livre des Rois," *Mélanges d'archéologie et d'histoire*, 45 (1928), 38 ff; H. Buchthal, *The Miniatures of the Paris Psalter* (London, 1938), pp. 20, 23, 28 and figs. 51, 71; Weitzmann, *Roll and Codex*, pp. 132 ff., 175 ff., 178 ff., 194 ff. and figs. 174, 183–84, 186; Idem, "The Psalter Vatopedi 761—Its Place in the Aristocratic Psalter Recension," *Journal of the Walters Art Gallery*, 10 (1947), pp. 40 ff. and figs. 27f; Idem, "Illustration der Septuaginta," p. 105 and fig. 7; p. 110 and fig. 13. [Translated and reprinted herewith, pp. 55 ff. and Fig. 34; p. 62 and Fig. 40.] Idem, *Geistige Grundlagen und Wesen der Makedonischen Renaissance* ("Arbeitsgemeinschaft für Forschung des Landes Nordrhein-Westfalen. Geisteswissenschaften," 107 [Cologne and Opladen, 1963]), 13 and fig. 4. [Translated and reprinted herewith, p. 182 and Fig. 164–65.]

Fig. 59 *Dura-Europos, Synagogue. Fresco.*
Destruction of the Temple of the Dagon

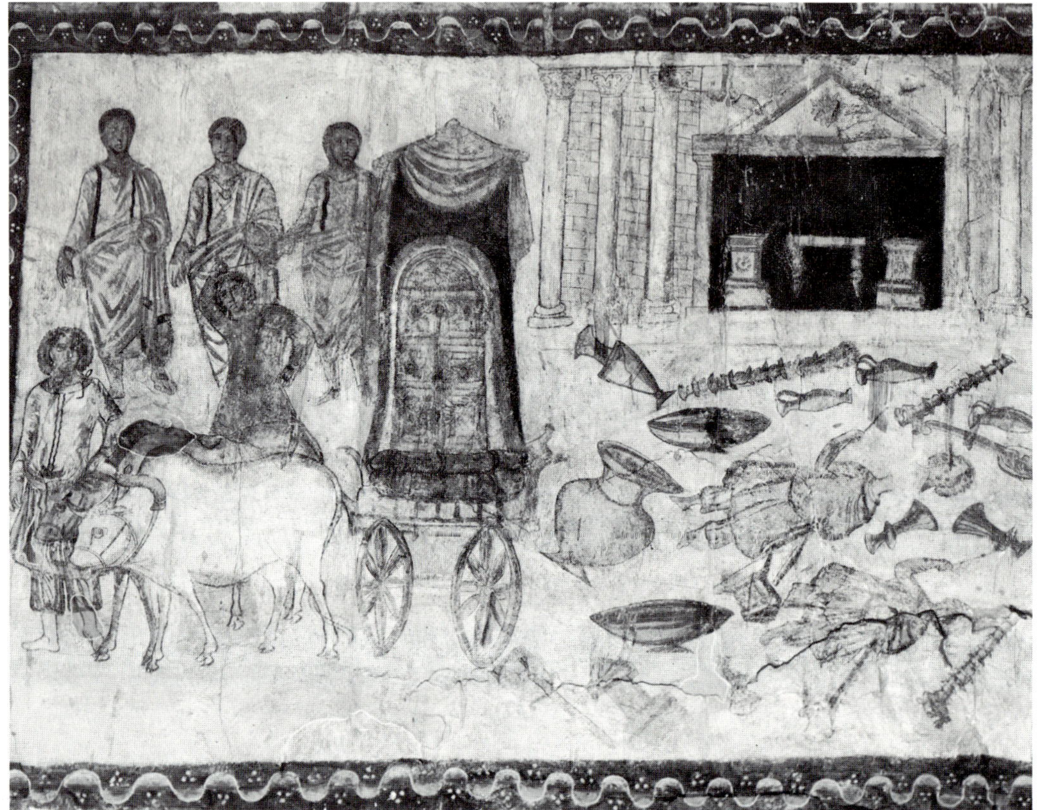

the Dura fresco are represented. The first (Fig. 60) shows the idol of Dagon in a double arcade on a pedestal at the left and an empty pedestal at the right. Near the vacant pedestal the statue is shown falling with its arms hanging down; and one can distinguish still another representation of the fallen statue lying diagonally in the foreground as in the Dura fresco. Here, then, the simultaneous method is carried a step further in that the statue is depicted thrice: overturned, set up again, and falling down once more. Shortly after the discovery of the Dura frescoes, H. Gute made a watercolor copy which

clearly shows a statue on the pedestal to the left; this statue, no longer visible on the fresco, I am informed,[16] could hardly have been invented by the copyist. Instead, presumably as the result of weathering, it has disappeared. It is difficult to imagine that the duplication of the pedestal and the threefold rendering of the Dagon statue in the simultaneous method could have been devised independently two different times; accordingly we draw what is, a priori, the more probable inference: both representations derive from a common

16 Professor Kraeling transmitted this information orally.

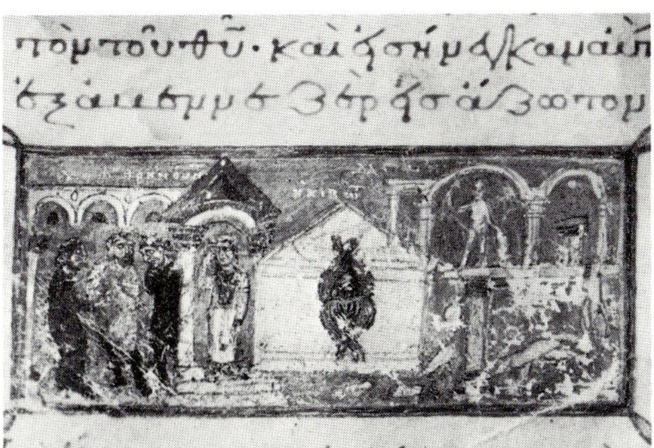

Fig. 60 *Vatican, Biblioteca. Cod. gr. 333, fol. 9ᵛ. Destruction of the Temple of Dagon*

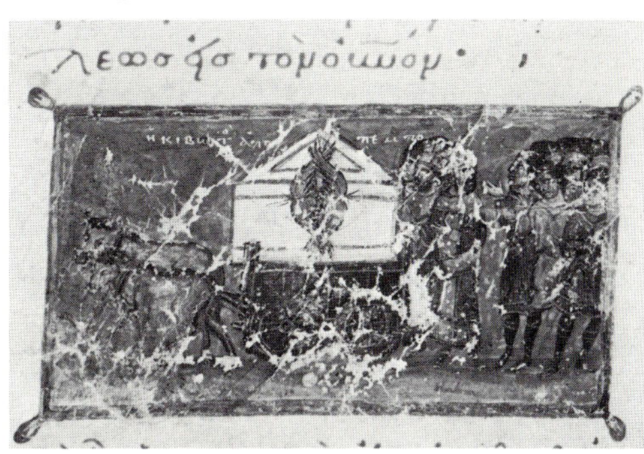

Fig. 61 *Vatican, Biblioteca. Cod. gr. 333, fol. 10ʳ. Departure of the Ark of the Covenant*

archetype. Furthermore, in both pictures the temple is divided in much the same way into an exterior and interior view, except that in the miniature the outside of the temple is to the left of the interior, while in the fresco, in order to save space and to center the composition the exterior view of the temple surrounds the interior like a frame. To be sure, the tiny miniature which measures 3.3 by 7.5 centimeters lacks the scattered temple implements; but to compensate for this and to clarify the scene, the ark of the covenant, adorned with a cherub, is displayed in the temple. This, as well as the group of lamenting Philistines, may well have been depicted in the archetype; and thus we may conclude that the miniature is a closer copy of the original composition than is the fresco where spatial considerations made alterations unavoidable.

In the Dura scene of the removal of the ark, the wagon with its precious contents is rendered in front view but the oxen are depicted in side view. Surely this should not be interpreted realistically, as if at this moment the procession is turning left; but rather it should be understood as a makeshift solution necessitated by the lack of space.

One would expect, therefore, that the archetype showed the wagon with the ark in side view as, in fact, we find it in the corresponding miniature of the Vatican manuscript (Fig. 61) where, moreover, the Philistine lords, in accord with 1 Kings 6:12, move along behind the ark, suggesting that the grouping of the lords in the background of the fresco is to be understood as yet another change made in order to use the available space in the best way. The miniature reproduces a composition which is more organic than that of the fresco and which is, in the last analysis, nearer Hellenistic art and thus closer to the original. Furthermore, between the two miniatures already described, the Vatican manuscript has yet another scene which shows the destruction of the Philistines, not by means of boils, but by a column of fire sent down from heaven. The five Philistine leaders lament this catastrophe caused by the ark which again is rendered as large as a man.

If, as we believe, the frescoes and the miniatures, in fact, do represent the same iconographical tradition, we gain new insight into the origins of both the synagogue frescoes and the Christian manuscript. With regard to the fresco, one is compelled to assume the existence of an extensive archetype from which the fresco painter chose two out of three available phases of a story, not making literal copies of single episodes but compressing them in the manner described above. The comparison demonstrates further that in the archetype the events were rendered spatially, as in Greco-Roman art, while the frescoes are orientalized through a stronger use of frontality and by the adaptation of the local Mesopotamian costume tradition. On the other hand, just as we demonstrated earlier in the case of scenes from the Pentateuch, we may conclude that the Christian illustrations of the Books of Kings derive from a Jewish pictorial tradition. The next step, which would take us beyond the limits of this study, would be a similar investigation of the synagogue scenes that go back to the Prophets and other biblical books and of their possible connection with Christian manuscripts.

The Octateuchs

The question of a Jewish Bible illustration has become an actuality because of the Dura synagogue. But even if Dura had not been unearthed, we would have had to postulate the existence of Jewish book illustration on the basis of the considerable traces it left in Christian manuscript illumination. Not only do scenes in the Octateuchs such as Jacob's Blessing, mentioned above, share a common tradition with the Dura frescoes, but they contain iconographic elements which can be explained only by Jewish sources. Here I refer briefly to an example from the Istanbul Octateuch,[17] in which the temptation of Eve is represented, most curiously, with a serpent on the back of a camel (Fig. 56), thus following exactly the passage in *Pirkê Rabbi Eliezer*: "'Now the serpent was more subtil than any beast of the field' (Gen. 3:1). It's appearance was something like that of the camel, and he [Satan] mounted and rode upon it." This is by no means a unique case within the Octateuch of iconography based on Jewish sources; and, at this point, I should like to add another example from the Book of Genesis. Whereas the Bible text tersely describes the sacrifice of Cain and Abel, "And the Lord had respect unto Abel and his offering; but unto Cain and his offering he had not respect" (Gen. 4:4), the Haggadic texts[18] answer the troublesome question of how God's pleasure and displeasure over the sacrifices were made visible. According to these Jewish commentaries, God sent down a column of fire to consume Abel's sacrifice; and in the depiction of this event in the Vatican Octateuch 747 (Fig. 62) which, as mentioned above, is nearest to the archetype, we see such a column of fire pouring down from the segment

[17] Weitzmann, "Illustration der Septuaginta," p. 119 and fig. 26. [Translated and reprinted herewith, p. 74. For further discussion of this scene and of the problem of Jewish elements in Christian art see G. Kretschmar, "Ein Beitrag zur Frage nach dem Verhältnis zwischen jüdischer und christlicher Kunst in der Antike," in *Abraham unser Vater: Festschrift für Otto Michel* (Leiden and Cologne, 1963), pp. 295 ff. and C.-O. Nordström, "Rabbinic Features in Byzantine and Catalan Art," *Cahiers Archéologiques*, 15 (1965), 179 ff.]
[18] L. Ginzberg, *The Legends of the Jews* (Philadelphia, 1947), 1:107, and 5:135, n. 10.

Fig. 62 *Vatican, Biblioteca. Cod. gr. 747, fol. 25^v. Cain and Abel*

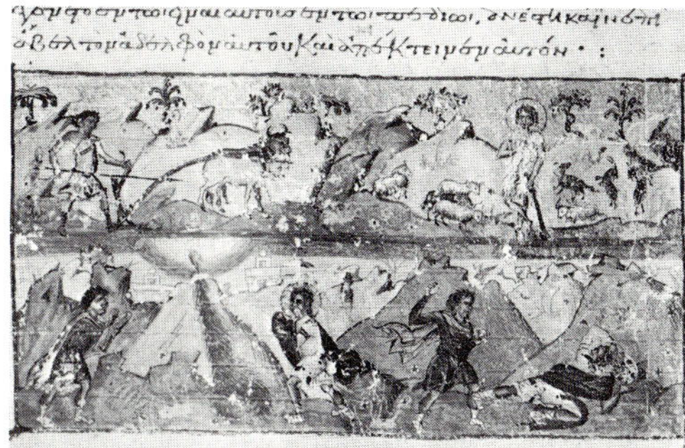

Fig. 63 *Vatican, Biblioteca. Cod. gr. 746, fol. 153^r. Finding and Childhood of Moses*

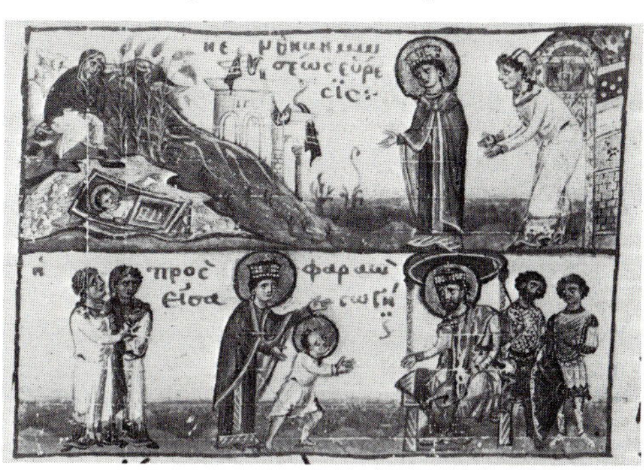

of sky onto the sacrifice on the ground in front of the nimbed Abel.

Following the sacrifice is the scene of the murder of Abel, which reveals even more unequivocally a Jewish source. Again the Bible text, "Cain rose up against Abel his brother and slew him" (Gen. 4:8), is not detailed enough to suggest to the artist the manner in which the killing was accomplished; and consequently the slaying is depicted in Christian art in various ways. The Haggadah texts, however, comment on the fact that there was no precedent for the killing of a man and, taking this circumstance into account, one of the texts describes the event as follows:[19] "The manner of Abel's death was the most cruel conceivable. Not knowing what injury was fatal, Cain pelted all parts of his body with stones, until one struck him on the neck and inflicted death." The illustrator of the Vatican Octateuch, following this text precisely, pictured Cain attacking with a stone in each hand and showed Abel, with a bleeding wound in his neck, already fallen to the ground.

A scene in the Book of Exodus[20] in the second Vatican Octateuch (cod. gr. 746, of the twelfth century, Fig. 63) may serve to demonstrate that the Jewish elements in the Octateuchs are not limited to the Book of Genesis and, furthermore, that the Haggadic texts were not the sole Jewish sources. The Finding of the Infant Moses in the Nile is followed by a scene which no text in the Bible elucidates: Pharaoh's daughter brings Moses to her father; and, with a joyful gesture, the boy runs into the open arms of the ruler of Egypt enthroned under a baldachin. In this case it is the *Antiquitates Judaicae* of Flavius Josephus (II. ix, 7)[21] that best clarifies the extra-biblical scene: "Such was the child whom Thermuthis [the name of Pharaoh's daughter] adopted as her son, being blessed with no offspring of her own. Now one day she brought Moses to her father and showed him to him and told him how she had been mindful for the

[19] Ginzberg, *Legends*, 1:109.

[20] J. Wilpert, *Die römischen Mosaiken und Malereien der kirchlichen Bauten vom IV–XIII. Jahrhunderts*, 1 (Freiburg i.B., 1916), 448 and fig. 160.
[21] A. St. J. Thackeray (trans.), *Josephus* (London, 1930), 4:264.

succession, were it God's will to grant her no child of her own, by bringing up a boy of divine beauty and generous spirit, and by what a miracle she had rescued him of the river's bounty, 'and methought' she said 'to make him my child and heir to thy kingdom.' With these words she led the child into her father's arms." Here the text corresponds so closely to the picture that one can posit an early illustrated Josephus manuscript as the source for this miniature.

The existence of illustrated Josephus manuscripts, the *Antiquitates Judaicae* as well as the *Bellum Judaicum,* can be demonstrated also by means of several scattered miniatures in the Paris manuscript of the *Sacra Parallela* (Bibliothèque Nationale cod. gr. 923) assignable to the ninth century.[22] In this manuscript we deal with "migrated" miniatures which imply the existence of older, surely pre-iconoclastic, models.

VIENNA GENESIS

As we stressed at the outset, in investigating the possibility of Jewish sources for manuscript illustrations, each unit of text should be examined separately. What is more, in cases where a single book, for example the Book of Genesis, has different pictorial recensions, we must raise anew the question of Jewish sources for each recension. The well-known Vienna Genesis obviously belongs to a recension different from the Genesis

cycle in the Octateuchs,[23] as is evidenced, for example, by the totally different treatment of Jacob's blessing (compare Figs. 58 and 138).

Nordström, in one of his many studies of the Jewish pictorial sources,[24] has already called attention to the angel who accompanies Joseph on the way to his brothers and has identified him as the archangel Gabriel whom Jewish legends mention at this point in the narrative. Pächt took up this point and adduced a whole series of further examples which show that the angel is not an isolated case and that the cycle of the Vienna Genesis is in fact permeated with pictorial elements based on Jewish legends.[25] He rightly emphasized that almost all of the figures not based on the Bible text and previously considered to be "anecdotal additions" were to be explained by Jewish legends. One of the most striking examples adduced by Pächt is the second scene of Joseph interpreting dreams to Pharaoh;[26] here the court official going through a gate—formerly considered to be a "free invention"[27]—

---

[22] Weitzmann, *Roll and Codex,* p. 134 and pl. 115.

[23] For the problem of the different picture recensions consult Weitzmann, "Illustration der Septuaginta," pp. 101 ff. [Translated and reprinted herewith, pp. 49 ff. Also H. Fillitz, "Die Wiener Genesis: Résumé der Diskussion," in *Akten zum VII. Internationalen Kongress für Frühmittelalterforschung* (Graz and Cologne, 1967), pp. 44 ff.]

[24] C.-O. Nordström, "Some Jewish Legends in Byzantine Art," *Byzantion,* 25–27 (1955–57), 489.

[25] O. Pächt, "Ephraimillustration, Haggadah und Wiener Genesis," in *Festschrift Karl M. Swoboda* (Vienna, 1959), pp. 213 ff.

[26] Ibid., p. 219.

[27] Gerstinger, *Wiener Genesis,* p. 106 and fol. XVIII, pl. 36.

is identified, on the basis of Jewish texts, as Potiphar who slips off to let his wife know about Joseph's rise to eminence.

In order to consolidate Pächt's findings and at the same time to focus sharply on the Jewish pictorial elements transmitted in the Vienna Genesis, we would like to examine yet another instance, also from the Joseph cycle, where Jewish legend seems to have penetrated the iconography. In the scene of Joseph interpreting the dreams of the butler and the baker (Fig, 64),[28] a woman, wearing a purple cloak over a brown garment trimmed with segmenta, stands behind the guard sitting outside the prison walls. She approaches the guard from behind, turning to him with an urgent gesture that underlines her words as if she were asking him for something. The guard turns toward the woman and, as indicated by his tranquilly raised right hand, replies. Who is this woman who plays an important role in this scene but who cannot be explained by the Bible text?

According to Jewish legend,[29] Joseph was not safe from the wiles of Potiphar's wife (whose name is given as Zuleika) even in prison. She had persuaded her husband not to kill Joseph but to throw him in prison so that she would have the chance to visit him there and seduce him.

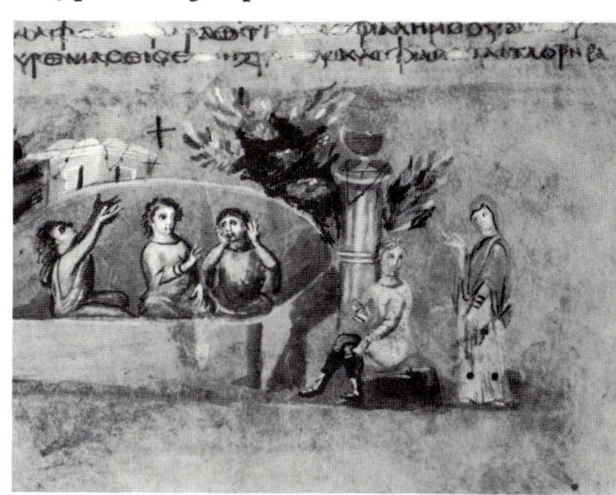

Fig. 64 *Vienna, Nationalbibliothek. Cod. theol. 31, pict. 33. Joseph in Prison*

Neither Zuleika's threats nor her promises to arrange his release could bring Joseph to the point of succumbing to her wishes. Thus, it seems natural to identify the woman depicted in the Vienna Genesis as Zuleika, Potiphar's wife. In comparison with the preceding miniature she wears a simpler costume. In our opinion, the reason for this is that Zuleika embarked on her escapade inconspicuously clad and veiled.

THE MANUSCRIPT OF THE SACRA PARALLELA IN PARIS

Until now our examples of miniatures incorporating features of Jewish legend have been taken from the Books of Genesis and Exodus; and, a priori, it is to be expected that, precisely in these two books, legendary elements would have penetrated most strongly. The extra-biblical elements are by no means limited to the Pentateuch, however, but can also be found in other books of the Old Testament. To demonstrate this, we have

[28] Fr. Wickhoff, *Die Wiener Genesis* (Vienna, 1895), p. 118, p. 131 and pl. 33; Gerstinger, *Wiener Genesis*, p. 103 and fol. XVII, pl. 33; P. Buberl, *Die byzantinischen Handschriften 1* ("Beschreibendes Verzeichnis der illuminierten Handschriften in Österreich," 8, Part IV [Leipzig, 1937]), 115 and pl. 37, no. 33.
[29] Ginzberg, *Legends*, 2:58 ff. and 5:341, n. 138 ff. [Nordström, "Rabbinic Features," p. 182. Also G. Strauss, "Jüdische Quellen frühchristlicher Kunst: Optische oder liter-

arische Anregung?" *Zeitschrift für die Neutestamentliche Wissenschaft*, 62 (1966), 114 ff.]

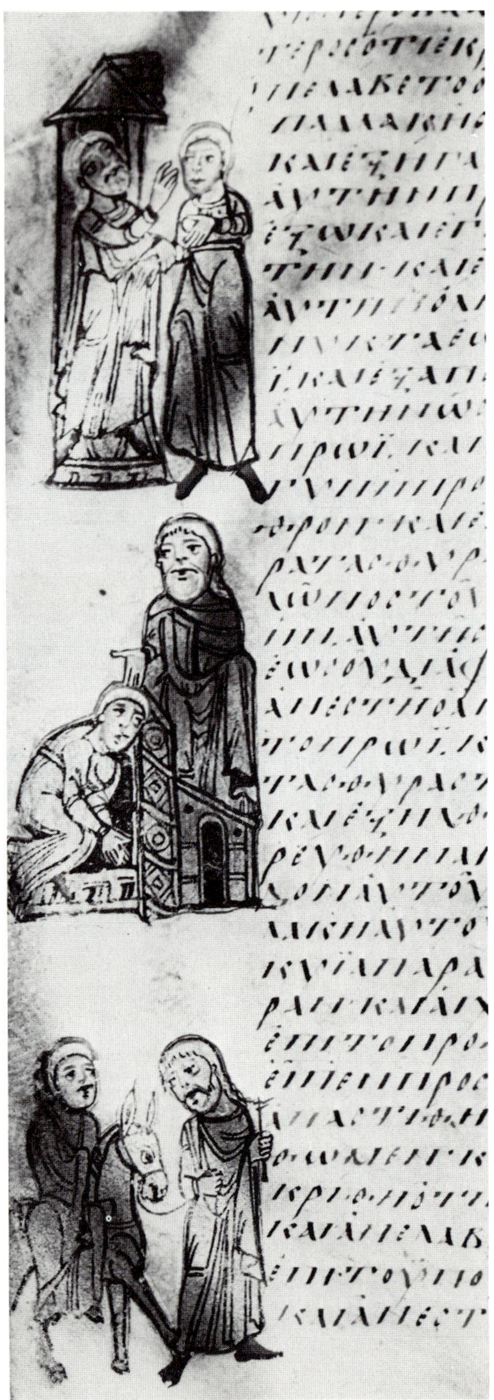

Fig. 65 *Paris, Bibliothèque Nationale. Cod. gr. 923, fol. 371ᵛ. Story of the Levite and His Concubine*

chosen two instances from a manuscript with particular importance for the reconstruction of Early Christian book illumination, the *Sacra Parallela* of John of Damascus which has come down to us, most richly illustrated, in the ninth-century copy in Paris.[30] This manuscript is especially important because the scenes from the first eight books of the Old Testament scattered throughout its margins clearly belong to a recension other than that of the Octateuchs already discussed.[31]

Our first example (Fig. 65), drawn from the Book of Judges (19:25–28), presents in three stages the story of the Levite and his concubine: in the first the Levite hands over the girl to the Benjamites; in the second he finds her the next morning lying before the house door; and in the third he goes off with her seated on a donkey. These representations, especially the second and third, so far as they depict the concubine clearly as being alive, contradict the Septuagint text according to which she should be

[30] J. R. Harris, *Fragments of Philo Judaeus* (Cambridge, 1886); Weitzmann, *Die byzantinische Buchmalerei des IX. und X. Jahrhunderts* (Berlin, 1935), pp. 80 ff. and pl. 86. (The author no longer maintains his former view that Italy was the place of origin; a Palestinian origin is now thought to be more probable.) Idem, *Roll and Codex*, pp. 115 ff., 133 ff., 150 ff., and figs. 103, 114–15. Idem, "Illustration der Septuaginta," pp. 105 ff. and figs. 8 f., 14, 16 f. [Translated and reprinted herewith, pp. 56 ff. and Figs. 35, 36, 41, 43, and 44.] The author is preparing a monograph on this manuscript in which he will treat more fully the question of the various models and the elements derived from Jewish legends which some of them contain.

[31] We shall attempt to offer the evidence for this conclusion in the forthcoming publication referred to in the preceding note.

dead. The passage in the *Sacra Parallela* (in common with the Vaticanus) has the phrase ὅτι ἦν νεκρά whereas the Alexandrinus uses the phrase ἀλλὰ τεθνήκει. Plainly, then, one would expect a representation in which the concubine lies dead on the threshold and her corpse is carried off on the donkey as, in fact, the event is rendered in the Octateuchs.[32] The phrase "that she was dead" is an addition in the Septuagint text, not occurring in the Hebrew text which is so vague and ambiguous that it elicited the addition in the Septuagint. The Hebrew text merely states that the concubine did not answer, in itself no proof that she was dead, although this fact emerges in subsequent verses. Therefore, we must assume that the miniature was originally composed for the Hebrew and subsequently taken over unchanged for the Septuagint text. This sort of migration of pictures from one text to another occurs with extraordinary frequency in book illumination; and often it can be pinned down only when the copyist has not troubled to adapt his miniature to a new text which has changed or supplemented the original.

Two episodes from the Books of Kings provide our second example (Fig. 66). The first episode depicts the execution of Agag, the king of the Amalekites (1 Kings 15:32 ff), in a manner contrary to the Septuagint text which strongly emphasizes that Samuel himself carried out the execution, whereas in the miniature an executioner

32 As, for example, in the Octateuch of Smyrna (Evangelical School, cod. 8). D. C. Hesseling, *Miniatures de l'Octateuque grec de Smyrne* (Leiden, 1909), pl. 95, no. 331.

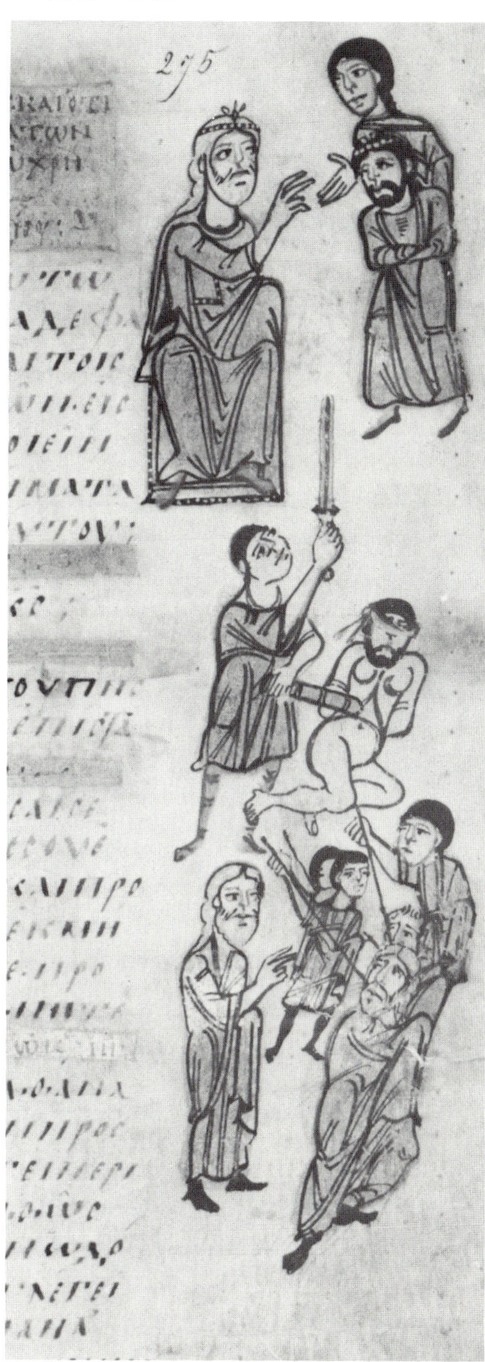

Fig. 66 *Paris, Bibliothèque Nationale. Cod. gr. 923, fol. 275ʳ. Executions of Agag and of the Baalite Priests*

with a drawn sword does the killing. It will not do to explain away the discrepancy merely as artistic license. According to the Haggadic texts[33] the difficulty was that a Nazirite, such as Samuel, was forbidden to touch a dead body. Flavius Josephus (*Ant. Jud.* VI. vii, 5) sought to solve the problem by having Samuel give an express command to have Agag put to death, thereby implying clearly that Samuel himself was not the executioner. Thus, the miniature in the *Sacra Parallela* is in full agreement with the text of Josephus, which, on the basis of the depiction of the childhood of Moses in the Octateuchs, we had already postulated was illustrated.

The miniature immediately following the Execution of Agag presents an analogous situation. Here it is the priests of Baal that are executed. According to the Septuagint (3 Kings 18:40) this was done by Elijah himself, "And Elijah brought them down to the brook Kishon and slew them there." That the prophet used a sword is confirmed in 3 Kings 19:1, "how he had slain all the prophets of Baal with a sword," but in the miniature Elijah gives the command for the execution which is carried out by some Israelites who pierce their victims with lances. In this case, too, the pictorial representation can be best explained by the text of Josephus (*Ant. Jud.* VIII. xiii, 6) which, emending the text of the Septuagint, specifies that at Elijah's command the Israelites seized the prophets of Baal and killed them. The manner of killing is not described, however, so that the use of lances, which

is at variance with the Septuagint text, may be taken to be artistic liberty.

The Recension of the Cotton Genesis

Whereas all indications suggest that the miniatures of the Octateuchs and the Vienna Genesis and the biblical representations which underlie the *Sacra Parallela* originated in Syrian and Palestinian territory, whence they spread to Constantinople, scholars unanimously consider Alexandria to be the home of the archetype of the extensive miniature cycle of the sixth-century Cotton Genesis in the British Museum, almost totally destroyed by fire in 1731.[34] Since Tikkanen proved that the thirteenth-century mosaics in the atrium cupolas of San Marco in Venice derive from the same archetype (in our opinion it is more than likely that the Cotton manuscript itself served as the model in Venice), these mosaics, despite their late date, may be considered as more or less exact copies of a miniature recension harking back to Alexandria.

[33] Ginzberg, *Legends*, 4:68 and 6:233, n. 65.

[34] The text was published by C. Tischendorf, *Monumenta sacra inedita* (nova collectio II; Leipzig, 1857) and was supplemented by F. W. Gotch, *A Supplement to Tischendorf's Reliquiae ex incendio ereptae codicis celeberrimi Cottoniani* (London, 1881). The fundamental but by no means comprehensive treatment of the miniatures, is by J. J. Tikkanen, "Die Genesismosaiken von S. Marco und ihr Verhältnis zu den Miniaturen der Cottonbibel," *Acta Societatis Scientiarum Fennicae*, 17 (1889), 99 ff. Recently, Weitzmann, "Observations on the Cotton Genesis Fragments," *Late Classical and Mediaeval Studies in Honor of Albert Mathias Friend, Jr.* (Princeton, 1955), pp. 112 ff.

If the illustration of Jewish texts was in fact as extensive as the examples discussed above suggest, one would expect to find traces of it transmitted in Alexandrian illumination; for Alexandria had what was perhaps the largest Jewish colony in the Hellenistic world; and Alexandrian Jews had completely assimilated Greek culture and had adopted as their own its material and artistic creations. Consequently the miniatures of the Cotton Genesis would be a natural place to search for subject matter derived from Jewish legend. This has not yet been systematically attempted,[35] and the following comments are intended only as the stimulus to further research rather than as the results of a thorough investigation.

In the pendentive of one of the narthex cupolas in San Marco the death of Pharaoh's baker (Fig. 67)[36] is not represented as Joseph had prophesied in the Septuagint (Gen. 40:18 f.) and as it later came to pass (Genesis 40:22), namely by hanging (ἐκρέμασεν is the expression used in the Septuagint). Instead, the baker is shown crucified in the manner often used for the thieves in the crucifixion of Christ, i.e., not nailed to the cross but with his arms bent over the crosspiece and tied in back. Again the source is Flavius Josephus, who plainly states that the baker was crucified (*Ant. Jud.* II. v, 3; ἀνεσταύρωσε).

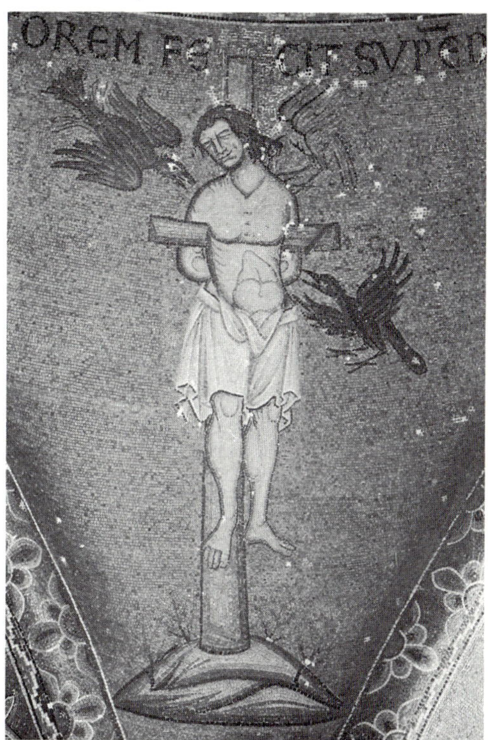

Fig. 67 *Venice, San Marco. Atrium Mosaic. Execution of the Baker*

The mosaic representation agrees so precisely with this text that the likelihood of an illustrated Josephus is enhanced, since the number of cases in which this text corresponds to the pictorial representations increases.

The Crucifixion of the Baker occurs also in the Octateuchs, although in another form.[37] There, a real nailing to the cross is combined with a beheading; and the decapitated head is shown lying on the ground. Despite this variation in treatment, the Octateuch representation also agrees more closely with the text of Josephus than with the Septuagint. Therefore, we may assume in this case the

[35] Pächt, "Ephraimillustration," p. 220, observes, "Die Cottonbibel ist, soviel ich sehe, eine reine Septuaginta-Illustration, die Vorlage der Wiener Genesis war es nicht." He apparently considers Jewish sources unlikely in the case of the Cotton Genesis.

[36] O. Demus, *Die Mosaiken von San Marco in Venedig* (Vienna, 1935), fig. 46.

[37] Cf. the Octateuch in Smyrna, Hesseling, *Octateuque de Smyrne*, pl. 42, no. 128.

existence of an illustrated *Antiquitates Judaicae*, especially since we have already interpreted another scene in the same manuscript, the Presentation of Moses to Pharaoh (Fig. 63), by means of the Josephus text. Nevertheless, the Cotton manuscript and the Genesis cycle of the Octateuchs undoubtedly belong to different recensions, and we can only conclude that an illustrated Josephus infiltrated into more than one recension of the illustrated Septuagint. (In this connection the question of whether or not the illustration of Josephus could have existed in more than one recension is left unanswered.) This leads to the conjecture that the illustrated text of Flavius Josephus, particularly the *Antiquitates Judaicae*—although it can be shown that the *Bellum Judaicum* was also illustrated[38]—enjoyed a special popularity and wide circulation.

The Latin West

In choosing new examples to substantiate the proposition that pictorial elements based on Jewish sources had a broad influence on Bible illustration, for a number of reasons we have purposely confined ourselves primarily to the Greek East and to the Septuagint tradition. To begin with, because the Septuagint was a pre-Christian Greek translation of the

Hebrew writings, it would be logical to assume that the conditions prerequisite for the illustration of the Old Testament existed much earlier in the Greek East than in the Latin West. Furthermore, we must realize that the illustrator of Greek books maintained a much more conservative attitude than artists in the Latin West. There is no doubt that manuscripts such as the Greek Octateuchs of the eleventh to thirteenth centuries, in spite of many alterations, reflect early archetypes more faithfully than contemporary Romanesque or early Gothic manuscripts, even though these, too, certainly require careful investigation in connection with the interrelated questions raised here. And finally, the material from the West so far has eluded a really systematic treatment because no serious attempt has yet been made to attack the problem of the different pictorial recensions; whereas at least a serious beginning to a solution has been made for the eastern material.

A typical example of the uncertainty prevailing in questions of this kind is the often discussed cycle of mosaics in the nave of S. Maria Maggiore in Rome.[39]

---

[38] Examples are to be found in the manuscript of the *Sacra Parallela* in Paris (Bibliothèque Nationale cod. gr. 923), mentioned previously. Cf. Weitzmann, *Roll and Codex*, p. 134 and fig. 115. Even though they date to the ninth century, the illustrations of this manuscript, which are all borrowings, derive from pre-iconoclastic archetypes.

[39] We cite only the following works from the extensive bibliography on the subject: J. P. Richter and A. C. Taylor, *The Golden Age of Classical Christian Art* (London, 1904); Wilpert, *Die römischen Mosaiken*, 1:412 ff. and 3, pls. 8 ff.; M. van Berchem and E. Clouzot, *Mosaiques chrétiennes du IVe au Xe siècle* (Geneva, 1924), pp. 11 ff.; L. de Bruyne, "Ricerche iconografiche sui mosaici dell' arco triomfale di S. Maria Maggiore," *Rivista di archeologia cristiana*, 13 (1936), 239 ff.; K. Schefold, "Altchristliche Bilderzyklen: Bassussarkophag und S. Maria Maggiore," *Rivista di archeologia cristiana*, 16 (1939),

Many scholars have pointed out parallels in Roman art for single figures and for whole compositions; while Morey,[40] comparing the mosaics with the miniatures of the Octateuchs and especially of the Vatican Joshua Roll, has assumed an archetype for the mosaics ultimately of eastern origin or, to put it more precisely, an archetype of the recension to which the Octateuchs belong. In our opinion, however, the relationship of the S. Maria Maggiore mosaics to illustrated manuscripts, which must be assumed to be the ultimate source, is by no means clear. The parallels with the Octateuchs are too vague and, to a large degree, they can be accounted for by the common textual source they share. In our opinion the differences so outweigh the similarities that the hypothesis that S. Maria Maggiore reflects another recension, perhaps a western one after all, must be seriously taken into consideration.

In one of the many articles in which he has tracked down Jewish sources, Nordström[41] elucidated one of the Moses scenes of S. Maria Maggiore with greater precision than hitherto had been attained when he found the clue in Jewish legends. We refer to the scene where the Israelites throw stones at Moses, Joshua, and Caleb, but the stones glance off an aureole surrounding the three men (it is the column of cloud in which the glory of the Lord is revealed).

Among the texts cited by Nordström the biblical paraphrase known as the *Targum Pseudo-Jonathan* most precisely explains this very detail. Naturally the artist who created the archetype of the mosaic did not necessarily use this very Targum, but Nordström certainly has discovered the type of text for which illustrated examples must be assumed. Consequently, if a Jewish pictorial source has been recognized in a work, the question of its recension gains significance. For if the mosaics were an offshoot of Septuagint illustration as presented in the Octateuchs,[42] one would have to assume that the elements of Jewish legend were already present in the archetype; and since we have already been able to demonstrate the influence of Jewish legend in several cases in the Octateuchs themselves, no new understanding would have been achieved in this instance. On the other hand, if the mosaic cycle of S. Maria Maggiore is a western creation, one would have to assume that independent of what occurred in the East, Jewish pictorial sources were also available to western artists. This is not the place to attempt to solve this problem which we consider sufficiently important to deserve separate attention.

In this connection it is important to note that it was a Latin manuscript, the Ashburnham Pentateuch (Paris, Bibliothèque Nationale, Nouv. acq. lat. 2334), and not a Greek one, that first posed the question of the existence of Jewish book illustration and which has subsequently received the most scholarly attention with

---

298 ff.; C. Cecchelli, *I mosaici della Basilica di S. Maria Maggiore* (Turin, 1956).

[40] C. R. Morey, *Early Christian Art* (2d ed.; Princeton, 1953), pp. 146 ff.

[41] C.-O. Nordström, "Rabbinica in frühchristlichen und byzantinischen Illustrationen zum 4. Buch Mose," *Figura*, N.S. 1 (1959), 28 ff.

[42] Nordström, relying on Morey's verdict here, did not investigate the problem further.

regard to this problem. More than half a century ago, Strzygowski,[43] on the basis of general features—mainly artistic and antiquarian details such as costume—postulated a Jewish source for the miniatures. Later the decoration of the title page was thoroughly discussed and connected with a Torah niche or Ark of the Covenant.[44] Recently Gutmann[45] and Hempel[46] have identified concrete examples of Jewish legend in the narrative miniatures. We still do not know where this richly illustrated luxury manuscript was produced, but there can scarcely be a doubt that it originated in a Latin milieu. Granted that eastern elements have repeatedly been pointed out in it, it is not out of the question that these found their way to a western scriptorium via an illustrated Jewish text.

North Africa and Spain have been the most frequently suggested places of origin for the Ashburnham Pentateuch, partly because reflections of the style

and iconography of this manuscript have been observed in Catalan Bibles.[47] Nordström has called attention to an iconographical detail in the cyclical representation of the story of Jonah[48] in one of these Catalan manuscripts, the Paris Bible of S. Père de Roda (Bibliothèque Nationale, lat. 6, III), which can best be explained by the text of a Midrash. Before Jonah is swallowed up by the fish, he is represented as a young man with wavy hair; afterward he is shown completely bald. "The intense heat in the belly of the fish had consumed his garments and made his hair to fall out," states the Midrash.

These widely scattered examples permit the conclusion that the content of Jewish legend in pictorial form, i.e., in illustrated manuscripts, also circulated in the western Mediterranean region. The same holds true north of the Alps, and I wish to end the series of examples with an English miniature of the twelfth century, now in the Morgan Library in New York (M 724), which may have been made in Bury Saint Edmunds. The miniature belongs to a series of Old and New Testament representations that seem to have preceded a Psalter text. After the depictions of the exposure and finding of Moses, we find the scene where the child is brought to Pharaoh (Fig. 68).[49] The representation shows

[43] J. Strzygowski, *Orient oder Rom* (Leipzig, 1901), pp. 32 ff.; A. Bauer and J. Strzygowski, "Eine alexandrinische Weltchronik," *Denkschriften der K. Akademie d. Wissenschaften, Phil.-hist. Kl.*, 51, Part II (1906), p. 184.

[44] J. C. Sloane, "The Torah Shrine in the Ashburnham Pentateuch," *Jewish Quarterly Review*, N.S. 25 (1934), 1 ff.; H. Rosenau, "Some Aspects of the Pictorial Influence of the Jewish Temple," *Palestine Exploration Fund Quarterly*, 1936, pp. 157 ff.; J. Leveen, *The Hebrew Bible in Art* (London, 1944), pp. 15 and 64.

[45] J. Gutmann, "The Jewish Origin of the Ashburnham Pentateuch Miniatures," *Jewish Quarterly Review*, N.S. 44 (1953), 55 ff. The giants in the flood, mentioned in the Midrash, are only one of several examples.

[46] H. L. Hempel, "Zum Problem der Anfänge der AT-Illustration," *Zeitschrift für die Alttestamentliche Wissenschaft*, 69 (1957), 124 ff.

[47] W. Neuss, *Die katalanische Bibelillustration um die Wende des ersten Jahrtausends und die altspanische Buchmalerei* (Bonn, 1922), pp. 59 ff.

[48] Nordström, "Some Jewish Legends," p. 505 and pl. 8. [Nordström, "Rabbinic Features," 181 ff., 196 ff. and *passim*.]

[49] M. R. James, "Four Leaves of an English Psalter of the Twelfth Century," *Walpole Society*, 25 (1937), 1 ff. and pl. 1.

Fig. 68 *New York, Morgan Library. Cod. 724,*
fol. 1ʳ. Finding and Childhood of Moses

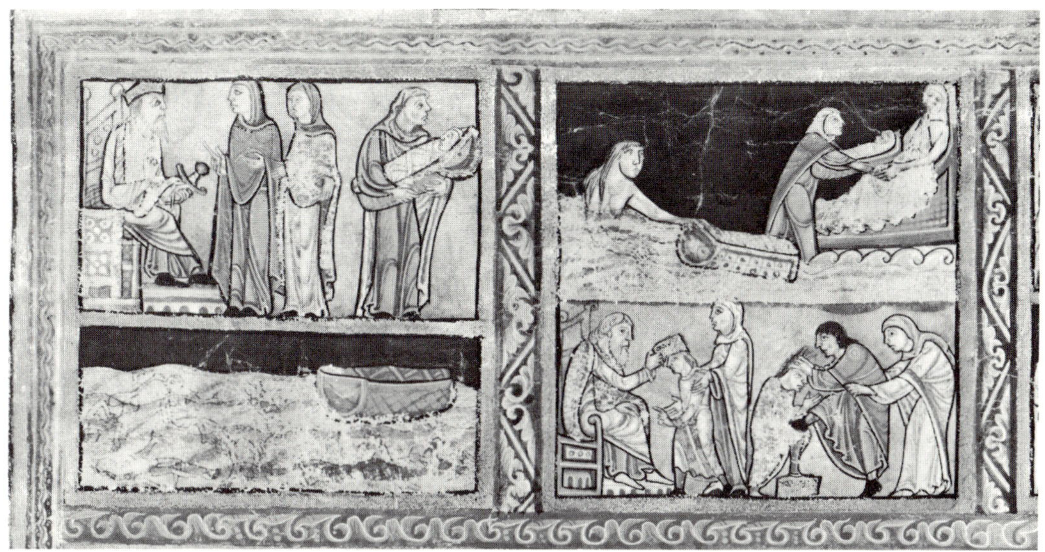

two phases which directly follow the moment illustrated in the Vatican Octateuch, cod. gr. 746 (Fig. 63) where a picture based on Flavius Josephus shows Thermuthis, Pharaoh's daughter, introducing the child Moses to her father. The passage in the text (*Ant. Jud.* II, ix, 7)[50] continues, "and Pharaoh took him to his breast, embraced him lovingly and, to please his daughter, placed his diadem on Moses' head. But Moses tore it off and in sheer childishness threw it on the ground and trampled it underfoot; this was seen as an evil omen for the kingdom. Seeing this, the holy scribe who had prophesied that the birth of the child would lead to a downfall of the Egyptian kingdom ran up with a terrible cry in order to kill him . . . But Thermuthis forestalled him, snatching the child away; Pharaoh postponed killing him, for God providentially watching over Moses' life

caused him to hesitate." Every detail of this text is illustrated.

At the left, the enthroned Pharaoh sets his crown on the head of the boy whom Thermuthis brings to him; to the right, the scribe rushes toward the boy who tramples on the crown while Thermuthis tries to restrain the man. Although this event is also recounted with but minor variations in several Midrashim, the miniature does, in fact, best agree with the Josephus text; hence, we assume that the miniature was taken from an illustrated codex of the *Antiquitates Judaicae*. It is by no means impossible that we are dealing with the same recension from which the miniature in the Greek Octateuch derives. Nevertheless, as in all such cases, before the probability of this conjecture is weighed it is necessary to check whether or not it can be verified by further examples.

[50] Thackeray translation, 4:267.

SUMMARY

We are fully aware of the fact that our selected examples, which could be multiplied in each of the manuscripts cited, raise more questions than they settle. We stand at the beginning of research on a new set of interrelated questions which cannot be completely worked out until important manuscripts such as the Octateuchs and the *Sacra Parallela* are fully published. In these lines our concern has been to build the broadest possible foundations for future research and to focus attention on the extraordinarily wide distribution which illustrated Jewish texts must have had to have exerted so extensive and lasting an influence on almost all Christian illustration of the Old Testament. The Octateuchs were produced in Constantinople, the Vienna Genesis and the *Sacra Parallela* point to Syria and Palestine as their place of origin, and the Cotton Genesis recension, rooted in the Alexandrian tradition, exercised a very strong influence in the Latin West. S. Maria Maggiore proves that illustrations of Jewish legend had traveled to Rome; the Ashburnham Pentateuch leads us perhaps to North Africa; the Catalan Bibles indicate circulation in the far West; and the emergence of Jewish pictorial elements in an English manuscript of the twelfth century obliges us to search for Jewish sources in the iconography of the whole of Early Christian and early medieval art even in the far north.

We are still a long way from being able to pinpoint the texts for which illustrations of biblical legend were first devised and from which Christian book illumination could draw. Nordström has correctly perceived that the chief sources may well have been illustrated Targumim and Midrashim,[51] and he has in mind two particular works, the *Targum Pseudo-Jonathan* for the Pentateuch and the *Pirkê Rabbi Eliezer* among the Midrashim. The evidence in favor of this mounts up, but these sources by no means appear to be the only ones. The example from the *Sacra Parallela* with the representation of the Levite and his concubine suggests that the Hebrew Bible text itself was also illustrated. Since the differences between the Hebrew and the Greek texts of the Old Testament are relatively slight, one may scarcely hope to find many examples where these differences show up in pictures; and therefore it will remain difficult to gauge the extent to which the Hebrew text of the Bible may have been illustrated. The *Antiquitates Judaicae* of Flavius Josephus is in a different category. Evidence that this work was illustrated, primarily the examples of scattered miniatures in various Bible manuscripts, is accumulating (Figs. 63, 66, 67, and 68); and at the same time the existence of an illustrated Josephus can be demonstrated from excerpted citations and their accompanying miniatures. The *Antiquitates Judaicae*, a chronicle rather than a work of religious edification, prepares the way for the type of historical illustration which

[51] Nordström, "Rabbinica," pp. 26 ff. [Nordström discusses fully "the largest series of rabbinically influenced illuminations which exists anywhere," those in the fifteenth-century Alba Bible, as well as many of the earlier monuments discussed by Weitzmann, in *The Duke of Alba's Castilian Bible* ("Figura," n.s. 5 [Uppsala, 1967]).]

became popular in the general histories of the world and which can be traced back in preserved monuments of the fourth/fifth century.[52] The hypothesis of an illustrated Hebrew Bible and of an illustrated Josephus has widened the angle of our vision but has not established its limits. We are confident that future research will find additional illustrated sources.

What were the conditions for the extensive production of illustrated books which we would like to assume for Hellenized Jewry on the basis of the evidence presented here? The Jews certainly did not invent the narrative technique which found its continuation in Byzantine Bible illustration. The credit for this goes to the Greeks of Alexandria who, in Hellenistic times, illustrated at length their great classics, especially Homer and Euripides.[53] The Jews borrowed this method of illustration from the Greeks much as Jewish writers imitated the different types of Greek literature.[54] Here we only need mention an epic written in Homeric hexameter Περὶ ᾽Ιουδαίων by a certain

Theodotos and the drama written in Euripidean style ᾽Εξαγωγή by one Ezekiel. Fragments of both of these poems by Jewish authors, 47 hexameters of the first and 269 iambic trimeters of the latter, are preserved in the *Praeparatio evangelica* of Eusebius (ix, 22 and ix, 28, 29).[55]

[55] Eusebius Pamphilus *Praeparatio Evangelica*, trans. T. Gaisford (4 vols.; Oxford, 1893), 2:385 ff., 404 ff.

[52] H. Lietzmann, "Ein Blatt aus einer antiken Weltchronik," in *Quantulacumque, Studies presented to Kirsopp Lake* (London, 1937), pp. 339 ff. and plate facing p. 140. [cf. Weitzmann, "Book Illustration of the Fourth Century," *Akten des VII. Internationalen Kongresses für Christliche Archäologie, Trier, 1965* (Rome, 1969) pp. 277 ff., herewith reprinted, pp. 96 ff. For further discussion of the question of an illustrated Josephus see Nordström, "Rabbinic Features", pp. 203 ff. and idem, *Alba Bible, passim.*]

[53] Weitzmann, *Ancient Book Illumination*, pp. 31 ff., 63 ff.

[54] Consult the observations of Kraeling, *Synagogue*, pp. 396 ff.

5

Book Illustration of the Fourth Century: Tradition and Innovation

THE long history of the book, its writing and its illustration, witnessed three revolutionary innovations of decisive consequence. The first was the invention of the papyrus scroll by the Egyptians, a medium which permitted the writing of lengthy texts and the insertion of diagrammatic and even scenic illustrations, of which the Books of the Dead (the earliest illustrated one dating from the Middle Kingdom) are our most conspicuous extant testimonies. The second was the invention of the parchment codex with "many-folded skins" which came into being at the end of the first century A.D., as proved by the epigrams of Martial,[1] and which, after a struggle of about two centuries, became the supreme ruler in the field of book production in the fourth century. The third was the invention of the printed book by Gutenberg in the fifteenth century when a new quantitative principle permitted the spread of written knowledge on an ever-increasing scale.

THE CHANGE FROM ROLL TO CODEX

It is the second revolutionary movement with which we are concerned. It affected the art of illustration even more than the art of writing: while it is true that in a codex the whole Aeneid could be written in a single volume, whereas twelve papyrus rolls were needed previously, the system of writing in vertical columns was not affected in principle. Yet for the illustrator, the clearly defined surface area of an individual parchment leaf provided entirely new possibilities which, as we shall try to prove, permitted him to develop a modest handicraft into an ambitious art on which, for centuries to come, some of the best painters concentrated their artistic efforts.[2] It may be said right at the beginning that the history of book illumination of the fourth century cannot be written on the basis of the few stray manuscripts remaining from this period, but that we can hope to reconstruct this history only by the archeological method of inference whereby close copies of a later period must be introduced in order to fill the gaps of the lost originals. The Roman marbles that are copies of lost Greek originals are, as far as their methodological treatment is concerned, the best-known parallel. As a case of analogy, later manuscripts, which reveal themselves as copies of very early models, provide our main evidence—notwithstanding the possibility of errors and

Reprinted with permission from *Akten des VII. Internationalen Kongresses für Christliche Archäologie, Trier, 1965* ("Studi di Antichità Cristiana. Pontificio Istituto di Archaeologia Cristiana," Vol. XXVII [Rome and Berlin, 1969]), pp. 257–81.

[1] Martial, *Epigrams* xiv, 184, 186, 190, 192.

[2] For the earliest phase of the illustrated book in the classical and early Christian period see G. Thiele, *De Antiquorum Libris Pictis Capita Quattuor* (Marburg, 1897); Th. Birt, *Die Buchrolle in der Kunst* (Leipzig, 1907); St. J. Gasiorowski, *Malarstwo Minjaturowe Grecko-Rzymskie* (Krakow, 1928); E. Bethe, *Buch und Bild im Altertum (aus dem Nachlass herausgegeben von Ernst Kirsten)* (Leipzig, 1945); Weitzmann, *Illustrations in Roll and Codex: A Study of the Origin and Method of Text Illustration* (2d ed. Princeton, 1970); idem, *Greek Mythology in Byzantine Art* (Princeton, 1951); idem, "Narration in Early Christendom," *American Journal of Archaeology*, 61 (1957), 83 ff.; idem, *Ancient Book Illumination* (Cambridge, Mass., 1959).

pitfalls which the use of such a method entails.

The method of illustration in Greek papyri can best be demonstrated by astronomical texts with constellation pictures, because in this branch of literature we possess not only the earliest extant example of an illustrated Greek papyrus roll but also a very considerable number of medieval copies.[3] To the second century B.C. belongs a papyrus roll two meters in length, now in the Louvre (Fig. 69),[4] containing instructions about the spheres based on propositions of a certain Eudoxus, whose text columns are intercalated with constellation pictures—the scarab for the sun, Osiris for Orion, the Claws, the Scorpion, and so on—which are placed, frameless, wherever the text requires them. The text predominates, and the pictures are subordinated. With a tenaciousness which is typical of conservative book art, this principle of illustration which we should like to term "papyrus style" persisted for centuries, even after new principles had developed. A manuscript in Munich (Staatsbibliothek, cod. 210) written

in the year 818 in Salzburg (Fig. 70)[5] shows exactly the same principle of illustration, except that the simple diagrams with partly Egyptian symbols were replaced by images essentially based on Greek mythology, images which surely were not invented for the *Phaenomena* of Aratus—although this whole group of texts is known as *Aratea*—but most likely for the *Katasterismoi* ascribed to Eratosthenes of Cyrene.[6] A typical example is the constellation picture of Andromeda fettered on two rocks which are rendered diagrammatically like stelae.

It was a revolutionary concept to separate text and picture and to enlarge each picture to the size of a whole folio, as in a manuscript in Leiden which was made in Reims in the second quarter of the ninth century.[7] The seminude Andromeda (Fig. 71) in a well-articulated, relaxed pose[8] derives from a very good classical model which, indeed, seems to have been copied so faithfully that the style of the model still shines through in the Carolingian picture. Nordenfalk[9]

[3] Cf. the very useful list of the illustrated astronomical manuscripts by A. W. Byvanck, "De platen in de Aratea van Hugo de Groot," *Mededeelingen der Koninklijke Nederlandsche Akademie van Wetenschappen, Afd. Letterkunde*, 12 (1949), 199 ff.

[4] M. Letronne and W. Brunet de Presle, *Notices et extraits des manuscrits de la Bibliothèque Impériale* (Paris, 1865), pp. 25 ff. and Album, pls. I–X; Weitzmann, *Roll and Codex*, pp. 49 ff. and fig. 37; Byvanck, "Aratea," pp. 205 ff., no. 1 (here fuller bibliography); Weitzmann, *Ancient Book Illumination*, p. 6 and pl. I, fig. 2.

[5] Weitzmann, *Roll and Codex*, p. 72.

[6] C. Robert, *Eratosthenis catasterismorum reliquiae* (Berlin, 1878).

[7] G. Thiele, *Antike Himmelsbilder* (Berlin, 1898), pp. 77 ff. and figs. 18–57; Byvanck, "Aratea," p. 214, no. 37 (here fuller bibliography).

[8] Thiele, *Himmelsbilder*, pp. 105 ff. and fig. 31; K. M. Phillips, Jr., "Perseus and Andromeda," *American Journal of Archaeology*, 72 (1968), 18 and fig. 51.

[9] C. Nordenfalk, *Der Kalender vom Jahre 354 und die lateinische Buchmalerei des IV. Jahrhunderts* ("Göteborgs Kungl. Vetenskaps och Vitterhets-samhälles Handlingar," Ser. A, V, 2 [Göteborg, 1936]), pp. 28 ff.

Fig. 69 *Paris, Louvre. Papyrus I. Constellations*

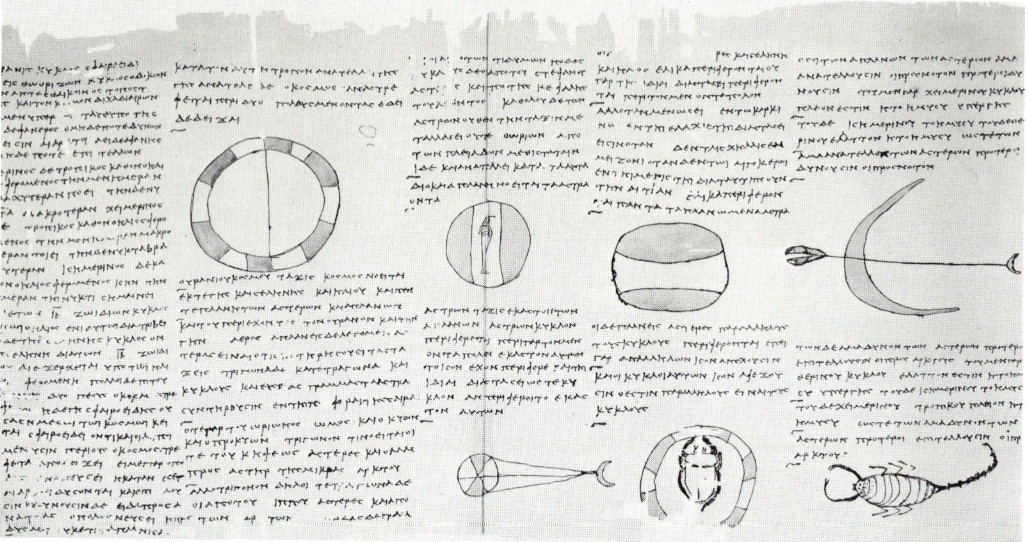

relates the miniatures of the Leiden manuscript to those of the Filocalus calendar of the year 354, a manuscript to be discussed later *in extenso*. The stylistic evidence fits that of the text. The accompanying verses in the Leiden manuscript are taken from Festus Rufus Avienus, who wrote a versified *Aratea Phaenomena* about the middle of the fourth century.

Yet the artistic transformation from column picture to full-page miniature in this case is not confined to an enlargement of the figure scale. Not only is a frame added, but this frame cuts through the rocks, thus giving the illusion that the rocky landscape continues beyond the limitations of the picture frame. In other words, the same rocks which in the Munich miniature are almost diagrammatically designed for mere iconographical reasons, in the Leiden miniature give the impression of a spatial landscape as if seen through a window,

and the blue ground adds to this illusion.

Here the miniaturist adapts principles which were developed in monumental painting previously. A fresco from Pompeii showing the liberation of Andromeda by Perseus (Fig. 72)[10] is laid out according to the very same principle of pictorially cutting the rock close to the left edge of the picture, thus stimulating the imagination of the beholder to conceive of a landscape continuing beyond the lateral limits. In the Leiden Aratus the Andromeda is a rather unique case of a miniaturist being inspired by monumental painting for the simple reason that no other constellation picture required landscape setting. It is obvious that in cases of scenic illustrations the opportunity of incorporating elements from monumental painting was much greater and

[10] A. Maiuri, *Roman Painting* (Geneva, 1953), figure on page 79.

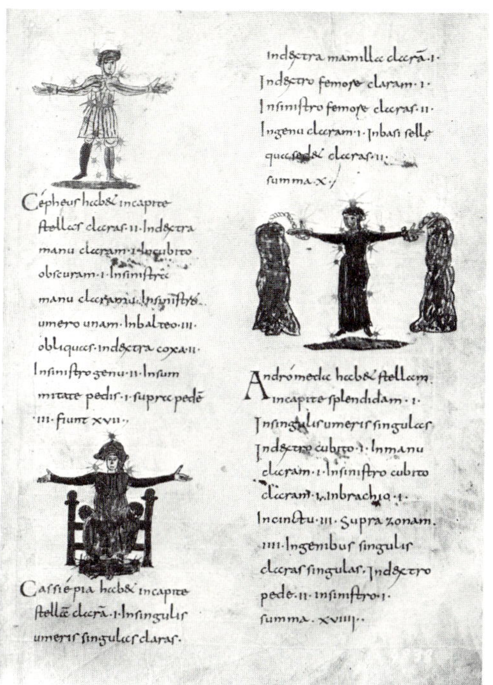

Fig. 70 *Munich, Staatsbibliothek. Cod. 210, fol. 118ᵛ. Constellations*

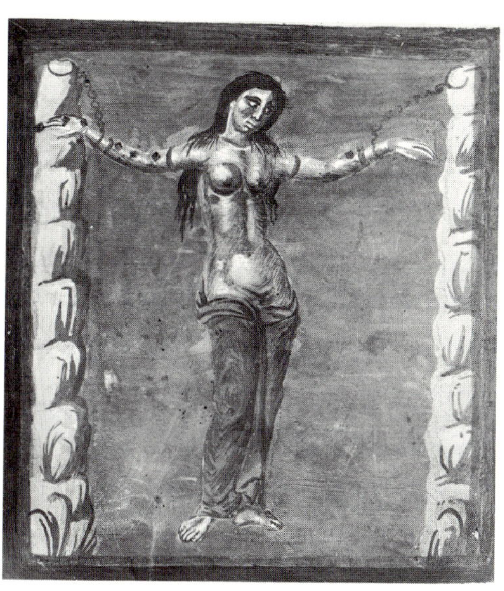

Fig. 71 *Leiden, Bibliotheek der Rijksuniversiteit. Cod. Voss lat. quart. 79, fol. 30ᵛ. Andromeda*

Fig. 72 *Naples, Museo Nazionale. Fresco from Pompeii. Perseus and Andromeda*

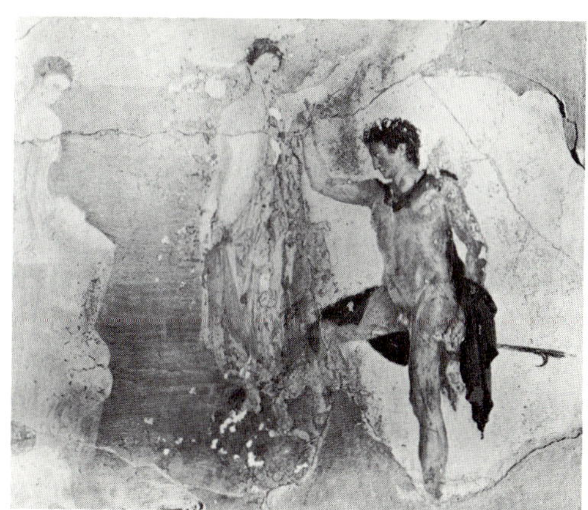

the addition of a landscape setting was one of the effective means of raising miniature painting to a higher artistic level.

Perhaps the best example to demonstrate the transition from a simple papyrus illustration to an elaborate codex miniature is the Milan Iliad (Ambrosiana, cod. F. 205 inf.), although what is left of its originally much more comprehensive picture cycle is from as late as the fifth or perhaps sixth century. Bianchi-Bandinelli, in a brilliant analysis of the Milan Iliad, has clearly demonstrated that there are different groups of miniatures which point to various models from earlier centuries.[11] The stylistically oldest group reaches back into the period of the papyrus roll and is most convincingly represented by the miniature in which Aphrodite, who is hurt, complains to Zeus (Fig. 73). The lining up of individual figures, void of background, reflects the very same system of illustration as that of the second-century Romance papyrus in Paris (Bibliothèque

[11] R. Bianchi-Bandinelli, *Hellenistic-Byzantine Miniatures of the Iliad* (Olten, 1955). Here the older bibliography.

Fig. 73 *Milan, Ambrosiana. Cod. F. 205 inf.,*
Pict. XIX. Aphrodite before Zeus
Fig. 74 *Paris, Bibliothèque Nationale. Cod.*
suppl. gr. 1294. Romance

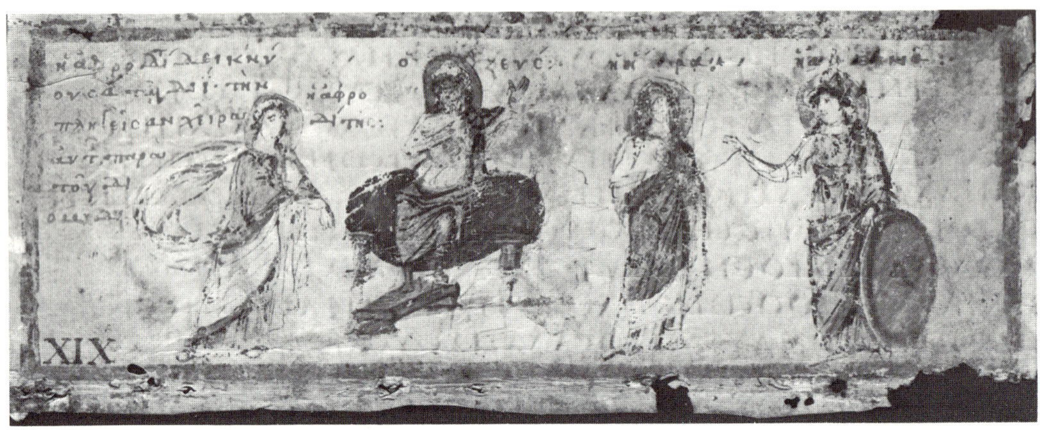

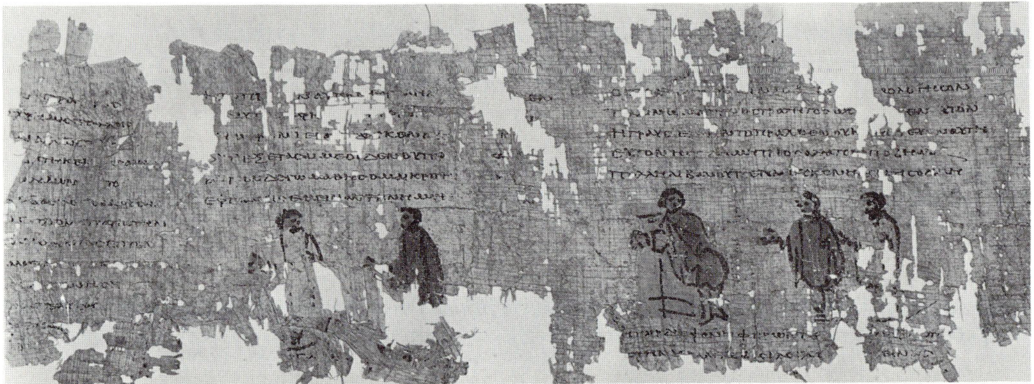

Nationale, Cod. suppl. gr. 1294. Fig. 74).[12]
The only addition of the Iliad painter is
the frame, which is the first step to
isolate a scene from the text and give it
a panel-like appearance.

That the complex battle scenes in the
Milan Iliad (Fig. 75) were derived from
monumental art hardly needs to be
argued. Bianchi-Bandinelli has attributed
this double miniature to his group C,
i.e., battle compositions that have their

closest parallels in Roman art of the
third century.[13] Yet, this does not
necessarily mean that at that time such
compositions were already adapted for
manuscripts. The answer to this problem
of adaptation depends essentially on
determining the time when the parchment codex was sufficiently popularized
so that artists would take advantage of
the new possibilities, and this was hardly
before the fourth century.

In one point we should like to elaborate on Bianchi-Bandinelli's opinion of

---

[12] Gasiorowski, *Malarstwo Minjaturowe,*
p. 17, V and fig. 2; Weitzmann, *Roll and Codex,*
p. 51 and fig. 40; idem, *Ancient Book Illumi-*
nation, p. 100 and fig. 107.

[13] Bianchi-Bandinelli, *Miniatures of the Iliad,*
pp. 62 ff. and 122 ff.

Fig. 75 *Milan, Ambrosiana. Cod. F. 205 inf.*
Pict. XX–XXI. Trojan Battle Scenes

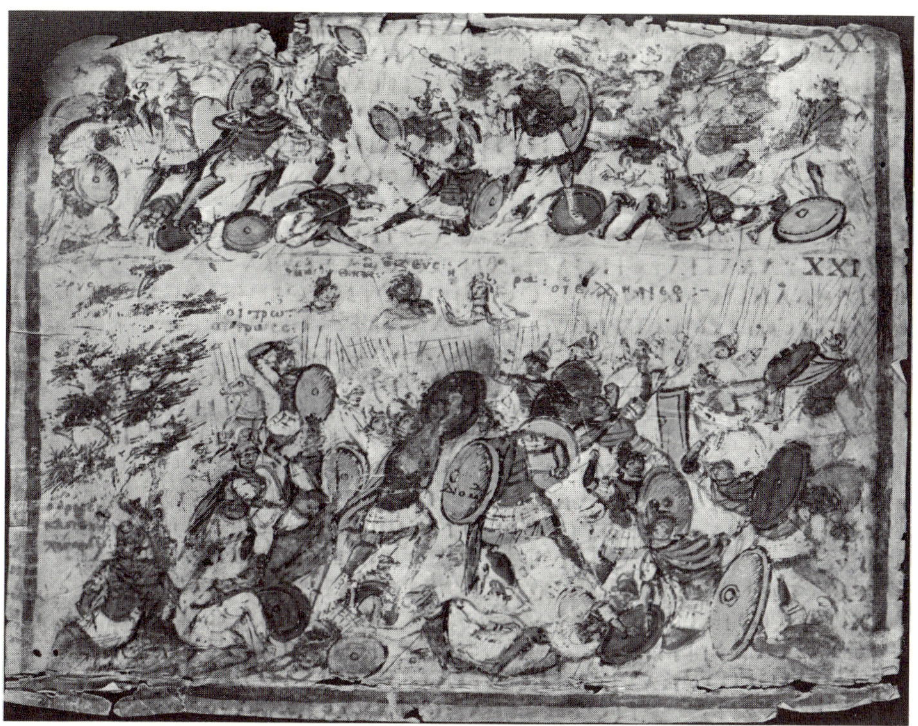

the genesis of the Milan Iliad cycle. According to him the different groups represent various manuscript traditions that were combined in the sixth century. If, however, the battle scenes of Group C come from one manuscript and the conversation scenes of group A, reflecting the papyrus tradition, from another, then A would have been without battle scenes and C without conversation scenes, which is not likely. We rather prefer the idea of a morphological growth of the picture cycle, whereby simple miniatures of group A at a certain state of development expanded both in size and compositional complexity under the impact of monumental painting. In other words, we think that the single combat group in the center, distinguished by a larger figure scale, is the one element that harks back to the papyrus tradition. The Megarian bowls, reflecting the early type of papyrus illustration (Fig. 76),[14] provide the evidence for this type of concise narrative scene, as demonstrated by a cup with three scenes from the Little Iliad[15] which easily fit into text columns of the type suggested by our reconstruction of a section of a papyrus roll. The illustrator of the Milan Iliad is thus not substituting one form of illustration for another but grouping

[14] Weitzmann, *Roll and Codex*, pp. 18 ff., 77 ff., and figs. A–B.

[15] C. Robert, *Homerische Becher* ("50. Berliner Winckelmannsprogramm" [Berlin, 1890]), pp. 30 ff., no. E.; U. Hausmann, *Hellenistische Reliefbecher* (Stuttgart, 1959), 54, no. 16.

Fig. 76 *Berlin, Staatliche Museen. Megarian
Bowl and Reconstructed Manuscript Model.
Three Scenes from the Little Iliad*

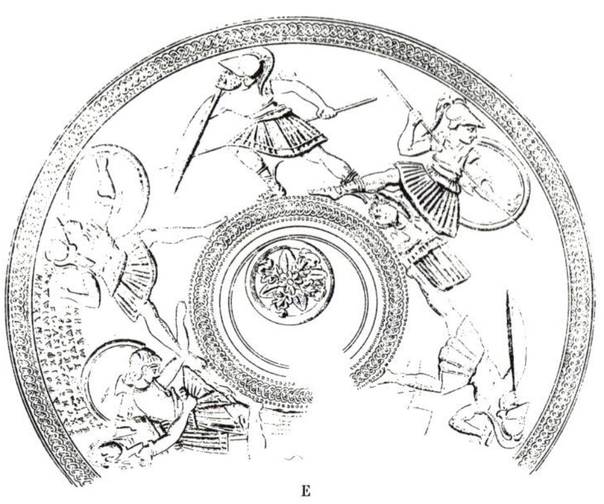

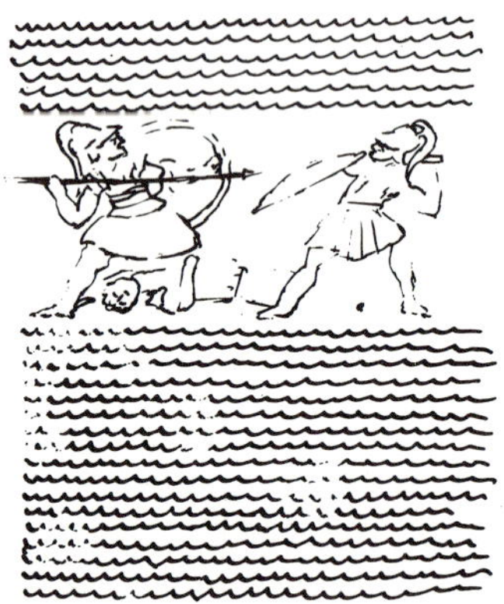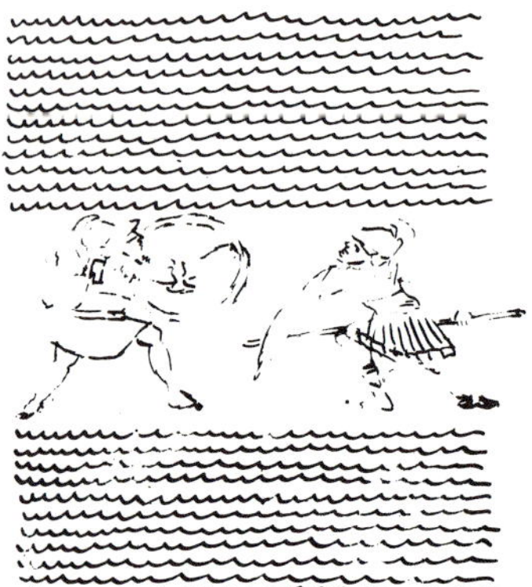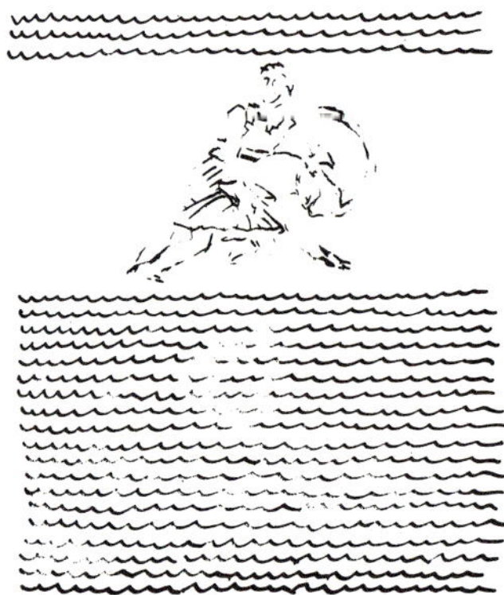

around the traditional nucleus additional
figures, landscape, and architectural
background. It is along these lines that
the illustrator seeks new solutions which
are aimed at combining a narrative
tradition with the embellishments of
panel paintings.

In his most informative study of the
substitution of the codex for the roll,
Colin Roberts[16] has clearly demonstrated
by statistics that in the second century
A.D. less than 3 per cent of the extant
books were codices; that not before the

fourth century did codices outnumber,
and then by far, papyrus rolls; and that
"with the opening of the fourth century
the codex is near its triumph."[17] Moreover, he provided the evidence that the
Christians took quicker advantage of the
new book form than did the pagans,
presumably because it was more economical. At the same time we now have
the evidence that very extensive picture
cycles of the Old Testament existed
before the third century, since several
panels of the frescoes of the synagogue
of Dura—the one with the Vision of

[16] C. H. Roberts, "The Codex," *Proceedings
of the British Academy*, 40 (1955), 169 ff.

[17] Ibid., pp. 184 ff. and 199.

Ezekiel in the Valley of the Dry Bones being the most characteristic example—point to an established tradition of vast narrative cycles which are typical of and must have originated in manuscripts[18] that were made for the Hellenized Jews of the Diaspora.[19] Thus the illustration of the Old Testament reaches back into a period in which the papyrus scroll was still supreme and, indeed, we still have evidence of biblical cycles in the papyrus style that have survived from the Middle Ages.

When at the turn of the fifth century Prudentius wrote his *Psychomachia* and, presumably, at the same time had added to the text miniatures which were to influence medieval art for centuries, the illustrator still used the papyrus style of inserting small concise scenes in the writing column, in spite of the fact that in all likelihood he was already using a codex. A Paris manuscript (Bibliothèque Nationale cod. lat. 8318) from the ninth/tenth century, of all extant copies, is the closest to this Early Christian archetype.[20] The very first miniature

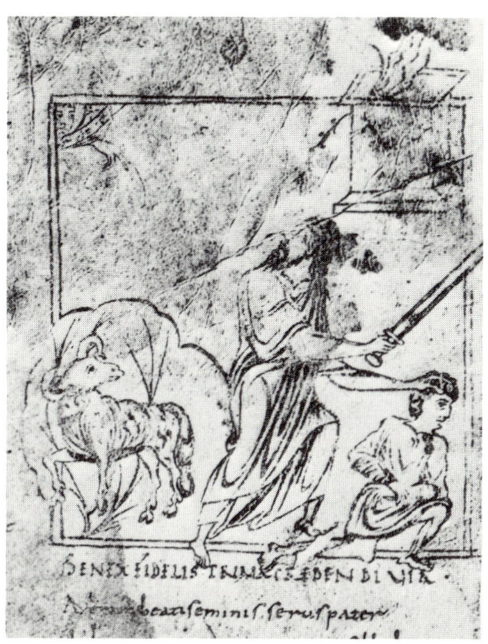

Fig. 77 *Paris, Bibliothèque Nationale. Cod. lat. 8318, fol. 49ᵛ. Sacrifice of Isaac*

shows a frame all around, but this is an exception; in most instances the Carolingian copyist began with the framing and then abandoned it;[21] even in the first miniature one will notice that the frame is an afterthought.

When the illustrator depicted the preface, which contains a mystical application of the Abraham story as told in Genesis XIV, he could and did rely on an existing tradition of Old Testament cycles. The very first miniature (Fig. 77) shows the sacrifice of Isaac with the latter placed not upon the altar but in front of it and rendered in movement as if he had tried to escape. We have demonstrated elsewhere that this very compositional scheme, which we find also in Byzantine manuscripts, is based

[18] C. Kraeling, *The Synagogue* ("The Excavations at Dura Europos. Final Report," 8, Part 1 [New Haven, 1956]), 398 ff.; Weitzmann, "Narration in Early Christendom," p. 89 and pl. 36, figs. 14–15.

[19] The illustrated Greco-Jewish books of the Old Testament, which were available to the earliest Christian illustrators, must, indeed, have been widespread. Cf. Weitzmann, "Zur Frage des Einflusses jüdischer Bilderquellen auf die Illustration des Alten Testamentes," *Mullus: Festschrift Theodor Klauser* (Münster, 1964), pp. 401 ff. (Here also the older bibliography on this subject.) [Translated and reprinted herewith, pp. 76 ff.]

[20] R. Stettiner, *Die illustrierten Prudentius-handschriften* (Berlin, 1895), pp. 3 ff., 167 ff., and pls. 1–12, 15–16.

[21] Weitzmann, *Roll and Codex*, p. 98 and fig. 83.

on a classical prototype which depicted the attempted, but not executed, sacrifice of the little boy Orestes by Telephus as told in the *Telephus* of Euripides.[22] The illustrated Book of Genesis, which the first illustrator of the *Psychomachia* used, with its papyrus style of illustration, may then hark back to a period when individual books of the Septuagint with very extensive cycles[23] were presumably still written on scrolls.

Due to the new possibilities of the parchment leaf of the codex, in the fourth century, Bible illustration underwent the same kind of changes we have noticed in the Milan Iliad. The proof rests on the fragments of the so-called Quedlinburg Itala (Berlin, Staatsbibliothek, cod. theol. lat. fol. 485) which can be dated to the very end of the fourth century.[24] No longer are the scenes interspersed in the columns of the text, but four scenes are united in one full-page miniature. Their framing still reveals that the original units would fit the two-column text if one wished to reinstate their former system. Samuel and Saul, from scenes that illustrate events from the fifteenth chapter of the first Book of Samuel (Fig. 78), stand out as silhouettes against a neutral gray-blue middle zone above which mountains and architecture are set against a pink dawn or sunset which gradually changes into a cooler blue. We would assume that this land-

scape, which is quite unrelated to the foreground, was added above the isocephalic figure composition by the very artist who combined the four scenes on one page and depicted for each pair of neighboring scenes a unifying, panoramic background.[25] Boeckler, in his publication of the Quedlinburg Itala, argued that these miniatures were the first formulation of the subjects they depict, and he saw a proof of this theory in the precepts for the painter written on the empty parchment before it was painted over. Such precepts, so Boeckler argued, would not have been necessary had the artist used an available model. Today, of course, we know from the frescoes of the Dura synagogue that extensive narrative cycles of the Books of Kings did exist before the middle of the third century. At the same time we believe that the precepts are sufficiently explained by the necessity to guide the painter, after the miniatures had lost their original close contact with the text and were grouped together on pages solely reserved for painting. Such a transfer has inherent possibilities for many errors, the avoidance of which was the concern of this particular illustrator. In other words, we believe that the illustrator of the Quedlinburg Itala did not invent a new biblical cycle but followed the same pattern as his colleague who illustrated the Milan Iliad when he converted an illustrated Books of Kings of the papyrus style into a sumptuous luxury edition with panel-like miniatures that show the

---

[22] Ibid., pp. 174 ff. and figs. 173 and 175.

[23] For the origin of the Septuagint illustration consult Weitzmann, "Die Illustration der Septuaginta," *Münchner Jahrbuch der bildenden Kunst*, 3/4 (1952/53), 96 ff. [Translated and reprinted herewith, pp. 45 ff.]

[24] H. Degering and A. Boeckler, *Die Quedlinburg Italafragmente* (Berlin, 1952).

[25] The very same device of unifying panoramic landscapes or architectural prospects was used by the illustrator of the Milan Iliad when he placed two scenes side by side. Cf. Weitzmann, *Roll and Codex*, p. 163 and fig. 159.

Fig. 78 *Berlin, Staatbibliothek. Cod. Theol. lat. fol. 485 fol. II^r. Samuel and Saul*

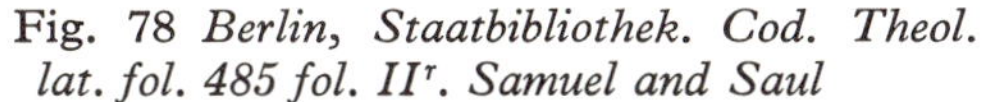

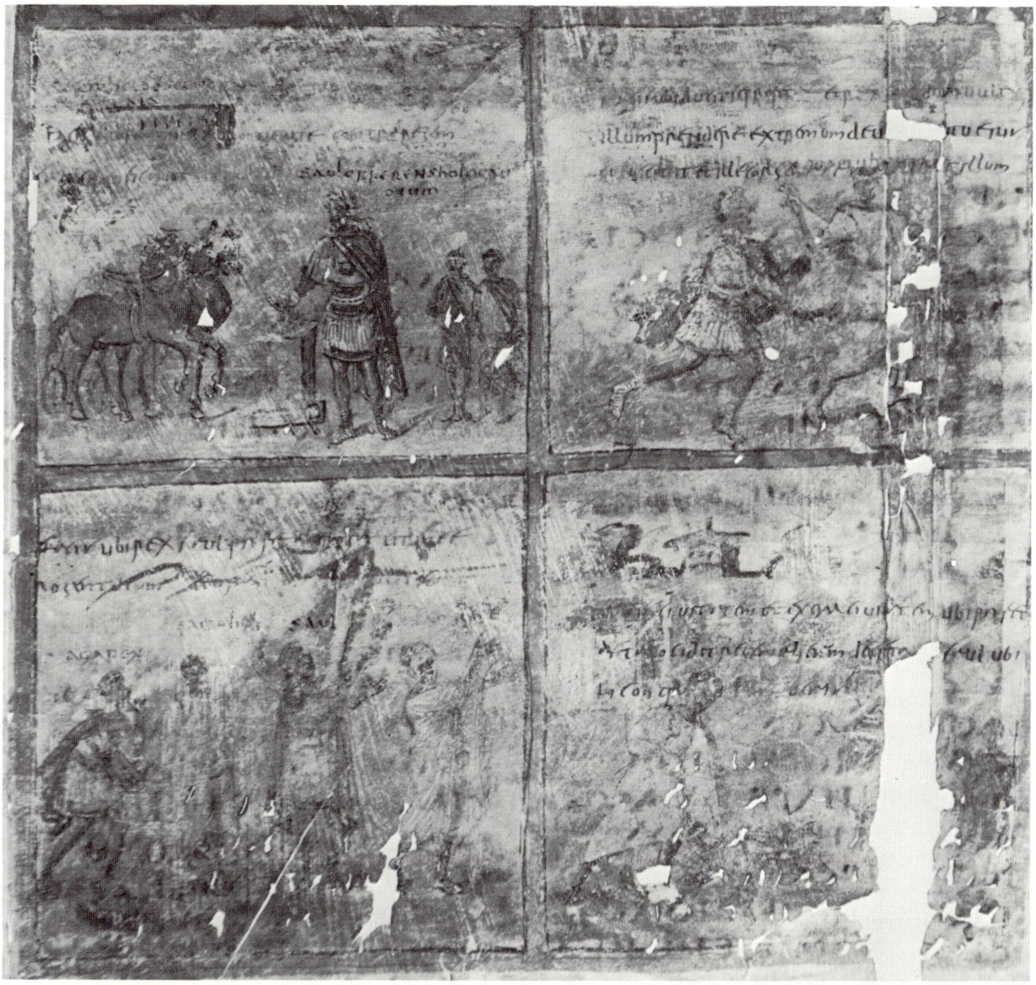

influence of monumental landscape painting.

THE FILOCALUS CALENDAR

One of the key monuments which gives us a varied insight into the process of transformation from roll to codex illustration is the Calendar of Filocalus, well known through the writings by Strzygowski[26] and Nordenfalk[27] and especially the exhaustive monograph by Henri Stern.[28] Its importance for our

[26] J. Strzygowski, "Die Calenderbilder des Chronographen vom Jahre 354," *Jahrbuch des kaiserlichen deutschen archaeologischen Instituts. Ergänzungsheft*, 1 (1888).

[27] Cf. n. 9.

[28] H. Stern, *Le Calendrier de 354. Étude de son texte et ses illustrations* (Paris, 1953).

investigation rests on the following points: 1) it is the only precisely dated manuscript of the fourth century; 2) though known today only from seventeenth-century drawings based on an intermediary copy of the Carolingian period, these very faithful and reliable copies reveal that the original must have been an ambitious, luxury manuscript of high quality; 3) it is a polycyclic manuscript, in which various sets of pictures from different traditions were combined, each set presenting different problems of transformation; and 4) the miniatures represent in part secular iconography and in part imperial iconography, but were made for a Christian named Valentinus. Thus we are led into a realm where various ideologies were fused and were not mutually exclusive.

A set of signs of the zodiac in small medallions accompanying the text are still thoroughly in the papyrus tradition.[29] In other words, in this case the illustrator did not make the step which is reflected in the constellation pictures of the Leiden Aratus, namely to enlarge them to the size of full-page illustrations.

The illustrator becomes aware of the possibilities of the format of the parchment leaf of the codex in another set of pictures where the representations of the months are depicted as personifications in full length (Fig. 79). The older tradition is reflected in the Alexandrian World Chronicle in Moscow (Pushkin Museum), which, though still written on papyrus, is nevertheless a codex which harks back to an archetype not older than

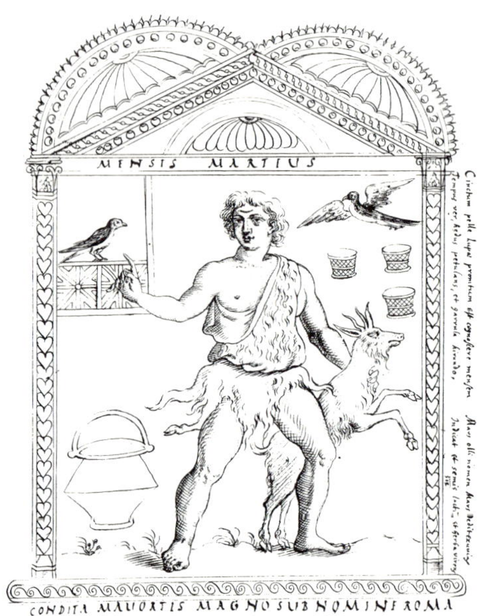

Fig. 79 *Vatican, Biblioteca. Cod. Barb. lat. 2154, fol. 18ʳ. Month of March*

the year A.D. 392, the year of the destruction of the Serapeion in Alexandria with which the chronicle ends. Here the months are represented as busts (only a few traces are left [Fig. 80]),[30] a form common in floor mosaics prior to the fourth century, as witnessed by the Monnus mosaic in Trier from the middle of the third century.[31] The illustrator of the Filocalus Calendar did not continue this tradition but rather turned to monumental art for inspiration.

It has generally been accepted that some floor mosaics from Rome reflect the same pictorial recension as the

[29] Strzygowski, "Calenderbilder," pls. XXIX, XXXI, XXXIII; Stern, *Calendrier*, pls. VII₂, XI₂, XII₂.

[30] A. Bauer and J. Strzygowski, *Eine alexandrinische Weltchronik* ("Denkschriften der kaiserlichen Akademie der Wissenschaften in Wien. Philosophisch-historische Klasse," 51, Part II [Vienna, 1906]), 144 ff. and pl. Iʳ.
[31] F. Hettner, "Das Mosaik des Monnus in Trier," *Antike Denkmäler*, 1 (1889), 35 ff. and pls. 47–49.

Fig. 80 *Moscow, Pushkin Museum. Alexandrian World Chronicle, fol. I*[r]. *Months*

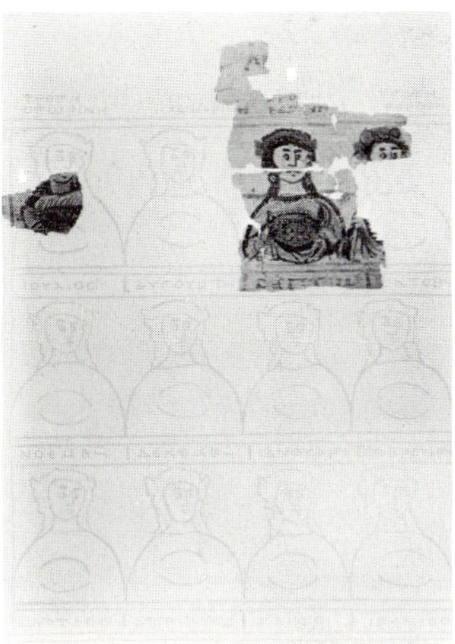

Fig. 81 *Rome, Antiquarium. Mosaic. Month of May*

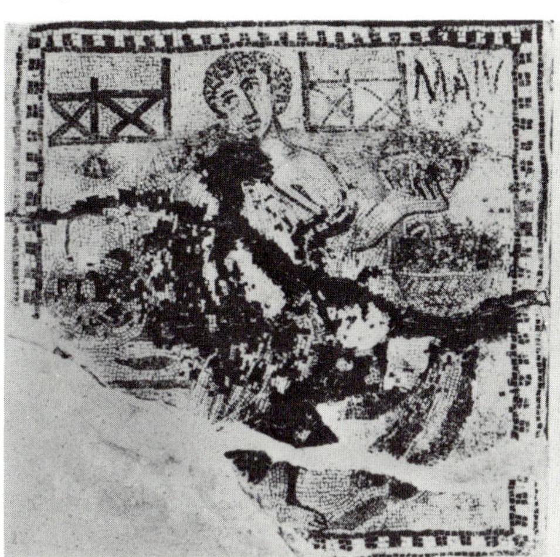

Calendar; and it has been made plausible by Stern that these mosaics themselves were not invented before the second quarter of the fourth century.[32] A representation of the month of May on a mosaic in the Antiquarium in Rome of approximately the same date (Fig. 81)[33] shows the same type of personification rather than an "Occupation with an agricultural task." Space and illusionistic effect are indicated by two windows with balustrades, and we notice this same motif in the picture of March in the Filocalus Calendar, where a swallow is perched on a similar window balustrade, a detail which indicates the dependence on the very same tradition of monumental painting on which the Roman mosaic is based.

The model, if it had any frame at all, most likely did not have more than a simple border like that of the mosaic. It was the book illustrator's idea to add a richer frame made up of architectural elements. But it also was in the tradition of book ornament to devaluate the structural elements, as the artist does in the present case by increasing the number of conches of the pediment and placing two over its oblique sides. Here we get a clear insight into the process of adapting human figures from monumental art and amalgamating them into the decorative art of the book.

Likewise derived from monumental painting are the four city personifications of Rome (Fig. 82), Alexandria (Fig. 83), Constantinopolis, and Treberis, i.e., Trier. The inclusion of Constantinople means, of course, that this set of the great capital cities of the Roman empire in this form could not be older than the second quarter of the fourth century. Certain elements, like the open windows in the Alexandria picture through which one can see boats sailing in the Mediterranean, are indicative of a survival of illusionistic effects rooted in the tradition of monumental painting. Here the miniaturist proves

[32] Stern, *Calendrier*, pp. 289 ff.
[33] Ibid., pl. XL2.

Fig. 82 *Vatican, Biblioteca. Cod. Barb. lat. 2154, fol. 2ʳ. Roma*

Fig. 83 *Vatican, Biblioteca. Cod. Barb. lat. 2154, fol. 3ʳ. Alexandria*

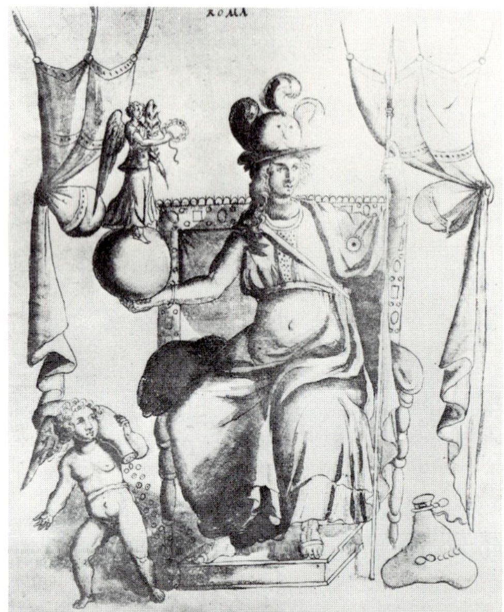

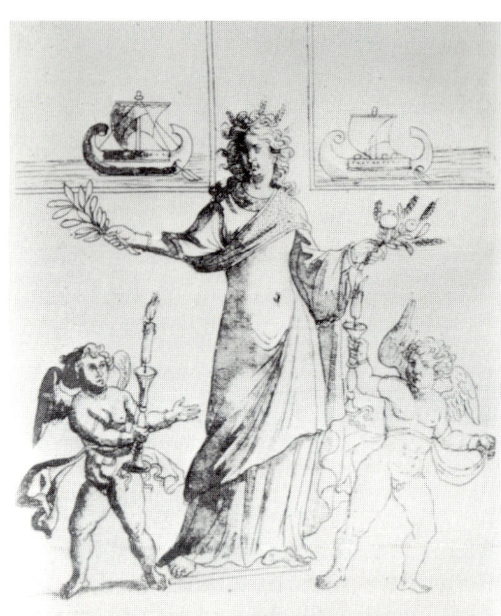

himself to be very much up to date in copying iconographical themes only recently created. Yet even before the invention of the codex, calendars, chronicles, and other texts on occasion required the illustration of cities. How were they depicted in the papyrus tradition?

Once more the Alexandrian World Chronicle gives us the answer. Where the illustrator was faced with the problem of finding a pictorial formula for the provinces of Asia Minor,[34] he chose the same formula which traditionally had been used exclusively for the representation of cities: a city wall flanked by towers and with a gate in the center (Fig. 84). This was the formula used in ancient maps, as can be seen in the numerous copies of the *Geography* of

Claudius Ptolemy.[35] The illustrator of the Filocalus Calendar discarded this tradition, which was eminently suitable for the papyrus illustrator, who had always looked for the briefest, most concise and diagrammatic formula.

Of course we no longer have the precise model of the Filocalus pictures, but there is a famous fresco, formerly in the Palazzo Barberini and now in the Terme Museum (Fig. 85), with a goddess enthroned in a frontal position who, like the personification of Rome in the Calendar drawing, holds a Victory in one hand and a spear in the other.[36]

[34] Bauer and Strzygowski, *Weltchronik*, p. 147 and pl. IIᵛ.

[35] J. Fischer, *Claudii Ptolemaei Geographiae codex Urbinas Graecus 82* ("Codices e Vaticanis selecti," 18 [Leiden, 1932]).

[36] J. Wilpert, *Die römischen Mosaiken und Malereien vom IV. bis XIII. Jahrhunderts* (Freiburg i. B., 1916), 1:127 ff. and 4, pl. 125; M. Cagiano de Azevedo, "La Dea Barberini," *Rivista dell'Istituto di Archeologia e Storia dell'Arte, Roma*, 3 (1954), 109 ff. with color plate.

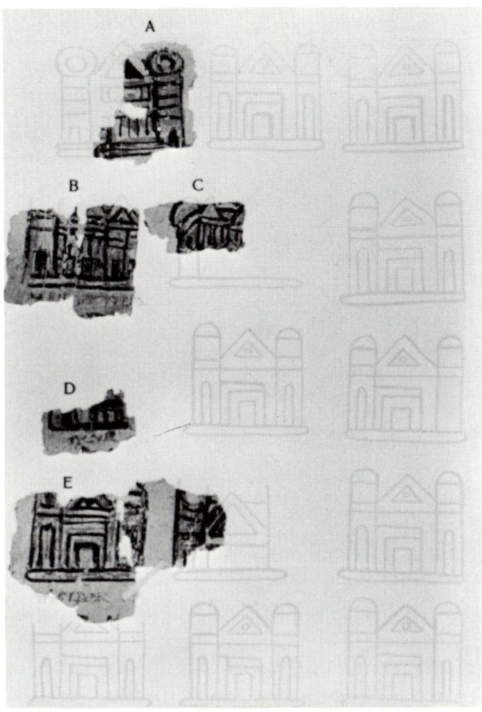

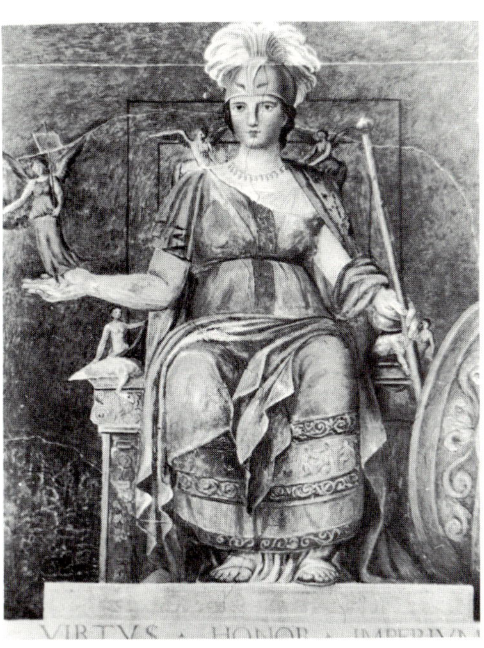

The type is sufficiently close to justify once more the assumption of a monumental painting as the inspiration for the Filocalus Calendar, and since the fresco can be dated around the turn of the fourth century[37] we must credit the miniaturist once more with having chosen as a model a type of the immediate past.[38]

To the fresco copy of an enthroned goddess the miniature painter made additions: iconographically he introduced a putto pouring coins, thus symbolizing the money gift of the consul, the *sparsio*, as seen similarly on the consular diptychs,[39] and for mere formal embellishment he added curtains which take the place of a picture frame, a motif we shall discuss more thoroughly in connection with the next set of pictures. Here we see as an antithetic pair of full-page miniatures the two Consuls

[37] A. Rumpf, *Stilphasen der spätantiken Kunst* ("Arbeitsgemeinschaft für Forschung des Landes Nordrhein-Westfalen. Geisteswissenschaft," 44 [Cologne and Opladen, 1957]), 25 and pl. 20.

[38] It is also very characteristic of the fourth century and of its desire of raising book illumination to a higher level that the famous Tabula Peutingeriana in Vienna (H. J. Hermann, *Die frühmittelalterlichen Handschriften des Abendlandes* ["Die illuminierten Handschriften der Nationalbibliothek Wien," N.F.I., Leipzig, 1923], pp. 5 ff.) which dates in the thirteenth century but harks back to an archetype of the second half of the fourth century, has the older type of diagrammatic walled city replaced by the enthroned city personifications of types very similar to those of the Filocalus Calendar.

[39] Stern, *Calendrier*, p. 132.

Fig. 86 *Vatican, Biblioteca. Cod. Barb. lat. 2154, fol. 13ʳ. Constantius II*

Fig. 87 *Vatican, Biblioteca. Cod. Barb. lat. 2154, fol. 14ʳ. Gallus Caesar*

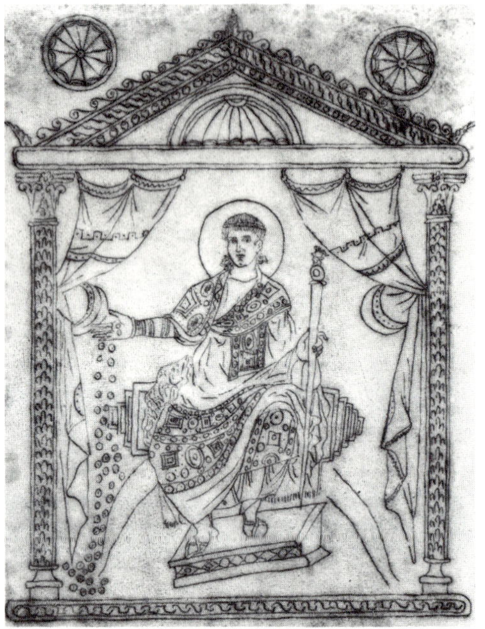

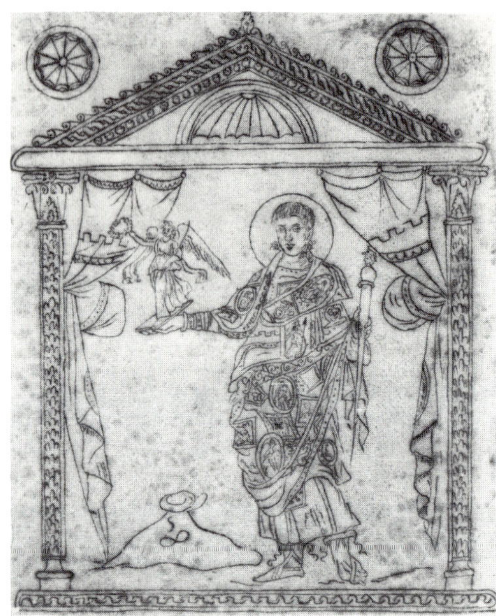

of the year 354, Constantius II (Fig. 86), the Augustus on the throne, distributing gold coins—the first mentioning of a *sparsio* like this is between A.D. 326 and 329[40]—and Gallus Caesar (Fig. 87), standing and holding in his extended hand a Victory who, on her part, offers a corona to the Augustus on the opposite page. In this way the artist makes a fine gradation of the order of rank and at the same time depicts a motion that leads the eye from one picture into the other. This is artistically the most progressive step in exploiting the possibilities of the full-page miniature, by going beyond the single page and perceiving the antithetic pair as an artistic unit. Once more we must raise the question as to whether such imperial portraits, like the subjects of all other

full-page miniatures of the Filocalus Calendar, also had existed previously in roll illustration and, if so, what their form had been.

There is in the Vatican Library a collective volume of treatises on surveying, the so-called *Agrimensores* (cod. Pal. lat. 1564), written toward the middle of the ninth century at Fulda[41] after a model which in its totality cannot be older than A.D. 540.[42] Yet several

---

[40] Ibid., pp. 156 ff.

[41] H. Zimmermann, "Die fuldaer Buchmalerei in karolingischer und ottonischer Zeit," *Kunstgeschichtliches Jahrbuch der K.K. Zentralkommission*, 4 (1910), 90 ff. and pl. XII; A. Goldschmidt, *German Illumination*, 1 (New York, 1928), 19 and pl. 16.

[42] A. W. Byvanck, "Een Antieke Miniatuur in het Handschrift Palatinus Latinus 1564 der Vaticaansche Bibliotheek," *Mededeelingen van het Nederlandsch Historisch Instituut te Rome*, 3 (1923), 123 ff. and especially p. 134.

of the individual treatises are considerably older, as for example the one entitled *De limitibus constituendis* by a certain Hyginus Gromaticus,[43] who lived in the time of Domitian or Trajan. Since this and other early treatises are prolifically illustrated, we can be certain that their pictures hark back to the papyrus period. Consequently the title miniature with two portraits of emperors, unfortunately not inscribed (Fig. 88), also may very well go back to such an early date. The intrinsic probability that, indeed, they reflect the papyrus tradition lies in their form as medallion busts, of which the second one is left unfinished. The busts of the personifications of the months and now the busts of the emperors suggest that, because of their abbreviated and concise form, they were most suitable for the heading of or the insertion into the narrow columns of writing of a papyrus roll, which imposed spatial limitations on the illustrator. For this very reason the bust was also chosen, as we have tried to demonstrate elsewhere, for the illustration of the 700 portraits in the *Hebdomades* of Varro.[44]

Returning to the imperial portraits in the Filocalus Calendar, we may assume,

Fig. 88 *Vatican, Biblioteca. Cod. Pal. lat. 1564, fol. 1ʳ, Two Emperors*

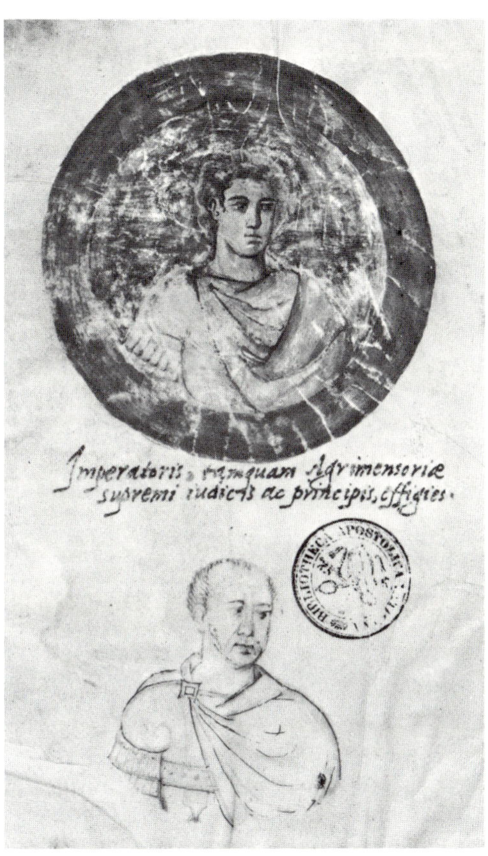

in analogy to the pictures of the months and the personifications of the cities, that the illustrator, while copying human figures from monumental painting, made a contribution of his own by framing them in a manner which reveals a certain ornamental complexity. The aedicula is structurally very clear and real and was obviously designed under the influence of some existing type of architecture which, in our opinion, can be determined. The characteristic adornments of the aedicula are the conch in the pediment and the parted curtains fastened to the columns. While both

[43] For the text of the Agrimensores in general consult F. Blume, K. Lachmann, and A. Rudorff, *Die Schriften der römischen Feldmesser* (Berlin, 1848–52); C. Thulin, *Die Handschriften des Corpus Agrimensorum Romanorum* ("Abhandlungen der königlich Preussischen Akademie der Wissenschaften. Philosophisch-historische Klasse," 1911 [Berlin, 1911]); idem, *Corpus Argrimensorum Romanorum*, B. G. Teubner (ed.) (Leipzig, 1913).

[44] Weitzmann, *Ancient Book Illumination*, pp. 116 ff.

elements occur in various types of Roman architecture, we believe it is plausible that in book illumination it derives from theater architecture and originally represented the Porta Regia.

Individually these two elements occur in aediculae which, as part of a *scenae frons*,[45] form the background in two Byzantine evangelist pictures of the tenth century. The first, from the Athos monastery Philotheu cod. 33 (Fig. 89),[46] depicts the Porta Regia, made up of two heavy columns of colored marble[47] that carry a semicircular architrave with a gable that includes a conch. This baldachin-like architecture is set against the colonnade of the *scenae frons* and rises above the proscenium wall, in front of which the Evangelist Mark is depicted enthroned in frontal position, just as in the ancient theater statues of poets were placed in niches of the hyposcenium wall.[48] The second picture, also representing the Evangelist Mark, is from a

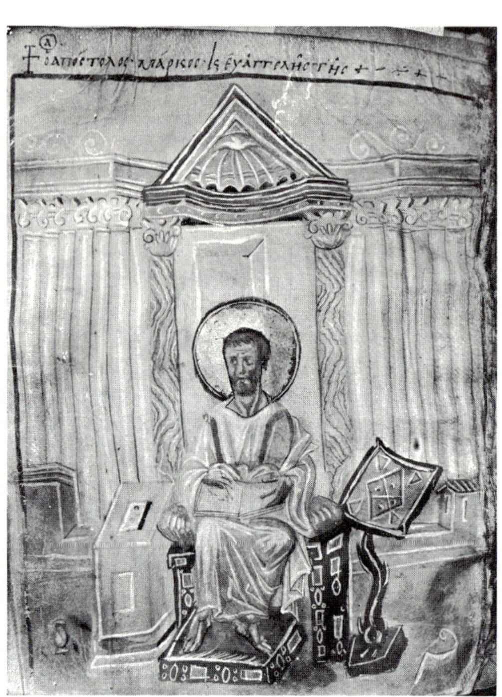

Fig. 89 *Mount Athos, Philotheu. Cod. 33. Mark*

tenth-century Gospel book in Oxford (Bodleian, cod. Auct. E.V.11. Fig. 90).[49] Here the hyposcenium wall is much more explicit and, as if seen in perspective from below, cuts off the bases of the two columns of colored marble to which the parted curtains are fastened. But due to the lack of space the crowning gable with the conch is cut off.[50] Both of these Greek manuscripts belong to the so-called Macedonian Renaissance of the tenth century and obviously copy very early models from a period in which these theater backgrounds were not yet ornamentalized; and the manuscripts still appear as an initial stage of trans-

[45] The relation of the background of certain Byzantine miniatures to the architecture of the ancient theater has been thoroughly discussed by A. M. Friend, "The Portraits of the Evangelists in Greek and Latin Manuscripts, Part II," *Art Studies* (1929), 4 ff. and especially 9 ff.

[46] Weitzmann, *Die byzantinische Buchmalerei des 9. und 10. Jahrhunderts* (Berlin, 1935), p. 46 and pl. LI, 302; idem, *Geistige Grundlagen und Wesen der Makedonischen Renaissance* ("Arbeitsgemeinschaft für Forschung des Landes Nordrhein-Westfalen, Geisteswissenschaft," 107 [Cologne and Opladen, 1963]), 26 and fig. 22. [Translated and reprinted herewith, pp. 196 ff.]

[47] Cf., for instance, the theater of Dugga in North Africa. M. Bieber, *The History of the Greek and Roman Theater* (2d ed.; Princeton, 1961), pp. 204 ff. and figs. 689 ff.

[48] Friend, "Portraits of Evangelists," p. 28 and pl. XII, 39.

[49] Weitzmann, *Byzantinische Buchmalerei*, p. 18 and pl. XXII, 120.

[50] Weitzmann, *Geistige Grundlagen*, p. 26 and pl. 5. [Herewith, p. 196.]

Fig. 90 *Oxford, Bodleian Library. Cod. Auct. E.V.11, p. 136. Mark*

Fig. 90 *Oxford, Bodleian Library. Cod. Auct. E.V.11, p. 136. Mark*

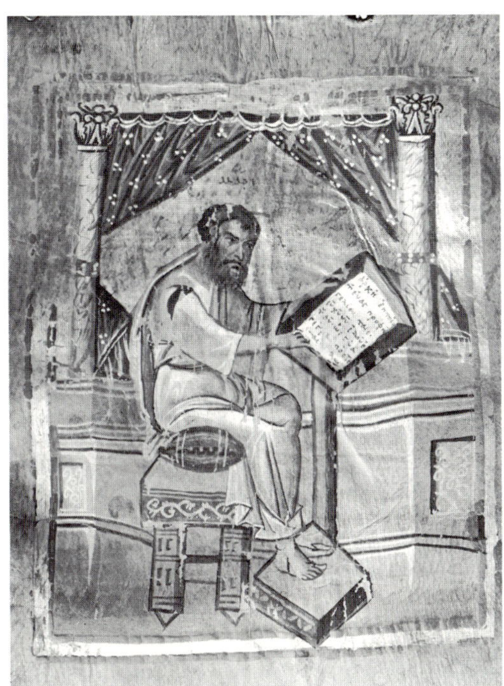

formation from monumental art—presumably fresco painting of architecture rather than existing architecture—into miniature painting. Most likely this happened in the first half of the fourth century,[51] because almost immediately thereafter the aedicula was isolated from the rest of the *scenae frons* and was used as a decoration for the canon tables of Eusebius. This must have taken place shortly before the middle of the fourth century, that is, before the death of Eusebius in A.D. 338 or 339.[52] The architectural setting of the Greek

Evangelists, the canon tables with the conch in the gable and the parted curtains,[53] and the architectural frames of the imperial portraits in the Filocalus Calendar are thus all derived from the same source.

In the light of this evidence one may well ponder whether the introduction of the *scenae frons* into miniature painting must not be accredited to Christian rather than pagan book illuminators of the fourth century. Yet we hesitate to draw such a conclusion from the meager evidence we have. The strong parallelism of the same architectural forms in secular and Christian book illumination speaks, in our opinion, rather in favor of imperial scriptoria which, in the first half and until well after the middle of the fourth century, produced secular and Christian luxury manuscripts side by side.

AUTHOR AND DEDICATION PICTURES

While the Filocalus Calendar is perhaps the most diversified example we have through which the changes from roll to codex illustration can be demonstrated, at the same time we must remember that it represents a rather exceptional illustrated text. By far the majority of Early Christian and medieval miniature paintings can readily be

---

[51] A third manuscript of the Macedonian Renaissance, the Gospel book in Stauronikita on Mount Athos, codex 43, from the middle of the tenth century, will be discussed *infra*, p. 115 f..

[52] For the history of the canon tables consult the basic study by C. Nordenfalk, *Die spätantiken Kanontafeln* (Göteborg, 1938).

[53] For a conch in a canon table see the tenth-century Gospel book in the Vatican (cod. Palat. grec. 220) Weitzmann, *Die armenische Buchmalerei des 10. und beginnenden 11. Jahrhunderts* (Bamberg, 1933), pl. V, 16; and for the curtains, see the tenth-century Abyssinian Gospel book of Abba Garima, J. Leroy, "L'Evangeliaire Ethiopien du Couvent d'Abba Garima," *Cahiers Archéologiques*, 11 (1960), 131 ff; Weitzmann, *Geistige Grundlagen*, p. 26 and fig. 21. [Herewith, p. 196 and Fig. 179.]

Fig. 91 *Vatican, Biblioteca. Cod. lat. 3867, fol. 14ʳ. Virgil*

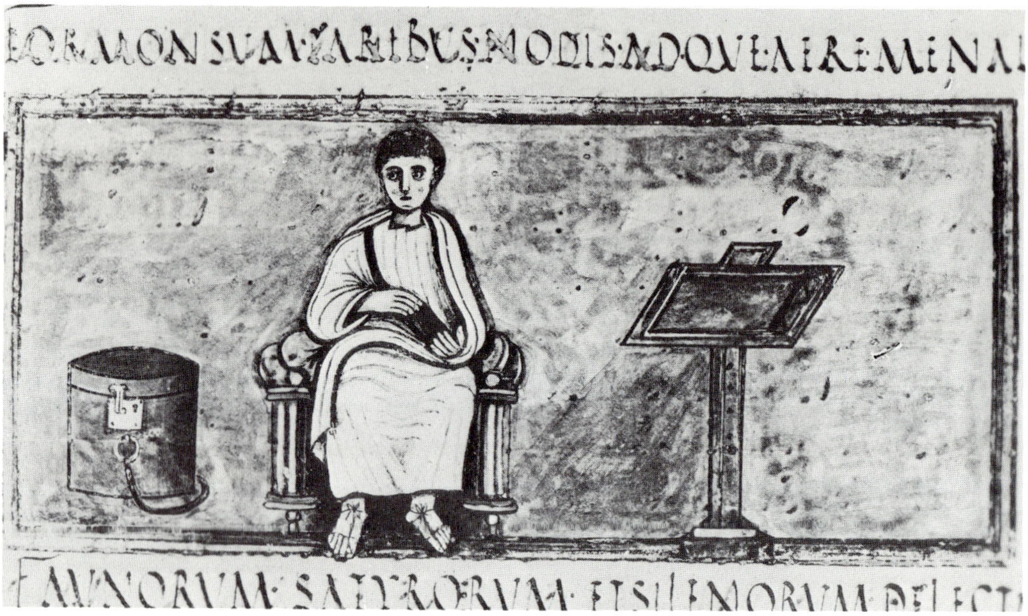

divided into two groups: the frontispieces with the figures of either an author, a donor, a person to whom the manuscript is dedicated, or the ruler in whose time it was executed (a category represented in the Filocalus by the two emperor portraits) and the narrative cycles (not represented in the Filocalus Calendar).

Our contention that portrait painting in papyrus rolls started with busts, usually in medallion form, finds its best support in the author portrait of Virgil. The "Codex Vaticanus" (lat. 3225),[54] from either the end of the fourth[55] or the early fifth century,[56] contains at the end

of Book VI of the Aeneid the offset of a lost medallion which can only have been a bust of Virgil that preceded the text of Book VII, the beginning of which is now lost. If Book VII had such a portrait, then each of the other eleven books must have had one too.[57] But such a system of illustration is meaningful only in the context of separate rolls, each containing one book, whereas for a codex containing all twelve books bound together[58] one author portrait at the

[54] *Fragmenta et Picturae Vergiliana Cod. Vat. lat. 3225* ("Codices e Vaticanis selecti," 1 [Rome, 1930]).

[55] Dated still in the fourth century by E. A. Lowe, *Codices Latini Antiquiores*, 1 (Oxford, 1934), no. 11.

[56] J. de Wit, *Die Miniaturen des Vergilius Vaticanus* (Amsterdam, 1959), pp. 153 ff.

[57] Weitzmann, *Ancient Book Illumination*, p. 116.

[58] Such a codex must have existed as early as the end of the first century A.D. as indicated by the epigram of Martial (xiv, CLXXXVI)

Quam brevis inmensum cepit membrana Maronem ipsius vultus prima tabella gerit.

The "face" of the author on the first page we assume, in analogy to the Vergilius Vaticanus, to have been once more a medallion portrait.

beginning of the total Aeneid would normally have been sufficient.

The second Virgil in the Vatican, the so-called Vergilius Romanus (lat. 3867)[59] which, though not much later than the former,[60] is executed in a rather provincial style, shows the same phenomenon of repeating the author portrait, though not in front of each book of the Aeneid, but of each Eclogue. Three of the original six are preserved, consisting in this case not of medallion portraits but of frontally seated author figures (Fig. 91) who almost seem to float on a surface area much too broad for them. They were apparently conceived to fit narrower writing columns, and this suggests—although this has to remain a hypothesis—that the seated portrait, presumably frameless, also existed in papyrus rolls,[61] though to what extent we do not know.

To fill the empty space the illustrator added a capsa for scrolls and a lectern but, significantly, no writing table, because the poet is depicted meditating, holding the finished product, a roll, in his hands, and is not occupied with

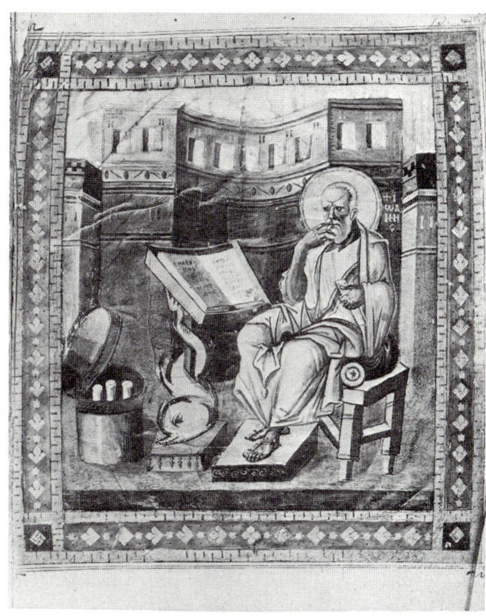

Fig. 92 *Mount Athos, Stauronikita. Cod. 43, fol. 13ʳ. John*

writing. These very same additions, the capsa and the lectern, were made in an evangelist portrait of John in a tenth-century Gospel book at Stauronikita on Mount Athos, the most characteristic representative of the Macedonian Renaissance (Fig. 92).[62] John sits in front of the hyposcenium wall, which has been turned into an exedra, and he not only has a very statuesque appearance but is depicted in the pose of a meditating philosopher.[63] Indeed, we have reason to believe that we have before us a faithful copy of a very early

---

[59] *Picturae Ornamenta-complura scripturae specimina codicis Vaticani 3867 qui Codex Vergilii Romanus audit* ("Codices e Vaticanis selecti" [Rome, 1902]).

[60] In an earlier study C. Nordenfalk (*Der Kalender*, pp. 31 ff.) proposed a date as early as the fourth century, relating the miniatures to monuments of "Constantinian expressionism" but more recently (*Early Medieval Painting* [Geneva, 1957], p. 97), he preferred a date in the first half of the fifth century, a date which is more in agreement with the paleographical evidence (Lowe, *Codices Latini*, Part I, p. 7, no. 19).

[61] Weitzmann, *Ancient Book Illumination*, p. 121 and fig. 130.

[62] Friend, "Portraits of the Evangelists, Part I," *Art Studies* (1927) p. 134 and pl. VIII, 95–98. Weitzmann, *Byzantinische Buchmalerei*, p. 23 and pl. XXX.

[63] One of the evangelists of the same manuscript, Matthew, could actually be derived from an ancient statue of Epicurus (Weitzmann, *Geistige Grundlagen*, p. 30 and figs. 23–24). [Herewith, p. 199 f. and Figs. 180–181.]

Fig. 93 *Madrid, Biblioteca Nacional. Cod.
A.16, fol. 55ʳ. Aratus*
Fig. 94 *Trier, Landesmuseum. Monnus Mosaic.
Aratus*

type of evangelist from the period when
the transition was made from an ancient
poet or philosopher into an evangelist,
who is not yet concerned with writing
down his Gospel. The more or less
simultaneous appearance of capsa and
lectern in a pagan and a Christian miniature, at about the time of the transition
from a striplike picture such as that of
the Virgil miniature into a full-page
miniature with a very illusionistic
background,[64] points once more to an
interrelated development of pagan and
Christian book illumination. This parallelism I should like to demonstrate also
in the following example.

The almost square format typical of
the early codex gave the illustrator the
chance to copy from monumental painting
more complex compositions with other
figures being added to that of the author.
One such instance is the group in which
a man of letters is inspired by a muse.
A twelfth-century Aratus manuscript
in Madrid (Fig. 93)[65] shows the seated
poet with the muse Urania standing in
front of him, both holding scrolls and
pointing at the celestial globe between

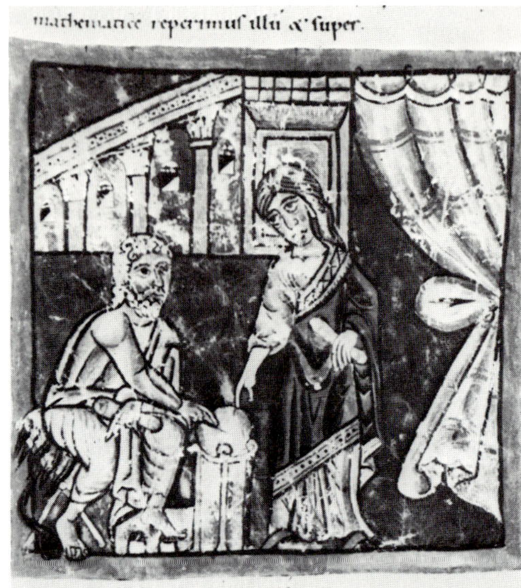

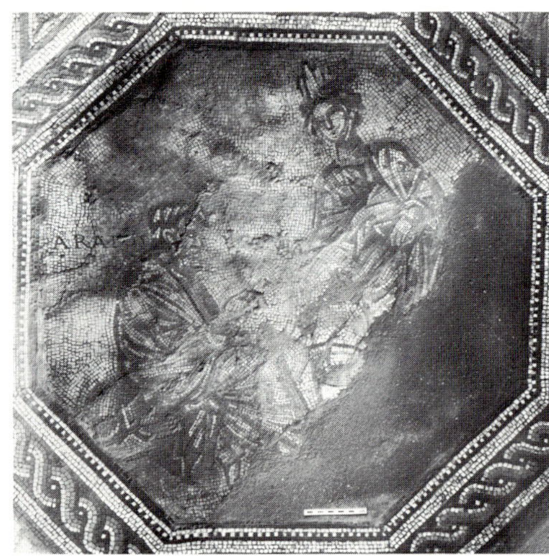

them. As was recognized long ago,[66] this
composition is very similar to the Aratus-
Urania group in the Monnus mosaic in
Trier (Fig. 94) which dates from the
middle of the third century,[67] and thus

[64] Because of the very illusionistic, painterly
treatment of the landscape background in all
four miniatures of this Gospel book, we have
been tempted (*Geistige Grundlagen*, p. 30
[herewith, p. 200]) to ascribe the archetype to
the pre-Constantinian period, but in the light
of our present study it hardly seems likely that
any full-page miniatures and especially such
luxurious ones could have been made before
Constantine. The illusionistic elements, in our
opinion, can be sufficiently explained by the
use of monumental paintings which either
were of an earlier date or, if later, reflected
models of an earlier date.

[65] Byvanck, "Aratea," p. 216, no. 44.

[66] E. Bethe, *Buch und Bild*, pp. 84 ff. and
figs. 52–54.

[67] F. Hettner, "Mosaik des Monnus";

we are led to believe that the illustrator of the archetype of the Madrid codex, for which Thiele suggested a date in the fourth/fifth century,[68] copied a monumental painting. This, of course, need not have been a mosaic but more likely was a fresco. The effect of an open window in the upper left corner we met in one of the representations of the months in the Filocalus Calendar, and a similarly heavy curtain we noticed in its pictures of the city personifications. In both instances we should like to consider the curtains to be additions of the miniature painters. The archetype of the Aratus miniature therefore must be assumed to have been close in date to the Filocalus Calendar.

Almost a twin sister to the muse Urania is the personification who inspires the Evangelist Mark in the well-known Rossano Gospels (Fig. 95)[69] and points at the scroll on his lap instead of the celestial globe. But while the twelfth-century Aratus miniature can be taken as a fairly faithful copy of a fourth-century archetype, at least in composition if not in stylistic detail, the Rossano miniature of the sixth century, which likewise can be traced to an early archetype, has undergone considerable changes.

How, in particular, the two emperor miniatures of the Filocalus (Figs. 86 and 87) had established a type of frontispiece that continued through the Middle Ages, though some significant changes and

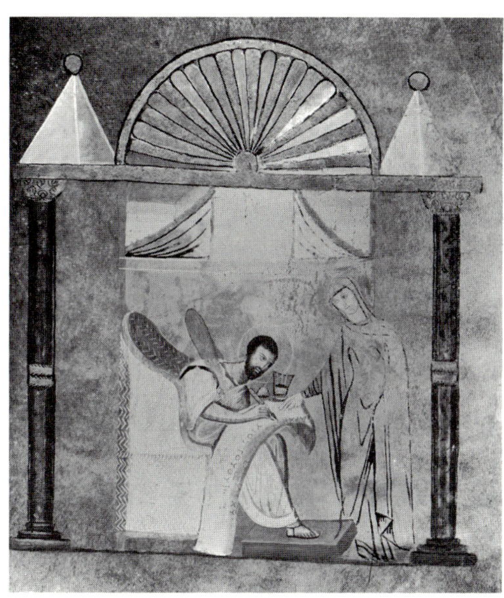

Fig. 95 *Rossano, Cathedral. Codex Purpureus, fol. 121ʳ. Mark*

adjustments were made, may be demonstrated by a title miniature to the *Bellum Judaicum* of Flavius Josephus in a manuscript in Paris (Bibliothèque Nationale, cod. lat. 5058) from the end of the eleventh century executed in or around Toulouse (Fig. 96).[70] Here we also see two emperors in frontal position: Vespasian at the right turns to Titus at the left and offers to his son the orb, apparently an indication that he had secured his son's succession. This offering of the orb should be compared compositionally with the offering of the *Nike* by Gallus Caesar. The basic difference is that in the Josephus miniature both emperors

---

K. Schefold, *Die Bildnisse der antiken Dichter, Redner und Denker* (Basel, 1943), 168 and 169, no. 5.

[68] Thiele, *Himmelsbilder*, p. 146.

[69] A. Muñoz, *Il codice purpureo di Rossano* (Rome, 1907), p. 5 and pl. XV.

[70] *Les manuscrits à peintures en France du VIIᵉ au XIIᵉ siècle* (catalogue of an exhibition, Bibliothèque Nationale, Paris, 1954), p. 107, no. 313; *Byzance et la France médiévale* (catalogue of an exhibition, Bibliothèque Nationale, Paris, 1958), p. 63, no. 114 and pl. XXXI; J. Porcher, *Medieval French Miniatures* (New York, 1959), p. 28 and pl. XIX.

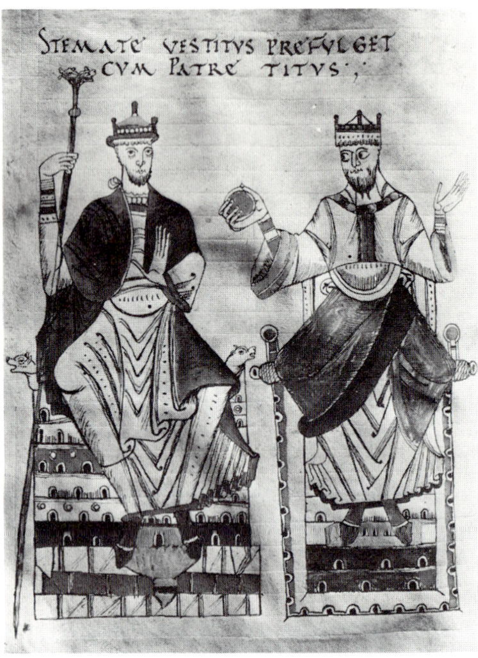

Fig. 96 *Paris, Bibliothèque Nationale. Cod. lat. 5058, fol. 2ᵛ. Vespasian and Titus*

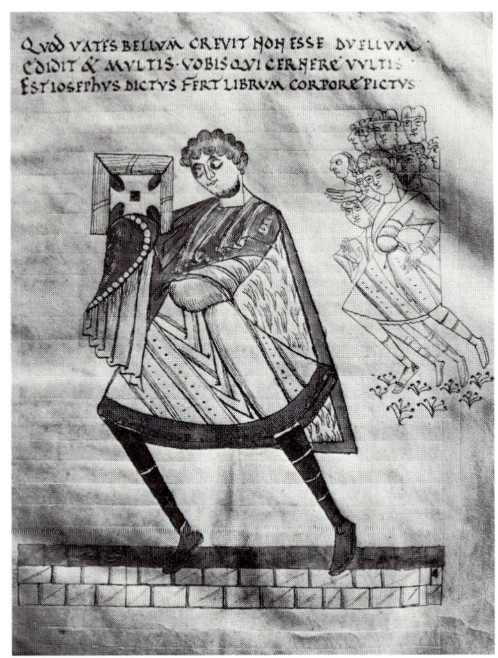

Fig. 97 *Paris, Bibliothèque Nationale. Cod. lat. 5058, fol. 3ʳ. Flavius Josephus*

are seated on thrones, as it should be, since both are Augusti. Yet Titus is artistically singled out as the more prominent one by holding a scepter, wearing an imperial mantle and, like Constantius II in the Filocalus, he is seated on what in the model must have been a folding chair with lion heads but was turned by the medieval copyist into a solid, bench-like throne. Moreover, the emperors are no longer seated under a baldachin, and we venture to suggest that the canopies had once existed in a more elaborate model but were omitted when the emperor portraits, originally facing each other on opposite pages as in the Filocalus, were condensed by the medieval illustrator into one full-page miniature. This condensation apparently happened at the time the figure of Flavius Josephus was introduced on the opposite

page, thus occupying the space that once had been taken by the second emperor. By depicting the author offering his opus with veiled hand (Fig. 97), the archetype, which we believe originally had presented only a pair of antithetic emperor portraits, was turned into a dedication scene. When this conceptual expansion happened still remains to be determined.

Quite a different solution of fusing the emperor and the author into a dedication scene can be seen in the antithetic pair of title miniatures in the late Carolingian Pseudo-Apuleius herbal in the Landesbibliothek, Kassel (cod. phys., fol. 10, Figs. 98–99) that was probably written in Fulda.[71] Gold-

[71] Ch. Singer, "The Herbal in Antiquity," *Journal of Hellenic Studies*, 47 (1927), 43 ff. and figs. 29, 40, 45; E. Howald and H. Sigerist,

Fig. 98 *Kassel, Landesbibliothek. Cod. phys. fol. 10, fol. 1ᵛ. Constantine*

Fig. 99 *Kassel, Landesbibliothek. Cod. phys. fol. 10, fol. 2ʳ. Apuleius*

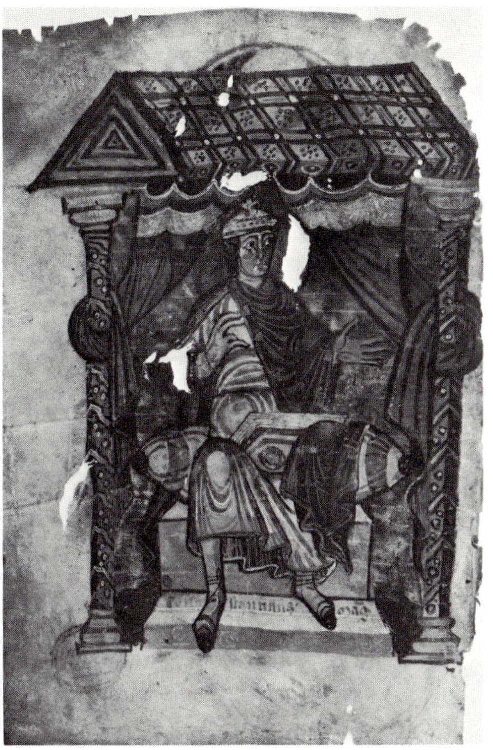

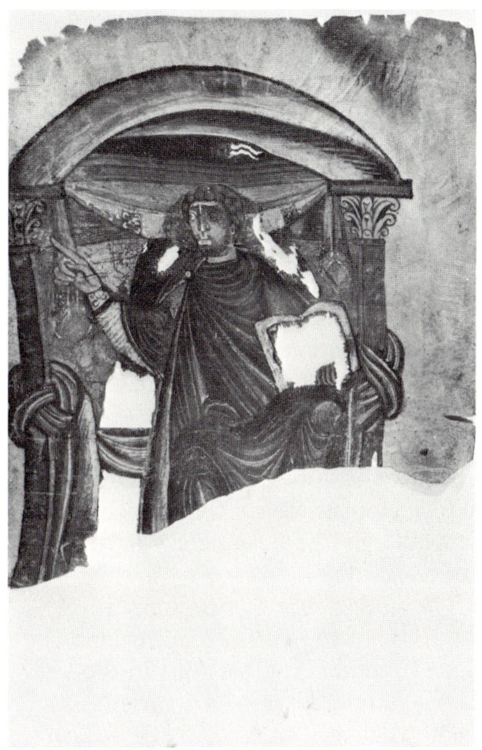

schmidt[72] described the two figures as "two disputing authors," although the figure at the left wears a crown and is thus clearly marked as an emperor. An inscription *Constantinus Mag.* was read by Goldschmidt as *Magister*, although he admits that a physician of Salerno by that name cannot be the person depicted

in the miniature, because he lived in the eleventh century. One wonders whether it should not be read *Constantinus Magnus*, but since this inscription is later than the miniature there is no way of knowing whether the Carolingian illuminator had any such idea about the identification of the emperor.

Even more problematical is the figure of Apuleius who explains his book, which he holds open in his left hand, to the emperor while the latter listens and at the same time has the dedication copy resting on his lap. It is irreconcilable with Roman court ceremonial that a writer should be seated in the presence of the emperor, that he should sit under a similar canopy, and that he should

Antonii Musae De herba vettonica liber . . . ("Corpus medicorum latinorum," 4 [Leipzig and Berlin, 1927]), xiii. According to these authors, the archetype of the Pseudo-Apuleius herbal was written before the fifth century but not before the fourth, and this date would seem to fit also the archetype of these dedication miniatures. Bethe, *Buch und Bild*, p. 35 and fig. 11; p. 39.

[72] Goldschmidt, *German Illumination*, p. 21 and pls. 19–20.

wear a similar type of chlamys. All these obvious incongruities can most easily be understood as an act of conflation of a second emperor portrait with that of an author, a conflation we should like to ascribe to the Carolingian miniaturist. Yet the basic concept that the figure at the right pays homage to the figure at the left is maintained. A late-Roman miniature would no doubt have the author depicted standing in front of the enthroned emperor like Epictetus the philosopher standing in front of the enthroned Hadrian as seen in the copy of the *Notitia Dignitatum* whose archetype leads us into the fourth century,[73] or like Oppian facing the enthroned Caracalla in the *Cynegetica* of that author.[74]

The importance of title miniatures like those of the Paris Josephus and the Kassel Pseudo-Apuleius lies in the fact that each one of them is a variant of a theme that was created in the fourth century. At the same time one should be aware that the antithetic pair of emperors is only one of many types of frontispieces whose origin can be traced to the fourth century.

NARRATIVE CYCLES

The one category of illustration not represented in the Filocalus Calendar is the narrative cycle. On the evidence of extant fragments of illustrated papyri, contemporary copies of miniatures in other media like terra-cotta bowls, and

copies in later manuscripts, in which the system of papyrus illustration has survived, we know today that the Homeric poems as well as the other poems of the epic cycle, the dramas of Euripides and others, romances of every conceivable type, and other prose texts were illustrated in papyrus rolls with extensive cycles.[75] Moreover, at the beginning we demonstrated in the case of the Milan Iliad how the individual pictures of these cycles were enriched as soon as they were taken over into the codex. The same process we assumed for the Bible or at least for the Old Testament, which from the beginning was illustrated with cycles so rich that they could have been conceived only for individual books of the Old Testament and not for its entirety.[76] The fragments of the Quedlinburg Itala, for instance, belong to a codex which surely never contained anything but the Books of Kings. We have today good reason to believe that the illustration of the Septuagint began with the Jews of the Diaspora and not only in one, but in many centers.[77] Yet to characterize the change from narrative papyrus to narrative codex illustration only with illustrated pagan and Christian texts would give an incomplete picture.

[73] H. Omont, *Notitia dignitatum imperii Romani; Bibl. Nat. MS. lat. 9661* (Paris, n.d.), pl. 14.
[74] K. Weitzmann, *Greek Mythology in Byzantine Art* (Princeton, 1951), p. 96 and pl. XXIX, 100.

[75] In *Roll and Codex* the author has laid out the method by which ancient book illumination can be reconstructed, and in *Ancient Book Illumination* a historical sketch was attempted with the aim of demonstrating what an extraordinary variety of texts with illustrations must have existed in classical antiquity prior to the invention of the codex.
[76] Weitzmann, "Illustration der Septuaginta" [herewith, pp. 45 ff.].
[77] Weitzmann, "Zur Frage," pp. 401 ff. Here the older bibliography [herewith, pp. 76 ff.].

Fig. 100 *Berlin, Staatliche Museen. Papyrus 13296. World Chronicle*

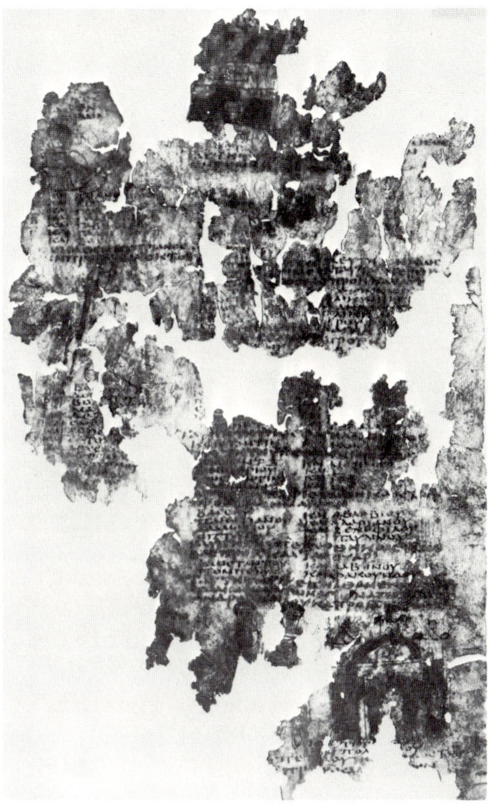

Fig. 101 *Moscow, Pushkin Museum. Alexandrian World Chronicle, fol. VI^v. Emperor Theodosius, Patriarch Theophilus, etc.*

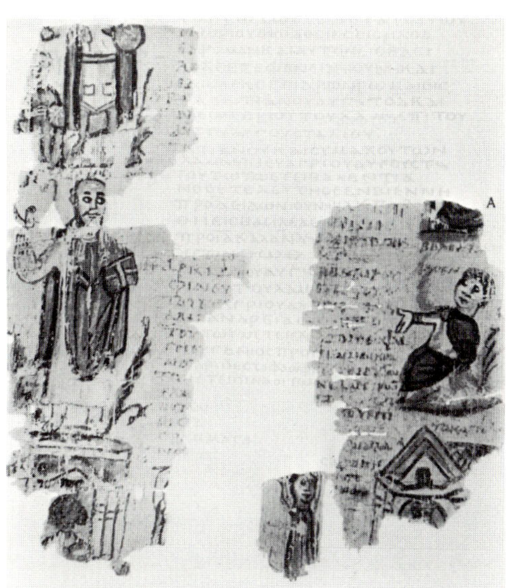

There existed a third artistic province, namely the imperial realm, which developed its own iconographical repertory and its own ceremonial style. In book illumination it found an outlet in world chronicles, *Historiae Ecclesiasticae,* and other kinds of historical texts of a popular and episodical character. A papyrus leaf in Berlin (No. 13296) from the fourth/fifth century has five very abbreviated colored pen drawings distributed over three writing columns (Fig. 100),[78]

while in the Alexandrian World Chronicle in Moscow the pictures were removed from within the text column and placed in the inner and outer margins (Fig. 101). What the leaves of both papyrus codices have in common with the older papyrus roll tradition is the abbreviated nature of the illustration. In the Alexandrian Chronicle we see on the best preserved leaf[79] not scenes proper but simply figures: at the left the emperor Theodosius with the young Honorius and underneath the patriarch Theophilus, at the right the feet of the emperor Valentinian and underneath the rival emperor Eugenios, while at the bottom the Serapeion is depicted with whose destruction the Chronicle breaks off.

There is good reason to believe that as soon as luxury codices were produced, a change took place from the almost pictographic type of illustration into a scenic one with variegated actions that

[78] H. Lietzmann, "Ein Blatt aus einer antiken Weltchronik," *Quantulacumque: Studies Presented to Kirsopp Lake* (London, 1937), pp. 339 ff. and plate facing p. 140.

[79] Bauer and Strzygowski, *Weltchronik,* p. 122 and pl. VI^v.

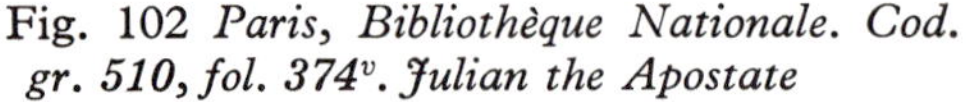

Fig. 102 *Paris, Bibliothèque Nationale. Cod. gr. 510, fol. 374ᵛ. Julian the Apostate*

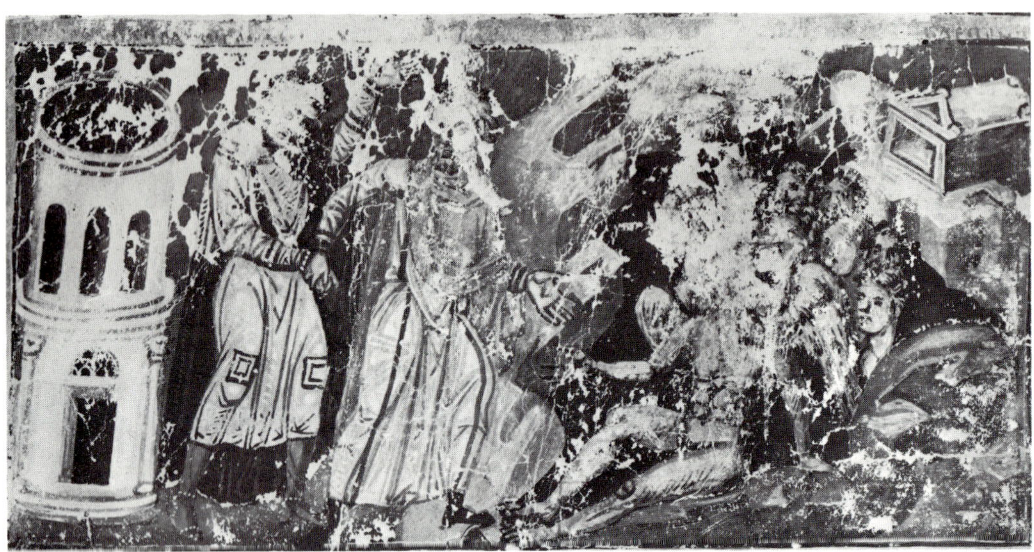

were set into a spatial landscape with architecture wherever the situation called for it—a change parallel to the one from single combat into multifigured battle scenes in the illustration of the Iliad. It is true that the only illustrated Byzantine chronicle we possess today, the John Scylitzes in Madrid with its more than four hundred miniatures, is not older than the fourteenth century,[80] but there is evidence for the existence of illustrated chronicles at a much earlier period. The ninth-century codex of the homilies of Gregory of Nazianzus in Paris (cod. gr. 510),[81] for example, contains a series of illustrations of historical events which were not invented for the homilies with which they are now connected but for texts which explain the details of the pictures more thoroughly. The series of six scenes from the life of Julian the Apostate (Fig. 102), for instance, begins with the emperor's visit to a demon in a cave, and at the upper right there is a sarcophagus, the tomb of the martyr Babylos, which is not mentioned by Gregory, but is referred to in the *Historia Ecclesiastica* of Sozomenos, the fifth-century chronicler.[82] Other scenes in Gregory can be explained by passages in Theodoret and Malalas, and from this we conclude that all these chronicles existed with extensive narrative cycles, most likely as early as the fifth century and in the case of Malalas, the sixth

[80] G. Millet, *La collection chrétienne et byzantine des Hautes Études* (Paris, 1903), p. 26, nos. B 369–75; p. 54, nos. C 869–1277; G. Schlumberger, *L'épopée byzantine à la fin du dixième siècle* (Paris, 1896–1905), vols. II and III, *passim*; S. Cirac Estopañán, *Skyllitzes Matritensis, 1* (Barcelona, 1965).

[81] H. Omont, *Miniatures des plus anciens manuscrits grecs de la Bibliothèque Nationale* (2d ed.; Paris, 1929), pp. 10 ff. and pls. XV–LX.

[82] Weitzmann, "Illustrations for the Chronicles of Sozomenos, Theodoret and Malalas," *Byzantion*, 16 (1942–43), 87 ff. and especially 100 ff.

century. So far we have no evidence that any fourth-century chronicle existed with rich cycles of a similar nature. It is tempting to speculate that if Theodoret was illustrated then also the *Historia Ecclesiastica* of Eusebius, that is the very chronicle which was continued by Theodoret, might have existed with pictures. Nevertheless, that richly illustrated chronicles must have existed alongside the simpler papyrus tradition in the fourth century can be inferred by the impact they had on other branches of illustrated texts.

In his painstaking analysis of the miniatures of the Vergilius Vaticanus, de Wit pointed out that most compositions were not invented for the text of the Aeneid, but that the illustrator borrowed figure types as well as whole schemes from representations of a different context and adjusted them to the text of Virgil's poems. Aeneas himself is consistently depicted as a Roman emperor rather than a Trojan hero,[83] and for scenes of an adlocution or a battle de Wit points to the triumphal columns of Trajan and Marcus Aurelius and other historical reliefs as the closest extant parallels. Perhaps the most striking example of such a borrowing can be seen in the miniatures of the nightly council presided over by Ascanius, who sits on a faldistorium, presumably the "sella castrensis" (Fig. 103)[84] which de Wit compared with scenes of judgment and negotiations with foreign tribes on the Marcus Aurelius column.

Very similar observations were made by Boeckler in connection with the miniatures of the Quedlinburg Itala.[85] He too noticed that Saul was depicted as a Roman emperor (Fig. 78), that adlocution, libation, battles, and so on, were rendered in compositional schemes that were borrowed from the iconography of Roman history, and he pointed to the very same monuments as the most suitable parallels, namely the triumphal columns. Not that he or de Wit had suggested the columns were the immediate source, but they are our richest and most complex extant repertory of compositional schemes for the illustration of historical events. Furthermore, it had not escaped Boeckler that the compositional schemes as well as the individual types were, indeed, the same as those used in the Vergilius Vaticanus.

Now it would seem highly unlikely that the illustrators of an epic poem and of a book from the Old Testament would walk around Rome and sketch the same triumphal columns. We rather have to imagine a common source available in a scriptorium, particularly in the case of the Vergilius Vaticanus and the Itala which, as Boeckler made plausible,[86] are stylistically so close to each other that the same scriptorium can be assumed, that is a scriptorium which produced illustrated pagan and Christian manuscripts side by side. What was this common source? In the light of our observations about illustrated world chronicles and related historical writings, it seems to us more than likely that it is in this category of illustrated texts that we have to look for

---

[83] De Wit, *Vergilius Vaticanus*, pp. 159 ff.
[84] Ibid., pp. 146 ff. and pl. 27, no. 1.

[85] Degering and Boeckler, *Italafragmente*, pp. 150 ff.
[86] Ibid., pp. 169 ff.

Fig. 103 *Vatican, Biblioteca. Cod. lat. 3225,*
fol. 73ᵛ. Aeneid. Council

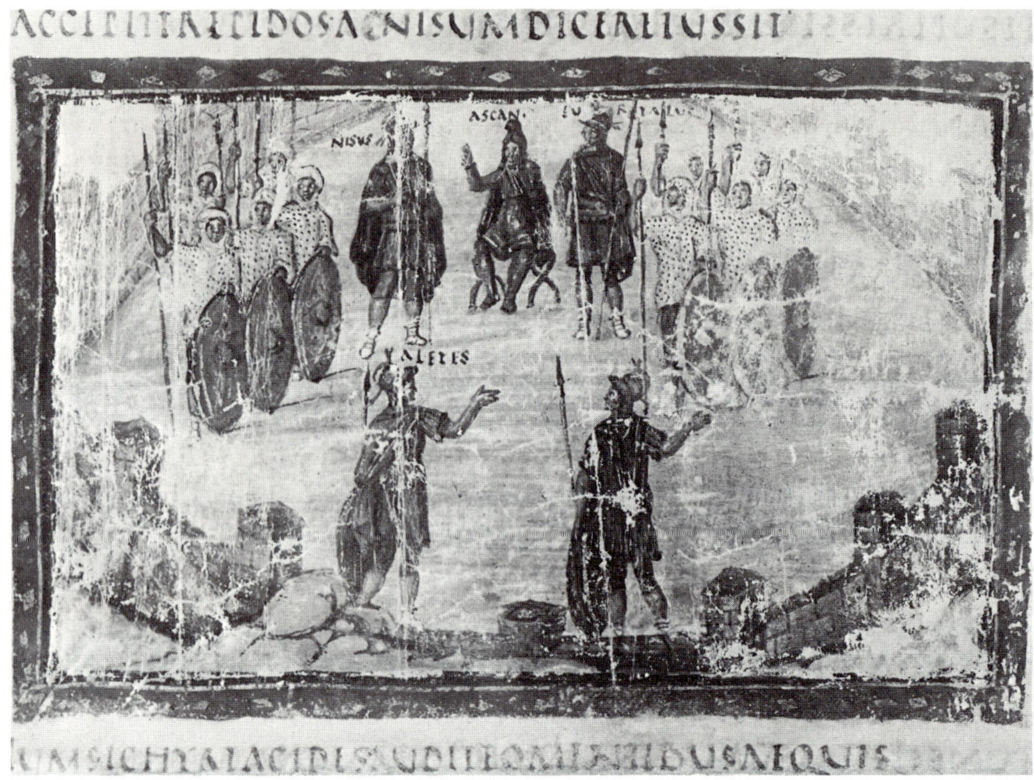

the common source that was utilized
by the illustrators of the Vatican Virgil
and the Bible.

Nothing more than a mere sketch in
its barest outlines can be attempted
here; it must be left for the future to
write a more coherent and more fully
documented history of book illumination
in the fourth century. At present it was
our intention to focus on the following
three aspects:

1) the juxtaposition of the codex illustration to the older papyrus illustration.
Only after the latter had been studied
more extensively within the last years and
the evidence for its existence on a wide
scale established was it possible to see
the achievements of fourth-century codex
illustration in their right perspective.
Actually it was the time when almost
every conceivable type of full-page
miniature came into being, and when
narrative cycles became embellished as
if to rival the effect of panel and fresco
painting, under whose influence they
had come. No essential type of illustration has been added since, and book
illumination of the present day still
profits from the inventions of the fourth
century;

2) the emergence of the imperial iconography as the dominating realm. The
fact that so little of early chronicle
illustration has survived obscures the

historical role it played, but its importance can still be sensed by the impact it had on all other branches of book illumination, pagan and Christian alike;

3) the lucky coincidence that the great technical innovation of the parchment codex came to fruition at a juncture in history when a climate prevailed in which pagan, Christian, and imperial illustrations could be produced side by side in the same scriptorium and influence each other mutually. Already at the end of the fourth century a work like the Calendar of Filocalus could hardly have been produced for a Christian.

In view of the great splendor and luxuriousness of fourth-century manuscripts like the Vergilius Vaticanus, the Quedlinburg Itala, the archetype of the Filocalus, and many others, it is safe to assume that the imperial court as patron must have played an essential role, although we are in no position to claim for any of the extant codices an imperial commission.

When in the Middle Ages the two most conspicuous revival movements, the Carolingian Renaissance in the Latin West and the Macedonian Renaissance in the Greek East, looked for early models to copy, they found them essentially in books and to such an extent that one could almost speak of "book renaissances." In both revival movements we find a similar close parallelism of pagan and Christian miniatures as we had found in the fourth century, and the explanation for this phenomenon may well be sought in the fact that their best products, like the Leiden Aratus, the Filocalus of the ninth century on which the later drawings are based, the Kassel Pseudo-Apuleius in the West, and

the various tenth-century Gospel books in the East, all hark back to fourth-century models, thus recreating similar conditions under which these models themselves were made, and in this way the achievements of the early codex illustration were kept alive and perpetuated as long as precious parchment codices were produced.

6

The Classical Heritage in the Art of Constantinople

THE survival of classical antiquity during the Middle Ages for a long time has been the subject of intensive art historical research, especially among German scholars. The point of departure and the aim of these studies is the demonstration that the Middle Ages did not make a complete break with the ancient world; but that, in fact, the classical heritage remained alive as an undercurrent and filtered into Christian culture, often changed, coarsened, or misunderstood, but at certain times contributing to the brilliant accomplishments of periods variously characterized Renaissance, *renovatio*, renascence, or simply revival.[1]

This study, which originally appeared as "Das klassische Erbe in der Kunst Konstantinopels," in *Alte und Neue Kunst*, 3 (1954), 41–59, is the shortened version of a lecture which the author delivered as the guest of the Österreichische Byzantinische Gesellschaft in November 1953 at the University of Vienna and shortly thereafter repeated at the University of Marburg in response to an invitation from the Kunsthistorisches und Archaeologisches Institut on the occasion of the commemoration of Winckelmann's birthday, and again at the Kunstgeschichtliches Institut at the University of Bonn. It has been translated and is reprinted with the permission of Anton Schroll & Company, Vienna.

[1] A good compilation of the voluminous literature on this theme is to be found in an article by R. Hamann-Maclean, "Antikenstudium in der Kunst des Mittelalters," *Marburger Jahrbuch für Kunstwissenschaft*, 15 (1949/50), 157 ff. Hence I cite only the most important older literature and the most recent works: A. Goldschmidt, "Das Nachleben der antiken Formen im Mittelalter," *Vorträge der Bibliothek Warburg*, 1 (1921/22), 40 ff.; E. Panofsky and F. Saxl, "Classical Mythology in Mediaeval Art," *Metropolitan Museum Studies*, 4 (1932/33), 228 ff.; J. Adhémar,

Although previous investigations have made fundamental contributions by defining and evaluating much relevant material, unfortunately, in our opinion, they have suffered from one drawback: all have virtually neglected the one center uniquely destined to preserve the classical heritage, Constantinople. We need only recall one fact: when barbarians overran the Latin West and an unclassical element was infused into Western culture and art, and when a great part of the Christian East was overtaken by the victories of Islam which facilitated a strong penetration of oriental elements, the walls of Constantinople remained intact—withstanding the attacks of barbarians and Muslims for almost one thousand years. This historical situation provided conditions indispensable for the continuity of the Greek inheritance, present even when recast in a Christian mold.[2]

Why have scholars not paid sufficient attention to the central role of Constantinople as preserver of ancient tradi-

Influences antiques dans l'art du moyen âge français (London, 1939); E. Panofsky, "Renaissance and Renascences," *Kenyon Review*, 6 (1944), 201 ff.; H. von Einem, "Die Monumentalplastik des Mittelalters und ihr Verhältnis zur Antike," *Antike und Abendland*, 3 (1948), 120 ff.; W. Paatz, "Renaissance oder Renovatio ?" *Beiträge zur Kunst des Mittelalters; Vorträge der ersten deutschen Kunsthistorikertagung auf Schloss Brühl, 1948* (Berlin, 1950), pp. 16 ff. [E. Panofsky, *Renaissance and Renascences* (2d ed., Stockholm, 1965).]

[2] Here I call attention to the brilliant formulations in a published lecture by Norman H. Baynes, *The Hellenistic Civilization and East Rome* (Oxford, 1946) [reprinted in *Byzantine Studies and Other Essays by N. Baynes* (London, 1955)].

tion? We believe that there are three principal reasons for this. First, there is Vasari's dominating formulation, according to which the *maniera greca*, i.e., the Byzantine tradition, was viewed as a stagnating art which Renaissance artists attempted to avoid by turning directly to antiquity.[3] In the light of this theory, would it not seem paradoxical to claim that Byzantine art transmitted the classical tradition? Even though contemporary art historians realize that Vasari's interpretation was conditioned in part by the prejudices of the Renaissance Florentines who no longer understood the formal language of either Western medieval or Byzantine art and that it is to be taken *cum grano salis*, Vasari's prejudice against Byzantine art, though often unconsciously, until recently has continued to make a deep impression.

The second factor is an inadequate knowledge of the works of Constantinopolitan art. Even today there remain many gaps in our knowledge which perhaps will never be entirely bridged and which virtually preclude a complete understanding and total judgment. Nevertheless, during the last decades significant advances in the investigation of Constantinopolitan art have provided a far more complete picture. For the Early Byzantine period we draw attention here only to a relief sarcophagus

for a child found in Istanbul in 1933,[4] the mosaic uncovered in the imperial palace shortly before the last war,[5] and the splendid silver bowls found in Russia, which were only recently recognized as products of Constantinopolitan workshops in the excellent publication by Matzulevich.[6] As for the Middle and Late Byzantine periods, our knowledge of Constantinopolitan art continues to grow as the mosaics of Hagia Sophia and the mosaics and frescoes of the Kariye Djami and other churches in Constantinople are uncovered[7] and as illuminated manuscripts become known, especially those in Greek monasteries which formerly were less accessible, including

[3] J. Schlosser has repeatedly stressed the role played by the concept of "maniera greca" in Renaissance writing, beginning with Ghiberti. [See also E. Kitzinger, "The Byzantine Contribution to Western Art of the Twelfth and Thirteenth Centuries," *Dumbarton Oaks Papers*, 20 (1966), 27 ff.]

[4] A. Müfid, *Ein Prinzensarkophag aus Istanbul* (Istanbul, 1934); J. Kollwitz, *Oströmische Plastik der Theodosianischen Zeit* (Berlin, 1941), pp. 132 ff. and pls. 45–47.

[5] G. Brett, "The Mosaic of the Great Palace in Constantinople," *Journal of the Warburg Institute*, 5 (1942), 34 ff.; G. Brett, W. J. Macauly, and R. B. K. Stevenson, *The Great Palace of the Byzantine Emperors* (Oxford, 1947), pp. 64 ff. and pls. 28–56. [D. Talbot Rice, *The Great Palace of the Byzantine Emperors, Second Report* (Edinburgh, 1958); review of *Second Report* by C. Mango and I. Lavin, *Art Bulletin*, 42 (1960), 67 ff.]

[6] L. Matzulevich, *Byzantinische Antike* (Berlin, 1929). [E. Cruikshank Dodd, *Byzantine Silver Stamps* ("Dumbarton Oaks Studies," 7; Washington, 1961).]

[7] A part of the mosaics of Hagia Sophia, which have been uncovered by T. Whittemore and his successor, P. Underwood, has been published in four preliminary reports: T. Whittemore, *The Mosaics of St. Sophia at Istanbul* (Oxford, 1933–52). [C. Mango, *Materials for the Study of the Mosaics of St. Sophia at Istanbul* ("Dumbarton Oaks Studies," 8; Washington, 1962); P. Underwood, *The Kariye Djami* (New York, 1966).]

many products of high quality manufactured in Constantinople.[8]

Previously, art historians had constructed a one-sided image of Early Byzantine art based on the mosaics of Ravenna, particularly those of San Vitale. In this connection the question has naturally arisen over and over again: to what degree do these mosaics truly mirror the style of Constantinople? The fact that the newly uncovered mosaics of Hagia Sophia have been assigned various dates, sometimes differing by hundreds of years, clearly reveals how uncertain our ideas of Middle and Late Byzantine style are. Because of recent discoveries, the view is gaining ground that different styles flourished side by side in Constantinople, as is to be expected of the artistic activity in a capital city at its zenith. In many cases the function of a specific artwork may explain its style. For example, a large-scale church mosaic often differs in style from contemporary minor arts which depend on another tradition, in many cases more closely on classical art.

The third reason is that in art historical writing Early Byzantine art from Constantinople has long been overshadowed by the art of the older centers such as Alexandria and Antioch, cities which were founded in Hellenistic times and which were flourishing centers of the Roman empire. These centers certainly played an outstanding role in continuing the classical tradition during early Christian times; but the question is how long Alexandria and Antioch were in a position to maintain their status as guardians of the classical tradition, exposed, as they were, to influences of the Egyptian and Syrian hinterlands which became conspicuous in late antiquity. Would not Constantinople, set in a Greek milieu, be in a position, from a certain period on, to compete with the older cities in this respect?

The survival of the classical tradition during the Middle Ages has two principal aspects: the continuation of ancient pictorial compositions retaining their original meaning (wherein one must take into account misunderstandings and intentional changes of content as well as a gradual penetration of medieval styles), and the influence of the classical on the Christian tradition. After all, it is because classical imagery so strongly affected Christian art that the strength and vitality of classical images made such a dominant impression. The author has already treated the influence of antiquity on the Christian art of Byzantium in several earlier studies[9]; therefore,

---

[8] In this connection, it may be noted that the author has photographed the illustrations of all accessible illustrated manuscripts of the various monasteries on Mount Athos during two expeditions carried out in 1935 and 1936 under the auspices of the Department of Art and Archaeology of Princeton University. Furthermore, after the last World War, the Library of Congress participated in an expedition which photographed the illustrated manuscripts of the Greek Patriarchate in Jerusalem and of the monastery of Saint Catherine at Sinai. [This has been supplemented by Weitzmann more recently during four expeditions to Mount Sinai.]

[9] Weitzmann, "Der Pariser Psalter MS. Grec. 139 und die mittelbyzantinische Renaissance," *Jahrbuch für Kunstwissenschaft* 6 (1929), 178 ff.; idem, "Probleme der mittelbyzantinischen Renaissance," *Archäologischer Anzeiger* (1933), 336 ff.; "The Psalter Vatopedi 761—Its Place in the Aristocratic Psalter Recension,"

in this essay we shall deal exclusively with the problem of the continuation of classical images with their original meanings.

THE PRE-ICONOCLASTIC PERIOD

When the emperor went from the Chrysotriklinos to one of the churches near the Pharos within the palace complex, he stepped across the splendid mosaic of the peristyle floor which was uncovered shortly before the last war in an excavation conducted by the University of Saint Andrews and which the British excavators have dated to the first half of the fifth century, i.e., during the reign of Theodosius II.[10] Originally, this mosaic was of an extraordinary size; and even though only a part of the pavement has come down to us, both the character and the scheme of the

mosaic can be ascertained on the basis of the preserved portions (Fig. 104). The main scenes are of hunting, catching, and killing animals, of the habits of animals, and of their natural destruction and domestication for work and play. One whole series of these animal scenes, loosely distributed over three strips, surely goes back to a single source.

The *Cynegetica*, a didactic poem on hunting with dogs by the Pseudo-Oppian, has illustrations of similar scenes, for example, of hunting hares—this treatise, an eleventh-century manuscript, derived from an ancient archetype, is preserved in the Marciana in Venice (cod. gr. 479. Fig. 105).[11] Because the miniatures of this manuscript do not depict the hare hunt with exactly the same composition as that of the mosaic,[12] it is not possible to prove that an illustrated manuscript of the *Cynegetica* of Pseudo-Oppian was the model for the mosaicist. However, it is likely that a similar treatise on animals, belonging to the same category of ancient didactic poems, was the model for the mosaic. On the other hand, so far as we may generalize from its fragmentary state, there are very few traces of mythological representations in the mosaic. Of the

---

The Journal of the Walters Art Gallery, 10 (1947), 20 ff.; idem, *The Joshua Roll: A Work of the Macedonian Renaissance* ("Studies in Manuscript Illumination," 3 [Princeton, 1948]); idem, *Greek Mythology in Byzantine Art* ("Studies in Manuscript Illumination," 4 [Princeton, 1951]); idem, *The Fresco Cycle of S. Maria di Castelseprio* (Princeton, 1951). [Idem, "The Survival of Mythological Representations in Early Christian and Byzantine Art and their Impact on Christian Iconography," *Dumbarton Oaks Papers*, 14 (1960), 43 ff.; idem, *Geistige Grundlagen und Wesen der Makedonischen Renaissance* (Cologne and Opladen, 1963), translated and reprinted herewith, pp. 176 ff.; idem, "The Classical in Byzantine Art as a Mode of Individual Expression." *Byzantine Art—An European Art* (Athens, 1966), pp. 149 ff., reprinted herewith, pp. 151 ff.]

[10] See n. 5. [In the second report, the excavators proposed a new date during the reign of Marcian (451–57), but this was rejected by Mango and Lavin who prefer a late sixth-century date.]

[11] A. W. Byvanck, "De geïllustreerde Handschriften van Oppianus' Cynegetica," *Mededeelingen van het Nederlandsch Historisch Instituut te Rome*, 5 (1925), 34 ff.; Weitzmann, *Greek Mythology* (here the older literature). [Idem, *Ancient Book Illumination* ("Martin Classical Lectures," 16 [Cambridge, Mass., 1959]), pp. 26 ff., 53 ff. and *passim*; idem, *Geistige Grundlagen*, p. 19 and *passim*, herewith, pp. 189 ff. and *passim*.]

[12] Cf. Byvanck, "Cynegetica," fig. 4 (fol. 18v). There is another hare hunting scene on fol. 17v.

Fig. 104 *Istanbul, Imperial Palace. Mosaic.*
Hunting Scenes

Fig. 105 *Venice, Marciana. Cod. gr. 479, fol.*
54ᵛ. Hare Hunt

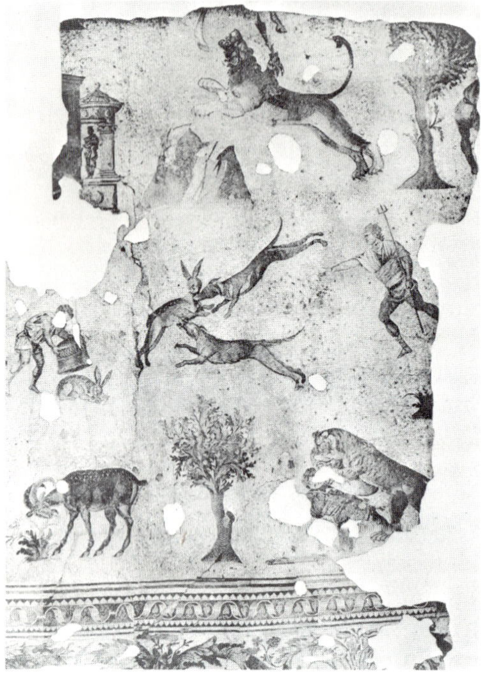

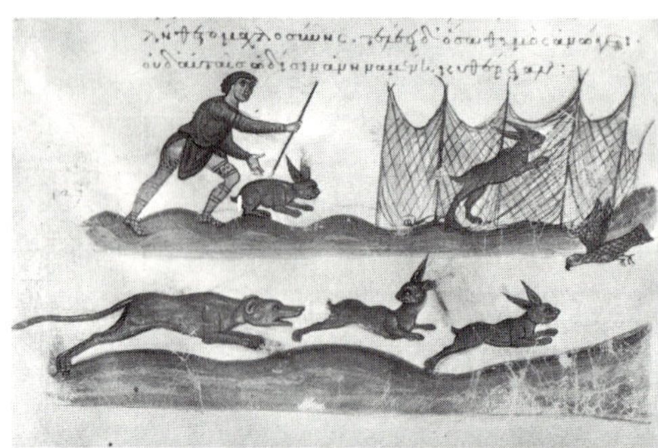

noteworthy depiction of the fight of
Bellerophon against the chimera (Fig. 104),
only the legs of Pegasus and the tip
of Bellerophon's lance are preserved.
This very representation is found
between two animal scenes in the Venice
manuscript of the Pseudo-Oppian,[13]
where, in keeping with the contents of
the didactic poem, the fight of Bellerophon interested the poet not because
of its mythological content but because
of the fantastic form of the monstrous
chimera. This strengthens our view
that the mosaicist used as his model a
didactic poem about animals and explains
the presence of a lone mythological
scene in the overall program of the
mosaic.

[13] Byvanck, "Cynegetica," fig. 2; Weitzmann,
Greek Mythology, pl. XXXII, 112.

In view of the fact that the subjects
of classical pictures, like those of written
works, may be divided into two groups—
learned treatises and literary works—
the selection of a didactic model for
a mosaic in such a prominent place is
quite remarkable. Even during Christian
times, scholarly texts, including the
didactic poems and their illustrations,
had had an enduring practical value, and
since their outlook was not offensive,
they were copied throughout the centuries. On the other hand, the prerequisite for copying works of poetry
and their illustrations is a tolerant
attitude toward the ancient tradition,
an attitude which has wavered between
neglect and conscious revival. In the
light of this general observation, we
may consider the choice of hunting and
animal scenes from a didactic poem to
reflect a conscious preference for a
scientific and, thereby, neutral subject
matter, which could not offend the
Christian emperor, Theodosius II,
when he strode over this mosaic on his
way to one of the palace churches. This
conforms very well to our picture of
this period. In 425 Theodosius II had
founded the University of Constantinople

Fig. 106 *Antioch. Mosaic. Hunting Scenes*

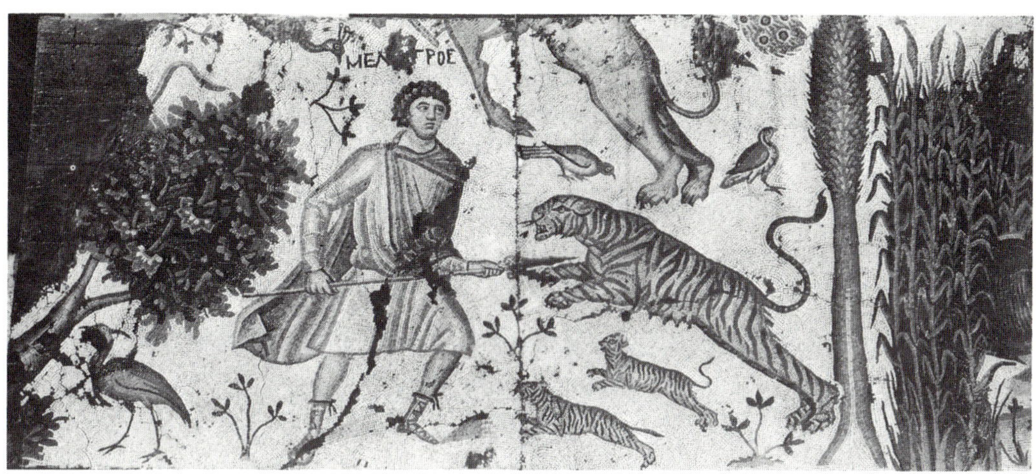

where, under Christian patronage, classical learning was cultivated.

Of high artistic quality, the mosaic is the product of an unbroken classical tradition. In spite of its highly classical character, however, it has features— quite apart from the loss of depth prevalent in late antiquity—that were determined by the development of Byzantine style in Constantinople. These features include the accentuated slenderness of people and animals, a tendency to a hard, almost creased rendering of folds of drapery, and, especially, the serious, tensely nervous facial expressions which, in works such as the palace mosaic, do not accord with the atmosphere of hunting and bucolic life. All of these features may be explained as a natural development of Hellenistic style and do not need the assumption of the influence of foreign, non-Greek styles. The spiritualizing tendency, which strengthened as the Christian outlook prevailed, sufficiently explains this transformation in style.

It is instructive to compare the style of the palace mosaic with that of a nearly contemporary mosaic from Antioch-on-the-Orontes, where the excavations of Princeton University have brought to light a wealth of mosaics so that for the first time in the history of ancient art we obtain an almost unbroken sequence of painting from the first to the sixth century. The Megalopsychia mosaic from Yakto which is dated to the time shortly after the death of Theodosius II has hunting scenes in which the hunters have been given mythological names such as Meleagros (Fig. 106).[14] Like the hunting scenes of the Constantinople mosaic, the scenes of the Antioch mosaic derive from good classical prototypes, to which the copyist owes his understanding of the lively

[14] J. Lassus, "La mosaïque de Yakto," *Antioch-on-the-Orontes*, 1 (Princeton, 1934). 114 ff.; D. Levi, *Antioch Mosaic Pavements* (Princeton, 1947), 1: 323 ff.; 2: pls. LXXVII–LXXVIII. [I. Lavin, "The Hunting Mosaics of Antioch and their Sources," *Dumbarton Oaks Papers*, 17 (1963), 181 ff.]

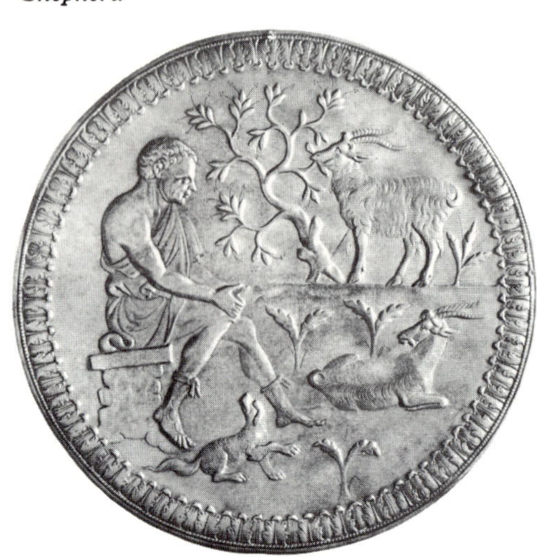

Fig. 107 *Leningrad, Hermitage. Silver Plate. Shepherd*

action and of the articulation of the bodies which, all in all, is still rather good. At the same time, the Antioch mosaic has nonclassical elements which cannot be explained away by the lesser quality of the mosaic but comes from another *Kunstwollen,* to use Riegl's vivid expression. The bodies are heavier and fleshier, the drapery folds are reduced to very broad smooth linear shadows, so that the figures convey the impression of softness in contrast to the muscularity of the hunters in the Constantinople mosaic. The growing influence of the art of the Syrian hinterlands, based on Palmyran and Persian styles, is revealed in these features of the art of Antioch.[15]

This comparison between the two hunting mosaics provides evidence that during the course of the fifth century Constantinople, in contrast to Antioch, preserved the classical tradition with comparatively greater purity. The reason for this is easily found in the fact that Constantinople had Greece and Greek Asia Minor as hinterlands, regions which at all times were relatively less exposed to oriental influence than was Antioch.

A silver plate found in Russia (Fig. 107) with stamps dating it in the reign of Anastasius or Justinian may serve to demonstrate that even as late as the sixth century classical form and content remained alive and astoundingly vigorous. Matzulevich, as we have previously mentioned, had good reason to attribute these and other silver plates

to Constantinople, contrary to earlier views according to which these plates were manufactured in Syria.[16] Two silver bowls, each with a representation of the communion of the apostles, survive from the same period; both were found in Syria and were certainly made there: the one from Stuma (North Syria) is now in the Istanbul Museum[17] and the other from Riha (also North Syria) is in the Dumbarton Oaks Collection in Washington.[18] A comparison between

[15] For the problem of Syrian style in the first century A.D. consult the first of three articles by G. de Francovich, "L'arte siriaca e il suo influsso sulla pittura medioevale nell'Oriente e nell'Occidente," *Commentari,* 2 (1951), 3 ff.

[16] For this controversy consult Francovich, "L'arte siriaca," 13 ff. where the relevant literature is cited.

[17] H. Peirce and R. Tyler, *L'art Byzantin,* 2 (Paris, 1934), p. 114 and pl. 140. [Cruikshank Dodd, *Silver Stamps,* p. 94 ff.; M. Ross, *Catalogue of the Byzantine and Early Mediaeval Antiquities in the Dumbarton Oaks Collection* (Washington, 1962), I, 12 ff.; E. Kitzinger, "Byzantine Art in the Period between Justinian and Iconoclasm," *Berichte zum XI. Internationalen Byzantinisten-Kongress* (Munich, 1958), pp. 18 ff.]

[18] Peirce and Tyler, *L'art Byzantine,* p. 115, pl. 144. [Cruikshank Dodd, *Silver Stamps,* pp. 94 f. and 108 f.; Kitzinger, "Byzantine

the Syrian silver bowls and the Leningrad shepherd plate show that they differ from each other in the same way that the two hunting mosaics differ from each other. The Syrian bowls reveal an uncertain articulation of the bodies and a rendering of the drapery which from a naturalistic point of view is imprecise, whereas the classical character of the shepherd bowl is apparent immediately.

In a spaceless landscape where the trees and plants are decoratively distributed in the manner of late antique style, a robust, well-modeled shepherd sits on a rock in a nervous pose, ready to leap up, and looking ahead tensely as if he were pondering something other than his pasturing goats. Because the facial features appear so individual, Studniczka once thought that one could descry a portrait of Theocritus in this figure.[19] The parallels with the hunters and farmers in the palace mosaic, however, clearly show that here we are dealing with a general tendency in Byzantine art to achieve a tenser and thus more spiritual expression by contracting the eyebrows thereby reducing the cheerful, carefree atmosphere of bucolic life.

Works such as the shepherd bowl

present a style that is hard to reconcile with that of the nearly contemporary mosaics of San Vitale in Ravenna customarily regarded as the true artistic expression of the Justinianic period.[20] We must learn to realize that in a thriving metropolis like Constantinople different traditions flourished side by side and that one tradition may be found in monumental church mosaics and another in luxury articles of precious metals for secular purposes. This wide range of different tendencies was also present in the literary culture of the time. While the emperor himself was interested mainly in theology and jurisprudence and closed the pagan schools of philosophers in Athens in 529, the writings of Procopius were influenced by Herodotus and Thucydides; Paul the Silentiary used the descriptions of pictures by Philostratus as patterns for his ekphrasis of Haghia Sophia; and Agathias composed epigrams in the classical manner. In such an aristocratic culture products like the shepherd bowl which continue the classical style are thoroughly understandable.

Despite certain mannerisms, the well-formed shepherd emanates a classical style and spirit which would be hard to find in any other metropolitan city of the eastern Mediterranean in the time of Justinian. At the same time, as we saw from the mosaics uncovered there and from the silver plates found not far away, Antioch fell more and more under the influence of the Syrian hinterlands;

Art," pp. 19 ff.; Ross, *Dumbarton Oaks Collection,* pp. 12 ff. On the basis of hallmarks, these scholars have now accepted the Stuma and Riha patens both to be Constantinopolitan products from the reign of Justin II (565–78). Because it has never been proven that silver with hallmarks necessarily must have been produced in Constantinople, Weitzmann does not consider the issue closed.]

[19] F. Studniczka, "Imagines Illustrium," *Jahrbuch des deutschen Archäologischen Instituts,* 38/39 (1923/24), 57 ff. and *Philologische Wochenschrift,* 54 (1924), 1276 ff.

[20] For the unclassical element of unreality in the art of the mosaics of S. Vitale see the observations of K. M. Swoboda, "Die Mosaiken von San Vitale in Ravenna," *Neue Aufgaben der Kunstgeschichte* (1935), 27 ff.

and half a century ago Strzygowski proved from the chancel reliefs at Aachen what had happened to classical representation in Alexandria at this time.[21] Dionysus (Fig. 108) is depicted, with a fleshy, thick-set body and an oversized head, enmeshed in an ornamental grape vine. Abstract and decorative values compensate for the loss of organic modeling. In Hellenistic times and during the Roman imperial period the great metropolis at the Canopic Nile had created works with a feeling for pure Greek style; but when a general tendency toward abstraction began to set in everywhere in late antiquity, Alexandria absorbed the particular abstract forms which seeped in from the Egyptian and Coptic hinterlands,[22] to which the ivory reliefs in Aachen bear such eloquent witness.

In Constantinople an elegant imitation of classical art persisted into the seventh-century reign of Heraclius, as we may learn from a silver plate with representations of Meleager and Atalante (Fig. 109) dated to this time by its stamp.[23] The figures standing at ease have lost nothing of their mobility or correctly understood proportions, but in accord with the general development

[21] J. Strzygowski, *Hellenistische und koptische Kunst in Alexandria* (Vienna, 1902), pp. 19 ff.
[22] For the intrusion of Egyptian style in contemporary Alexandrian book illustration see Weitzmann, "Observations on the Cotton Genesis Fragments," *Late Classical and Mediaeval Studies in Honor of Albert M. Friend, Jr.* (Princeton, 1954), pp. 112 ff.; idem, "Observations on the Milan Iliad," *Nederlands Kunsthistorisch Jaarboek*, 5 (1954), 241 ff.
[23] Matzulevich, *Byzantinische Antike*, pp. 9 ff. and *passim*, pl. 1. [Cruikshank Dodd, *Silver Stamps*, p. 176 f.]

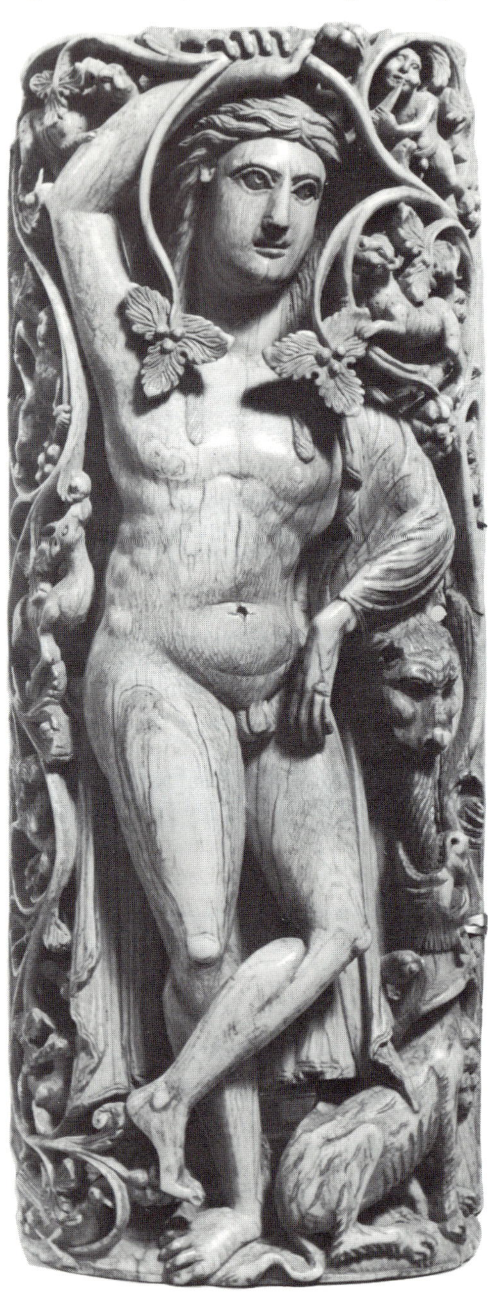

Fig. 108 *Aachen, Cathedral. Pulpit. Dionysus*

Fig. 109 *Leningrad, Hermitage. Silver Plate. Meleager and Atalante*

Fig. 110 *Vienna, Nationalbibliothek. Cod. med. gr. 1, fol. 4ᵛ. Dioscurides (Crateuas) and Heuresis*

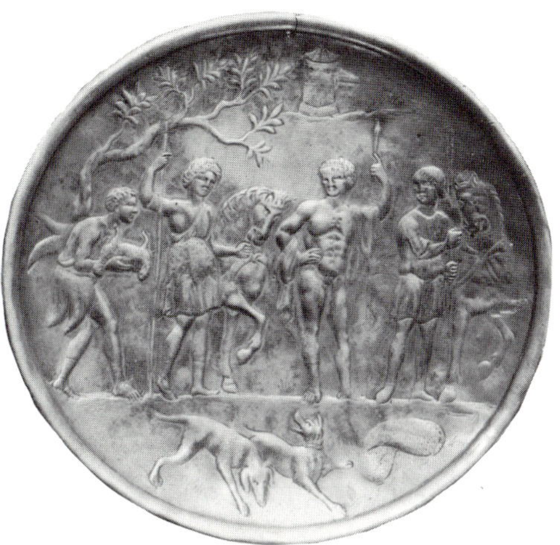

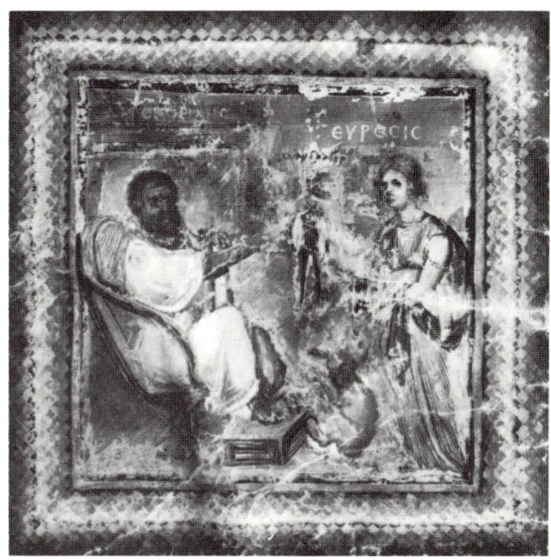

of Byzantine art, they betray a growing tendency to make bodies less corporeal by outlining them with deeply incised grooves and at the same time flattening the relief. In order to understand how two styles based on different traditions can exist side by side and yet be poles apart, one has only to recall the nearly contemporary mosaics in the Church of Saint Demetrios in Thessalonica.

The classical tradition was best preserved in book illumination which had an innate tendency to be conservative. This can be seen from the one luxury manuscript of early Byzantine times which is demonstrably Constantinopolitan: the well-known Dioscurides herbarium of the National Library in Vienna (cod. Med. gr. 1) which was made about 512 for Juliana Anicia, who came from the imperial family and was the daughter of one consul and wife of another. Of the two full-page author portraits in the Vienna Dioscurides, the one showing a pharmacologist with the personification of Heuresis holding a

mandrake (Fig. 110)²⁴ clearly reflects an artistic tradition having affinities with Pompeian wall painting as indicated by the handling of the flesh tints, the painterly rendering of the drapery of the author, and the architectural background dextrously laid on with a broad brush. Wickhoff's analysis of the Vienna Genesis has brought home to us how important the aesthetic values of this

²⁴ A. von Premerstein, K. Wessely, and J. Mantuani, *Dioscurides, Codex Aniciae Julianae, picturis illustratis, nunc Vindobonensis Med. gr. 1, phototypice editus* (Leiden, 1906), fol. 4ᵛ; H. Gerstinger, *Die griechische Buchmalerei* (Vienna, 1926), pp. 19 ff. and pl. VI; P. Buberl, "Die antiken Grundlagen der Miniaturen des Wiener Dioscurideskodex," *Jahrbuch des deutschen archäologischen Instituts*, 51 (1936), 129 ff.; idem, *Die byzantinischen Handschriften*, ("Beschreibendes Verzeichnis der illuminierten Handschriften in Österreich," 8, Part IV, 1 [Leipzig, 1937]), 22 ff. and pl. III. [*Der Wiener Dioscurides* (Codex Vindobonensis Med. gr. 1) Introduction by H. Gerstinger (Graz, 1965); Weitzmann, *Ancient Book Illumination*, pp. 122 ff.; idem, "Classical in Byzantine Art," pp. 154 ff., reprinted herewith, pp. 154 ff.]

tradition were for painting in late antique and early Christian times. At the same time such details as the golden highlights on the drapery of Heuresis are to be attributed to the sixth-century copyist.

Premerstein has ascertained[25] that this author, in spite of the inscription "Dioscurides," does not have the features of this pharmacologist but rather those of Crateuas; as a result he conjectured that the model had originally served as the frontispiece for the herbal by a predecessor of Dioscurides. Buberl, who accepted Premerstein's hypothesis,[26] inferred that this frontispiece had been made for the archetype of the Crateuas herbal which was written in the first century B.C. This picture, which is set in a broad, almost square frame, presupposes the existence of the codex which was not invented before the end of the first century of the Christian era.[27] Consequently this picture, at least as it is now with its elaborate frame, cannot date earlier than the beginning of the second century; and therefore we assume that it originated when a papyrus roll was converted into a parchment codex. Presumably above the first column of writing the papyrus archetype had only the figure of the seated author; the figure of Heuresis

with the mandrake and the dying dog were added when the full-page miniature of the first parchment codex was made. This conjecture removes the difficulty seen by Buberl, namely, that the superstition about the mandrake shown in the miniature is not known before the time of Aelian and Flavius Josephus, i.e., the first century of the Christian era.

A considerable part of the best and most naturalistic plant pictures of the so-called Index class, for example the iris and the violet (Figs. 111–112), does go back to the original Crateuas herbal of the first century B.C. The slightly asymmetrical drawing of the leaves, the irregular formation of the root fibers of the iris, and especially the elegant indolence of the violet stems and the casual arrangement of the leaves reveal the persistence of the ancient tradition of sharp observation of nature even in this copy which is separated from the archetype by more than half a millennium.

Another manuscript of Dioscurides dating to the seventh century, now in Naples, has pictures which probably derive directly from the Vienna codex or, at least, from a common source.[28] The plant illustrations in this manuscript (Fig. 113) are also of consistently high quality but reveal a different sense of style. The strict symmetry of the iris leaves and the ornamental treatment of the roots, the violet blossoms geometri-

---

[25] *Dioscurides*, p. 60.

[26] Buberl, *Handschriften*, p. 23.

[27] For the invention of the codex see the comments in Weitzmann, *Illustrations in Roll and Codex* ("Studies in Manuscript Illumination," 2d ed.; Princeton, 1970), 69 f. [More recently, idem, "Book Illustration of the Fourth Century: Tradition and Innovation," *Akten des VII. Internationalen Kongresses für Christliche Archäologie, Trier, 1965*, (Rome, 1969), pp. 257 ff., reprinted herewith, pp. 96 ff.]

[28] Ch. Singer, "The Herbal in Antiquity," *The Journal of Hellenic Studies*, 47 (1927), 24 and fig. 16: [Weitzmann, *Ancient Book Illumination*, p. 13; M. Anichini, "Il Dioscuride di Napoli," *Atti della Accademia Nazionale dei Lincei, Rendiconti. Classe di Scienze morali, storiche e filologiche*, Ser. VIII, Vol. XI (1956), 77 ff.]

Fig 111 *Vienna, Nationalbibliothek. Cod. med. gr. 1, fol. 147ᵛ. Iris*

Fig. 112 *Vienna, Nationalbibliothek. Cod. med. gr. 1, fol. 148ᵛ. Violet*

Fig. 113 *Naples, Biblioteca Nazionale (olim cod. Vind. suppl. gr. 28), fol. 42ʳ. Iris and Violet*

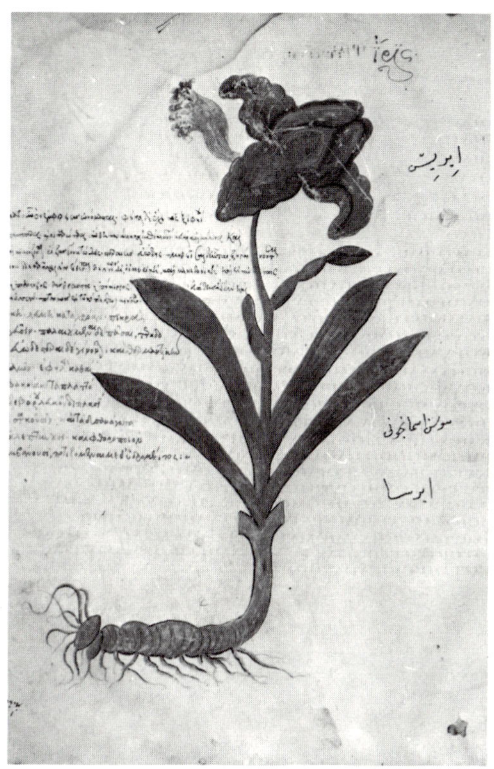

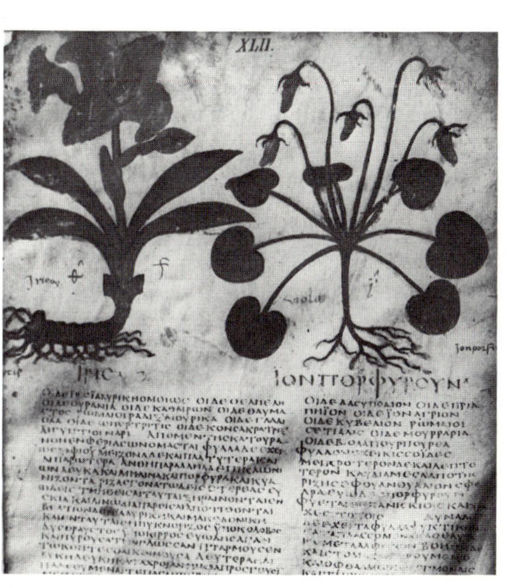

cally distributed in two triangles fitted together, and the wreathlike arrangement of the leaves are strikingly noticeable features. The patterning of the plants is perceptible here and is even clearer in the herbals of the Pseudo-Apuleius from the Latin West, as, for example, the Leiden codex also assigned to the seventh century.[29]

[29] Singer, "Herbal in Antiquity," pp. 43 ff. and figs. 28, 30, 44, 46; St. J. Gasiorowski, *Malarstwo Minjaturowe Grecko-Rzymskie* (Krakow, 1928), p. 68, XIII and figs. 19–22; A. W. Byvanck, "Les principaux manuscrits à peintures du royaume des Pays-Bas," *Bulletin de la Société français de reproductions de manuscrits à peintures*, 15 (1931), 58 and pl. XVII.

THE MACEDONIAN RENAISSANCE

The influence of the Vienna Dioscurides miniatures can be followed further. The Morgan Library in New York owns a luxury manuscript of Dioscurides (cod. 652) whose highly stylized, slightly affected minuscule writing indicates a date in the first half of the tenth century and is certainly Constantinopolitan.[30] That this manuscript was produced in an imperial scriptorium is highly probable. Moreover, it can be demonstrated, not only that whole groups of plant pictures in the New York manuscript have been copied directly from the Vienna manuscript, but also that they are considerably nearer to the Vienna manuscript than are the plant pictures in the Naples codex of the seventh century. In the pictures of the iris and the violet (Figs. 114–115), to keep to the same examples, there is no trace of a tendency toward geometric forms; rather, the casual way in which the flowers and leaves are arranged, resembling those in the Vienna codex, reflects a similarly strong feeling for the naturalistic rendering of classical plant pictures in this later copy.

The sequence we have just described —direct contact with antiquity evident

Fig. 114 *New York, Morgan Library. Cod. 652, fol. 66ᵛ. Iris*

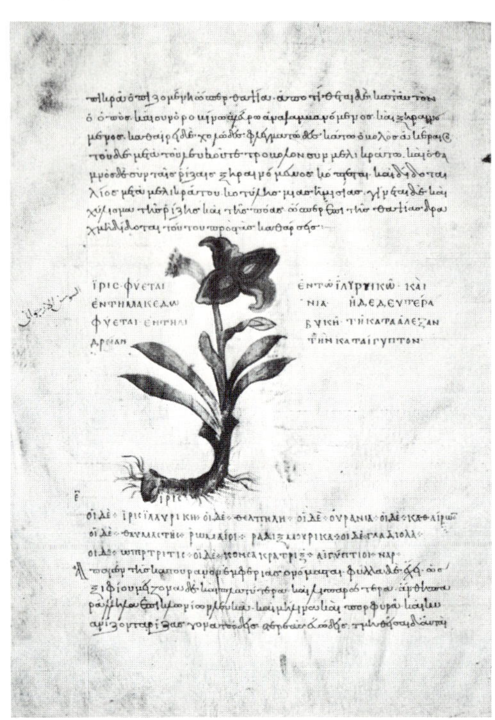

in the plant pictures of the Anicia codex of the sixth century, about to be lost in the plant pictures of the Naples copy of the seventh century, again to be seen in a tenth-century manuscript—is not an isolated case in the history of the illustration of Dioscurides but is connected with a revival of the classical tradition, which began very soon after the end of Iconoclasm and, at present, is usually called the Macedonian Renaissance. Our knowledge of the works of art which are associated with this movement is limited, primarily though not exclusively, to illustrated manuscripts;[31] and scholars are gradually beginning to have a clearer picture of the course of this movement which started with a

---

[30] Singer, "Herbal in Antiquity," pp. 25 ff. and figs. 35, 42; cf. facsimile: *Pedanii Dioscuridis Anazarbaei de Materia Medica*, 2 (Paris, 1935); B. da Costa Greene and M. Harrsen, *The Pierpont Morgan Library. Exhibition of Illuminated Manuscripts held at the New York Public Library* (New York, 1933–34), p. 6, no. 12 and pl. XI; Weitzmann, *Die byzantinische Buchmalerei des 9. und 10. Jahrhunderts* (Berlin, 1935), p. 34 and pl. XLI, 231–33. [Idem, *Ancient Book Illumination*, p. 13; idem, *Geistige Grundlagen*, p. 16, reprinted herewith, p. 186.]

[31] See bibliography cited in n. 9.

Fig. 115 *New York, Morgan Library. Cod. 652, fol. 67ʳ. Violet*

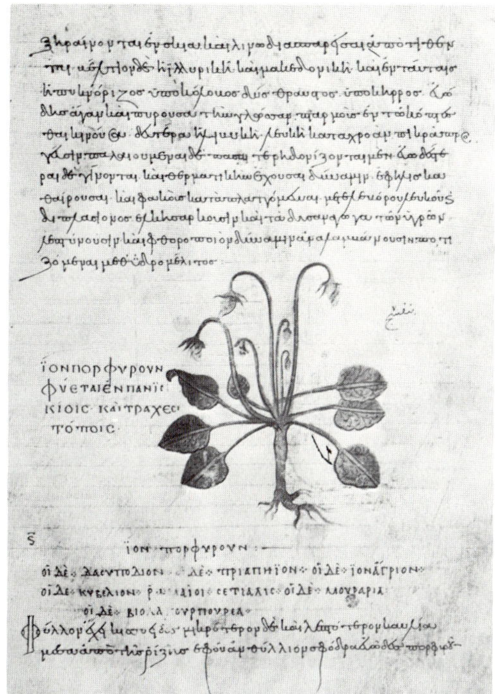

revival of classical literature. Shortly after Iconoclasm came to an end, the learned patriarch Photius collected a considerable body of texts, Christian and classical, and discussed them critically in his *Myriobiblon.*[32] His student Arethas, the bishop of Caesarea, more of a philologist than a literary critic, set himself to improve the classical texts; and several of the texts, which were copied for him with extreme care and provided with extensive commentary, still form the basis for modern editions.[33] Constantine Porphyrogenitus, the scholar on the imperial throne, with all the resources at his disposal, began an extensive program of publishing encyclopedias for the purpose of making available to the general public a steadily increasing body of literature in the form of summaries, as the emperor himself remarks in the almost modern sounding foreword to one of his writings.[34]

The New York Dioscurides manuscript is an outstanding example of a scholarly edition of a text at the beginning of the tenth century. In evaluating it, it is important to know that it reintroduces the original division of the Dioscurides text into five books, although each individual book, as became usual later, keeps to the alphabetical order of the plants—a distinguishing feature also of the Vienna codex which, however, is shortened and limited to *one* book. In spite of this, the Vienna codex was certainly the model for a part of the pictures in the New York manuscript, clear proof that it was known and regarded highly in tenth-century Constantinople. One can appreciate all the more in what high esteem the Anicia codex was held at that time if one considers the fact that other plant pictures in the New York manuscript derive from far inferior models and that no models at all were to be found for certain descriptions of plants so that the artist had to leave blank the spaces provided for those illustrations.

Another luxurious compendium of the same time, obviously produced in

<hr>

[32] Photius, *Opera Omnia* ("Patrologiae cursus completus," J. P. Migne [ed.], 103/104 [Paris, 1860]).

[33] Σ. Β. Κουγεᾶ, Ὁ Καισαρείας Ἀρέθας καὶ τὸ ἔργον αὐτοῦ (Athens, 1913), pp. 27 ff.

[34] A. Rambaud, *L'empire grec au dixième siècle, Constantin Porphyrogénète* (Paris, 1870), pp. 51 ff.; K. Krumbacher, *Geschichte der byzantinischen Literatur* (2d ed.; Munich, 1897), pp. 252 ff.

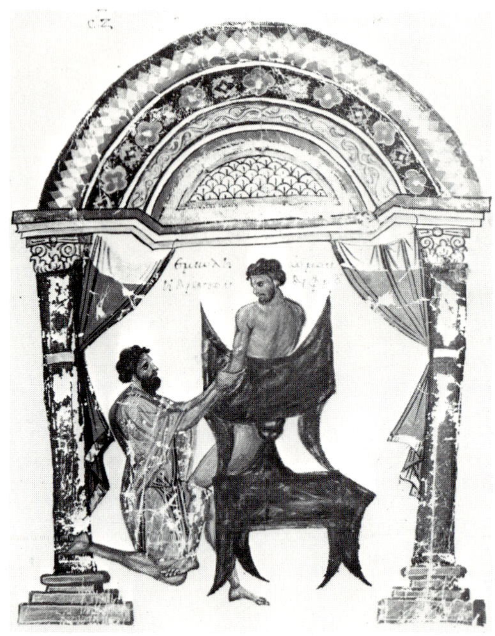

Fig. 116 *Florence, Laurenziana. Cod. Plut. LXXIV, 7, fol. 190ʳ. Medical Scene*

the same imperial scriptorium and now in the Laurentian Library in Florence (cod. Plut. LXXIV, 7), contains fifty medical treatises on the subject of Hippocratic methods of treatment, of which only two are illustrated. One of these has illustrations for the treatise by Apollonius of Citium on the treatment of dislocated bones, as, for example, the picture of a physician holding the dislocated arm of his patient over the back of a chair (Fig. 116).[35] The type of chair in the illustration, with a concave back raised on narrow supports, is to be found in Pompeian wall paintings, good proof that the model of this miniature belongs to the imperial Roman period or even earlier, probably to the first century B.C. when the archetype was written in the only book form used at that time, a papyrus roll. In this archetype, the healing scenes were certainly within the columns of text and not framed and the arch of Fig. 116, which is so similar to those of the canon tables of Gospel manuscripts that it must be derived from them, was added after the papyrus roll model was transformed into the codex.[36] The repertoire of patterns used in these arches, for example the wavy band done in perspective and painted the colors of the rainbow,[37] includes patterns which do not appear on dated mosaics before the fifth or sixth century, so that

we assume that the arches were not added before then.

As in the case of Dioscurides, we are able to trace a similar sequence of copies in the Hippocratic corpus. In both cases a manuscript of the early imperial period was copied in the fifth or sixth century; and this copy, in turn, was the model for the illustrations of the tenth century. In this way, we have established the different stages in which the copying of good scholarly texts with their illustrations was carried out and at the same time defined the place of these respective copies in the renaissance movements of these epochs. During the time of Justinian, if our judgment of this period is correct, outstanding models were available for scientific illustrations, but apparently not to the same degree for those of literary texts. Although no illustrated literary texts of the period

---

[35] H. Schöne, *Apollonius von Kitium* (Leipzig, 1896), pl. VIII.

[36] Weitzmann, *Roll and Codex*, pp. 73 ff., 108 ff., fig. 94 and the sketch, fig. F, in which we have attempted to reconstruct an idea of the original appearance of illustration in a papyrus roll. [Idem, *Geistige Grundlagen*, pp. 26 ff., reprinted herewith, pp. 197 ff.]

[37] Schöne, *Apollonius*, pl. XI.

of Justinian or of the tenth century have been preserved, we may suggest that in the Macedonian period illustrated literary texts were used as models and also that the available models go back directly to the Roman imperial period, presumably because there were none available from the period of Justinian.

For example, the availability of a very early model can be inferred from a richly illustrated, tenth-century copy of the *Theriaca* and the *Alexipharmaca* of Nicander now in the Bibliothèque Nationale in Paris (cod. suppl. gr. 247),[38] which probably was made in Constantinople although this cannot be proven. In the tenth century the style of Constantinople was so dominant and local variations had become so slight that the differences between the capital city and the provinces are no longer as important as they were in the Early Byzantine period. This manuscript contains not only purely scientific illustrations of venomous snakes and plants which heal poisonous bites, but also human figures and other elements which cannot be shown to have existed in ancient herbals[39] and which, on the basis of internal

evidence, can be shown to be later additions. Thus, for example, the illustration of the plant labeled ἀλκίβιον and the snake beneath it (Fig. 117) has obviously been shifted to one side to make room for a shepherd seated under a tree, who is in a style quite different from that of the scientific plant picture. The text[40] speaks about a youth named Alkibios, after whom the plant is named, who was bitten in the thigh by a viper while he was sleeping on the threshing floor; whereupon he leapt up, tore the roots of the healing plant out of the ground, bit it into pieces, sucked out the sap, and put the remains on his wound. Clearly, the picture does not agree with this story in a number of respects. The youth has not been sleeping on the threshing floor, has not been bitten in the thigh, and his comfortable, seated position is not the pose for expressing the action of ripping up roots needed in a great hurry. Without preconceived notions, one would describe the scene as a shepherd sitting peacefully under a tree, not unlike the shepherd on the Leningrad plate (Fig. 107). The figures clearly derive from similar models, which we conjecture to have been an illustrated bucolic poem along the lines of Theocritus' verses. The free brush

---

[38] H. Omont, *Miniatures des plus anciens manuscrits grecs de la Bibliothèque Nationale* (2d ed.; Paris, 1929), pp. 34 ff. and pls. LXV–LXXII; E. Bethe, *Buch und Bild im Altertum* (Leipzig, 1945), pp. 24, 70, and figs. 2 and 42; Weitzmann, *Roll and Codex*, pp. 144 ff., 195 ff., and figs. 131 and 162. [Idem, *Ancient Book Illumination*, p. 14 and *passim*; idem, "Mythological Representations," pp. 49 ff.; idem, *Geistige Grundlagen*, pp. 15 ff., reprinted herewith, pp. 184 ff.]

[39] They are lacking not only in the early Dioscurides herbals but also, and more significantly, in the paraphrase of Nicander's

Theriaca and *Alexipharmaca*, written by a certain Eutecnius and preserved in the Vienna Anicia Codex (folios 393ʳ–437ᵛ) and in the Morgan Manuscript (folios 338ʳ–360ᵛ and 375ʳ–384ᵛ). See also Weitzmann, "The Greek Sources of Islamic Scientific Illustrations," *Archaeologica Orientalia in Memoriam Ernst Herzfeld* (New York, 1952), pp. 258 ff. [reprinted herewith, pp. 35 ff.].

[40] Nicander, *Theriaca*, in *Nicandrea, Theriaca et Alexipharmaca*, O. Schneider (ed.) (Leipzig, 1856), pp. 541 ff.

Fig. 117 *Paris, Bibliothèque Nationale. Cod. suppl. gr. 247, fol. 16ᵛ. Alkibion*

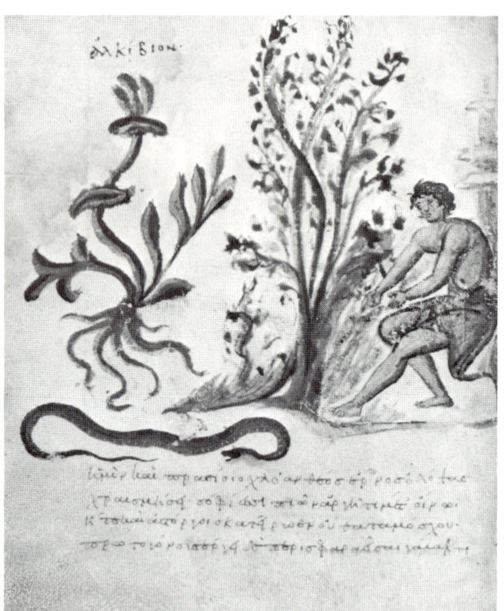

Fig. 118 *Paris, Bibliothèque Nationale. Cod. suppl. gr. 247, fol. 47ʳ. Giants*

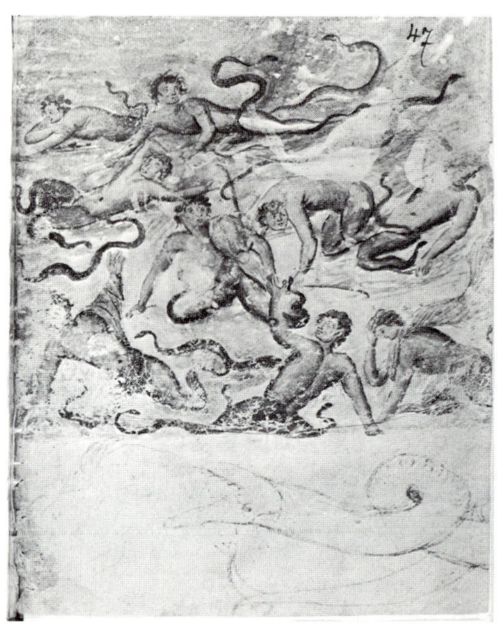

technique of the Nicander miniature presupposes a model which was considerably older than the silver plate of the sixth century, which is more abstract than the tenth-century miniature with regard to the absence of space in general and the stylization of the trees in particular. The disclosure that an ancient illustrated manuscript of a bucolic poet was available[41] not only clarifies the way in which the tenth century transmitted the classical tradition but also focuses on a subject of book illumination that archeologists have not considered sufficiently.[42]

At the beginning of the *Theriaca* Nicander mentions that malignant spiders, creeping worms, snakes, and other harmful beasts are supposed to

have issued from the blood of Titans, if, as the author skeptically adds, one can place any faith in Hesiod.[43] At the end of the Paris codex is a miniature (Fig. 118) which obviously refers to this passage in the text, although the details of the picture cannot be explained fully by the text of Nicander. The giants are not spawning spiders and snakes from their blood but are engaged in another activity. While some raise their arms with extremely lively gestures as if to defend themselves against invisible attackers, others writhe and look as if they had been struck down. Doubtless this was a representation of the gigantomachia which, in the archetype, must have included the victorious gods. That this type of abbreviated gigantomachia existed as early as ancient times is witnessed by the newly excavated mosaic in Piazza

[41] On this subject see also Weitzmann, *Greek Mythology*, pp. 183 ff.

[42] [Weitzmann, *Ancient Book Illumination*, p. 14 and pl. VIII, 16.]

[43] Nicander, *Ther.*, pp. 8 ff.

Fig. 119 *Piazza Armerina. Mosaic. Giants*

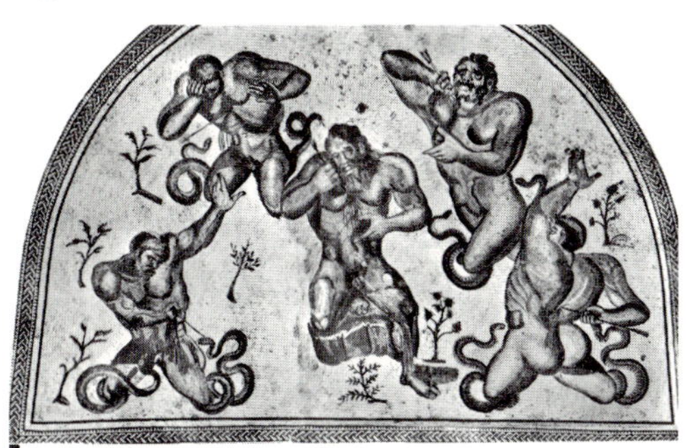

Armerina, Sicily (Fig. 119),[44] which shows giants writhing in somewhat similar poses.

With which text was the giants miniature of the Nicander originally associated? Since Nicander quotes it as a source, would it have been an illustrated Hesiod? A priori, this is not out of the question, although we believe there was another source. The legs of the giants terminate as snakes; this is an important detail which is not mentioned in Hesiod[45] but which is recorded in the mythological handbook of the Hadrianic period which goes under the name of Apollodorus.[46] Therefore, we would like to suggest that an illustrated Apollodorus was the source for the illustrator of Nicander's text, a conjecture which is supported by two considerations: first, mythological scenes in various Middle Byzantine manuscripts can be best explained by the

text of Apollodorus,[47] and second, the *Bibliotheke* of Apollodorus was demonstrably the best known and the most used handbook of classical mythology in the Middle and Late Byzantine periods.[48] In the Paris miniature the liveliness of the gestures, the assurance in the modeling of the nudes, and, in particular, the spatial depth indicate a good source for the miniature, which to all appearances was earlier than the flatter, more patterned Piazza Armerina mosaic which dates to the third/fourth century. Bucolic poetry and the mythological handbook were not the only sources for the Nicander illuminator, nor is the way in which he excerpted single miniatures from ancient manuscripts an isolated case; on the contrary, it can be shown that the migration of pictures from one text to the other was quite common practice in the Middle Ages.[49]

The already cited richly illustrated *Cynegetica* manuscript by Pseudo-Oppian in the Marcian Library in Venice (cod. gr. 479) is another example of this kind.[50] This codex, certainly a product of Constantinople, is to be dated as early as the eleventh century and certainly goes back to a model of the tenth

[44] G. V. Gentili, "Piazza Armerina," *Notizie Scavi*, 4 (75) (1951), 291 ff. and fig. 10; idem, "I mosaici della Villa Romana del casale di Piazza Armerina," *Bolletino d'Arte*, 37 (1952), 33 ff. and pl. 1a.

[45] *Theogony*, pp. 183 ff.

[46] Apollodorus, *Bibliotheca*, 1.6.1, J. G. Frazer (ed.) (London, 1921), 1:42.

[47] Weitzmann, *Greek Mythology*, pp. 78 ff., 143 ff., 195 ff. and *passim* [idem, *Ancient Book Illuminations*, pp. 96 ff.; idem, *Geistige Grundlagen*, pp. 17 ff.; reprinted herewith, pp. 185 ff.].

[48] Weitzmann, *Greek Mythology*, p. 83.

[49] Weitzmann, *Roll and Codex*, pp. 134 ff., 143 ff.

[50] See n. 11. [Also, Weitzmann, *Ancient Book Illumination*, pp. 26 ff., 53 ff., and *passim*; idem, *Geistige Grundlagen*, pp. 19 ff.; reprinted herewith, pp. 188 ff.]

century,[51] in which, we would like to
assume, a series of mythological scenes
not based on the text of Pseudo-Oppian
had been inserted. Only the purely
didactic pictures, for example the horse
grieving over his fallen rider (Fig. 120),
originally accompanied this text. The
subsequent scene on the same page,
showing a charioteer on a war chariot,
refers to a passage in the text about a
horse who has violated natural law by
assuming a human voice. The Byzantine
illuminator was alert enough to catch
an allusion to the horse Xanthus in the
Iliad who warned Achilles not to go into
battle whereupon he consulted an illustrated manuscript of the Iliad, copied
this scene from the nineteenth book, and
even included the charioteer Autome-
don[52] who is not mentioned in the text
of Pseudo-Oppian. The third scene
was also created for another text. In
referring to Bucephalus, Pseudo-Oppian
says only that he was the horse of the
soldier king of Macedonia and that he
fought against armed men. In the miniature, on the other hand, we see a groom
bringing the untamed Bucephalus to
King Philip, in precise agreement with
a passage in Pseudo-Callisthenes. Thus,
in this picture we may recognize the
oldest preserved illustration of the
Alexander Romance.[53]

[51] This is evident particularly in the paleography which imitates a tenth-century minuscule so closely that various scholars believed
it was necessary to date the Venetian copy as
early as the tenth century.
[52] Weitzmann, *Greek Mythology*, pp. 98 ff.
and pl. XXX, 103.
[53] Ibid., pp. 102 ff. and pl. XXXI, 108. [A
mosaic of the fourth/fifth century, with scenes
from the Alexander Romance, has been found
near Baalbek, cf. M. Chéhab, "Mosaïques du

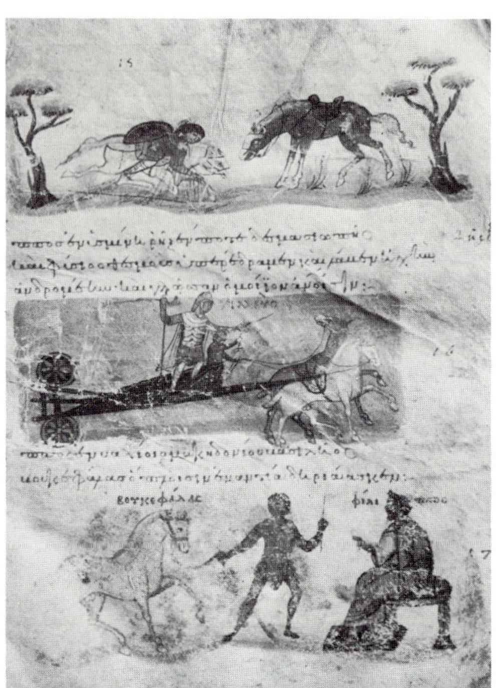

Fig. 120 *Venice, Marciana. Cod. gr. 479, fol.
8[r]. Scenes from the Cynegetica, Iliad, and
Alexander Romance*

In order to attain a more complete
picture of the spread of the classical
revival in the tenth century, we should
not limit ourselves to manuscripts, even
though they were the main vehicle for the
perpetuation and diffusion of ancient
tradition. We must also take into account
the media which are dependent upon the
miniatures, for example a series of ivory
caskets with secular representations, the
best of which date from the tenth century.[54] Even though the scenes of these
casket reliefs, separated from their texts,
were soon fragmented in the copying

Liban," *Bulletin du Musée de Beyrouth*, 14
(1958), 29 ff., 15 (1959), pls. XXI–XXV.]
[54] A. Goldschmidt and K. Weitzmann, *Die
byzantinischen Elfenbeinskulpturen des X. bis
XIII. Jahrhunderts* (Berlin, 1930) I, Kästen;
Weitzmann, *Greek Mythology*, pp. 152 ff.

Fig. 121 *London, Victoria and Albert Museum. Veroli Casket. Sacrifice of Iphigenia*

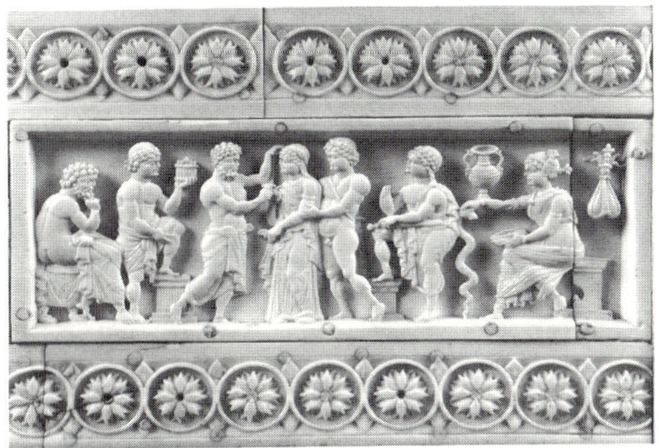

Fig. 122 *Florence, Uffizi Museum. Drawing after the Altar of Cleomenes. Sacrifice of Iphigenia*

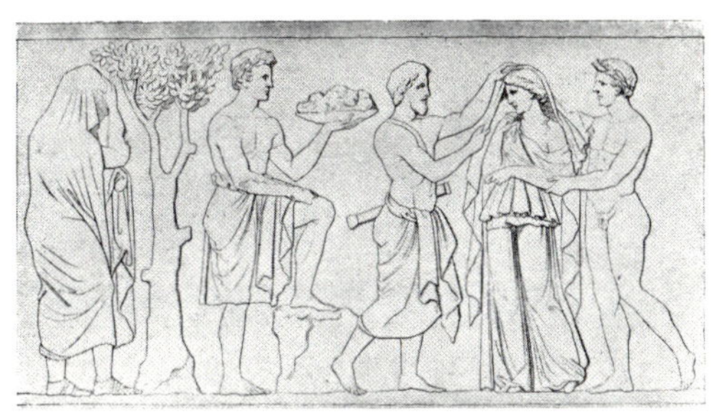

process whereby the excerpted figures lost their original meaning, several complete scenes have been preserved on one of the earliest and finest of the caskets, now in London, the Veroli Casket. One scene of the sacrifice of Iphigenia (Fig. 121) illustrates the end of the Euripidean tragedy and has been treated at great length by Löwy and other archeologists in connection with the Timanthes problem, as yet unsolved in our opinion.[55] Calchas, the seer, approaches Iphigenia in order to cut off a lock of her hair, while a youth, probably the herald Talthybius, leads her to him. Two men, each with one foot propped up, frame the central group of three, to the left Achilles with the basket of barley and to the right, presumably, Menelaus. In our

opinion, the model for this scene was an illustrated manuscript of Euripides, and this assumption is supported by the fact that there are other figures from Euripidean tragedies in the repertoire of ivory caskets, figures from the *Hippolytus* and other tragedies.[56]

The style of the ivory plaque with the sacrifice of Iphigenia is important because, as a product of the tenth century, it reflects the classical style much more directly than the eleventh-century miniatures of the Pseudo-Oppian. This becomes instantly clear when we compare the ivory with the so-called Ara of Cleomenes (Fig. 122), a Neo-Attic work of the first century. Whereas it is true that the ivory figures do look rather like putti, at the same time the fleshy treatment of the body and the clinging drapery reveal a good understanding of classical form. If only we had the tenth-century model for the Venetian Pseudo-Oppian and other tenth-century copies of ancient literary texts with their illustrations, how much clearer and more vivid our picture of the Macedonian Renaissance would be. It is impossible, of course, in the present context to give a rounded picture corresponding to the

[55] E. Pfuhl, *Malerei und Zeichnung der Griechen* (Munich, 1923), II, 697 and III, fig. 639; E. Löwy, "Der Schluss der Iphigenie in Aulis," *Jahreshefte des Österreichischen archäologischen Instituts*, 24 (1929), 4 and fig. 3; Weitzmann, "Euripides Scenes in Byzantine Art," *Hesperia*, 18 (1949), 177 ff. and pl. 27, 7; idem, *Greek Mythology*, pp. 169 ff. and pl. LIV, 214. [Idem, *Geistige Grundlagen*, pp. 21 ff., reprinted herewith, pp. 191 ff.; E. Simon, "Nonnos und das Elfenbein kästchen aus Veroli," *Jahrbuch des deutschen archäologischen Instituts*, 79 (1964), 279 ff.]

[56] Weitzmann, "Euripides Scenes," pp. 192 ff. and pls. 29–31: idem, *Greek Mythology*, pp. 174 ff. and pls. LV–LVI.

present state of investigations of the illustrated ancient manuscripts available in Constantinople in the tenth century; but we have mentioned here the most important and widely diffused examples: bucolic poetry, the mythological handbook, Homeric epics, Euripidean dramas, and the Alexander Romance.

PALAEOLOGAN ART

Until the fall of Constantinople and even afterward the attainments of the tenth century in absorbing the classical tradition were never entirely lost, although there were considerable fluctuations during different centuries. Particularly in the thirteenth and early fourteenth centuries, the ancient tradition was turned to with new zeal; and the results continued to be fruitful in the later fourteenth and fifteenth centuries, to such a degree that one may rightly speak of a Palaeologan Renaissance.

The relation between Palaelogan copies of ancient illustrated texts and the models available at that time can be set forth especially clearly with regard to the Dioscurides herbal. The copies of the eleventh and twelfth centuries, for example, codex Athos Lavra Ω75, show a certain curtailment of the illustrations,[57] whereas a manuscript in the Vatican (Chis. grec. F. VII 159) of the Palaeologan period—perhaps as late as the early fifteenth century—has truly magnificent pictures, though no text.[58]

[57] Weitzmann, *Roll and Codex*, pp. 86 ff. and fig. 68; idem, "Greek Sources," pp. 253 ff. and pl. XXXV, 9 [reprinted herewith, pp. 30 ff. and Fig. 13].

[58] It is not out of the question that this codex was originally made for an Italian humanist, which perhaps would explain the lack of text.

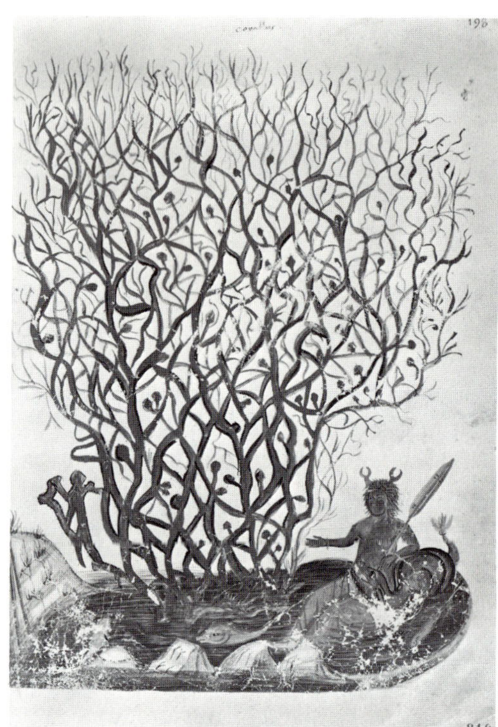

Fig. 123 *Vatican, Biblioteca. Cod. Chis. F.VII 159, fol. 210ʳ. Coral*

Penzig realized that the majority of the pictures are full-scale replications of the pictures in the Vienna Anicia codex; and a comparison of the coral picture in both manuscripts (Fig. 123–124) leaves not the slightest doubt that this is so. The fifteenth-century copyist devoted himself to the task of copying with archeological precision, although he simplified somewhat the filigree of the coral branches and enlarged, for the sake of emphasis, the personification of Thalassa with the sea monster.

For the manuscript see P. Fr. de Cavalieri, *Codices graeci Chisiani et Borgiani* (Rome, 1927), pp. 104 ff.; O. Penzig, *Contribuzioni alla storia della botanica* (Genoa, 1904), pp. 239 ff. and pls. I–V; A. Muñoz, *I codici Greci miniati delle minori Biblioteche di Roma* (Florence, 1906), pp. 45 ff. and pls. 11–14.

Fig. 124 *Vienna, Nationalbibliothek. Cod. med. gr. 1, fol. 391ᵛ. Coral*

Fig. 125 *Vatican, Biblioteca. Cod. Chis. F. VII 159, fol. 224ʳ. Processing Oil and Pitch*
Fig. 126 *New York, Morgan Library. Cod. 652, fol. 225ᵛ. Processing Oil*
Fig. 127 *New York, Morgan Library. Cod. 652, fol. 240ʳ. Extraction of Pitch*

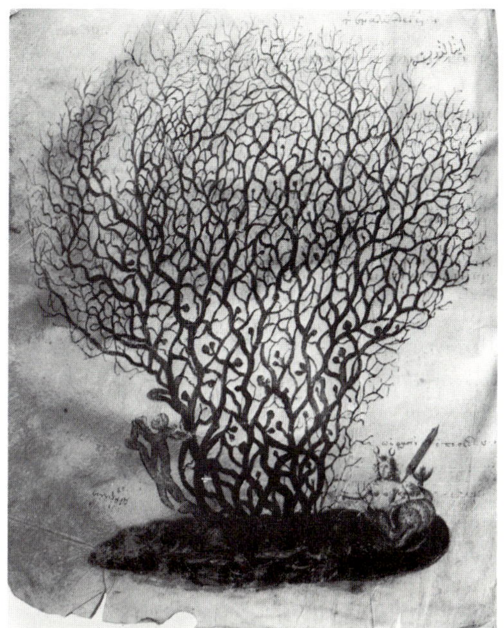

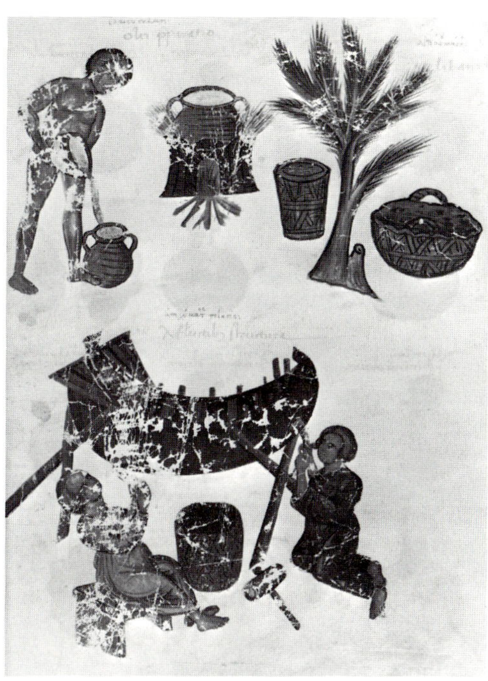

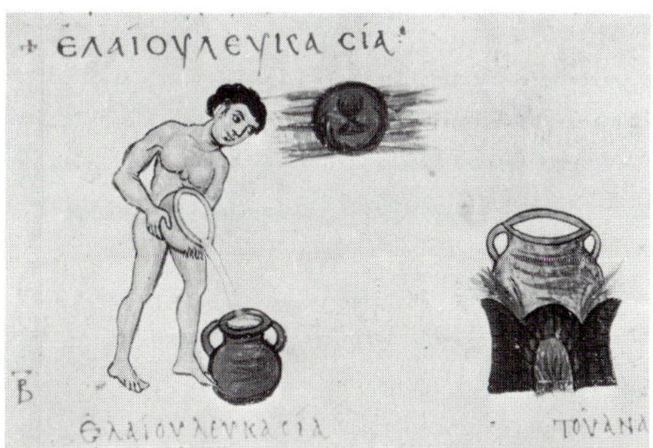

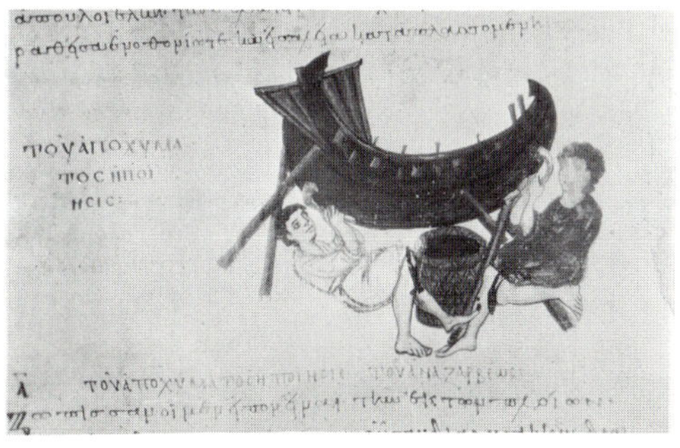

The Vatican manuscript has a second group of illustrations which cannot be derived from the Anicia codex and for which Penzig was not able to name the source. The second source is obviously the Morgan manuscript which in Penzig's time was virtually unknown. One glance at the representation showing how to produce white oil by means of continuous decanting and how to scrape a certain kind of pitch, zopissa, from boats (Fig. 125) dispels any doubt about the direct dependence of the Chigi codex on the Morgan manuscript (Figs. 126–127). The Vatican miniature shows a more marked turning away from the classical original only in details, for example, for convenience one workman is sitting on a bench and both workmen have exchanged the short tunic for longer garments.

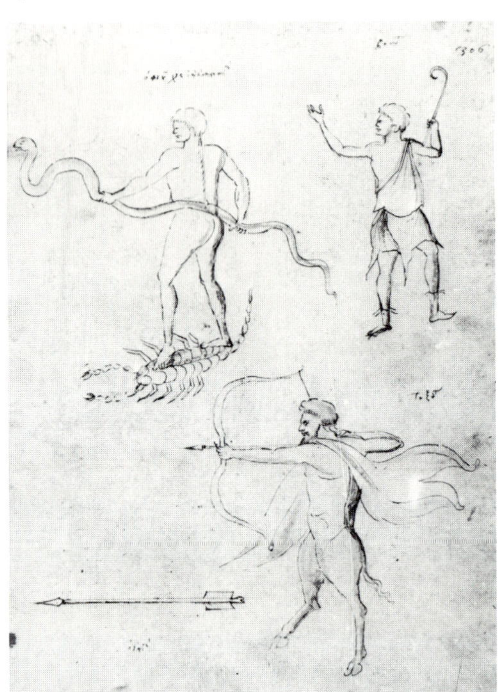

Fig. 128 *Vatican, Biblioteca. Cod. gr. 1087, fol. 306^r. Constellations*

Thus, it becomes crystal clear that the Anicia codex of the sixth century as well as the Morgan codex of the tenth century were both available to the illustrator of the Chigi manuscript at the same place, namely at Constantinople, and that just as they are today, both were regarded as the outstanding heirlooms of herbal illustration. In this way, we gain a profound insight into the method of copying during the Middle Ages. Whenever possible the *best*, not necessarily the most recent copies, were used as models; and since the best copies were the ones produced in times of conscious return to the classical traditon, all the classical-renaissance manuscripts of the Early, Middle and Late Byzantine periods share a common impulse and are related to each other.

One may assume that it was quite common for artists in Palaeologan times to use good Early or Middle Byzantine models, and that only rarely, when no older Byzantine manuscripts were available, did they turn directly to the classical sources. The start of the chain and the intervening links are not always preserved, however, and thus certain Palaeologan manuscripts attain a special significance as the last links in an otherwise lost sequence. For example, we have only a single Greek manuscript with constellations of the stars, and that one lacks the text, which must have been one of the many commentaries to the *Phaenomena* of Aratus. The jaunty pen drawings of the Vatican manuscript (cod. gr. 1087, Fig. 128)[59] from the fifteenth

century apparently go back to a ninth or tenth century model which, in turn, derives from a late classical work. Only if we assume that such manuscripts were copied at long intervals, that is during times of special interest in ancient texts and pictures, are we able to explain the fact that, as late as the fifteenth century, pictures such as the ones of the constellations Serpentarius, Boötes, and Sagittarius preserve fairly intact the feeling for ancient form.

It would be wrong, however, to judge the Byzantines merely as clever copyists and to deny them any inventive faculty. Where no classical pictorial tradition existed, during both the Middle and Late Byzantine times, they were quite

---

[59] Fr. Boll and W. Gundel, "Die Sternbilder der Griechen und Römer," in W. H. Roscher (ed.), *Ausführliches Lexikon der griechischen und römischen Mythologie*, 6 suppl., cols. 869 ff.

and figs. 1–13, 15–19; Weitzmann, *Roll and Codex*, pp. 96 and 144 and figs. 80 and 132.

capable of creating pictures in the classical style. There is a group of six *carmina figurata* which comes under the heading of bucolic poetry, a branch of literature which was obviously highly esteemed by the Byzantines; of the six the best known is the *Syrinx* of Theocritus. In the tenth century these figured poems (i.e., poems with lines so arranged as to form the silhouette of an object) were incorporated into the so-called Palatine Anthology,[60] and at the end of the thirteenth century interest in them was aroused anew when a certain Manuel Holobolos wrote a commentary on them. For the thirteenth-century edition, the figured poems were enriched with human figures[61] for which, to judge from the Palatine Anthology, no ancient pictorial tradition was known; and one may justifiably doubt if one had ever existed. A Florentine manuscript of the fourteenth century (Laurenziana Cod. Plut. XXXII, 52 Fig. 129)[62] contains a pen-and-ink wash drawing of an Eros on whose wings the poem by Simias, *Pteryges*, is written—the writing filling up the area of the wings. Apparently this figure does not belong to the Holobolos edition, but the artist was certainly stimulated by it, and thus the drawing may be considered as an invention of the thirteenth or fourteenth century. Although a certain feeling for classical form and content is present, the

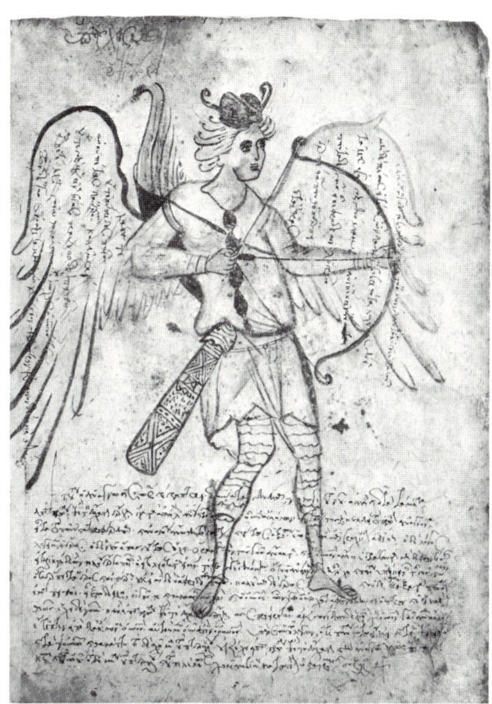

Fig. 129 *Florence, Laurenziana. Cod. Plut. XXXII, 52, fol. 119ᵛ. Carmen Figuratum*

peculiarities of a late period should not be overlooked: the overly slender proportions, the cut of the unclassical, long-sleeved tunic buttoned down the front, the odd headcovering, and other details.

One has only to think of contemporary Gothic drawings to realize the distance that separates the style of the Latin West —constantly changing since the Romanesque period—from the style of Constantinople and the Byzantine East— where contemporary art at no time developed an antagonism toward the antique. Constantinople was qualified as no other Mediterranean metropolis to carry on the classical heritage; and, as we have attempted to show in this short sketch, this task was accomplished successfully. At the same time Constantinople rendered an invaluable service to

[60] *Anthologia graeca*, W. Paton (ed.) (London, 1926); *Anthologia Palatina; codex palatinus et codex parisianus phototypice editi*, K. Preisendanz (ed.) (Leiden, 1911).
[61] C. Wendel, "Die Technopägnien-Ausgabe des Rhetors Holobolos," *Byzantinische Zeitschrift*, 16 (1907), 460 ff.; 19 (1910), 331 ff.; Omont, *Manuscrits grecs*, p. 60 and pl. CXXX.
[62] Wendel, "Technopägnien-Ausgabe," 16, 463, n. 1.

the whole of Western culture; for at the times when the Latin West came to grips with classical art, the catalyst not infrequently was Constantinople.

The Classical in Byzantine Art as a Mode of Individual Expression

HAT Byzantine art is deeply indebted to the classical tradition in more than one way, using its formal vocabulary and often being inspired by its content, is common knowledge and can no longer be disputed. What is still controversial is the extent of the classical impact, the means of the transmission of the classical forms, and the reason—or rather the variety of reasons—for continued dependence on the classical tradition. So far scholarship has concentrated mainly on two aspects. The first is the conscious revival at certain periods, when the copying of works of art was part of a broader humanistic movement which tried to reawaken understanding of classical poetry, philosophy, and learning in general. Such a period is the tenth century, and since two of the emperors of the Macedonian Dynasty Leo VI the Wise and Constantine VII Porphyrogenitus, were actively involved as patrons, there is some justification for calling this movement the "Macedonian Renaissance." To the tenth century belong our best texts of Homer, Plato, and Aristotle, as well as a whole series of treatises in a number of scientific fields such as medicine and mathematics.[1]

In this spirit of reawakening the past, the illustrator of a tenth-century Gospel book in the Athos monastery Stauronikita (cod. 43) searched for the best classical model he could find from which to copy his evangelist portraits. Mark (Fig. 203), like a statue transformed into a painting, sits in a niche, reminiscent of the proscenium wall of a Roman theater.[2] Like a philosopher, Mark holds his hand raised as if addressing a group of disciples; and the background is filled with architecture and landscape elements, a pergola, rocks, and trees, painted in a delicate way to which parallels should be sought in classical painting of the second to third century A.D.

Equally close to a classical model are the other evangelists of this Gospel book, including Matthew (Fig. 180), who holds his left arm in the sling of his mantle and raises the right in a gesture of pensiveness to his mouth, revealing that once more the archetype was a philosopher.[3] So exactly are the pose and every detail of the drapery copied that the archetype can still be identified. It is Epicurus, as preserved in a statue in the Palazzo Margherita in Rome (Fig. 181), though the present head is not the original one.[4] The portrait features of Epicurus are well known: he wore a long, parted

---

Reprinted with permission from: *Byzantine Art an European Art, Ninth Exhibition held under the auspices of the Council of Europe. Lectures* (Athens: Office of the Minister to the Prime Minister of the Greek Government, Department of Antiquities and Archaeological Restoration, 1966), pp. 149-77.

[1] For the most recent treatment of the problem of the Macedonian Renaissance and its sources consult Weitzmann, *Geistige Grundlagen und Wesen der makedonischen Renaissance* ("Arbeitsgemeinschaft für Forschung des Landes Nordrhein-Westfalen," 107 [Cologne and Opladen, 1963]); here also the older bibliography. [Translated and reprinted herewith, pp. 176 ff.]

[2] Weitzmann, *Die byzantinische Buchmalerei des 9. und 10. Jahrhunderts* (Berlin, 1935), p. 23 and pl. XXX, 170.

[3] Ibid., pl. XXX, 169.

[4] Weitzmann, "Probleme der mittelbyzantinischen Renaissance," *Archäologischer Anzeiger* (1933), 346 and figs. 5 and 7; idem, *Geistige Grundlagen*, p. 30 and figs. 23–24. [Translated and reprinted herewith, pp. 199–200]

beard[5] not unlike that of the evangelist whose representation, even in such a detail, is a very exact and reliable copy. Once more the philosopher is placed before a very painterly background: a temple in perspective view whose columns cast shadows on the cella wall, and above the temenos wall one looks, as in the Mark picture, into an illusionistic landscape of great purity. It seems inconceivable that there could have been many, if any, intermediary copies, and we believe that the tenth-century miniaturist must have had available one of the very first illustrated Gospel books ever made; presumably it may have been as early as the second century and not later than the third. Some alterations, however, were made in the copies, as for example in the inclusion of the lectern and table which allude to the writing of the Gospel by the evangelists, but are not needed by contemplative philosophers; nevertheless, the Gospel book of Stauronikita is one of the most characteristic products of the Macedonian Renaissance.

The second aspect much discussed by Byzantine scholars is that of an uninterrupted classical undercurrent in Byzantine art.[6] The idea is that the thread of the classical tradition was never cut entirely and that the classical style is, to a greater or lesser degree, prevalent in all phases. Here a sharper definition of what is meant by "classical tradition" is necessary. If by "classical tradition" one means the fully developed Late-Hellenistic and

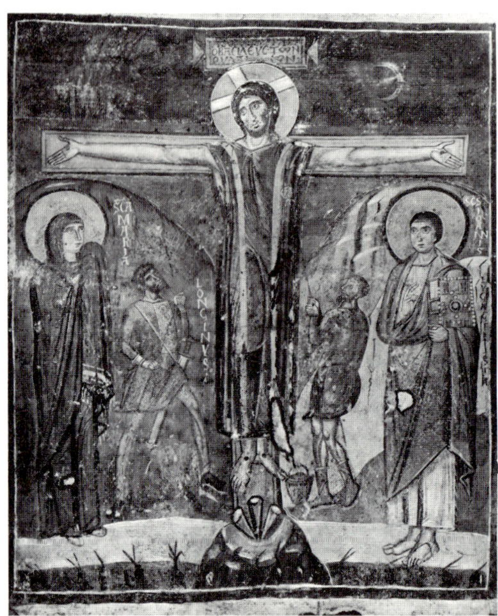

Fig. 130 *Rome, Sta. Maria Antiqua. Fresco. Crucifixion*

Roman style with all its illusionistic features of a rich landscape setting, just like that seen in the background of the Stauronikita evangelists, then the idea of an uninterrupted undercurrent, in our opinion, can not be sustained.

What we know for instance of the eighth century does not justify the assumption that an illusionistic mode of expression had been continued from the late classical period. A fresco of the Crucifixion in S. Maria Antiqua in Rome (Fig. 130),[7] executed at the time of Pope Zacharias in the middle of the eighth century under the impact of a Byzantine wave which had swept the art of Rome, and likewise a stylistically similar Crucifixion icon on Mount Sinai

---

[5] K. Schefold, *Die Bildnisse der antiken Dichter, Redner und Denker* (Basel, 1943), pp. 118 ff.
[6] E. Kitzinger, "The Hellenistic Heritage in Byzantine Art," *Dumbarton Oaks Papers*, 17 (1963), 97 ff.

[7] J. Wilpert, *Die römischen Mosaiken und Malereien der kirchlichen Bauten vom IV–XIII. Jahrhunderts* (Freiburg i B., 1916), 2:687; 4, pl. 180; E. Kitzinger, *Römische Malerei vom Beginn des 7. bis zur Mitte des 8. Jahrhunderts* (Munich, 1934), pp. 26 ff.

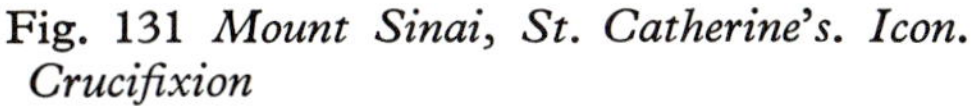

Fig. 131 *Mount Sinai, St. Catherine's. Icon. Crucifixion*

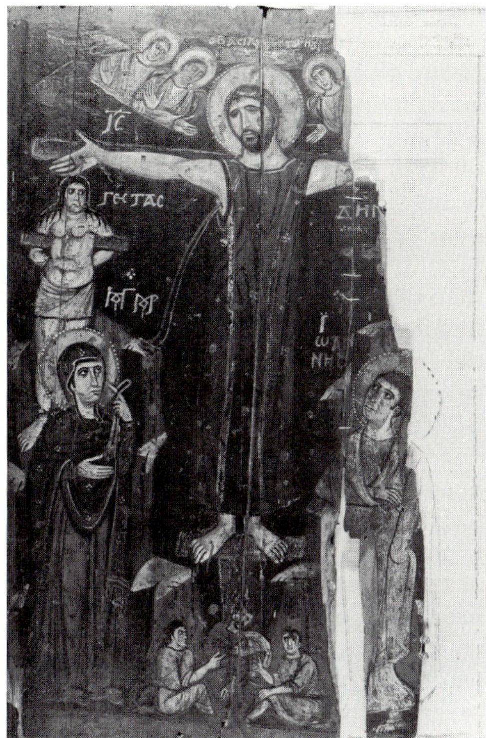

of about the same period (Fig. 131),[8] which we believe to be a work of a Palestinian workshop, do show elements of landscape, but space and atmosphere are lost and the mountains have been reduced to a linear, almost two-dimensional design.

However, if by "persistence of a classical undercurrent" scholars think first of all of the clear articulation and organic structure of the human body, then indeed we fully subscribe to this concept. From all we know, the eighth century is comparatively one of the most abstract in the history of Byzantine art, and these two Crucifixion pictures, one made in the East, the other under Eastern influence in the West, show, it is true, a great simplification of the body structure: the proportions are slightly thick-set, the poses stiff, some of the faces fleshy and round, and yet the artists were quite capable of conveying the impression that under the simplified garments the bodies have a physical reality.

This sustained sense for corporeal values will come into focus all the more in comparison with a Western miniature of about the same period, i.e., the middle of the eighth century, executed by an Irish artist and now in Saint Gall (Chapter Library cod. 51).[9] This Crucifixion also, like the Roman fresco, harks back ultimately to an East Christian prototype with a figure of Christ dressed in the so-called colobion, a sleeveless long tunic, but here the artistic conception of the human figure is basically different. The colobion is transformed into decorative ribbons like the wrappings of a mummy, and into this mass of whirling bands the limbs of the body seem to have been added afterward. In other words, this artist does not start out from the concept of an organic human body and then drape it, but follows the opposite procedure.

Our present concern is not with the problem of the renaissances nor with that of the uninterrupted classical undercurrent but with a third aspect of the classical tradition in Byzantine art. Classical elements occur often within the same work of art alongside nonclassical or even anticlassical elements. Some-

[8] G. and M. Sotiriou, *Icones du Mont Sinaï* (Athens, 1956–58), 1:39; 2, pl. 25.

[9] J. Duft and P. Meyer, *The Irish Miniatures in the Abbey Library of St. Gall* (Olten, 1954), p. 100 and pl. XIII.

times the differences can be explained simply by the use of models from different periods, but there are also instances where the two different modes seem to be chosen purposely for contrast. Such cases presuppose that the artist had, within certain limits, the freedom to choose his models. The classical in such instances need not be the artistically superior mode, and it occurs in periods which are not necessarily linked with a renaissance movement. In dealing with such cases we shall try wherever possible to find an answer to the question of what motivated the use of classical models and, if we succeed, we will have achieved a glimpse into the workshop procedures of some accomplished Byzantine artists who were greater individualists than scholarship has thus far realized. I propose to present the material not historically but methodologically according to certain categories and to confine myself to the Early and Middle Byzantine periods, implying that the same principles are also valid for Late Byzantine art.

THE COPYING OF THE CLASSICAL PICTURE COMPOSITION

I should like to start with a few examples from illustrated manuscripts where, within one codex, different modes are used for different types of frontispieces. In the well-known herbal of Dioscurides in the National Library of Vienna (cod. med. gr. 1) from the sixth century, we see the author, dressed in a white mantle with bluish shadows, pointing to the mandragora plant which the personification of EYPEΣIΣ—Invention—holds in her hand (Fig. 110).[10] The

[10] A. von Premerstein, K. Wessely, and J. Mantuani, *Dioscurides, Codex Aniciae Julianae,*

door frame is painted a purple color which seems to dissolve into the atmospheric blue, a blue that is light at the horizon and gains in intensity higher up. The illusionistic elements, quite well understood and by no means a common feature in the style of the sixth century, point to a very early model. This thesis is supported by the fact that the author with the full beard and sunburned face, in spite of the inscription Dioscurides, does not represent this famous pharmacologist of the second century A.D. who was the compiler of the botanical treatise under discussion, but Crateuas, an earlier botanist of the first century B.C. whose treatise Dioscurides had excerpted.[11] It is probable, therefore, that the illustrator of the archetype of Dioscurides already had incorporated the author portrait of an older herbal, trying to preserve the features of the model as best he could in order to give recognition to the older sources.

This same painter uses a different and nonclassical mode for the donor portrait of Juliana Anicia, seated in a frontal position in ceremonial garb, flanked by the personifications of Magnanimity (Megalopsychia) and Prudence (Phronesis) who seem as if they were posed as ladies in waiting (Fig. 132).[12] The throne

———

picturis illustratus, nunc Vindobonensis Med. gr. 1. phototypice editus (Leiden, 1906); H. Gerstinger, *Die griechische Buchmalerei* (Vienna, 1926), pl. VI (color). [*Der Wiener Dioscurides (Codex Vindobonensis Med. gr. 1)*, Introduction by H. Gerstinger (Graz, 1965).]

[11] P. Buberl, "Die antiken Grundlagen der Miniaturen des Wiener Dioscurideskodex," *Jahrbuch des deutschen archäologischen Instituts,* 51 (1936), 131; compare figs. 5 and 9.

[12] Idem, *Die byzantinischen Handschriften,* 1 ("Beschreibendes Verzeichnis der illuminier-

Fig. 132 *Vienna, Nationalbibliothek. Cod. med. gr. 1, fol. 6ᵛ. Juliana Anicia*

Fig. 133 *Copenhagen, Kongl. Samml. Cod. 6, fol. 83ᵛ. Solomon and Jesus Sirach*

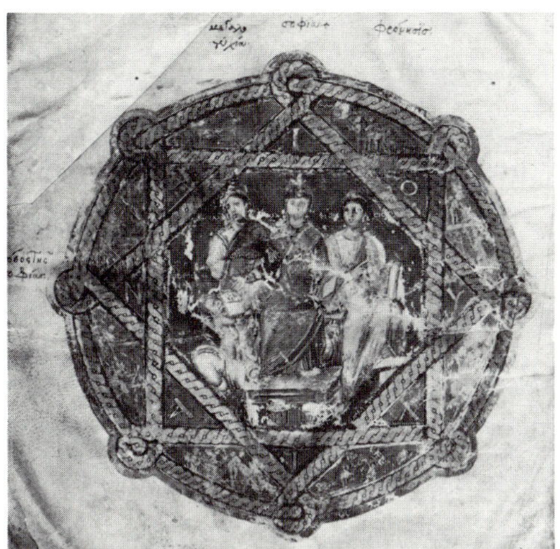

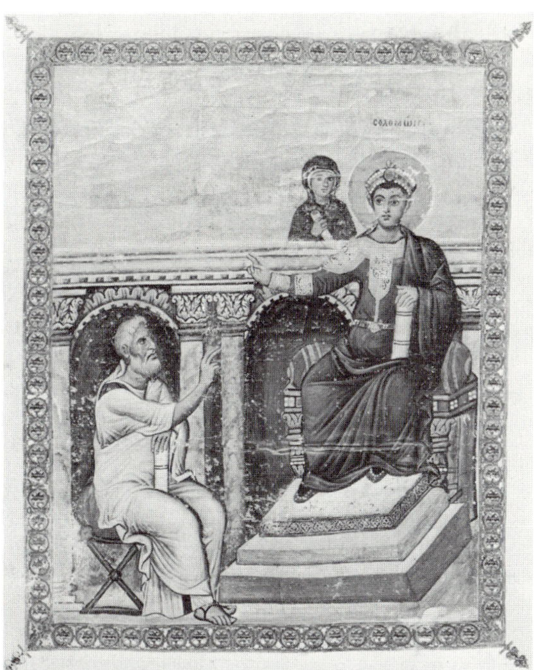

seems almost as if it were suspended against a neutral nonatmospheric blue, while at the same time the whole scene is tightly fitted into an ornamental frame: an octagonal star within a circle made of interlaced ropes. While quite certainly both miniatures were made by the same painter, we begin to sense that he was indeed capable of working in almost contradictory modes, using a spatial illusionistic setting in one case and a more abstract compositional pattern in the other. The artistic aim was obviously to contrast the past and the present, being traditional in one instance and using up-to-date conventions in the other. Surely, this is an individual solution only to a limited extent. Similar juxtapositions were repeated in principle by other artists and at different times.

An example of the tenth/eleventh century is the title miniature of a codex in Copenhagen (Kongl. Samml. cod. 6

Fig. 133),[13] which contains various poetical books from the Old Testament. What we see is actually a fusion of two author figures, each of which most likely existed at one time as a separate miniature, and the wall in the background does not quite achieve its aim of binding them together into a unified composition. To the left, Jesus Sirach is depicted resting one hand on a scroll and extending the other in a gesture of speech, very much like Crateuas in the Vienna Dioscurides. Solomon, on the other hand, is depicted in the garb of a Byzantine emperor and in a stately, frontal pose, stiffer and

ten Handschriften in Österreich," 8, Part IV [Leipzig, 1937]), 26 ff. and pl. V.

[13] M. Mackeprang, V. Madsen, and C. S. Petersen, *Greek and Latin Illuminated Manuscripts: X–XIII Centuries in Danish Collections* (Copenhagen and London, 1921), p. 1 and pl. 1 (color).

somewhat less corporeal. Once more we deal with two different modes which can be explained by the difference of iconographical realms in which these author figures are rooted: like the evangelists of the Stauronikita Gospel, Jesus Sirach harks back to an ancient man of letters—a poet or philosopher—while the figure of Solomon is an adaptation of the portrait of a contemporary Byzantine emperor around whose image a court style had developed, in which more abstract forms were required to express ceremonial dignity and unapproachability.

Yet, classical and imperial realms are not the only ones to be juxtaposed in such a way that a comparatively more naturalistic and a more abstract mode confront each other. In the sixth-century Gospel book of the Cathedral of Rossano which contains the only Early Byzantine evangelist portrait preserved today (Fig. 95), Mark is depicted sitting in a wicker chair leaning forward in order to write in a scroll on his lap while an inspiring personification in front of him dictates.[14] This group is placed in front of a wall with a square on top of it. The wall is hung with draperies and is set against an atmospheric sky. It is true that these classical elements are rather abstracted and ornamentalized, notwithstanding the fact that we are dealing with an ambitious product in the form of a luxurious purple manuscript. The classical models all being lost, we have to turn to a picture of John in a tenth-century manuscript, a Gospel book in the Vatican Library (cod. grec. 364, Fig. 182), in

order to realize that the archetype was a contemplative philosopher seated in front of a garden gate, on which draperies are hung which flow down upon the wall.[15] Thus, while the Rossano miniature would not qualify as the expression of a renaissance movement, as indeed the Vatican miniature does, nevertheless what is important in our context is the fact that it is the only miniature in the whole codex which has elements of a classical setting at all, and thus we can only conclude that the miniaturist applied them deliberately in the case of an author portrait, while abstaining from their use in the christological scenes.

How different in concept is the pair of miniatures depicting the Communion of the Apostles;[16] evenly spaced in single file, the apostles approach Christ in a rhythmic procession, silhouetted against the purple ground. The fact that this scene could not be accommodated on a single leaf suggests that it was not invented as a miniature but adapted from monumental painting, and therefore the miniature had to be cut in two halves. In many Byzantine churches this scene is located in the apse of the bema, and the miniature must be derived from such a monumental composition; consequently it can be postulated that in the sixth century at the latest this subject was a common feature in the church program. In the case of the Rossano Gospels the

---

[14] A. Muñoz, *Il codice purpureo di Rossano* (Rome, 1907), p. 5 and pl. XV.

[15] A. M. Friend, Jr., "The Portraits of the Evangelists in Greek and Latin Manuscripts, Part I," *Art Studies* (1927), 136 and pl. X, figs. 103–06; Weitzmann, *Geistige Grundlagen*, p. 31 and fig. 25. [Translated and reprinted herewith, p. 201]

[16] Muñoz, *Codice purpureo*, p. 4 and pls. VI–VII.

use of two different modes of expression once more can be explained by prototypes from different realms; the Christian author portraits had remained steeped in the tradition of classical portraiture while liturgical representations had developed in time more abstract devices for the sake of ceremonial dignity.

CLASSICAL PERSONIFICATIONS IN CHRISTIAN ART

In the cases mentioned so far, the artist had employed different modes side by side in two separate pictorial units, the classical one for author portraits, the more abstract mode for imperial and Christian iconography, and only in the Copenhagen miniature (Fig. 133) are they already united. The next step is to elaborate on the parallelism of two different modes within the same pictorial unit, which raises the problem of artistic homogeneity. One of the most frequent instrusions of the classical mode into the Christian is the insertion of classical personifications in biblical illustrations.

The largest of the David plates from Cyprus, made in the early seventh century under Heraclius and now in the Metropolitan Museum in New York (Fig. 134), represents the scene of the fight, and above, in smaller scale, the scene of the challenge.[17] David and Goliath, facing each other and exchanging threats, are separated by the personification of the Valley of Elath, a typically

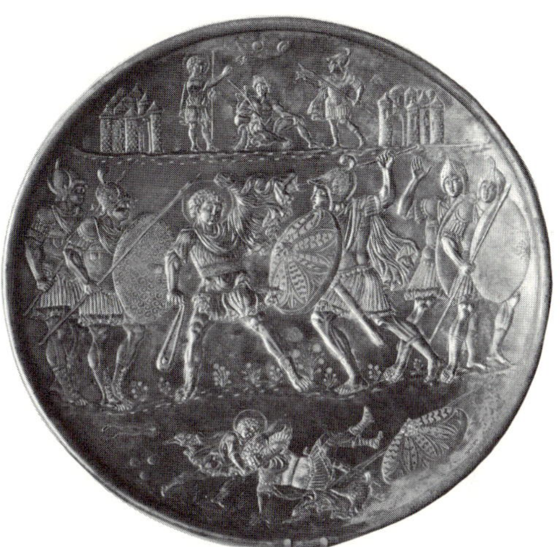

Fig. 134 *New York, Metropolitan Museum of Art. Silver Plate from Cyprus. David and Goliath* [*Gift of J. Pierpont Morgan, 1917*]

classical river god who leans on a vase and holds a reed. It will be noticed that this is the only figure in all three zones which is rendered in three-quarter pose, creating a sense of depth through foreshortening which no other figure has, including the decapitated Goliath whose contorted pose is flattened into a two-dimensional plane. Obviously the personification harks back to a different realm and most likely is an accretion of the very period when the silversmith adapted a miniature model—an illustrated Psalter manuscript of the aristocratic group, we believe—to the round format of the plate. We see support for this supposition in the fact that in the repetition of the same scene within the very same set of silver plates, also in the Metropolitan Museum,[18] this personification is, indeed, lacking.

[17] H. Buchthal, *The Miniatures of the Paris Psalter* (London, 1938), p. 21 and pl. XXI, no. 44; Weitzmann, "The Psalter Vatopedi 761," *Journal of the Walters Art Gallery*, 10 (1947), 39 and fig. 24; E. Cruikshank-Dodd, *Byzantine Silver Stamps* (Washington, 1961), p. 178, no. 58.

[18] O. M. Dalton, "Byzantine Plate and Jewellery from Cyprus," *Burlington Magazine*, 10 (1906/07), 361 and pl. I, no. 3; Cruikshank-Dodd, *Silver Stamps*, p. 190, no. 64.

While personifications as an expression of the classical spirit were available in almost every phase of Byzantine art, they were used with an increasing frequency during the Macedonian Renaissance and, at times, accumulatively within one picture. The best-known and most characteristic example in this respect is the Psalter in Paris (Bibliothèque Nationale cod. gr. 139) from about the middle of the tenth century, in whose title miniature David, as the author of the Psalter, is flanked by the two personifications of Wisdom and Prophecy (Fig. 135).[19] There are other Psalter manuscripts of the same aristocratic recension with the same David figure but without the two personifications as, e.g., the codex in the Theological Seminary of the University of Berlin.[20] Though this manuscript is later, twelfth century, its miniature cycle contains many features closer to the archetype,[21] and thus we believe that its simpler and more hieratic title miniature also reflects the original version.

It should be pointed out that the addition of classical personifications can, but does not necessarily, improve the artistic unity of a pictorial composition. In the present miniature the artist strug-

---

[19] H. Omont, *Miniatures des plus anciens manuscrits grecs de la Bibliothèque Nationale* (2d ed.; Paris, 1929), p. 7 and pl. VII; Weitzmann, "Der Pariser Psalter Ms. grec 139 und die mittelbyzantinische Renaissance," *Jahrbuch für Kunstwissenschaft* 6 (1929), 182; Buchthal, *Paris Psalter*, p. 25 and pl. VII.
[20] G. Stuhlfauth, "A Greek Psalter with Byzantine Miniatures," *Art Bulletin*, 15 (1933), 321 and fig. 9.
[21] Weitzmann, *Geistige Grundlagen*, p. 13 and figs. 4–5 [translated and reprinted herewith, p. 182 and Figs. 164–66].

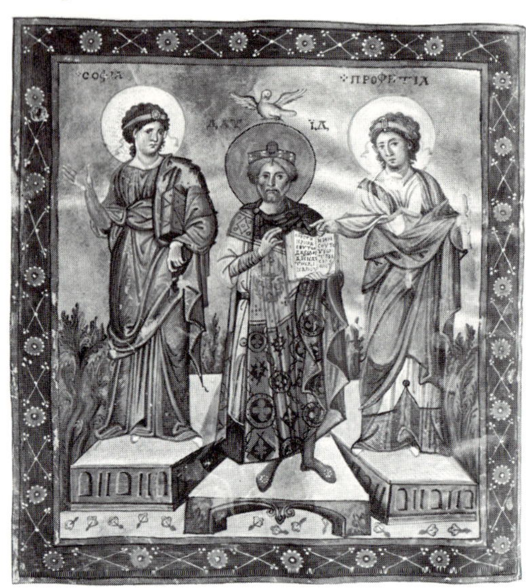

Fig. 135 *Paris, Bibliothèque Nationale. Cod. gr. 139, fol. 7ᵛ. David between Sophia and Prophetia*

gles, not very successfully, with the problem of amalgamation, and the result is not entirely satisfactory. As his model for the *Prophetia* he chose the gigantic lower part of a female statuary type which, if continued at the same scale, would touch or even penetrate the upper border. The small bust and crippled right arm do not quite fit. In the case of the *Sophia* the artist likewise tampered with his classical model and squeezed a codex under her arm which led to an awkward gesture of her left hand. It is essential to realize that the desire to add personifications, however, did not necessarily oblige the artist to use a model in the classical style. The miniature of the Copenhagen Old Testament (Fig. 133) includes, next to Solomon's head, a woman appearing from behind the wall who likewise may be identified as a personification of Wisdom, although she is not inscribed as such. Like the *Prophetia* in the Psalter miniature, she holds a scroll in her hand as an allusion to her role as an inspirer of a man of letters, but otherwise she rather resembles a Virgin type with the typical *maphorion* over her head. Some critics may consider this artistic solution more satisfactory and more in harmony with the author portrait. Be this as it may, our main point in this context is the realization that the artist had a choice in the selection of the mode for the depiction of a personification.

CLASSICAL SETTING IN CHRISTIAN ART

The addition of personifications is the result of a literary as much as an artistic endeavor. When we turn to the discussion of how either an architectural or a landscape background was added to the figure composition, however, we move primarily in the realm of formal problems.

I should like to start once more with an author portrait from the Vienna Dioscurides, this time the portrait really being that of Dioscurides himself (Fig. 136).[22] He is depicted reading a codex, while an artist sitting in front of an easel is painting a mandrake on a parchment sheet, and the personification of Epinoia, having the same meaning and function as Heuresis in the preceding miniature (Fig. 110), is holding up the plant so that the illustrator can paint it from nature. What interests us here is the setting: a colonnade with Corinthian columns, interrupted by a niche with a conch—architectural elements which are related to a Roman *scenae frons* with the *porta regia* in the center. With the ceiling

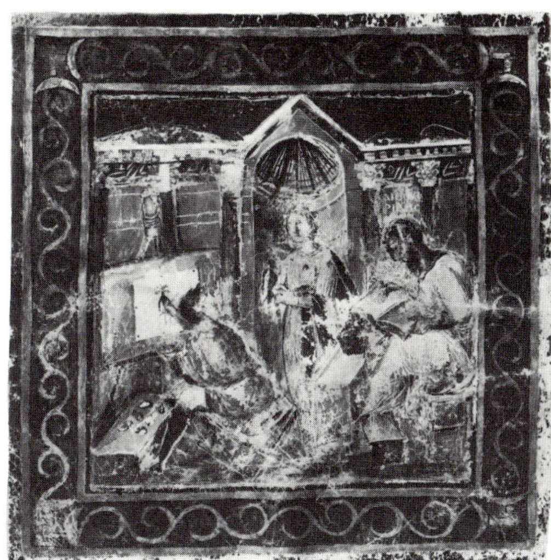

Fig. 136 *Vienna, Nationalbibliothek. Cod. med. gr. 1, fol. 5ᵛ. Dioscurides and Epinoia*

coffers designed in perspective, it is a well-constructed piece of architecture which, there seems hardly any reason to doubt, was included in the illustration of the archetype, from perhaps as early as the second century A.D.

It comes almost as a surprise to see in another title miniature of the same manuscript, executed by the same artist, no background features at all, but a plain gold ground, against which seven portrait figures of physicians are effectively placed like silhouettes that seem to be suspended (Fig. 137).[23] Each figure sits on a little hillock which is depicted like a floating island. The center is occupied by Claudius Galenus, the court physician of Marcus Aurelius, testifying to the fact that the archetype of this group of physicians cannot be older than the second century A.D.; he is flanked by

---

[22] Buberl, *Byzantinischen Handschriften*, I, 24 and pl. IV.

[23] Ibid., p. 16 and pl. II; Weitzmann, *Ancient Book Illumination* (Cambridge, Mass., 1959), p. 122 and pl. LXII, no. 131.

Fig. 137 *Vienna, Nationalbibliothek. Cod. gr. 1, fol. 3ᵛ. Seven Physicians*

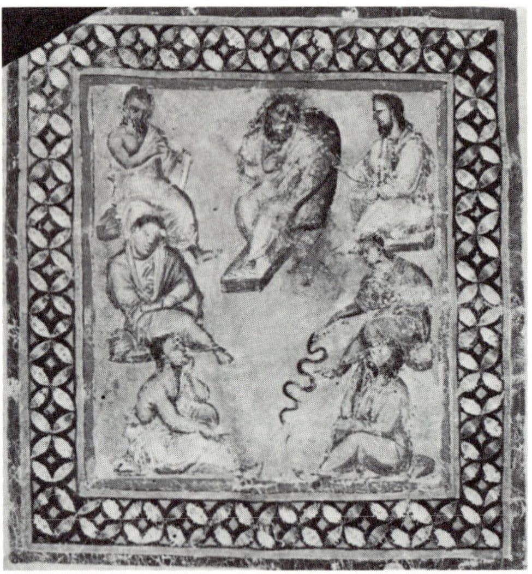

Crateuas and Dioscurides, who show the same portrait features as the two pharmacists in the two title miniatures already discussed (Figs. 110 and 136). Each of these seven physicians is rendered in the same painterly style and if, as seems quite likely, each of them originally formed a separate title miniature, just like those of Crateuas and Dioscurides, then they may originally have had the same rich architectural setting. We believe that it was the idea of the painter of the Vienna codex in the sixth century to assemble seven portrait figures on a single sheet, and lack of space forced him to abandon all architectural or landscape elements and to use the then contemporary convention of the plain gold ground, which was a dominant feature in sixth-century mosaic and miniature painting.

Had a model been available in the classical tradition that depicted a gathering of seven famous men, it would most likely have looked like a gathering of the Seven Wise Men as they are depicted in the first-century mosaic from Torre Annunciata in the Naples Museum.[24] The spatial arrangement of the figures, the sparse but characteristic landscape and architectural elements, would harmonize quite well with the backgrounds found in the Crateuas and Dioscurides miniatures. What the juxtaposition of miniatures with single authors and groups of authors within the same manuscript once more proves is the artistic freedom of the painter, who could at will use contradictory principles in the arrangement and setting of human figures.

A similar dichotomy exists, though as we shall see for different reasons, in another sixth-century miniature cycle, that of the Genesis fragment in Vienna (National Library, cod. theol. gr. 31). In the scene of the Blessing of Ephraim and Manasseh by Jacob in the presence of Joseph and his Egyptian wife Asenath (Fig. 138),[25] the background, a rocky landscape, is depicted in a very painterly style, as a matter of fact in such a free brushstroke technique that one is tempted to call it impressionistic. Only in the Roman frescoes of Pompeii and the very earliest Christian catacombs will one find parallels in which the change of color from green to brown to blue under the influence of atmospheric conditions is so clearly understood, and this feature more than anything else led Wickhoff to

[24] Schefold, *Dichter, Redner und Denker,* pp. 154 ff.
[25] H. Gerstinger, *Die Wiener Genesis* (Vienna, 1931), p. 109 and pl. 45; Buberl, *Byzantinischen Handschriften,* I, 125 and pl. XLIII, no. 45; Weitzmann, *Illustrations in Roll and Codex: A Study in the Origin and Method of Text Illustration* (2d ed. Princeton, 1970), p. 101 and fig. 86.

Fig. 138 *Vienna, Nationalbibliothek. Cod. theol. gr. 31, pict. 45. Jacob's Blessing*

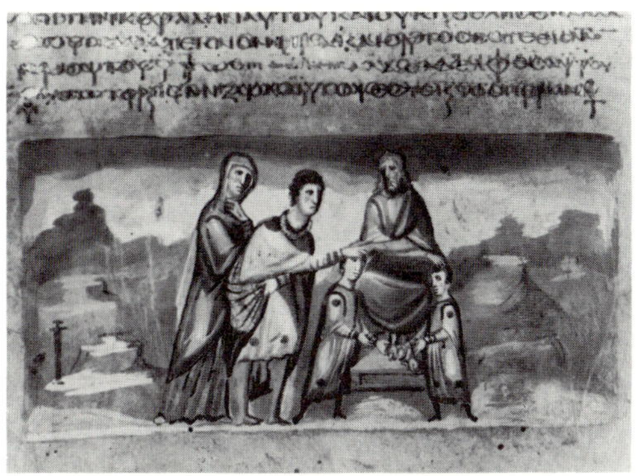

believe that the Vienna Genesis belonged to the third century. This picture, however, has to be viewed not only from the formal but also from the iconographical point of view. The blessing of Jacob's grandchildren is an action which surely did not take place in the open, but must be imagined as having taken place in an interior, and thus it is, indeed, depicted in all parallel representations of this event.

Moreover, such illusionistic backgrounds are by no means a common feature but rather the exception in the Vienna Genesis. In the scene of the Temptation of Joseph by Potiphar's wife (Fig. 139),[26] the colonnade behind the couch is an iconographical item essential to leading the beholder to understand that the scene took place in a palace, and the open door at the right is also required for the clarification of the content, but otherwise the figures are silhouetted against the plain purple-stained background of the parchment leaf. Now, in contrast to the Vienna Dioscurides, the

Genesis pictures with the Hellenistic background do not represent the older tradition. All we know of the earliest narrative illustrations, when the medium for writing was still papyrus, is that landscape settings as well as frames were avoided,[27] and from this point of view the Temptation miniature is actually the more traditional one. But why would the illustrator of the blessing scene add the landscape which iconographically was not required? The reason, if we are not mistaken, is a formal one: in the earlier miniatures there are usually two, and often three or four scenes lined up either in one or in two superimposed zones. The blessing scene, being the only one in the predetermined picture area, had to be enlarged, but even so, the figure composition did not fill the whole surface area provided for the illustrator and the landscape was introduced as a space filler, not a very good choice considering the content of the scene. It seems almost paradoxical that the one illuminator who is by far the weakest and the least classical in his design of the human figure should, of his own volition, select such a strikingly illusionistic setting.

As is to be expected in the tenth century at the time of the Macedonian Renaissance, elements of classical landscape appear more frequently and are much better understood in detail than in the sixth century. In a miniature of the Paris Psalter with David playing the harp (Fig. 160)[28] there are at the upper

[26] Gerstinger, *Genesis*, p. 101 and pl. 31; Buberl, *Byzantinischen Handschriften*, I, 113 and pl. XXXVI, no. 31; Weitzmann, *Roll and Codex*, p. 166 and fig. 161.

[27] *Roll and Codex*, pp. 47 ff. (The Physical Relation between the Miniature and the Text).
[28] Omont, *Manuscrits grecs*, p. 6 and pl. I; Buchthal, *Paris Psalter*, p. 13 and pl. I; Weitzmann, *Geistige Grundlagen*, p. 9 and color plate 3 [translated and reprinted herewith, p. 178].

Fig. 139 *Vienna, Nationalbibliothek. Cod. theol. gr. 31, pict. 31. Joseph and Potiphar's Wife*

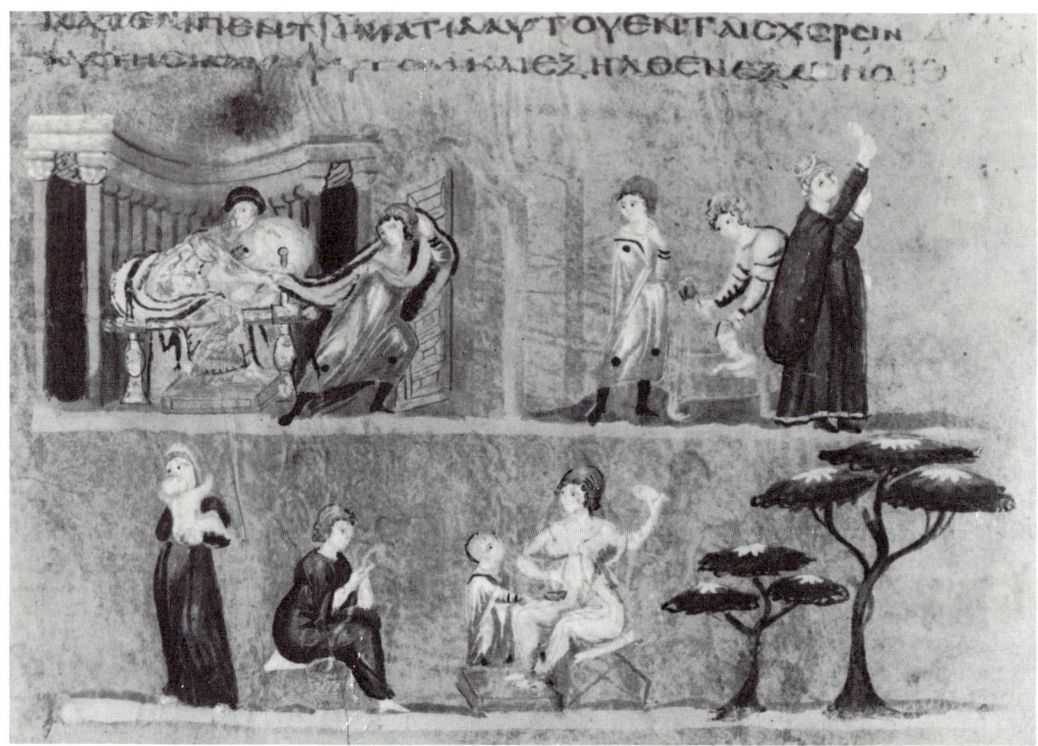

left some architectural features reminiscent of a Greco-Roman country villa, painted in blue to suggest an atmospheric change of color caused by distance; at the right is a column with a vase and a ribbon tied around it to fasten a votive gift, a feature common in Pompeian landscape painting, and further to the right one will notice a rock formation consisting of cubes. These landscape elements do not form a very homogeneous setting. It is a pasticcio, and the Psalter illustrator apparently found the various elements in different models.

Now there are other miniatures in the Paris Psalter in which the artist uses plain gold as the background color instead of utilizing a classical setting, as for example in the Prayer of Isaiah (Fig. 158).[29] One cannot accuse this miniaturist of being less a lover of the classical mode; the figure of the personification of Nyx is perhaps the finest single figure in the whole manuscript, as far as the recapturing of the classical form and spirit are concerned. Should we consider the appearance side by side of a classical and an anticlassical background as a wavering in taste, or can we make it plausible that the artists purposely used two different modes? David pasturing

[29] Omont, *Manuscrits grecs*, p. 9 and pl. XIII; Buchthal, *Paris Psalter*, p. 42 and pl. XIII; Weitzmann, *Geistige Grundlagen*, p. 8 and color plate 2 [translated and reprinted herewith, p. 177].

his flocks belongs essentially to the bucolic genre, and the similarity of this scene to Orpheus soothing the wild passions of the animals with his music has often been stated. Apparently, then, it is the affinity to a related iconographical realm in ancient art which induced the Psalter illustrator to assemble so many classical elements and thus to suggest the happy, carefree shepherd's life which David led before he became the leader of his people, at which time the imperial ceremonial realm begins to influence the depiction of the scenes from his life. On the other hand, the Prayer of Isaiah, visualized as a communication with God, is transposed into another sphere. In spite of some trees and plants, the gold ground eliminates the feeling of space and reality. There are other scenes within the same manuscript cycle which likewise involve an interrelation between heaven and earth, be it a prayer, a divine command or a vision, set against the neutral gold background, while in the case of simple narrative events the scene is usually set against a landscape or architectural backdrop in order to create the impression of space and depth. This leads us to believe that Byzantine illustrators, even at the height of the Macedonian Renaissance, had no intention of classicizing Byzantine art as a whole, but rather that they remained conscious of the artistic expressiveness of such abstractions as the gold ground and its usefulness for special purposes.

THE CLASSICAL AS EXPRESSION OF PHYSICAL REALITY

So far we have seen the classical mode introduced into Christian iconography in the form of personifications and landscape setting, that is as additive elements that did not touch the core of a Christian scene or figure. In the following lines I should like to deal with instances where the antithesis between the classical and nonclassical mode is operative within the core of a Christian scene.

Byzantine artists, as we shall try to demonstrate, used artistic devices which they borrowed from classical art for special purposes, and one of these is the human figure shown with a particularly high degree of physical reality. As an example from the Early Byzantine period I have chosen two figures from the Metamorphosis mosaic (Fig. 140) in the apse of the basilica of Saint Catherine's monastery on Mount Sinai, a building which was erected by Justinian toward the end of his long reign, and, we believe, also decorated in his lifetime.[30] Moses stands to the right raising his hand in a gesture of speech toward Christ (Fig. 141).[31] His feet are placed firmly on the ground and by turning the body the artist succeeded in giving a high degree of physical reality to the figure. The free leg in particular gives the effect of three-dimensionality and motion in space. These sculptural values call to mind ancient statues of philosophers, poets, or orators. Not that the mosaicist was

[30] The most numerous reproductions of the mosaic can be found in G. Sotiriou, "Τὸ μωσαϊκὸν τῆς Μεταμορφώσεως τοῦ Καθολικοῦ τῆς Μονῆς τοῦ Σινᾶ," *Atti dello VIII Congresso Internationale di Studi Byzantini, Studi Bizantini e Neoellenici*, 8 (Rome, 1953), 246 ff. [K. Weitzmann, "The Mosaic in St. Catherine's Monastery on Mount Sinai," *Proceedings of the American Philosophical Society*, 110 (1966), 392 ff.]
[31] Sotiriou, "Τὸ μωσαϊκὸν," pl. LXXVIa.

Fig. 140 *Mount Sinai, St. Catherine's. Mosaic.*
Transfiguration

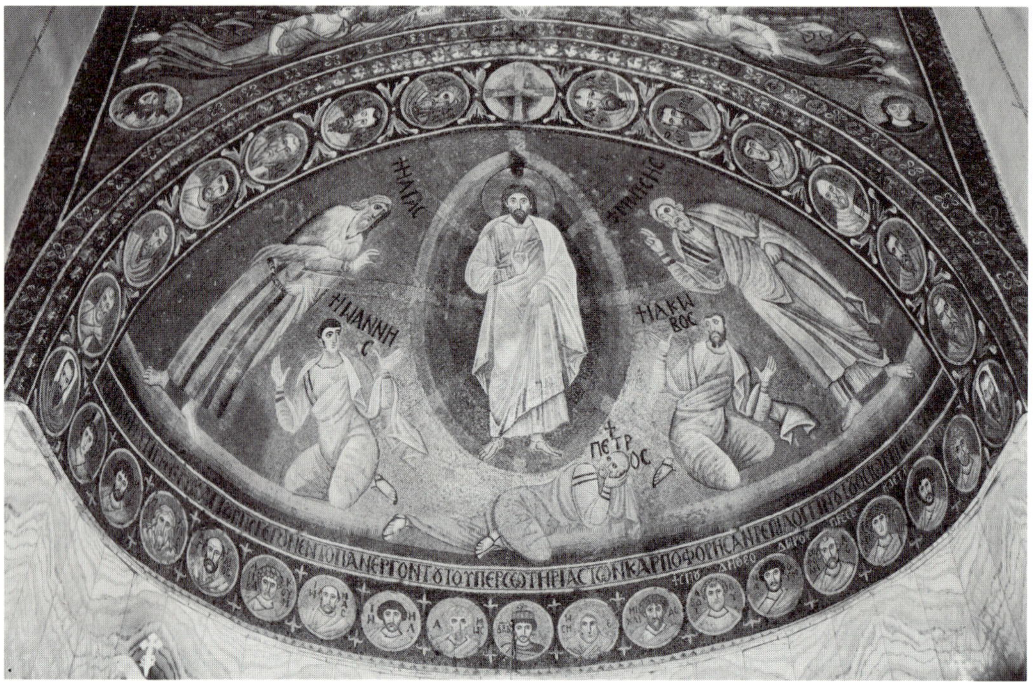

necessarily inspired by a piece of sculpture; the classical tradition more likely was transmitted through painting. The fingers of the left hand are bent, obviously meant to hold a scroll, and this strengthens our thesis that indeed the model was a man of letters from antiquity.

The high degree of corporeality in the Moses figure is effectively contrasted with the immateriality of the body of Christ (Fig. 142)[32] which is achieved by such devices as frontality, axiality, suspension, as there is no groundline, and the sparsely folded garment which tends to flatten the body. Classical corporeality and Christian abstractionism are no doubt purposely used in order to distinguish between the human and the divine. This example shows the difficulty and dangers inherent in reducing the concept of the artistic trend of a certain period to a simple formula of a development from the naturalistic to the abstract or vice versa.

We find similar juxtapositions of the classical and anticlassical mode in other phases of Byzantine art and also in other media. A lectionary on Sinai (cod. 204) which might be dated around the year 1000 has, at the beginning, a set of four standing evangelists even more classical than the Moses of the Sinai mosaic, a fact not surprising since we are dealing with a product of the Macedonian Renaissance. Matthew (Fig. 143)[33] is

[32] Ibid., pl. LXXV.

[33] Weitzmann, *Byzantinische Buchmalerei,* p. 28 and pl. XXXVIII, no. 211.

Fig. 141 *Mount Sinai, St. Catherine's. Mosaic. Transfiguration (det. of Moses)*

Fig. 142 *Mount Sinai, St. Catherine's. Mosaic. Transfiguration (det. of Christ)*

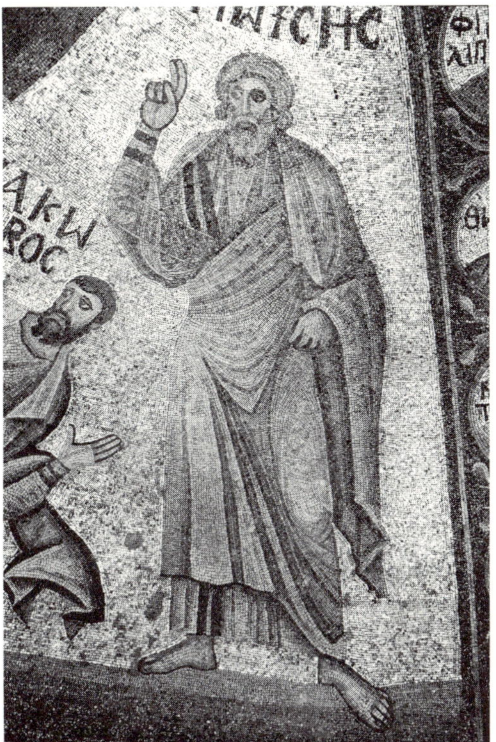

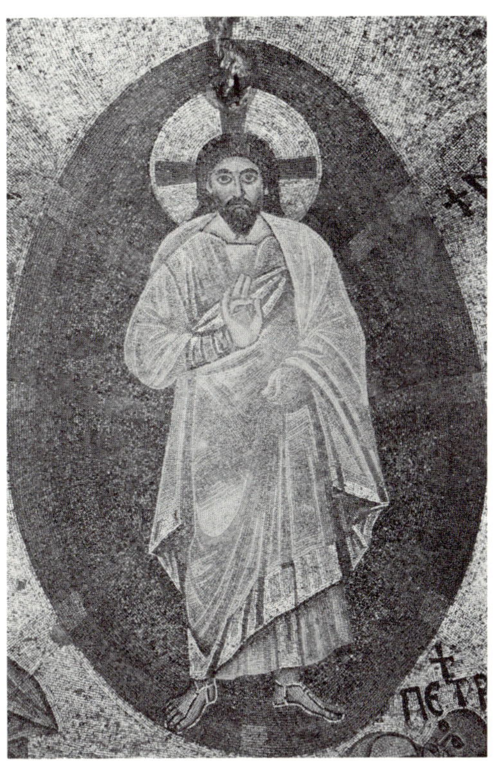

once more the typical man of letters from the classical past in a relaxed stance, the right arm, in classical fashion, held in the sling of his mantle; but instead of holding a scroll the artist has placed a jewel and pearl-studded Gospel book in his veiled left hand. The head has a distant affinity to that of Sophocles in the well-known Lateran statue. The elegant miniature is the product of a highly aristocratic art which was much appreciated at the imperial court, and although we cannot prove it, the manuscript, written throughout in golden uncials, seems to be the product of an imperial scriptorium, that is of a milieu where the taste for the classical had remained particularly strong.

Between the introductory miniatures of Christ and the Virgin, on the one hand, and the four evangelists on the other, there is the picture of a monk inscribed Ο ΟΣΙΟΣ ΠΕΤΡΟΣ (Fig. 144),[34] about whom we know only that this Peter was a monk of Monobata, a monastery whose location is unknown, and that he was commemorated on 7 February. In contradistinction to the evangelists he is depicted in strict frontality and in monastic garb so flat that it completely hides the body underneath. While in the mosaic (Figs. 141 and 142) the contrast was between the human and the divine, in the present case it is

[34] V. Beneševič, *Monumenta Sinaitica* (Leningrad, 1925), fasc. I, 47 and pl. 28.

Fig. 143 *Mount Sinai, St. Catherine's. Cod. 204, fol. 4^v. Matthew*

Fig. 144 *Mount Sinai, St. Catherine's. Cod. 204, fol. 3^r. Monk Peter*

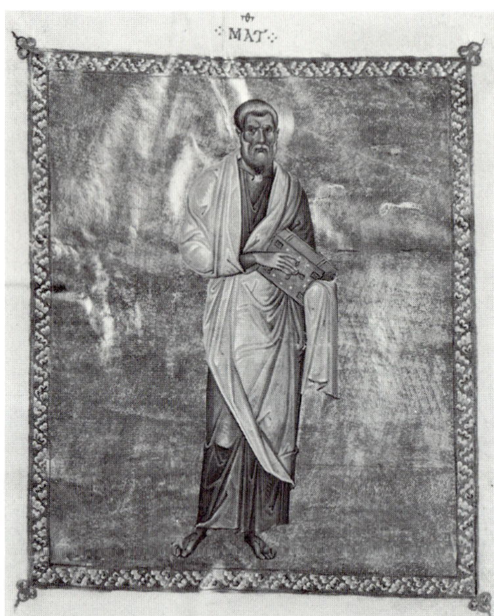

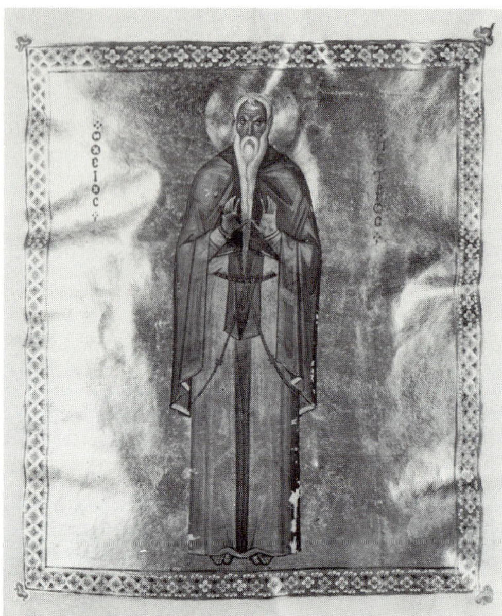

between the human and the ascetic. This figure of Peter visualizes the mortification of the flesh, supposed to make the monk susceptible to the transcendental and to develop his visionary powers. The faces of both figures, Matthew and Peter, have a spiritual quality, but that of the monk again stresses the ascetic.

It should not be assumed that the classical mode of stressing corporeality was restricted to periods of revival movements. For instance, in the twelfth century the general classicizing trend of the Macedonian Renaissance had somewhat worn off, while the Palaeologan Renaissance had not yet begun: nevertheless, for individual figures the classical mode continued to be used. One of the finest icons of the twelfth century in the rich Sinai collection depicts the miracle of the archangel Michael at Chone (Fig. 145).[35] The angel is shown saving

[35] G. and M. Sotiriou, *Icones*, I, 79 and pl. 65.

the abode of the pious monk Archippus by diverting the river which, according to the design of the devil, was to sweep away his hut. Michael is rendered as a youth of Apollonian beauty, gracious in the movement of the body, which is shown in full plasticity under a garment which clings to the body in classical fashion and whose folds combine a rhythmic flow with modeling power. In contrast, like the monk Peter of the Sinai miniature, Archippus' body seems weightless under the monastic garb, whose vertical folds do not detract but lead the beholder immediately to the expressive, ascetic head. That the angel, in spite of the high degree of physical reality, is not a being of this world is indicated by the marked difference in scale in relation to the monk. Why, then, is Michael depicted here with such a high degree of corporeality?

It must be pointed out that in Byzan-

Fig. 145 *Mount Sinai, St. Catherine's. Icon.
St. Michael at Chone*

Fig. 146 *Mount Sinai, St. Catherine's. Icon.
Two Archangels*

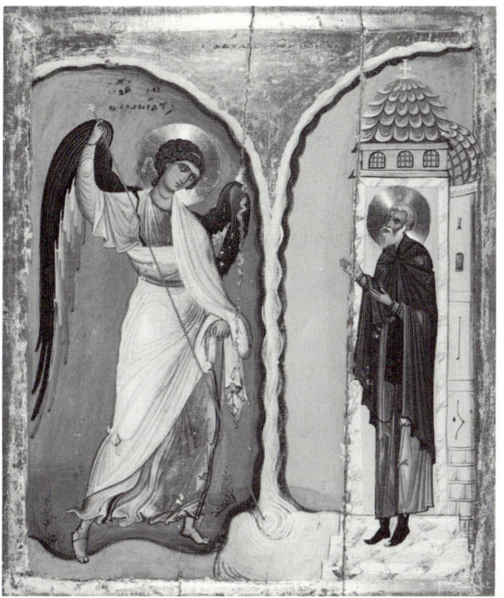

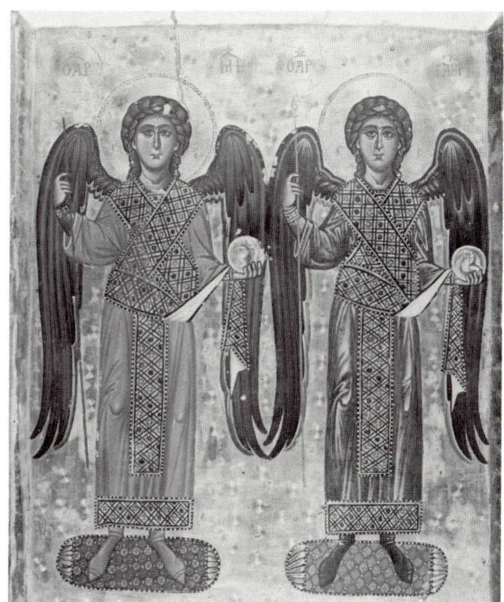

tine art Michael is not always rendered
so corporeally. Another Sinai icon, a
little later and apparently belonging to
the thirteenth century (Fig. 146),[36]
depicts him together with Gabriel,
dressed in the imperial *loros*, stiff and
motionless and with a rather dematerialized body. How is the use of two different
modes for the same angel figure to be
explained? In the first icon Michael is
involved in a heroic action performed in
this world, while in the second he is a
member of the synaxis of the archangels
which has its abode in heaven. In other
words, the angel takes on a more human
form while being active on earth, and this
aim the artist achieved by employing the
classical mode, which strives at a corporeal appearance.

THE CLASSICAL AS EXPRESSION OF MOTION

There are reasons for adopting the
classical mode other than merely to
stress corporeality. Classical art, at the
end of the Hellenistic period, had
achieved the facility to represent the
human figure in every imaginable pose
and under every conceivable emotional
stress. Consequently, when Byzantine
artists wanted to represent a human
figure in an unusual pose they did not
study it from nature but were confident
of finding some fitting type in the classical
repertory which could be adapted to
their special needs.

I should like to demonstrate this point
by choosing one particular and clearly
defined classical type and showing its
adaptation for very different purposes.
This type is a maenad dancing a
pirouette and seen from the back, a type
well known from the statue of Scopas,

[36] Unpublished.

which by the Hellenistic period had
become common in relief sculpture and
also in painting. In one of the richly
illustrated Bible manuscripts that contain
the first eight books of the Septuagint,
the so-called Octateuchs, an eleventh-
century copy in the Vatican Library
(cod. gr. 747) shows "Miriam and all the
women that went out after her with
timbrels and with dances" (Ex. 15:20)
after the Crossing of the Red Sea
(Fig. 147).[37] The woman at the left beats a
drum, standing quietly—rather a medieval type—while the two in the center,
joining hands, dance ecstatically and the
one at the right plays the cymbals. It is
the one seen from the back and rendered,
in classical fashion, with one breast bare,
who reflects the classical model in
greatest purity. Obviously, the artist who
first introduced a maenad type for this
scene was sufficiently familiar with
representations of Dionysian revelry and
knew perfectly well where to find the
most appropriate model for a joyful
dance. Yet that the adaptation of a
classical maenad was not the only possible solution becomes clear in looking
at the parallel miniature from another
Octateuch, likewise in the Vatican
Library (cod. gr. 746), from the twelfth
century, a manuscript which undoubtedly
belongs to the same recension (Fig. 148).[38]
The two musicians flanking the
central group are basically identical, but

Fig. 147 *Vatican, Biblioteca. Cod. 747, fol. 90ᵛ. Dance of Miriam*

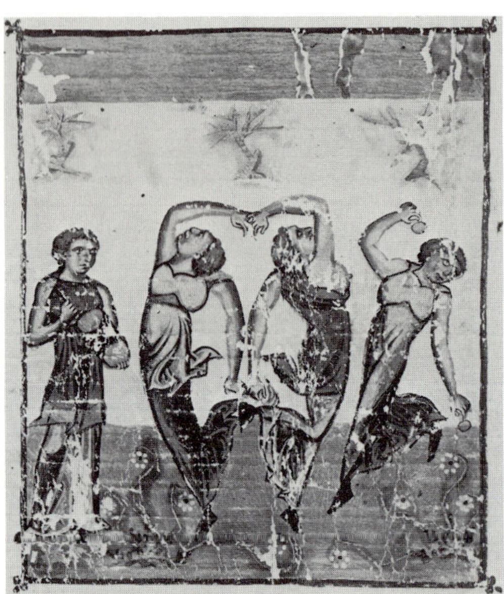

the two women in the center are calmer
and dance by moving only their feet, a
dance which corresponds more to a type
of Greek folk dance.

While in the scene of Miriam and the
Israelite women dancing form and
content were not basically changed in
the process of adapting a maenad for a
biblical dancer, in the next instance to be
discussed only the classical form is
preserved, while the content is changed.
On the lid of an ivory casket in Stuttgart
that represents the Ascension of Christ
(Fig. 149)[39] we see one of the apostles,
the second from the left, in the dancing
pose of a maenad. Obviously it was not
the intention of the artist to show the
apostle dancing; he was looking for a
formula that expressed excitement and

---

[37] For the place of this manuscript within the
group of illustrated Octateuchs consult
Weitzmann, *The Joshua Roll* (Princeton,
1948), pp. 31 ff.

[38] For the parallel scene in the Octateuch of
Smyrna, now destroyed, consult D. C.
Hesseling, *Miniatures de l'Octateuque grec de
Smyrne* (Leiden, 1909), pl. 59, no. 180.

[39] A. Goldschmidt and K. Weitzmann, *Die
byzantinischen Elfenbeinskulpturen des X. bis
XIII. Jahrhunderts* (Berlin, 1930–34), 2:30
and pl. VII, no. 24a.

Fig. 148 *Vatican, Biblioteca. Cod. 746, fol. 194ᵛ. Dance of Miriam*

Fig. 149 *Stuttgart, Schlossmuseum. Ivory Casket. Ascension*

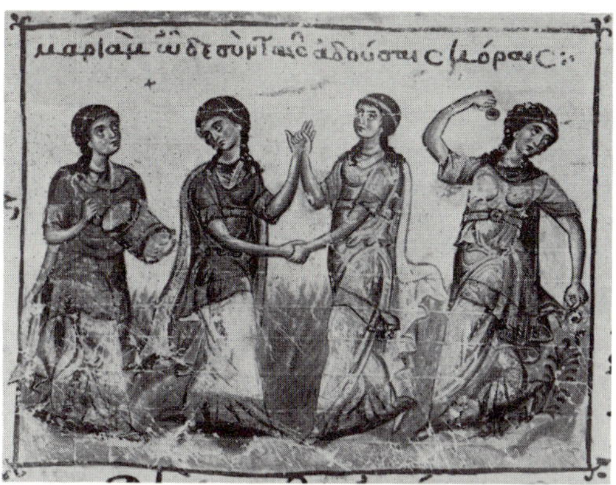

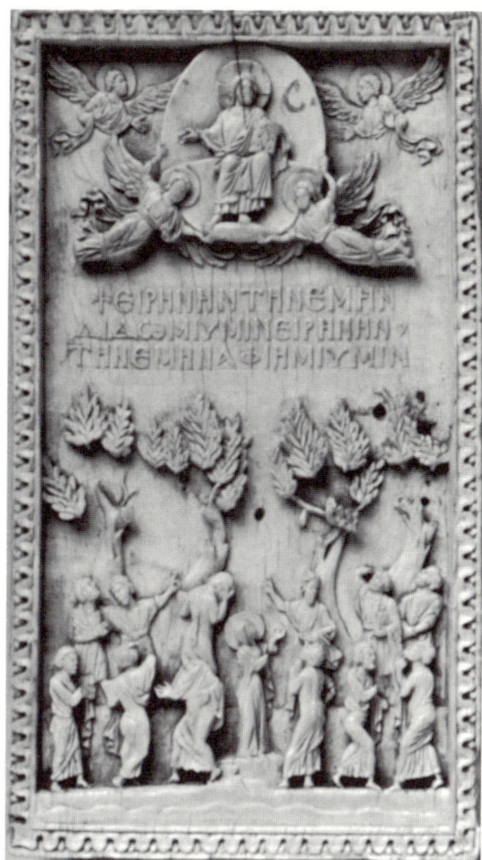

agitation, and at the same time he wanted a pose that conveyed the impression of a movement spiraling upward. The maenad type must have seemed to him to fulfil all these requirements.[40] Perhaps his contemporaries found this artist to be a bit too eccentric, and this may have been the reason why, as far as we know, this classicized version of the Ascension was not imitated, and if it was, surely not frequently. The more common type of Ascension of the same period, i.e., the tenth century, is represented by an ivory plaque of equally high quality in Florence.[41] It too shows one of the apostles seen from the back, but he is not a particularly classical type. The Stuttgart ivory is just another example of an individualistic artist's attempt to reintroduce the classical mode for the

purpose of expressive motions, attempts that were usually checked by the average Byzantine artist's preference for more measured poses that were in closer conformity to his sense of hieratic dignity.

In a third instance, the maenad type is used in yet a different context and for a different purpose in an Annunciation icon from Sinai (Fig. 150)[42] which belongs to the end of the twelfth century,

[40] Weitzmann, "The Survival of Mythological Representations in Early Christian and Byzantine Art and their Impact on Christian Iconography," *Dumbarton Oaks Papers*, 14 (1960), 62 and figs. 34 and 36. Here the maenad in an ivory pyxis in Zurich is reproduced as a parallel to the apostle of the Stuttgart casket.

[41] Goldschmidt and Weitzmann, *Elfenbeinskulpturen*, 2:42 and pl. XXIII, no. 58.

[42] Weitzmann, "Eine Spätkomnenische Verkündigungsikone des Sinai und die zweite byzantinische Welle des 12. Jahrhunderts," in *Festschrift Herbert von Einem* (Berlin, 1965), pp. 299 ff., color plate and pl. 70.

Fig. 150 *Mount Sinai, St. Catherine's. Icon.*
  Annunciation

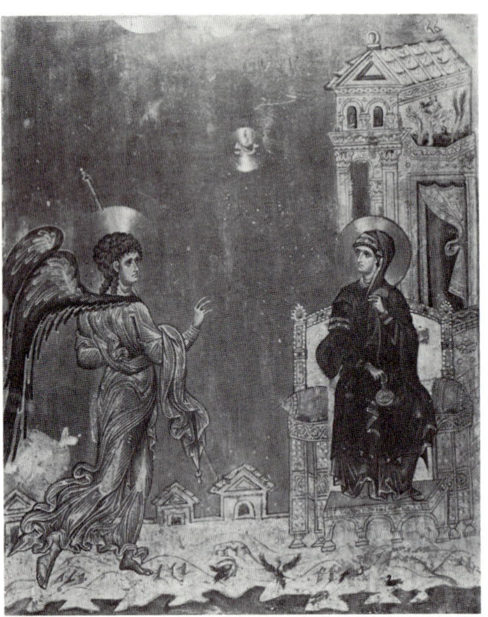

that is to that manneristic phase of Late
Comnenian art which has been much
discussed recently in connection with
the frescoes of Kurbinovo, Agioi
Anargyroi in Kastoria, and Lagoudhera
on Cyprus, all belonging to the last
decade of the twelfth century. But while
all these frescoes contain some elements
of provincialism, the icon does not;
therefore we believe that it is a product
of a Constantinopolitan workshop. The
slender, sensitive Virgin seems to shrink
back slightly at the approach of the angel,
who senses her embarrassment and,
stopping very suddenly, turns around in
a movement which once more resembles
that of the Scopasian maenad. Thus,
while making use of a classical type to
express a highly spirited motion, the
artist at the same time tries to devaluate
other aspects of the classical mode. The

over-elongated proportions and the
technique of gold grisaille help to de-
materialize the body. This Annunciation
angel is not without parallels: we
mentioned already the frescoes of Lagoudhera which contain a very similar Annunciation group. Yet the more common and
more traditional type of Annunciation
shows a stately matron being approached
by an angel who unhesitatingly steps
forward with a firm stride. A good
example of approximately the same
period, that is from about the second
half of the twelfth century, may be seen
on one of those iconostasis beams which
have come to light in the Sinai collection
(Fig. 151).[43] This is just another example
which demonstrates that the classical
mode as expressed in the maenad type
made deep inroads into the Christian
iconography but was not able to displace
the traditional, more hieratic, and less
classical mode. Once more we arrive at
the conclusion that at various phases of
Byzantine art a considerable degree of
freedom of choice permitted the artist
to select a classical model only when he
desired to do so.

THE CLASSICAL AS AN EXPRESSION OF
EMOTIONAL STATES

In analyzing the Annunciation icon of
Sinai we have already touched upon
another aspect, namely emotional expression as visualized by the reflective
behavior of both the Virgin and the
angel. This psychological aspect can
best be studied in facial expressions, and
I should like to demonstrate in a last
series of examples how the classical mode
was used for this purpose. I return to the

43 G. and M. Sotiriou, *Icones*, 1:107 and
pl. 100.

Fig. 151 *Mount Sinai, St. Catherine's. Iconostasis Beam. Annunciation*

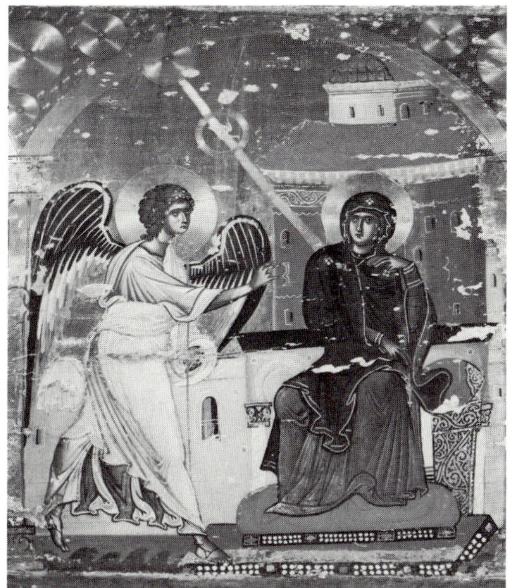

Christ of the Metamorphosis mosaic (Fig. 142) which we have already discussed as an example of a dematerialized body in contrast to the corporeal figure of Moses, which was derived from a classical statuary type of a philosopher or poet. For the facial expressions I should like to compare the head of Christ with that of Elijah on the other side (Fig. 140).[44] The abstract treatment of the head of Christ corresponds to the dematerialization of the body. The wide open eyes, the arched eyebrows, the massive, bell-shaped hair, and the slightly parted beard are designed symmetrically and with an almost geometric clarity. The effect of this pronounced emphasis on abstract design is the utter lack of any human quality. This Christ is neither the severe judge as we know him from Later Byzantine art nor the benevolent savior of mankind.

[44] Sotiriou, "Tὸ μωσαϊκὸν," p. 248 and pl. LXXVIb.

In contrast to the frontal Christ head, that of Elijah is given in three-quarter pose with a deep shadow falling on the hair flowing down over his left shoulder. Here an element of ancient illusionism is employed with great subtlety in that the shadow is not black but purple and lightened by occasional amber-colored and green cubes. Not only does Elijah perceive the outside world, his face reveals deep emotion, which one might interpret as awe at the vision or worry. This expression is achieved by steep, contracted brows and the oblique setting of the eyes.

There can be no doubt that both heads are by the same hand and that the use of more abstract forms for the Christ head is not the result of a lack of understanding of a more naturalistic form but an act of volition. What did the artist want to achieve by such a conscious juxtaposition? If we are not mistaken, his aim was to express by pictorial means the difference between the human and the divine. Christ had changed on Mount Tabor before the eyes of the apostles from the human to the divine nature, and it is one of the greatest achievements of Byzantine art to have succeeded in rendering the divine in pictorial form. We find the same distinction between the human and the divine again and again in Byzantine art, and it is by no means an individual solution of the Sinai artist, who also made full use of this juxtaposition in another part of the same mosaic.

On the triumphal arch we see the earliest representation of the Deesis known so far: the Virgin and John the Baptist, rendered as medallion busts set against a silver background (Fig. 140), flank Christ, who is, rather uniquely in

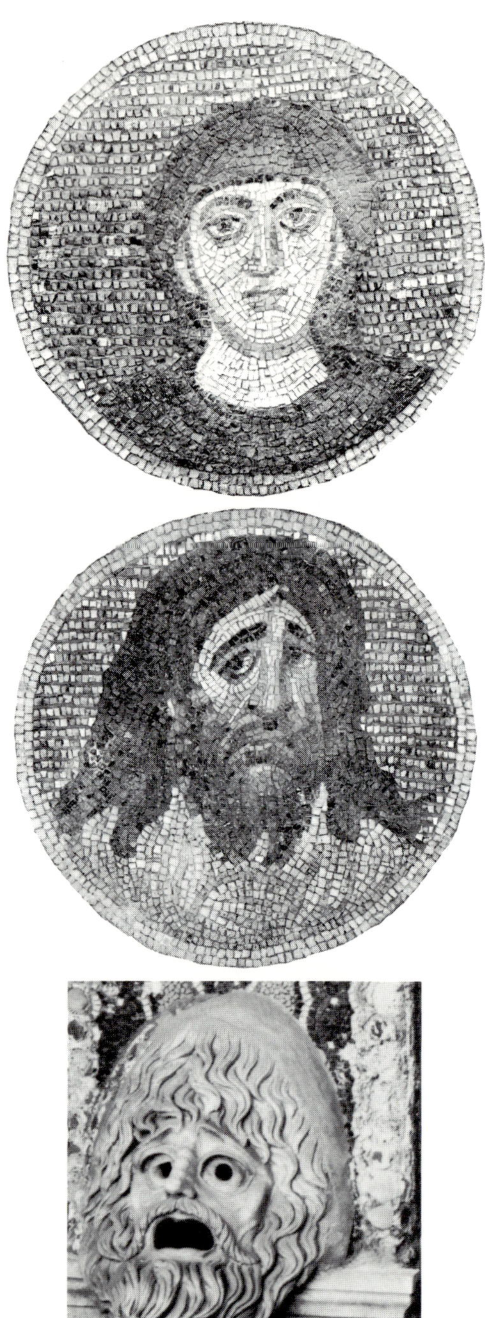

this context, represented as the Lamb of God.[45] For the depiction of the Virgin (Fig. 152) the same abstract means are used as in the case of the Metamorphosis Christ: strong symmetry, clear geometric lines for the staring eyes and the arched eyebrows. In the strongest possible contrast, John (Fig. 153) is turned in three-quarter view and the expression of great pathos shows an even higher degree of emotion than the comparable head of Elijah in the Metamorphosis. The eyebrows are even steeper and the impression of pathos more pronounced. The eyes are more deeply set in the sockets and the mass of somewhat disheveled hair falls upon his shoulders.

Essentially these are the very elements on which the emotional impact of the tragic mask is based. A marble mask from a fountain in Pompeii (Fig. 154)[46] has a very similar design with the steep, contracted eyebrows and the high *onkos* with the flowing hair; not much adaptation was required to fill in the eyes and to close the mouth. It seems to us more than likely, indeed, that the artist of the mosaic not only used a tragic mask of antiquity as his model, but did so with the full realization that this was the most effective way to express in pictorial form the tragic genius of John the Baptist. In juxtaposing this type of John with the abstract Virgin, the artist once more succeeds in expressing by pictorial means the difference between the divine and the human.

As a last example I should like to introduce two icons which are companion pieces and were surely painted for

[45] Ibid., p. 251 and pls. LXXVII–LXXVIII.
[46] M. Bieber, *The History of the Greek and Roman Theater* (rev. ed.; Princeton, 1961), p. 243 and fig. 800.

Fig. 155 *Mount Sinai, St. Catherine's. Icon. Elijah Fed by the Raven*

Fig. 156 *Mount Sinai, St. Catherine's. Icon. Moses Receiving the Law*

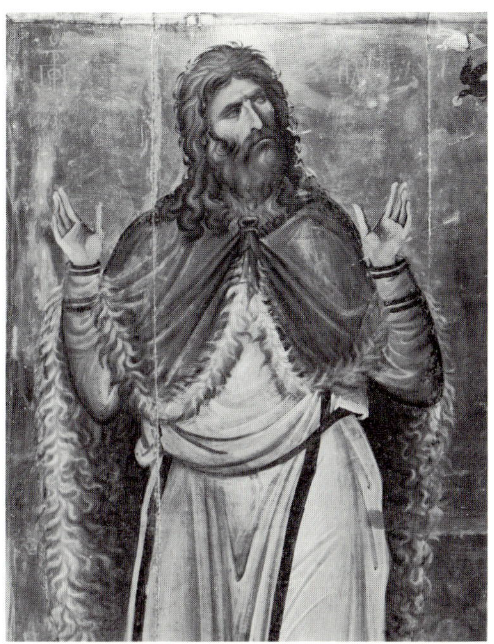

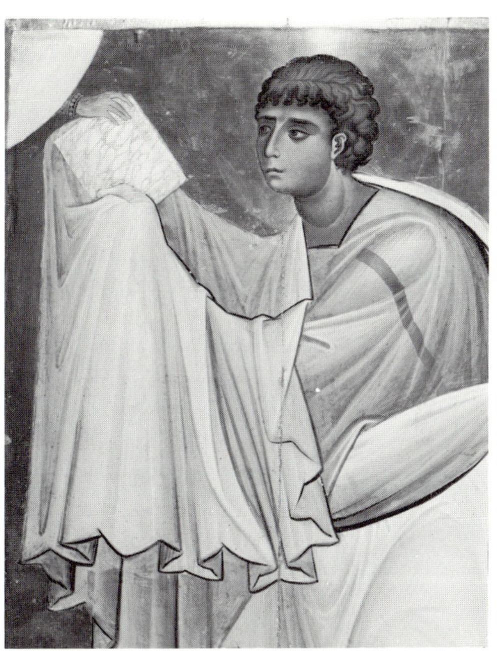

Mount Sinai since they represent the two Sinaitic prophets: Moses receiving the tablet of the law and standing before the burning bush, and Elijah fed by a raven (Figs. 155 and 156).[47] They are depicted almost life-size in a style which points toward the end of the twelfth century, as is revealed especially by Moses' garment with the mannered zigzag folds so typical of the Late Comnenian style; and the paleography of the bilingual inscription in Greek and cufic Arabic agrees with this date.

[47] G. and M. Sotiriou, *Icones*, 1:88 ff. and pls. 74–75. Here the icons are, as we believe, correctly dated in the end of the twelfth century; in a previous study ("Ελληνο-ἀραβικαὶ εἰκόνες τοῦ Μωϋσέως καὶ τοῦ προφήτου Ἠλιοῦ τῆς Μονῆς Σινᾶ," *Tome commémoratif du Millénaire de la Bibliothèque Patriarchale d'Alexandrie* [Alexandria, 1953], pp. 153 ff.) Sotiriou had dated them not older than the fifteenth century.

While Moses is rendered in a rather traditional iconographic manner, the figure of Elijah shows greater originality, particularly in the impressive gesture of the raised hands. The most characteristic features are the unkempt hair and the fur cloak. Both are typical of the itinerant Cynic philosopher, like the one in a fresco from the garden of the Farnesina in Rome (Fig. 157) in which the philosopher with disheveled hair, identified as Crates,[48] has his fur thrown over his shoulder instead of wearing it. This parallel is, of course, not proof enough that indeed the portrait of a Cynic philosopher was the prototype of our Elijah. Yet an ultimate descent from some

[48] H. Fuhrmann, "Krates und Hipparchia," *Mitteilungen des deutschen archäologischen Instituts: Römische Abteilung*, 55 (1940), 86 ff. and pl. 9.

Fig. 157 *Rome, Museo Nazionale. Fresco from the Farnesina. Philosopher Crates*

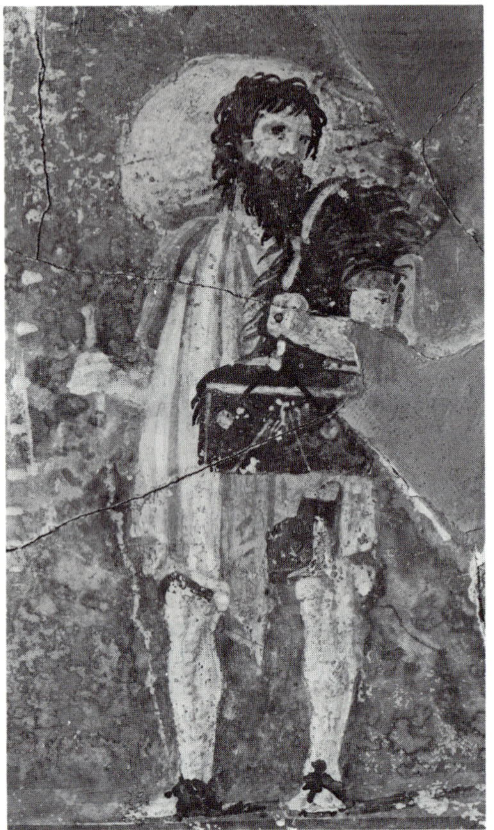

such type of classical antiquity is by no means unlikely, not only because of the external features mentioned above, but also because of the similarity of concept of an itinerant philosopher and an itinerant prophet, both of whom denied the value of worldly goods and went unkempt.

What interests us primarily in the present context is the rendering of the faces. The youthful Moses has a calm, smooth face, and while looking at the tablets he is about to receive his face does not show much emotion save for a slight contraction of the eyebrows. In contrast, the face of Elijah is based on the classical formula of pathos not unlike that used for the Elijah in the Metamorphosis mosaic, save that the icon painter individualizes the face to a much higher degree by means of more subtle modeling. One gets the impression that in the icon a great artist used the classical formula of pathos very freely, and that one would search in vain for a very precise model. Actually he has absorbed the classical mode so thoroughly that it has become second nature to him. Similarly, shortly thereafter, a great sculptor in Reims created a Visitation group which would not have been possible without a careful study of classical art; and yet precise models have not been and most likely never will be found. With the highly emotional expression in the face of Elijah juxtaposed to the rather calm face of Moses, the Byzantine artist of this later period demonstrated the same kind of freedom in the selection of different modes of facial expressions as his predecessor of the Early Byzantine period who made the Metamorphosis mosaic. By claiming a general validity of the various principles discussed for the Early and Middle Byzantine periods we assume that this validity applies also to the Late Byzantine period.

While emphasizing the ever-present use of the classical mode in different forms in all phases of Byzantine art, it also must be reaffirmed that Byzantine art is by no means a mere extension of classical art. There is a continuous interplay with more abstract and nonclassical forms, some of which were stimulated by oriental influences, while others were created by Byzantine artists as an expression of a spiritual, ascetic, and sometimes mystical trend in a basically Christian culture. One of the reasons for the great inner strength of Byzantine art is that the two strands, the classical and the nonclassical, are often used for artistic contrast, but nonetheless they never seem to be in conflict with each other.

One rightly may ask whether the use of different modes in the same work of art does not endanger its artistic unity. No doubt the archaic, the classical, and even the Hellenistic period show in their artistic creations a relatively greater cohesion. On the other hand, in Neo-Attic art this cohesion begins to dissolve and in its creations different modes are often used in a rather eclectic manner, as the result of copying models from different periods of the past. This is not quite the same, however, as what we experience in Byzantine art: here we have seen side by side the corporeal and the uncorporeal, agitation and noble restraint, a high pitch of emotion and utter calm, not for reasons of mixing styles but for the characterization of the physical and the spiritual, the human and the divine. Seen from this point of view, Byzantine art reflects the most harmonious interpenetration of the classical and the Christian ever achieved in the Middle Ages.

8

The Character and Intellectual Origins of the Macedonian Renaissance

THE most striking characteristic of Byzantine art—in contrast to Western art—is its unbroken continuity of the Greek heritage which always remained potentially formative. It is precisely because of this continuity that many scholars have not admitted the possibility of a renaissance movement in Byzantium. However, it would be an unbalanced evaluation to consider Byzantine art solely as a persistence of the ancient tradition. Oriental influences and an innate tendency to give Christian subject matter a spiritual form interacted to produce a feeling for a more abstract art which, operating within certain limits, veered from the naturalism of the antique—at certain times more sharply than at others. In contrast to the Latin West, the rendering of the body always remains more organic in Byzantium: essentially, the variable factors are the degree of physical reality and the relationship of the human figure to its environment. In spite of this qualification, the concept of a "renaissance" in the art of the late ninth and tenth centuries is—on the strength of an intensified study of the classical repertory of forms—beginning to take root, a renaissance which is called "Macedonian" after the ruling dynasty. Art historians have defended or attacked this concept with equal vehemence; and it seems to us that the time has come to give an account of this controversy and

Translated and reprinted with permission from *Geistige Grundlagen und Wesen der Makedonischen Renaissance* ("Arbeitsgemeinschaft für Forschung des Landes Nordrhein-Westfalen" 107 [Cologne and Opladen: Westdeutscher Verlag, 1963]). Foreword, Discussion and Résumé omitted.

to place the renaissance movement in a broader frame of reference, in the belief that new evidence for its existence can be adduced.

THE PARIS PSALTER

Within the field of art history, the concept of the Macedonian Renaissance evolved in connection with an important Psalter manuscript which, for a long time, was the center of the controversy almost exclusively: the Paris Bibliothèque Nationale, codex graecus 139. The full-page pictures of this manuscript evoke such an immediate impression of a good understanding of classical form that it is easy to understand why this manuscript occupies a key position. In the first systematic treatment of book illumination, Kondakov, the real founder of Byzantine art history, had already discussed in detail the Paris Psalter and, on the whole, had evaluated it correctly.[1] To be sure, he did not use the expression "renaissance"; but his sound characterization of the miniatures as a mixture of typical classical and equally typical Byzantine types and his dating in the tenth century go directly to the heart of what is the very essence of the renaissance.

At first Kondakov's penetrating observations found no favorable response; and his idea that an artist of the tenth century had revived very early classical models was met with counter arguments which were very largely subjective so far as they presumed that such a relatively pure rendition of classical types was possible only in a tradition which had never been interrupted and could not

[1] N. Kondakov, *Histoire d'Art byzantin*, 2 (Paris, 1891), 30 ff.

Fig. 158 *Paris, Bibliothèque Nationale. Cod. gr. 139, fol. 435ᵛ. Prayer of Isaiah*

Fig. 159 *Rome, Museo Capitolino. Endymion Sarcophagus. Selene*

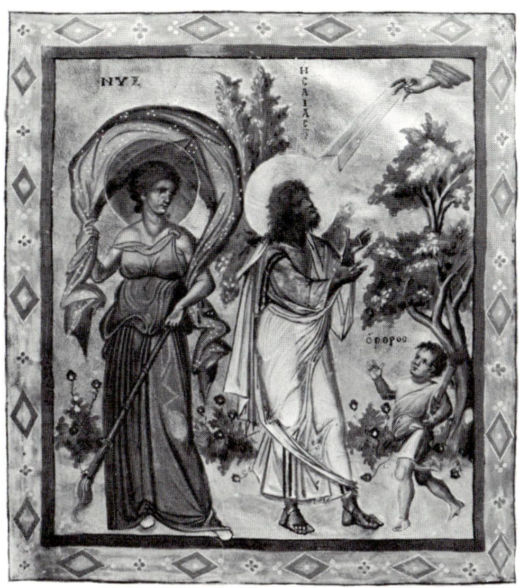

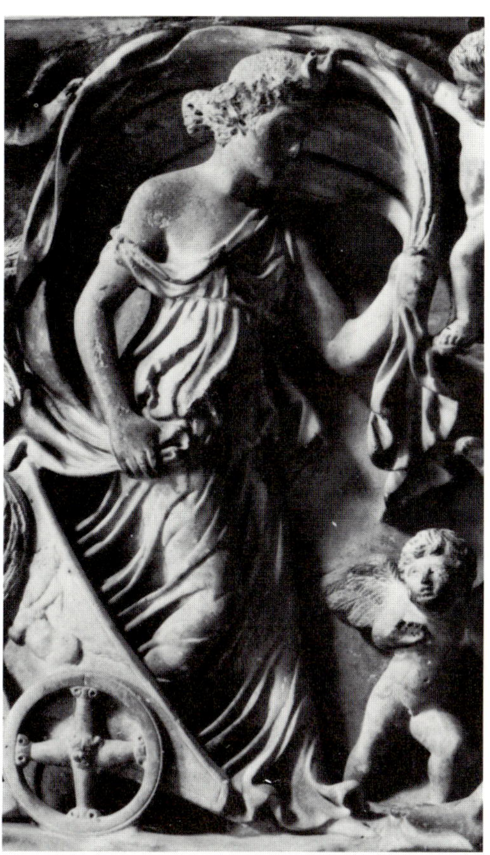

result from harking back anew to early models.

A study by Alois Grünwald,[2] in which he exhaustively analyzed the ancient sources of two miniatures, gave rise to the controversy which is concerned with a fundamental judgment concerning the nature of Middle Byzantine art. He assumed that, for the miniature in which the praying Isaiah is flanked by the personifications of Nyx and Orthros (Fig. 158)[3], a Roman Endymion sarcophagus (Fig. 159)[4] was the model. According to his argument, the upper part of Nyx

[2] A. Grünwald, *Byzantinische Studien. Zur Entstehungsgeschichte des Pariser Psalters Ms. grec. 139* ("Schriften der philosophischen Fakultät der deutschen Universität in Prag," fasc. I [Brünn, 1929]).
[3] H. Omont, *Miniatures des plus anciens manuscrits grecs* (2d ed.; Paris, 1929), pl. XIII and color plate; H. Buchthal, *The Miniatures of the Paris Psalter: A Study in Middle Byzantine Painting* (London, 1938), pl. XIII.
[4] Grünwald, *Pariser Psalter*, pp. 11 ff. and fig. 3.

was copied from a Selene figure, not the one on this particular Endymion sarcophagus in the Capitoline Museum but from a similar one, while a classical Demeter statue[5] of the fifth century B.C., preserved in several replicas, was the model for the calm, statuesque lower body. From the analysis of this and other figures Grünwald concluded that the Byzantine artist produced pastiches, combining with varying degrees of skill parts taken from different figures, and that the obvious discrepancies in many of the figures of the Psalter are explained by this method

[5] Ibid., figs. 4–5.

of working. Grünwald called this process a *gewaltsames Antikisieren* and concluded that it could have occurred only during the Middle Byzantine "renaissance."

Of course, one might ask whether or not the painter of the Psalter picture really made use of an Endymion representation and if a Roman sarcophagus was the direct source. It is highly unlikely that a painter who worked during the tenth century in Constantinople—and the Paris Psalter certainly originated in that eastern capital—would have used Roman sarcophagus reliefs. On the contrary, his good understanding of an impressionistic brush technique virtually guarantees that his model was a painting. In spite of these objections, we think that in principle Grünwald correctly evaluated the origin of the Paris Psalter miniatures.

In 1929, the same year as Grünwald's essay, my own study on the Paris Psalter appeared, in which I analyzed the whole cycle of fourteen miniatures along the same lines and traced their ancient sources.[6] At that time perhaps the closest parallel which I was able to produce was for the Melodia of the introductory miniature (Fig. 160)[7] grouped with the harp-playing David in a landscape which still preserves an atmosphere of bucolic serenity. In a Pompeian fresco of Io guarded by Argus, surviving in several replicas (Fig. 161),[8] Io is depicted in pose

and garments so similar to that of Melodia that it seemed necessary for us to assume that the illustrator of the Psalter turned almost certainly to a good model from Roman times. In other words, the ancient type was not dulled by constant copying but, to a large extent, has preserved its pure classical character. The center of this miniature is not the group, however, but David alone, who pays little or no attention to the personification of Melodia sitting behind him. Therefore, we have assumed that Melodia is an addition of the tenth-century renaissance, though not necessarily appearing in this very manuscript for the first time. We thought then, as we still do today, that not all of the personifications were added to a Christian-Byzantine core of Psalter illustration but only those which, like Melodia, have an active part in the composition. The representation of localities as personifications had never died out; and thus it is probable that the mountain god, Bethlehem, was a traditional element of the picture.[9] A whole series of similar observations gave rise to the conception of an eclectic artistic movement in which ancient elements, consisting of human figures as well as landscape and architecture, were brought into association with Christian elements and fused together into a new whole. In some cases, for example the picture of the harp-playing David, these amalgamations are quite successful and artistically satisfactory; while in miniatures where lesser masters were at work, the quality of a pastiche is quite evident.

---

[6] Weitzmann, "Der Pariser Psalter ms. grec. 139 und die mittelbyzantinische Renaissance," *Jahrbuch für Kunstwissenschaft*, 6 (1929), pp. 178 ff.

[7] Omont, *Manuscrits grecs*, pl. I; Buchthal, *Paris Psalter*, pl. I.

[8] P. Herrmann (ed.), *Denkmäler der Malerei des Altertums* (Munich, 1904–50), series I, pl. 53.

[9] In this case certain details indicate that a river god has probably been transformed into a mountain god. Cf. Weitzmann, *Pariser Psalter*, p. 179.

Fig. 160 *Paris, Bibliothèque Nationale. Cod. gr. 139, fol. 1ᵛ. David and Melodia*

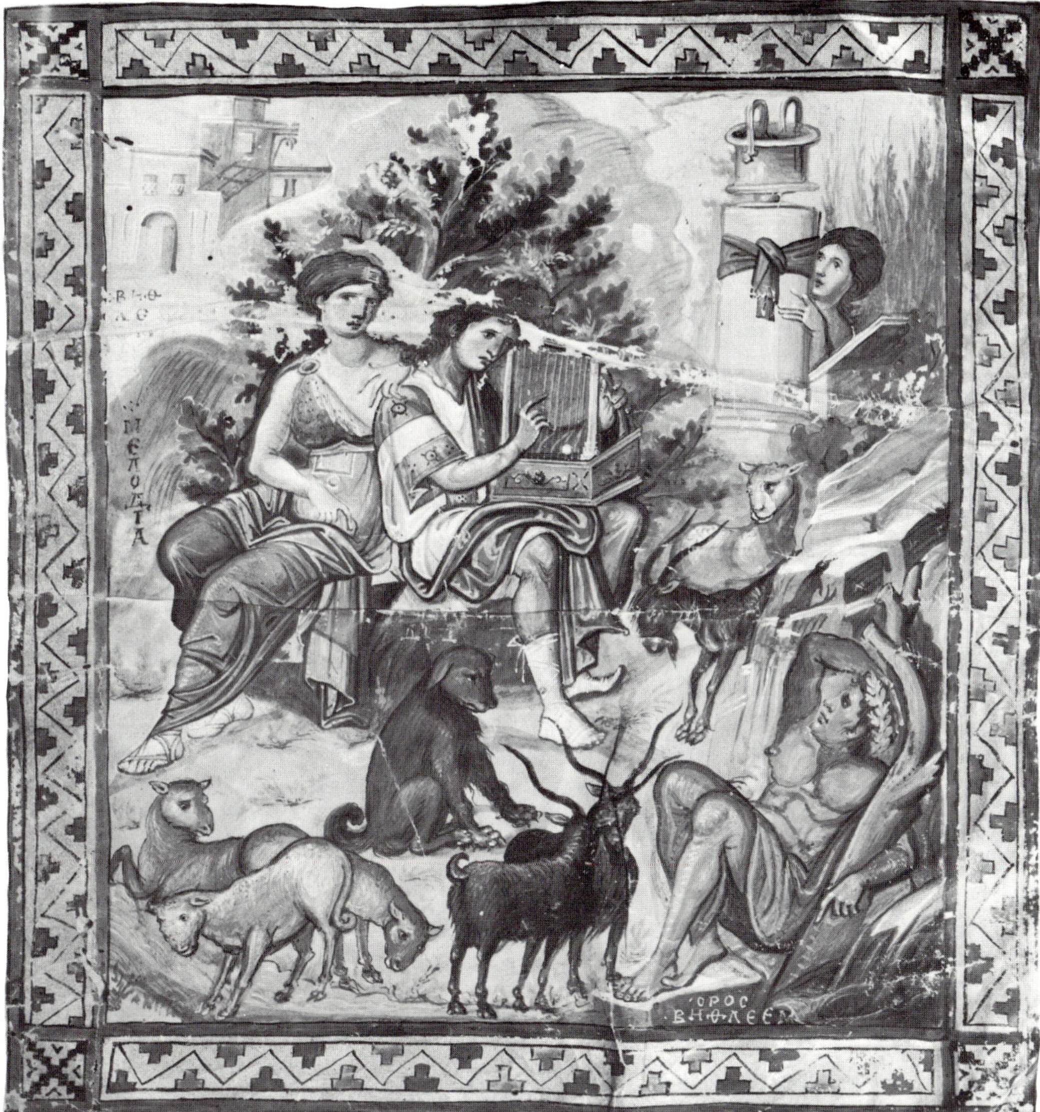

In 1938 Hugo Buchthal's comprehensive monograph on the Paris Psalter appeared[10] and dealt with the question of ancient prototypes within a broader frame of reference. Buchthal accepted the essential characteristics of the concept of a Middle Byzantine Renaissance; but he took exception to several ideas in my study of the Psalter. Buchthal had

[10] Cf. n. 3. In 1933 Buchthal's dissertation for the University of Hamburg had appeared under the title *Codex Parisinus Graecus 139.*

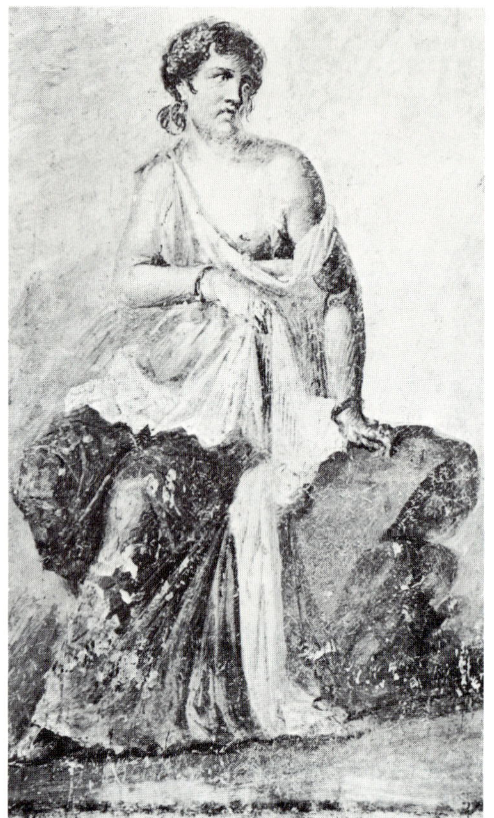

Fig. 161 *Pompeii, Macellum. Fresco. Io*

three main objections to which, because of their importance for the understanding of the nature of this renaissance, I would like to reply briefly. First of all, Buchthal disapproved of the view that a figure might be a pastiche pieced together from parts of other figures, for it seemed to him that this destroyed the artistic unity of the Psalter pictures. However, the method of work which we ascribe to the illustrator of the Psalter is not unusual and is by no means confined to this manuscript; it is possible to demonstrate its use throughout medieval painting, in the East and in the West, and

even as early as the classical period.[11]

His second objection was directed against deriving classical elements from heterogeneous sources which would conflict with the at least partially consistent character of the Psalter illustrations which in turn presupposes more homogeneous sources. According to Buchthal, in the case of David and Melodia, similar groups had existed as early as the classical period and therefore, despite the formal similarities, the borrowing of an isolated Io as she appears in the Pompeian fresco does not appear convincing. No doubt Buchthal is right in asserting that in the classical period it was not unusual for a certain type to turn up in various iconographical contexts; and in connection with the Melodia of the Paris Psalter we, ourselves, have found confirmation of this observation in a mosaic from Antioch (Fig. 162)[12] where the nymph Oenone, in a pose like that of Melodia, forms a group with Paris. Even though the details do not agree with each other as closely

[11] As one example among many, I refer here to an observation made by Boeckler, who showed that the painter of a figure of Christ in a Weingarten manuscript at Manchester combined the lower body of the evangelist Mark, which he took from a Liège Gospels, with the upper body of another figure. A. Boeckler, "Unerkannte Weingartner Bildhandschriften," in *Adolph Goldschmidt zu seinem 70. Geburtstag* (Berlin, 1935), p. 36 and pl. XII.

[12] *Antioch-on-the-Orontes. III The Excavations 1937–1939* (Princeton, 1941), p. 189, no. 135E and pl. 64; D. Levi, *Antioch Mosaic Pavements I* (Princeton, 1947), p. 210; II, pl. XLVIa; Weitzmann, "The Survival of Mythological Representations in Early Christian and Byzantine Art and their Impact on Christian Iconography," *Dumbarton Oaks Papers*, 14 (1960), 67 and figs. 42–44.

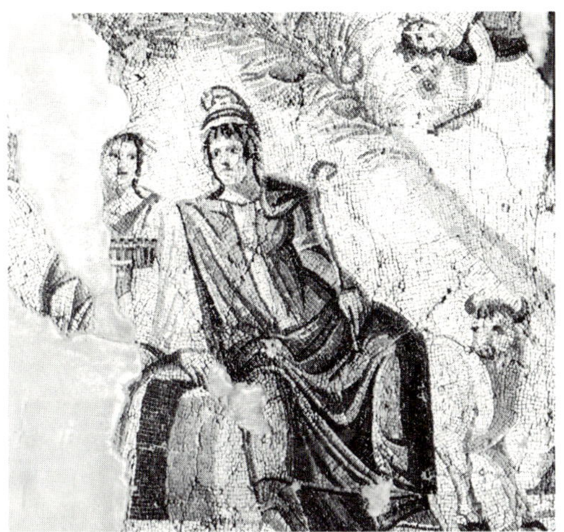

Fig. 162 *Princeton, University Art Museum. Mosaic from Antioch. Paris and Oenone*

as in the case of Io,[13] the Oenone figure does have the advantage that she is holding a syrinx in her hand and thus could have furnished the Psalter painter, who was searching for a prototype, with an idea of how to represent his Melodia, and that she does belong to a group. In general, our continued study of the problems of the Byzantine Renaissance has led us to the result that, in many cases, though not invariably, the painters of this period were quite conscious of the content of their ancient sources and, consequently, they chose their models carefully—not only for form but also for iconography. Our discussion will support this assertion with further concrete evidence.

[13] The summary treatment of the Oenone in the mosaic, which dates to the third century A.D., compared with the Pompeian fresco of the first century may generally be explained by the differences between Early and Late Roman Style. We can only conclude that the source of the Psalter illuminator was closer in style to the Pompeian wall-paintings of the first century than to the Antioch mosaics of the so-called House of Menander.

The third difference of opinion, which has considerable bearing on the final appraisal of the renaissance, concerns the personifications. Whereas, in our view, most of the personifications are additions of the renaissance, Buchthal assumed that they were present in the Early Byzantine archetype of the Psalter. In other words, while we are inclined to grant the Middle Byzantine painter an individual role in fusing traditional biblical elements of Byzantine style with classical elements, Buchthal supposed that the fourteen Paris Psalter pictures are extremely precise copies of early Christian pictures and that certain inconsistencies can be explained as mere technical incompetence on the part of the copyist.

This raises the question of the relationship of the Paris Psalter to the archetype, and here I cannot refrain from reproaching all those, the present author included, who have treated this subject thus far, for neglecting to do what a philologist, working on the manuscript tradition of a given text, would have done first of all, namely, to collate the main texts and to make the results of his comparison of texts graphic by means of a stemma.[14] In the case of the Paris Psalter, it turns out that the pictures were not invented for a Psalter manuscript at all, but that, with the single exception of the title-page illustration, which depicts David as the author of Psalms between Sophia and Prophetia (Fig. 135), all were taken over

[14] For the problem of the extent to which similar principles can be applied to text criticism and picture criticism see Weitzmann, *Illustrations in Roll and Codex: A Study of the Origin and Method of Text Illustration* (2d ed. Princeton, 1970), pp. 182 ff.

Fig. 163 *Paris, Bibliothèque Nationale. Cod. gr. 139, fol. 4ᵛ. David and Goliath*

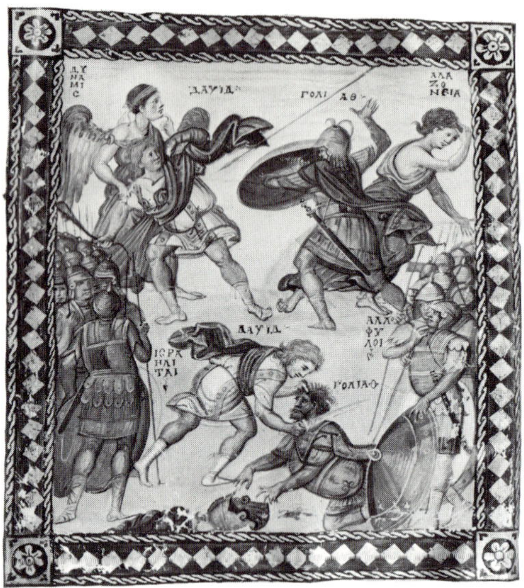

from other books of the Bible: the David scenes from the Books of Kings and the Ode pictures from the Pentateuch, the Prophets, and the New Testament. Strictly speaking, the question of the archetype of these pictures is not a matter for a Psalter recension but should be treated in connection with the biblical books for which the pictures were created.[15]

The David and Goliath miniature may serve to demonstrate this. In the Paris

Psalter, David's battle with Goliath is shown in two scenes (Fig. 163)[16] which, however, are not separated from each other, so that the impression of a unified space is conveyed, intensified by the way in which the onlooking armies of the lower zone intrude into the upper. David is spurred on to battle by a personification entitled *Dynamis*, while the personification inserted as *Alazoneia* abandons Goliath and flees. Relevant is the Vatican codex gr. 333, an illustrated manuscript of the four Books of Kings with over 100 miniatures comprising more than 160 scenes.[17] Although this manuscript is as late as the twelfth century, we may assume that an extensive cycle was not copied as often as a Psalter cycle and that therefore the Vatican manuscript preserves the character of an Early Christian narrative Bible illustration in a relatively pure state. Here the two battle scenes are shown with exactly the same iconography (Figs. 164–165)[18] so that there can be no doubt that it belongs to the same recension as the Paris Psalter, but the scenes are separate units and the personifications are lacking. Were only one case involved, it might be possible to maintain that the personifications had indeed existed in the archetype and had been eliminated by the illustrator of the Vatican Book of Kings. However, with a single exception, which only proves the rule,[19] the voluminous

---

[15] In several cases Buchthal has indicated the connection with the Books of Kings and with other biblical books. For a more systematic treatment of the question of the illustration of the aristocratic Psalter in connection with the migration of pictures from text to text see Weitzmann, "The Psalter Vatopedi 761—Its Place in the Aristocratic Psalter Recension," *The Journal of the Walters Art Gallery*, 10 (1947), 21 ff. The author has embarked on a comprehensive treatment of the Paris Psalter and its place in the aristocratic Psalter recension.

[16] Omont, *Manuscrits grecs*, pl. IV; Buchthal, *Paris Psalter*, pl. IV.

[17] J. Lassus, "Les miniatures byzantines du Livre des Rois," *Mélanges d'archéologie et d'histoire*, 45 (1928), 38 ff.

[18] Ibid., figs. 6–7.

[19] The exception is the Anointment of David (Lassus, "Livre des Rois," Fig. 4) in

Fig. 164 *Vatican, Biblioteca. Cod. gr. 333, fol. 23ᵛ. David and Goliath*

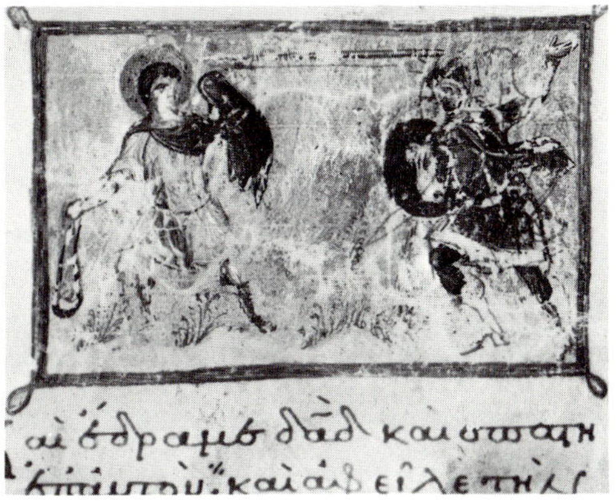

Fig. 165 *Vatican, Biblioteca. Cod. gr. 333, fol. 24ʳ. David and Goliath*

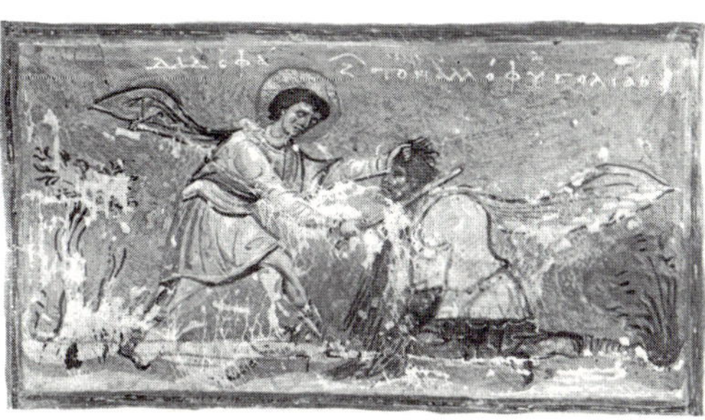

cycle of the Vatican manuscript is without personifications and other classicizing elements, whereas the Paris Psalter miniatures are literally crowded with them. Furthermore, it is worth noting that a whole series of Psalters belonging to the "aristocratic recension"

which the personification of *Praotes*, Gentleness, performs the same function as in the corresponding miniature of the Paris Psalter (Omont, *Manuscrits grecs*, pl. III; Buchthal, *Paris Psalter*, pl. III). Therefore, we assume that the Vatican Book of Kings, which dates as late as the twelfth century, in its turn has been influenced by an aristocratic Psalter, an assumption strengthened by the fact that a second cycle of the Book of Kings, preserved in the manuscript of the *Sacra Parallela* of John of Damascus in Paris (Bibliothèque Nationale, cod. gr. 923), has the same scene without the personification (Weitzmann, "Psalter Vatopedi," p. 38 and fig. 25). The Paris manuscript is as early as the ninth century and, as a florilegium, includes excerpts from a cycle of the Book of Kings. Even though the cycle is heavily excerpted, it is still worth noting that among the more than eighty scenes from the Book of Kings, certainly belonging to the same recension as Vatican gr. 333, not a single scene has been enriched with a personification.

has full-length pictures which correspond more closely to the Vatican Books of Kings than to the Paris Psalter. For example, a twelfth-century Psalter in the Theological Seminar of Berlin University represents David's battle (Fig. 166)[20] with the same division into two zones but with the personifications once more missing. On the basis of this and a great number of analogous cases, we come to the conclusion that the classical elements of the Paris Psalter were present neither in the prototype of the relevant Bible manuscripts nor in the archetype of the aristocratic Psalter which literally had copied its David scenes from these Bible manuscripts. The personifications, actively participating in the narrative, make their first appearance only in an advanced stage of the development of the Psalter; and it follows that in a stemma of this Psalter recension, the Paris manuscript would not represent the prototype from which all other manuscripts are derived[21] but rather would find its

[20] G. Stuhlfauth, "A Greek Psalter with Byzantine Miniatures," *Art Bulletin*, 15 (1933), 325 and fig. 13.

[21] This was G. Millet's considered judgment. G. Millet and S. Der Nersessian, "Le Psautier arménien," *Revue des Études Arméniennes*, 9 (1929), 167, 175, and 180, characterize the Paris Psalter as "l'ancêtre de toute une famille" and "l'oeuvre maîtresse dont tout dépend."

Fig. 166 *Berlin, Universität. Psalter, fol. 231^r.*
David and Goliath

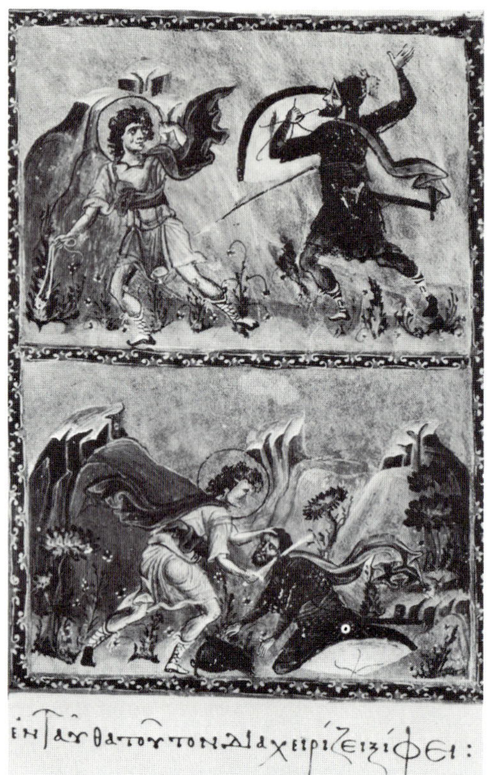

proper place in a branch of the stemma.

Charles Rufus Morey contested most vehemently our view of the Paris Psalter and the concept of the Macedonian Renaissance which it involves.[22] He went so far as to argue against the existence of the Byzantine Renaissance on the grounds of lack of evidence from preserved material. He confined himself to four manuscripts, of which he dated the two most important, the Paris Psalter and the closely related Joshua Roll, to the end of the seventh and the be-

ginning of the eighth century[23] and connected them with a survival of Hellenistic art in Alexandria and with the style of certain frescoes in S. Maria Antiqua in Rome. Instead of recapitulating the arguments against the early dating of these two key manuscripts,[24] which few at present would still maintain, it seems to us more profitable to raise the question whether or not the Paris Psalter really occupies such a vital position and whether the existence of a Middle Byzantine Renaissance depends on the evaluation of its style. Was it really only the whim of a Byzantine miniature painter who infused classical elements into a few biblical representations—in which case we would be dealing with the mere caprice of an antiquarian eccentric—or is it not possible, after all, that the Paris Psalter is the expression of a widely sustained effort to bring ancient art and literature into the cultural life of the ninth and tenth centuries?

THE ILLUSTRATION OF CLASSICAL TEXTS

For classical and Byzantine philologists, the art historian's question about the existence of a classical revival following the end of Iconoclasm must seem like tilting at windmills, because for them it

---

[22] C. R. Morey, "The 'Byzantine Renaissance,'" *Speculum,* 14 (1939), 139 ff.

[23] Morey had previously set forth his arguments for this dating in an article, "Notes on East Christian Miniatures," *Art Bulletin,* 11 (1929), 21 ff. The other two manuscripts which he mentions in the *Speculum* article are the Paris Gregory (Bibliothèque Nationale, cod. gr. 510), dating to the ninth century, and the Stauronikita Gospel (cod. 43), about which we shall have more to say. See pp. 199 ff.
[24] For the dating cf. Weitzmann, *The Joshua Roll. A Work of the Macedonian Renaissance* (Princeton, 1948), pp. 39 ff.

is a solid fact. In the year 963, when Caesar Bardas founded the university which bears his name, a chair for Homeric studies was established which was held by the grammarian Cometas about whom the Palatine Anthology—itself a tenth-century compilation of epigrams in the classical spirit—says, "Great-souled Homer, Cometas who found your books completely antiquated restored them to youth and after he had removed the dust of ages he presented them in new splendor to whomever understands such things" (XV, 37).[25] Furthermore, the subsequent epigram emphasizes that Cometas rejuventated Homer. At about the same time, the learned patriarch Photius wrote his *Myriobiblon*,[26] 280 critical essays and information about the contents of the books in his library, which contained almost as many classical as Christian texts. This activity represents the first phase of the classical revival which we would like to designate as the "collecting phase."

In his library Photius also had a mythological handbook, the *Bibliotheke* (volume 186), which he was the first to attribute to Apollodorus the Athenian grammarian of the second century B.C.,[27] though Carl Robert has shown that this book is not earlier than the Hadrianic period.[28]

Wilamowitz once said about the *Bibliotheke* that "from the ninth century on it was the handbook for ancient heroic legends"[29] because it can be shown that the *Bibliotheke* often was used by later Byzantine scholars.[30]

When we find a miniature (Fig. 118)[31] in a tenth-century manuscript in Paris (Bibliothèque Nationale, suppl. gr. 247) which is best elucidated by the text of Apollodorus, one naturally thinks of a connection between the miniature and the new popularity of this mythological text. The miniature shows giants whose legs terminate as snakes, a feature especially mentioned in Apollodorus. The style, by comparison with the giants of the very similar mosaic at Piazza Armerina dated to the fourth century (Fig. 119),[32] produces a more "painterly" and thereby a more classical effect, which leads to the conclusion that the source for the tenth-century miniature is earlier than the mosaic.

Remarkably enough, the giants miniature does not illustrate a mythological text but accompanies the *Theriaca* of Nicander of Colophon, a treatise on the antidotes for snake poisons, written in the

[25] *Anthologia graeca*, W. Paton (ed.) (London, 1926), 5:143.
[26] Photius, *Opera Omnia* ("Patrologiae cursus completus," J. P. Migne (ed.), 103/104 [Paris, 1860]); J. H. Freese, *The Library of Photius*, 1 (London, 1920).
[27] Apollodorus, *Bibliotheca*, J. C. Frazer (ed.), (London, 1921).
[28] C. Robert, *De Apollodori bibliotheca* (Berlin, 1873).

[29] "Sitzungsberichte der archäolog. Gesellschaft zu Berlin. Dezember, 1898," *Archäologischer Anzeiger*, 13 (1898), 228.
[30] Among others, by John Tzetzes in the twelfth century and John Pediasimos in the fourteenth century.
[31] Omont, *Manuscits grecs*, p. 40 and pl. LXVIII, 2.
[32] Weitzmann, "Das klassische Erbe in der Kunst Konstantinopels," *Antike und Neue Kunst. Wiener Kunstwissenschaftliche Blätter*, 3 (1954), 54 ff. and pl. VIII, 15–16. [Translated and reprinted herewith, pp. 126 ff.] Idem, "Survival of Mythological Representations," p. 49 and figs. 7–8.

second century B.C. Because this text does
not fully explain all the details in the
representation of the giants, we must
conclude that the miniature was borrowed
from another text, which most probably
was the *Bibliotheke* of Apollodorus. The
question is at what point was the mythological miniature taken over into the
medical-pharmaceutical text of Nicander?

We have a sixth-century paraphrase of
Nicander's text by a certain Eutecnius as
part of the famous Dioscurides herbal of
Juliana Anicia in the Vienna National
Library (cod. med. gr. 1 [Fig. 167]),[33]
and the illustrations of this text are
limited to pictures of snakes and creatures
with fatally poisonous bites and to the
plants used for healing venomous bites.
This same restriction to the bare necessi-
ties—so typical of ancient scientific
illustration—also characterizes the illustrations of a tenth-century luxury manuscript based on the Anicia codex in the
Morgan Library in New York.[34] In the
Dioscurides herbal, preserved in numerous copies, we meet the same situation:
in all the early manuscripts the illustrations are limited to pictures of plants,
and not until Middle Byzantine times
were human figures and explanatory

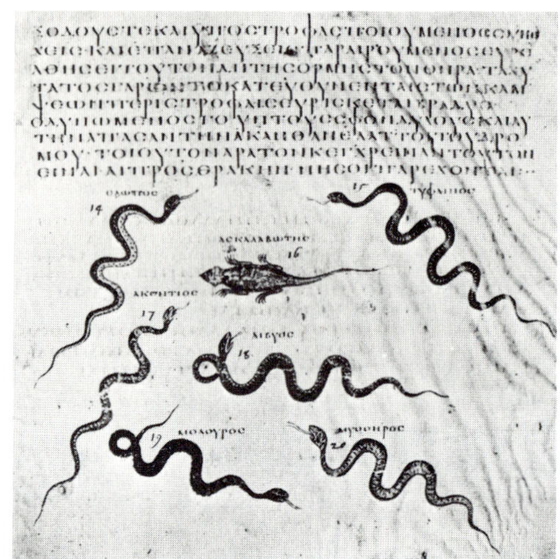

Fig. 167 *Vienna, Nationalbibliothek. Cod. med.
gr. 1, fol. 411ʳ. Snakes*

scenic representations added.[35] By
analogy we may assume that in the Paris
Nicander manuscript the giants miniature and several other scenes with mythological and bucolic content were not
added until the Middle Byzantine period,
not improbably appearing first in the
Paris codex. Thus, the Paris Nicander
manuscript is seen to be the product of
the same mental attitude as the Paris
Psalter, in that classical elements were
added to a set of traditional pictures.

Apart from the scattered mythological
miniatures in manuscripts such as the
Nicander, there is also an illustrated
Middle Byzantine mythological text,
namely a commentary to four homilies
of Gregory of Nazianzus, attributed to a

---

[33] A. von Premerstein, K. Wessely, and J.
Mantuani, *Dioscurides, Codex Aniciae Julianae,
picturis illustratus, nunc Vindobonensis Med. gr.
1., phototypice editus* (Leiden, 1906), fols. 393
ff.; P. Buberl, *Die byzantinischen Handschriften* ("Beschreibendes Verzeichnis der illuminierten Handschriften in Österreich," 8,
Part 4 [Leipzig, 1937]), I, 52 ff. [*Der Wiener
Dioscurides* (Codex Vindobonensis Med. gr. 1),
Introduction by H. Gerstinger (Graz, 1965)]
[34] Codex 652. *Pedanii Dioscuridis Anazarbaei
de Materia Medica* (Paris, 1935).

[35] Weitzmann, "The Greek Sources of Islamic Scientific Illustrations," *Archaeologica
Orientalia in Memoriam Ernst Herzfeld* (New
York, 1952), pp. 250 ff. [reprinted herewith,
pp. 20 ff.]; idem, *Ancient Book Illumination*
("Martin Classical Lectures," 16 [Cambridge,
1959]), pp. 15 ff.

certain Nonnus[36] and based to a large extent on the *Bibliotheke* of Apollodorus. Of the two illustrated manuscripts of this text, the better one in the Patriarchal Library in Jerusalem (cod. Taphou 14)[37] is dated to the second half of the eleventh century and adorned with illustrations which not only can be derived from ancient sources but which include details that can be elucidated better by the text of Apollodorus than by the text of Pseudo-Nonnus.[38] The chariot race of Pelops and Oenomaus is a typical example (Fig. 168).[39] In spite of the Byzantinizing garments, designed to look like imperial costume, the types and the composition can be associated with the classical tradition represented on Roman sarcophagi. In this eleventh-century miniature not much is left of the feeling for classical style which characterizes the tenth-century giants miniature; and this indicates that the lively response to ancient art, experienced in the tenth century, had diminished and stiffened by the eleventh century. A somewhat earlier ivory relief in the Archaeological Museum in Madrid (Fig. 169),[40] dating to the end of the tenth or early eleventh century, demonstrates that we are indeed justified

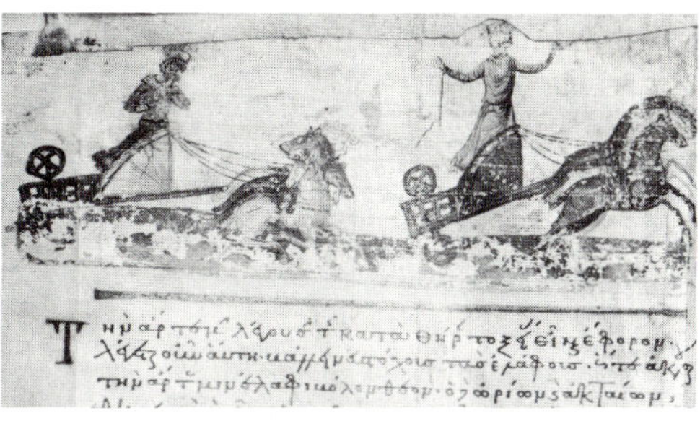

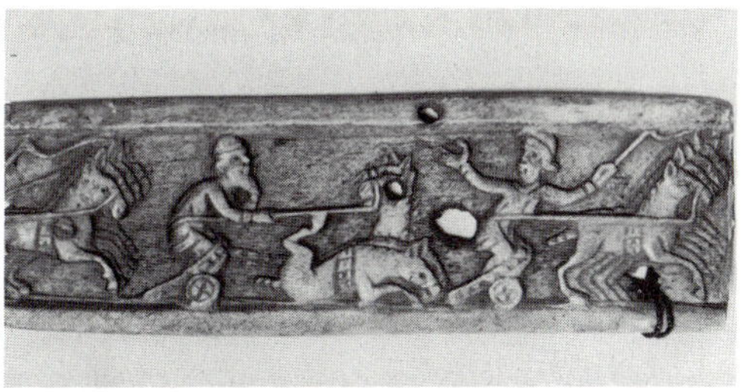

Fig. 168 *Jerusalem, Patriarchal Library. Cod. Taphou 14, fol. 307ᵛ. Pelops and Oenomaus*
Fig. 169 *Madrid, Museo Arqueológico. Ivory Relief. Pelops and Oenomaus*

in assuming classical sources for the Jerusalem miniatures, because the ivory figures, in spite of their putti-like appearance, are relatively closer in style to an earlier renaissance version. During this period, mythological scenes occasionally also occur in the Latin West, but we may be certain that their content was still better understood in Byzantium because of the closer connection with the mythological texts.

The initial phase of collecting ancient texts was followed by the second, which we may call the "consolidating phase." Not only did material continue to be collected even more systematically than heretofore, but new and improved editions of the texts were produced. The most outstanding representative of this second phase is Arethas, the learned bishop of Caesarea and student of Photius.[41] Certain texts in which Arethas

---

[36] E. Patzig, *De Nonnianis in IV orationes Gregorii Nazianzeni commentariis* ("Jahresbericht der Thomasschule in Leipzig" [Leipzig, 1890]).

[37] Weitzmann, *Greek Mythology in Byzantine Art* (Princeton, 1951), pp. 9 ff.

[38] Ibid., pp. 74 ff.

[39] Ibid., p. 12, p. 81 and pl. II, 2.

[40] A. Goldschmidt and K. Weitzmann, *Die byzantinischen Elfenbeinskulpturen des X. bis XIII. Jahrhunderts* (Berlin, 1930–34), 1:41 and pl. XXV, 46; Weitzmann, *Greek Mythology*, p. 154 and pl. XLVI, 167.

[41] We owe the most comprehensive study on Arethas to S. V. Kougeas, Ὁ Καισαρείας

took an interest were not to be found in Constantinople either because they had been destroyed during the period of Iconoclasm or because they had never existed in Constantinople. Correctly concluding that papyrus rolls would furnish older and better versions of the texts, he sent agents to Egypt and Syria to seek such rolls; and he, himself, went to Syria at the behest of the emperors Leo the Wise and Romanus Lecapenus, both of whom were patrons of this campaign to acquire books. In a well-organized scriptorium where Arethas was the προιστάμενος, copies of these texts with an extensive apparatus of commentaries in the wide margins were made. We actually know the names of several scribes who worked in this scriptorium; and we have a whole series of the copies which they made—the earliest complete texts of the classics that have been preserved (only papyrus fragments have survived from earlier centuries). Stephanos produced the Oxford Euclid dated A.D. 888, the calligrapher John did the two Plato manuscripts in Oxford (one of them dates from A.D. 895), a Vatican Aristides manuscript from 907, and an Athenaeus in Venice. A certain Gregorios copied the *Categoriae* of Aristotle around 901; Baanes did the London Lucian, and so on. A page of the Vatican Aristotle manuscript (codex Urb. grec. 35 [Fig. 170])[42] may serve to give an idea

of these carefully written texts, for whose large-scale production, the minuscule, increasingly employed at this time, was the suitable script.[43] Occasionally text and commentary were provided with explanatory sketches with decorative flourishes which did not originate in contemporary ornamentation but which find their closest parallels in ancient vase-painting and to all appearances go back to the unpretentious but elegant vignettes in ancient papyri. The pursuit of learning in Byzantium begins with editions of texts such as these; and this undertaking brought forth a virtually unbroken series of outstanding learned men and philologists from Arethas to Bessarion in the fifteenth century.

The famous earliest Iliad manuscript, codex Venetus A, Marciana gr. 454 (Fig. 171),[44] has been connected with Arethas[45] and, more recently, even has been attributed directly to him.[46] It can be dated in the first half of the tenth century[47] not only on paleographic grounds,

---

ʼΑρέθας καὶ τὸ ἔργον αὐτοῦ (Athens, 1913), which forms, in the main, the basis for our statements. Cf. pp. 107 ff., pp. 114 ff. and *passim*.

[42] Ibid., p. 100; L. Lefort and J. Cochez, *Palaegraphisch Album* ("Tydschrift voor classieke philologie. Université catholique, Louvain," 1 [Louvain, 1932]), pl. 13.

[43] Dain has made it clear, however, that the minuscule script was not invented for the purpose of transcribing classical texts but had existed earlier. Cf. A. Dain, "La transmission des textes littéraires classiques de Photius à Constantin Porphyrogénète," *Dumbarton Oaks Papers*, 8 (1954), 36 ff.

[44] Dom. Comparetti, *Homeri Ilias cum scholiis, Codices Graeci et Latini*, Tom. VI (Leiden, 1901), fol. 12ʳ.

[45] Kougeas, ʼΑρέθας, p. 102.

[46] A. Severyns, "Aréthas et le Venetus d'Homère," *Bulletin Royale de Belgique. Classe des Lettres, Sciences, Morales et Politiques*, 5ᵉ serie, 37 (1951), 279 ff.

[47] Weitzmann, *Die byzantinische Buchmalerei des 9. und 10. Jahrhunderts* (Berlin, 1935), p. 58. Dain, "Transmission des textes," p. 45, dates the beginning of the copying of poetical texts around 960 at the earliest. If our dating

Fig. 170 *Vatican, Biblioteca. Cod. Urb. gr. 35, fol. 23ʳ. Aristotle*

Fig. 171 *Venice, Marciana. Cod. gr. 454, fol. 12ʳ. Iliad*

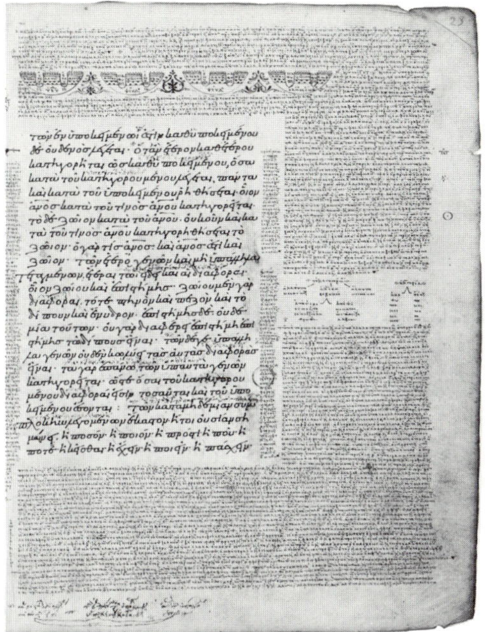

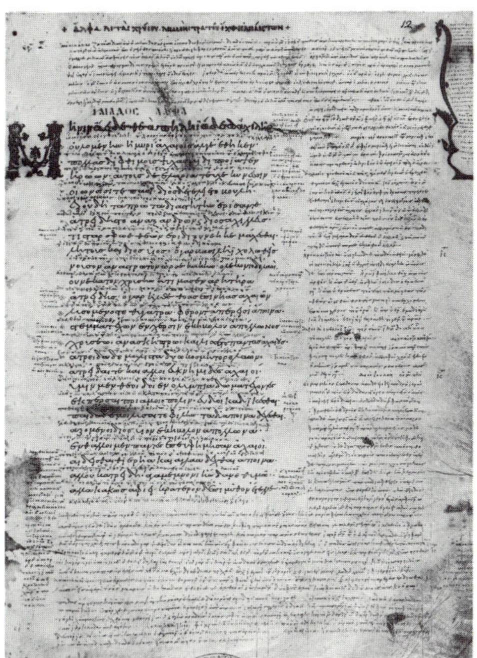

but specifically because of the "jigsaw" decoration which is typical of this period; and it shows that the interest in Homer, newly kindled by the grammarian Cometas, had born fruit and had resulted in a scholarly text edition. The Venetus A manuscript was not meant to be illustrated,[48] however; and the sudden appearance of Iliad illustrations in tenth- and eleventh-century Byzantine art can only be explained by supposing that there existed an illustrated Iliad among the copies of ancient texts associated with Arethas' activities. In an eleventh-century manuscript in Venice (Marciana

gr. 479) of the *Cynegetica* attributed to Oppian, there is a representation of the scene from the nineteenth book of the Iliad (Fig. 120)[49] where the talking horse Xanthus warns Achilles against going into battle. Here again parallels in classical art such as a Pompeian fresco in the Casa di Loreio Tiburtino[50] show that we are dealing with an ancient pictorial tradition and not with a Byzantine invention. The *Cynegetica* is a didactic poem dedicated to the Emperor Caracalla, the archetype of which certainly

---

of the Venetus A is correct, one would have to assume that these texts began to be copied somewhat earlier than 960.

[48] The illustrations on fols. 1ʳ–9ᵛ in Venetus A (Comparetti, *Ilias cum scholiis,*) do not go with the text of the Iliad; they illustrate the preceding *Chrestomathis* of Proclus and belong

to a considerably later period, approximately to the fifteenth century. Cf. Weitzmann, "Survival of Mythological Representations," p. 56 and fig. 22.

[49] Weitzmann, *Greek Mythology*, pp. 98 ff. and pl. XXX, 103; idem, "Klassische Erbe," p. 55 and pl. IX, 17 [reprinted herewith, p. 141].

[50] *Greek Mythology*, pl. XXX, 107.

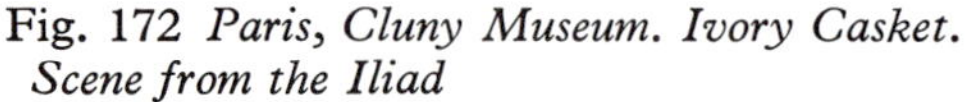

Fig. 172 *Paris, Cluny Museum. Ivory Casket.*
Scene from the Iliad

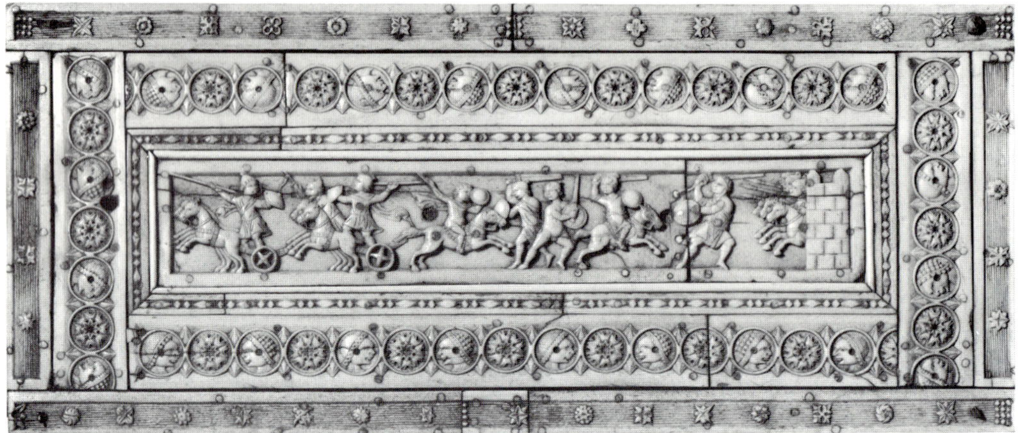

had illustrations having to do with hunting. By analogy with the Nicander manuscript considered above, the mythological scenes must be considered later insertions which, we would suppose, were made for the first time during the period between Arethas and the Venice manuscript, i.e., in the tenth century. It is also possible to point out echoes of an illustrated Iliad in tenth-century ivories which are dependent on miniatures. A rosette casket in the Cluny Museum in Paris (Fig. 172),[51] has among other representations a scene from the eleventh book of Hector forcing Diomedes to retreat.

This Oppian manuscript also contains several scenes from Euripidean tragedies (Fig. 173),[52] of which those referring to

the *Peliades* and the *Medea* in the lower frieze are easily identifiable; one depicts the ill-fated attempt, made on Medea's advice, to rejuvenate the old father; and the other presents the infanticide of the infamous sorceress. The scenes on the upper frieze refer to the *Aegeus* and the *Ion.* The fact that, of the four tragedies mentioned, only the *Medea* is preserved, is important. There are indications that in Middle Byzantine times more Euripidean tragedies were known than the few that survive today in the selection supposedly made during the third century for school use.[53] The Oppian manuscript furnishes proof that there must have been several illustrated Euripides manuscripts from which copies could have been made. To be sure, no Euripides from Arethas' times is preserved and, apart from a tenth-century fragment in Jerusalem, the earliest and

[51] Ibid., p. 168 and pl. LIII, 212; Goldschmidt and Weitzmann, *Elfenbeinskulpturen,* I, p. 39 and pl. XXIII, 41a.

[52] Discussed in detail in Weitzmann, "Euripides Scenes in Byzantine Art," *Hesperia,* 18 (1949), 159 ff. and pls. 25–26. Cf. idem, *Greek Mythology,* p. 131 and pl. XLIV, 159; and idem, "Klassische Erbe," p. 55 and fig. 17 [herewith reprinted, p. 141. Also, idem, "Eine

Darstellung der Euripideischen Iphigenie auf einem koptischen Stoff," *Antike Kunst,* 7 (1964), 42 ff.].
[53] U. von Wilamowitz-Moellendorf, *Einleitung in die griechische Tragödie* (Berlin, 1907), p. 210.

Fig. 173 *Venice, Marciana. Cod. gr. 479, fol. 47ᵣ. Euripidean Tragedies*

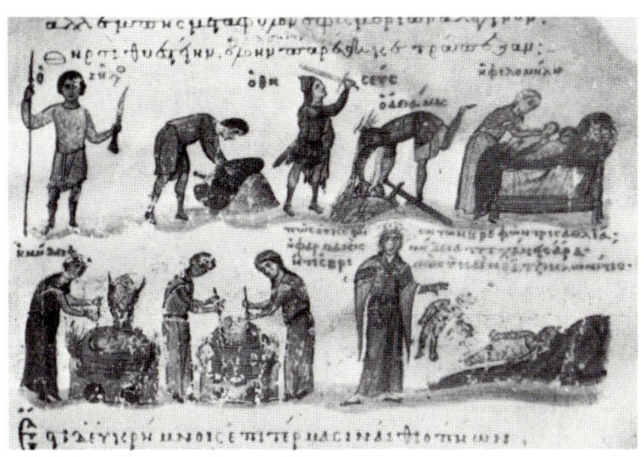

most important manuscript (Marciana cod. gr. 471 [=M]), is not earlier than the twelfth century. The most significant clue to the situation prevailing in the transmission of classical literary texts has been provided by Alexander Turyn, the outstanding expert for the text transmission of Euripides, who postulated a medieval edition (the σ in his stemma) which must have been made in the ninth/tenth century in the time of Photius and Arethas and was based on the edition produced in the third century.[54] The Oppian miniature and other works of art support Turyn's thesis; they help to fill in the gap in our knowledge of tenth- and eleventh-century texts; and they indicate that Euripides illustrations were fairly widespread at this time.

The rosette ivory caskets once again fill the gap for the tenth century. The most famous of these ivory carvings is the often discussed representation of the sacrifice of Iphigenia on the Veroli casket in the Victoria and Albert Museum in London (Fig. 121), one of the very

few Byzantine artifacts to which the classical archeologists have paid attention, particularly because it has a classical parallel in the so-called Ara of Cleomenes in the Uffizi (Fig. 122).[55] In these ivory relief figures, it is possible to detect the beginnings of a transformation which turned the figures in the miniatures of the prototypes into putti-like creatures intended for decorative purposes; nevertheless, the classical types still lead a a vigorous existence in this representation, and one may guess that the miniature prototype for the Iphigenia reliefs was in no way inferior in style to the giants miniature of the Nicander manuscript (Fig. 118).

In demonstrating that in the time of the Macedonian Renaissance illustrated exemplars of a mythological handbook of the Iliad and of Euripidean drama were copied and their illustrations taken over into other texts by no means have we exhausted the repertoire of classical illustrated texts with literary content. Other heroic epics, bucolic poetry, and the Alexander Romance are only a few of the texts with illustrations that turn up in Middle Byzantine book illumination; and we gain the impression that the classical revival was carried out on a broad basis in writing and in painting.

[54] A. Turyn, *The Byzantine Manuscript Tradition of the Tragedies of Euripides* ("Illinois Studies in Language and Literature," 43 [Urbana, 1957]), 311.

[55] Cf. E. Löwy, "Der Schluss der Iphigenie in Aulis," *Jahreshefte des österreichischen archäologischen Instituts in Wien*, 24 (1929), 4 and fig. 3; Goldschmidt and Weitzmann, *Elfenbeinskulpturen*, 1:31 and pl. IX, 21b; Weitzmann, "Euripides Scenes," p. 177 and pls. 27-28; idem, *Byzantine Mythology*, p. 169 and pl. LIV, 214-18; John Beckwith, *The Veroli Casket* (London, 1962). [E. Simon, "Nonnos und das Elfenbeinkästchen aus Veroli," *Jahrbuch des deutschen archäologischen Instituts*, 79 (1964), 279 ff.]

Necessary conditions for the large-scale production of classical texts existed at the moment the center of patronage shifted from the academy of the patriarchate to the imperial court. In this third phase of the renaissance which we would like to call the "expanding phase," the *spiritus rector* of an extensive plan for editing texts was none other than the emperor himself, Constantine VII Porphyrogenitus, the scholar on the throne.[56] An able writer like his grandfather Basil I whose *Vita* is one of the best writings of the tenth century,[57] Constantine VII is associated particularly with the preparation of comprehensive encyclopedias, clearly intended not only to renew knowledge of ancient writings but also to create a new basis for future scholarship and, at the same time, to make this knowledge available to a wider audience.

We know of three such encyclopedias associated with the name of the Emperor Constantine Porphyrogenitus. The first one deals with treatises on military tactics, for example the Τακτικά of Aelian, the text of which is illustrated with diagrams as we know from an eleventh-century exemplar in the Vatican (cod. gr. 1164 [Fig. 174]).[58] These dia-

grams have a system for indicating various types of troops with different symbols, scientific illustration in its purest form, typical of the classical period.[59] These symbols were first replaced by little figures of soldiers in the renaissance manuscript of Vergetius,[60] thus transforming a manuscript intended for purely practical purposes into a display copy, a type of change, which in many other cases, for instance the Nicander manuscript mentioned above and several Dioscurides manuscripts, had already occurred in Middle Byzantine times.[61]

The second encyclopedic collection deals with treatises on agriculture, the

[56] A. Rambaud, *L'empire grec au dixième siècle. Constantin Porphyrogénète*: 2, "Histoire littéraire" (Paris, 1870), 51 ff.; A. Dain, "L'encyclopédisme de Constantin Porphyrogénète," *Bulletin de l'Association G. Budé. Lettres d'Humanité*, 12 (1953), 64 ff.

[57] R. J. H. Jenkins, "The Classical Background of the Scriptores post Theophanem," *Dumbarton Oaks Papers*, 8 (1954), 11 ff. One of the influences on the imperial author Jenkins points out here is that of Isocrates.

[58] A. Dain, *Histoire du texte d'Élien le Tacticien. Des origines à la fin du Moyen Age* (Paris, 1946).

[59] For the nature of ancient scientific illustration in general see chap. I, "Scientific and Didactic Treatises" in Weitzmann, *Ancient Book Illumination*.

[60] Paris, Bibliothèque Nationale, cod. gr. 2523, dated 1564, and the undated manuscript cod. gr. 2525. Cf. A. Dain, "Les manuscrits des Constitutions Tactiques," *Scriptorium*, 1 (1946), 48.

[61] In distinction to the manuscript in Florence (Laurenziana, cod. Plut. LV, 4) which is as early as the tenth century which has Aelian's text bound together with other treatises on tactics, the Vatican manuscript is a compendium comprising a whole series of treatises on the science of besieging cities (poliorcetica), such as Athenaeus, Biton, Heron of Alexandria, Apollodorus of Damascus, etc. These treatises too are illustrated with drawings showing how to construct and how to operate machines ready for use. Whereas the purely classical type of scientific illustration is used in the Vatican manuscript, on the other hand there are Middle Byzantine treatises on the subject of sieges with human figures working the machines. C. Wescher, *Poliorcétique des grecs* (Paris, 1867); Weitzmann, "Islamic Scientific Illustrations," p. 245 [reprinted herewith, p. 20].

Fig. 174 *Vatican, Biblioteca. Cod. gr. 1164, fol. 8ʳ. Aelian*

Fig. 175 *Florence, Laurenziana. Cod. Plut. LIX, 32, fol. 11ʳ. Geoponica*

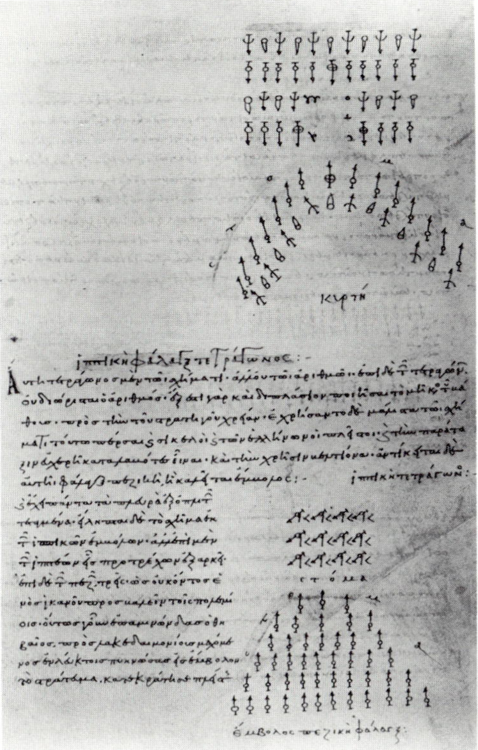

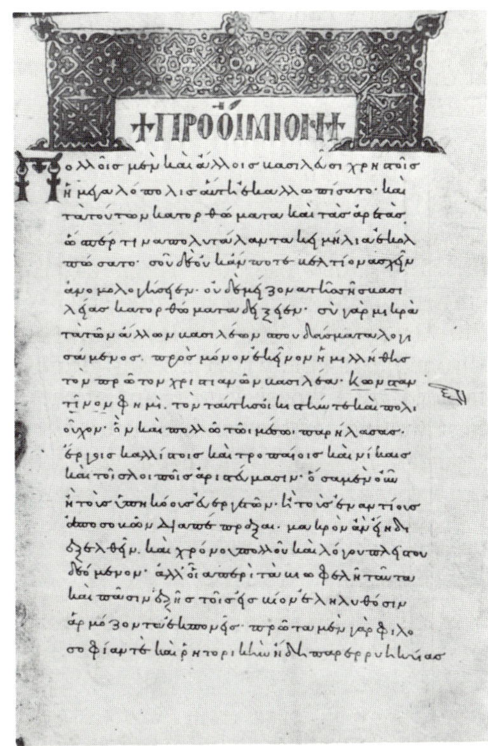

so-called *Geoponica*.[62] As we know from the script and from the typical "jigsaw" decoration of the heading on the title page, the earliest copy in Florence (Laurenziana cod. Plut. LIX, 32 [Fig. 175]),[63] falls in the period of the Emperor Constantine.[64] One must ask whether this manuscript could not be the exemplar dedicated to the emperor, for it is the only one of about forty copies which contains the important preface which extols the emperor for sponsoring a restoration of all the arts and sciences —καινισμός is the expression here used for renaissance.[65]

This is not an isolated statement; it expresses the contemporary view of the emperor as the patron of the renaissance movement, as we learn from a similar homage in the prologue of the *Chronographia* of Theophanes Continuatus where the terms παλινζωία and παλιγγενεσία are used for the emperor's endeavors to create a classical revival.[66] It is only the

[62] Constantine VII Porphyrogenitus, *Geoponica*. H. Beckh (ed.) (Leipzig, 1895).

[63] A. Bandini, *Catalogus codicum manuscriptorum Bibliothecae mediciae laurentianae*, 2 (Florence, 1764–70), col. 554.

[64] For the dating of this type of decoration see Weitzmann, *Byzantinische Buchmalerei*, pp. 118 ff. and pls. XXII–XXVIII.

[65] ἔπειτα δὲ καὶ πᾶσαν ἄλλην ἐπιστήμην τε καὶ τέχνην πρὸς καινισμὸν ἐπανήγαγες.

[66] *Patrologiae cursus completus*, J. P. Migne [ed.], 109, col. 16. καὶ τοῦτο πάντως τῶν σῶν, ὦ φιλοσφώτατε βασιλεῦ, καλῶν, μετάγε

fact that the Florentine *Geoponica* manuscript lacks the elegant script and the refined ornament which one would expect to find in the exemplar dedicated to the emperor that speaks against its being such a copy.

It would appear, however, that a dedication copy has been preserved among the medical manuscripts associated with the third encyclopedia. The Berlin Library possesses the earliest copy of the *Hippiatrica* (cod. Phill. 1538) a veterinary's handbook on the treatment of ailing horses (Fig. 176),[67] a codex which is a real luxury manuscript, written in an affected, elegant minuscule and brilliantly decorated with imitations of cloisonné enamels. In the first publication, this manuscript was associated with Constantine Porphyrogenitus,[68] but later scholars have dated it in the ninth century and have connected it with Michael III.[69] Since the type of ornament allows of no dating other than the middle of the tenth century,[70] the case is decided in favor of

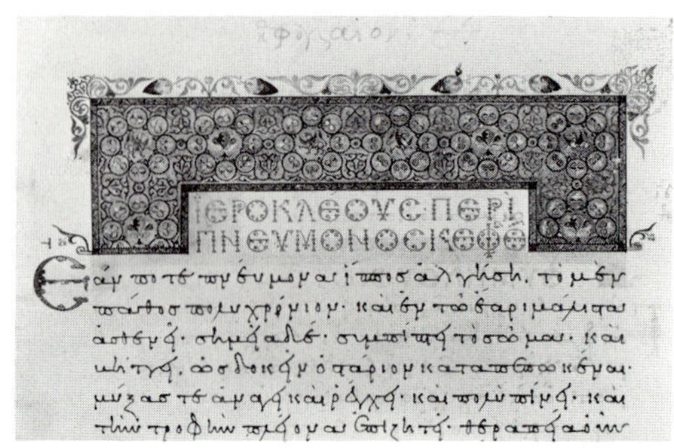

Fig. 176 *Berlin, Staatsbibliothek. Cod. Phill. 1538, fol. 29*[r]. *Hippiatrica*

Constantine. Only one thing is lacking in the Berlin manuscript, which in all other respects must have met the high standards of the cultivated bibliophile emperor, and that is the illustrations which are almost indispensable for scientific treatises of this nature. In some later *Hippiatrica* manuscripts, for instance in a fourteenth-century manuscript in Paris (Bibliothèque Nationale cod. gr. 2244), there are, in fact, very lively illustrations of the treatment of sick horses (Fig. 177);[71] and there is no reason to doubt that these go back to a classical archetype. Since the dedicatory poem at the beginning is missing in the Berlin manuscript, it is entirely possible that the text was once preceded by a set of illustrations, now lost. In medical manuscripts miniatures are often separated from the text and put together at the beginning, presumably because it made them easier to use for teaching purposes.[72] If the Berlin manuscript

---

πολλῶν ἄλλων τε καὶ μεγάλων, τὸ τὰ τῷ χρόνῳ παραρρυέντα καὶ κεχωρηκότα πρὸς τὸ μὴ ὂν πρὸς παλινζωΐαν αὖθις καὶ παλιγγενεσίαν ἀναγαγεῖν, καὶ τοῦ τῆς ἱστορίας ἐπιμεληθῆναι καλοῦ, ἀλλὰ μὴ τοῖς πρὸ τοῦ τὴν βασιλικὴν ἐπειλημμένοις ἀμεληθῆναι ἀρχήν.

[67] J. Kirchner, *Beschreibendes Verzeichnis der Miniaturhandschriften der preussischen Staatsbibliothek zu Berlin* (Leipzig, 1926–28), I Phillipps Handschriften, pp. 16 ff.

[68] L. Cohn, "Bermerkungen zu den konstantinischen Stammelwerken," *Byzantinische Zeitschrift*, 9 (1900), 158 ff.

[69] E. Oder, "Beiträge zur Geschichte der Landwirtschaft bei den Griechen, III," *Rheinisches Museum für Philologie*, 48 (1893), 33 ff.; E. Oder and C. Hoppe, *Corpus Hippiatricorum Graecorum* (Leipzig, 1924).

[70] Weitzmann, *Byzantinische Buchmalerei*, pp. 16 ff. and pls. XIX–XXI.

[71] M. Laignel-Lavastine, *Histoire générale de la médecine*, 1 (Paris, 1936–49), 652; Weitzmann, *Ancient Book Illumination*, p. 22 and pl. XIII, 27.

[72] For several examples see K. Sudhoff, *Beiträge zur Geschichte der Chirurgie im Mittelalter* (Leipzig, 1914).

Fig. 177 *Paris, Bibliothèque Nationale. Cod. gr. 2244, fol. 54ʳ. Hippiatrica*

Fig. 178 *Florence, Laurenziana. Cod. Plut. LXXIV, 7, fol. 197ʳ. Apollonius of Citium*

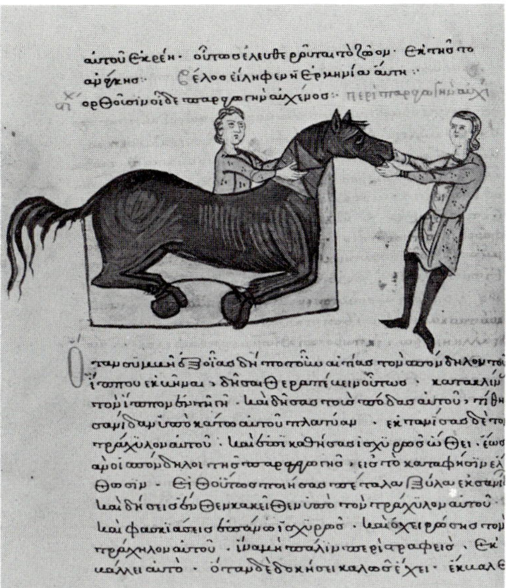

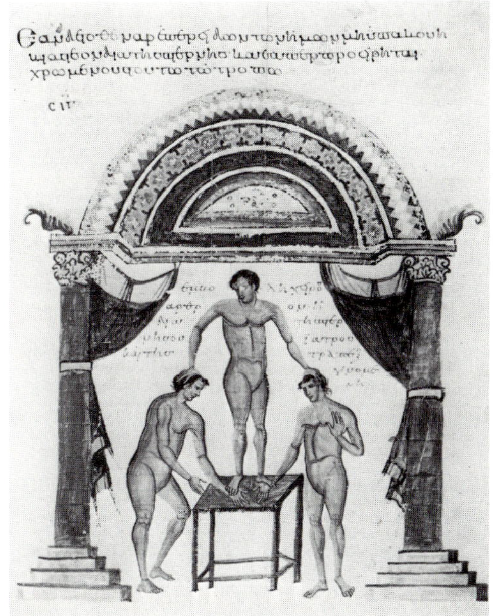

ever had pictures, they were surely of a quality far superior to that of the Paris manuscript and in a more purely classical style, as may be judged from the style of another medical manuscript.

Among the numerous Greek manuscripts of this period, a medical compendium in the Laurentian Library in Florence (codex Plut. LXXIV, 7) containing various treatises on Hippocratic methods of treatment by approximately a dozen authors may be considered as a product of the imperial scriptorium. Two of these treatises are illustrated: the book on dislocations of bones (περὶ ἄρθρων) by Apollonius of Citium (Fig. 178),[73] and another on the application

of bandages (περὶ ἐπιδέσμων) by Soranus of Ephesus.[74] Three epigrams precede the text; and because they are by three different hands, they are rightly considered to be autographs. Schöne, the editor of the Apollonius text, has held that one of them, praising for his services a physician named Nicetas, is an autograph of the emperor. The style of the miniatures dates the manuscript to about the second quarter of the tenth century and, thus, the emperor in question can once again only be Constantine Porphyrogenitus. In one of the Apollonius miniatures showing the setting of the wrist bone, the doctor standing on a table and the two patients are naked and, in conformity with the spirit of the

[73] H. Schöne, *Apollonius von Kitium* (Leipzig, 1896). Weitzmann, *Byzantinische Buchmalerei*, p. 33 and pl. XLI, 227; idem, "Klassische Erbe," p. 52 and fig. 13 [translated and reprinted herewith, p. 140]; idem, *Ancient Book Illumination*, p. 21 and pl. XIII, 26.

[74] Sudhoff, *Chirurgie*, p. 5 and figs. 1–4; J. Ilberg, *Soranus* ("Corpus Medicorum Graecorum," 4 [Leipzig, 1927]); Weitzmann, *Ancient Book Illumination*, p. 19 and pl. XI, 22.

Byzantine age, are shown sexless.

Although the figures, which are rendered in a wholly classical, "painterly" style, certainly go back to a classical archetype, the framing arch is a decorative element which was surely not present in the prototype, a papyrus roll of the first century B.C.[75] Whereas the individual patterns have their parallels in floor mosaics of the fifth/sixth century, the structure of the arch is so similar to that of canon tables in Middle Byzantine Gospels that we would like to assume a direct borrowing from a tenth-century Gospels. The curtains, fastened to the solid porphyry columns with Corinthian capitals, are an unusual feature of the arched frame in the Florentine manuscript. This motif is repeated on canon table arches, and the best example from a tenth-century manuscript is in an Ethiopian Gospel in Abba Garima (Fig. 179)[76] which has copied the Greek source with a considerable degree of precision. This motif is particularly important because it indicates the architectural milieu from which the structure was taken. These are the curtains which were hung on the sumptuous columns in

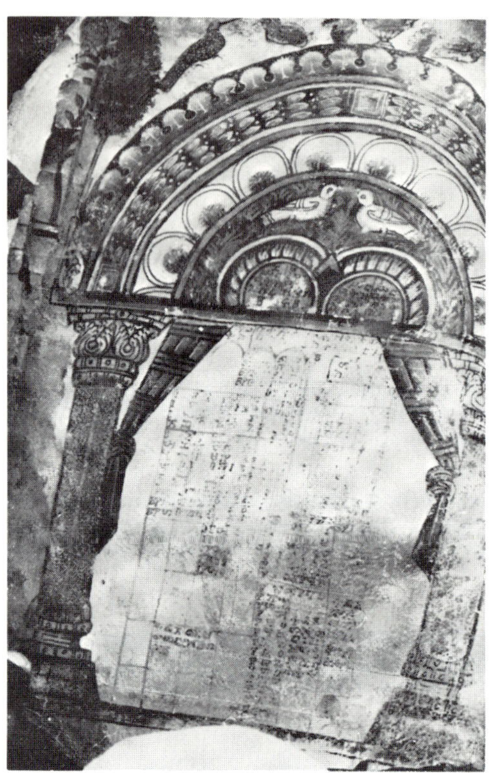

Fig. 179 *Convent of Abba Garima. Gospels. Canon Table*

front of the *porta regia* of the Roman *scenae frons*. The background of a picture of Mark in a tenth-century Gospel in Oxford (Bodl. cod. Auct. E.V.11 [Fig. 90])[77] clearly shows the columns and curtains above the proscenium wall; the evangelist sits in a niche in this wall like the statues of poets which were set up in the same place in ancient theaters.[78]

---

[75] See Weitzmann, *Roll and Codex*, p. 108 and fig. F which, in an effort to reconstruct the original state of the papyrus illustration, presents a sketch of the model without the arcade. [Idem, "Book Illustration of the Fourth Century: Tradition and Innovation." *Akten des VII. Internationalen Kongresses für Christliche Archäologie, Trier, 1965* (Rome, 1969), pp. 257 ff., reprinted herewith, pp. 96 ff.]

[76] J. Leroy, "L'évangeliaire Éthiopien du couvent d'Abba Garima," *Cahiers Archéologiques*, 11 (1960), 131 ff. [idem, "Un nouvel évangeliaire éthiopian illustré du monastère d'Abba Garima," *Synthronon* ("Bibliothèque des Cahiers Archéologiques," 2 [Paris, 1968]), 75 ff.].

[77] Weitzmann, *Byzantinische Buchmalerei*, p. 18 and pl. XXII, 120.

[78] For theater backgrounds in Byzantine portraits of the evangelists cf. A. M. Friend, Jr., "Portraits of the Evangelists in Greek and Latin Manuscripts," *Art Studies*, 2 (1929), 9 ff. [Weitzmann, "Book Illustration of the Fourth Century," pp. 269 ff., reprinted herewith, pp. 112 ff.].

By far the best example of such a *scenae frons* is preserved in a picture of Mark in a Gospel in the Monastery of Philotheu on Mount Athos (cod. 33 [Fig. 89]),[79] dated approximately to the early tenth century. Towering above the proscenium wall, here somewhat atrophied, is the *scenae frons* with its separate inset consisting of two larger columns of variegated marble and a pediment decorated with a scallop shell on a bent architrave. This is a typical feature of the Roman *scenae frons* particularly in the theaters of North Africa, for instance at Dugga.[80]

We are now able to explain how the framing arch became an established feature in the Apollonius illustrations of the Florence manuscript (Fig. 178). During the Macedonian Renaissance early pictures of the evangelists with theater backgrounds were copied; and at the same time the central motif of ornamental columns with curtains was used to give the canon arches a more classical appearance than they had had in the Gospels of the sixth to seventh centuries.[81] The illustrator of a medical

manuscript then borrowed such widely known canon arcades for no other reason than to enrich the decoration of his picture. Hence, it follows with regard to the medical manuscript that the originally plain illustrations in scientific treatises were enriched with additions, a common procedure in manuscripts of the Macedonian Renaissance. Furthermore, it could be demonstrated that decorative pagan motifs like the *scenae frons* were not only used in Gospel books as backgrounds for the evangelists and canon tables, but that these motifs had a retroactive influence from a Gospel book back into a classical text.

Because of the elaborate embellishments lavished on some of the scientific treatises of the tenth century, they are no less important for the history of the Macedonian Renaissance than are the illustrations of literary texts. There is an important difference, however, in the history of the transmission. Whereas very early sources are indicated for the literary texts, as was clearly noticeable in the case of the giants miniature which goes back to a source earlier than the third century, for the scientific treatises almost invariably one must assume that there was an intermediate stage around the fifth and sixth centuries, at a time when, as in the Macedonian Renaissance, there were vigorous attempts at making encyclopedias. In the case of Aelian, Dain has pointed out the "Minor Aelian corpus" of the fourth/fifth century;[82] the *Geoponica* is based on a collection of the same name which was compiled by a certain Cassianus Bassus in the sixth

[79] Cf. Weitzmann, *Byzantinische Buchmalerei*, p. 46 and pl. LI, 302, where an attempt is made to place the provenance in Asia Minor. We no longer maintain this but prefer a Constantinopolitan origin for the Athos manuscript and for the Joshua Roll which is related in style. It is this connection with the Joshua Roll which justifies dating the Philotheu evangelist in the tenth century.

[80] M. Bieber, *The History of the Greek and Roman Theater* (2d ed.; Princeton, 1961), pp. 204 ff. and pls. 689 ff.

[81] Cf. the fragments of fine canon arcades of the pre-iconoclastic period, conjecturally of the seventh century, in London (British Museum, cod. Add. 5111); C. Nordenfalk, *Die spätantiken Kanontafeln* (Göteborg, 1938), pp. 127 ff. and pls. 1–4.

[82] Dain, *Elien le Tacticien*, pp. 68 ff.

century;[83] and the work of Hierocles who lived in the fifth or sixth century forms the intermediary link for the veterinary manuscripts.[84] Therefore, it is more than probable that most scientific illustrations are based on manuscripts of this intermediate period during which the illustrators, as we well know from the famous Dioscurides herbal of Juliana Anicia in Vienna,[85] were so competent at reproducing the classical heritage that scholars are beginning to use the expression "Justinianic Renaissance."[86]

The illustrations of classical texts have purposely been treated here at some length because they reveal with special clarity the nature of the Macedonian Renaissance; they disclose its sources; and they provide a clear view of the different phases of its historical development. Above, we spoke of the three phases: *preparation, consolidation,* and *expansion.* These correspond more or less to a natural morphological process, and it will scarcely be a surprise to discover that there was a very similar development under similar circumstances in Alexandria more than a millennium earlier.[87] When Ptolemy I called Demetrius of Phaleron to the newly founded metropolis on the Canopic Nile, he gave him a free hand to collect on a large scale books of all periods, from Homer to contemporary literature, for the library which he was about to establish. This phase of collecting corresponds to the activity of Photius who, like Demetrius, was both a scholar and statesman. Demetrius' successor, Zenodotus, the first librarian of the museum library, represents the consolidating phase. He was the first to make an ἔκδοσις, that is an edition, of the Homeric poems; and he was the first to divide them into 24 books. Would it not be natural to compare his activity with that of Arethas, to whom the codex Venetus A has recently been attributed? Callimachus and Eratosthenes are outstanding among the successors of Zenodotus; under them the great library catalogue in 120 volumes, the so-called *Pinakes,* was begun with the idea of making the accumulated writings available to the specialist as well as to the general public. Eratosthenes, the first to call himself φιλόλογος, wrote about Attic comedy, geography, mathematics, and astronomy; and thus he represents a type of scholar, not unlike those who worked together with Constantine Porphyrogenitus to make encyclopedias, under imperial patronage similar to that of the Ptolemies.

---

[83] K. Krumbacher, *Geschichte der byzan-. tinischen Literatur* (2d ed., Munich, 1897), pp. 261 ff.

[84] Oder and Hoppe, *Corpus Hippiatricorum Graecorum.*

[85] The author has shown in "Klassische Erbe," pp. 49 ff. and figs. 8–10 [reprinted herewith, pp. 136 ff. and Figs. 111–13], how the pictures of plants in the period following the Anicia codex became artistically inferior and then are truer to nature again in the tenth century under the direct influence of the Anicia codex.

[86] E. Kitzinger, "Mosaic Pavements in the Greek East and the Question of a 'Renaissance' under Justinian," *Actes du VIIme Congrès International d'Études Byzantines Paris, 1948* (Paris, 1951), pp. 209 ff.

[87] The following observations on the activity of the Alexandrian scholars are mainly based on F. Susemihl, *Geschichte der griechischen Literatur in der Alexandrinerzeit* (Leipzig, 1891); cf. E. A. Parsons, *The Alexandrian Library, Glory of the Hellenic World* (Amsterdam, 1952).

The artistic interests of the emperor explain why the art of illustration apparently was the object of particular attention in the imperial scriptorium under the patronage of Constantine Porphyrogenitus. Such varied historical sources as Theophanes Continuatus,[88] Sigebert of Gembloux,[89] and Liudprand of Cremona[90] are unanimous not only in praising Constantine Porphyrogenitus for his interest in the arts but also in extolling him as a practicing artist. Here I would like to quote Liudprand: "Constantine spent his spare time in conversation and reading . . . and he sought to maintain himself by means of his own handiwork. ζωγραφία, that is painting, he exercised most beautifully." Whatever his own artistic accomplishments may have been, it is extremely likely, at any rate, that the series of manuscripts which have been presented here were done under the emperor's own supervision, that is to say, under the eyes of a man whom his contemporaries associated with the idea of a renewal of the arts.

THE RENAISSANCE AND CHRISTIAN ART

The many-sided classical revival had achieved penetrating insights into the classical past. Even so, had it been confined to the copying of classical texts and their illustrations, it would have to be judged merely as the activity of a humanistic court circle with limited influence.

The copies of mythological and other classical miniatures, however, attracted the illustrators of Christian books so powerfully that Byzantine art as a whole took a new turn. This interpenetration of reintroduced classical and traditional Christian forms took place in different modes.

Just as scribes copied classical as well as patristic texts under the direction of Arethas, Byzantine illuminators painted classical and Christian miniatures in the same workshops. The process of copying ancient miniatures must have opened the eyes of these artists also to the classical values of the earliest Christian miniatures, many of which were as old and may have been painted in the same style as many of the classical miniatures accessible in that period. Close tenth-century copies, such as the evangelist portraits of a Gospel (cod. 43) in the Stauronikita Monastery on Mount Athos, prove that there were early pictures of evangelists scarcely distinguishable from representations of ancient philosophers. The seated Matthew (Fig. 180)[91] not only preserves the character and type of a classical figure clad in a *pallium* but also reproduces a particular meditating philosopher so faithfully that the source can be definitely identified as a representation of Epicurus. A statue in the Palazzo Margherita in Rome (Fig. 181)[92]

88 Theophanes Continuatus, *Opera*, VI, 22 ("Corpus scriptorum historiae byzantinae," 33 [Bonn, 1838]), 450.

89 *Sigebertus Gemblacensis*, L. K. Bethmann (ed.) ("Monumenta Germaniae historica Scriptores," 6 [Hanover, 1844], p. 346.

90 Luidprandus episcopi cremonensis, *Opera Omnia*, E. Dümmler (ed.) ("Scriptores rerum germanicarum," 27 [Hanover, 1877]), 69 f.

91 Friend, "Portraits of the Evangelists," p. 134 and pl. VIII, 95–98; Weitzmann, *Byzantinische Buchmalerei*, p. 23 and pl. XXX.

92 Friend, "Portraits of the Evangelists," p. 142 and pl. XVI, 156–157, where the Ince Blundell Hall Epicurus is illustrated and the

Fig. 180 *Mount Athos, Stauronikita. Cod. 43, fol. 10ʳ. Matthew*

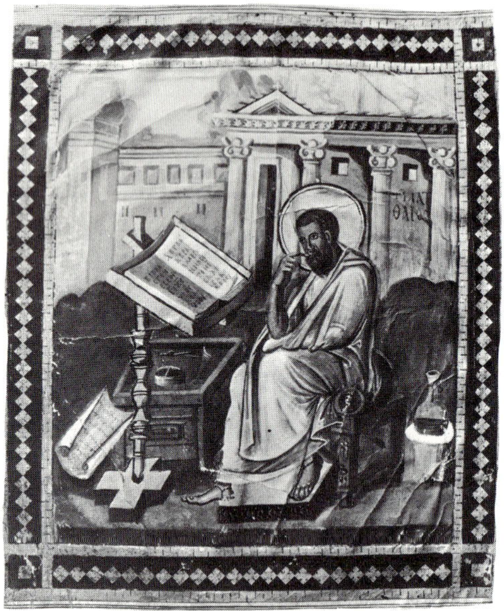

Fig. 181 *Rome, Palazzo Margherita. Statue. Epicurus*

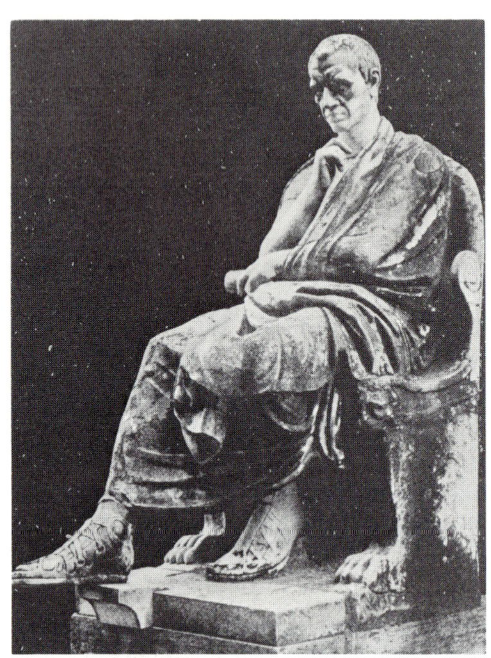

agrees in all essential details of pose and treatment of drapery with the evangelist; and Lippold has shown that the Roman portrait head does not belong to this statue and that the original head must have been that of Epicurus.[93] The portrait of this philosopher is sufficiently well-known,[94] and the slight parting of the beard is a typical detail which has been preserved in the miniature. The table, lectern, and everything which refers to the writing activity of the author are, of course, medieval additions. The

background has a special picturesque charm: a temple with columns throwing shadows on the cella wall placed within the wall of a temenos, and cypresses and gnarled trees set off against a sky painted in the most delicate colors. The illusionistic element is so genuine that it is safe to assume that the Athos miniatures copy directly, with no intermediary stage, a pre-Constantinian source. On the basis of the ornament which includes strongly classicizing elements, the Stauronikita Gospel can be securely dated to about the middle of the tenth century.[95] If we had no Paris Psalter, this manuscript by itself would be sufficient to demonstrate the existence of a Macedonian Renaissance.

statue in the Palazzo Margherita is mentioned. Weitzmann, "Probleme der mittelbyzantinischen Renaissance," *Archäologischer Anzeiger* (1933), p. 346 and figs. 5 and 7.

[93] G. Lippold, *Griechische Porträtstatuen* (Munich, 1912), p. 79 and fig. 17.

[94] Cf. the fine head in the Metropolitan Museum, New York. K. Schefold, *Die Bildnisse der antiken Dichter, Redner und Denker* (Basel, 1943), pp. 118–19.

[95] Weitzmann, *Byzantinische Buchmalerei*, pl. XXXI.

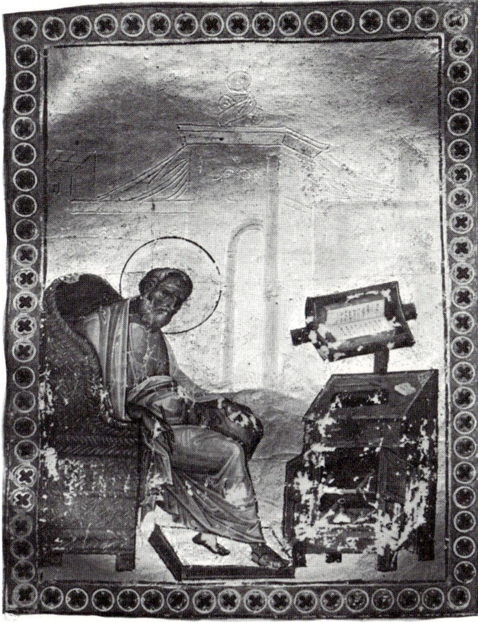

Fig. 182 *Vatican, Biblioteca. Cod. gr. 364, fol. 205ʳ. John*

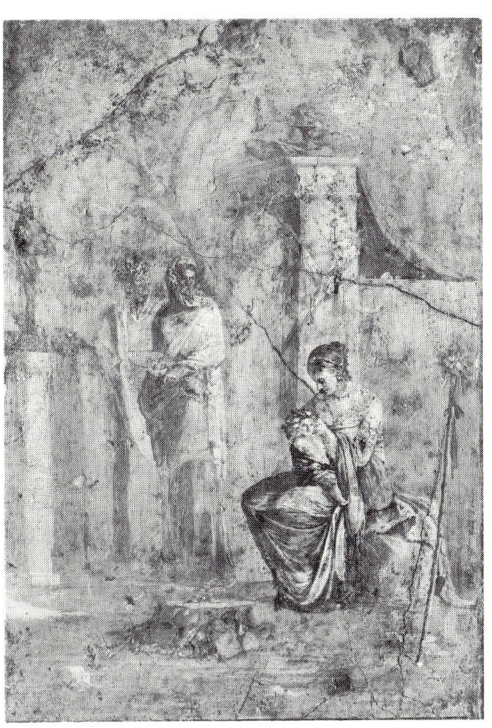

Fig. 183 *Rome, Villa Farnesina. Fresco. Rearing the Child Bacchus*

An important question remains to be answered: was the statuesque philosopher-evangelist together with the architecture, set in a picturesque landscape, present in the source of the Roman period, or were the two main elements first brought together in the tenth century as a pastiche of the type we know from the Paris Psalter? Another miniature may be brought to bear on this question, the figure of John (Fig. 182) in a Vatican Gospel book (codex gr. 364) dated to the end of the tenth century.[96] Even though his drapery has a tendency to crumple and bunch up, he presents an ancient philosopher type, i.e., a meditating thinker just as genuine as the Matthew

of Stauronikita. In this case not only the table and the lectern but also the pen in his hand are later additions, although obviously John appears to have had no intention of making use of his pen. Again there is a classicizing landscape in the background but this time, in conformity with a late phase of the renaissance, the illusionistic painting of the original has been transformed into a drawing incised on a gold background. The background is a garden gate, seen in perspective, set in a temenos wall with drapery attached to the cornice above the gate and falling softly. In a central wall-painting from the Villa Farnesina (Fig. 183),[97] which shows the bringing up

[96] Friend, "Portraits of the Evangelists," 1: 136 and pl. X, 103–6; Weitzmann, *Byzantinische Buchmalerei*, p. 25 and pl. XXXIV, 192–94.

[97] *Monumenti inediti*, 12 (1884–1885), pl. XVIII; G. E. Rizzo, *La Pittura Ellenistico-Romana* (Milan, 1929), pl. CVIII.

of the infant Bacchus, the figures are set against an architectural background which corresponds in every detail to the backdrop of the Vatican evangelist picture.[98]

From an earlier example, we know the type of evangelist who sits somewhat precariously at the edge of a wickerwork armchair and leans far forward. It is the type of Mark in the well-known Rossano Gospels (Fig. 95),[99] the sole Byzantine evangelist painting known to us from pre-Iconoclastic times. The Rossano Mark sits before a background with the same elements as the Vatican miniature: a wall topped by a central block-shaped object with a piece of drapery swinging out on both sides and set off from a striped sky.[100] We may conclude from the fact that the philosopher in the wicker chair and the garden architecture are found together in the Rossano codex that they were both present in the archetype and, furthermore, that classical evangelist pictures such as those in the Stauroni-kita and Vatican Gospel books are not pastiches of the Macedonian Renaissance but have preserved the classical quality in an unusually pure state.

The simplifications in the Rossano picture are by no means to be explained as a sign of inferior quality, for it is a luxurious purple manuscript of the sixth

century. The flatness and the patterning are the expression of a tendency toward abstraction, typical of this phase of pre-iconoclastic art; and accordingly, the physical reality of the evangelist and the drapery treatment are much less classical. Moreover, the miniature reveals a transformation into an author actively engaged in writing and thus a move away from the type of the meditating philosopher.[101] In other words, the evangelist miniatures of the Stauronikita and Vatican Gospels, with which those of other tenth-century Gospels may also be grouped,[102] are in every respect much more classical than those of the sixth

[98] I owe this reference to my departed friend, Professor A. M. Friend, who has written a comprehensive study on the Byzantine evangelist portraits for which posthumous publication is planned; it contains further identifications with ancient authors and goes far beyond his two articles in *Art Studies*.

[99] A. Muñoz, *Il codice purpureo di Rossano* (Rome, 1907), p. 5 and pl. XV.

[100] Cf. Friend, "Portraits of the Evangelists," 1:138 ff. and figs. 114, 148.

[101] Another manifestation of the tendency toward decorative effects is the framing arcade with the scallop shell niche which—as in the case of the arcades framing the pictures of bone-setting (Fig. 178)—is to be derived from canon table arcades. Characteristic of this picture as a whole, the arcade is much less convincing as a structure and, thus, less classical than the arch with curved architrave and curtains in the Florence manuscript. As a result of inserting the arcade in the Mark picture of the Rossano codex the original picture space is diminished and, in addition, the inspiring muse cuts into the right edge and so could not have belonged to the original composition, even though the idea for such an insertion evidently goes back to a group with poet and muse (cf. Friend, "Portraits of the Evangelists," pp. 141 ff.).

[102] Only the most important examples are named here: Paris, Bibliothèque Nationale, Cod. Coislin 195; Athens, National Library, cod. 56; Athos, Dionysiu, cod. 34; Vienna, Nationalbibliothek, cod. suppl. gr. 50*; Patmos, cod. 72; Leningrad, Public Library, cod. 21. Friend, "Portraits of the Evangelists," figs. 99–102, 107–10, 117–20, 129–31; Weitzmann, *Byzantinische Buchmalerei*, pls. XII, 59–60; XXVII, 151–52; XXXIII, 183–86; XXXV, 196–97; XLIX, 291–94.

century. This example shows in all clarity that we are dealing here not with a classical tradition that uniformly retained its vitality but rather—as in the case of the classical texts—with a conscious return to excellent, very early sources. Of course this verdict has far-reaching implications for the evaluation of the Paris Psalter to which we should like to return once more.

Our analysis of some of the Psalter pictures had led us to the conviction that they are not exact copies of pre-iconoclastic models but that, instead, a nucleus of Christian compositions was classicized and additional elements, borrowed directly from ancient art, were inserted. The question of where such elements as personifications, ancient architectural elements, and so on, originated and through what channels they were transmitted to Byzantine miniature painters, was left open. The answer to this question led us into the field of ancient text transmission because during the course of copying ancient texts, miniatures also were copied, which explains the sudden appearance of scenes from the Iliad, from Euripidean tragedies, and from other literary texts. That such miniatures were available to the illustrator of the Psalter may now be proven by means of an example.

In the picture of David's return home to Jerusalem (Fig. 184),[103] which is of lesser quality than the miniatures discussed previously, David stands somewhat apart and is seen from the back while Saul, contrary to the text, accepts the greeting. Instead of a whole chorus of

---

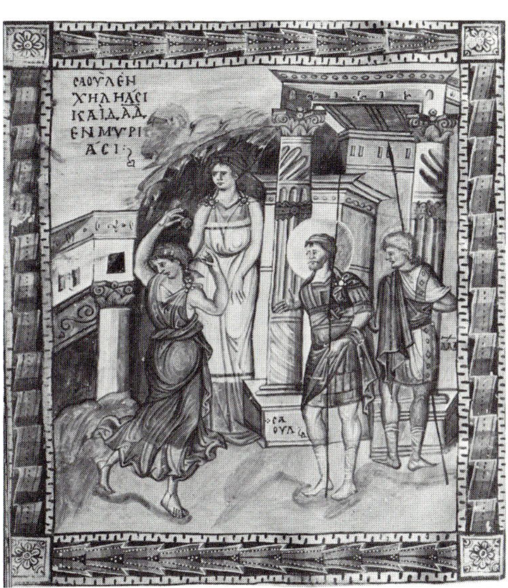

Fig. 184 *Paris, Bibliothèque Nationale. Cod. gr. 139, fol. 5ᵛ. David's Reception in Jerusalem*

dancing Israelite women,[104] the two warriors are welcomed by a single dancer while a second one stands indifferently in the background. Elements of columnar architecture substitute for the city of Jerusalem surrounded by a wall with an open gate in which one would expect to see the cheering Israelites. All these inconsistencies, which must be considered an attempt to replace the traditional composition with a newly created classicizing one, are elucidated by an ancient source which we believe to be a representation of the Euripidean *Iphigenia in Taurus*.[105] It is the scene where Iphigenia appears on the steps of the temple and confronts Orestes and Pylades, a moment preserved in several Pompeian

---

[103] Omont, *Manuscrits grecs*, pl. V; Buchthal, *Paris Psalter*, pl. V.

[104] As in the Vatican Book of Kings (cod. gr. 333). Weitzmann, "Psalter Vatopedi," p. 41 and fig. 27.

[105] K. Weitzmann, "Euripides Scenes," pp. 197 ff. and pls. 32–36 [idem, "Darstellung der Euripideischen Iphigenie," pp. 46 f.].

Fig. 185 *Naples, Museo Nazionale. Fresco from the House of Caecilius Jucundus. Iphigenia*

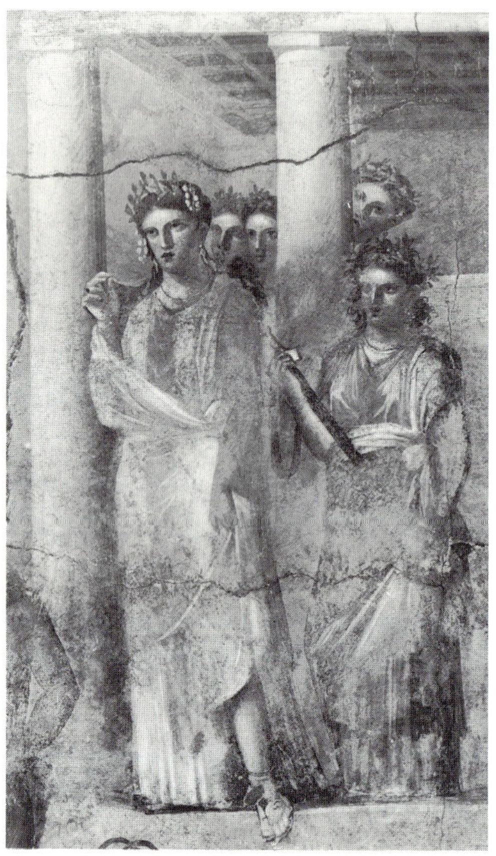

explained as Orestes, seen from the back, as he is depicted on another fresco from the Casa del Citarista[107] (as also in Fig. 186). The architecture in the miniature, however, is not a temple but is derived from the splendid columns placed in front of the *porta regia* of a *scenae frons* which we have also seen in other Byzantine miniatures (cf. Figs. 89, 90, and 178). Even the metal strips for holding the curtains back are copied.

Among the Pompeian frescoes the same Iphigenia representation appears also in the Casa del Pinario Ceriale where it is set against a theater background of the fourth style (Fig. 186);[108] here, however, in keeping with this phase of wall-painting, the columns look like stones and the architecture as a whole is less realistic. There also existed painted theater backgrounds which corresponded more closely to actual theater architecture;[109] and with this in mind, we have attempted to visualize how the model of the Paris Psalter may have looked

frescoes, for example, in the fragmentary painting from the house of Caecilius Jucundus (Fig. 185),[106] where Iphigenia appears between the columns of the temple. The woman in the background of the Psalter picture can be identified with her, only here she stands beside, instead of between, the columns of a similar building. The bowdlerized figure of David can be

---

[106] P. Herrmann, *Denkmäler der Malerei des Altertums* (Munich, 1931), pp. 161 ff. and pl. 118; E. Löwy, "Iphigenie in Taurien," *Jahrbuch des deutschen archäologischen Instituts,* 44 (1929), p. 86 ff. and fig. 10.

[107] Herrmann, *Denkmäler der Malerei,* p. 158 and pls. 115–16; E. Löwy, "Iphigenie," p. 86 and fig. 1; L. Curtius, *Die Wandmalerei Pompejis* (Leipzig, 1929), p. 244 and figs. 142–43.

[108] V. Spinazzola, *Le arti decorative in Pompei* (Milan, 1928), pl. 119; G. E. Rizzo, *La pittura Ellenistico-Romano* (Milan, 1929), pl. XXV; Löwy, "Iphigenie," p. 102 and pl. I.

[109] See the floor mosaic in Antioch depicting the scene from the play of Euripides, *Iphigenia in Aulis,* where Iphigenia is confronted by Clytemnestra and Agamemnon: Weitzmann, "Illustrations of Euripides and Homer in the Mosaics of Antioch," *Antioch-on-the-Orontes,* III, *The Excavations* 1937–39 (Princeton, 1941), p. 242 and pl. 49; D. Levi, *Antioch Mosaic Pavements* (1947), p. 119 and pl. XXII; Weitzmann, "Euripides Scenes," p. 202 and pl. 36.

Fig. 186 *Pompeii, Casa di Pinario Ceriale.
Fresco. Iphigenia*

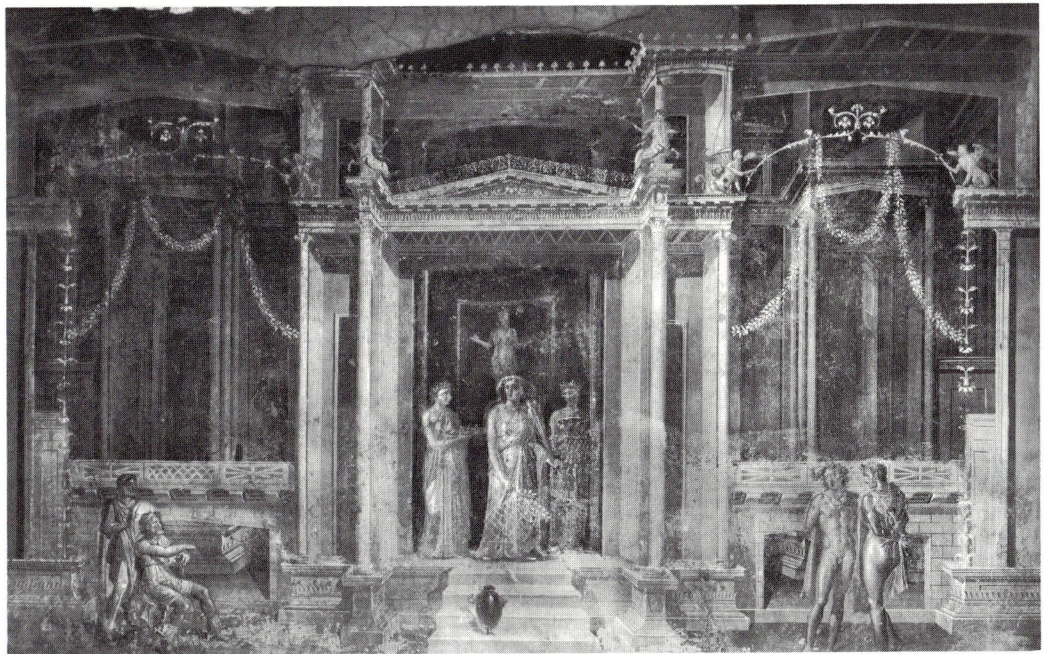

by making a reconstruction sketch (Fig. 187).[110] We envisage this model as a miniature in an illustrated Euripides of the late Roman Empire. The pastiche of the Paris Psalter is artistically not satisfactory, but precisely because the miniature is by a lesser artist it provides a clear idea of the working methods of the court atelier. If, at first, the idea of using a Euripides scene in this way comes as a surprise, it may be pointed out once more that such Euripides illustrations can be proven to have existed both in Middle Byzantine miniature painting (Fig. 173) and in the ivory carvings derived from it (Fig. 121).

We may accept from the start that the method of composing the Psalter pictures by assembling various elements from

different sources was not the whim of an individual artist but represents the working habits of a scriptorium during a certain period, and that this scriptorium —the "Palace school" as we may call this imperial atelier, borrowing the name of the scriptorium serving Charlemagne— used the same method in other manuscripts. Another of its products is the well-known Joshua Roll in the Vatican (cod. Palat. gr. 431 [Fig. 188])[111] which needs no lengthy discussion because its place within the renaissance has been thoroughly discussed elsewhere.[112] The

[110] Ibid., p. 203 and the figure on page 207.

[111] *Il Rotulo di Giosuè* ("Codices e Vaticanis selecti," 5 [Milan, 1905]).

[112] Weitzmann, *The Joshua Roll. A Work of the Macedonian Renaissance* (Princeton, 1948). In this book the reasons for dating the illustrations in the tenth century, in opposition to the early dating around 700, advocated mainly

Fig. 187 *Reconstruction of Iphigenia Scene*

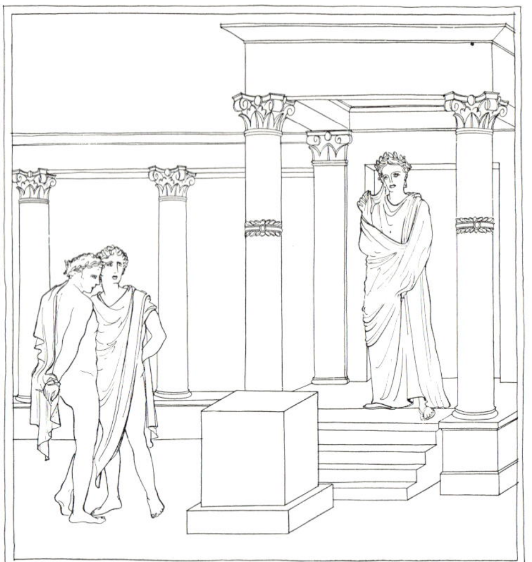

Joshua Roll is a parchment rotulus dominated by a picture frieze and containing a radically abbreviated Bible text. Joshua's acquisition of the Promised Land is depicted; and although the beginning and the end of the roll are missing, it is possible to prove definitely that the roll never had more than the first thirteen chapters of the Book of Joshua illustrated in this form. The triumphal frieze is related in many respects to the columns of Theodosius and Arcadius which were still standing in Constantinople during the tenth century.[113] The separate scenes of the Joshua Roll are based on the Octateuch tradition; but the biblical iconography has often been altered in order to intensify the general impression of military activity. This ex-

plains why the representations are iconographically further removed from the archetype than those of the Octateuchs.

The Joshua Roll and the Paris Psalter have in common an accumulation of personifications of which most either recline on hills in the upper area of the picture where no distinction is made between river and mountain gods, or they are inserted between scenes. For instance, above the scene of the building of the altar with twelve stones is a reclining youth with a cornucopia (Fig. 188) personifying the place Gilgal; and not far away is a second personification with a gesture of astonishment, identified by an inscription as the "Hill of Foreskins." As in the case of the Paris Psalter, a comparison with other manuscripts which preserve the archetype more faithfully shows that these personifications were not in the archetype but were inserted later. The eleventh-century Octateuch in the Vatican (cod. gr. 747), one such manuscript, entirely lacks the personifications which we consider insertions.[114]

The personification of the city of Gibeon (Fig. 189)[115] is of special interest because it agrees with the Melodia on the title page of the Paris Psalter down to the smallest details of pose, folds of drapery, and so on (cf. Fig. 160). This means that it is a copy of the same classical source used for Melodia, a source which must have contained a figure extremely close to the Io of the Macellum fresco in Pompeii (Fig. 161) and to the Oenone of the Antioch mosaic

---

by C. R. Morey ("Notes on East Christian Miniatures," p. 50) are also set forth in detail; M. Schapiro, "The Place of the Joshua Roll in Byzantine History," *Gazette des Beaux-Arts*, 35 (1949), 161 ff.

[113] Weitzmann, *Joshua Roll*, pp. 100 ff.

[114] Ibid., pp. 51 ff.

[115] Ibid., pp. 64 ff. and pl. XIX, 65–66.

Fig. 188 *Vatican, Biblioteca. Cod. Pal. gr. 431.*
Building the Altar

Fig. 189 *Vatican, Biblioteca. Cod. Pal. gr. 431.*
Personification of the Town of Gibeon

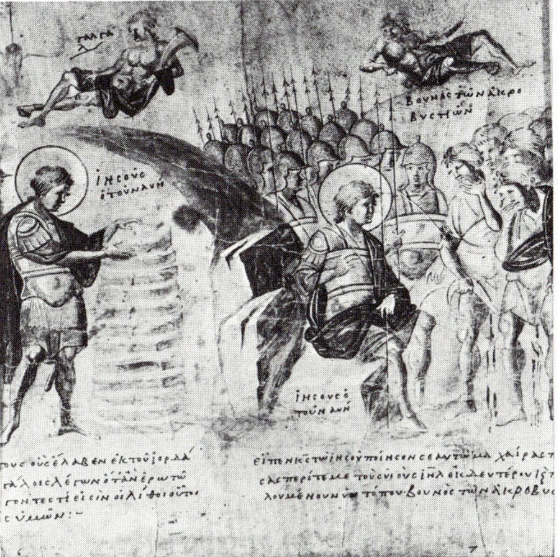

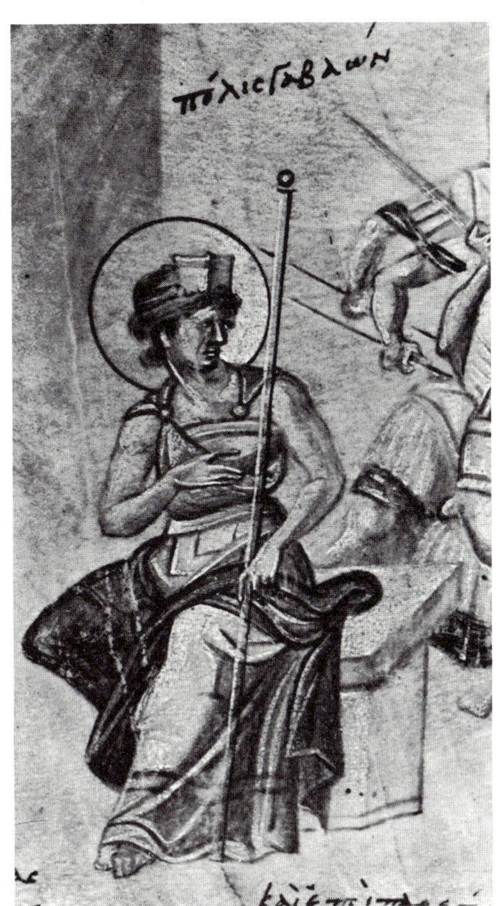

(Fig. 162).[116] The fact that the same classical sources must have been available to the painters of both manuscripts is a clear indication that the Paris Psalter and the Joshua Roll are the products of the same workshop. The homogeneity of the Joshua Roll frieze and the freshness of its execution make it likely that the painter of the Vatican roll was the very artist who undertook to transform a series of separate Octateuch scenes into a continuous frieze. Thus, we gain some idea of the personality of a noteworthy artist of the Macedonian Renaissance who understood how to blend, skillfully, imperial and classical mythological elements with the biblical and how to adapt them to the wholly unusual roll form. This contrasts with the Paris Psalter which, to all appearances, is not the first Psalter to be recast in the spirit of the Macedonian Renaissance but rather a copy, incomplete in many details.

116 On the relationship of the Joshua Roll to the Paris Psalter, ibid., pp. 73 ff.

So far as religious manuscripts were concerned, the Joshua Roll being a special case, the artistic energies of renaissance illuminators were concentrated on the most important liturgical books: Gospels, like the one at Stauronikita, which often were used in the liturgy, Psalters, and lectionaires. The lectionary, which as the book of lessons had its place on the altar table, was used in the liturgy, and therefore was provided with splendid covers (cf. Fig. 231). Understandably it occupies a leading position among the liturgical books,[117] and for this reason we may expect that artists paid particular attention to this all important service book. One would like to have a tenth-century lectionary which, as a creation of the Macedonian Renaissance, would have taken its place among the manuscripts previously discussed, but unfortunately no splendid display copy of this century has been preserved; nevertheless, the evidence from influences on other branches of art during the same period and from later manuscripts of the eleventh and twelfth centuries proves that such a manuscript once existed.

Lectionary illustration focuses on the representation of the twelve great feasts of the church,[118] which, as a liturgical cycle, extended far beyond miniature painting and had reverberations in icon painting and wall painting as well as in ivory carving. Among the ivories it is particularly those of the tenth-century *malerische Gruppe* which show the influx of classical elements. One would scarcely expect ancient personifications such as the Melodia in the David page of the Paris Psalter to be connected as closely with Christ; and yet the feast pictures do have clearly recognizable classical elements. On a tenth-century ivory plaque

in Berlin (Fig. 190),[119] beneath the hoof of the donkey carrying Christ to Jerusalem, we find a small figure removing a thorn from his foot. This figure is not to be considered merely as a decorative motif taken from a classical source; but rather it is a symbol of pagan idolatry[120] over which Christ, as Triumphator, is riding—an inconography which had also spread to Western art.[121] Furthermore, just as in the case of the Paris Psalter and the Joshua Roll, the traditional biblical figures have undergone a classicizing treatment, the most evident signs of this being the arm in the loop of the mantle and the tendency toward contrapostal stance.

A Crucifixion plaque in the Metropolitan Museum in New York (Fig. 191)[122] has this tendency; both John and the well-modeled Christ on the cross have a lightness and elegance of movement which can only be due to renewed classical influence. The renaissance character of the scene appears even more forcefully in the Adam figure which replaces the usual skull at the same spot and which

[117] On the artistic layout of lectionaries see Weitzmann, "The Narrative and Liturgical Gospel Illustrations," *New Testament Manuscript Studies*, M. M. Parvis and A. P. Wikgren (eds.) (Chicago, 1950), pp. 151 ff. [reprinted herewith, pp. 247 ff. Now also, Weitzmann, "Byzantine Miniature and Icon Painting in the Eleventh Century," *The Thirteenth International Congress of Byzantine Studies* (Oxford, 1967) pp. 207 ff., reprinted herewith, pp. 271 ff.].

[118] G. Millet, *Recherches sur l'iconographie de l'Évangile* (Paris, 1916), pp. 15 ff.

[119] Goldschmidt and Weitzmann, *Elfenbeinskulpturen*, 2:25 and pl. I, 3; E. Panofsky, *Renaissance and Renascences in Western Art* (Stockholm, 1960), p. 58 and fig. 23.

[120] W. S. Heckscher, "Dornauszieher," *Reallexikon zur Deutschen Kunstgeschichte*, 4 (1958), 294.

[121] For instance, the Entry into Jerusalem in a thirteenth-century manuscript from Saint Martin in Cologne [Brussels, Bibliothèque Royale, MS 466 (9222)] in H. Swarzenski, *Die lateinischen illuminierten Handschriften des XIII. Jahrhunderts in den Ländern am Rhein, Main und Donau* (Berlin, 1936), p. 85 and pl. 3, 11; idem, *The Berthold Missal* (New York, 1943), pp. 41 ff. and note 45.

[122] Goldschmidt and Weitzmann, *Elfenbeinskulpturen*, 2:26 and pl. II, 6.

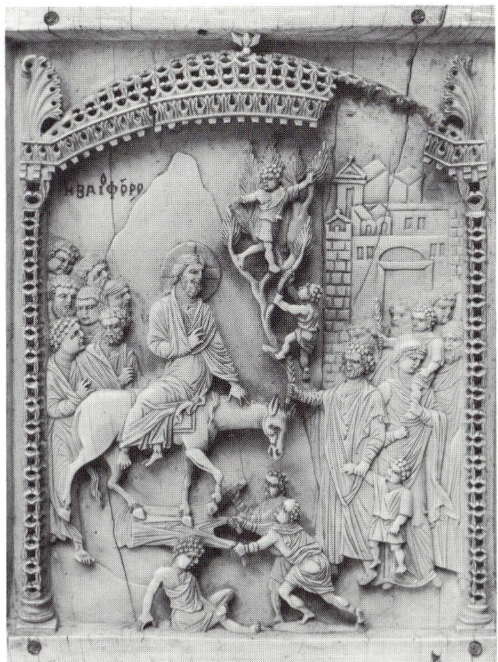

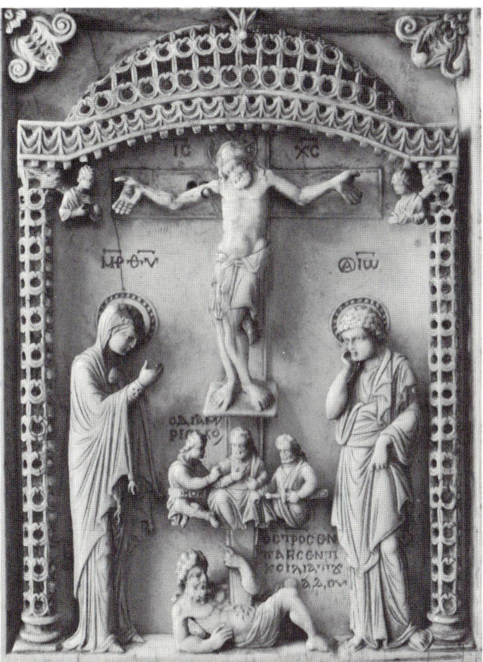

has caused the artist to push higher up the group of soldiers casting lots for the garments. This figure of Adam, clad only in a loincloth, is very similar to the river and mountain gods in the Joshua Roll (Fig. 188); and indeed, it is most probable that the same classical models were available to the artists in the imperial workshops and to the ivory carver who made the figure of Adam. It is interesting that Schlumberger[123] once interpreted this figure as Hades; the ambiguity of the inscription ΕΝ ΤΗ ΚΟΙΛΙΑ ΤΟΥ ΑΔΟΥ accounts for his explanation. Although this interpretation is open to question, it is not entirely unfounded, for the idea of Hades may have played a part in the choice of the type for Adam.

The infiltration of ancient types was not limited to subordinate figures such as Adam and the Spinario. It extends to the core of Christian representations, resulting either in the alteration or in the replacement of traditional types.

Gradually around the tenth century the Burial of Christ—which together with the Deposition from the Cross formed a feast picture—was transformed into the Bewailing of Christ, a scene of changed significance that, in turn, was the starting point for a further development which crystallized into the creation of the Pietà.[124] The end of the first stage of this

---

[123] G. Schlumberger, *L'épopée byzantine à la fin du Xe siècle*, 2 (Paris, 1900), 13.

[124] Weitzmann, "The Origin of the Threnos," *De Artibus Opuscula XL. Essays in Honor of Erwin Panofsky* (New York, 1961), pp. 476 ff. [H. Hunger, "Die byzantinische Literatur der Komnenenzeit. Versuch einer Neubewertung," *Anzeiger der phil-hist. Klasse der Österreichischen Akademie der Wissenschaften* (1968), 59 ff.]

Fig. 192 *Vatican, Biblioteca. Cod. gr. 1156,
fol. 194ᵛ. Threnos*

Fig. 193 *Paris, Louvre. Sarcophagus. Lamen-
tation for Actaeon*

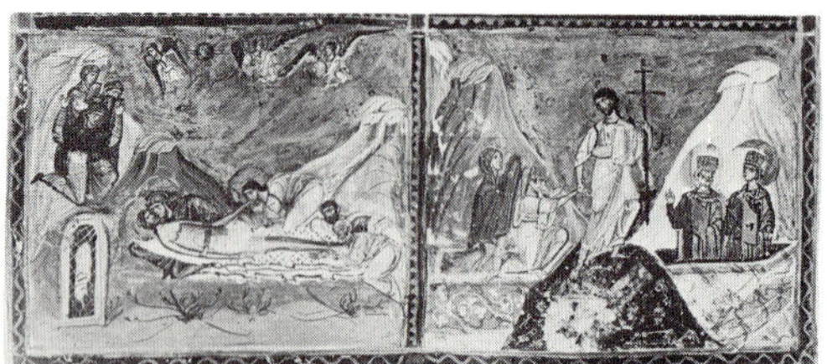

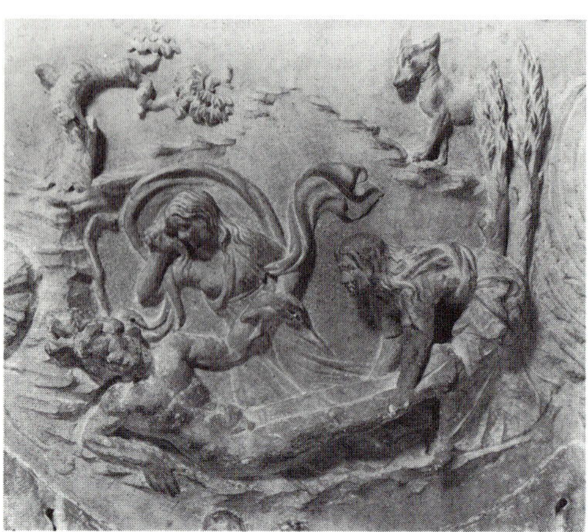

transformation was reached when the
body of the dead Christ was placed on
the ground, as in a miniature of the
Vatican Lectionary (cod. gr. 1156
[Fig. 192]).[125] At this point it is possible to
observe the influence of an ancient representation of Actaeon, best preserved on
a Roman sarcophagus in the Louvre
(Fig. 193).[126] Mary takes on the traits of
Autonoë who pours out her grief for her
dead son in words similar to those of
Mary mourning the dead Christ as recorded in the Gospel of Nicodemus.
In the Threnos the beloved disciple
John raises aloft the slack arm of Christ
and then bends to kiss the hand. Nicodemus and Joseph of Arimathia, like the
woman in the sarcophagus relief, correctly or not called the nurse of Actaeon,
lower the feet to the ground. The remarkable thing is that the Byzantine painter
not only was stimulated by the composition of the lament for Actaeon, he also
realized that the ancient source had a
similar content; and this is not an isolated
case of an artist displaying a remarkable
empathy into the antique.

In a magnificent lectionary of the
eleventh century in the monastery of

Lavra on Mount Athos the first of three
icon-like miniatures represents the
Anastasis (Fig. 194)[127] in a new iconography which may have originated in the
tenth century and which takes its place
beside the two older types. The first, a
pre-iconoclastic type, represents Christ
striding toward Adam and extending his
hand;[128] the second, most likely a post-
iconoclastic type, shows Christ frontally
on an elevated platform and Adam and
Eve placed symmetrically and kneeling
out of Christ's reach.[129] In the Lavra
Lectionary, on the other hand, Christ
pulls Adam out of limbo just as Heracles
had dragged Cerberus out of the under-
world. A representation of this deed of
Heracles actually appears to have been

[125] Millet, *Recherches*, p. 494 and fig. 533.
[126] C. Robert, *Die antiken Sarkophag-Reliefs*,
3 (Berlin, 1897), 1, 1 ff. and pl. I, 1; J. M. C.
Toynbee, *The Hadrianic School, A Chapter in
the History of Greek Art* (Cambridge, 1934),
pp. 213, 230, and pl. XLVIII, 1.

[127] Weitzmann, "Das Evangelium im Skevophylakion zu Lawra," *Seminarium Kondakovianum*, 8 (1936), 83 ff. and pl. II, 1. [idem,
"Miniature and Icon Painting," pp. 216 ff.,
reprinted herewith, pp. 290 ff.].
[128] For the iconography of the Anastasis see
C. R. Morey, *East Christian Paintings in the
Freer Collection* (New York, 1914), pp. 45 ff.
[129] Weitzmann, "Aristocratic Psalter and Lectionary," *Record of the Art Museum Princeton
University*, 19 (1960), 98 ff.

Fig. 194 *Mount Athos, Lavra, Skevophyla-kion. Lectionary, fol. 1ᵛ. Anastasis*

Fig. 195 *London, British Museum. Sarcoph-agus. Heracles*

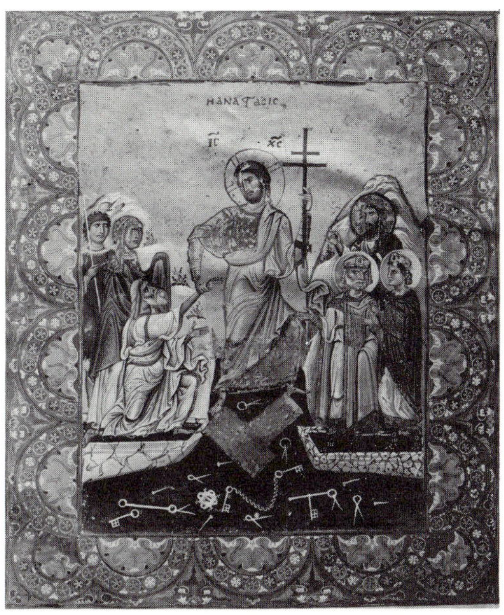

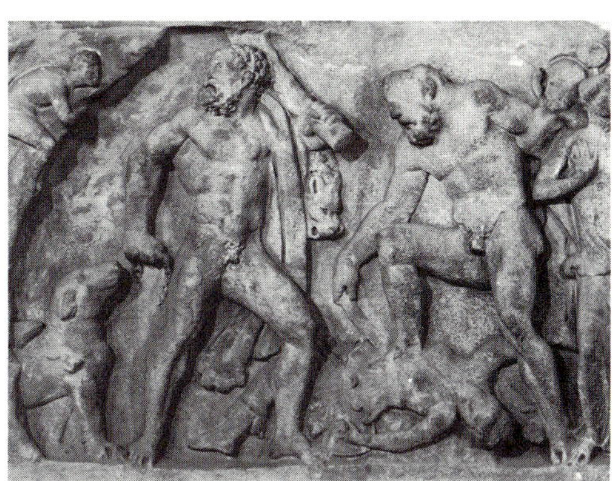

the source for the renaissance type, as a comparison with a sarcophagus relief in the British Museum reveals (Fig. 195).[130] Again, it is not merely a matter of assimilating a formal composition but also of a parallelism of ideas. In both scenes the victor over death is shown as he triumphantly holds aloft in his left hand the attribute of victory, Christ the cross and Heracles the club.

This example, although most characteristic, by no means conveys the full range of classicizing in the cycle of church feasts. In the Nativity of the same lectionary at Lavra (Fig. 258) the washing of the newborn child can be plainly and distinctly traced back to a representation of the bathing of the child Dionysus;[131]

on a tenth-century ivory plaque of the Ascension of Christ[132] in Stuttgart (Fig. 149) one of the apostles, instead of looking up to the ascending Christ, is shown in the attitude of a brooding Agamemnon;[133] and such examples could be multiplied. These separate observations clearly lead to the conclusion that there must have existed a renaissance lectionary with a miniature cycle which, from start to finish, was permeated with features drawn from classical sources. Judging by the originality, the versatility of the artist in solving his problems, and the sensitive feeling displayed in harmonizing classical elements with the sacred themes of the great christological feasts, the lost archetype must have been one of the most brilliant accomplishments of this renaissance.

From all this there is scarcely reason to doubt that magnificently illustrated manuscripts occupy a central place in the Macedonian Renaissance and that these

---

[130] Robert, *Sarkophag-Reliefs*, 3:1, figs. 113a, 120, and others.
[131] Weitzmann, "Evangelium," pp. 89 ff. and pl. IV, 3.

[132] Goldschmidt and Weitzmann, *Elfenbein-skulpturen*, 2:30 and pl. VII, 24.
[133] Weitzmann, "Survival of Mythological Representations," p. 62 and figs. 34–37.

were made in Constantinople, stimulated by a leading palace school. The renaissance movement was by no means confined to miniature painting, however, but spread to other branches of art. We have repeatedly mentioned ivory carvings such as the rosette caskets which were decorated with classical subjects (Figs. 121, 169, and 172) and the plaques with religious representations which served as icons (Figs. 190 and 191). Without going into detail, suffice it to mention that the reliefs of the classicizing caskets were widely distributed; in the Latin West they were imitated in stone and metal;[134] and they also had an influence on Russian church façades.[135] In the latter case, they were used to create an imitation of classical types, though in most cases the artist seems unaware of their meaning. The virtually total destruction of one major class of monuments, Byzantine icons, accounts for the fact that it is possible today to show the influence of the renaissance on icon painting only in a few isolated cases. As might have been expected, of the very few tenth-century icons which recently came to light in the Monastery of Saint Catherine on Sinai, one clearly shows the classicizing influence (Fig. 210). The

apostle Thaddaeus, who converted the people of Edessa, is shown in classical drapery opposite King Abgarus, who has the facial features of Constantine Porphyrogenitus.[136] In the frescoes of Castelseprio, on the other hand, if our dating to the tenth century is correct,[137] we even have painting on a monumental scale. These frescoes have some of the same classical elements as the Paris Psalter, and their compositions are constructed according to similar principles. We can only conclude that our almost exclusive concentration on book illumination does not do justice to the extent of the influence of the renaissance movement on contemporary art.

THE SIGNIFICANCE OF THE
MACEDONIAN RENAISSANCE

In order to evaluate the significance of the Macedonian Renaissance in the history of Byzantine art, it is not only important to investigate the range of its influence upon the art of its time, but also to ask whether it remained confined to the period of the Macedonian Dynasty or if the transmission of ancient culture had a decisive effect

---

[134] Weitzmann, "Abendländische Kopien byzantinischer Rosettenkästen," *Zeitschrift für Kunstgeschichte*, 3 (1934), 89 ff.

[135] For instance, a relief of a reclining figure in a chariot drawn by lions (V. N. Lazarev, *Geschichte der Russischen Kunst*, 1 [Dresden, 1957], 111 and fig. 113) is evidently to be derived from a rosette casket plaque which, in turn, copies a miniature such as the one preserved in the Venice Oppian manuscript where the reclining figure is named Rhea. Weitzmann, *Greek Mythology*, p. 129 and pls. XLII, 153–XLIII, 155.

[136] Weitzmann, "The Mandylion and Constantine Porphyrogennetos," *Cahiers Archéologiques*, 11 (1960), 163 ff. and figs. 2–3 [here reprinted pp. 224 ff. K. Weitzmann, M. Chatzidakis, K. Miatev, S. Radojčić, *A Treasury of Icons—Sixth to Seventeenth Centuries* (New York, 1967), p. xi and pl. 11.]

[137] Weitzmann, *The Fresco Cycle of S. Maria di Castelseprio* (Princeton, 1951). In the first publication, this fresco cycle was dated in the seventh century (G. P. Bognetti, G. Chierici, A. de Capitani d'Arzago, *Santa Maria di Castelseprio* [Milan, 1948]) whereas M. Schapiro has suggested a date in the Carolingian period (*Art Bulletin*, 34 [1952], 148 ff.).

on the later course of Byzantine art. For the literary historian this is an academic question, because it is a solid fact that the studies of ancient texts taken up by Photius and Arethas were continued without interruption. For evidence of the continuity of the Byzantine humanistic movement one need only recall such names as Michael Psellus in the eleventh century, Anna Comnena and John Tzetzes in the twelfth, Maximus Planudes and Theodore Methochites in the thirteenth and fourteenth centuries, and Georgios Gemistos Plethon in the fifteenth century, along with a whole series of other distinguished learned men. The best way to show how the achievements of the Byzantine Renaissance survived in Byzantine painting is to examine the illustrations of those texts which played a vital part in the assimilation of ancient art in the tenth century, the Joshua Roll, the aristocratic Psalter, and the lectionary or Gospel manuscripts.

The Vatican Joshua Roll had an enduring influence on most, but not all, of the Octateuchs of the post-renaissance period. In an imperial manuscript of the early twelfth century in the Library of the Seraglio in Istanbul (cod. 8), the scene of the circumcision of the Israelites (Fig. 196)[138] not only agrees with the iconography and composition of the corresponding scene in the Joshua Roll (cf. Fig. 188) but both have the same hill personification,[139] except that in the

later manuscript it has become a plump, putto-like figure in a pose betraying no great understanding of ancient form. This evidences a hardening of style at a time when the sensitivity to the classical style had virtually disappeared. If we look at the same scene in the Octateuch from the Athos Monastery of Vatopedi, (cod. 602 [Fig. 197]),[140] it becomes immediately apparent that the illustrator of this thirteenth-century manuscript[141] has succeeded in recapturing the antique atmosphere—a fact which can only be explained by the assumption that the artist made direct use of the Vatican roll. This roll apparently was available to him in the imperial library, and thus it would be reasonable to infer that the Vatopedi Octateuch is also a product of the imperial scriptorium. The mountain god again reclines indolently on the ridge and, in accord with classicizing taste, a cornucopia has been placed in his hand (the mountain god in the Joshua Roll does not hold one); the soldier next to Joshua rests his left hand on his shield which is supported on the ground; and in the landscape of cliffs, resembling the landscape of the Joshua Roll only in general contour, the illustrator has filled in detailed rock formations and other landscape elements like those in the Paris Psalter (cf. Fig. 160), elements which are based on Greco-Roman landscape painting.

---

[138] T. Ouspensky, *L'octateuque de la Bibliothèque du Sérail à Constantinople* (Sofia, 1907), p. 163 and pl. XXXV, 231.

[139] Vatican codex gr. 747 (fol. 220ʳ) does not have this personification and is, as mentioned above, free from any influence of the Joshua Roll.

[140] Photo, Princeton-Athos Expedition, 1935.

[141] For the dating of the Vatopedi Octateuch in the thirteenth century see Weitzmann, "Constantinopolitan Book Illumination in the Period of the Latin Conquest," *Gazette des Beaux-Arts*, 86 (1944), 208 and figs. 11–12 [reprinted herewith, pp. 327 ff. and Figs. 317-318].

Fig. 196 *Istanbul, Seraglio. Cod. 8, fol. 480*[r]. *Circumcision*

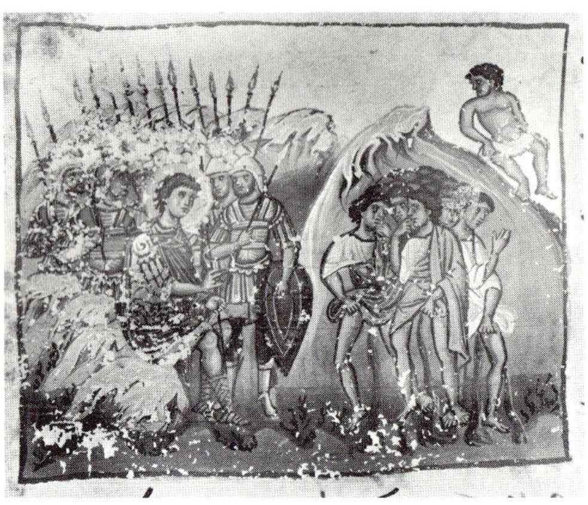

Fig. 197 *Mount Athos, Vatopedi. Cod. 602, fol. 349*[v]. *Circumcision*

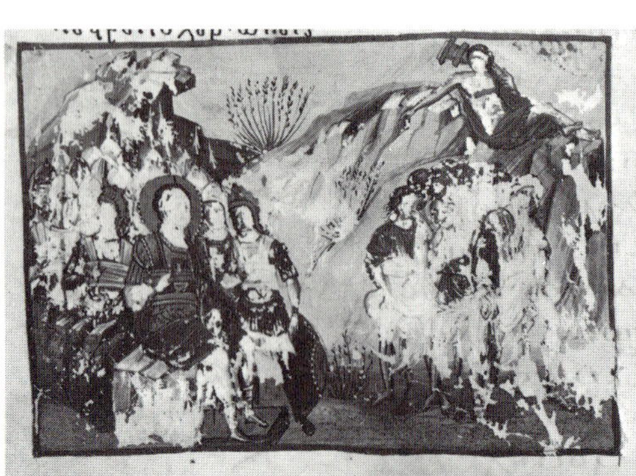

The aristocratic Psalter recension furnishes even clearer proof that there was a direct return to tenth-century works during the thirteenth century. Eleventh-century copies of the Paris Psalter or of its immediate renaissance prototype exist as, for example, the copy in the Athos monastery of Pantokratoros (cod. 49 [now in Dumbarton Oaks Washington])[142] dated to ca. 1084; and the manuscript in the Vatican Library (cod. Barb. gr. 320), dated to 1177, is a typical twelfth-century example. In the title miniature of the latter (Fig. 198)[143] all three personifications of the Paris Psalter are present; yet, in the course of two centuries the figures have become meager, brittle, and lifeless. A miniature in the Public Library in Leningrad (cod. 269

[Fig. 199]),[144] cut out of a Psalter in the Sinai Monastery and certainly to be dated in the thirteenth century, is ever so much closer to the Paris Psalter.[145] The atmosphere of a Hellenistic landscape, a certain liveliness of motion, and a wealth of forms have been retrieved, even though the figures are more elongated and have certain drapery mannerisms which are characteristic of late Byzantine art. This repeated classical revival in the thirteenth century reaching into the fourteenth is a phenomenon that has been known for some time; some scholars have called it "Neo-Hellenism"[146] while more generally it is called the "Palaeologan Renaissance." At present many scholars advocate the theory that the creators of this late classical revival returned directly to ancient sources. In this connection, the

[142] Buchthal, *Paris Psalter*, pp. 28, 38–39, 41 and pls. XXII, 53, XXV, 68, XXVI, 76 and 78; Weitzmann, *Roll and Codex*, pp. 111, 149, 152, 162, 170, 185 and figs. 140, 157, 164.
[143] A. Venturi, *Storia dell'arte italiana*, 2 (Milan, 1901–14), 442 and fig. 311; J. J. Tikkanen, "Die Psalterillustration im Mittelalter," *Acta Societatis Scientiarum Fennicae*, 31 (1903), 128 and fig. 109; Buchthal, *Paris Psalter*, p. 15 and pl. XVI, 21; Weitzmann, *Greek Mythology*, p. 68 and pl. XXV, 85.

[144] V. N. Lazarev, *Istoriia vizantiiskoi zhivopisi* (Moscow, 1948), p. 110 and pl. 140a [translated and revised as *Storia della pittura bizantina* (Turin, 1967)].
[145] Weitzmann, "Eine Pariser Psalter-Kopie des 13. Jahrhunderts auf dem Sinai," *Jahrbuch der österreichischen byzantinischen Gesellschaft*, 6 (1957), 129 and fig. 3.
[146] P. Muratoff, *La peinture byzantine* (Paris, 1928), p. 127.

Fig. 198 *Vatican, Biblioteca. Cod. Barb. gr. 320, fol. 2ʳ. David and Melodia*

Fig. 199 *Leningrad, Public Library. Cod. 269, fol. 1ʳ. David and Melodia*

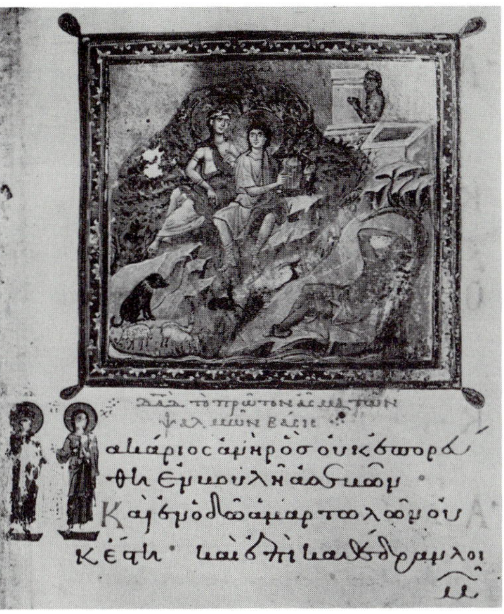

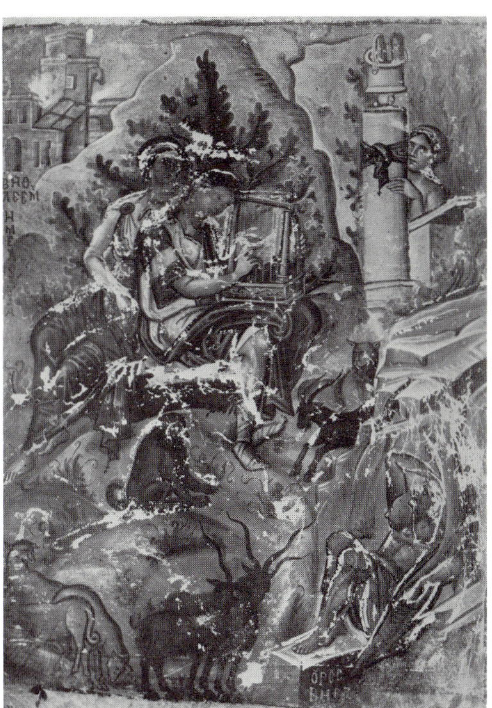

manuscripts treated here have scarcely been discussed[147] because most scholars have dated them incorrectly in the eleventh century, an attempt to make them as close as possible in time to the Paris Psalter. Precisely because we do have numerous concrete examples of direct dependence on tenth-century manuscripts in the Late Byzantine period, the ways in which the Macedonian Renaissance acted as a transmitter of classical art should receive closer attention.

Thirteenth- and fourteenth-century miniatures in renaissance style do exist,

however, for which prototypes are no longer preserved; therefore in analogy with the preceding examples we may assume that these prototypes are also tenth-century manuscripts which, in turn, represented the first stage of the process of assimilating ancient sources.

A pocket-size Psalter manuscript in the Vatican (cod. Barb. gr. 285) has an inserted leaf depicting the combat of David and Goliath (Fig. 200)[148] with a composition typical for the aristocratic Psalters. This scene is set in an aedicula-like frame, the details of which clearly reveal the influence of the fourth

[147] Otto Demus is an exception; in his basic paper on Byzantine painting of the thirteenth century he correctly placed the manuscripts in question within the general framework of the development of that time. Cf. O. Demus, "Die Entstehung des Paläologenstils in der Malerei," *Berichte zum XI. Internationalen Byzantinisten-Kongress München 1958* (Munich, 1958).

[148] E. T. DeWald, "A Fragment of a Tenth-Century Byzantine Psalter in the Vatican Library," *Mediaeval Studies in Memory of A. Kingsley Porter* (Cambridge, Mass., 1939), pp. 139 ff. and fig. 2.

Fig. 200 *Vatican, Biblioteca. Cod. Barb. gr. 285, fol. 140ᵛ. David and Goliath*

Fig. 201 *Naples, Museo Nazionale. Fresco. Dionysus and Silen*

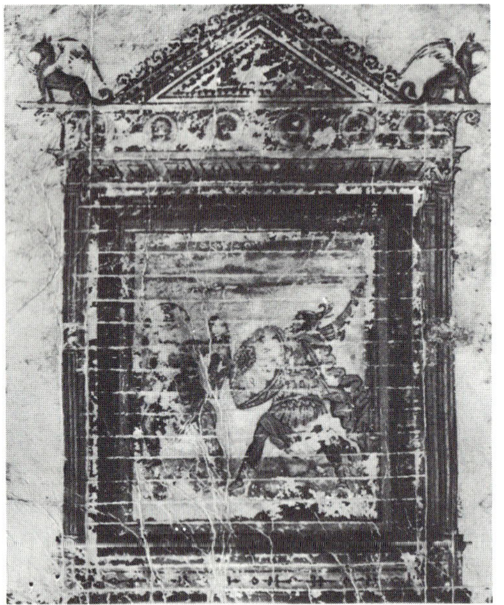

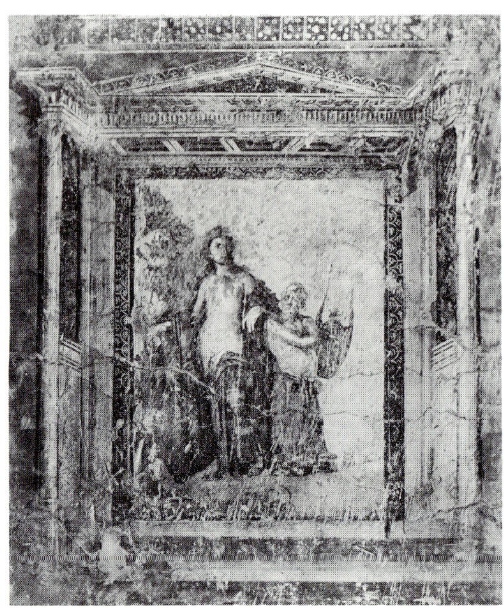

Pompeian style, complete with sphinx acroteria at the corners. The closest parallel is a Pompeian fresco of Dionysus and Silenus (Fig. 201)[149] also with an aedicula which is not part of a larger fresco decoration but forms an independent frame. Chiefly on the basis of the genuinely classical architecture, otherwise unparalleled in Byzantine times, DeWald thought that this miniature was a work of the Macedonian Renaissance and dated it in the second half of the tenth century. The form of Goliath's helmet and the mannered treatment of his fluttering mantle, however, point unquestionably to an origin not earlier than the thirteenth century, and thus we are clearly dealing with a copy made directly

from a tenth-century source with no intervening link.

After all this, it is not surprising to discover that the most faithful copies of the Gospel manuscript with the most distinctively renaissance character, the Stauronikita Gospels, do not date from the eleventh and twelfth centuries but from the time of the Palaeologues. For instance, the Matthew in a London Gospels (British Museum cod. Add. 22506 [Fig. 202]),[150] dated to 1305, reproduces the Mark of the Athos manuscript (Fig. 203),[151] not only in all the elements of the sculpturesque philosopher figure but also in the details of the back-

---

[149] Herrmann, *Denkmäler der Malerei*, p. 265 and pl. 194; reproduced again in DeWald, "Tenth-Century Byzantine Psalter," fig. 3.

[150] Friend, "Portraits of the Evangelists," 2: 13 ff. and figs. 14 and 19. Here a connection is made between the pictures in the background and the *pinakes* of the Hellenistic theater.
[151] Ibid., Part I, p. 134 and pl. VIII, 96; Weitzmann, *Byzantinische Buchmalerei*, p. 23 and pl. XXX, 170.

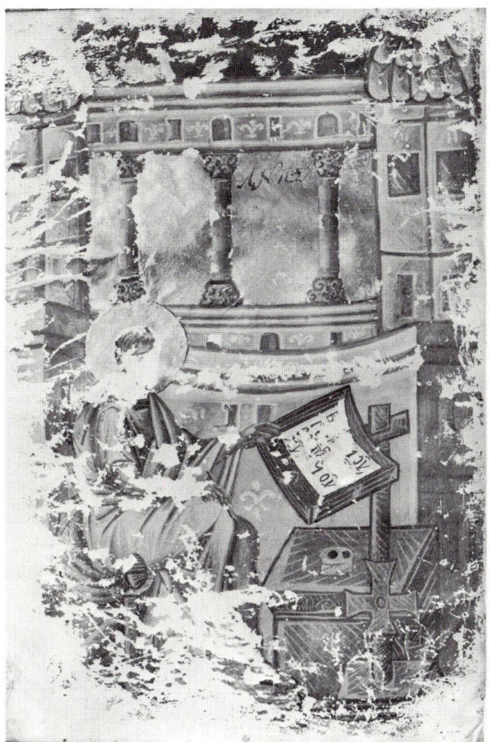

Fig. 202 *London, British Museum. Cod. Add. 22506, fol. 5ᵛ. Matthew*

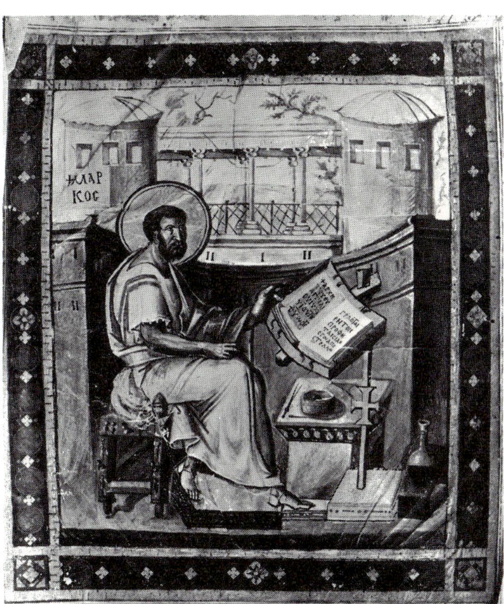

Fig. 203 *Mount Athos, Stauronikita. Cod. 43, fol. 11ʳ. Mark*

ground which reflects a statue set in a niche of the proscenium wall of a Roman theater. The architectural background of a pergola flanked by towers, partly concealed by the niche, is also repeated down to the last detail, even though the drawing in this not too elegant, rather provincial, copy appears to be slightly less polished and flattened out—an impression intensified by the substitution of the gold background (which prevailed more and more over the ancient landscape) for the delicately painted cliffs and trees of the Stauronikita picture.

There are also several late pictures of evangelists which, by analogy with the London Gospels just considered, presumably have tenth-century sources no

longer extant. An examination of these pictures therefore serves a twofold purpose: not only does it provide deeper insight into the revitalizing of ancient art, but also it rounds out our picture of the Macedonian Renaissance itself. A thirteenth-century Gospels in Athens (cod. 118), shows Matthew (Fig. 204)[152] absorbed in reading an inscribed roll, whereby the evangelist may be recognized immediately as a copy of an ancient literary figure. In the emphasis on physical, three-dimensional reality this figure is scarcely inferior to the best tenth-century miniatures, even though the accumulation of creased drapery folds leaves no doubt about the late date.

[152] P. Buberl, "Die Miniaturhandschriften der Nationalbibliothek in Athen," *Denkschriften der Wiener Akademie, Phil.-Hist. Kl.,* 60 (1917), 23, no. 24 and pl. XXX, 82; Weitzmann, "Constantinopolitan Book Illumination," p. 197 and fig. 2 [reprinted herewith, p. 317].

Fig. 204 *Athens, National Library. Cod. 118, fol. 1ᵛ. Matthew*

Fig. 205 *Rome, (Drawing after a) Fresco from the Villa Farnesina. Tragic Poet*

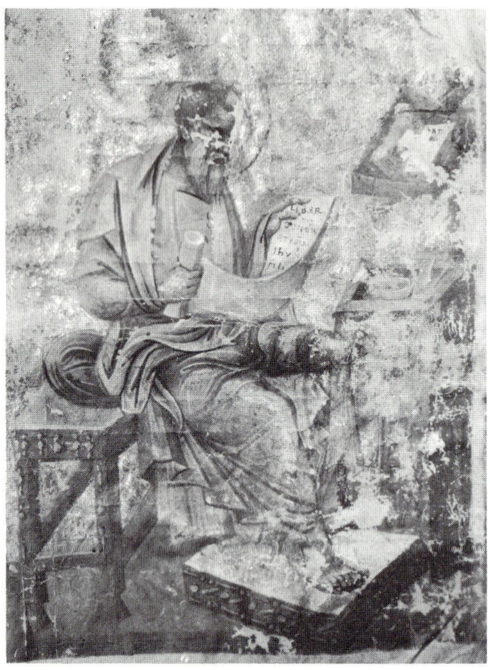

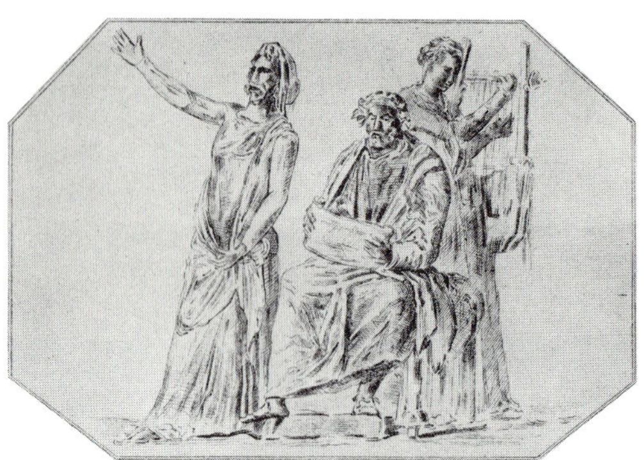

We can trace this type back to ancient times; a fresco in the Villa Farnesina (Fig. 205)[153] portrays a laureate poet in a very similar pose but seen from a different angle. We may suppose from the presence of an actor wearing a tragic mask and declaiming that this is a tragic poet; and thus we may conclude that not only philosophers such as Epicurus (cf. Figs. 180–81) but also poets were models for paintings of the evangelists.

There is a telling detail in the Athens evangelist picture, namely that the beginning of the Gospel of Matthew written on the roll is in Latin. Because this Gospel dates from the period when Constantinople was ruled by the Latins

and when there was a lively exchange between East and West just as in the Latin kingdom of Jerusalem, it would seem likely that the Athens Gospels, even though its pictures were executed by a Greek artist, was commissioned by a Latin patron. This is all the more likely because a closely related manuscript in Paris[154] is bilingual, i.e., it is written in Greek and Latin.

In addition, it can be shown that either the Athens manuscript or a very similar one from the same workshop was copied by a Western artist. In the well-known model book from Wolfenbüttel there is a page showing two evangelists (Fig. 206);[155] the one on the left is such a close copy of the Athens Matthew, the drapery folds being reproduced line for line, that one is almost tempted to think that it was done by tracing. This also is true of the second evangelist, a strikingly close parallel to the Athens Mark

[153] *Monumenti inediti publicati dall instituto di corrispondenza archeologica*, 12 (1884-85), pl. XXII, 3; T. Birt, *Die Buchrolle in der Kunst* (Leipzig, 1907), p. 114 and fig. 78.

[154] Bibliothèque Nationale, cod. gr. 54; Omont, *Manuscrits grecs*, pls. XC–XCVI.
[155] F. Rücker and H. R. Hahnloser, "Das Musterbuch von Wolfenbüttel," *Mitteilungen der Gesellschaft für vervielfältigende Kunst* (Vienna, 1929), p. 8 and fig. VII [cf. R. W. Scheller, *A Survey of Medieval Model Books* (Haarlem, 1963), pp. 78 ff.].

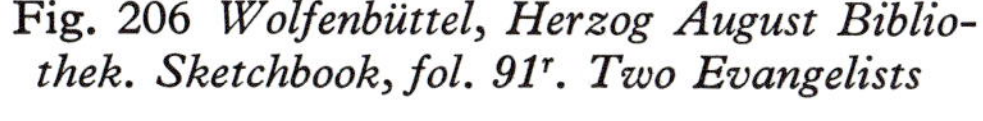

Fig. 206 *Wolfenbüttel, Herzog August Biblio-thek. Sketchbook, fol. 91ʳ. Two Evangelists*

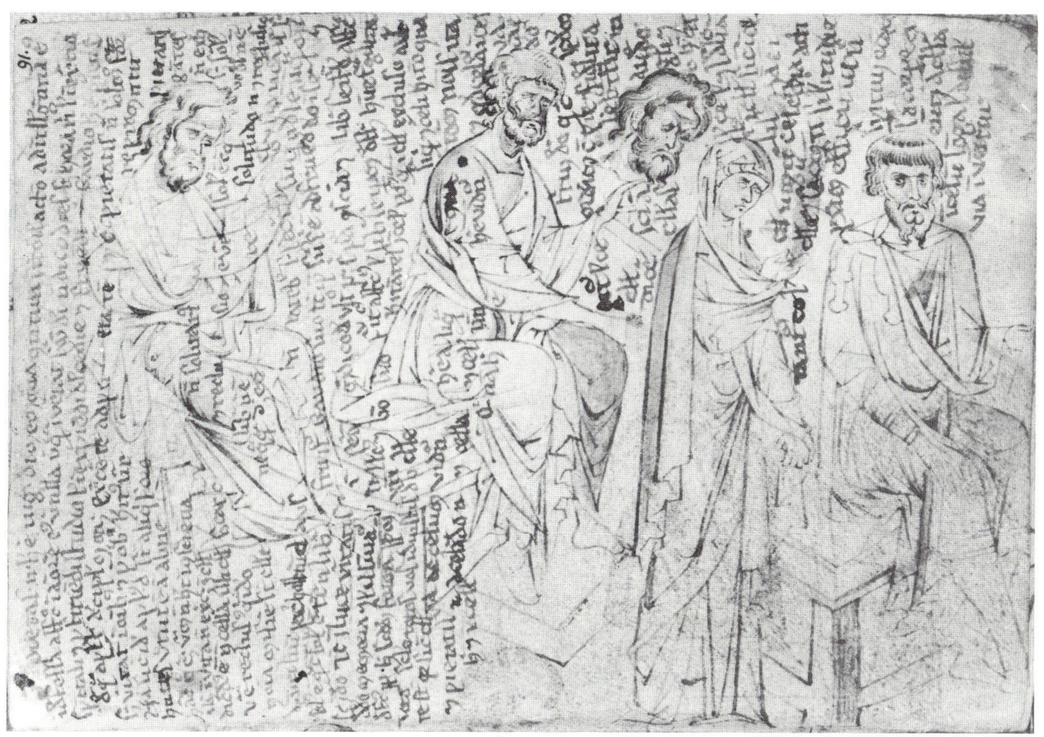

(Fig. 309).[156] Model books such as this one done by a Saxon painter ca. 1230–40 played a decisive part in passing on to the West the wealth of Byzantine types; and the Wolfenbüttel model book allows us to see clearly how this process of transmission must be envisioned.

The Wolfenbüttel model book contains a second series of evangelists (Fig. 207)[157] which by analogy with the preceding series we may assume were also copied with painstaking accuracy from Byzantine miniatures because its draftsman used mainly, and perhaps even

exclusively, Byzantine sources.[158] The exaggerated heaping-up of folds on the lap of the figure on the left, the change from manuscript roll to banderole, and the additional book on the lap are signs of deviation from the pure renaissance types although, on the whole, this figure still retains much of the proportions, plasticity, and bearing of the ancient archetype. John in the Goslar Rathaus Gospels (Fig. 208)[159] repeats this figure in all details though with even more exaggeration of the excited pose and

[156] Buberl, *Miniaturhandschriften*, pl. XXX, 83; Weitzmann, "Constantinopolitan Book Illumination," p. 197 and fig. 3.
[157] Rücker and Hahnloser, "Musterbuch von Wolfenbüttel," p. 6 and fig. IV.

[158] Weitzmann, "Zur byzantinischen Quelle des Wolfenbütteler Musterbuches," *Festschrift Hans R. Hahnloser* (Basel and Stuttgart, 1961), pp. 223 ff.
[159] A. Goldschmidt, *Das Evangeliar im Rathaus zu Goslar* (Berlin, 1910), p. 13 and pl. 10.

Fig. 207 *Wolfenbüttel, Herzog August Biblio-thek. Sketchbook, fol. 89ʳ. Two Evangelists*

Fig. 208 *Goslar, Rathaus. Gospels. John*

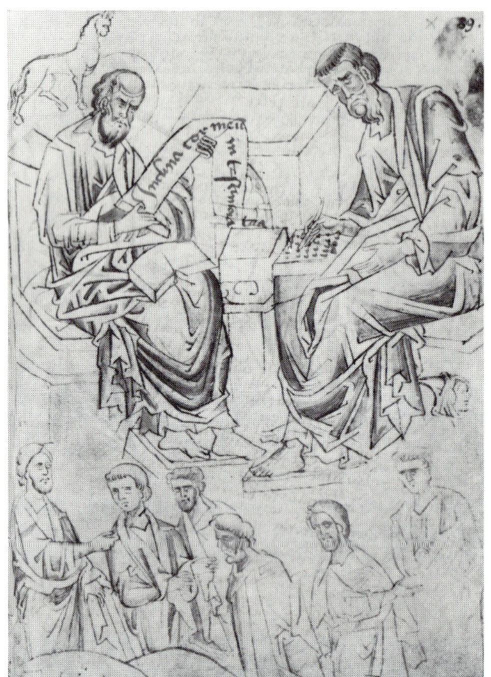

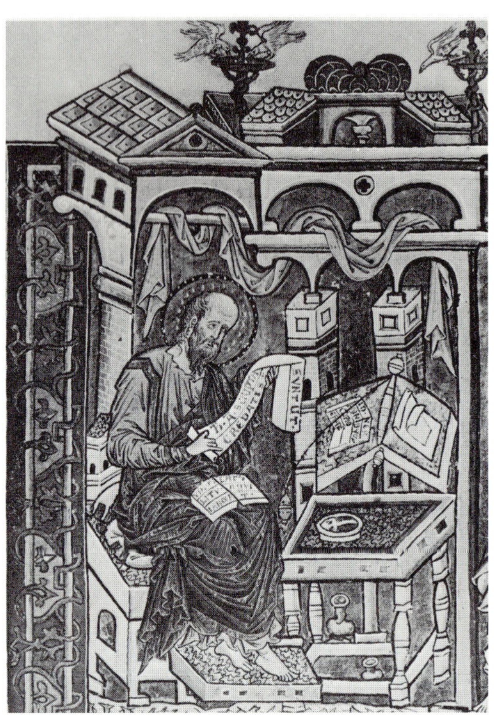

treatment of drapery; and not only the evangelist pictures but also the other miniatures of the manuscript, produced in Saxony around 1270, betray an extensive Byzantine influence. The minia-tures of the Goslar Gospels are remark-able in that the figures are extremely close to Byzantine prototypes whereas the background architecture and the frames are entirely Romanesque, and the same holds true more or less for all of the manuscripts of the Thuringian-Saxon school of art. The explanation for this discrepancy is that the artists used model books such as the one in Wolfenbüttel and that these contained only separate figures and groups of figures. Conse-quently, the Western miniature painters had to supply the other elements from

their own workshop tradition.[160]

Byzantium taught the Western and especially the German painters of the thirteenth century a livelier, more natural, and more three-dimensional figure style, most closely paralleled in manuscripts such as the Athens Gospels. Thus, the stimulus was contemporary Byzantine painting, that is to say miniatures in manuscripts which show the fully developed Late Byzantine style charac-teristic of the thirteenth century. There-fore, we may no longer explain away all Byzantine reflections in Western art by the booty of the year 1204, as has been done so often. Since we have seen that

[160] Cf. Weitzmann, "Icon Painting in the Crusader Kingdom," *Dumbarton Oaks Papers*, 20 (1966), 75 ff.

Late Byzantine manuscripts with a distinctly classical character are to a large degree exact copies of Macedonian Renaissance manuscripts, in the last analysis it is this Macedonian renaissance —although it was only in rare instances the immediate source—that fostered the renewed understanding of ancient art in the Latin West in a way which proved decisive.

SUMMARY

What is, in summary, the importance of the Macedonian Renaissance for art and the history of civilization in general? Soon after Iconoclasm came to an end and cultural interest turned to a study of the ancient world, the patriarch Photius wrote in his *Myriobiblon* critical essays about the ancient authors he had collected, in which his attitude was not preponderantly apologetic as that of the early church fathers had been. Christianity had finally triumphed and paganism was no longer a real threat. He and his contemporaries were in a position to accept the study of the ancient world as a part of one's education. This tolerant attitude not only allowed ancient culture to exist alongside the Christian but even permitted to a certain degree the fusion of the two cultures. When Leo the Wise wrote his homilies he mentioned ancient myths not only in apologia but also to display his cultivation and erudition in so referring to ancient authors.

Fundamentally the same attitude led to the fusion of Christian and ancient elements in such works as the Paris Psalter, the Joshua Roll, and the reconstructable renaissance lectionary. The process was twofold: first personifications and other classical pictorial elements were added to the biblical figures, and second the biblical figures themselves like David or Christ were transformed into the classical. Sixth- and seventh-century silver plates from the imperial workshops show most clearly how these two spheres existed independently in early Byzantine times. The series of David plates found in Cyprus (Fig. 134),[161] their iconography deriving from the same archetype as that of the Paris Psalter,[162] make sparing use of ancient elements; whereas a contemporary workshop, perhaps even the same one, manufactured mythological plates in a purely classicizing style.[163]

In many respects the artist of the Macedonian period was less constrained than the writer in blending the Christian and classical worlds. I know of no literary parallel for equating the Christ of the resurrection triumphing over death with Heracles; and I have the impression that one would seek in vain for such a parallel.

The artistic accomplishment of the Macedonian Renaissance consists not only in the precise copying of and a strong feeling for the style and content of ancient art works, but also in the blending of Christian themes and styles

[161] O. M. Dalton, "Byzantine Plate and Jewellery from Cyprus in Mr. Morgan's Collection," *Burlington Magazine*, 10 (1906–1907), 361 ff.; idem, "A Second Silver Treasure from Cyprus," *Archaeologia*, 60 (1906); M. Rosenberg, *Der Goldschmiede Merkzeichen*, 4 (Berlin, 1928), 640 ff.; E. Cruikshank Dodd, *Byzantine Silver Stamps* ("Dumbarton Oaks Studies," 7 [Washington, 1961]), 178 ff.

[162] Weitzmann, "Psalter Vatopedi," pp. 38 ff.

[163] L. Matzulevich, *Byzantinische Antike* (Berlin, 1929); Cruikshank Dodd, *Silver Stamps*.

with those of the ancient world. The purpose was to unite the ancient physical world with Christian unworldliness and to bring the classical idea of beauty into harmony with Christian transcendentalism.

One of the most consummate creations of this process of amalgamation are the evangelists of a lectionary at Sinai (cod. 204), dated to the end of the tenth century and considered to be a product of the imperial scriptorium. Mark (Fig. 209)[164] stands in the pose of an ancient orator, his roll replaced by a codex studded with gems. The assurance of the classical contrapostal stance is counterpoised by the slender proportions of the figure placed against the gold background as if hovering over the ground, which is indicated only by an incised line. The painting of the head, down to the last detail, has been accomplished in a painterly brush technique derived from ancient art but, at the same time, a strongly spiritual cast has been imparted to the features. The antitheses between the pagan and Christian worlds are abolished here; and a rare harmony is achieved, a harmony to which the West also aspired and which it first attained, in a different manner, during the Italian Renaissance.

Hans Kaufmann once drew attention to the fact that Donatello's tondi of the evangelists in the Old Sacristy of San Lorenzo are, in the last analysis, inspired by Byzantine evangelist portraits.[165]

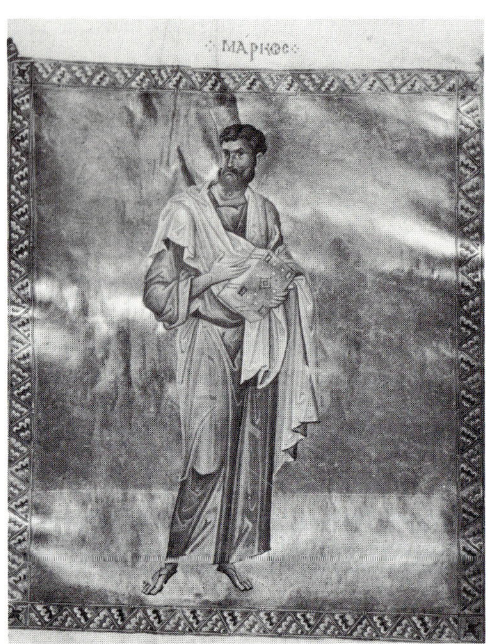

Fig. 209 *Mount Sinai, St. Catherine's. Cod. 204, fol. 5ᵛ. Mark*

Significantly, he illustrated as parallels the evangelist portraits of the Stauronikita Gospel, that is, precisely with those pictures of philosopher-evangelists that we hold to be the most distinctive representatives of the Macedonian Renaissance. Thus Byzantine art makes its appearance as a source of inspiration in the Italian Renaissance along with an antiquarian influence, as when during the sixteenth century apparently no less an artist than Primaticcio copied the pictures of the treatment of dislocated bones, discussed above, from the Florentine manuscript of Apollonius of Citium (Fig. 178).[166]

The Laurenziana is especially rich in

---

[164] V. Beneševič, *Monumenta Sinaitica*, 1 (Leningrad, 1925), 47 ff. and pls. 26–28; Friend, "Portraits of the Evangelists," 1:125 and pl. I, 5–8; Weitzmann, *Byzantinische Buchmalerei*, figs. 211–12.

[165] H. Kauffmann, *Donatello. Eine Einführung*

---

in sein Bilden und Denken (Berlin, 1935), p. 89 and pl. 19.

[166] H. Omont, *Collection de chirurgiens grecs avec dessins attribués au Primatice* (Paris, n.d.).

classical texts, and many of them, especially the early ones of the tenth and eleventh centuries, were acquired by John Laskaris, an excellent connoisseur of manuscripts, sent by Lorenzo the Magnificent to Sultan Bayezid II to conduct the negotiations for the acquisition of Greek manuscripts for the Laurenziana. Thus the Florentine humanists had as sources the manuscripts of the Macedonian Renaissance. The beginnings of what we call humanism lead us back to Constantinople and the time of the Macedonian emperors, and the literary circle which discussed classical texts in the patriarchate of the learned Photius may be regarded as the precursors of the Medicean academy. It would be a distortion of history, of course, to regard the Italian Renaissance merely as a continuation of the Macedonian Renaissance. Nonetheless, the humanistic movement in the East, limited to a small circle of learned men, which began at the end of the ninth century and had a more or less unbroken tradition until the fifteenth century, had an influence on the literary and artistic life of Italy which should not be underestimated, an influence which received a strong impetus especially during the years of the Council of Florence. If today we still are able to read Plato, Homer, and Euripides in the original texts, we owe this primarily to those excellent Greek scholars who in the tenth century saved many texts from destruction by making new copies; and if today we again enjoy a close contact with Byzantine art, this is chiefly due to the harmony of classical and Christian forms attained at the time of the Macedonian Renaissance.

9

The Mandylion and Constantine Porphyrogennetos

OUT of the great wealth of icons in Saint Catherine's monastery on Mount Sinai about one hundred were selected, after the erection of a modern wing against the south wall, for a permanent home in a special room, marked "Picture Gallery." About twenty of them, by reason of their small size, early origin, high quality, or endangered condition of preservation, are exhibited in a glass case, and one of these is the icon which is the subject of the present study (Fig. 210).[1] It was first published by George and Maria Sotiriou in their recent book on the icons of Mount Sinai, in which an essential part of this extraordinary collection was made known for the first time. Here they proposed for the icon under consideration a date in the late ninth century and a localization in Edessa.[2]

It is divided into two zones, the upper of which, being higher and thus more important than the lower, depicts at the left the apostle Thaddaeus (Fig. 211) seated on a throne with a simple, draped back and with his name inscribed in red letters on the gold ground.[3] He is dressed in a white tunic with a purple clavus and a white mantle, and his youthful head is directed toward the center just like that of King Abgarus opposite him (Fig. 212), whose identity is likewise established by an inscription. Dressed in a dark blue tunic and a chestnut-colored mantle, he sits on a throne of similar shape but with a more prominently displayed cushion. His dignified head is marked by a rather long and full beard and the Byzantine imperial crown with the pendulia, and on his feet he wears the pearl-studded purple shoes which are the prerogative of the Byzantine emperor. In his hands he prominently displays the Mandylion,

Reprinted with permission from *Cahiers Archéologiques*, XI (1960), pp. 163–184.

[1] I wish to express my sincere thanks to His Eminence, Archbishop Porphyrios III, his learned secretary, the Archimandrite Gregorios, and the late Pater Christophoros, the skevophylax and librarian, for their continuous support of the expedition organized by the universities of Michigan, Princeton, and Alexandria in the summer of 1958, whose investigations included the study of the icons. This will be the first publication of several essays on individual icons prior to their more comprehensive publication. [See subsequent publications by Weitzmann: "Thirteenth-Century Crusader Icons on Mount Sinai," *Art Bulletin*, 45 (1963), 179 ff.; "Fragments of an Early St. Nicholas Triptych on Mount Sinai," *Deltion Archaiologikēs Hetaireios*, 4th ser., 4 (1964), 1 ff.; "Eine Spätkomnenische Verkündigungsikone des Sinai und die zweite byzantinische Welle des 12. Jahrhunderts," *Festschrift für Herbert von Einem zum 16. Februar 1965* (Berlin, 1965), pp. 299 ff.; "Eine vorikonoklastische Ikone des Sinai mit der Darstellung des Chairete," *Tortulae. Studien zu altchristlichen und byzantinischen Monumenten*, 30 (1966), 317 ff.; "An Encaustic Icon with the Prophet Elijah at Mount Sinai," *Mélanges offerts à K. Michalowski* (Warsaw, 1966), pp. 713 ff.; "Icon Painting in the Crusader Kingdom," *Dumbarton Oaks Papers*, 20 (1966), 49 ff.; and "Byzantine Miniature and Icon Painting in the Eleventh Century," *Proceedings of the XIIIth International Congress of Byzantine Studies. Oxford. 5–10 September 1966* (Oxford, 1967), pp. 207 ff., reprinted herewith, pp. 271 ff.]

[2] G. and M. Sotiriou, *Icones du Mont Sinaï* (Athens, 1956–58), 1:figs. 34–36, 2:49–51.

[3] [A color reproduction of the Thaddeus wing is to be found in Weitzmann, "Sinai Peninsula. Icon Painting from the Sixth to the Twelfth Century," in *A Treasury of Icons* (contributions by K. Weitzmann, M. Chatzidakis, K. Miatev, and S. Radojčić (New York, 1967)), pl. 11.]

Fig. 210 *Mount Sinai, St. Catherine's. Icon.*
Abgarus Story and Saints

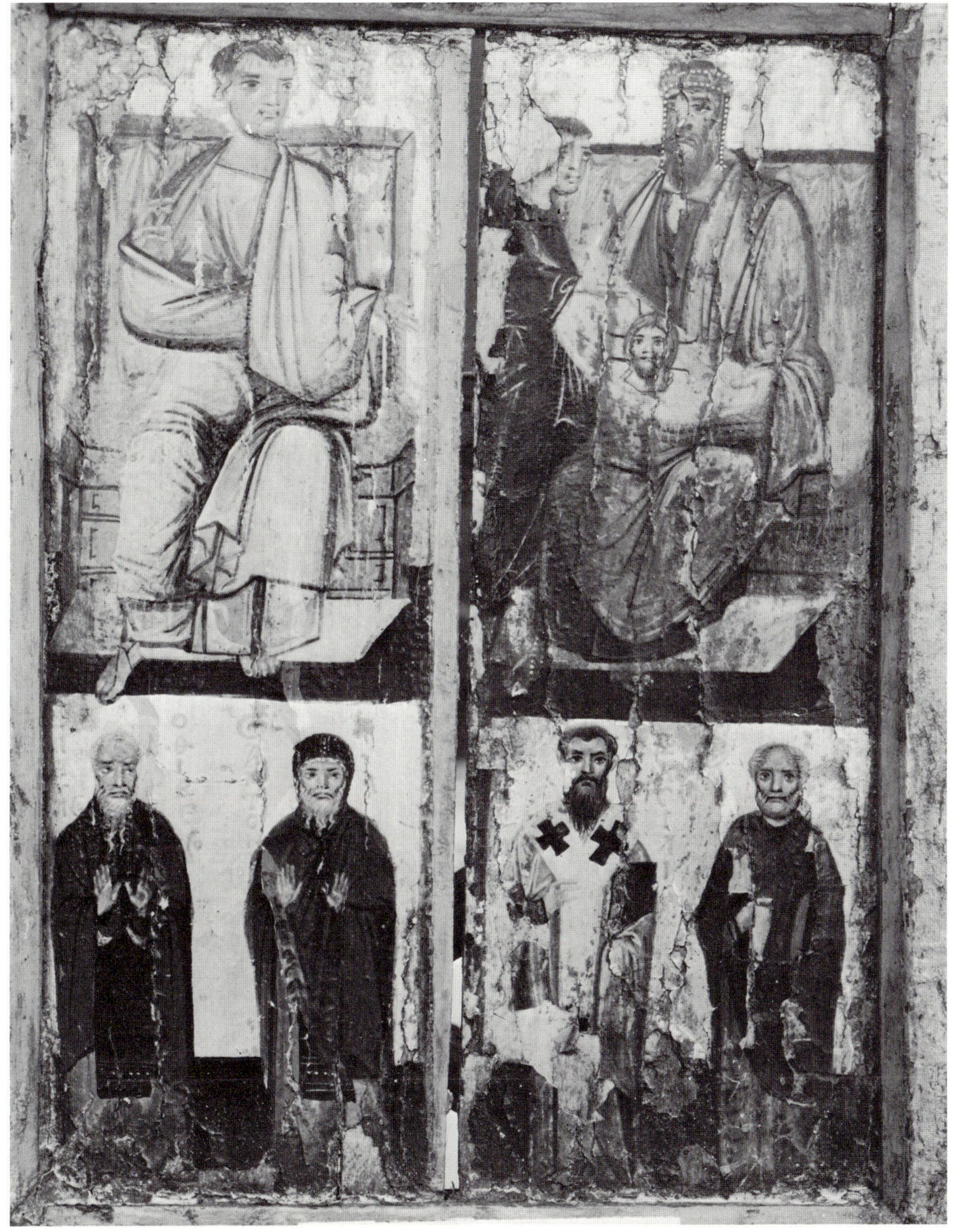

Fig. 211 *Mount Sinai, St. Catherine's. Icon. Abgarus Story and Saints (det. of Apostle Thaddaeus)*

Fig. 212 *Mount Sinai, St. Catherine's. Icon. Abgarus Story and Saints (det. of King Abgarus)*

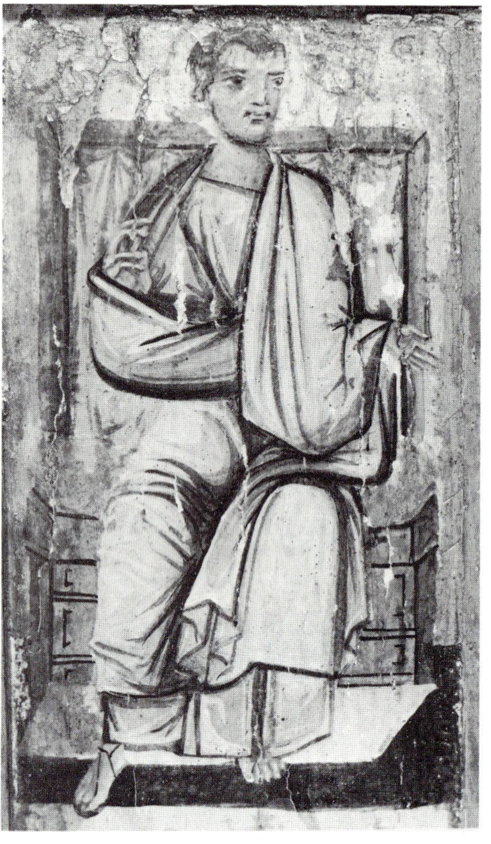

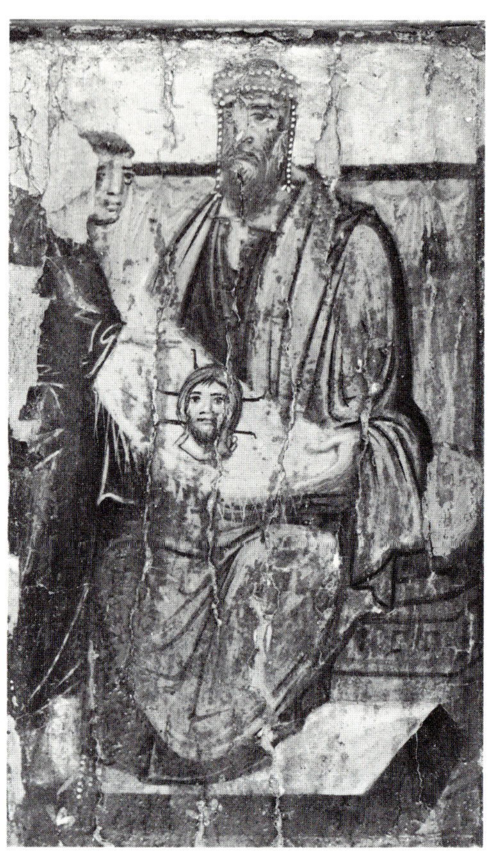

the holy image of Edessa,[4] which has just been delivered to him by a messenger in a dark blue garment to whom the name Ananias is given by some sources.[5] In the lower row (Fig. 213) are

four standing saints: three are monks in light brown and chestnut-colored garb of whom the two at the left, inscribed Paul of Thebes and Antonios, wear, in addition, the so-called megaloschema, while the third at the extreme right, inscribed Ephraim the Syrian, holds a huge codex just like his neighbor Basil, the founder of organized Greek monasticism, who is depicted in bishop's vestments. The surface of the icon, particularly around the edges, is somewhat damaged through flaking, but there are no restorations—save for a slightly discoloring varnish.

[4] For the first and comprehensive art historical study of the Mandylion consult A. Grabar, *La Sainte Face de Laon, le Mandylion dans l'Art orthodoxe* (Prague, 1931). [Most recently, C. Bertelli, "Storia e vicende dell' Immagine Edissena di San Silvestro in Capite a Roma," *Paragone*, 217 (1968), 3 ff.]

[5] The fullest account of the Abgarus legend, its various versions and critical evaluation, is given by E. von Dobschütz, *Christusbilder, Untersuchungen zur Christlichen Legende* (Leipzig, 1899), pp. 102 ff., 158* ff., 29** ff.

Fig. 213 *Mount Sinai, St. Catherine's. Icon. Abgarus Story and Saints. (det. of Four Monastic Saints)*

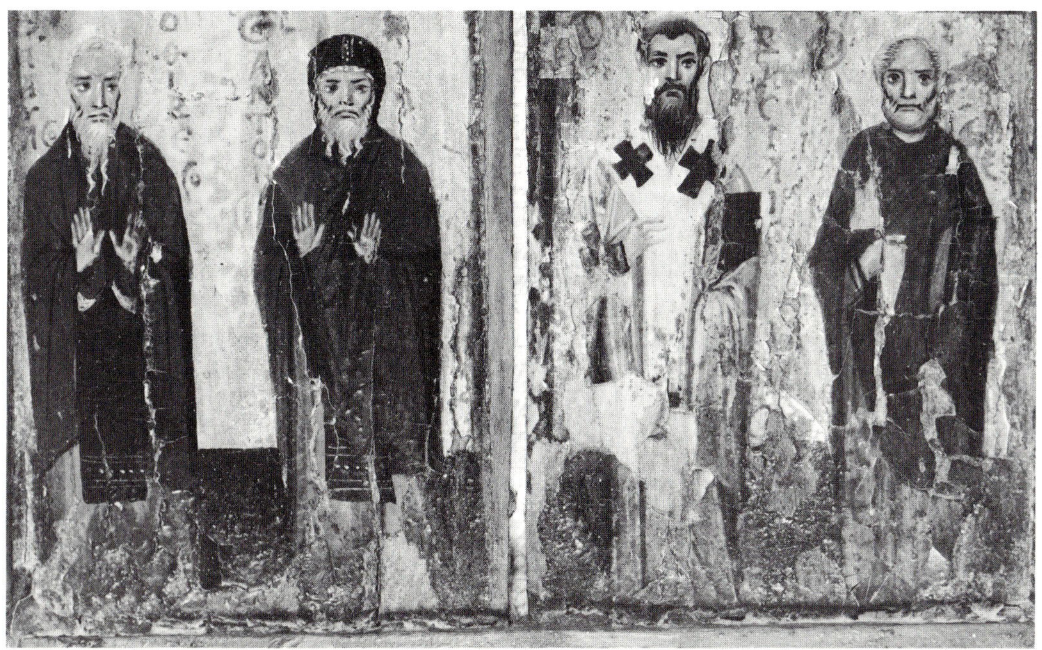

The icon is set into a broad frame which, as the Sotirious have already noticed, is worked separately.[6] In good Middle-Byzantine icons picture area and frame are as a rule worked in one piece, and the present frame of this icon is obviously of a rather recent date. If the frame were removed, one would immediately realize that the icon is made up of two separate vertical panels of equal size and, moreover, that these are two wings, apparently from a triptych. Unfortunately they are so tightly set in the frame that one cannot see the edges and analyze the mechanism by which the wings were once connected with the now-lost central plaque. Yet there are other triptych wings in the Sinai collec-

tion that give the clue. There is a pair with the standing figures of Peter, Paul, John Chrysostom, and Nicholas which the Sotirious with good reason date as early as the seventh/eighth century.[7] This, too, is set in a modern frame of which the lower part, however, is lost, laying bare the lower edges of the wings.

[6] With the frame the icon measures 34.5 × 25.2 cm and each of the two vertical panels of the icon proper 28 × 9.5 cm.

[7] *Sotiriou, Icones*, 1, pls. 21, 23 and color pl. III; 2: 36 ff. For other examples of very early triptych wings consult O. Wulff and M. Alpatoff, *Denkmäler der Ikonenmalerei* (Dresden, 1925), p. 15, fig. 5 and p. 32, fig. 13. A painted wing found in Dura and depicting a Victory proves the existence of such triptychs in classical antiquity. See M. J. Rostovtzeff and P. V. C. Bauer, "Victory on a Painted Panel found at Dura," in *The Excavations at Dura-Europos: Preliminary Report of the Second Season of Work* (New Haven, 1931), pp. 181 ff. and frontispiece and pl. I. Another panel from Berlin is reproduced here on pl. XXII.

Here one sees in the corners protruding pegs, made to fit holes in horizontal strips that were worked separately and nailed upon the top and bottom frame of the central panel. In this way the wings could be turned in front of the central panel instead of alongside it. This is exactly the mechanism common in Byzantine ivories that are contemporary with the Abgarus icon, a mechanism which because of its fragility and apparent impracticality has survived intact in only two instances.[8]

Aside from the narrow, high format, the organization in two superimposed scenes is also typical of triptych wings, as can be seen in a great number of Byzantine ivories. Most commonly they are filled with frontally standing saints, similar to those that occupy the lower zone of the Sinai icon. But how was the missing central part organized? By analogy with the ivories, our richest comparative material as far as contemporary triptychs are concerned, there are two possibilities: either it contained one single subject or it was horizontally divided in the same way as the wings. About the theme of the missing center of the Sinai icon there can be, in our opinion, little doubt: it must have contained a depiction of the Mandylion, the holy image that was not made by human hands—an ἀχειροποίητος. This image exists in a considerable number of copies,[9] but what did it look like?

Dobschütz assumed[10] that the various representations of the Mandylion, which differ considerably from each other, are ultimately not based on an autopsy of the famous relic, which apparently was very rarely to be seen without its protective cover, but were made on the basis of the legendary texts for the illustration of which the artists, while using earlier models, at the same time depended on the ideal of the Christ head that prevailed in their own time.

In this case one can justifiably assume that the Mandylion which Abgarus holds in his hands is but a miniature version of the bigger one in the lost central plaque. The head of Christ shows a comparatively round face, framed by somewhat loose strands of hair and a rather full, rounded beard. This Christ type is quite comparable to other tenth-century Christ heads,[11] while for the original relic, rediscovered in A.D. 544, we would assume quite a different type, i.e., the Syrian-Palestinian type with the pointed beard. The one point which the face of the Mandylion of the icon must have shared with the original is the absolute frontality, though this is a feature, of course, not confined to the Mandylion type of Christ. How the head of Christ began to change under the influence of the style of the time may be seen in eleventh/twelfth century representations of the Mandylion, chiefly

---

[8] A. Goldschmidt and K. Weitzmann, *Die byzantinischen Elfenbeinskulpturen*, 2 (Berlin, 1930–34), pl. XXVIII, no. 72 (Berlin); pl. LIV, no. 155 (Liverpool).
[9] Several copies are reproduced by Grabar, *Sainte Face*, pls. I–III, VII.

[10] *Christusbilder*, p. 169.
[11] Compare, for example, the Christ head in the narthex of Hagia Sophia, presumably from the time of Leo VI. Reproduced most recently in A. Grabar, *L'iconoclasme byzantine. Dossier archéologique* (Paris, 1957), fig. 121.

Fig. 214 *Alexandria, Greek Patriarchal Library. Cod. 35, p. 286. Mandylion*

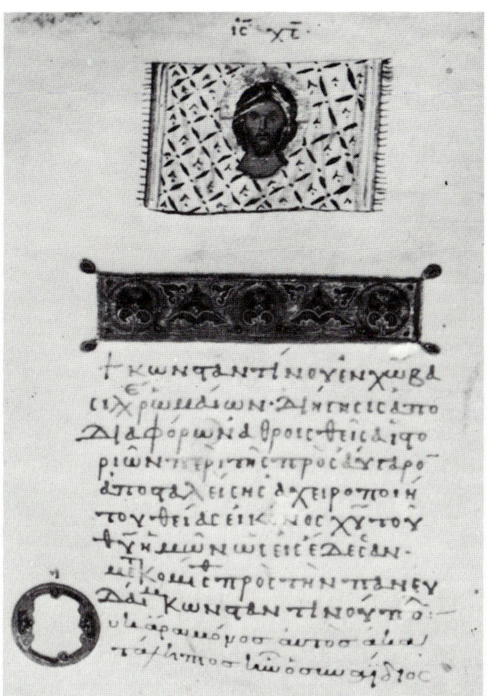

miniatures,[12] including the one of a hitherto unpublished eleventh-century menologion in the Greek Patriarchal Library of Alexandria (Fig. 214).[13] All of them depict a more ascetic type with leaner cheeks and a more pointed beard, in conformity with the stylistic tendencies and general concepts of these centuries. At the same time what these miniatures have in common with the image on the icon is the accentuated line which sets off the neck from the collar of the tunic, a feature which, presumably,

did not exist in the holy image. This, then, would be yet another indication that our pictorial representations are not based on a familiarity with the great relic kept in the imperial palace church.

Assuming, then, a representation of a Mandylion like that in King Abgarus' hands as the subject of the lost central panel of the triptych, we come back to the question: did it occupy the whole panel or simply the larger, upper half? While neither of the two possibilities can be discarded in principle, nevertheless we prefer the second alternative, because the Mandylion, normally, has a shape that is wider than it is high and, therefore, would better fit a two-part central panel. Moreover, Thaddaeus and Abgarus are both turning toward something between them, whereas the standing saints show no such orientation.

If the second alternative is accepted, then one has to raise the question as to the most likely subject in the narrower, lower strip of the central panel. In our opinion there can be little doubt that here were depicted other standing saints, four or rather five in number, in similar, frontal positions, thus giving an effect of a rhythmic alignment comparable to that in the three most splendid ivory triptychs of the tenth century.[14] Yet, in spite of this similar, formal arrangement, the iconography must have been different from that of the ivories. The latter have an abbreviated set of Apostles, five in number, who form a liturgical unity with the Deesis above and with the other saints on the wings, illustrating

[12] For example, in Vatican cod. Rossianus 251. J. R. Martin, *The Illustration of the Heavenly Ladder of John Climacus* (Princeton, 1954), p. 110 and pl. LXXXIV, no. 231; Grabar, *Iconoclasme*, p. 20 and fig. 67.

[13] T. D. Moschonas, Κατάλογοι τῆς Πατρι-αρχικῆς Βιβλιοθήκης (Alexandria, 1945), I Χειρόγραφα, 51–54.

[14] Goldschmidt and Weitzmann, *Elfenbein-skulpturen*, pl. X, no. 31 (Rome, Palazzo di Venezia); XI–XII, no. 32 (Vatican, Museo Cristiano); XIII, no. 33 (Paris, Louvre).

the prayer of intercession of the Greek liturgy.[15] For the lost center of the Sinai icon we propose, instead, the depiction of other Church fathers. The main reason is the presence of Basil who, whenever grouped with other saints in Middle Byzantine art, usually appears together with John Chrysostom and Gregory of Nazianzus. Who the other two or three missing saints were—most likely bishops—is difficult to say. Nicholas is a very likely choice, but any additional suggestion must appear arbitrary. A rough sketch (Fig. 215) may help to visualize the general impression of the reconstructed triptych.

Such an arrangement of saints drawn up in a row with the Church fathers in the center and the monastic saints flanking them has its parallels in miniature painting. There is in the splendid lectionary in Dionysiu on Mount Athos (cod. 587) from the eleventh century a picture (Fig. 216)[16] in which five Church fathers—the four in the front row clearly indentifiable as Basil, Nicholas, John Chrysostom, and Gregory of Nazianzus and the fifth, placed in the second row, most likely as Gregory of Nyssa—are flanked by monastic saints with crosses of martyrdom. Unfortunately the specific meaning of this miniature is not quite clear since it heads the lection of the Sunday before Christmas the title of

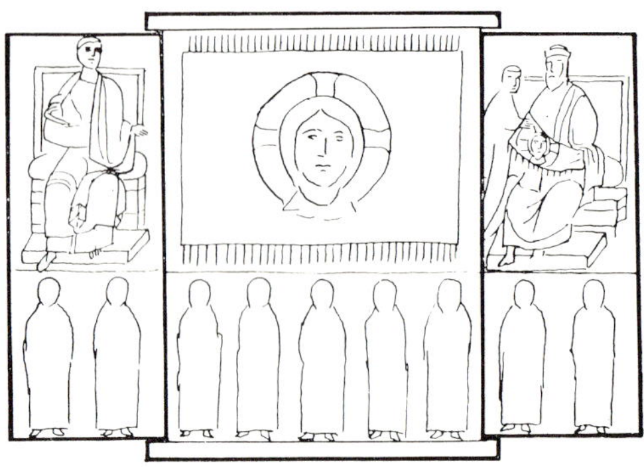

Fig. 215 *Reconstruction of the Sinai Triptych*

which, τῶν ἁγίων πατέρων (in other manuscripts given more precisely as τῶν ἁγίων προπατέρων), was apparently misinterpreted by our illustrator as Church fathers rather than as forefathers. Other manuscripts correctly illustrate Abraham, Isaac, and Jacob in in this place.[17] Another picture with an assembly of various saints appears on folio 40[v] in the Dionysiu Lectionary as an illustration of All Saints Day, but here Church fathers and monks are joined by a third group, the soldier saints, who are lacking in the first mentioned miniature of the Dionysiu Lectionary and, in all likelihood, were not included in the Sinai icon. There is no point in trying to push the comparison between icon and miniature any further. The purpose of introducing the latter is merely to aid our visual impression of what the Sinai icon must have looked like in its original state and to define the iconographical layout within a larger framework.

---

[15] E. H. Kantorowicz, "Ivories and Litanies," *Journal of the Warburg and Courtauld Institutes*, 5 (1942), 56 ff.

[16] For this manuscript see Weitzmann, "The Narrative and Liturgical Gospel Illustrations," *New Testament Manuscript Studies*, M. M. Parvis and A. P. Wikgren (eds.) (Chicago, 1950), p. 157 and *passim* (here given as cod. 740, but the more correct signature is 587) [reprinted herewith, pp. 247 ff.].

[17] As, for instance, in the eleventh-century lectionary in the Vatican (cod. gr. 1156, fol. 273[r]).

Fig. 216 *Mount Athos, Dionysiu. Cod. 587, fol. 126ʳ. Holy Fathers*

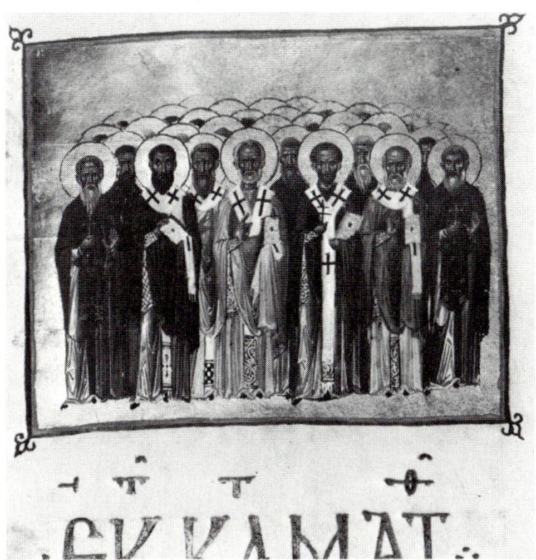

Narrative Illustrations of the Abgarus Legend

The handing over of the Mandylion to King Abgarus by a messenger (Fig. 212) is a storytelling feature which suggests that the icon is dependent on a narrative illustration of the Abgarus legend. It is to be expected that our richest pictorial source for a lengthier depiction of the Abgarus story should be neither frescoes, where it is rare, nor icons, where usually the image of the Mandylion alone occurs, but miniature painting. Here it is important to realize that the stimulus to a rich and diversified literary as well as pictorial narration was provided by the transfer of the famous relic to Constantinople in 944. Shortly thereafter, perhaps for the first anniversary on 16 August 945, or not long thereafter, a feast homily was written which in the titles of many copies, including the menologion of Alexandria (Fig. 214), is attributed to the Emperor Constantine Porphyrogennetos. Dobschütz, who edited this text, argues that it was not written by the emperor himself but surely by a court cleric under his close supervision.[18] About the same time or shortly thereafter a variant of the story was written for the menaeon, and with these two texts a firm tradition was established now that the bringing of the Mandylion to the capital had become an important calendar feast. Yet while menaea in general are rarely illustrated—no illustration of the Abgarus story is preserved in any of those known to us—there are several Metaphrastian menologia in which the imperial feast homily was incorporated with a set of pictures. In all probability this narrative picture cycle was made for the first publication of the homily or very soon thereafter, i.e., quite likely before the homily was incorporated into the Metaphrastian menologion. Whether this cycle, even in part, harks back to an older Edessene tradition or whether any such tradition existed at all, of which no trace is left,[19] is impossible to say, while on the other hand there is much to be said for the hypothesis that the pictures were made for the new homily for the same purpose as the text itself, namely to propagate the newly established feast.

Aside from the manuscript in Alexandria in which the Mandylion is the only decoration of the feast homily (Fig. 214), there are two more menologia that possess a set of narrative scenes. The one in Paris (Bibliothèque Nationale cod. gr. 1528) from about the second

[18] Dobschütz, *Christusbilder*, pp. 160 ff. and pp. 39** ff.

[19] Grabar, *Sainte Face*, p. 23.

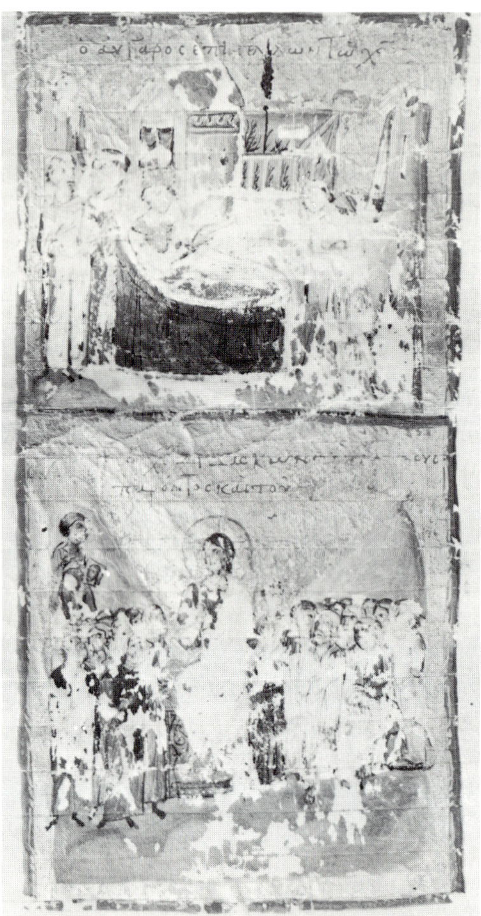

Fig. 217 *Paris, Bibliothèque Nationale. Cod. gr. 1528, fol. 181ᵛ. Abgarus Sends Letter and Christ Teaching*

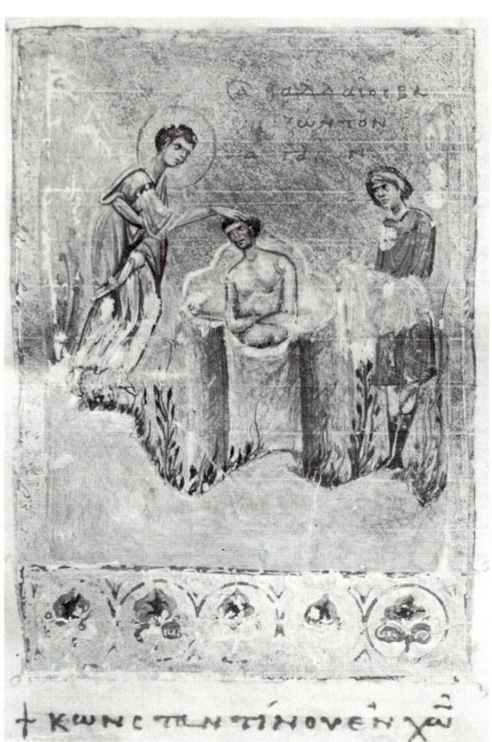

Fig. 218 *Paris, Bibliothèque Nationale. Cod. gr. 1528, fol. 182ʳ. Baptism of Abgarus*

half of the eleventh century[20] contains three episodes which, damaged as they are, nevertheless still leave the layout of the compositions clearly recognizable. In the first (Fig. 217) Abgarus, on a sickbed, sends a letter to Christ which he hands over to a messenger. King Abgarus is depicted like a Byzantine emperor, attended by two court officials in front of a house suggesting the palace and an enclosed garden. All this breathes an air of court setting and court art. In the second, Christ on the throne teaches to a crowd gathered around Him, while the painter with the Mandylion in his outstretched hands stands at a respectful distance. In the third (Fig. 218) Thaddaeus baptizes King Abgarus in a font while a servant—like the angels in Christ's baptism—holds a towel in his covered hands. Another menologion in Moscow (Historical Museum, cod. 382), from the year 1063,[21] has four scenes

[20] H. Omont, *Inventaire sommaire des manuscrits grecs de la Bibliothèque Nationale* (Paris, 1886–98), 2:80; K. Weitzmann, *Ancient Book Illumination* (Cambridge, Mass., 1959), pp. 120 ff. and pl. LXI, no. 129.

[21] A. Vladimir, *Sistematičeskoe opisanie rukopisi Moskowskoi Sinodalnoi Biblioteki* (Moscow, 1894), 1:575; *Exempla codicum graecorum*

Fig. 219 *Moscow, Historical Museum. Cod. 382, fol. 192ᵛ. Abgarus and Mandylion*

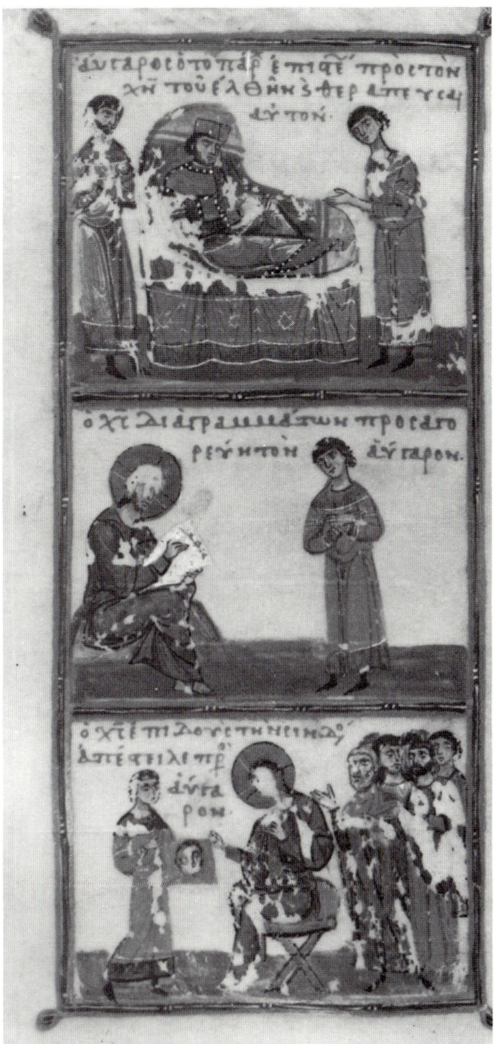

which are simpler and confined to fewer figures (Fig. 219).[22] The first shows once more King Abgarus on the sickbed, sending out the messenger, but there is only one court official and the architectural setting is omitted altogether. In the second, Christ, sitting on a hillock, is writing a letter while the messenger with crossed arms is facing Him, standing in an attentive pose; in the third, the messenger holds the Mandylion enfolded before Christ who sits on a folding chair, surrounded by the citizens of Jerusalem. The fourth, of which no photograph was available, depicts the bringing of the veil to Abgarus (Fig. 220). The Paris and the Moscow manuscripts agree only in the first scene and differ in all subsequent ones. Der Nersessian ascribed these differences to different redactions, but, in our opinion, there is another explanation possible, namely that there existed one archetype with a rather lengthy narrative cycle from which the copyists in Moscow and Paris made different selections, while copying in only one case, at the very beginning, the same episode.

There is evidence for the existence of an archetype with a rather extensive cycle. The Morgan Library in New York possesses a unique scroll (cod. 499)

litteris minisculis scriptorum, etc. ed. G. Cereteli and S. Sobolevski (Moscow, 1911–13), I, pl. XIX; *Dated Greek Minuscule Manuscripts to the Year 1200*, K. and S. Lake (eds.) (Boston, 1936), 6, pls. 408–11; V. Lazarev, *Istoriia Vizantiiskoi Zhivopisi* (Moscow, 1947), 1, pp. 109 and 313; and 2, pl. 132. I am very grateful to Professor Sirarpie Der Nersessian for giving me permission to publish the photograph she owns of the Moscow miniature.

[22] For a discussion of this and related manuscripts see S. Der Nersessian, "La légende d'Abgar d'après un rouleau illustré de la bibliothèque Pierpont Morgan à New York," in *Actes du IVᵉ Congrès internationale des Études byzantines* in *Bull. de l'Inst. Arch. Bulgare*, X (1936), p. 105; idem., "The Illustrations of the Metaphrastian Menologium," *Late Classical and Mediaeval Studies in Honor of Albert M. Friend, Jr.* (Princeton, 1955), p. 229.

Fig. 220 *Moscow, Historical Museum. Cod. 382, fol. 192^v. Abgarus and Mandylion*

Fig. 221 *New York, Morgan Library. Cod. 499, pict. III. Thaddaeus*

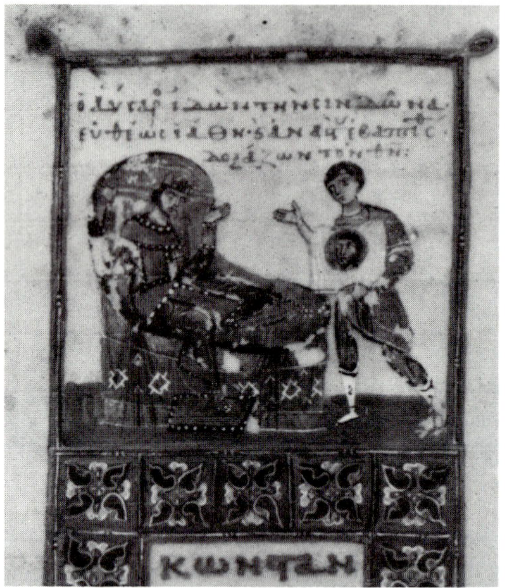

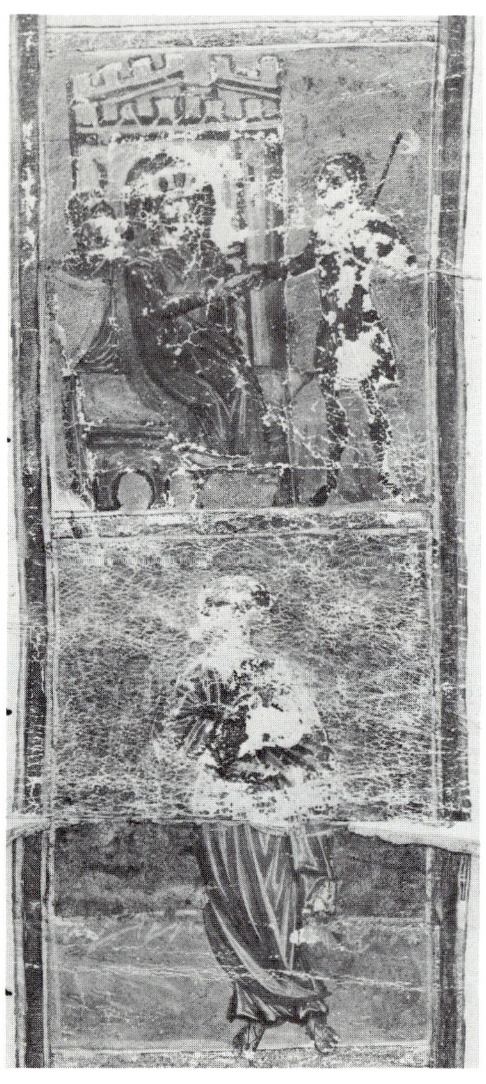

that contains the exchange of letters between Abgarus and Christ concerning the depiction of Christ's face. This text that tells the Abgarus legend in an abbreviated form[23] was written about 1032, the year when this autograph letter of Christ also was sent as a relic to Constantinople.[24] In the Morgan scroll this *Epistola Abgari* is illustrated with no less than fourteen miniatures which were first published and discussed *in extenso* by Der Nersessian, who dated the scroll in the end of the fourteenth or beginning of the fifteenth century.[25] The cycle begins with a miniature in

which King Abgarus gives the letter destined for Christ to a messenger (Fig. 221) and it ends with the messenger, after his return, handing over the Mandylion to Abgarus (Fig. 222). The former corresponds to the initial miniature in the Moscow and Paris menologia, save that Abgarus in the scroll is sitting on a

[23] E. von Dobschütz, "Der Briefwechsel zwischen Abgar und Jesus," *Zeitschrift für wissenschaftliche Theologie*, 43 (1900), pp. 422 ff.

[24] [Cf. the narrative scenes on the thirteenth/fourteenth century Byzantine frame in San Silvestro in Capite, Rome. Bertelli, *Imagine Edissena*, figs. 7–11.]

[25] Der Nersessian, "Legende d'Abgar."

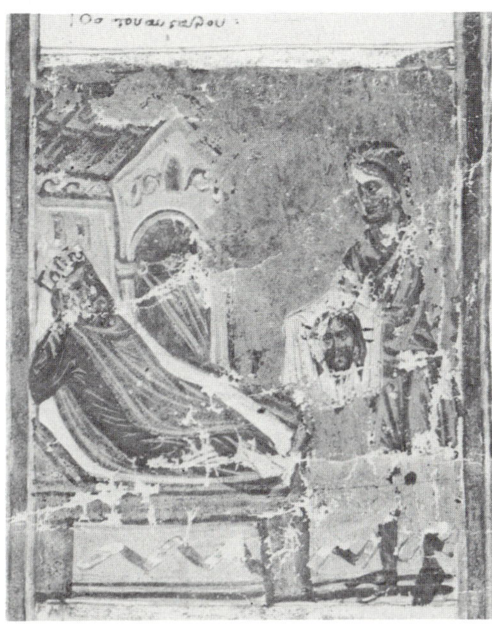

Fig. 222 *New York, Morgan Library. Cod. 499, pict. XIV. Abgarus and Mandylion*

bench-like throne and not lying on a sickbed, and the final miniature with the handing-over of the Mandylion has its parallel in the fourth miniature of the Moscow menologion.[26] One gets the impression that just as the Epistola Abgari is an abbreviation of the lengthier feast homily, so is the miniature cycle, rich as it is, reduced as compared with the archetype behind the Moscow and Paris menologia, since in the Epistola there is no place for the Baptism of Abgarus (Fig. 218).

What, then, is the relation between this narrative tradition and the Sinai icon? The scene of the handing-over of the Mandylion to King Abgarus is the very

one with which the cycles of the Moscow menologion and the New York scroll (Figs. 220 and 222) end. There are formal differences which can be explained, however, by the icon-painter's dual purpose of condensing the narrative model into a steeper format that is higher than it is wide and of giving to the main protagonist a more hieratic appearance in conformity with the icon tradition, i.e., of casting a temporal event into forms that suggest greater permanency.

First of all, in order to orient the flanking figures on the triptych wings toward the now missing center, the icon-painter was forced to depict Abgarus in mirror reversal, looking toward the left, whereas in the narrative miniatures he almost always turns to the right, since the action normally moves in that direction. This change of orientation affected the placing of the messenger; in the miniatures he approaches or leaves from the right side, but in the icon he is moved to the opposite side. Furthermore, by reason of the changed format, the artist had to condense the scene and consequently placed the Mandylion, which in the model is held by the messenger, in the hands of Abgarus. The abruptness of this change can still be seen in some rough spots which the artist did not succeed in smoothing over. It will be noticed that Abgarus holds the Mandylion only with the left hand, there being no space left for the right. The hand seen in the upper corner of the Mandylion is that of the messenger; it does not hold the relic but is extended in a gesture of speech and protrudes from an arm that is much too short. The whole figure of the messenger is very tightly

---

[26] Since I have not seen the manuscript the extent of the agreement of formal details cannot be discussed. [The fourth scene, is herewith reproduced through the courtesy of M. Tschepkina, Fig. 220.]

squeezed, because the icon-painter clearly wanted to place the king in the very center of the composition, whereas in the miniature king and messenger balance each other. Still another change, resulting from the same desire for a more iconic effect, is that Abgarus is seated on a throne rather than lying on the sickbed (Fig. 222). But since in the miniature tradition the seated type also occurs at times (Fig. 221), the icon-painter might have been inspired by some such scene of the same cycle. In both miniature and icon, King Abgarus wears the imperial Byzantine crown, in the latter even with the typical pendulia. Yet, since in Byzantine art any king or ruler—biblical, legendary, or historical—may be characterized by the regalia of the Byzantine emperor, no particular significance can be attached to this point.

Opposite King Abgarus we see Thaddaeus (Fig. 211), one of the seventy disciples, who preached in Edessa, according to some tradition, converted Abgarus and the Edessenes to Christianity, and baptized the king, as depicted in the final miniature of the Paris menologion (Fig. 218). He sits on a throne like that of Abgarus, blessing with the right hand and extending the left toward the Mandylion we believe to have formed the center of the triptych. The forcefulness of the gesture of the left hand, which in comparison to the right one is much too small, makes us believe that it results from the icon-painter's intent to adjust the figure to the present context. The basic concept is that of an author portrait, and originally Thaddaeus may well have held a scroll or a codex in his left hand. An isolated figure of Thaddaeus in the form of an author portrait exists in the tradition of the narrative cycle and occurs in the Morgan scroll directly after the introductory miniature (Fig. 221). Indeed, here he is depicted holding a codex in his left hand. It is quite conceivable that the icon-painter actually made the alteration from a standing to a seated figure for no other reason than to create a companion figure to King Abgarus enthroned. The idea of such a transformation is supported by the rather weak organic relationship between the upper and the lower parts of the body. The making-up of a human figure from heterogeneous parts is not infrequent in miniature painting of the Macedonian Renaissance. Unfortunately the face of the apostle in the Morgan miniature is badly flaked, but to judge from the scene of Abgarus' baptism (Fig. 218) Thaddaeus was depicted in miniature and icon alike as beardless and very youthful.

Now, if the icon wings depend, indeed, as we have tried to demonstrate, on the narrative tradition as manifested in the illustrated manuscripts, then certain conclusions will have to be drawn which will make a date of the icon in the ninth century and its origin in Edessa highly unlikely. If we are right that the miniature tradition started with the feast homily, attributed to Constantine Porphyrogennetos and written at the earliest in 945, then this would also be the earliest possible date for the icon; furthermore, it would bring all derivative monuments, including the icon, into the orbit of Constantinopolitan art. Yet, the dating and localizing of the Sinai wings should not be based exclusively on their iconographical relation to the miniature tradition but on independent, stylistic evidence.

THE DATE OF THE SINAI ICON

As was said at the beginning, the Sotirious have dated the Sinai icon at the end of the ninth century, i.e., before the Mandylion was brought to Constantinople. They base this date on stylistic similarities with the miniatures of the Cosmas Indicopleustes in the Vatican (cod. gr. 699), the homilies of Gregory of Nazianzus in Paris (Bibliothèque Nationale, cod. gr. 510), and the homilies of John Chrysostom in Athens (National Library, cod. 210). But since the date of the latter is controversial and a tenth- rather than a ninth-century origin a high probability,[27] the case for a ninth-century date of the icon would have to rest on comparisons with the other two manuscripts, one of which, the Gregory, is dated between 880 and 886, while the other, the Cosmas, appears to be slightly earlier, but not before the second half of the ninth century.

For comparison with the enthroned Abgarus the Sotirious pointed particularly to the figure of Solomon in the Judgment scene of the Paris Gregory.[28] In both icon and miniature we deal no doubt with very articulate figures in which the classical heritage of organic body treatment is strongly felt. Yet there are essential differences too. In the Solomon figure the garment clings to the body, revealing the shape of the legs, while in the figure of King Abgarus the garment is slightly billowing, disassociating itself from the body underneath in such a way that the folds gain a greater fluency. It looks as if it were the artist's intention to increase the voluminosity of the figure beyond its corporeal limitations. This tendency is even stronger in the Thaddaeus figure. The motif of the arm in the sling is, of course, a common motif of any classical revival style. But while in many figures of the Paris Gregory an articulated arm appears under the sling of the mantle, in the case of the Thaddaeus the sling is bulging, and the same is even more true for that part of the mantle that falls down from the left shoulder. Here certain tendencies begin to develop which in the later tenth century are again arrested, only to reappear with even greater vigor in the thirteenth century.

The peculiar emphasis or even slight over-emphasis on three-dimensional values, so apparent in the Sinai icon, has its closest parallels in miniature-painting of about the middle of the tenth century. The best representative of this phase is the Gospel book in Stauronikita on Mount Athos (cod. 43) which on the basis of script and ornament can be dated quite precisely at about that time.[29] Particularly in the figures of Matthew (Fig. 180) and Mark (Fig. 203), the plasticity of the rounded bodies and the enveloping drapery in which the hard, broken folds (which are so strong in the Paris Gregory, the Vatican Cosmas, and again in illuminated manuscripts from the end of the tenth century) are to a very essential degree eliminated, point-

[27] P. Buberl, *Die Miniaturhandschriften der Nationalbibliothek in Athen* (Vienna, 1917), p. 5, No. 2 and pls. II–III; Weitzmann, *Die byzantinische Buchmalerei des 9. und 10. Jahrhunderts* (Berlin, 1935), p. 61 and pl. LXVII, 399; pl. LXVIII, 401.

[28] H. Omont, *Miniatures des plus anciens manuscrits grecs de la Bibliothèque Nationale du VIe au XIVe siècle* (2d ed.; Paris, 1929), pl. XXXIX.

[29] Weitzmann, *Byzantinische Buchmalerei*, pp. 23 ff. and pls. XXX–XXXI.

ing, in our opinion, to a date for the Sinai icon not before the middle of the tenth century. As for the exaggerations of the drapery motifs in the icon, one might point to the two miniatures of an Isaiah manuscript in the Vatican (cod. gr. 755) from the second half of the tenth century, one with the standing prophet and the other with the scene of his martyrdom,[30] as even closer parallels.

Yet while the figures of Thaddaeus and Abgarus share with the Byzantine miniatures cited above a high degree of plasticity, they are at the same time painted with a broader brushstroke. In this respect they reflect even more strongly the flavor of the classical tradition than the miniatures just quoted, in which linear design counteracts the painterly effects. On occasion, however, one also meets the soft, painterly style in tenth-century miniatures. In the Athos codex Vatopedi 456,[31] there are two medallion busts of the martyrs Gurias and Samonas (Fig. 223), dressed in very soft blue and red tunics, whose flesh color—light steel-blue and pink— is very smooth without any sharp highlights, as is also the treatment of the hair. This Vatopedi manuscript, on the basis of its script, a rather stylized minuscule, and its ornament, a golden fretsaw ornament on blue ground, can be dated fairly precisely around the

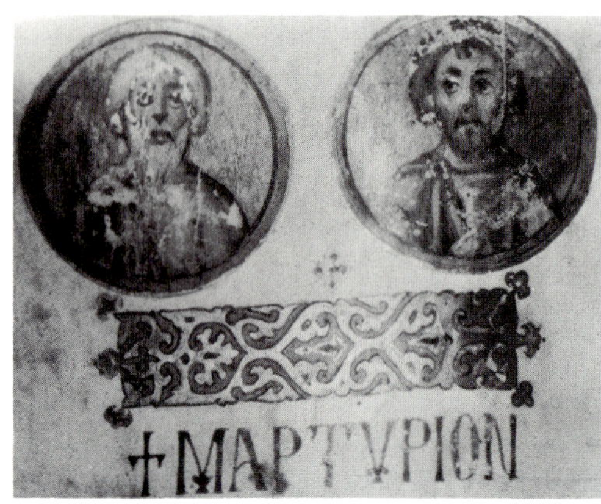

Fig. 223 *Mount Athos, Vatopedi. Cod. 456, fol. 221ʳ. Gurias and Samonas*

middle of the tenth century and localized in Constantinople.[32] Thus all our comparisons with Byzantine miniatures suggest for the Sinai icon, from the stylistic point of view, a date not earlier than the middle of the tenth century.

The other problem concerns the suggestion by the Sotiriou that the Sinai icon may have been made in Edessa. If this were true then one would have to assume that the classicizing style, typical of Constantinople and so well expressed in the Thaddaeus figure, had spread from the capital to eastern Syria without being blended with East Byzantine local tradition. Since our knowledge of icon-painting of this period is much too fragmentary, some light can be thrown on this problem only by illustrated manuscripts, about which we are somewhat better informed. We introduced

---

[30] A. Muñoz, *I codici greci miniati delle minori biblioteche di Roma* (Florence, 1905), p. 24 and pl. 6; Weitzmann, *Byzantinische Buchmalerei*, p. 12 and pl. XII, no. 62.

[31] S. Eustratiades and Arcadios, *Catalogue of the Greek Manuscripts in the Library of the Monastery of Vatopedi on Mt. Athos* (Cambridge, Mass., 1924), p. 91; Weitzmann, *Byzantinische Buchmalerei*, pp. 20 ff. and pl. XXV, No. 140; XXVI, no. 142.

[32] In the original layout miniatures were not contemplated, and the few that were added later could only be accommodated in the upper margins. Yet their addition cannot have been made much later since the inscriptions alongside the medallions show a stylized minuscule very similar to that of the text proper.

above the Gospel book Stauronikita 43 as the most characteristic Constantinopolitan Renaissance manuscript of the middle of the tenth century. It can be shown that its particular set of evangelist pictures quickly spread into the eastern provinces; a copy made close to the middle of the tenth century is preserved in the lectionary fragment in Leningrad (cod. 21) which may have been made in the region around Trebizond.[33] As closely as these copies of the evangelist portraits follow, iconographically and stylistically, Constantinopolitan models, they also show reflections of a local provincial tradition that is visible in the hardening and linearization of the folds—thus revealing the fading of the classical flavor. Would one not expect in a manuscript made in Edessa, a place still further removed from the capital and, besides, located on Moslem territory, an even stronger infiltration of local and probably even Islamic elements? The evangelist portraits of a Gospel book in Paris (Bibliothèque Nationale, cod. gr. 48) help us to envisage what Greek art on Islamic territory was like at this period,[34] though admittedly their particular style may reflect only one of many possibilities of interpenetration of Byzantine and Islamic elements.

To illustrate this point I may be permitted a slight deviation for which I find a justification in that it involves a parallel problem relating to Edessa. It concerns the codex Vatopedi 456, already introduced (p. 238). Textually it is

affiliated to that group of hagiographical texts which Ehrhard[35] called the *Jahrespanegyriken*. Of its twenty-seven homilies, twelve are on christological feasts, three on John the Baptist and the remaining twelve on feasts of various saints. Here a marked emphasis is noticeable on the three confessors and martyrs and patron saints of Edessa, Gurias, Samonas, and Abibos, to whom no less than five homilies are dedicated. Moreover, when a few miniatures were added in the upper margins, as already mentioned, they were confined exclusively to the homilies on the Edessene saints, thus giving an even stronger emphasis to this section of the manuscript. The two pre-Metaphrastian texts of the martyrion of Gurias and Samonas[36] and of the martyrion of Abibos[37] are decorated with bust medallions of the saints, the former with those we have already discussed (Fig. 223) and the latter with that of the youthful deacon Abibos (Fig. 224), who wears a lightly colored gray-white dalmatic with the stole over the left shoulder. The third homily is the encomium of Arethas, archbishop of Caesarea, which deals jointly with all three martyrs[38] and is

---

[33] Weitzmann, *Byzantinische Buchmalerei*, pp. 59 ff. and pls. LXVI, 392 and LXVII, 398 (here the older bibliography).

[34] *Byzantinische Buchmalerei*, p. 72 and pl. LXXXII, 516–517.

[35] A. Ehrhard, *Überlieferung und Bestand der hagiographischen und homiletischen Literatur der griechischen Kirche*, 1 (Leipzig, 1938), Vol. IV, 3 ff. Here I found no mention of the Vatopedi codex, which has no exact parallel to any of the types described by him.

[36] O. von Gebhard and E. von Dobschütz, "Die Akten der Edessenischen Bekenner Gurjas, Samonas und Abibos," *Texte und Untersuchungen zur Geschichte der altchristlichen Literatur*, 37 (1911), 2 ff.

[37] Ibid., pp. 132 ff.

[38] Ibid., pp. 210 ff.

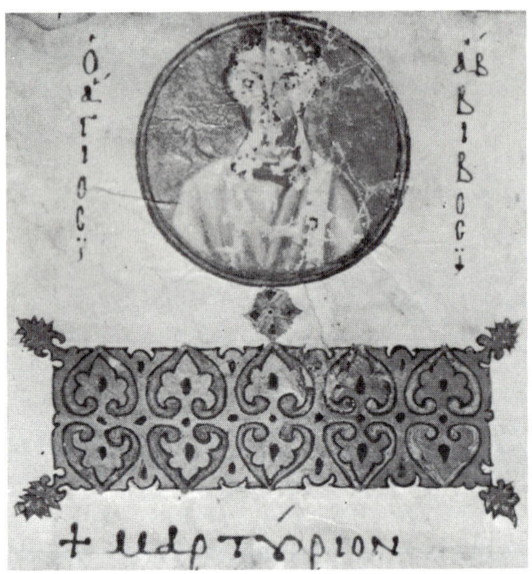

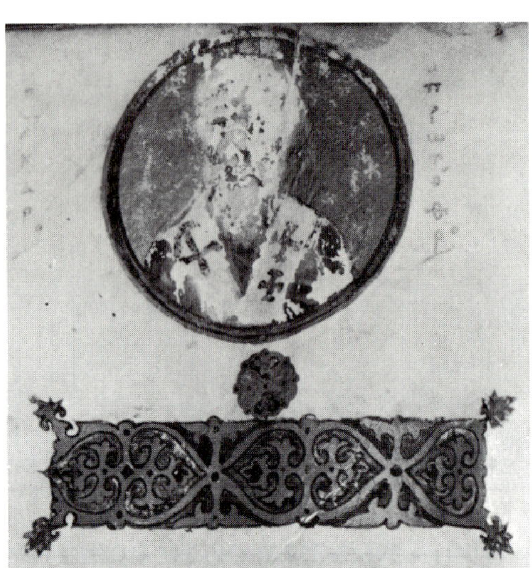

headed by a medallion portrait of the author (Fig. 225) inscribed ὁ μακάριος ὁ πρωτόθρονος.[39] It is not only the earliest but, as far as our knowledge goes, the only portrait of this prominent pupil of the great scholar Photios to whom classical scholarship owes so much with regard to the preservation of good classical texts. All the more deplorable is the poor condition of this badly flaked miniature, which shows an aged bishop with pinkish flesh and gray hair and beard—particularly if we realize that Arethas died some time after 932 and that this miniature portrait was made about a generation later, when the memory of his actual features might still have been alive. The fourth homily deals with the miracle[40] in which the three

saints, after their death, save an Edessene woman; a captain of the Goths had bigamously married her and later buried her alive in the tomb of his lawful wife, who had been poisoned by the Edessene woman after having first poisoned the latter's son. This dramatic story, which reads like a Greek novel, reaches its climax when the three Edessene saints free the woman from the prison tomb and bring her miraculously back to Edessa and to her mother. This homily likewise has a miniature (Fig. 226) which, however, contains nothing that could be related to the miracle story as just told. It is made up of three ingredients: a procession of clerics, the last of whom is a deacon with pyxis and censer; a little shrine, presumably a reliquary, which the leader of the procession holds in his outstretched hands; and a church building with an entrance at the left and an apse at the right. These are the elements of which representations of a

---

[39] For the title πρωτόθρονος consult Dom. DuCange, *Glossarium ad scriptores mediae et infimae Graecitatis* (Lyon, 1688), s.v. θρόνος.
[40] Von Gebhard and von Dobschütz, *Akten der Edessenischen Bekenner*, pp. 148 ff.

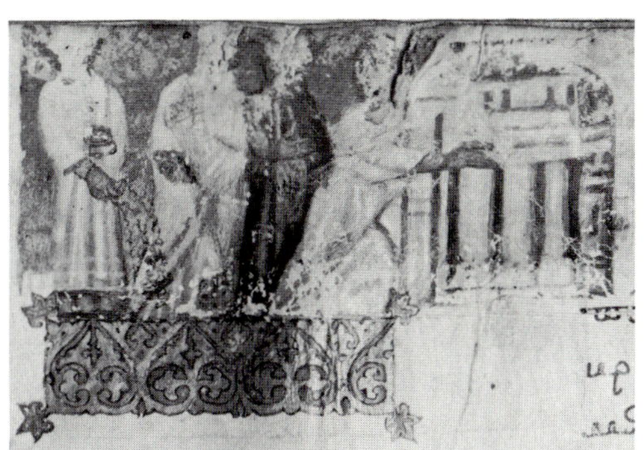

Fig. 226 *Mount Athos, Vatopedi. Cod. 456, fol. 253*[r]*. Translation of Relic*

transfer of relics are composed.[41] Now the fifth text, according to the catalogue of the Vatopedi manuscripts, is described as "Translation of the head of Abibos to the monastery of the martyrs Abibos, Gurias and Samonas" and a remark is added that the beginning is missing.[42] We have been unable to find a reference to such a text in the bibliography about the three saints and it is, perhaps, not printed; but there can be little doubt that the miniature would perfectly fit a text of this description, and that here obviously we have to do with the misplacement of a scene, destined for the fifth homily but erroneously attached to the fourth.

Taking together all the textual and the pictorial evidence, what scholar would not have been tempted to conclude that the Vatopedi manuscript was made in the locality where the cult of the three confessors and martyrs was centered,

i.e., in Edessa? Yet the script, ornament, and style of the miniatures speak, as we have tried to demonstrate, for an origin in Constantinople. There is, of course, still the alternative that the manuscript, while made in the capital, might have been commissioned by and destined for the Church of the Three Confessors in Edessa. There were two establishments in this East Syrian metropolis dedicated to them: one a martyrion of the fourth century on a hill outside the walls, to which a monastery was later added, and the other in the city proper.[43] Although such a possibility cannot be excluded entirely, it must at the same time be pointed out that Constantinople also had a chapel dedicated to the three martyrs of Edessa which was located near the forum Constantini,[44] and as early as 536 there existed in the capital a monastery of Abibos, an establishment of Syrian monks,[45] and consequently the Vatopedi manuscript could have been made for either one of them. So it seems that the cult of the Edessene martyrs had early taken root in Constantinople and acquired new importance in the tenth century, when, at its beginning, Arethas wrote his homily and when, at

[41] See for instance, *Il Menologio di Basilio II: Codex Vaticanus Greco 1613* ("Codices e Vaticanis selecti," 8 [Turin, 1907]), pls. 341, 344, 353, 355.

[42] Eustratiades and Arcadios, *Greek Manuscripts of Vatopedi*, περὶ τῆς μεταφορᾶς τῆς κάρας τοῦ μάρτυρος Ἀββίβου εἰς τὴν μονὴν τῶν μαρτύρων Ἀββίβου, Γουρία καὶ Σαμωνᾶ (ἄνευ ἀρχῆς).

[43] Von Gebhard and von Dobschütz, *Akten der Edessenischen Bekenner*, p. LXII; see also A. Baumstark, "Vorjustinianische kirchliche Bauten in Edessa," *Oriens Christianus*, 4 (1904), 171 ff.

[44] Von Gebhard and von Dobschütz, *Akten der Edessenischen Bekenner*, p. LXII; R. Janin, *La géographie ecclésiastique de l'Empire, byzantin*, 3 (Paris, 1953), 84.

[45] As against von Gebhard-von Dobschütz, Janin argues that Abibos is not the martyr of Edessa but rather the name of the founder of a monastery by this name.

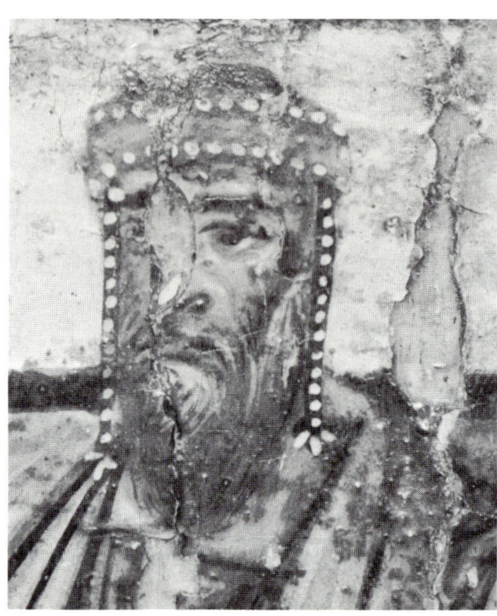

Fig. 227 *Mount Sinai, St. Catherine's. Icon. Abgarus Story and Saints (det. of Head of Abgarus)*

its end, Simeon Metaphrastes incorporated the story of the three saints in his hagiographic corpus.

It is perhaps more than mere coincidence that the two great cults of Edessa, that of the Mandylion and that of the three confessor-martyrs, had gained widespread interest in the capital in the tenth century. Of this interest we now possess two almost contemporary pictorial testimonies: one is the Sinai icon and the other is the Vatopedi codex. In the case of the Mandylion the point of departure, as already mentioned, is the bringing of the relic to Constantinople in 944 or, even more precisely, the writing and illustrating of the pseudo-Constantinian feast homily in or shortly after 945. If our dating of the Sinai icon on stylistic grounds not before the middle of the tenth century and its placing within the orbit of the Constantinopolitan style are accepted, then our thesis that the Sinai icon presupposes the narrative picture cycle of the feast homily receives very strong support. But there exists, as we believe, one even more conclusive piece of evidence for linking the Sinai icon with Constantinople and more directly with the imperial court.

EMPEROR CONSTANTINE VII

Comparing the heads of Thaddaeus and Abgarus (Figs. 211 and 212) one will notice a marked difference between them: while that of the former is rather impersonal and would fit other apostles, like Philip or Thomas, quite as well, that of the latter with the impressive beard and pensive look (Fig. 227) shows character and personality and gives the impression of a portrait head. The painter's emphasis on the crown and the

exact rendering of the pendulia with the triple pearls suggest that he actually used an emperor's portrait as model. If he chose what, a priori, seems to be a reasonable assumption, that of the contemporary emperor, it could be, in accordance with the dating of the icon by style, only Constantine VII Porphyrogennetos. Pictorial evidence and historical considerations strongly support this identification.

A survey of the coins of this period reveals that only two emperors wore such stately beards, Leo VI the Wise and his son Constantine Porphyrogennetos, i.e., the two litterati on the throne. Within the Middle Byzantine period, Leo was the first to wear this type of long, rounded, and cultivated beard.[46] But since he is

[46] W. Wroth, *Catalogue of the Imperial Byzantine Coins in the British Museum*, 2 (London, 1908), 444 and pl. LI, 8.

Fig. 228 *London, British Museum. Solidus. Constantine VII Porphyrogennetos*

Fig. 229 *Moscow, Historical Museum. Ivory. (det. of Constantine VII Porphyrogennetos)*

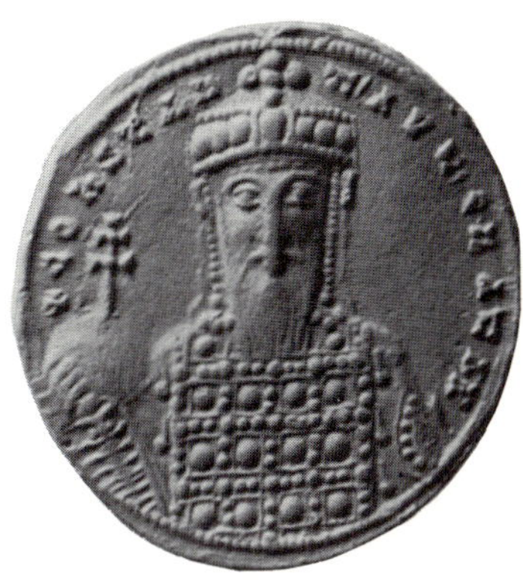

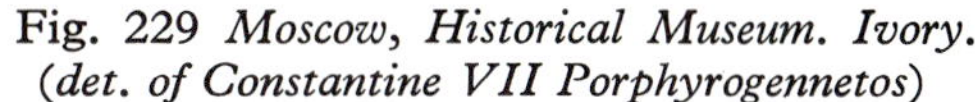

too early for this icon and also has no particular connection with the Mandylion, the only alternative is Constantine. The closest parallel is with a solidus (Fig. 228)[47] which dates within the short period from 27 January to 6 April of the year 945, after he had imprisoned the two young sons of Romanos I, Constantine and Stephen, and before he had made his own young son Romanos II his co-emperor, i.e., the short period during which, at almost forty years of age, he became the sole ruler of the empire. The almost equal length and fullness of the beard compares well with that of Abgarus in the icon.

This very coin in the British Museum led A. Goldschmidt and me to identify as the same personage the portrait of an emperor inscribed Constantine on a Byzantine ivory relief in Moscow (Fig. 229).[48] It was again the shape of the beard that was decisive in making this identification, which generally seems to

have been accepted.[49] Seen in three-quarter pose and looking pensively from under heavy brows, the ivory portrait shows an even closer similarity to the emperor head of the Sinai icon. The Moscow ivory depicts Christ placing the crown on the emperor's head, an action symbolizing monarchy as a divine institution. It is generally assumed,[50] however, that Constantine Porphyrogennetos was crowned in 911 when he

[47] Ibid., p. 462 and pl. LIII, 7.
[48] Goldschmidt and Weitzmann, *Elfenbein-skulpturen,* p. 35, and pl. XIV, no. 35.

[49] A. Grabar, *L'Empereur dans l'art byzantin* (Paris, 1936), p. 116 and pl. XXV, no. 1; H. Peirce and R. Tyler, "Three Byzantine Works of Art," *Dumbarton Oaks Papers,* 2 (1941), 17 ff. and pl. 18 A.
[50] S. Ostrogorsky, *Geschichte des byzantinischen Staates* (Munich, 1952), p. 209.

was only five years old and when Leo VI, his father, was much interested in having the dynastic succession secured in this manner, i.e., two years before Constantine became emperor in 913 at the age of seven. It is true that a Byzantine emperor, even when crowned as a child, will not be represented as such but as a full-grown man for reasons of great dignity, as can be seen in the coronation ivory of Romanos II and Eudokia in Paris,[51] where they are represented as of mature age, although in reality they were six and four years old. To satisfy the sense of greater dignity the change of size alone would have sufficed, whereas the long beard clearly points to the emperor's advanced age. Actually the close similarity with the London coin suggests that the Moscow ivory, too, was made in the year 945 in order to commemorate not the first coronation of the emperor in his childhood but the event of his sole rulership.[52]

The comparison of the London coin with the Moscow ivory makes us believe that for the head of King Abgarus not only was a portrait head of Constantine Porphyrogennetos used but the very one which is connected with his sole rulership in the year 945. From the historical point of view one could not wish for a more opportune date. As may be recalled, it was in this or one of the years immediately following that the feast homily dealing with the transfer of the Mandylion from Edessa to Constantinople and into the palace chapel was written at the instigation of this very emperor. What might have been the reason for the painter to go as far as to equate King Abgarus with the emperor Constantine? Let us recall the historical circumstances under which the transfer of the famous relic took place.

In 944 John Curcuas, the great general of Romanos I, laid siege to the city of Edessa without being able to conquer it. He made a pact with the Emir whereby the Mandylion was given to the imperial army for a price of 12,000 silver pieces, while the Byzantines returned their Muslim prisoners. In great triumph the relic was brought to Constantinople where it arrived on August 15, the feast day of the Koimesis. So far, every action connected with the transfer of the Mandylion was made at the initiative of Romanos I Lecapenos, Constantine's energetic and pious co-emperor. Does this, then, not speak against the identification of the emperor on the icon as Constantine and should one not rather expect Romanos to be represented as the receiver of the holy image? In the chronicle of John Scylitzes, of which an illustrated fourteenth-century copy exists in Madrid, there is a miniature (Fig. 230)[53] which indeed depicts the historical event of Romanos, followed by the patriarch and other dignitaries, receiving with veiled hands the Mandylion.

---

[51] Goldschmidt and Weitzmann, *Elfenbeinskulpturen*, pp. 15 ff., 35 and pl. XIV, no. 34.

[52] The same line of argument, to be sure, must have induced Beckwith to suggest in the catalogue of the Byzantine Exhibition in London (*Masterpieces of Byzantine Art* [London, 1958], p. 33, no. 63) the date *ca.* 945 for the Moscow plaque. The catalogue of the same exhibition in Edinburgh (p. 32, no. 63) had proposed a date *ca.* 920.

[53] Grabar, *Sainte Face*, p. 24 and pl. VI, no. 5.

Fig. 230 *Madrid, Biblioteca Nacional. Cod. 5.3.N.2, fol. 131ʳ. Romanos Receiving the Mandylion*

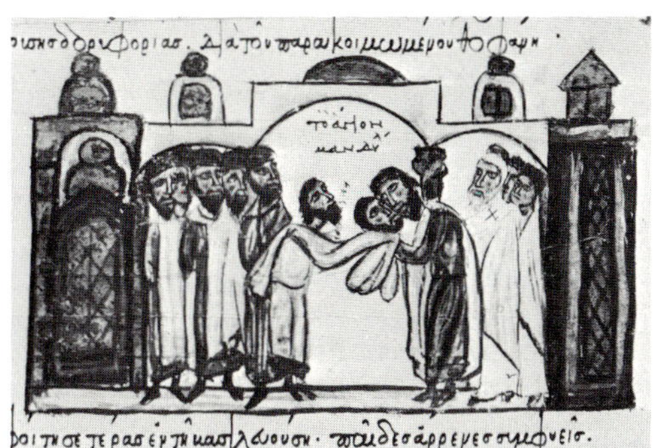

A few months after this event, on 16 December, Romanos was dethroned by his two sons, Constantine and Stephen, and imprisoned in the monastery on the island of Prote, only to be followed a few weeks later, on 27 January 945, by the two usurpers themselves whom Constantine Porphyrogennetos had succeeded in expelling, thus achieving finally his independent rulership. Perhaps in the very same year, and very probably for the first anniversary of the Mandylion's transfer to Constantinople, the feast homily celebrating this event was written. While Constantine may not, as some manuscripts claim (Fig. 214), be the author, there can be little doubt that it was written not only on his initiative but with the explicit desire to claim the credit for the relic's transfer, which historically belongs to Romanos, for himself. Among the many miracles that, according to the feast homily, took place during the transport of the relic there is the story of the healing near the Theotokos monastery of Eusebiu in Bithynia of a demoniac who is supposed to have predicted the impending sole rulership of Constantine.[54] In the

light of these historical events the Sinai icon can have only one meaning: to represent Constantine in the guise of King Abgarus as the new recipient of the Mandylion. Thus the icon was made with the same intention as the writing of the feast homily: to disseminate the idea of Constantine as the pious emperor whose spiritual concern is the collection of famous relics in the palace chapel of the Virgin of the Pharos.[55]

The Sinai icon is hardly the archetype of the newly invented Mandylion triptych which we believe to have been made not only at the instigation of the emperor but most probably even in a workshop controlled by him. After all, the emperor's interest in painting is not only well-documented, but the sources tell us that he was a painter of renown himself.[56] Yet the small size of the triptych wings and the fact that the style, though purely Constantinopolitan, is not of the very first quality speak against their being the original creation. Since their stylistic analysis indicated a date not long after the middle of the tenth century, they must be very early and presumably faithful copies.

This raises a new problem: does the Sinai triptych, as we have reconstructed it, reflect the archetype in its entirety or is the correspondence perhaps restricted

---

[54] Von Dobschütz, *Christusbilder*, p. 79**.

[55] The transfer of the relic of the hand of John the Baptist in 956 from Antioch to Constantinople, i.e., to the treasury of the Pharos church in the palace, is one of the other instances that shows Constantine's sustained interest in the collection of famous relics. J. Ebersolt, *Sanctuaires de Byzance* (Paris, 1921), p. 80, n. 4.

[56] Weitzmann, *The Joshua Roll* (Princeton, 1948), p. 88.

to the upper zone only? It will be noticed that the part related to the Abgarus story is, through the feast homily, iconographically linked with Constantinople, whereas no such relation exists with regard to the saints in the lower zone.

A triptych, consisting of only the Mandylion in the center and the figures of Thaddaeus and Abgarus on the flanking wings, constitutes a perfect unity in concept and form, and it seems, therefore, quite conceivable that the lower zone is an addition made for the present replica. What could have been the purpose of such an addition? Ephraim the Syrian's chief place of activity was Edessa; Paul of Thebes and Anthony are two of the holy fathers of the Egyptian Desert, the latter being the patriarch of the monastic and the former of the eremitical life; and Basil wrote the monastic rules that still govern Eastern monasticism. From this selection one might deduce that the triptych was made as a gift for an Eastern monastery.

It is, of course, a tempting speculation that it may actually have been made for Sinai. One must remember that Sinai is an imperial foundation of Justinian which persisted as a stronghold of Chalcedonian orthodoxy in the surroundings of monophysite Christianity. Here gifts from Constantinople should be expected. The choice of the monastic saints, at least in part, could be explained in relation to Sinai. Anthony and Basil had special chapels within the monastery, of which that of Anthony still exists, while the chapel of Basil was in that part of the complex which is now occupied by a modern wing. The Abgarus icon is a very competent piece of painting, but

it does not reach the high level that one might expect of a personal gift of an emperor. Even so, it is, from the stylistic point of view, a touchstone since it is the first icon which with a fair degree of certainty can be dated around or shortly after the middle of the tenth century, thus becoming the focal point for further attributions and datings of icons of a similar style.[57] Equally important is its iconographic value since it has given us not only the earliest representation of the Abgarus legend and of the Mandylion but also a new portrait of the art-loving emperor Constantine Porphyrogennetos.

[57] [For other tenth-century icons see Weitzmann, *Treasury of Icons*, pp. ix ff. and pls. 13–16 and especially, Weitzmann, "An Encaustic Icon." For the Macedonian Renaissance cf. Weitzmann, *Geistige Grundlagen und Wesen der Makedonischen Renaissance* (Cologne and Opladen, 1963), especially p. 41, translated and reprinted herewith, pp. 176 ff.]

10

The Narrative and Liturgical Gospel Illustrations

COMPARED with textual criticism, the history of the art of the Middle Ages is a fairly recent discipline still in the state of collecting, organizing, and editing the documents, many of which, including very basic ones, are still unpublished.[1] Moreover, art history has only started to develop a critical method through which the monuments can properly be related to each other and through which a clearer and more coherent picture of historical and artistic trends ultimately may be achieved. Of course, such a method has to be flexible and adjusted to the basic character of the Middle Ages. Contrasted with the highly individualized art of the Italian Renaissance, a methodical treatment of medieval works of art has to take into account the artist's primary concern with the iconographi-

cally accurate rendering of the content, which loomed larger in his mind than formalistic problems, and also his adherence to an established, sanctified tradition of rendering certain themes which goes hand in hand with self-imposed limitations on his invention of new subject matter. To be sure, the process of continued copying was by no means mechanical and permitted ample opportunity for new stylistic and even iconographical interpretations, but this traditionalism, by which the iconography of a certain scene retains for centuries, basic features of an archetype is evident and can be studied most successfully in the field of book illumination for a number of reasons: the comparative wealth of the extant material; the usually good state of preservation of miniatures; their high quality in its best products; and, what is perhaps the most important factor, the association of miniatures with a text, which permits a control over the iconographic accuracy of the picture.

Pictures and text in manuscripts often travel together over long stretches of time, so that obviously the process of copying one must have a bearing on that of the other. Thus a comparison between the method of textual criticism and of what we should like to call picture criticism becomes imperative. It has become quite obvious that each resembles the other in principle to a remarkable degree,[2] and that every kind of evidence as defined by Westcott and Hort in connection with the text of the New Testa-

Reprinted with permission from *New Testament Manuscript Studies*, M. M. Parvis and A. P. Wikgren (eds.) (Chicago, University of Chicago Press, 1950), pp. 151–74, 215–19.

[1] When this lecture was delivered at the meeting held at the University of Chicago in 1948 to honor Edgar J. Goodspeed and to discuss matters preliminary to the preparation of a new critical apparatus of the Greek New Testament it was not intended to be published. This explains its preliminary character; many of its assertions would need a fuller documentation than limited space permits. [Weitzmann returned to a number of points adduced in this study in his article, "Byzantine Miniature and Icon Painting in the Eleventh Century," *Proceedings of the XIIIth International Congress of Byzantine Studies. Oxford 5–10 September, 1966* (London, 1967) pp. 207 ff.; here the recent literature. Reprinted herewith, pp. 271 ff. Special attention might also be drawn to Weitzmann, "The Constantinopolitan Lectionary, Morgan 639," *Studies in Art and Literature for Belle da Costa Greene* (Princeton, 1954), pp. 358 ff.]

[2] Weitzmann, *Illustrations in Roll and Codex, A Study of the Origin and Method of Text Illustration* (2d ed. Princeton, 1970), pp. 182 ff.

ment[3]—the internal evidence of readings, the internal evidence of documents, and the genealogical evidence—operate in pictures in much the same way as in texts; though picture criticism has, of course, its peculiarities due to the difference of the medium. But long before these problems were discussed from the methodological point of view, the realization of an interrelation between text and picture was the working basis for many scholars in the field of book illumination. I need here only refer to the various publications of illustrated New Testament manuscripts in the University of Chicago collection as one of the many instances in which the editors were fully aware of the parallel trends in the two disciplines of textual and pictorial criticism.[4]

The complexity of problems arising from a methodical study of miniatures can best be studied in those manuscripts in which pictures are compiled from different sources, as for instance in the Homilies of Gregory of Nazianzus in Paris (cod. gr. 510), in the Christian Topography of Cosmas Indicopleustes in the Vatican (cod. gr. 699), and in various Psalter manuscripts.[5] To this type of illustrated manuscript, which we should like to call polycyclic, the lectionary of the Gospels also belongs and

is, in fact, one of the most characteristic examples. But there are still other reasons for closely examining the lectionary. One is its importance as the chief liturgical book of the Eastern Church which is reflected in the splendor of its illustration and another is the enrichment of our knowledge of illustrated lectionaries in recent years by a number of manuscripts from Mount Athos, some of which are still unpublished.[6]

In many instances the lectionary, kept in the church, was never opened for reading during the service. It was deposited on the altar as the most sacred possession and taken from it only for the Little Entrance in the Divine Liturgy when the deacon proceeds to the center of the church, raises the "Holy Evangelion," saying with a loud voice Σοφία ὀρθοί, and then carries it back through the royal doors, depositing it again on the altar. A book of such importance deserves special attention, not only as far as its rich and splendid illumination is concerned, but also for its covers. The earliest and at the same time artistically the most outstanding Byzantine book cover we possess is, characteristically

---

[3] B. F. Westcott and F. J. A. Hort, *The New Testament in the Original Greek. Introduction and Appendix* (New York, 1882), pp. 19 ff.

[4] E. J. Goodspeed, D. W. Riddle, and H. R. Willoughby, *The Rockefeller McCormick New Testament* (Chicago, 1932); E. C. Colwell and H. R. Willoughby, *The Four Gospels of Karahissar* (Chicago, 1936); H. R. Willoughby and E. C. Colwell, *The Elizabeth Day McCormick Apocalypse* (Chicago, 1940).

[5] Weitzmann, *Roll and Codex,* pp. 198 ff.

[6] The photographs of the three Athos lectionaries from which examples are reproduced in this article, i.e., the one in the *skevophylakion* of Lavra (Figs. 231, 258, 259), Iviron cod. 1 (Fig. 249), and Dionysiu cod. 587 (*olim* 740; Figs. 239, 241–42, 246, 248, 251–53) were made by the author during his trips to Mount Athos in 1935 and 1936. ["Miniature and Icon Painting," pp. 214 ff.; herewith pp. 285 ff. and idem, "Zur byzantinischen Quelle des Wolfenbüttler Musterbuches," *Festschrift Hans R. Hahnloser zum 60. Geburtstag, 1959* (Basel and Stuttgart, 1961), pp. 223 ff.]

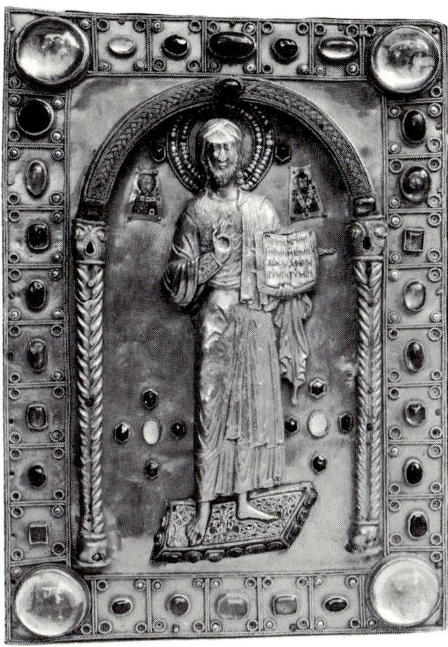

Fig. 231 *Mount Athos, Lavra, Skevophy-lakion. Lectionary. Front Cover. Christ*

enough, on a lectionary (Fig. 231).[7] Kept as a relic in the *skevophylakion* of the Great Lavra on Mount Athos, this manuscript, according to a local tradition, was given by the emperor Nicephorus Phocas to Saint Athanasius, the founder and the first abbot of this imperial monastery. Restored though it is, the cover still conveys the impression of great splendor, which results from the employment of the most refined techniques of Byzantine craftsmanship. The figure of Christ is executed in gold repoussé, the nimbus is studded with pearls, the book in the hand of Christ and the footstool are made in the most delicate enamel cloisonné technique with brilliant translucent colors, and two small enamels with the busts of Saint

Gregory and Saint Basil are probably only remnants of an originally still richer enamel decoration.[8]

It must be made clear at the outset that miniatures make no contribution to the much debated question as to when the lectionary in its present form came into being. The oldest illustrated lectionaries we possess with pictures other than the portraits of the four evangelists belong to the tenth century,[9] a period when its present form was firmly established. With very few exceptions,[10] all extant illustrated lectionaries were made either in Constantinople itself or under the influence of a Constantinopolitan model, so that the evidence from the pictures bears out fully the contention of textual critics that the majority of lectionaries belong to a Constantinopolitan recension which achieved an ecumenical character in the Greek Church as early as the ninth century or perhaps a little earlier.[11]

---

[7] N. P. Kondakov, Ламятники христіанскаго искусства на Афонѣ (St. Petersburg, 1902), pp. 95 ff. and pls. XXVI–XXVII.

[8] The frame with its stones and filigree and the stones on the ground within the arch are modern as are the filling of the arch, the left corner of the footstool, and the Christ. Originally, all of these were filled with small enamel plaques.

[9] They are: Patmos cod. 70; Leningrad, Public Library, cod. 21; Mount Athos, Lavra, cod. A.86. Cf. Weitzmann, *Die byzantinische Buchmalerei des 9. und 10. Jahrhunderts* (Berlin, 1935), pp. 46, 59, 66, and pls. LII–LIV, LXVI–LXVII, LXXI–LXXIII.

[10] As, for instance, Patmos cod. 70, which originated most probably in Asia Minor, and Milan, Ambrosian Library, cod. D.67 sup., a southern Italian manuscript of the thirteenth century. Cf. A. Muñoz, *L'art byzantin à l'exposition de Grotta Ferrata* (Rome, 1906), p. 93 and figs. 61–63.

[11] A. Ehrhard, *Überlieferung und Bestand der hagiographischen und homiletischen Literatur*

Manuscript Sources of Lectionary
Illustrations

When the lectionary was first illustrated, the painters obviously saw no need
to invent a new set of illustrations of the
life of Christ but took over pictures
from an illustrated Gospel book, just as
the lectionary text itself is a derivation of
the continuous Gospel text. We believe
that already in the early Christian period
the four Gospels were illustrated with a
very extensive picture cycle which could
be read, to use a modern simile, like a
comic strip or somewhat in a cinematographic fashion. It is true that we have
only a few fragments of early Byzantine
Gospel illustration,[12] but two very
prolifically illustrated Gospel books from
the eleventh century, one in Paris
(Bibliothèque Nationale cod. gr. 74)[13] and
the other in Florence (Laurenziana

cod. Plut, VI, 23),[14] show very clearly
the early Christian system of a densely
spaced, narrative illustration as it exists
similarly in two fragments of early
Christian manuscripts of the Septuagint, the Genesis in Vienna[15] and
the so-called Cotton Genesis in the
British Museum in London,[16] and
likewise in Middle Byzantine copies
which hark back to Early Byzantine
models like the Octateuchs[17] and the
Books of Kings.[18]

A typical example of narrative Gospel
illustration may be chosen from the

---

der griechischen Kirche, 1 (Leipzig, 1937),
I, 27.

[12] They are: The Gospels of Rossano. Cf.
O. v. Gebhardt and A. Harnack, Evangeliorum
Codex graecus purpureus Rossanensis (Berlin,
1880); A. Haseloff, Codex purpureus Rossanensis (Berlin, 1898); and A. Muñoz, Il codice
purpureo di Rossano e il Frammento Sinopense
(Rome, 1907). The fragment from Sinope
(Paris, Bibliothèque Nationale, cod. suppl. gr.
1286). Cf. H. Omont, Peintures d'un manuscrit grec de l'Évangile de Saint Matthieu
("Monuments E. Piot," 7 [Paris, 1900]), 175 ff.
and pls. XVI–XIX; idem, Miniatures des
plus anciens manuscrits grecs de la Bibliothèque
Nationale (2d ed.; Paris, 1929), pp. 1 ff. and
pls. A–B; A. Grabar, Les Peintures de l'Évangile de Sinope (Paris, 1948). [Weitzmann,
"Miniature and Icon Painting," p. 216, reprinted herewith, p. 290.]

[13] H. Omont, Évangiles avec peintures byzantines du XIe siècle (Paris [1908]). G. Millet,
Recherches sur l'iconographie de l'Évangile
(Paris, 1916), pp. xxxvii ff. and passim.

[14] Millet, Recherches.

[15] W. Ritter von Hartel and F. Wickoff, Die
Wiener Genesis (Vienna, 1895); H. Gerstinger,
Die Wiener Genesis (Vienna, 1931); P. Buberl,
Die byzantinischen Handschriften ("Beschreibendes Verzeichnis der illuminierten Handschriften in Österreich," 8, [Leipzig, 1937]),
IV, 65 ff. and pls. XXI–XLIV. [cf. Weitzmann, "Die Illustration der Septuaginta,"
Münchner Jahrbuch der bildenden Kunst, 3/4
(1952/53), 96 ff., translated and reprinted herewith, pp. 45 ff.]

[16] Vetusta Monumenta Rerum Britannicarum
(London, 1747), 1, pls. LXVII–LXVIII; C.
Tischendorf, Monumenta sacra inedita (nova
collectio; Leipzig, 1857), 2:92 ff.; J. J.
Tikkanen, "Die Genesismosaiken von S.
Marco in Venedig und ihr Verhältnis zu den
Miniaturen der Cotton Bibel," Acta Societatis
Scientiarum Fennicae, 17 (1889), 99 ff.

[17] So far, only two have been published completely: Smyrna, Evangelical School, cod.
A.1 (now destroyed); cf. D. C. Hesseling,
Miniatures de l'Octateuque grec de Smyrne
(Leiden, 1909). Istanbul, Seraglio, cod. 8;
cf. Th. Ouspensky, L'Octateuque de la
Bibliothèque du Serail à Constantinople (Sofia,
1907).

[18] Only one illustrated copy exists today, the
Vatican codex grec. 333. Cf. J. Lassus, "Les
miniatures Byzantines du Livre des Rois,"
Mélanges d'archéologie et d'histoire, 45 (1928),
38 ff.

Fig. 232 *Paris, Bibliothèque Nationale. Cod. gr. 74, fol. 4ᵛ. Flight into Egypt*

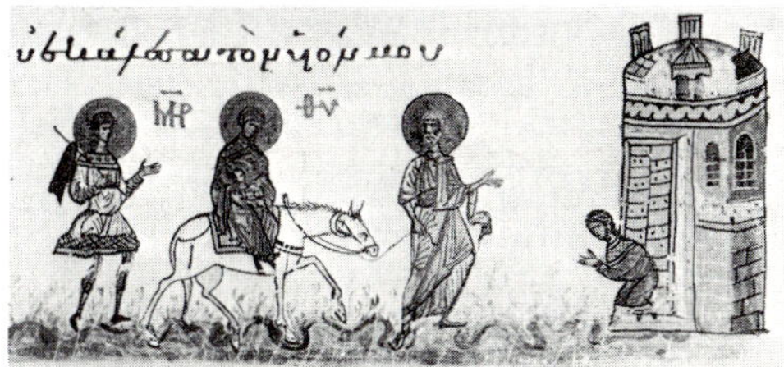

Fig. 233 *Paris, Bibliothèque Nationale. Cod. gr. 74, fol. 5ʳ. Massacre of the Innocents*
Fig. 234 *Paris, Bibliothèque Nationale. Cod. gr. 74, fol. 5ᵛ. Dream of Joseph and Return from Egypt*

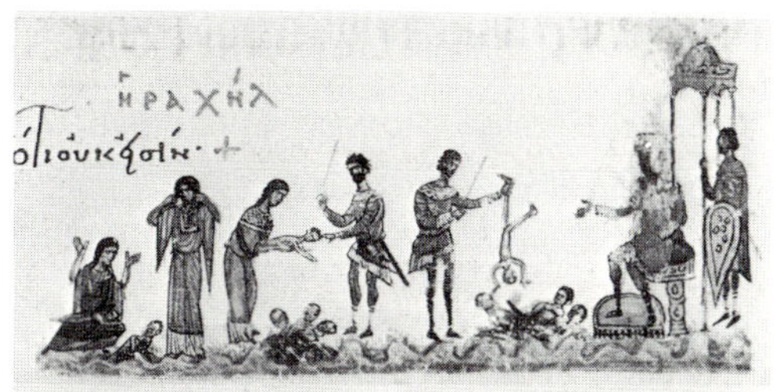

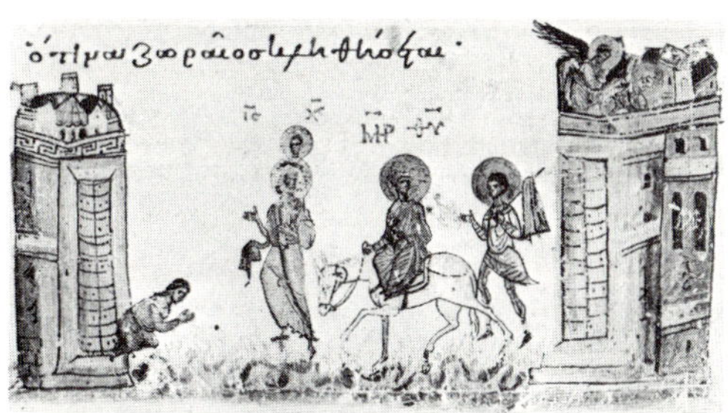

above-mentioned manuscript in Paris. It illustrates the episode of the Flight to Egypt in the following four phases (Figs. 232–234):[19] (1) The Flight to Egypt proper, in which the Holy Family consisting of Joseph, the Virgin and Child, and (in accordance with the apocryphal Gospels) a son of Joseph, are received by the personification of Egypt in front of a walled city; (2) The Massacre of the Innocents; (3) The Dream of Joseph, where he is told by the angel to return. Because of lack of space, this scene is placed on top of a walled city; and (4) The Return to Nazareth, in which Joseph, carrying the Christ Child on his shoulders, is followed by the Virgin on the ass and by one of his sons and is received by the personification of the the city of Nazareth.

It may be noticed that these four scenes cover only ten verses (14–23) of the second chapter of Matthew. Taking this density of scenes more or less as a norm, one can well imagine the extent of the miniature cycle in a fully illustrated Gospel book whose scenes would have to be counted by the hundreds.

It seems only natural that, to the extent permitted in a service book, an illustrator of a lectionary should adapt

this type of illustration. That this is, indeed, the case can be demonstrated by the eleventh-century Vatican Lectionary (cod. gr. 1156)[20] where the same scenes occur in the lection of 26 December (Figs. 235–238), and in part with the same peculiarities: (1) The Flight to Egypt, in which the son of Joseph, because of lack of space, is lacking, but where we meet also the receiving personification of Egypt, not in front of the Holy Family, but, because of lack of space, kneeling on top of the walled city; (2) The Massacre of the Innocents; (3) The Dream of Joseph, in this case as a separate picture; and (4) The Return to Nazareth, where, once more, Joseph's son is lacking while the city personifica-

---

[19] Omont, *Evangiles*, pls. 7–8.

[20] Millet, *Recherches*, p. 13 and *passim*. [Weitzmann, "Miniature and Icon Painting," p. 219 and pl. 32 and 33 a–b, herewith, p. 295; V. Lazarev, *Storia della pittura bizantina* (Turin, 1967), p. 188; here the more recent literature.]

Fig. 235 *Vatican, Biblioteca. Cod. gr. 1156, fol. 280ʳ. Flight into Egypt*

Fig. 236 *Vatican, Biblioteca. Cod. gr. 1156, fol. 280ᵛ. Massacre of the Innocents*

Fig. 237 *Vatican, Biblioteca. Cod. gr. 1156, fol. 281ʳ. Dream of Joseph*

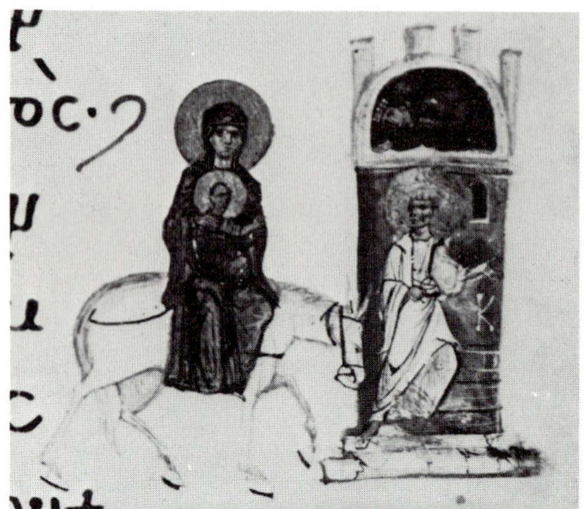

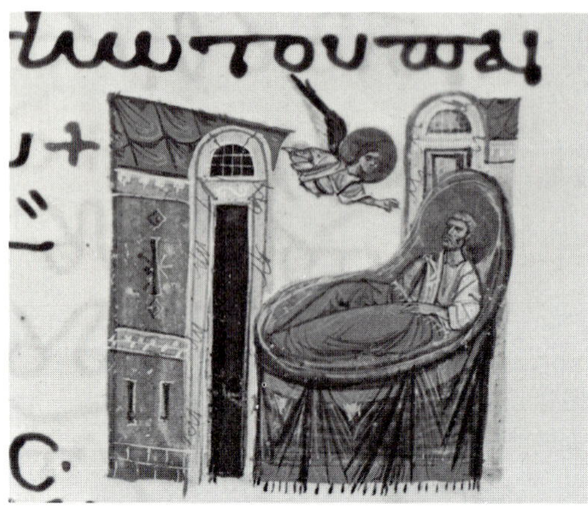

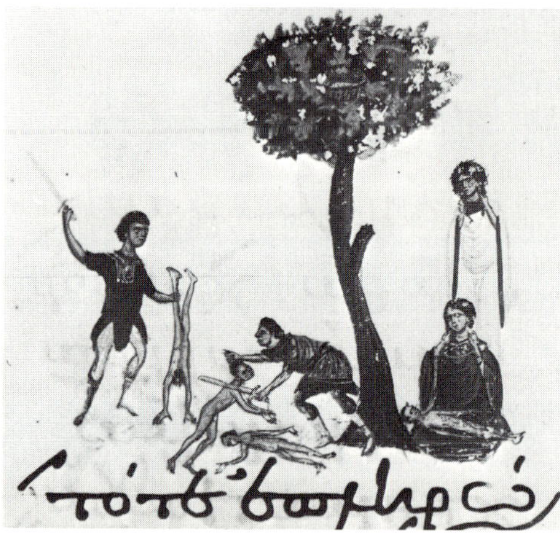

tion kneels on top of the city.[21]

Yet this kind of narrative illustration is not frequent in lectionaries and soon the peculiar nature of the liturgical book becomes apparent. A pericope is an inviolate unit, and for this reason artists

respect its unity by not inserting pictures within the text of a lection—the example just shown from the Vatican manuscript is one of the very few exceptions. Normally they select the beginning of the lection as the most suitable place for its illustration.

Since it was the tradition of narrative illustration to have a picture physically connected as closely as possible with the text it illustrates, there was a natural tendency to depict a scene which is related to the very first verses of the lection. In an eleventh-century lectionary from Dionysiu on Mount Athos (cod. 587 [olim 740] Fig. 239),[22] for instance, we find a picture of Christ meeting the blind man as the title miniature to the lection of the fifth Sunday after Easter (John 9:1–38). In the Gospel book in Paris, this episode is illustrated in no less than ten phases, beginning with the

[21] A full illustration of this episode would also include the first dream of Joseph, which precedes the flight (verse 13), and although this is lacking in the Paris Gospels, it is represented in the Vatican Lectionary (cf. Millet, *Recherches*, fig. 96). It also exists in the Florence Gospels (Millet, *Recherches*, fig. 111), which proves that this scene, too, is part of the full narrative Gospel cycle.

[22] [See the most recent discussion: Weitzmann, "The Wanderings of the Imperial Lectionary on Mt. Athos," *Revue des Études Sud-Est Euro-péenes*, 7 (1969), pp. 239 ff. A number of color plates are presented in Weitzmann, *Aus den Bibliotheken des Athos* (Hamburg, 1963), pp. 65 ff.]

Fig. 238 *Vatican, Biblioteca. Cod. gr. 1156, fol. 281ʳ. Return from Egypt*

Fig. 239 *Mount Athos, Dionysiu. Cod. 587, fol. 26ᵛ. Healing of the Blind Man*

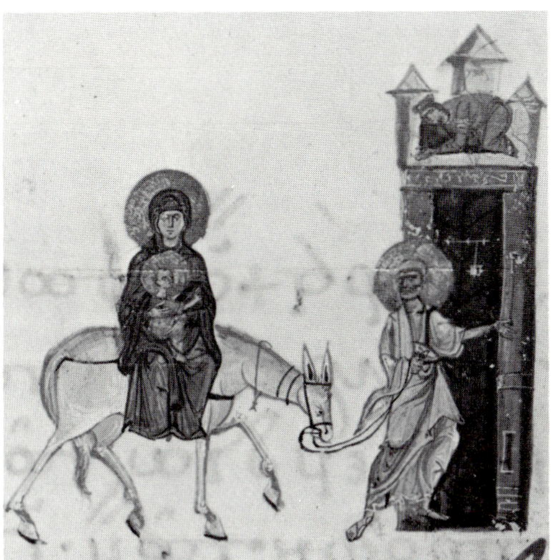

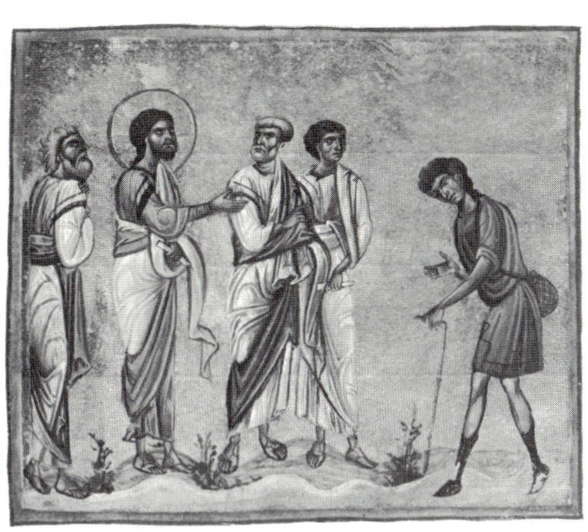

healing proper and ending with the healed blind man worshipping Christ,[23] while the Florentine Gospel book has only four,[24] the first of which, representing the meeting before the healing, is not duplicated in the Paris codex, so that altogether the narrative cycle exists in at least eleven phases. One might have expected that the illustrator of the Dionysiu Lectionary would select the most important phase, the actual healing in which Christ touches the eyes of the blind man, as the headpiece of the lection. Instead he chose the very first phase, the meeting before the healing as represented in the Florentine Gospel. The space between the dignified figure of Christ and the slender blind man, who is depicted in an expressive silhouette, is filled by Peter standing in an elegant contrapposto beside a second Apostle, and the general effect of this very balanced composition is an enhance-

ment of the hieratic element in comparison with the same scene in the Florentine Gospel where it is part of a continuous story.

Scholars studying the text of the lectionary are familiar with the incipits or opening formulae like τῷ καιρῷ ἐκείνῳ and εἶπεν ὁ κύριος which were added to the Gospel readings when, after their cutting up into lections, they needed an introductory phrase.[25] On occasion these phrases are quite lengthy, like that to the lection for 14 September which reads τῷ καιρῷ ἐκείνῳ συμβούλιον ἐποίησαν οἱ ἀρχιερεῖς καὶ οἱ πρεσβύτεροι κατὰ τοῦ ἰησοῦ ὅπως αὐτὸν ἀπολέσωσιν καὶ παρεγένοντο πρὸς πιλᾶτον λέγοντες ἆρον ἆρον σταύρωσον αὐτόν. In a twelfth-century lectionary in the Morgan Library in New York (cod. 692. Fig. 240)[26] this very phrase

---

[23] Omont, *Évangiles*, pls. 159–61.

[24] Millet, *Recherches*, fig. 663 (where the first three phases are reproduced).

[25] E. C. Colwell and D. W. Riddle, *Prolegomena to the Study of the Lectionary Text of the Gospels* ("Studies in the Lectionary Text of the Greek New Testament," 1 [Chicago, 1933]), pp. 1 ff.

[26] B. da Costa Greene and M. P. Harrsen, *The Pierpont Morgan Library. Exhibition of*

Fig. 240 *New York, Morgan Library. Cod. 692, fol. 222ᵛ. Council of the Chief Priests*

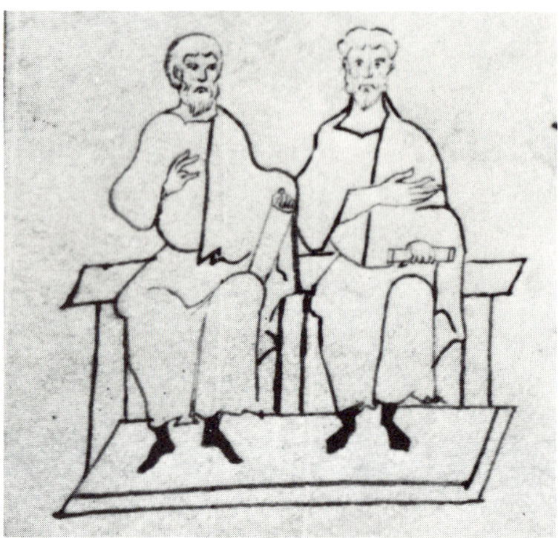

is illustrated by two drawings in the lower corners of the cruciform text page, one representing two chief priests seated and holding council, and the other two more priests on their way to Pilate to demand Christ's crucifixion. Obviously, these representations could not have existed in a Gospel book where the phrase quoted above does not occur; and it thus becomes apparent that on occasion the illustrator of the lectionary had to invent new narrative scenes, similar in character to those he found in Gospel books.

In the course of time, however, the lectionary illustrator centered his attention on the most important phase of the story instead of clinging to the initial verses of the lection for his choice of the subject. On 1 January, the story of Christ among the Doctors is read (Luke

2:40–52), an event which in the narrative cycle of the Florentine Gospel book, for example, is illustrated with epic breadth in four phases:[27] (1) Joseph and Mary go to the feast of the Passover (verse 42); (2) they leave while Christ tarries behind (verses 43–44); (3) Christ teaches among the doctors (verses 46–47). This scene is conflated with (4) Christ speaking to his mother, who stands outside with Joseph (verses 48–50).[28] Of these four phases, the illustrator of the Dionysiu codex (Fig. 241) selected not the first, which in the traditional way would have connected the picture closely with the beginning of the text of the lection, but the third because of its greater significance, and he added to it the parents from the fourth. Since we have already met a similar conflation of phases three and four in the Paris Gospels, its invention cannot be credited to the illustrator of the Dionysiu codex. But the latter related the two parts in a new and original way by using the picture frame of the main scene simultaneously as a division between interior and exterior.

Gradually a system of selection and gradation was worked out by reducing the number of scenes and by elaborating with great splendor those of liturgical significance. While the miniatures in the Dionysiu Lectionary normally occupy only the width of one of the two text columns, in a few places we find larger miniatures extending over both columns,

---

Illuminated Manuscripts Held at the New York Public Library (New York, 1934), p. 20, no. 36 and pl. 36; K. W. Clark, *A Descriptive Catalogue of Greek New Testament Manuscripts in America* (Chicago, 1937), pp. 162 ff. and pl. XXXI.

[27] Millet, *Recherches*, fig. 656.
[28] In the codex gr. 510 of the Bibliothèque Nationale in Paris the third and fourth phases are still separate scenes and Christ is represented in each of them. Cf. Omont, *Miniatures des manuscrits grecs*, pl. XXXV.

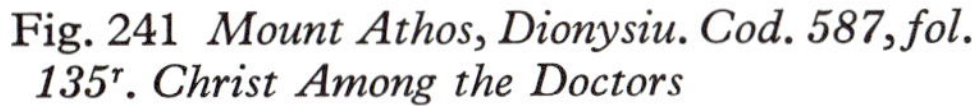

Fig. 241 *Mount Athos, Dionysiu. Cod. 587, fol. 135ʳ. Christ Among the Doctors*

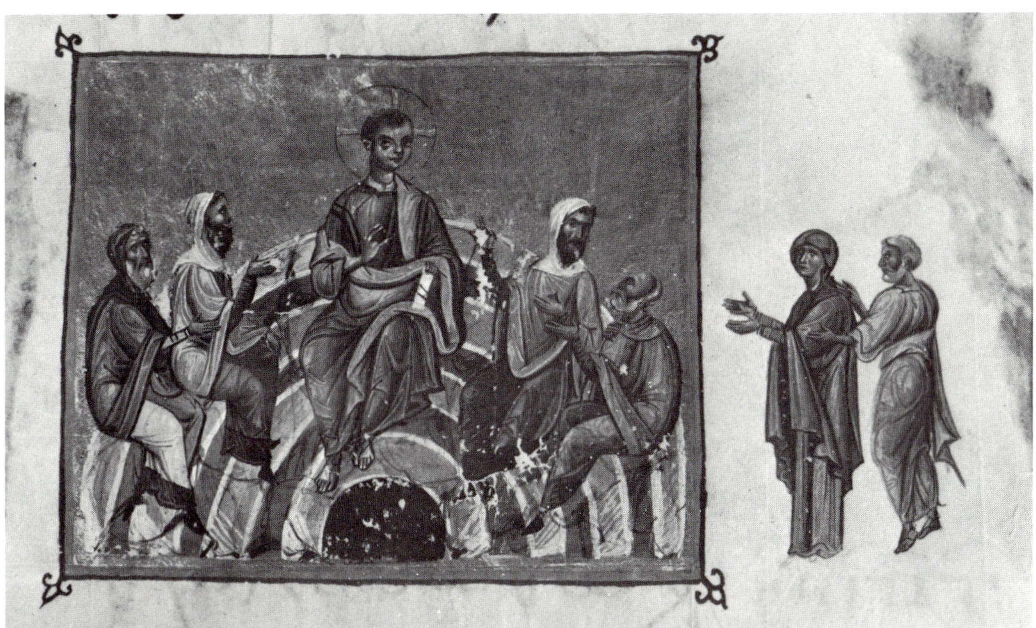

as for instance the picture of Christ in Gethsemane (Fig. 242). Within a richly ornamented frame Christ appears three times: (1) ascending the mountain and praying, (2) praying once more in *proskynesis*, and (3) speaking thereafter with his disciples. The root of this picture is still recognizable as a section out of a continuous narrative, but by regrouping the three phases, the artist unified them into a single picture— using most intelligently the ascending ridge of the mountain for the Christ praying to heaven, the slope beyond the peak for the sliding posture of Christ in *proskynesis* (whereby he created the effect of utter dejection), and the mountain as a whole as a backdrop for the group of the disciples whom he represented with a keen sense of observation in various stages of sleepiness, drowsiness, and wakefulness. Although this miniature

heads a group of twelve Passion readings preceding Good Friday, neither the first of these lections (John 13:31–18:1) to which our miniature is attached, nor any of the following contains the Geth-semane episode, which occurs in the lection read on Maundy Thursday (Matt. 26:40–27:2). As far as we can see, the transfer of this picture to its present location was governed by purely artistic reasons since the first lection, beginning with John 13:31, has no striking event which, as an introductory miniature to the story of the Passion, would have been as suitable and effective as Christ's prayer in Gethsemane.

While reducing the number of scenes from the Gospels, the illustrator of a lectionary of the same time often added scores of miniatures from other sources, particularly for the pictorialization of those feasts which are not based on

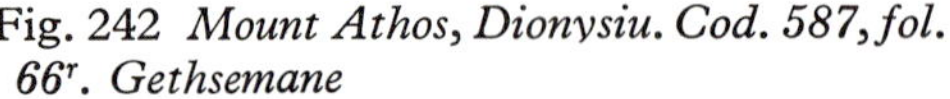

Fig. 242 *Mount Athos, Dionysiu. Cod. 587, fol. 66ʳ. Gethsemane*

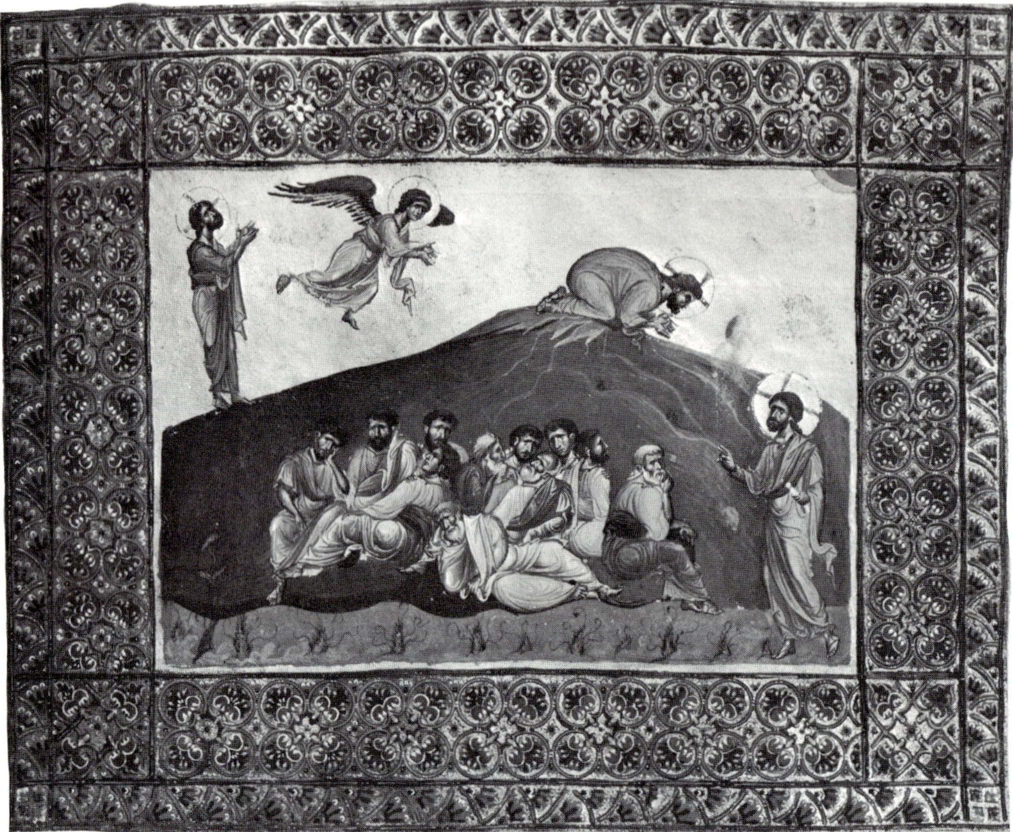

Gospel events. There are, for example, the various feasts from the life of the Virgin, among them her Birth, commemorated on 8 September, and her Presentation in the Temple, celebrated on 21 November. In the Vatican Lectionary mentioned above, the illustration of the Virgin's birth resembles and surely is ultimately derived from a Birth of Christ (Fig. 243). The artist has omitted the figure of the Child's father, while keeping the typical Washing of the Child by two midwives. The Presentation (Fig. 244) shows a greater originality and does not seem to be dependent on any other Gospel scene for its compositional layout. Here Joachim and Anna, followed by the candle-bearing daughters of the Hebrews, present the Virgin to the priest in the Temple, and the Virgin is repeated sitting on the upper step of the semicircular marble benches of the apse of a Christian church while the angel offers her the wafer. As is well-known, the textual basis for these miniatures is the Protevangelium of James (5, 7, and 8). There is good reason to believe that the text of this apocryphal Gospel was provided at a rather early time with an extensive cycle of narrative

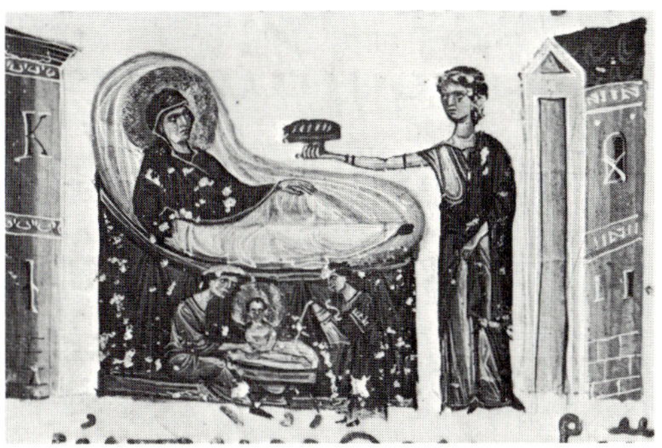

Fig. 243 *Vatican, Biblioteca. Cod. gr. 1156, fol. 246ᵛ. Birth of the Virgin*

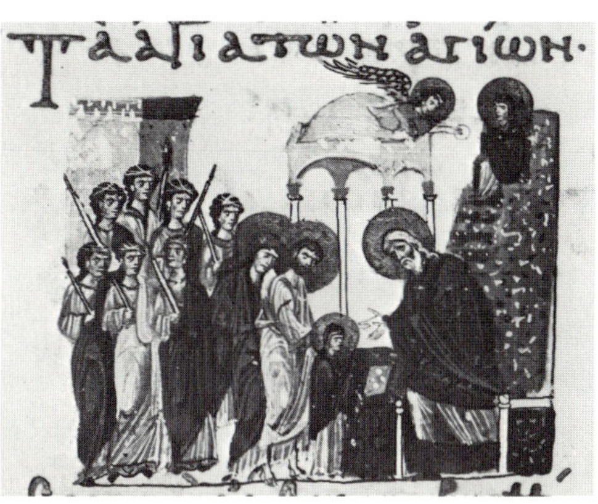

Fig. 244 *Vatican, Biblioteca. Cod. gr. 1156, fol. 268ᵛ. Presentation of the Virgin in the Temple*

miniatures. Although no such copy exists today, a certain number of scenes from such a cycle had migrated into other texts,[29] copies of which are preserved from the Middle Byzantine period; and a fairly complete cycle, which, in our opinion, depends on miniature models, is preserved in relief on the alabaster columns of Saint Mark's in Venice.[30] The pictorial evidence points to a considerable popularity of the Protevangelium in the Middle Byzantine period, and the same can also be demonstrated by the writings of that time, as for instance the Homilies of George of Nicomedia, in which the Protevangelium plays an important role.[31]

The situation is much the same with regard to the Gospel of Nicodemus. That this apocryphal Gospel, too, was originally illustrated in an extensive narrative cycle we know in this case not only from the Saint Mark's columns which contain several scenes based on it but also from a thirteenth-century Latin manuscript of the Gospel of Nicodemus itself, the miniatures of which surely go back to a Byzantine model.[32] Of all the scenes based on the text of Nicodemus, only the Anastasis was copied very frequently, because it was the feast picture for Easter Sunday and as such had gained a widespread popularity. In the lectionary fragment in Leningrad (Fig. 245),[33] which in our opinion belongs to the tenth

[29] For the principle of migration of miniatures from one text to another consult Weitzmann, *Roll and Codex*, pp. 130–53.

[30] H. v. d. Gabelentz, *Mittelalterliche Plastik im Venedig* (Leipzig, 1903); G. Costantini, "Le colonne del ciborio di San Marco a Venezia," *Arte Cristiana*, 3 (1915), 8 ff., 166 ff., 235 ff; E. Weigand, "Zur Datierung der Ciboriumsäulen von S. Marco in Venedig," *Studi Byzantini e Neoellenici*, 6 (1940), 440 ff. [For a thorough, recent treatment of this problem consult J. Lafontaine-Dosogne, *Iconographie de l'enfance de la vièrge dans l'empire byzantin et en occident* ("Memoires de l'Académie Royale de Belgique. Classe des Beaux-Arts," 11 [Brussels, 1964]).]

[31] J. P. Migne (ed.), *Patrologiae cursus completus . . . series graecus* (Paris, 1857–66), 100, cols. 1335 ff.

[32] A. v. Erbach-Fürstenau, "L'evangelo di Nicodemo," *Archivio storico dell'arte*, 2 (1896), 225 ff.

[33] C. R. Morey, "Notes on East Christian Miniatures," *Art Bulletin*, 11 (1929), 57 and fig. 63. [Consult: Lazarev, *Storia della pittura*, pp. 139 ff., 173, n. 53 and figs. 116–18.]

Fig. 245 *Leningrad, Public Library. Cod. gr. 21, fol. 1ᵛ. Anastasis*

Fig. 246 *Mount Athos, Dionysiu. Cod. 587, fol. 124ᵛ. St. Nicholas*

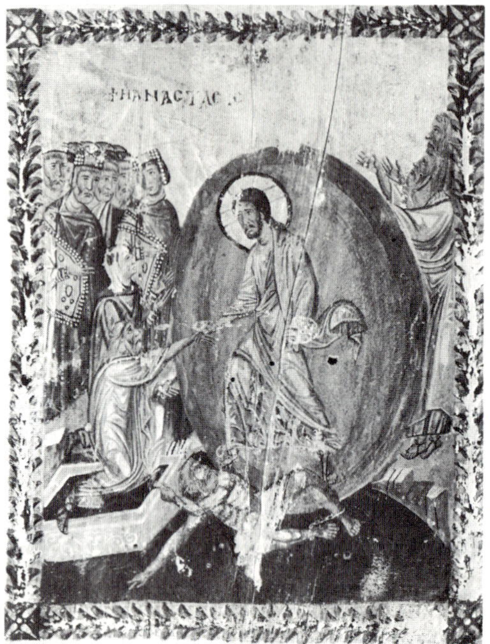

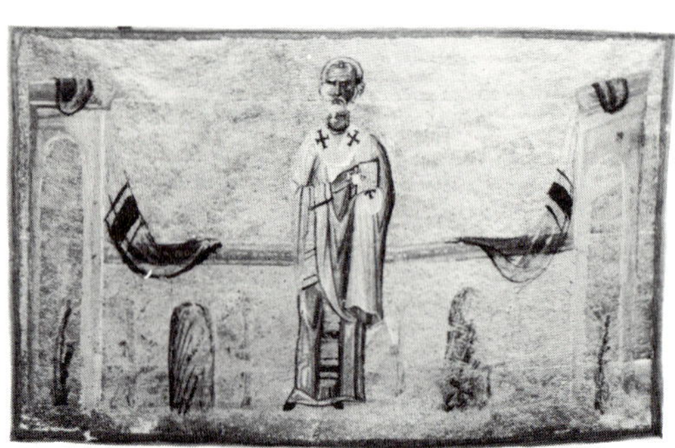

century,[34] Christ is represented in a mandorla trampling over Hades as he grasps the hand of Adam. Apparently it was from the lectionary, where it is often the frontispiece miniature preceded on occasion only by the evangelist portrait of John, that the Harrowing of Hell spread into other media (icons, frescoes, mosaics, and the like) and developed into what one might call a canonical rendering of the Easter Feast.

The illustrated text most prolifically exploited by the lectionary painters was the menologion, which contains the lives of saints in the same order as the second part of the lectionary—also usually called a menologion—i.e., both begin 1 September. It was an easy procedure for an illustrator of a lectionary to copy

from a menologion proper the picture of a saint which preceded the account of his life or martyrdom and to transfer it to the corresponding place in the second part of the lectionary in front of the Gospel lection of the day the saint is commemorated. In certain lectionaries the pictures of the saints take an even more important place in the artistic decoration than the feast pictures from the life of Christ. Representations of martyrdom are rare, and usually the saints are depicted standing in a frontal attitude facing the spectator. In the lectionary from Dionysiu most saints, such as Saint Nicholas of Myra (Fig. 246), stand in front of a background that is ornamentalized and degenerated from an architectural point of view, but whose derivation from the *scenae frons* of the Roman theater can still be recognized. This type of background behind the standing saint is typical also of the famous menologion in the Vatican Library (cod. gr. 1613) which was made around the year 1000 for the emperor Basil II, as may be seen in its corresponding miniature of the same saint (Fig. 247).[35] Since the

---

[34] Weitzmann, *Byzantinische Buchmalerei*, pp. 59 ff.

[35] *Il menologio di Basilio II* ("Codices e Vaticanis selecti," 8 [Turin, 1907]), 226.

Fig. 247 *Vatican, Biblioteca. Cod. gr. 1613, p. 226. St. Nicholas*

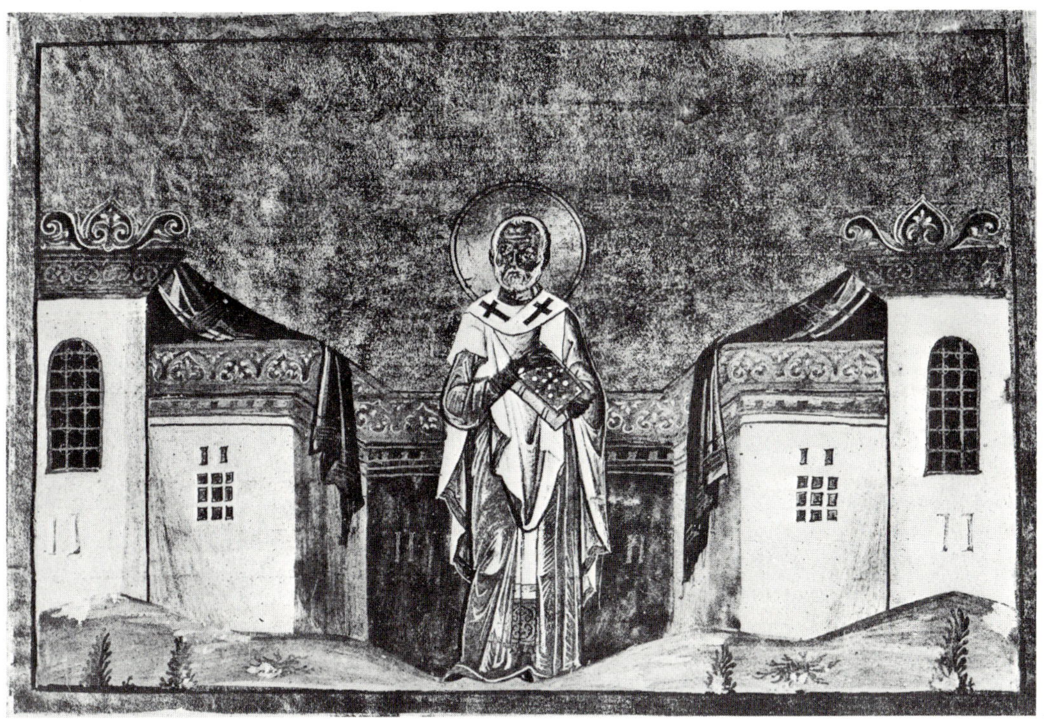

Vatican manuscript, because of its dedication to Basil II, is obviously the product of the imperial scriptorium, it is more than probable that the illustrator of the Dionysiu Lectionary, who must have studied the Vatican menologion, also worked in the same scriptorium. Here the pictures supply evidence for the localization of the manuscript which could not be gained on the basis of textual study alone—one of those cases where the textual critic has to incorporate

[Weitzmann, "Miniature and Icon Painting," p. 208 and *passim*, herewith, p. 272; idem, "Imperial Lectionary," pp. 242 ff. See also I. Ševčenko, "The Illuminators of the Monologium of Basil II," *Dumbarton Oaks Papers*, 16 (1962), 245 ff.; here the recent literature on the Vatican manuscript.]

art-historical information for a more complete gathering of the internal evidence of the documents.

Other pictures in the lectionary seem not to be derivative from other sources, but rather are inventions which neither illustrate the text of the lection to which they are attached nor any other text with which they might originally have been connected and from which they were subsequently transferred. One of the great feasts of the Orthodox Church is the Elevation of the Holy Cross, celebrated on 14 September.[36] In the Dionysiu and several other lectionaries this feast is illustrated by a miniature (Fig. 248) which can be explained on the basis of the

[36] "Miniature and Icon Painting," pp. 218 ff. and pls. 31–33.

Fig. 248 *Mount Athos, Dionysiu. Cod. 587, fol. 119ᵛ. Elevation of the Holy Cross*

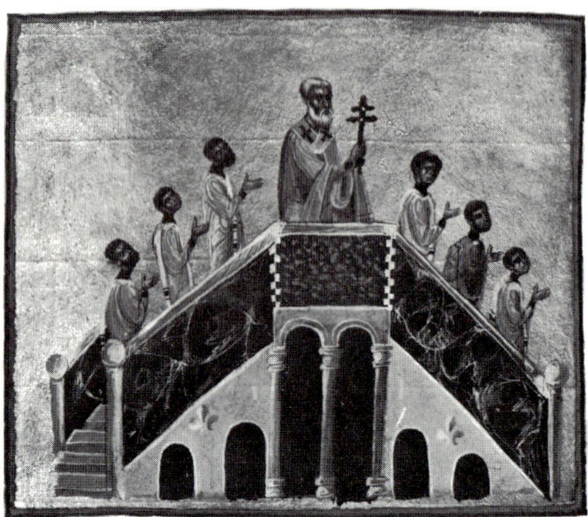

Book of Ceremonies of the emperor Constantine VII Porphyrogenitus, though there is no evidence that this book itself was ever illustrated. Here we read (1, 31)[37] that the emperor in person takes part in the celebration of the feast in Hagia Sophia, in the course of which the patriarch mounts the ambo with the venerated relic of the Holy Cross that was kept in this church and lifts it over his head four times toward the four sides of the ambo. It is this very moment when the patriarch, accompanied by several deacons, lifts the cross while standing on the ambo of Hagia Sophia which is depicted in the Dionysiu miniature.

For many pictures of the great feasts which had become the focus of the illustrated lectionary, the post-iconoclastic period developed new iconographical schemes that were accepted as almost canonical solutions, so much so that following generations saw no need to change them in any essential point. Although the lectionary provides a proper setting for the pictures of the great feasts, some of them were apparently not invented for this service book but for the mosaic decoration of great churches in Constantinople.

Most famous for its mosaics was the Church of the Holy Apostles whose five domes, arches, and adjacent lunettes were covered mostly with New Testament scenes, as we know from the tenth century poem of Constantinos Rhodios and from their description by Nicolaos Mesarites, who around 1200 described them in considerable detail. Unfortunately, the one manuscript of the Mesarites text preserved today is fragmentary.[38] The program of these lost mosaics, as becomes clear from its reconstruction based on the literary sources, was not a mere narration of the life of Christ. Only certain scenes were chosen and these for particular reasons in some ways similar to the theological purposes of the lectionary, and this explains in a large measure the close relationship between the two. Mesarites describes in detail the Metamorphosis mosaic, with which a miniature in an eleventh-century lectionary in the Athos monastery Iviron (cod. 1 Fig. 249)[39] agrees to such an astonishing

---

[37] Constantine VII Porphyrogenitus, *Le Livre des Cérémonies*, 1, trans. A. Vogt (Paris, 1935), 116 ff. and 141 ff.

[38] A. Heisenberg, *Grabeskirche und Apostelkirche, 2, Die Apostelkirche in Konstantinopel* (Leipzig, 1908). [Cf. R. Krautheimer, "A Note on Justinian's Church of the Holy Apostles in Constantinople," *Mélanges Eugene Tisserant* ("Studi e Testi," 232, Vatican, 1964), 2: 265 ff.]

[39] H. Brockhaus, *Die Kunst in den Athos Klöstern* (Leipzig, 1891; 2d ed., 1924), pp. 189 ff. and pl. 25; A. Xyngopoulos, *Evangiles avec miniatures du monastère d'Iviron au Mont Athos* (Athens, 1932), pp. 6 ff. and pls. I–II.

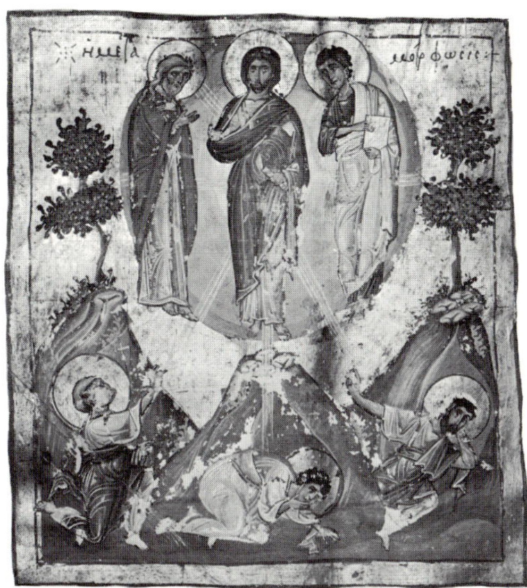

Fig. 249 *Mount Athos, Iviron. Cod. 1, fol. 305ᵛ. Metamorphosis*

degree[40] that its derivation from the lost work in the Apostles Church can hardly be doubted. He tells us[41] that in the mosaic, which occupied the northern cupola, the three disciples who had gone with Christ to Mount Tabor fell prostrate, covering their faces with their hands; that then Peter, the strongest of them, stood up as far as he could; that one of them, the older one (i.e. James), knelt with difficulty upon one knee and held his heavy head with his left arm while the greater part of his body was still earthbound; and that John did not even want to look upward, but, like a man who did not care or think of the world, a virginal man, seems to inhabit Mount Tabor as in a house and to lie in deep sleep. Important also is Mesarites' remark that Christ was not alone in the cloud of light but Moses and Elijah stood with him. While the Iviron miniature is surely not the first copy ever made from the lost mosaic, nevertheless it seems to be the best one among the preserved monuments, and the few details which deviate from the description can be explained as changes due to the process of repeated copying.

The western cupola was occupied by a representation of the Pentecost[42] as is the case in Saint Mark's in Venice,[43] which in many respects resembles the Apostles Church. This mosaic, with its peculiar compositional layout adapted to the hemispheric shape of the cupola, became the archetype of all Pentecost pictures in the Middle and Late Byzantine periods. The difficulties which arose from transforming a dome composition to a two-dimensional picture plane can still be realized by looking, for instance, at the miniature in the tenth-century lectionary fragment in Leningrad (cod. 21 Fig. 250).[44] The Apostles, who in the dome were seated in a full circle, had to be squeezed into a semicircle, and the rays descending on their heads are therefore slightly curved as they would have appeared to a spectator looking from below into the dome. The φύλαι, the representatives of the various nations

[40] Heisenberg, *Apostelkirche*, pp. 183 ff., has already enumerated this miniature among the reflections of the Apostle Church mosaic.
[41] Heisenberg, *Apostelkirche*, pp. 32 ff. [For a more detailed discussion of the Iviron miniature cf. Weitzmann, "Wolfenbüttel Musterbuch," pp. 227 ff.]

[42] Heisenberg, *Apostelkirche*, pp. 38 ff., 196 ff.
[43] O. Demus, *Die Mosaiken von S. Marko in Venedig* (Baden bei Wien, 1935), pp. 18 ff. and figs. 2–3.
[44] Morey, "East Christian Miniatures," p. 73 and fig. 85; O. Demus, *Byzantine Mosaic Decoration* (London, 1947), pp. 83 ff. and fig. 64.

Fig. 250 *Leningrad, Public Library. Cod. gr. 21, fol. 14ᵛ. Pentecost*

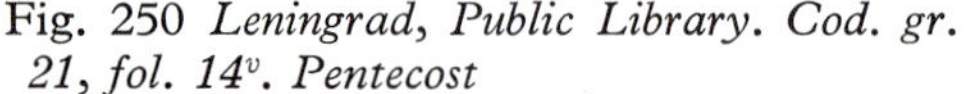

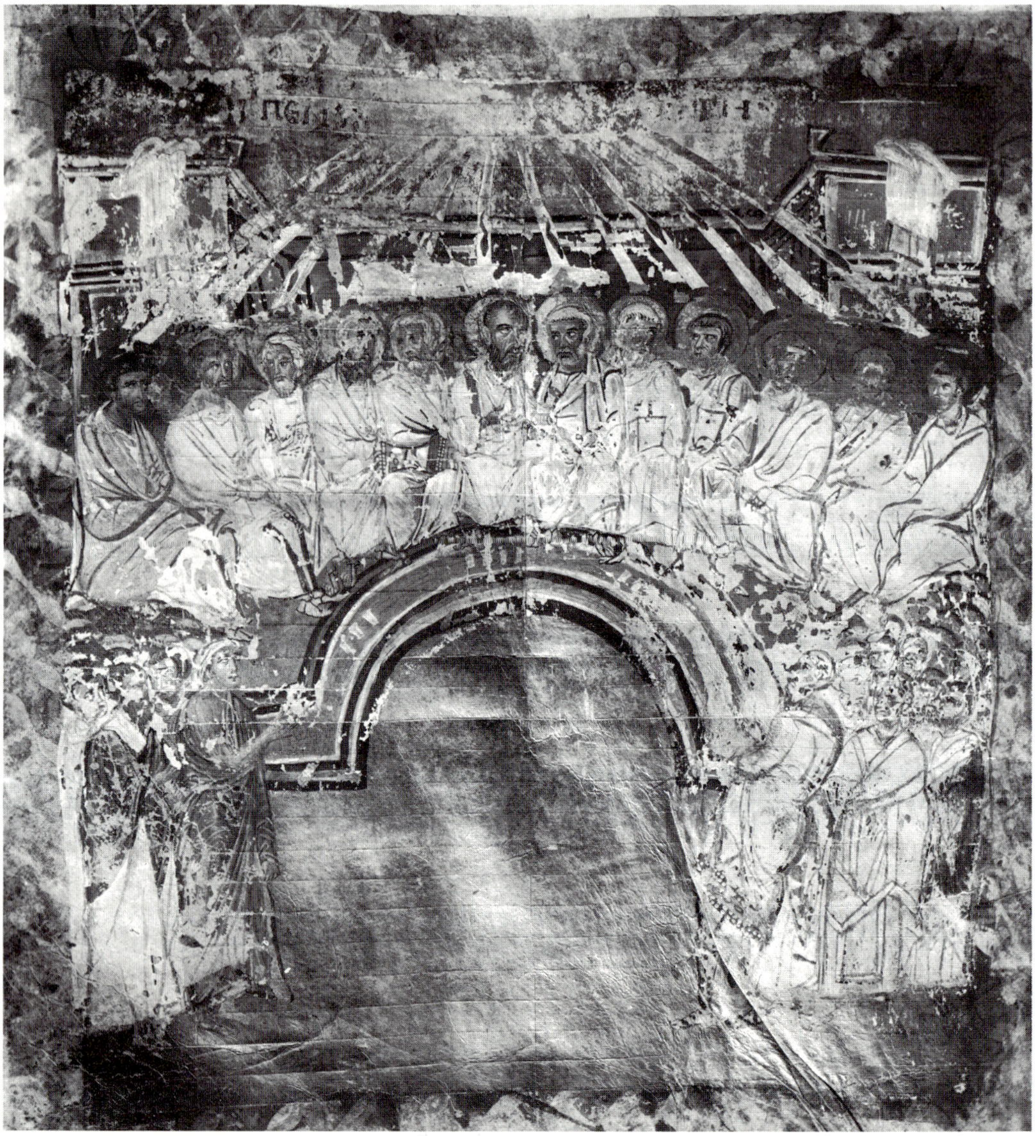

(Acts 2:9–11) who in the mosaic were represented in the four pendentives supporting the dome, are in the miniature reduced to two and placed in the corners. Thus, from looking at the Metamorphosis and Pentecost miniatures it becomes obvious that monumental art had a considerable share in the formation of what one might call the canonical rendering of the great feasts which in the lectionaries and elsewhere developed into a feast cycle.

New formulations of New Testament scenes in mosaic art, a medium which lends itself to hieratic compositional schemes, were not confined to the cupolas (where special formal conditions prevail) but originated also in other parts of the wall surface, such as the broad arches and the adjacent lunettes. There are quite a number of miniatures in the Dionysiu Lectionary which, because of of their hieratic quality, one feels must have derived from a monumental archetype such as the strongly symmetrically composed Mission of the Apostles (Fig. 251), in which Christ stands in the center in a dignified position elevated on a pearl studded footstool while the Apostles, six on either side and headed by Peter and Paul, approach Christ in a devoted attitude. The fact that we deal here with an intrusion into the lectionary from an outside source is supported by the fact that the miniature is associated with the wrong text passage. Its present location is before the lection for Ascension day, on which Luke 24:36–53 is read. The proper picture for this passage would be a representation of the appearance of Christ in which he shows his stigmatized hands and feet to his disciples.

Still, the reason for the misplacement can be surmised. The proper lection of the Mission of the Apostles (Matt. 28:1–20) is read on the Sabbath of Holy Week, i.e., at the very end of the first part of the lectionary with the movable feasts, and part of it (verses 16–20) is repeated as the first of the so-called ἑωθινά. But in the latter place the Dionysiu Lectionary already had a picture of the Mission (Fig. 252) which the illustrator apparently did not want to abandon by substituting for it the monumental composition of

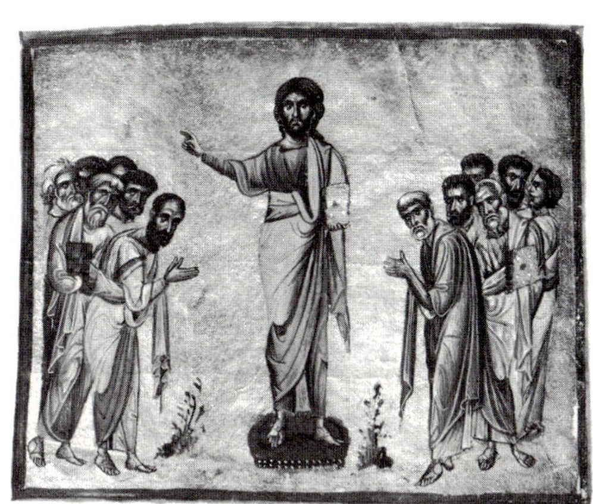

Fig. 251 *Mount Athos, Dionysiu. Cod. 587, fol. 32ᵛ. Mission of the Apostles*

the same theme. Therefore, he inserted the borrowed form elsewhere, where it was not totally out of place since a composition of Christ among the Apostles also fits the Ascension passage to some degree, if not in detail, at least in its more general meaning. It is very instructive, indeed, to compare the two representations of the Missions of the Apostles. The one preceding the ἑωθινά is a typical narrative picture in the tradition of Gospel illustration. Christ stands at the right on a hill while giving the command of the mission to the Apostles, who are represented with a keen sense of psychological observation. They are divided into two groups: one is leaning forward (προσεκύνησαν), the other is standing aside with signs of doubt (ἐδίστασαν). Here we have a particularly illuminating example of how two representations of the same theme may differ between a purely narrative illustration and a hieratic rendering influenced by a monumental composition.

The hieratic compositional schemes developed in monumental art had such an impact on the illustration of the

Fig. 252 *Mount Athos, Dionysiu. Cod. 587, fol. 168ʳ. Mission of the Apostles*

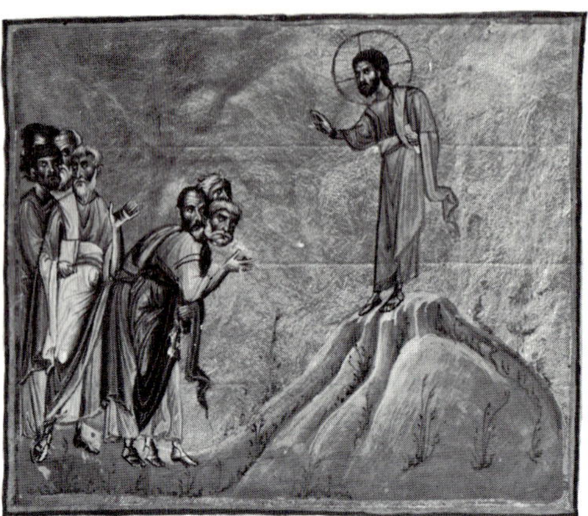

Fig. 253 *Mount Athos, Dionysiu. Cod. 587, fol. 19ᵛ. Christ Speaking about the Circumcision*

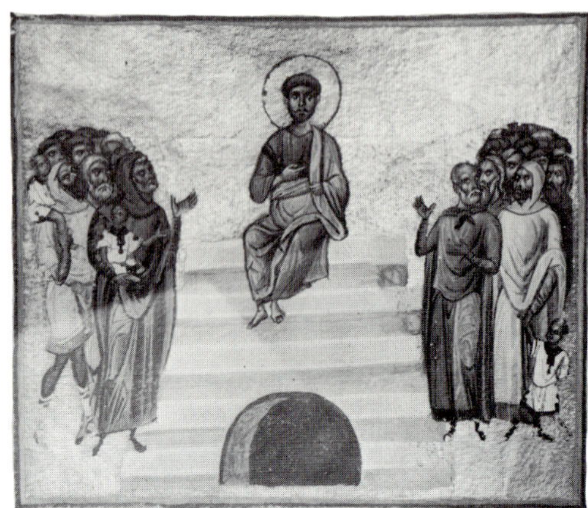

lectionary that they were adopted by the miniaturists even in scenes which, so far as we know, never existed in a fresco or mosaic. On Wednesday of the fourth week after Easter, the lection deals with Christ speaking in the Temple about circumcision on the Sabbath (John 7:14–30). In a narrative Gospel book like cod. gr. 74 in Paris this passage is illustrated by a picture in which Christ sits on one side, in front of an architectural structure suggesting the synagogue, and faces the Jews on the other while a few disciples stand between them.[45] But in the Dionysiu Lectionary (Fig. 253) Christ is seated in the center, not on a chair but on top of a flight of marble steps which are meant to represent the semicircular benches in the apse of a Christian church, while the Jews are divided into two groups, creating thereby a symmetrical and at the same time monumental and hieratic composition. This change from a narrative into a hieratic rendering is a sign of the growing independence from the Gospel model and of the establishment of a new type

of New Testament picture which emphasizes the liturgical aspect of the scene and imbues it with a sense of greater authority and permanency.

INFLUENCE OF LECTIONARY ILLUSTRATIONS

To such an extent does the lectionary of the Middle Byzantine period become the focus of New Testament illustration that a retroactive influence upon the illustration of the canonical Gospels can be observed. This process is in full harmony with the textual development. Colwell in his *Prolegomena* has demonstrated that the opening formulae, invented as incipits of the lections, were sometimes taken over by reverse process, into the running Gospel text.[46] The very Gospel book in Paris which exemplifies the characteristics of narrative illustration at the same time has a considerable number of miniatures which were taken over from a lectionary. For example, toward the end of the Gospel of Matthew the Crucifixion is represented

[45] Omont, *Évangiles*, pl. 156a.

[46] Colwell and Riddle, *Prolegomena*, pp. 18 ff.

Fig. 254 *Paris, Bibliothèque Nationale. Cod. gr. 74, fol. 58ᵛ. Crucifixion*

Fig. 255 *Paris, Bibliothèque Nationale. Cod. gr. 74, fol. 59ʳ. Crucifixion*

Fig. 256 *Paris, Bibliothèque Nationale. Cod. gr. 74, fol. 59ᵛ. Crucifixion*

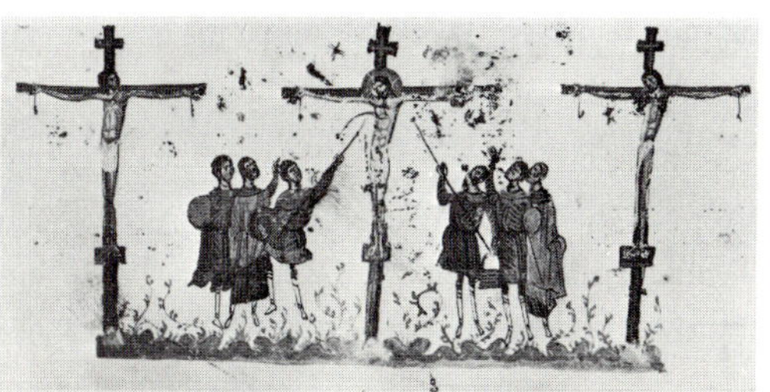

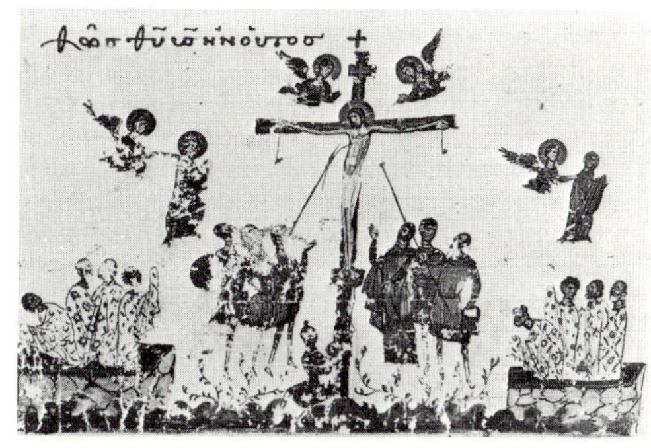

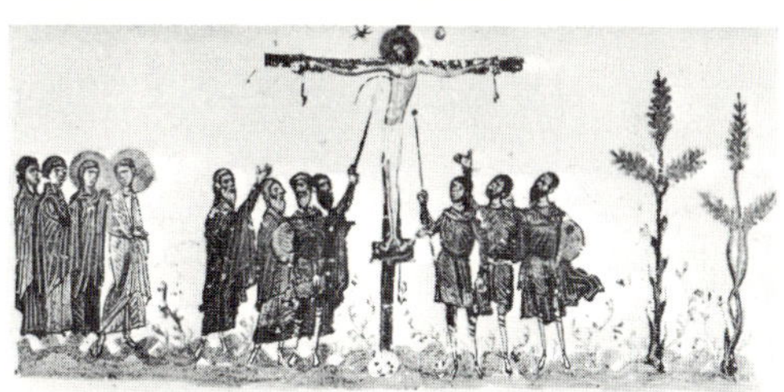

three times (Figs. 254–56)[47] although one picture would have been sufficient. Of these the second (Fig. 255) is most typical for the Gospel of Matthew which alone mentions the resurrection of the dead, who in the miniature stand in open sarcophagi, whereas the third Crucifixion (Fig. 256), which represents at the left John, the Virgin, and two other Marys, is clearly based on the Gospel of John (John 19:25–27). The presence of the latter in this place cannot be explained by a misplacement within the Gospel book because in the text of the Gospel of John it is not only repeated but we find once more three Crucifixion scenes where one would have been sufficient.[48] The most reasonable assumption is that a lectionary was used as a model in which each of the four consecutive lections of the Passion (Nos. 6–9), which have the cognate readings of the Crucifixion story according to Mark (15:16–32), Matthew (27:33–54), Luke (23:32–49), and John (19:25–37), had a title miniature of the Crucifixion.

Lectionary pictures, for their content as well as for their compositional schemes, were copied not only in Gospel books but also in other texts. The Basil menologion in the Vatican starts the miniature cycle for 1 September with an illustration of the Luke passage (4:16–22) in which the Book of Isaiah is given to Christ in the synagogue (Fig. 257).[49] In the narrative representation of this scene in the Gospel book in Paris[50] Christ, holding the book, sits on one side and the Jews face him from the other, and a very similar composition is found in the lectionary fragment in Leningrad,[51] which obviously depends on the Gospel tradition. The composition in the Vatican menologion is totally different: here Christ stands in the center on a jewel-studded footstool showing the open book to the beholder, while the Jews, divided symmetrically into two groups, approach Christ from either side in a

---

[47] Omont, *Évangiles*, pls. 50–52.

[48] Ibid., pls. 178–80

[49] *Il menologio di Basilio II*, p. 1.

[50] Omont, *Évangiles*, pl. 101.

[51] Morey, "East Christian Miniatures," p. 79 and fig. 94.

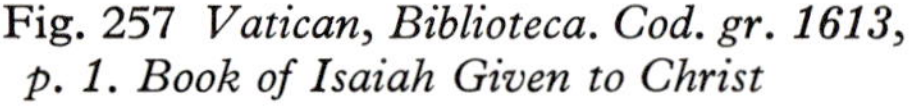
Fig. 257 *Vatican, Biblioteca. Cod. gr. 1613,*
p. 1. Book of Isaiah Given to Christ

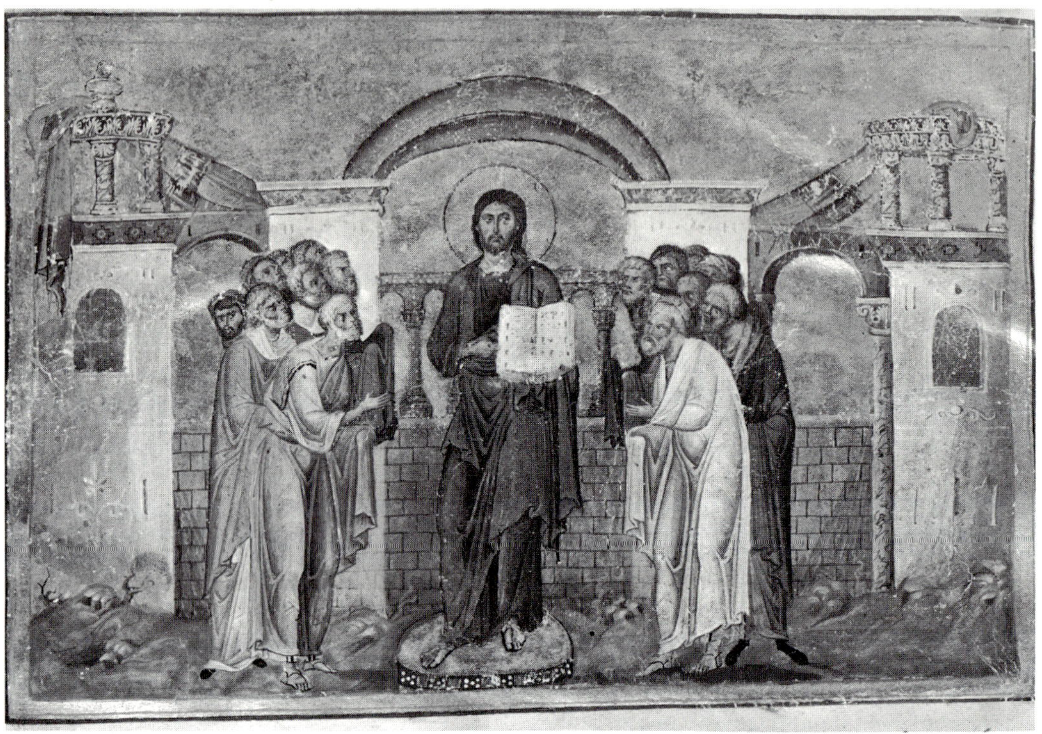

devout attitude with veiled hands. This is obviously an adaptation of the compositional scheme invented for the Mission of the Apostles (cf. Fig. 251). It so happens that in a lectionary, the lection for 1 September is preceded by that for Saturday of Holy Week which contains the Matthew passage of the Mission. This suggests that the illustrator of the menologion used as a model a lectionary in which these two scenes followed each other, so that a fusion between the compositional scheme of the first and the content of the second could easily be achieved.[52]

It must be the aim of the art historian to work out, by means of a comparative method, a stemma of illustrated manuscripts and, on the basis of picture criticism, to establish families in a manner similar to that used by the text critic. One such family would comprise those lectionaries which show a decisive influence of the mosaics of the Apostles Church, such as Iviron cod. 1 with its lofty Metamorphosis (Fig. 249) and the fragment in Leningrad (cod. 21) with its Pentecost transformed under the influence of a cupola composition (Fig. 250). It must have been a splendid lectionary which first absorbed the influence of monumental art and showed its hieratic quality in stately full-page miniatures.

[52] Weitzmann, *Roll and Codex*, pp. 180 ff. and figs. 190–91.

CLASSICAL INFLUENCES

In surveying the extant material of illustrated lectionaries we come across still another type of picture which reveals quite a different outside influence. Its chief characteristic is a strong classical appearance which manifests itself in different forms. In the so-called Phocas Lectionary in the *skevophylakion* of Lavra, of which we have already seen the splendid cover (Fig. 231), the first full-page miniature prefacing the Easter lection (John 1:1–7) represents the Anastasis with a new type of Christ (Fig. 194).[53] In the traditional iconography as seen in the lectionary fragment in Leningrad (Fig. 245)[54] Christ approaches Adam and, slightly inclining to him, takes his hand in order to raise him out of Hades. The new type shows Christ dragging Adam out of Hell just as Heracles dragged Cerberus out of Hell, and in his left hand Christ holds the cross as a sign of victory just as Heracles holds his club. The only conclusion which can be drawn from this coincidence of types, which surely is not accidental, is that a Heracles like that found on Roman sarcophagi (Fig. 195)[55]

is responsible for the alteration of the Anastasis iconography, though the prototype of the miniaturist—or rather of the artist who first introduced the new type into Middle Byzantine art—was surely not a marble relief but a classical miniature.

The reappearance of classical elements in Middle Byzantine book illumination is part of a widespread revival of classical learning which started at the end of the ninth century and reached its height in the tenth century under the emperor Constantine VII Porphyrogenitus, the scholar on the imperial throne. Under his guidance comprehensive encyclopedias of classical learning were made in which classical texts of all kinds were copied and excerpted, some of them surely with their pictures. From these copies the classical elements spread into Christian miniatures, into Psalters like the famous one in Paris (Bibliothèque Nationale cod. gr. 139) with its numerous personifications, into the well-known Joshua Roll in the Vatican (cod. Palat. gr. 431) and, as we learn now, also into lectionaries of which the Phocas manuscript in the Lavra is not the only one to show the impact of what we call the Macedonian Renaissance.[56]

The second full-page miniature of the Phocas Lectionary represents the Birth

---

[53] K. Weitzmann, "Das Evangelion im Skevophylakion zu Lawra," *Seminarium Kondakovianum*, VIII (1936), 83 ff.

[54] For the iconography of the Anastasis consult C. R. Morey, *East Christian Paintings in the Freer Collection* (New York, 1914), pp. 45 ff.

[55] Weitzmann, "Evangelion," p. 88 and pl. IV, no. 3. [For a more detailed discussion of classical influence on New Testament illustration consult K. Weitzmann, *Geistige Grundlagen und Wesen der Makedonischen Renaissance* (Cologne and Opladen, 1963), pp. 39 ff., translated and reprinted herewith, pp. 211 ff.]

[56] The evidence for this much debated renaissance has been adduced by the author in several works, most recently in a monograph on the Vatican Rotulus, *The Joshua Roll, a Work of the Macedonian Renaissance* (Princeton, 1948) and on a broader basis, including historical, literary, and philological evidence, in *Greek Mythology in Byzantine Art* (Princeton, 1951). [Weitzmann, *Geistige Grundlagen*, for a recent discussion of the Macedonian Renaissance, herewith, pp. 176 ff.]

of Christ as the feast picture of Christmas (Fig. 258). In the center lies the Virgin in a well-understood, almost elegant contrappostic attitude and in the foreground we see the Washing of the Child, resembling in many ways the Washing of the Child Dionysus by the nymphs from which it is ultimately derived,[57] just as the Christ of the Anastasis has its prototype in a figure of Heracles. There is no reason to assume that these classicizing changes were made for the first time by the illustrator of the Phocas Lectionary. Its miniatures, like those of other lectionaries, merely help to reconstruct a Renaissance archetype which we date in the first half of the tenth century.

EVIDENCE FROM LECTIONARY ILLUSTRATIONS

For the establishment of the internal evidence of documents, miniatures are important in still another respect. At times, they furnish independent evidence of where a manuscript was made and for which locality it was destined. The textual critic depends for information of this kind chiefly on the colophon, cursed and troublesome as it may be on occasion. But in cases where the manuscript has no colophon, pictorial evidence can fill a gap where the textual critic is at a loss. The third miniature of the Phocas Lectionary represents the Koimesis of the Virgin, which like other Virgin scenes is based on an apocryphal text (Fig. 259). In its present state the Phocas Lectionary contains only three miniatures, the Anastasis, the Nativity,

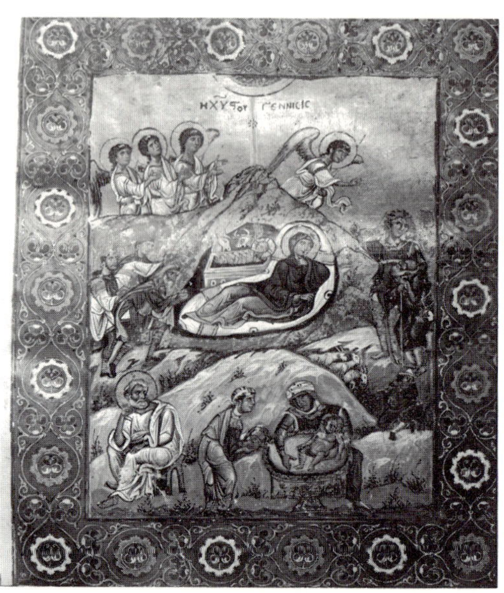

Fig. 258 *Mount Athos, Lavra, Skevophylakion. Lectionary, fol. 144ᵛ. Birth of Christ*

and the Koimesis, and since the manuscript is in an excellent and undamaged condition, there is no reason to assume that it ever contained other illustrations. Now it happens that Easter, Christmas, and the Day of the Dormition of the Virgin are the three feast days on which, at the time of Saint Athanasius, the founder of the Lavra, all the monks of Mount Athos came together to hold a common service in Karyaes, the capital of the little monastic republic.[58] Thus the selection of these three feast pictures provides the evidence that the Phocas Lectionary was actually made for Mount Athos.

Yet, this does not mean that it was also executed there. The style of the highly accomplished miniatures points to the leading scriptorium of Constantinople and not to Mount Athos. According to a

[57] Cf. the representation on a Roman sarcophagus. Weitzmann, "Evangelion," pp. 89 ff. and pl. IV, no. 4.

[58] K. Lake, *The Early Days of Monasticism on Mount Athos* (Oxford, 1909), p. 92.

Fig. 259 *Mount Athos, Lavra, Skevophyla-kion. Lectionary, fol. 134ᵛ. Koimesis*

Fig. 260 *Mount Athos, Dionysiu. Cod. 587, fol. 148ʳ. Finding of the Head of John the Baptist*

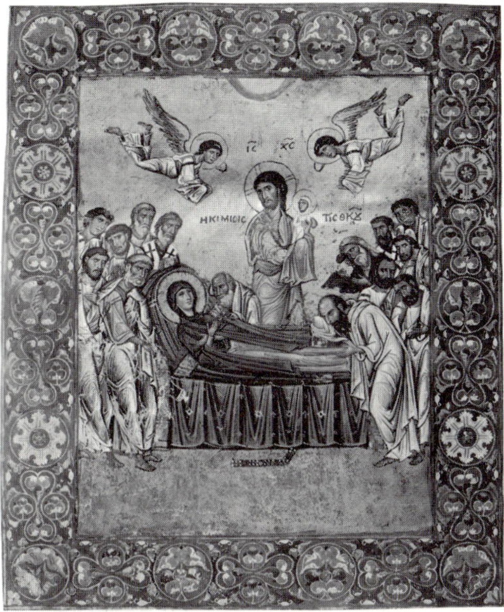

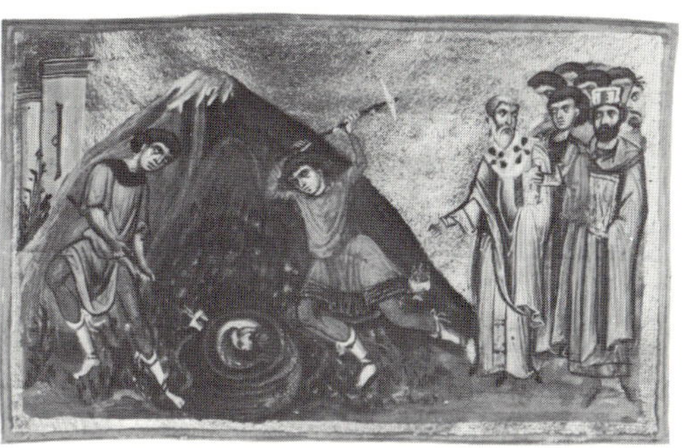

local tradition it was a gift of the emperor Nicephorus Phocas to Saint Athanasius, his personal friend. Phocas was already dead in 969, a date which in our opinion is too early for the miniatures from the stylistic point of view. But since Saint Athanasius survived his imperial friend by several decades and was still alive at the beginning of the eleventh century, the tradition that this treasured manuscript was an imperial gift to him is well borne out by the analysis of the picture style. But it was, as we believe, Basil II and not Phocas who gave the manuscript to the imperial monastery of the Great Lavra.[59]

Likewise, in the case of the Dionysiu Lectionary, which has no colophon, its place of origin and destination can be made out in large measure on the basis

of its pictures. We have already pointed out the dependence of its pictures of saints (Fig. 246) on those of the menolog-ion of Basil II (Fig. 247) and have drawn the conclusion that the Dionysiu manuscript is likewise a product of the imperial scriptorium, as we know for sure of the Vatican manuscript. More-over, there is a marked emphasis among the miniatures of the former on scenes from the life of John the Baptist, in-cluding among others a representation of the Finding of the Head of John in the ninth century (Fig. 260). The representation is of the third of the three findings which took place at the time of the emperor Michael III and the patri-arch Ignatius, both of whom appear in the picture. The most famous monastery of Constantinople, dedicated to John the Baptist, is without question the Studios. So in all probability the lectionary, which on stylistic grounds dates around the the middle of the eleventh century, was made as an imperial gift for this monas-tery. In 1059 Isaac Comnenus abdicated after a short rule of two years and retired as a monk into the Studios monastery. Therefore, it is an attractive hypothesis, though admittedly it lacks final proof, that the Dionysiu Lectionary was made

[59] [This thesis is expanded by Weitzmann in "Imperial Lectionary."]

by the order of this emperor at the time he retired to the Studios. In this manner the selection of the miniatures has to be judged in much the same way as the rubrication of local saints in the comes of Western manuscripts, whereby the locality for which it was made can often be determined.

In this brief sketch we have purposely centered on those aspects of the illustrated lectionary which have a bearing on similar problems of the textual critic, thus trying to make him conscious that miniatures in manuscripts, besides giving aesthetic enjoyment, can provide him at times with supplementary evidence which he cannot gather from the study of the text alone. It is true, as we said before, that the illustrations in lectionaries make no contribution to the establishment of the archetype of the Gospels in the way the text of the lectionaries promises to do whenever it will be more fully studied. But to those who are interested in the later history of Gospel and lectionary manuscripts and their place in various phases of Byzantine civilization, the pictures speak a language often just as clear and vivid as the text itself to show us the importance, function, and diffusion of the lectionary as the main service book of the Orthodox Church.

Byzantine Miniature and Icon Painting in the Eleventh Century

THE task of defining and characterizing Byzantine painting in the eleventh century immediately raises the question whether this century created a style sufficiently distinct from the preceding and following centuries to constitute a clearly discernible artistic identity of its own. We cannot assume, a priori, that history, for the convenience of the scholar, has done us the favor of changing style at the turn of each century. And even if one does notice changes at the beginning of a new century, are they more important and more decisive than those which occur naturally with each new generation within any given century? In order to answer this question, one has first to try to establish as precisely as possible a chronology of miniature and icon painting.

For each phase of the history of art, the analysis and reconstruction of the development of style has to be based on surely dated monuments, which may not always be works of art of the highest artistic merit but which offer incalculable service as focal points around which related works can be grouped. As for the eleventh century[1]—and this would be equally true for some other centuries of the Middle Ages—the most suitable

material for such a study is miniature painting, since in this medium, because of its association with texts, a higher percentage of monuments are either firmly dated or datable on historical or paleographical grounds. The study of icon paintings, as far as the eleventh century is concerned, has only very recently come into focus, after a certain number of icons of high quality were discovered at Mount Sinai.[2] These, however, do not contribute to the solving of the problem of precise dating since not a single icon of this period has a sure date or can be dated by internal evidence. Their dating therefore is conversely dependent on miniature painting. Monumental painting poses a lesser problem than icons, since at least a few of the major mosaic cycles—Nicaea, now destroyed, the Nea Moni of Chios, and S. Sophia in Kiev—can be dated within a fixed period of either a few years or a quarter of the eleventh century. But mosaics are more sporadically preserved than manuscripts and do not give a complete picture of the stylistic development of this century. Thus it seems justifiable to concentrate on book illumination for the sake of establishing a chronology.

STYLISTIC CHANGE IN THE ELEVENTH CENTURY

Miniature painting of the tenth century has a definite focus in the Macedonian Renaissance, which had reached its zenith around the middle of that century under Constantine VII Porphyrogenitus, the scholar and artist on the imperial throne. The Psalter (cod. gr. 139) in Paris, the

Reprinted with permission from, *The Proceedings of the XIIIth International Congress of Byzantine Studies. Oxford. 5–10 September, 1966*, J. M. Hussey, D. Obolensky, and S. Runciman (eds.) (London: Oxford University Press, 1967), pp. 207–24.

[1] The most comprehensive treatment of the history of Byzantine painting which does justice to all its branches is found in V. N. Lazarev, *Istoriya Vizantiiskoy Zhivopisi* (Moscow, 1947–48) [revised and translated, *Storia della pittura bizantina* (Turin, 1967)].

[2] G. and M. Sotiriou, *Icones du Mont Sinaï* (Athens, 1956–58).

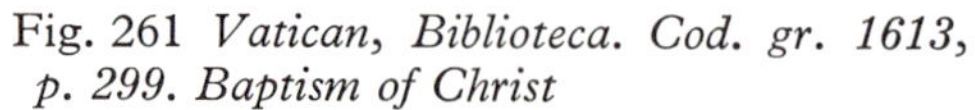

Fig. 261 *Vatican, Biblioteca. Cod. gr. 1613, p. 299. Baptism of Christ*

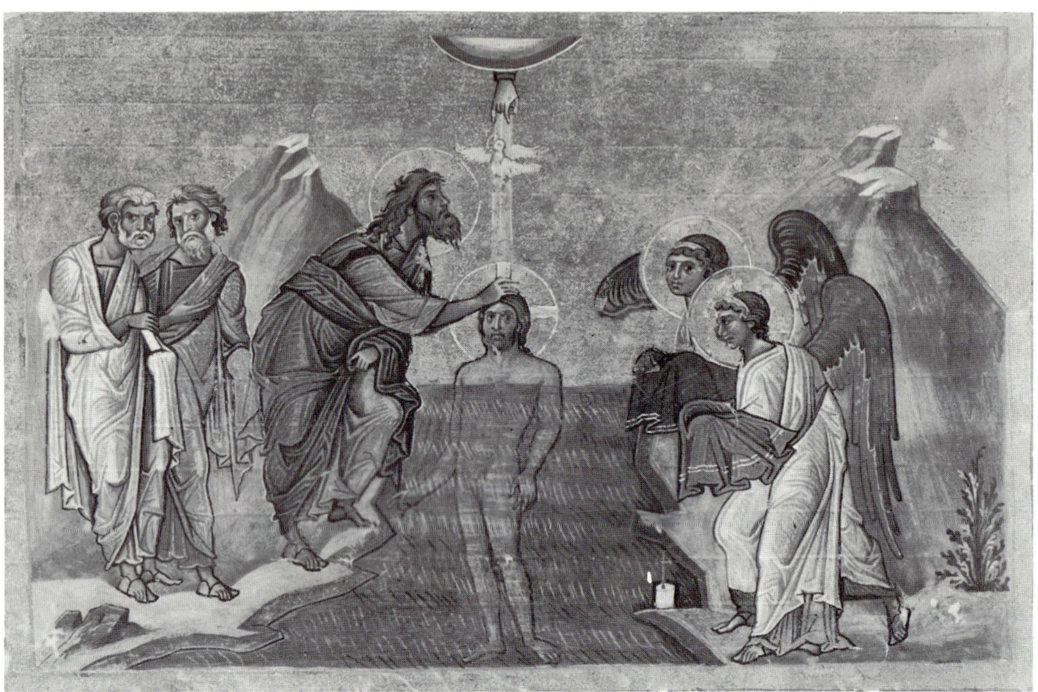

Joshua Roll in the Vatican (cod. Palat. gr. 431), and the classicizing evangelists of the Gospels in Stauronikita on Mount Athos (cod. 43) are the best known and most striking witnesses of this revival movement.[3] Toward the end of the tenth century the classicizing style began to run its course and to become somewhat mannered, as can be exemplified by the miniatures of the well-known menologion in the Vatican (cod. gr. 1613), a product of an imperial workshop made for Basil II.[4] The classical forms remained alive, however, especially in the scenes from the life of Christ which, we believe, hark back to a Gospel lectionary in which the Macedonian Renaissance had asserted itself most forcefully.[5] In the scene of Baptism (Fig. 261) Christ is well-proportioned; in the figure of John the Baptist, however, a sense of physical reality begins to be exaggerated or—to use another term—to be mannered;

---

[3] The most recent study of this Renaissance movement, where a more complete bibliography can be found, is Weitzmann, *Geistige Grundlagen und Wesen der Makedonischen Renaissance* (Cologne and Opladen, 1963) [translated and reprinted herewith pp. 176 ff.]

[4] *Il Menologio di Basilio II* ("Codices e Vaticanis Selecti," 8 [Turin, 1907]). As for the dating of this manuscript around the year 985 cf. S. Der Nersessian, "Remarks on the Date of the Menologion," *Byzantion*, 15 (1940–41), 104 ff.

[5] On the various sources of the miniature cycle in the Vatican menologion cf. Weitzmann, *Illustrations in Roll and Codex* (2d ed. Princeton, 1970), pp. 199 ff., esp. pp. 202–3.

Fig. 262 *Baltimore, Walters Art Gallery. Cod. W 521, fol. 38ʳ. Baptism of Christ*

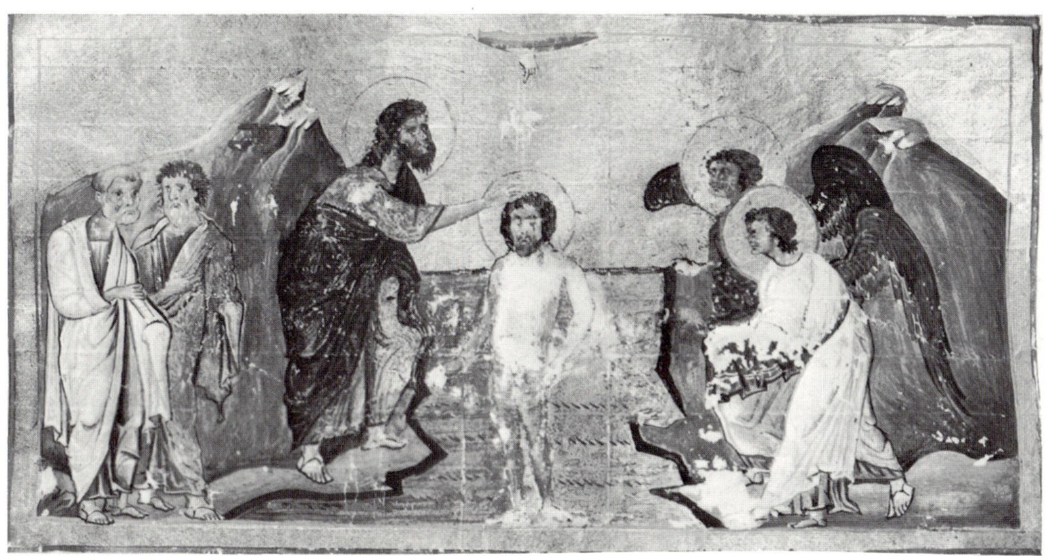

in the case of Andrew, the artist delights in creating a forceful turning of the body, while Peter, in spite of the unnatural craning of his neck, appears as the most classical figure, not unlike an orator with his arm in the sling of his mantle and holding a scroll. The mountains seem to recede from the foreground, whereby the painter—Georgios is his name[6]— tried to capture the illusion of depth, not from his own observation of nature but by his studies of classical models.

There is in the Walters Art Gallery in Baltimore a menologion of the month of January (cod. W521),[7] which once belonged to the Patriarchal Library of Alexandria,[8] whose miniatures are obviously copied directly from the Vatican menologion. Though they are not of the same quality, one would assume that these very faithful copies, such as that of the Baptism (Fig. 262), would have been executed in the same imperial scriptorium. The differences are very slight: one will notice that the figure of John the Baptist is not as massive or as vigorous,

---

[6] The problem of the various artists has more recently been discussed by I. Ševčenko, "The Illuminators of the Menologion of Basil II," *Dumbarton Oaks Papers*, 16 (1962), 243 ff. Cf. also A. Frolow, "L'origine des miniatures du Ménologe du Vatican," *Recueil des travaux de l'Institut d'Études byzantines*, 6 (Belgrade, 1960), 29 ff.

[7] *Arts of the Middle Ages 1000–1400* (catalogue of an exhibition [Boston, Museum of Fine Arts, 1940]), p. 3, no. 3 and pl. II; *Early Christian and Byzantine Art* (catalogue of an exhibition [Baltimore, The Walters Gallery, 1947]), p. 139, no. 707 and pl. XCIX; *Byzantine Art—An European Art* (catalogue of an exhibition [Athens; The Zappaion, 1964]), p. 342, no. 360 (the manuscript, however, was not exhibited in this exhibition). A facsimile of this manuscript is being prepared by S. Der Nersessian.

[8] F. Halkin, "Le mois de janvier du 'Ménologe Impérial' byzantin," *Analecta Bollandiana*, 57 (1939), 225 ff.

and that the movements of the two disciples are somewhat stiffer and the faces less expressive. At the end of each of the twenty-four lives which are contained in the Baltimore manuscript there is a poem with an acrostic which reveals that the manuscript had been written for a certain Michael Π, who is supposed to be Michael IV, the Paphlagonian (1034–41). If this is correct, which is not sure, the manuscript would be about half a century later than the Basil menologion, and thus would provide the evidence that in the span of the half century which lies between the execution of these two manuscripts no basic changes in style had taken place and that, consequently, the years around the turn of the millenium were not a starting point for a new trend in miniature painting.

More decisive are the changes one will notice in a miniature of the Baptism that decorates the Gospel Lectionary (cod. 587) in the Athos monastery of Dionysiu.[9] We believe this manuscript too to be a product of the same imperial scriptorium that produced the two aforementioned menologia, since quite a number of its miniatures belong to the same iconographic and artistic tradition. Moreover, we have previously[10] tried to establish

9 Weitzmann, "The Narrative and Liturgical Gospel Illustrations," *New Testament Manuscript Studies*, M. M. Parvis and A. P. Wikgren (eds.) (Chicago, 1950), p. 157 *passim* and pls. XIV, XVI–XVII, XX–XXI, XXIV–XXVI, XXXII [reprinted herewith, p. 247], A. Grabar, *L'Iconoclasme Byzantin* (Paris, 1957), p. 203 and fig. 142.
10 Ibid., p. 173. [See most recently, Weitzmann, "The Wanderings of the Imperial Lectionary on Mt. Athos," *Revue des Études Sud-Est Européenes*, 7 (1969), pp. 239 ff. For color reproductions of a number of miniatures consult idem, *Aus den Bibliotheken des Athos* (Hamburg, 1963), pp. 65 ff.]

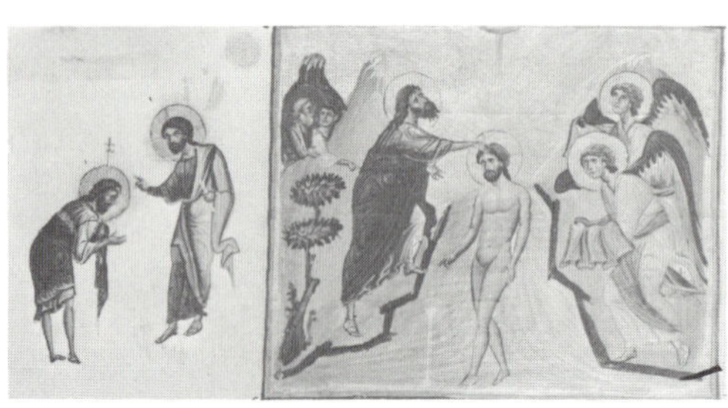

Fig. 263 *Mount Athos, Dionysiu. Cod. 587, fol. 141ᵛ. Baptism of Christ*

some evidence that the Dionysiu Lectionary was made for the emperor Isaac Comnenos when, in 1059, he retired to the Studios monastery. In this third miniature of Baptism (Fig. 263) not only have the proportions of the human figures changed toward greater slenderness, but John the Baptist and the angels lean forward so that their stance is unstable and they seem to sway. The cross-legged pose of Christ creates a similar effect. The aim of the artist is obviously to deprive the human figures, to a large extent, of their physical reality without altering the harmony of body proportions and without abandoning the formulae of classical drapery. The dates of the Baltimore menologion and the Dionysiu Lectionary, which are highly likely though not definitely proved, suggest that around the middle of the eleventh century, within a fairly narrow time span, a more fundamental change of style occurred than at the turn of the millennium. This change of style coincides with the downfall of the Macedonian Dynasty, and thus it seems more reasonable to group works of art of the tenth century together with those of the first half of the eleventh century under the heading of "Art of the Macedonian Dynasty," rather than to apply a purely mechanical division by centuries. This is not a new idea. Victor Lazarev, in his history of Byzantine painting, divided different periods by dynasties, and Sotiriou, in his treatment of the Sinai icons, arrived at similar divisions.[11] In introducing the Baltimore and the Dionysiu manuscripts, we have been able to bring into sharper focus the characteristic changes which took place in the transitional period and to narrow down its time limits to around the middle of the eleventh century.

Yet the turn from a classicizing emphasis to a comparatively more abstract one which produced a more spiritualizing style was not quite as abrupt as the Baptism miniatures may suggest. Within Byzantine miniature painting of that period, our examples thus far represent only one mode of expression, since the same three manuscripts contain other miniatures in a somewhat different mode.

The majority of pictures in most menologia depict frontally standing saints, who convey an impression of hieratic dignity. They are much less corporeal than the more plastic figures in the scenic compositions, but at the same time, as demonstrated by the portrait of Gregory of Nazinazus in the Vatican[12] (Fig. 264) and the Baltimore menologion (Fig. 265), the comparatively thick-set proportions are still in conformity with the Macedonian style. Characteristic also of this particular recension of menologion miniatures are the elaborate architectural backgrounds which ultimately are derived from the *scenae frons* of the Roman theater.[13] But while the background in

the Vatican miniature is reminiscent of a perspective rendering derived from the classical past, the architecture in the Baltimore miniature has become more two-dimensional. The Gregory figure in the Dionysiu Lectionary (Fig. 266) is more slender than the two previous ones, but otherwise the change is not as marked as in the case of the Baptism scenes, because in the case of these saints the earlier miniatures already reveal a tendency toward diminishing their physical reality. This dematerialization is also expressed in the architecture of the Dionysiu miniature; it is merely sketched in a brown color to give the impression of a grisaille, thus losing all suggestion of solidity.

In the third quarter of the eleventh century the abstract tendencies in the figure style are greatly intensified, as may be seen in the miniatures of a menologion in the Historical Museum of Moscow (cod. 382)[14] which is dated A.D. 1063. The scenes from the life of John the Baptist, his Birth, Decapitation, and the Finding of his Head (Fig. 267) are executed in a rather sketchy manner with a certain disregard for proportion, movement, and stance of the body, thereby moving further away from the classical tradition than any miniature of the Macedonian period. The same is true for the

---

[11] Cf. n. 1 and 2.

[12] *Menologio di Basilio II*, p. 349.

[13] H. Kenner, "Die frühmittelalterliche Buchmalerei und das klassische griechische Theater," *Österreichische Jahreshefte*, 39 (1952),

47 ff. For the use of theater backgrounds in evangelist miniatures cf. Weitzmann, *Geistige Grundlagen*, pp. 26 ff. [translated and reprinted herewith, pp. 196 ff.]

[14] G. Cereteli and S. Sobolevski, *Exempla Codicum Grecorum*, 1: *Codices Mosquenses* (Moscow, 1911), pl. XIX; K. and S. Lake, *Dated Greek Minuscule Manuscripts* (Boston, 1934–39), 6, pls. 408–11; Lazarev, *Istoriya Vizantiiskoy Zhivopisi*, pp. 109, 315, 324 and pl. 132.

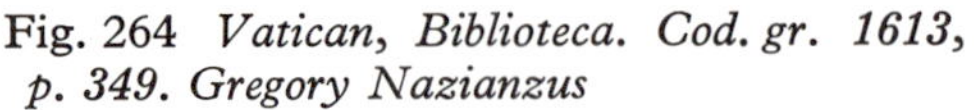

Fig. 264 *Vatican, Biblioteca. Cod. gr. 1613, p. 349. Gregory Nazianzus*

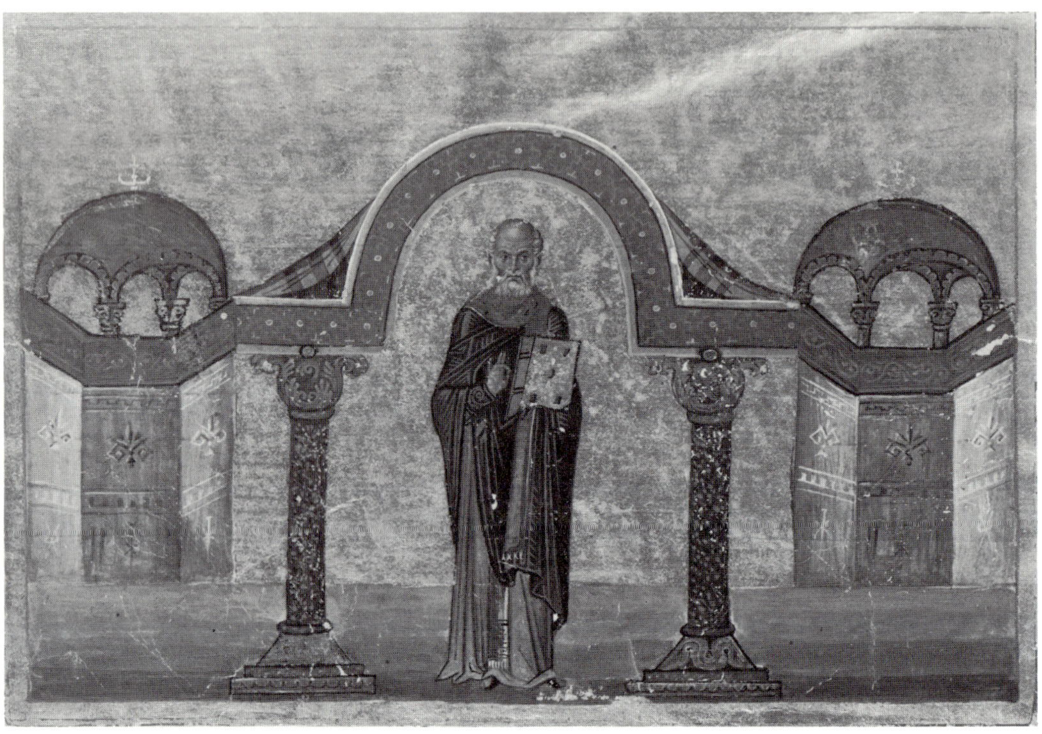

frontal figures of saints, as, for instance, Saint Procopius (Fig. 268), whose thin legs and arms have an almost doll-like quality. What had been two different modes of expression—one for scenic representations and one for single saint figures—have now been fused into one, wherein the abstract mode has gained the upper hand.

We have a considerable number of dated manuscripts from the fourth quarter of the eleventh century, with the beginning of the Comnenian Dynasty, one of the finest being a Psalter and New Testament which comes from the Athos monastery of Pantocratoros (cod. 49) and is now in Dumbarton Oaks in Washington.[15] The Easter tables begin

15 G. Millet, "Quelque représentations byzantines de la salutation angélique," *Bulletin de Correspondance Hellénique*, 18 (1894), 453 ff. and pl. XV; O. M. Dalton, *Byzantine Art and Archaeology* (Oxford, 1911), figs. 277–78; G. Millet and S. Der Nersessian, "Le Psautier arménien illustré," *Revue des Études Arméniennes*, 9 (1929), 165 and pl. IX; H. Buchthal, *The Miniatures of the Paris Psalter* (London, 1938), pp. 28, 38–41 and figs. 53, 68, 76, 78; F. Dölger, *Mönchsland Athos* (Munich, 1943), pp. 178 and 180 and figs. 98–101; Lazarev, *Istoriya Vizantiiskoy Zhivopisi*, pp. 111, 314, 339, and pl. 141; Weitzmann, *Roll and Codex*, pp. 111, 149, 152, 162, 170, 185, and figs. 140, 157, 164. [S. Der Nersessian, "A Psalter and New Testament Manuscript at Dumbarton Oaks," *Dumbarton Oaks Papers*, 19 (1965), 155 ff. For the birth of David, pp. 167 ff.]

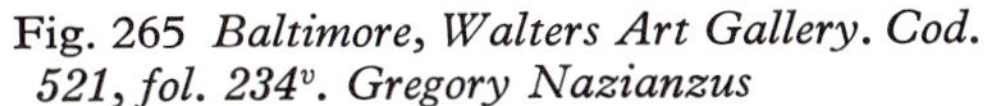

Fig. 265 *Baltimore, Walters Art Gallery. Cod. 521, fol. 234ᵛ. Gregory Nazianzus*

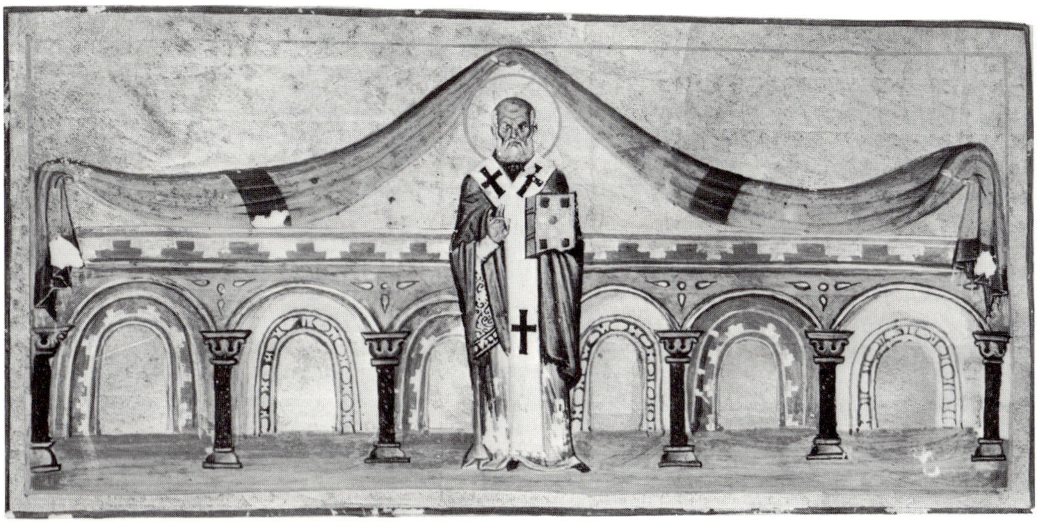

with the year 1084, and this can be assumed to be the date of the origin of the manuscript.

In the scene of the Birth of David (Fig. 269), obviously modeled after a composition of the Birth of John the Baptist or that of the Virgin, the figures are just as disjoined as those in the Moscow menologion, although they are more refined and not as sketchy. The same holds true if one compares Saint Peter of the former (Fig. 270)[16] with Saint Procopius of the latter. The basic difference between the miniatures of these codices is not so much that of a new direction toward greater solidity, but rather that the Pantocratoros Psalter is of higher quality and has realized a comparatively stronger assertion of the classical mode.

A return to greater solidity of the human body is discernible, however, in the early twelfth century, as exemplified by the miniatures of a Gospel book in the Vatican Library (cod. Urb. gr. 2), which was written in the time of John II Comnenos and his son Alexius (1119–43).[17] As in the miniature of the Birth of John the Baptist (Fig. 271), the outlines and highlights are more sharply delineated and, in certain cases, there is a tendency to overemphasize the plasticity of the human body and to treat highlights in a patterned fashion. This is not merely a return to the style of the Macedonian period, but the formulation of a new style which attempts to fuse the Macedonian heritage with the expressive element emphasized in the style of the second half of the eleventh century, i.e., the Early Comnenian style. The piercing eyes in the stern faces are indications of the development of a new vigor. Another

---

[16] This cut-out miniature was acquired by the Cleveland Museum of Art before the manuscript was sold to Dumbarton Oaks.

[17] C. Stornajolo, *Miniature delle Omilie di Giacomo Monaco e dell'Evangeliario Greco Urbinate* ("Codices e Vaticani selecti," ser. min. I [Rome, 1910]), pp. 19 ff. and pls. 83 ff.

Fig. 266 *Mount Athos, Dionysiu. Cod. 587, fol. 143ʳ. Gregory Nazianzus*

Fig. 267 *Moscow, Historical Museum. Cod. 382, fol. 210ʳ. Birth of John the Baptist*

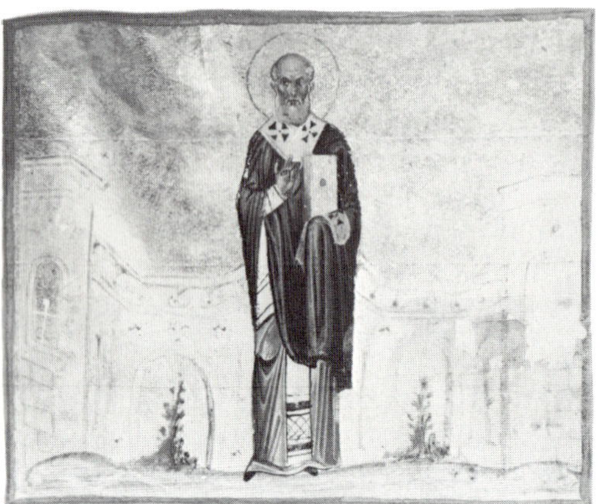

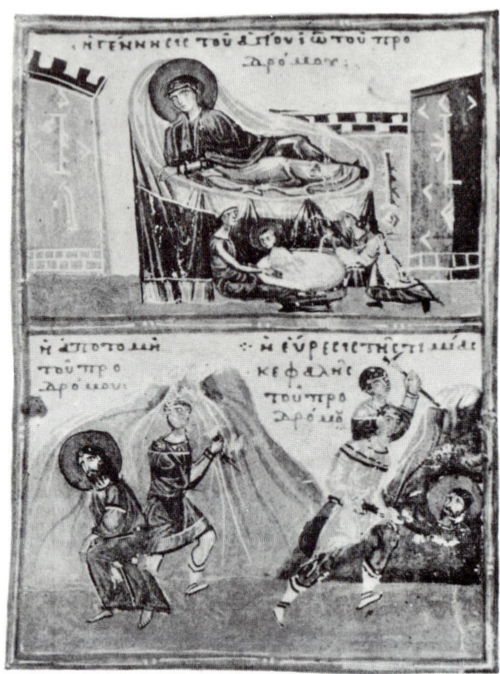

new trend is a certain ornamental quality achieved by dividing the miniature surface into smaller units on a two-dimensional plane with an almost complete disregard of spatial relationships. Although the style of the second half of the eleventh century shows a more dematerialized human figure than in the periods before and after, in order to define generally the style of the eleventh century we have chosen miniatures that represent what we would consider a "middle of the road" style. If one begins to study all the facets of the eleventh-century style, one will soon notice a wide range of modes of expression existing side by side. The style of the Macedonian Renaissance, though losing strength toward the end, nevertheless asserted itself quite strongly on occasion, even in the second half of the eleventh century, as may be demonstrated by another miniature of the Pantocratoros Psalter. Juxtaposed against the general tendency of this period to ignore spatial effects to a large degree, the miniature of Moses receiving the tablets (Fig. 272)[18] shows the prophet in a

landscape that has not lost its spatial quality, in comparison with the corresponding miniature in the Paris Psalter (Fig. 273),[19] one of the key monuments of the Macedonian Renaissance. The classical personification of Mount Sinai is perhaps not as fully fleshed and vital as its counterpart in the Paris miniature, yet it still conveys the flavor of the classical tradition.

On the other hand, the tendencies toward more abstract forms, as witnessed in the miniatures of the Moscow menologion (Figs. 267–68), are carried still further in a Psalter manuscript now in London (Brit. Mus. cod. add. 19352) which was written in 1066 in the Studios

[18] Buchthal, *Paris Psalter*, pl. XXV, 68.

[19] H. Omont, *Miniatures des plus anciens manuscrits grecs de la Bibliothèque Nationale* (2d ed.; Paris, 1929), p. 8 and pl. X; Buchthal, *Paris Psalter*, pp. 33 ff. and pl. X.

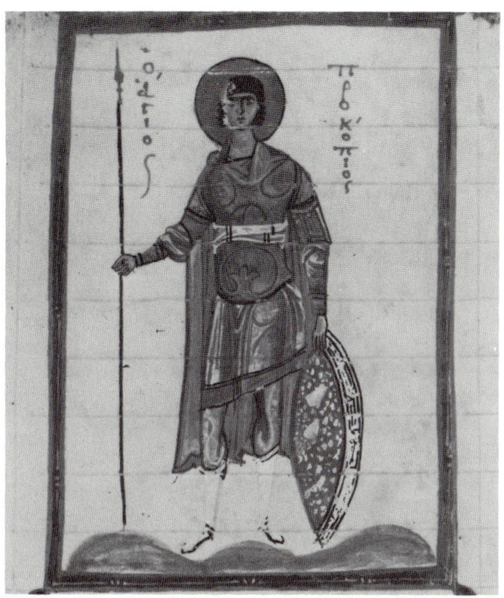

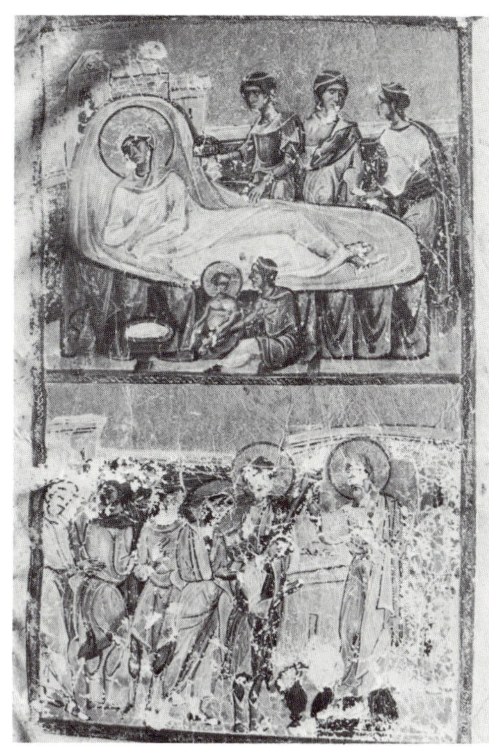

monastery by a monk, Theodore.[20] Here the scene of the Receiving of the Law (Fig. 274) is placed in a silhouette-like mountain landscape which lacks any illusion of depth. The human figures are over-elongated and flat, a quality which is enhanced by gold striations that have a decorative quality but do not suggest any highlights.

It is not without significance that this high degree of abstraction occurs in a

product of the leading monastery of Constantinople, and one may well deduce from this fact that the spiritual quality which is expressed pictorially through the weightlessness of the human body is an assertion of the ascetic spirit of monasticism. This is the period in which the Studios monastery in particular was the center of ascetic and mystic writing and where Symeon the New Theologian had started his career. Thus it seems logical that there would exist a close connection between the peculiarly ascetic style of the book illumination of the Studios monastery and the spiritual forces asserted in the literary production of this leading monastery of Constantinople. On the strength of close stylistic

[20] G. F. Warner, *Reproductions from Illuminated Manuscripts*, II Ser. (2d ed.; London, 1910), pls. II–III; G. Millet, *Recherches sur l'Iconographie de l'Évangile* (Paris, 1916): for page references cf. index, p. 742; also figs. 13, 33, 64, 87, 119, 142–43, 184, 241, 299, 343, 424, 460, 463; K. and S. Lake, *Dated Greek Minuscule Manuscripts*, 2, pls. 129–30. Lazarev, *Istoriya Vizantiiskoy Zhivopisi*, pp. 107–8, 321, and pl. 124. [S. Dufrenne, "Deux chefs-d'oeuvre de la miniature du XIe siècle," *Cahiers Archéologiques*, 17 (1967), 177 ff. Here also the older literature.]

Fig. 270 *Cleveland, Museum of Art (olim Pantocrator Cod. 49), fol. 254ʳ. Peter*

Fig. 271 *Vatican, Biblioteca. Cod. Urb. gr. 2, fol. 167ᵛ. Birth of John the Baptist*

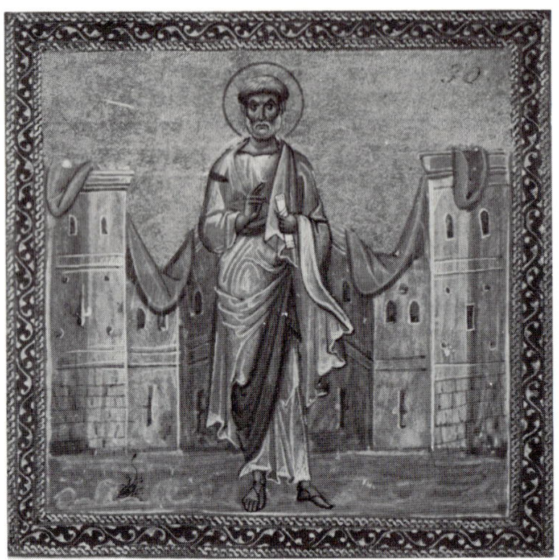

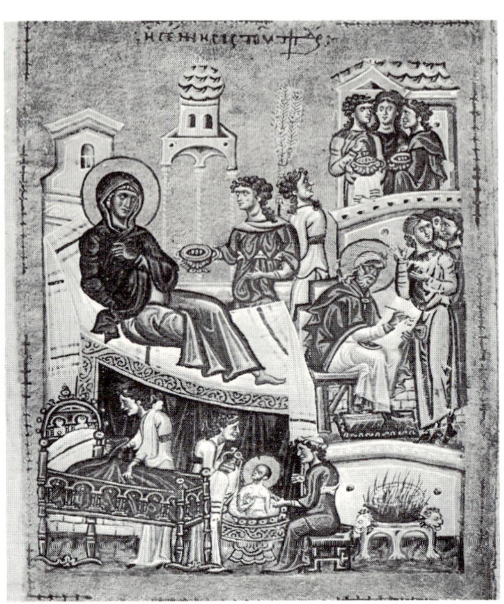

similarities, one of the richest illustrated manuscripts, a Gospel book in Paris (Bibliothèque Nationale cod. gr. 74), can be ascribed to the same date and, with a high degree of probability, to the same scriptorium in the Studios monastery.[21] As demonstrated once more by a Baptism scene (Fig. 275), the physical reality of the human figures is reduced almost to the degree where they become phantom-like. In this manuscript the abstract figure style has reached its climax.

If, indeed, our thesis is correct, that the ideals of monastic asceticism were a strong factor in shaping the outlook of painters of the second half of the eleventh century, then one would expect this style to be especially clearly expressed in illustrations for monastic writings; and this is indeed the case. The most popular

manual for the conduct of the monk is the *Heavenly Ladder* of John Climacus, which, as far as we can tell, was written in the seventh century on Mount Sinai, and was decorated for the first time with extensive cycles (and this is in itself symptomatic) in the eleventh century.[22] The richest and artistically most refined manuscript among a considerable number of copies, which indicates that this treatise became quite fashionable at that time, is in the Vatican (cod. gr. 394). It is surely a product of a Constantinopolitan monastery from the second half of the eleventh century. There is no need to emphasize once more the incorporeal quality of the human figure (Fig. 276), except to state that it seems a peculiarly fitting pictorial formula for the representation of a monk and that it was

[21] H. Omont, *Évangiles avec peintures Byzantines du XIᵉ siècle* (Paris, s.d.); Millet, *Recherches*, pp. and figs. cf. index, p. 746. Lazarev, *Istoriya Vizantiiskoy Zhivopisi*, pp. 107–8, 113, 242, 313, 321, 376, and pls. 125–26.

[22] J. R. Martin, *The Illustration of the Heavenly Ladder of John Climacus* (Princeton, 1954).

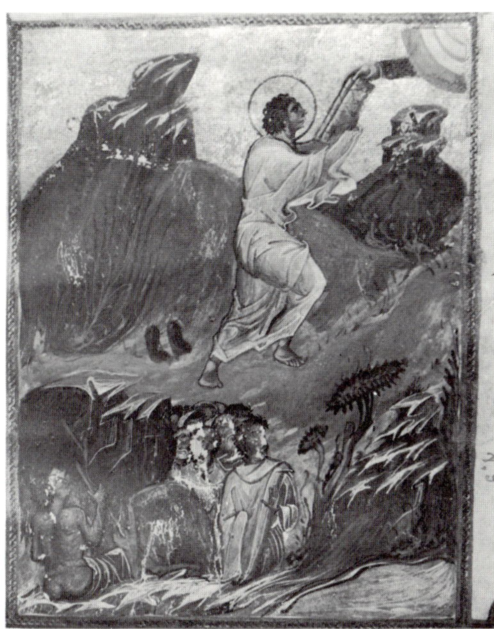

Fig. 272 *Washington, Dumbarton Oaks (olim Pantocrator Cod. 49), fol. 73ʳ. Moses Receiving the Law*

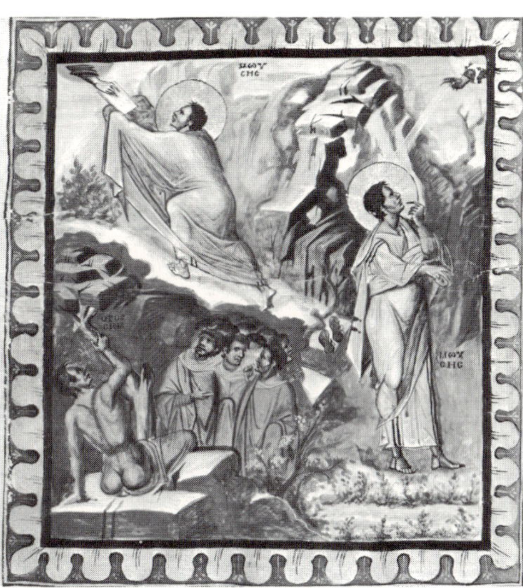

Fig. 273 *Paris, Bibliothèque Nationale. Cod. gr. 139, fol. 422ᵛ. Moses Receiving the Law*

applied even to classical personifications like Malice (μνησικακία) and Humility (ταπεινοφροσύνη),[23] i.e., even to figures derived from the classical tradition where one would least expect to find it. Moreover, the denial of physical reality applies also to the attenuated architectural details and to the impression of floating given by the human figures.

This illustration from the *Heavenly Ladder*, then, leads us to the more general problem of what miniature and icon painting as well contributed to the history of Byzantine art of the eleventh century from the iconographical point of view. In book illumination the great narrative cycles of the Old Testament, such as those of the Octateuchs, the Books of Kings, the Book of Job, and also of the Gospels, continued to be illustrated

with comparatively few changes. The major changes took place in the liturgical books. Of course the Psalter, the Gospel lectionary, and the menologion, to mention only the three most outstanding ones in the history of book illumination, had long existed with illustrations, but in the eleventh century some important innovations and enrichments were made which are not so much to be sought in the iconography of the single scene but in the organization of the miniature cycle as a whole, in which the individual scenes are often derived from various sources and then rearranged.

THE ILLUSTRATED MENOLOGION

I should like to deal briefly with all three service books and begin with the menologion. The older tradition was a selection of the lives of certain saints,[24]

23 Ibid., p. 66 and pl. XXXI, 102.

24 The main study where the older bibliography can be found is A. Ehrhard, *Überlieferung und Bestand der hagiographischen und homiletischen Literatur der griechischen Kirche*

Fig. 274 *London, British Museum. Cod. Add. 19352, fol. 193ᵛ. Moses Receiving the Law*

Fig. 275 *Paris, Bibliothèque Nationale. Cod. gr. 74, fol. 169ʳ. Baptism of Christ*

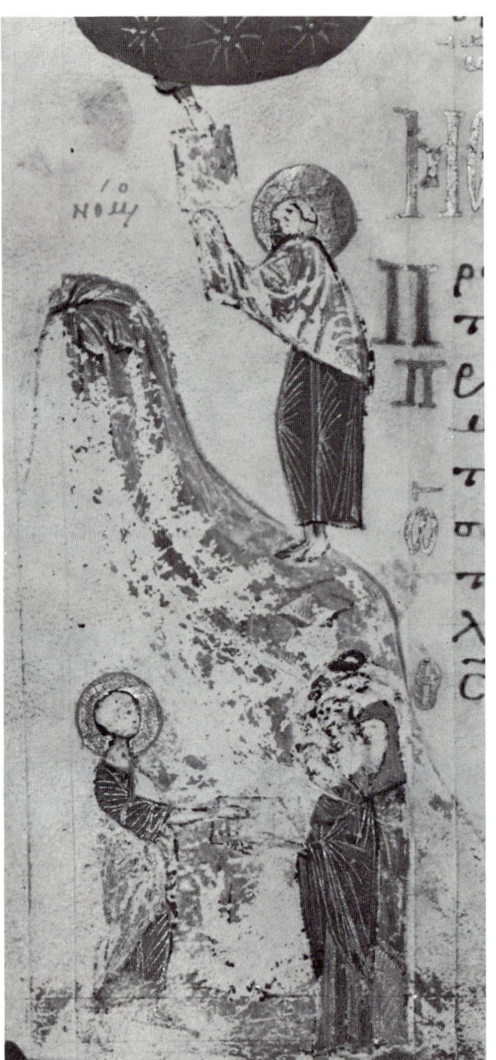

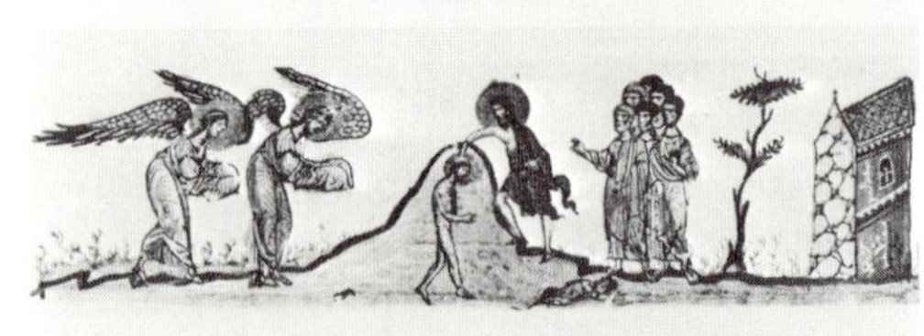

were, so it seems from later evidence, accompanied by more or less extensive narrative miniature cycles. This type of illustrated menologion has survived in the eleventh-century manuscript in Esphigmenu on Mount Athos (cod. 14),[26] which contains altogether eight *Vitae* from September to December, and each *Vita*, like that of Menas, Hermogenes, and Eugraphus (Dec. 10) (Fig. 277),[27] has at its beginning a narrative picture cycle which covers the recto and verso of a purple leaf. This system of illustration of a saint's life surely has a long history and still persists, in some instances like the Esphigmenu manuscript, in the Metaphrastes texts.

In the eleventh century these narrative cycles from the lives of saints invade icon painting, and the earliest example we know of is a triptych wing, now cut in two parts, which is preserved in the icon collection of Saint Catherine's monastery

and when these were illustrated[25] they

("Texte und Untersuchungen zur Geschichte der Altchristlichen Literatur," 50–52 [Leipzig, 1937–52]).
[25] For the illustration of the menologion cf. S. Der Nersessian, "The Illustrations of the Metaphrastian Menologium," *Late Classical and Mediaeval Studies in Honor of Albert M. Friend, Jr.* (Princeton, 1955), pp. 222 ff; P.

Mijović, "Une Classification Iconographique de Ménologes Enluminés," *Actes du XIIe Congrès International d'Études Byzantines*, 3 (Belgrade, 1964), 271 ff.
[26] H. Brockhaus, *Die Kunst in den Athosklöstern* (Leipzig, 1891), pp. 192, 228, and pl. 26; Dölger, *Athos*, p. 174 and fig. 94.
[27] Weitzmann, *Aus den Bibliotheken des Athos* (Hamburg, 1963), pp. 89 ff. and pls. on pp. 91, 95.

Fig. 276 *Vatican, Biblioteca. Cod. gr. 394, fol. 66ʳ. Malice and Humility*

Fig. 277 *Mount Athos, Esphigmenu. Cod. 14, fol. 294ʳ. Sr. Menas et al.*

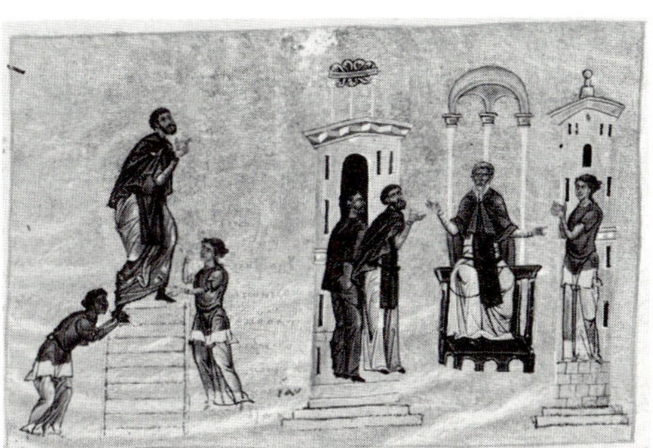

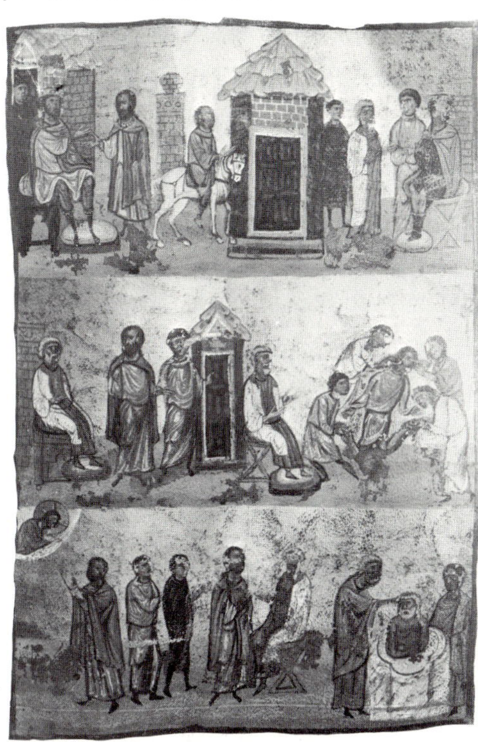

on Mount Sinai (Fig. 278).[28] The six scenes from the life of Saint Nicholas, including the early scenes of his ordination as priest and bishop, and the last one, his burial, belong to a cycle of twenty scenes which were originally distributed over the center and both wings of the triptych. The style of these delicately depicted scenes is so much in the tradition of the illustrated book that we must assume not only that a miniature cycle was the source, but that icons and miniatures in instances like this actually may have been executed by the same artist. Toward the end of the tenth century Simeon Metaphrastes compiled his extensive collection of the lives of saints with the intention of having, as a norm, one *Vita* for each day of the ecclesiastical year. A complete copy of this hagiographic encyclopedia consisted commonly of either twelve volumes, one for each month, or—and this is by no means a rare case—of twenty-four volumes, one

for each half month. This Metaphrastian compilation led to the need for standardization of its illustration. The norm would now be to have one picture at the beginning of each *Vita* and, on occasion, a second one at its end, and these pictures could be either scenic or consist of frontally standing saints. A characteristic example is the eleventh-century menologion in the Lavra monastery on Mount Athos (cod. Δ. 51),[29] which comprises only the lives from the second half of December, and thus must have been part of a twenty-four volume edition. A picture of either a scenic illustration or a standing saint precedes each *Vita*: the life of

[28] The lower part of the wing is published by G. and M. Sotiriou, *Icones*, p. 62 and pl. 46, the upper part by Weitzmann, "Fragments of an Early St. Nicholas Triptych on Mount Sinai," *Timētikos G. Sotiriou. Deltion Archaiologikēs Hetaireios*, 4th ser., 4, 1964–65 (Athens, 1966), 1 ff. and figs. 1–3.

[29] S. Der Nersessian, "Metaphrastian Menologium," p. 226 and pls. XXIV, 2; XXV, 7.

Fig. 278 *Mount Sinai, St. Catherine's. Icon. Life of St. Nicholas*

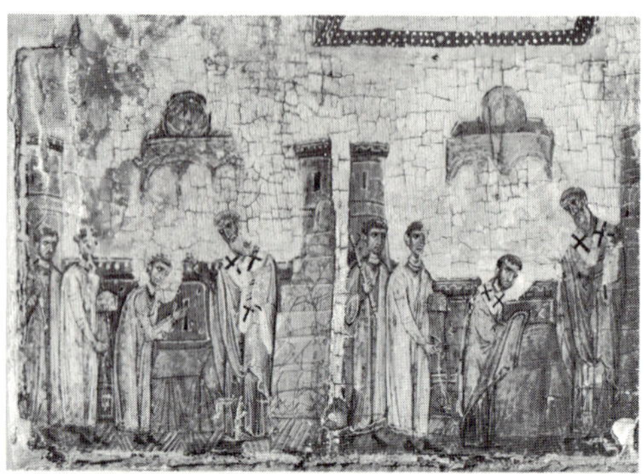

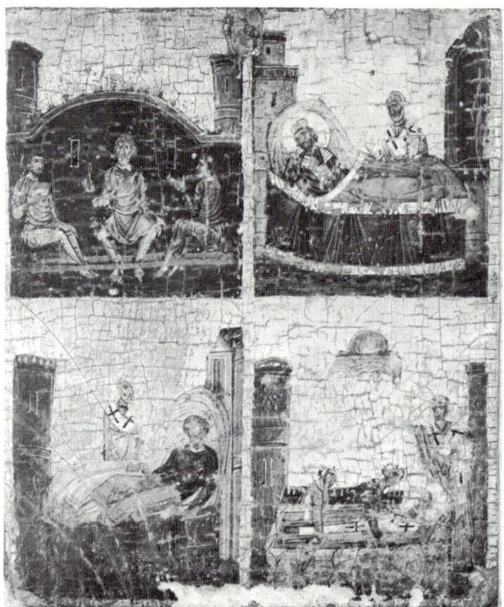

Fig. 279 *Mount Athos, Lavra. Cod. Δ.51, fol. 131ᵛ. Saints*

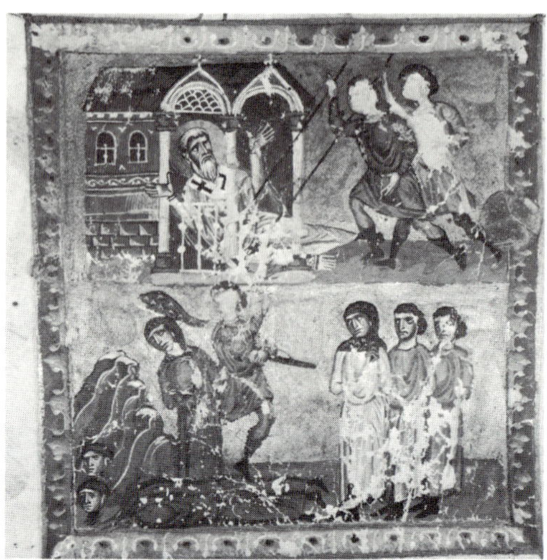

Saint Eugenia (Fig. 279) is preceded by a scene of her martyrdom which seems to be excerpted from a more richly illustrated *Vita*. In other instances, where narrative cycles did not exist or were not available, new pictures had to be invented, which did not always fit the narrative details of the text. In the case of the standing saints, like Saint Melane (Fig. 280), we deal with solitary figures which the artist repeats with a certain monotony. To extract from larger narra-

tive cycles and to add single miniatures is a procedure which was already used in the Basil menologion, which strictly speaking is not a menologion but a syn-axarion, and it is by no means unlikely that this famous manuscript was the first ever. to adopt this system.

Another variant is to collect on one title page all the individual miniatures of one volume and to line them up in rows. There is on Mount Sinai a menologion (cod. 512) with such a title miniature (Fig. 281), which comprises in three rows frontal standing saints as well as scenic representations like that of the killing of the forty martyrs of Mount Sinai and that of Saint Peter in prison. The depictions in this volume relate to the *Vitae* that begin 5 January and end 17 January, indicating that once more we are dealing with a manuscript from a twenty-four volume edition.

We find this very same arrangement on icons of that period. From a set on Mount Sinai which originally had twelve panels, one for each month, four remain,

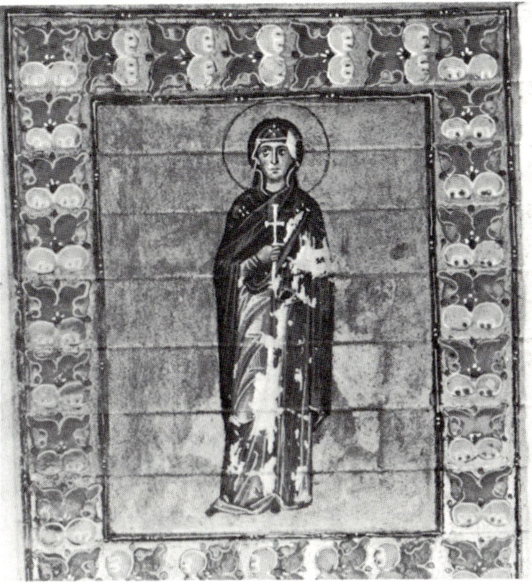

Fig. 280 *Mount Athos, Lavra. Cod. Δ.51, fol. 220ᵛ. Melane*

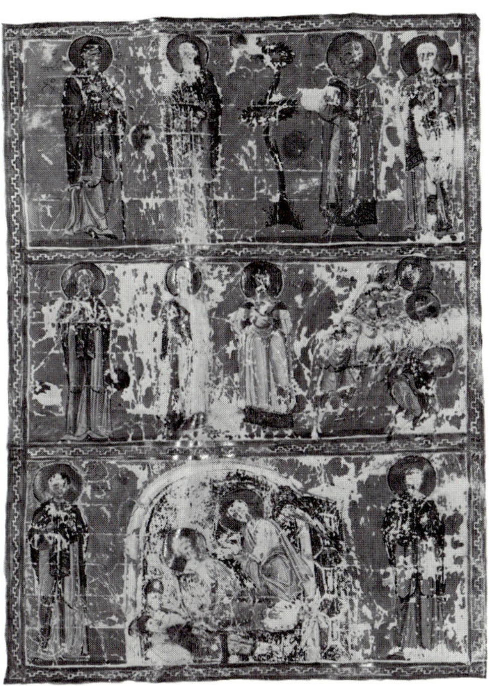

Fig. 281 *Mount Sinai, St. Catherine's. Cod. 512, fol. 2ᵛ. Saints of the Month of January*

including that of the month of February (Fig. 282).[30] In seven rows standing saints, scenes of martyrdom, and calendar feasts like the Presentation in the Temple in the top row are lined up in precisely the same fashion as in the Sinai miniature. There can be little doubt that the individual scenes and figures of saints ultimately hark back to an illustrated menologion, while, conversely, the idea of a "collective picture" very likely started out in icon painting and then was adapted for greater convenience by some miniature painters. Possibly we are dealing in both cases with an artist who was used to working in either technique.

PSALTER ILLUSTRATION

The second liturgical book containing profuse and varied illustrations, which surely reach back into the Early Byzantine period, is the Psalter. The changes

which took place in the eleventh century in its illustration are perhaps less spectacular than in the menologion but nevertheless add further new aspects to the iconographical development. The problem in the two basic picture recensions which Tikkanen[31] had once termed the "aristocratic" and the "monastic" is not so much that of a reorganization of the basic cycles but of the additions which were made in both recensions.

We have already introduced the Psalter which was once in the Pantocratoros monastery and is now in Washington, and which belongs to the aristocratic

[30] G. and M. Sotiriou, *Icones*, pp. 123 ff. and pl. 144.

[31] J. J. Tikkanen, "Die Psalterillustration im Mittelalter," *Acta Societatis Scientiarum Fennicae*, 31 (1903) [S. Dufrenne, *L'illustration des Psautiers grecs du Moyen Age* ("Bibliothèque des Cahiers Archéologiques," 1, Paris, 1966).]

recension, and we have also dealt with its miniature of the Birth of David (Fig. 269). The lower scene of the same page, the Anointing of David, is a literal copy of the corresponding miniature of the tenth-century Psalter in Paris.[32] The Birth scene does not exist in the Paris Psalter, however, and must therefore have been added to this recension later, and most likely not before the eleventh century. The rather novel intention of the artist is clear: to round out the David cycle in the fashion of a saint's *Vita* with a picture of his birth, although this event is not mentioned in the Books of Kings. The model was apparently a miniature of the Birth of the Virgin which the Psalter painter could have found in a Gospel lectionary,[33] where it headed the lesson for 8 September, the feast of the Birth of the Virgin. What is of primary importance is the fact that a New Testament composition had stimulated the imagination of an Old Testament illustrator. This is by no means an isolated case, but the expression of a general trend in the Middle Byzantine period which was intensified in the eleventh century.

Another addition to the recension is found in the composition of the folio preceding the one with the Birth and Anointing of David. It is also divided in two zones (Fig. 283);[34] the upper one shows the Virgin cut off below the waist and on a much larger scale than the flanking John the Baptist and the Archangel Michael, and the lower zone is occupied by the three church fathers, Gregory, Basil, and John Chrysostom. In this case the miniature painter was inspired by monumental art, to be precise, by an apse decoration in which the Virgin dominated the center of the conch (this explains the deviation in scale), and the church fathers occupied the lower regions of the apse wall. Other instances of an influence of monumental art upon book illumination have been known from earlier centuries,[35] but the point in which our miniature differs from these is that the influence is not confined to a single scene or figure but attempts to reflect a complex liturgical program typical of an apse composition. The depiction of the chief intercessors is based on the prayer of intercession of the liturgy[36]—only the Apostles are not represented. With this liturgical aspect we touch upon perhaps the most decisive element in eleventh-century Byzantine painting, about which more will be said later. It is all the more important since it appears here in an Old Testament manuscript. The second major recension of the illustrated Psalter, the so-called monastic one, also made some significant additions in the eleventh century.

---

[32] Omont, *Manuscrits grecs*, pl. III; Buchthal, *Paris Psalter*, pl. III. [Cf. n. 15.]

[33] As, e.g., in the Vatican Lectionary gr. 1156, fol. 246ᵛ, Weitzmann, "Narrative and Liturgical Illustration," p. 160 and pl. XVIII, fig. 1 [herewith, pp. 256 f. and Fig. 243.]

[34] This leaf has recently been cut out and its present whereabouts is unknown to me. I am reproducing a photograph I took when the manuscript was still in Pantocratoros.

[35] A striking example are some of the full page miniatures of the Rossano Gospels. W. C. Loerke, "The Miniatures of the Trial in the Rossano Gospels," *Art Bulletin*, 43 (1961), 171 ff.

[36] For the impact of the liturgy, especially the prayer of intercession, on the ivories of the tenth century, cf. E. H. Kantorowicz, "Ivories and Litanies," *Journal of the Warburg and Courtauld Institutes*, 5 (1942), 56 ff.

Fig. 282 *Mount Sinai, St. Catherine's. Icon. Month of February*

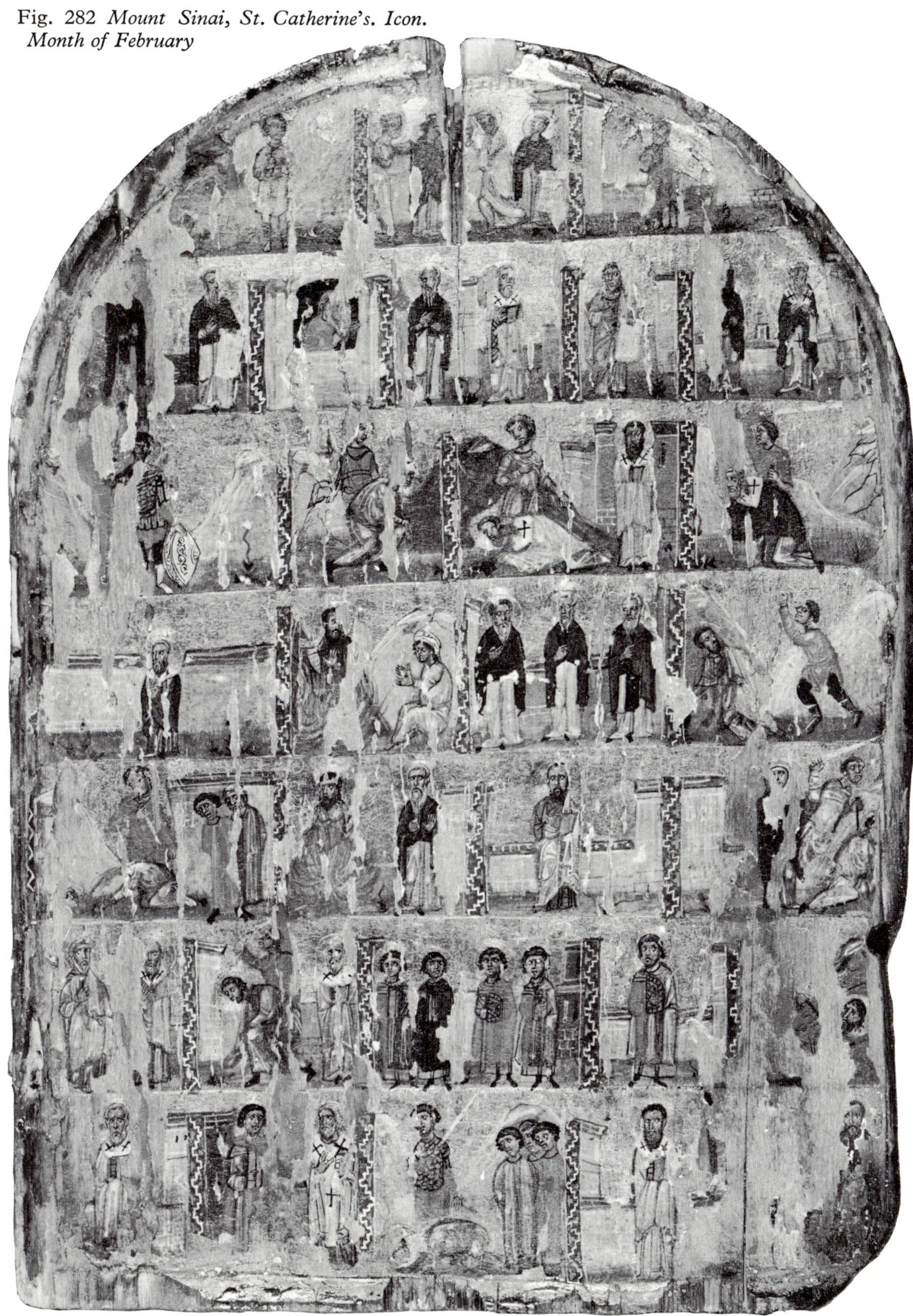

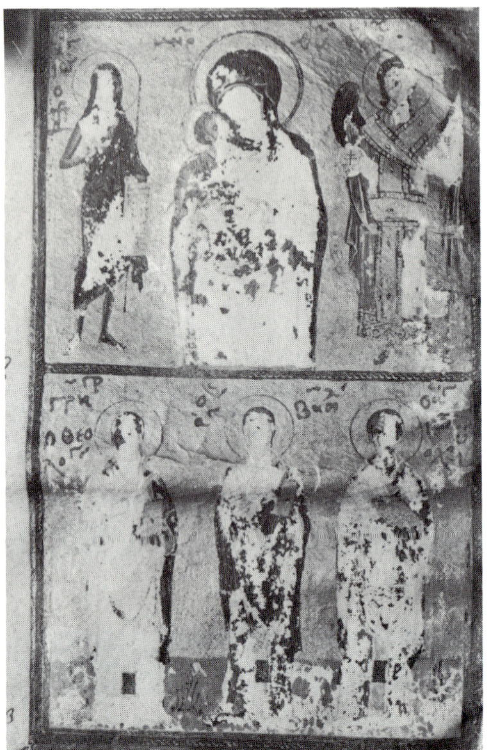

Fig. 283 *Washington, Dumbarton Oaks (olim Pantocrator Cod. 49), fol. 4ᵛ. Virgin and Saints*

The ninth-century Psalters with their extensive cycles of marginal illustrations, such as the one in the Pantocratoros monastery (cod. 61, Fig. 39)[37] and the Chloudov Psalter in the Historical Museum in Moscow (cod. 129, Fig. 38),[38] are

what I should like to call polycyclic, i.e., they contain whole sets of pictures from different sources, including a few from the lives of saints. The latter belong to an iconographic realm where the illustrator of the eleventh century expanded the pictorial cycle and added many more hagiographical illustrations,[39] which obviously were taken from a Simeon Metaphrastes menologion of the same type as the one in Lavra, of which I showed two illustrations, the standing Saint Melane and the martyrdom of Saint Eugenia (Figs. 279 and 280). Both these types of pictures occur in the Theodore Psalter in London, as may be demonstrated by the figure of Saint Stephen the Younger (Fig. 284),[40] whose picture the illustrator found in the Metaphrastes *Vita* of 28 November, and by the scene in which a servant of the emperor carves an inscription on the forehead of Saint Theodore Graptos, taken from the saint's *Vita* of 27 December (Fig. 285). It is significant that this new influx of iconographical subject matter should be taken from a Metaphrastes menologion, i.e., a liturgical book

---

[37] Tikkanen, "Psalterillustration," p. 11 and *passim*; Weitzmann, *Die Byzantinische Buchmalerei des 9. und 10. Jahrhunderts* (Berlin, 1935), pp. 54 ff. and pls. LIX–LXI. [Dufrenne, *Psautiers grecs*, pp. 1 ff.]

[38] N. Kondakov, *Miniatures du MS. grec du Psautier du IXᵉ siècle de la collection A. I. Chloudow à Moscou* (Moscow, 1878); Tikkanen, "Psalterillustration," p. 11 and *passim* and pls. 1–3; N. Maliskij, "Remarques sur la date des mosaïques de l'église des Saint Apôtres à Constantinople décrites par Mésaritès," *Byzantion*, 3 (1926), 123 ff. and

pls. 1–3; idem, "Čerty palestinskoj i vostočnoj ikonografii v vizantijskoi psaltiri," *Seminarium Kondakovianum*, I (1927), 49 ff; idem, "Le Psautier byzantine à illustrations du type Chludov est-il de provenance monastique?" *L'art byzantine chez les slaves, l'ancienne Russie, les slaves catholiques; deuxièmes recueil dédié à la mémoire de Théodore Uspenskij* (Paris, 1932), p. 235; Weitzmann, *Byzantinische Buchmalerei*, pp. 55 ff. and pls. LXI–LXII. [A. Grabar, "Les Psautiers grecs illustrés byzantins du IXᵉ siècle," *Cahiers Archéologiques*, 11 (1965), 61 ff.]

[39] L. Mariès, s.j., "L'Irruption des Saints dans l'Illustration du Psautier Byzantin," *Mélanges P. Peeters*, 2, *Analecta Bollandiana*, 68 (1950), 153 ff.

[40] Grabar, *Iconoclasme*, p. 202 and fig. 141.

Fig. 284 *London, British Museum. Cod. Add. 19352, fol. 117ʳ. Stephen the Younger*

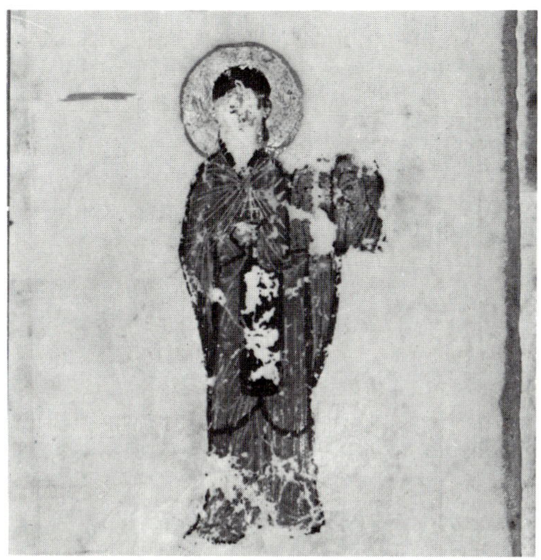

Fig. 285 *London, British Museum. Cod. Add. 19352, fol. 120ᵛ. Theodore Graptos*

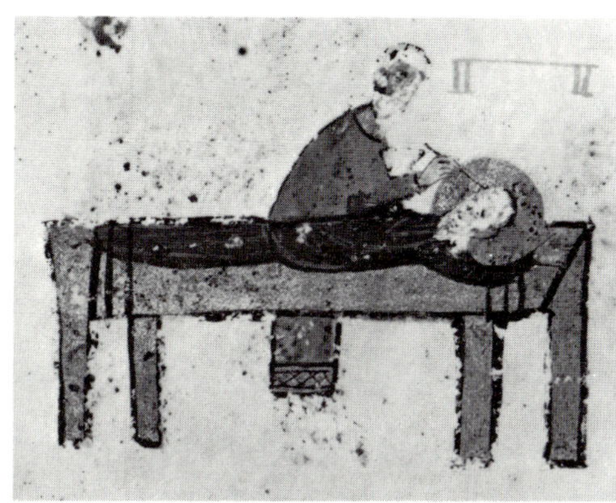

which itself is a creation of the end of the tenth century.[41]

THE ILLUSTRATED LECTIONARY AND ITS INFLUENCE

Of all the liturgical books the most important is the Gospel lectionary, which is used as an implement of the service, being carried around by the deacon in the Little Introitus of the Divine Liturgy, and for this reason it usually had a precious metal cover studded with jewels, pearls, and enamels, though only a few such covers are preserved (cf. Fig. 231). No wonder that miniaturists concentrated their greatest effort on the embellishment of this service book, and this applies to the refinement of the technique as well as the icono-

graphic richness.[42] Several illustrated lectionaries of high quality, like the fragment in Leningrad (cod. 21),[43] still survive from the tenth century; and these already concentrate on the liturgical pictures of the great feasts. Yet it is not before the eleventh century that lectionary illustration reaches the state of its fullest complexity, which will inspire all subsequent lectionary illustration.

The finest lectionary of the eleventh century which we possess today is the one in Dionysiu, of which I have already introduced two examples (Figs. 263 and 266). At the opening of the book the lesson of Easter Sunday is, as is normal, preceded by a picture of the Anastasis

[41] The increasing popularity of the full calendar in the eleventh century also finds expression in its versified form in the eleventh-century poet Christophoros of Mytilene. E. Follieri and I. Dujčev, "Il Calendario in Sticheri di Christoforo di Mitilene," *Byzantinoslavica*, 25 (1964), 1 ff.

[42] For the importance of the illustrated lectionary cf. Weitzmann, "Narrative and Liturgical Illustration," [herewith, pp. 247 ff.]. Idem, "The Constantinopolitan Lectionary Morgan 639," *Studies in Art and Literature for Belle de Costa Greene* (Princeton, 1954), pp. 358 ff.

[43] C. R. Morey, "Notes on East Christian Miniatures," *Art Bulletin*, 11 (1929), 53 ff. and figs. 61 *passim*; Weitzmann, *Byzantinische Buchmalerei*, pp. 59 ff. and pls. LXVI–LXVII; Lazarev, *Istoriya Vizantiiskoy Zhivopisi*, p. 81 and pls. 66–68.

Fig. 286 *Mount Athos, Dionysiu. Cod. 587, fol. 2ʳ. Anastasis*

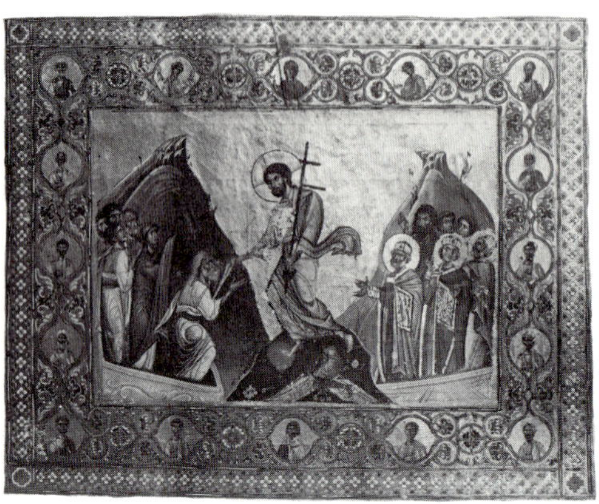

(Fig. 286),[44] a subject which, it will be remembered, is not based on a canonical Gospel but on the apocryphal Gospel of Nicodemus, in which text, therefore, this composition must have originated. Thus it is logical that the traditional narrative miniature cycle of the Gospels, on which the lectionary cycle is largely based, would not have this scene.

The richest illustrated Gospel book, with literally hundreds of iconographical units, is in the Laurentian Library in Florence (cod. Plut. VI, 23) and belongs to the end of the eleventh century.[45] The Gospel narrative is illustrated with a spirit of epic breadth, and at the end of Matthew's Gospel (Fig. 287)[46] the Deposition from the Cross and the Bewailing of Christ are followed by scenes of lesser importance: first the priests and Pharisees ask Pilate to have the tomb guarded, later the tomb is sealed and guards are posted. The last scene, which depicts the Holy Women at the Tomb, is again an important one. Each scene is a very literal illustration of the end of the twenty-seventh chapter and the beginning of the twenty-eighth chapter of Matthew.

The second Gospel book of this period, almost as richly illustrated as the one in Florence, is the better known one in Paris, of which I discussed the Baptism scene (Fig. 275). What is significant is that within the almost identical set of pictures of the Passion cycle (Figs. 288–290)[47] a representation of the Anastasis is added in the Paris Gospels ahead of that of the Women at the Tomb, and there can be little doubt that the intrusion of this scene is due to the influence of a lectionary. Nor is this the only instance of this kind in the Paris Gospels, while the Florentine Gospel book is free from strictly liturgical scenes.[48] Whereas Millet, in his *Recherches sur l'Évangile*, tried to explain the differences between the picture cycles of these two Gospel books in terms of a difference between an Antiochene and an Alexandrian recension, we rather believe that the basic distinction is that the Florentine cycle follows more strictly the narrative tradition of Early Christian art, while the Parisian cycle has undergone far-reaching changes under the impact of the liturgical lectionary cycle. It would seem to us to be no exaggeration to state that the crystallization of the lectionary illustration into a liturgical cycle of can-

[44] For the Anastasis iconography in general cf. C. R. Morey, *East Christian Paintings in the Freer Collection* (New York, 1914), pp. 45 ff.

[45] Millet, *Recherches*, pp. and figs.; cf. index, p. 739; Lazarev, *Istoriya Vizantiiskoy Zhivopisi*, pp. 115, 216, 374, 376, and pl. 159.

[46] Millet, *Recherches*, p. 493 and fig. 527.

[47] Omont, *Évangiles*, pls. 52–54.

[48] As for the influence of the lectionary cycle on the Paris Gospel book in other instances cf. Weitzmann, "Narrative and Liturgical Illustration," p. 168 and pl. XXVII [herewith, pp. 264 f. and Figs. 254–56].

Fig. 287 *Florence, Laurenziana. Cod. Plut. VI, 23, fol. 59ᵛ. Passion Scenes*

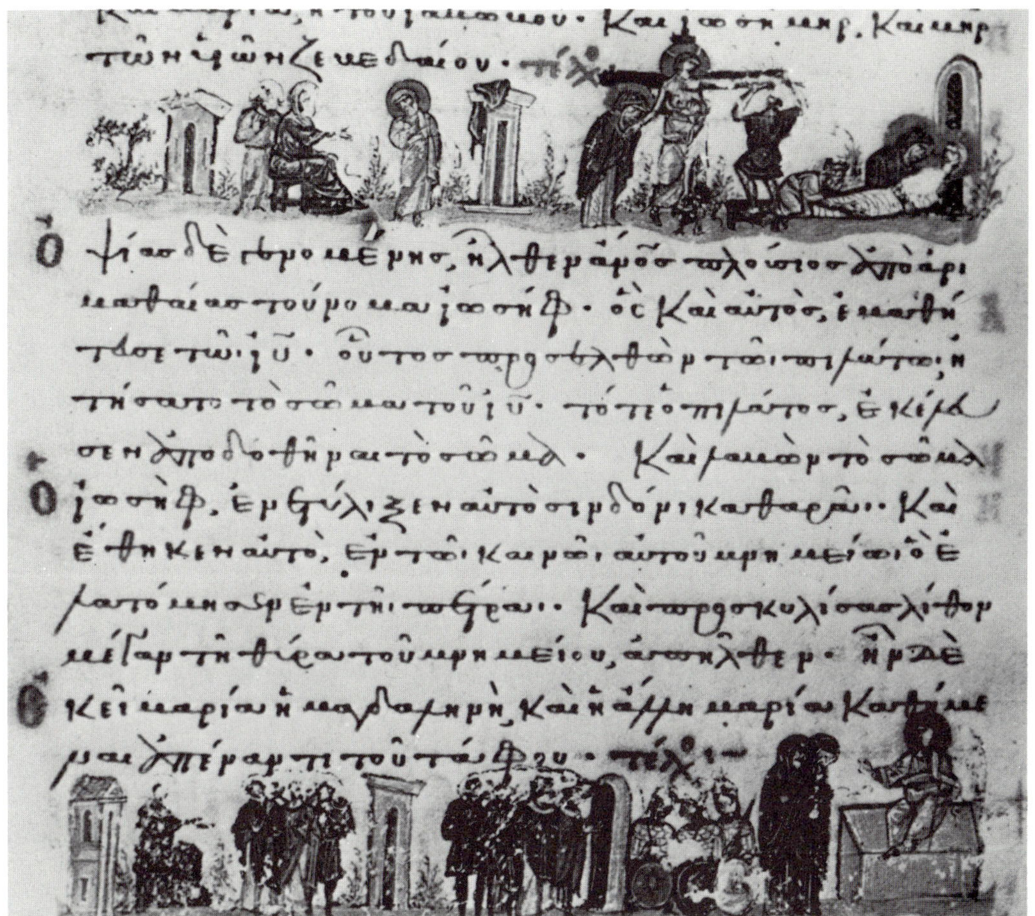

onical validity, and its spread into other manuscripts and a variety of media, are the most important aspects of eleventh-century book illumination.

One of the most striking examples of the wide distribution of lectionary miniatures is the appearance of the Anastasis picture in many different texts,[49] e.g., in the homilies of Gregory of Nazianzus, as a title miniature for the Easter homily—the codex in Jerusalem (Taphou 14) being a typical example (Fig. 291).[50] What makes the appearance of the Anastasis and other lectionary miniatures in the Gregory so significant is that they occur during the time of the establishment of a new textual recension.[51]

[49] For a case of an Anastasis miniature in a Psalter cf. Weitzmann, "Aristocratic Psalter and Lectionary," *Record of the Art Museum, Princeton University*, 19 (1960), 98 ff.

[50] W. H. P. Hatch, *Greek and Syrian Miniatures in Jerusalem* (Cambridge, Mass., 1931), pp. 58 ff. and pls. I–XVII; Lazarev, *Istoriya Vizantiiskoy Zhivopisi*, p. 108 and pls. 129–30.
[51] G. Galavaris, "The Illustrations of the

Fig. 288 *Paris, Bibliothèque Nationale. Cod. gr. 74, fol. 59ᵛ. Deposition and Entombment*

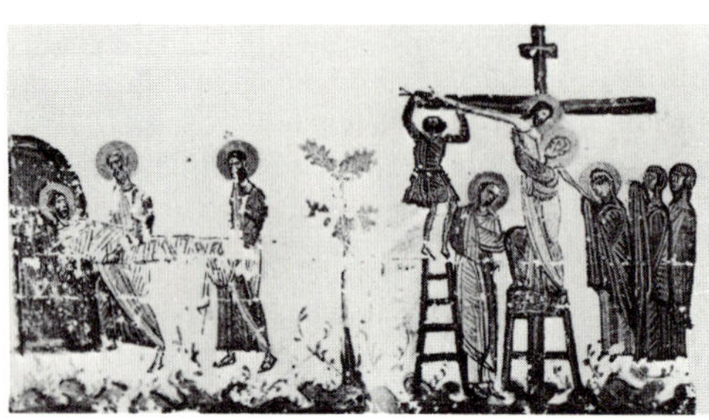

Out of the original 45 homilies that exist with illustrations in the well-known Paris cod. gr. 510 of the end of the ninth century,[52] a selection of 16 was made in the eleventh century, and these were arranged to be read in the liturgical order of the feast days. Consequently we now find the Easter homily placed at the beginning and illustrated with the Anastasis miniature. In this way the organization of the new edition of the illustrated homilies is very much the same as that of the Gospel lectionary proper, and this liturgical edition has survived as the accepted one.

The Anastasis is only one of the great feasts which in the Middle Byzantine period were crystallized in a cycle of twelve. There is nothing canonical about these twelve feasts and their selection is, to a certain extent, alterable, since a few feasts are interchangeable, but the cycle as such became a firmly established convention.[53] The time when the cycle

---

Liturgical Homilies of Gregory Nazianzenus" (Ph.D. thesis, Princeton University, 1955). The liturgical aspect is much stressed in this thesis. [G. Galavaris, *The Illustrations of the Liturgical Homilies of Gregory Nazianzenus* (Princeton, 1969).]

[52] Omont, *Miniatures*, pp. 10 ff. and pls. XV–LX bis.

[53] Millet, *Recherches*, pp. 15 ff.

Fig. 289 *Paris, Bibliothèque Nationale. Cod. gr. 74, fol. 60ᵛ. Tomb Sealing and Anastasis*

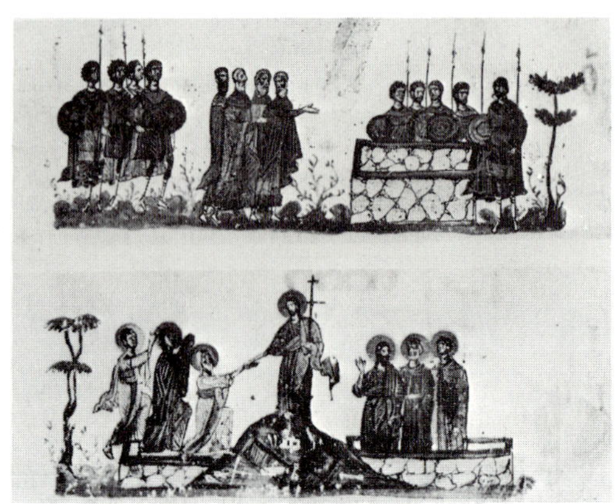

of the twelve feasts became fixed is not quite clear. The available evidence suggests that it might have existed already in the tenth century, although no complete cycle of that century has come down to us. We do have complete cycles from the eleventh century, although unfortunately none has survived in any Gospel lectionary, where above all one would have expected it. Most of the extant lectionaries have only a selection of feast pictures, in the form of splendid full-page miniatures. Our evidence for the full cycle rests on other eleventh-century manuscripts, whose miniatures are based on a lectionary, and also on works of art in other media.

A unique Psalter in the Vatican Library (cod. gr. 752), whose Easter tables begin with the year 1059, contains, inserted between the illustrated prefaces and the beginning of the first Psalm, a cycle of the twelve feasts, distributed over three pages (Fig. 292).[54] These individually

[54] E. T. DeWald, *Vaticanus Graecus 752* ("The Illustrations in the Manuscripts of the Septuagint," 3 [Princeton, 1942]), Part II, 6 ff. and pls. XI–XIII. Actually there are thirteen in the cycle, the Women at the Tomb being the supernumerary.

Fig. 290 *Paris, Bibliothèque Nationale. Cod. gr. 74, fol. 61ʳ. Women at the Tomb*

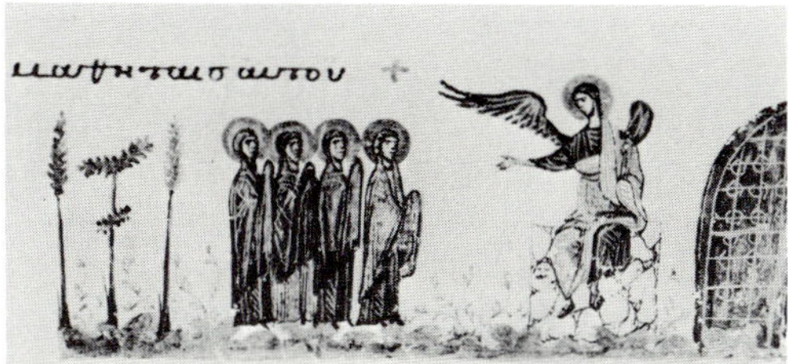

Fig. 291 *Jerusalem, Patriarchal Library. Cod. Taphou 14, fol. 3ʳ. Anastasis*

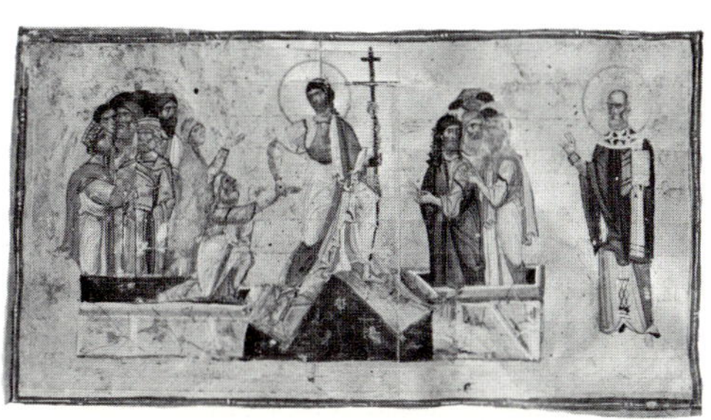

framed little feast pictures must ultimately have been derived from a lectionary, where the prototypes quite surely occupied full pages, and thus they provide the evidence for lectionaries with full feast cycles. The arrangement in rows in the Vatican Psalter resembles that of the previously discussed calendar icons, and thus it seems quite possible that the *direct* model in this case was an icon. This is just another instance of the easy interchange between these two media.

There exists on Mount Sinai a diptych (Figs. 293–294)[55] which on stylistic grounds can be dated, if we are not mistaken, not later than the middle of the eleventh century; it is the earliest icon with a cycle of the twelve feasts known to us. The scenes are executed in the most delicate miniature style and arranged in rows, which are unevenly subdivided; the latter feature may well be explained by the use of miniatures as models, where a variance of dimension is not uncommon. This cycle, although it has the normal number of twelve feasts, is irregular inasmuch as the Death of the Virgin is omitted at the end, and, instead, the *Chairete* inserted between the Anastasis and the Ascension. There are

other examples of feast cycles in which the Koimesis is missing, but there is no other instance known to me where the substitute scene is the *Chairete*. The event of Christ meeting the two Marys is included in the lesson for the Holy Sabbath (Matt. 28: 1–20), and this is the place where it occurs in illustrated lectionaries.[56] Its presence in the Sinai icon suggests that the conventional set of the twelve feasts had not yet been fully accepted at that time.

The innovations in the illustration of the lectionary, however, are not confined to turning narrative illustrations into feast pictures into which dogmatic and liturgical elements are injected in order to give them, by pictorial means, a greater significance. On occasion the painter went one step further and invented entirely new scenes, theological rather than narrative.

A characteristic example is an illustration of John 1:18, "No man hath seen God at any time; the only begotten Son, which is in the bosom of the Father, he

[55] G. and M. Sotiriou, *Icones*, pp. 52 ff. and pls. 39–41.

[56] So, e.g., in the fragment Leningrad cod. 21 (Morey, "East Christian Miniatures," p. 70 and fig. 83; Weitzmann, "Das Evangelion," pp. 94–95) and the lectionary Istanbul, Greek Patr. cod. 8, Fol. 254ᵛ (G. Sotiriou, Κειμήλια τοῦ Οἰκουμενικοῦ Πατριαρχείου [Athens, 1937], p. 88).

Fig. 292 *Vatican, Biblioteca. Cod. gr. 752, fols.*
17ᵛ–18ᵛ. Twelve Feasts

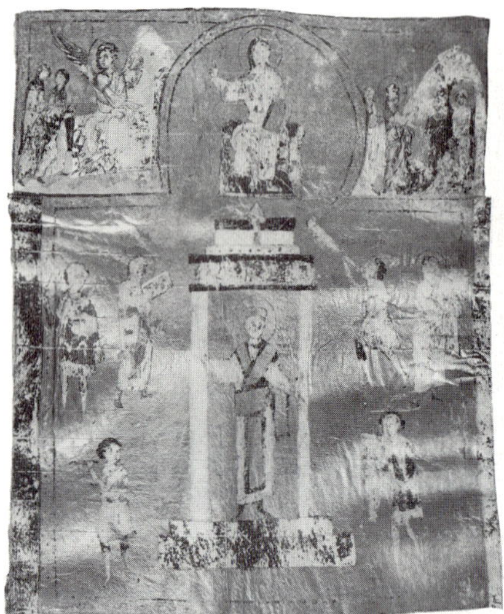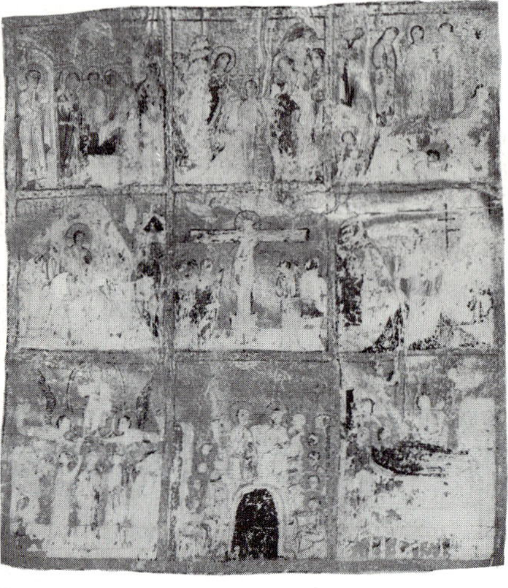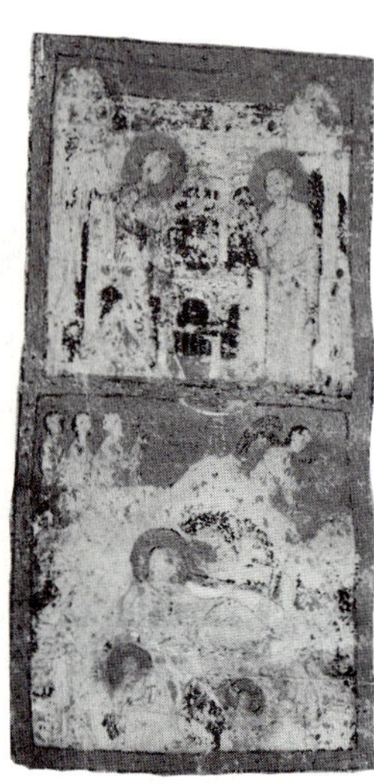

hath declared him," a verse which marks
the beginning of the lesson to be read on
the Monday after Easter. In a narrative
cycle of the four Gospels such a passage
seems to have had no appeal to the
illustrator,[57] but in a lectionary, such as
the one in Dionysiu (Fig. 295),[58] there
is an imaginative illustration of John the
Evangelist who dramatizes the truth of
his statement by pointing to heaven where
God, in the manifestation of Christ, is
depicted enthroned as the Ancient of
Days, holding a youthful Christ Emman-
uel in his lap. None of the lectionaries of
the tenth century has either this or any
other scene of a similar nature. While

there is no proof that the illustrator of
the Dionysiu Lectionary was the first to
invent this type of illustration, the probability is that it was an innovation of the
eleventh century.

Another type of illustration, which was
invented earlier, but which gained
increasing popularity in the eleventh
century, is the pictorial rendering of the
liturgical ceremonies proper. A characteristic example is the Elevation of the
Holy Cross as depicted in the Basil
menologion from the end of the tenth
century (Fig. 296).[59] The patriarch is
standing on the ambo of Saint Sophia and,
flanked by other clerics, he raises the
Holy Cross in his hands. There is a reason
to believe that the illustration of this feast
consisted originally of a historical
narrative, i.e., the Finding of the Holy
Cross by Helen. Such illustrations have
survived in the Syriac lectionaries.[60] The

[57] The only instance where it does occur in
a Gospel is in the Rockefeller McCormick
Gospel in Chicago (H. R. Willoughby, *The
Rockefeller McCormick New Testament*, 3
[Chicago, 1932], 207 ff., and I, pl. fol. 86ᵛ),
but here it is pictorially corrupt, using a
compositional scheme that was invented as an
illustration of John 1:37 where Christ meets
the first two disciples.
[58] Weitzmann, "Lectionary Morgan 639,"
p. 635 and fig. 294.

[59] *Il Menologio di Basilio II*, p. 35.
[60] London, Brit. Mus. Cod. add. 7169,
fol. 13r, and Berlin, Staatsbibl. Cod. Sachau
304, fol. 162v. J. Leroy, *Les Manuscits Syriaques*

Fig. 293 *Mount Sinai, St. Catherine's. Icon.*
Twelve Feasts

Fig. 294 *Mount Sinai, St. Catherine's. Icon.*
Twelve Feasts

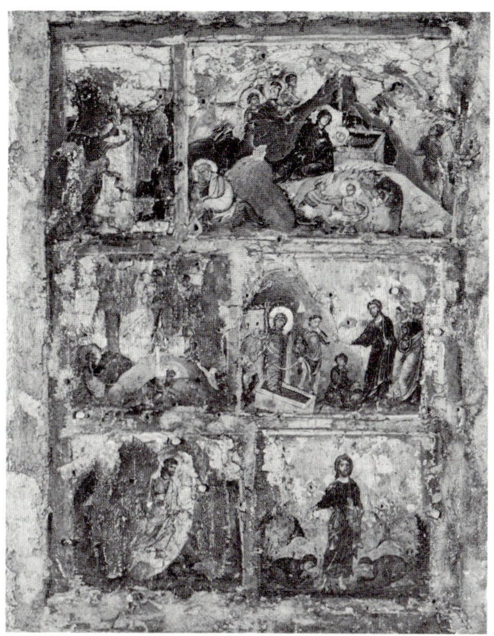

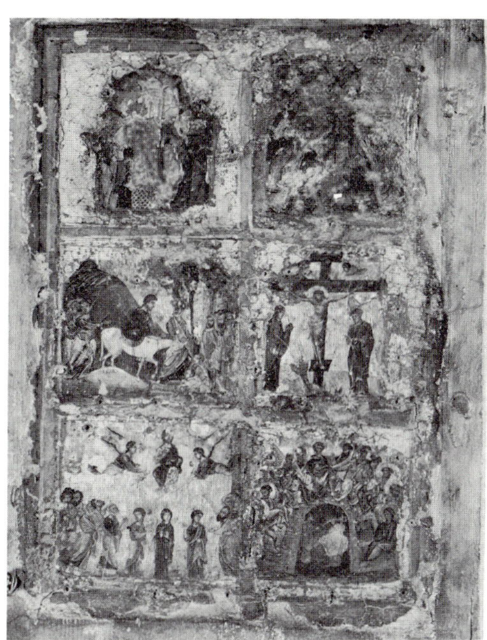

ambo picture occurs also in a richly
illustrated lectionary in the Vatican (cod.
gr. 1156; Fig. 297) of the third quarter of
the eleventh century.[61] This and the
picture of the Basil menologion seem to
be derived from the same archetype,
which was more likely a lectionary than
a menologion.

Now, in the Vatican lectionary this
ambo miniature is preceded by four
similar scenes, all of which have to do
with the feast of the Elevation of the Holy
Cross (Figs. 298–299); in each of them
worshippers, in the presence of one or
more bishops, are either bending over the
altar table to kiss the Cross upon it or
making a proskynesis. This proskynesis
is celebrated in four consecutive days
before the Feast of the Elevation on 14
September, and this accounts for the
repetition of the miniatures. This serial
representation must be understood as
an expression of the growing interest of
the eleventh-century illustrator in
liturgical ceremonies.

The most conspicuous enrichment of
the illustration of the lectionary is due
to an ever-increasing influence of the
menologion. True, tenth-century manuscripts like the Uncial Lectionary in
Lavra on Mount Athos (cod. A.86)[62]
already had a few saint figures in the calendar part, but in the eleventh century the

---

à Peintures (Paris, 1964), p. 355 and pl. 124,
2; p. 368 and pl. 126, 3–4.

[61] Millet, *Recherches*, pp. (cf. index, p. 749)
and figs. 76–77, 93–99, 141, 344, 426, 533;
Weitzmann, "Narrative and Liturgical Illus-
tration," pp. 156, 160, and pl. XIII, 1–4;
XVIII, 1–2 [herewith, pp. 251 ff. and
Figs. 235–38 and 243–44].

[62] Weitzmann, *Byzantinische Buchmalerei*,
pp. 46 ff., and pls. LII–LIV.

Fig. 295 *Mount Athos, Dionysiu. Cod. 587, fol. 3ᵛ. John the Evangelist*

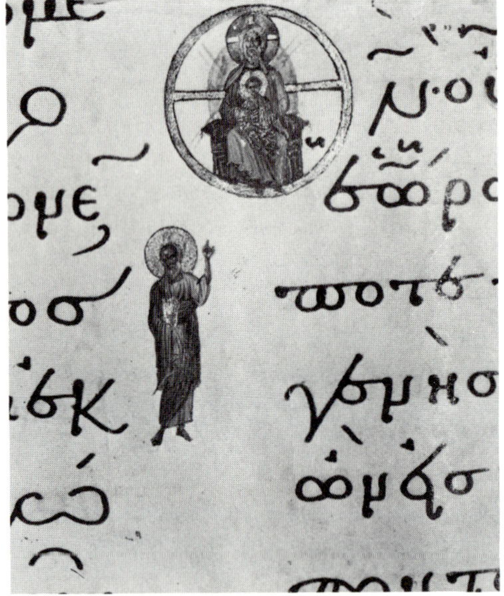

Fig. 296 *Vatican, Biblioteca. Cod. gr. 1613, p. 35. Elevation of the Holy Cross*

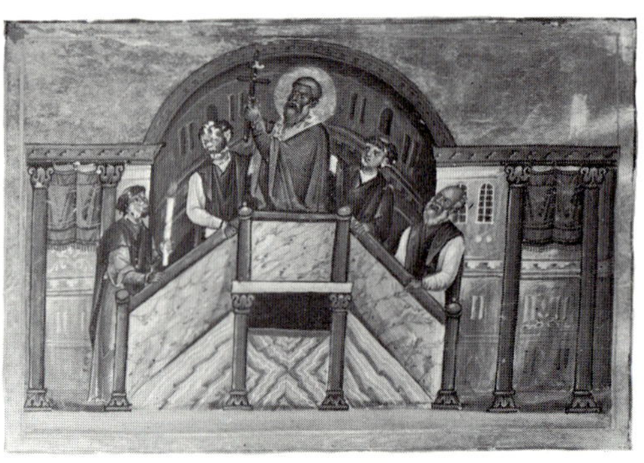

saint pictures in the lectionary increase in splendor and numbers. In the Vatican Lectionary, for example (Figs. 298–299), there exists, at least in its earlier part, a saint picture for every day of the month, and in this particular manuscript the menologion pictures by far surpass in number the christological ones.

What I should like to emphasize is that this mixture of primarily liturgical scenes based on the New Testament with the wealth of imagery coming from the menologion and additional material from other sources is not confined to the illustration of the Gospel lectionary nor to that of other liturgical manuscripts, such as the Theodore Psalter in London, but that it occurs equally in this period in other branches of the representational arts such as icon painting.

ICON PAINTING

I have already introduced the little

Sinai icon with a complete set of saints for the month of February (Fig. 282), which is only one of an original set of twelve. Preserved on Sinai are four altogether, namely those of January, February, March, and April. Now if one visualizes these four icons as a single unit and turns them over, the one on the far right now naturally becomes the first on the left: one will then see an extensive christological cycle which begins with the Birth of the Virgin and her Entry into the Temple and is followed by the Infancy of Christ. The next panel depicts the miracles of Christ and with the third one (Fig. 300)[63] begins the Passion, starting with the Entry into Jerusalem and ending, on the fourth panel, with the Koimesis. This cycle is in part narrative and in part liturgical, so far as it incorporated the great feasts, including of course the Anastasis, Pentecost, and Koimesis, which are not Gospel scenes. It is a mixture similar to the one which had developed in the illustration of the Gospel lectionary, and since the style of this icon is identical with that of miniature painting it can be taken for granted that the model was indeed a lectionary, and this may

[63] G. and M. Sotiriou, *Icones*, p. 123 and pl. 145.

Fig. 297 *Vatican, Biblioteca. Cod. gr. 1156, fol. 250ᵛ. Elevation of the Holy Cross*

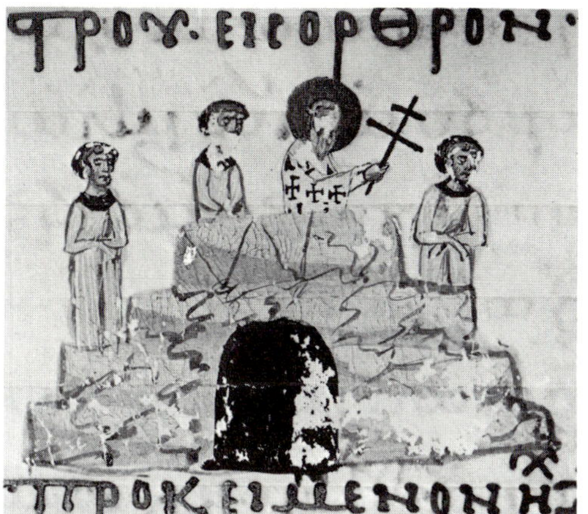

also apply to the menologion scenes. After all, we have seen that the Vatican Lectionary had an almost complete set of calendar pictures incorporated into its second part, i.e., the synaxary.

Since in the case of the four Sinai icons just discussed the christological part is complete, these panels of the calendar from January to April formed a central unit, a tetraptych, apparently preceded on the left by another tetraptych with the months of September to December, and, on the right, a similar one with the months of May to August. Did these two other tetraptychs, now lost, also have paintings on their backs, and, if so, what could their subject have been? This we do not know for sure, but we can at least make some suggestions on the basis of analogous cases. There are other such complex polyptychs among the Sinai icons, and it seems to us more than likely that this type of polyptych was actually invented in the eleventh century, in order to accommodate the increasingly elaborate liturgical programs, whereas previously diptychs and triptychs in icon painting, ivory carvings, metal

reliefs, and so on, had sufficed for the more limited programs.

There is at Sinai another set of four calendar icons,[64] almost intact,[65] which comprise the saints for every day of the year and depict the saints of three months on each icon with three rows allotted to each month, as may be seen in the first panel, which contains all the saints from September to November (Fig. 301). Compared with the previous set of calendar icons the style is somewhat earlier, i.e., quite assuredly still belonging to the second half of the eleventh century, and iconographically the narrative scenes from the lives of the saints make up a higher proportion of the illustrations, in contrast to the later calendar icons, in which the simple, frontally standing saints become preponderant. Now the far sides of the outer calendar icons have metal hinges, which proves that the first panel on the left and the fourth panel on the right were each connected to another panel, so that we are dealing here with a hexaptych rather than a tetraptych. These two outer panels also exist separately on Sinai. The one that should be on the far left shows again a mixture of the narrative and the liturgical illustration

---

[64] G. and M. Sotiriou, *Icones*, pp. 121 ff. and pls. 136–43. The inscriptions are in Greek and Georgian.

[65] The panel that contains the months of December, January, and February is cut through horizontally (Sotiriou, pl. 139) and at the right side a narrow strip is missing. I found it reproduced in N. P. Likhachev, *Materialy dlya Istorii Russkogo Ikonopisaniya* (St. Petersburg, 1906), pl. XII, 21. Apparently it is one of the Sinai icons which Porphyrius Uspensky brought to Russia in the middle of the nineteenth century.

Fig. 298 *Vatican, Biblioteca. Cod. gr. 1156,*
fol. 248ʳ. Holy Cross

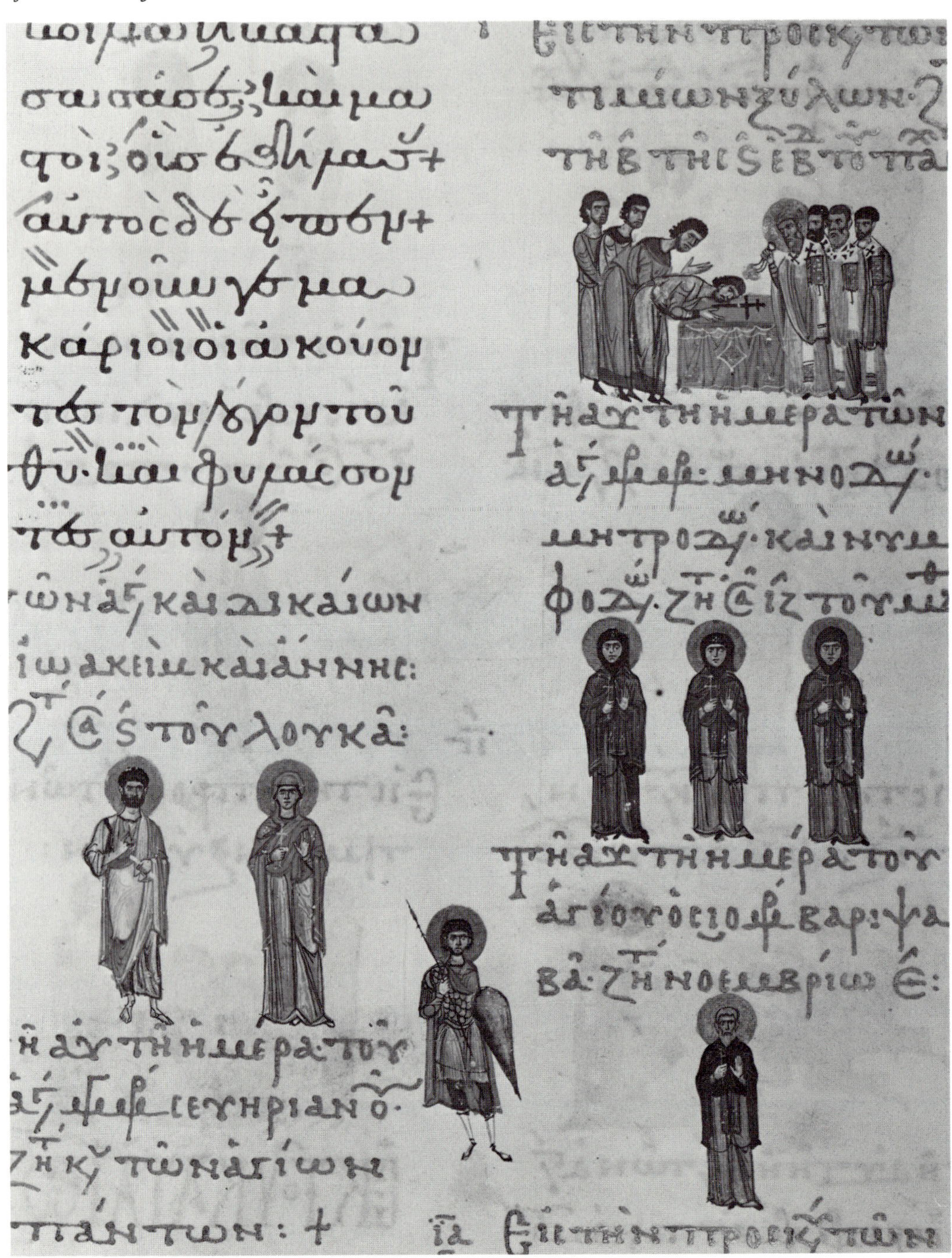

Fig. 299 *Vatican, Biblioteca. Cod. gr. 1156,*
fol. 248ᵛ. Holy Cross

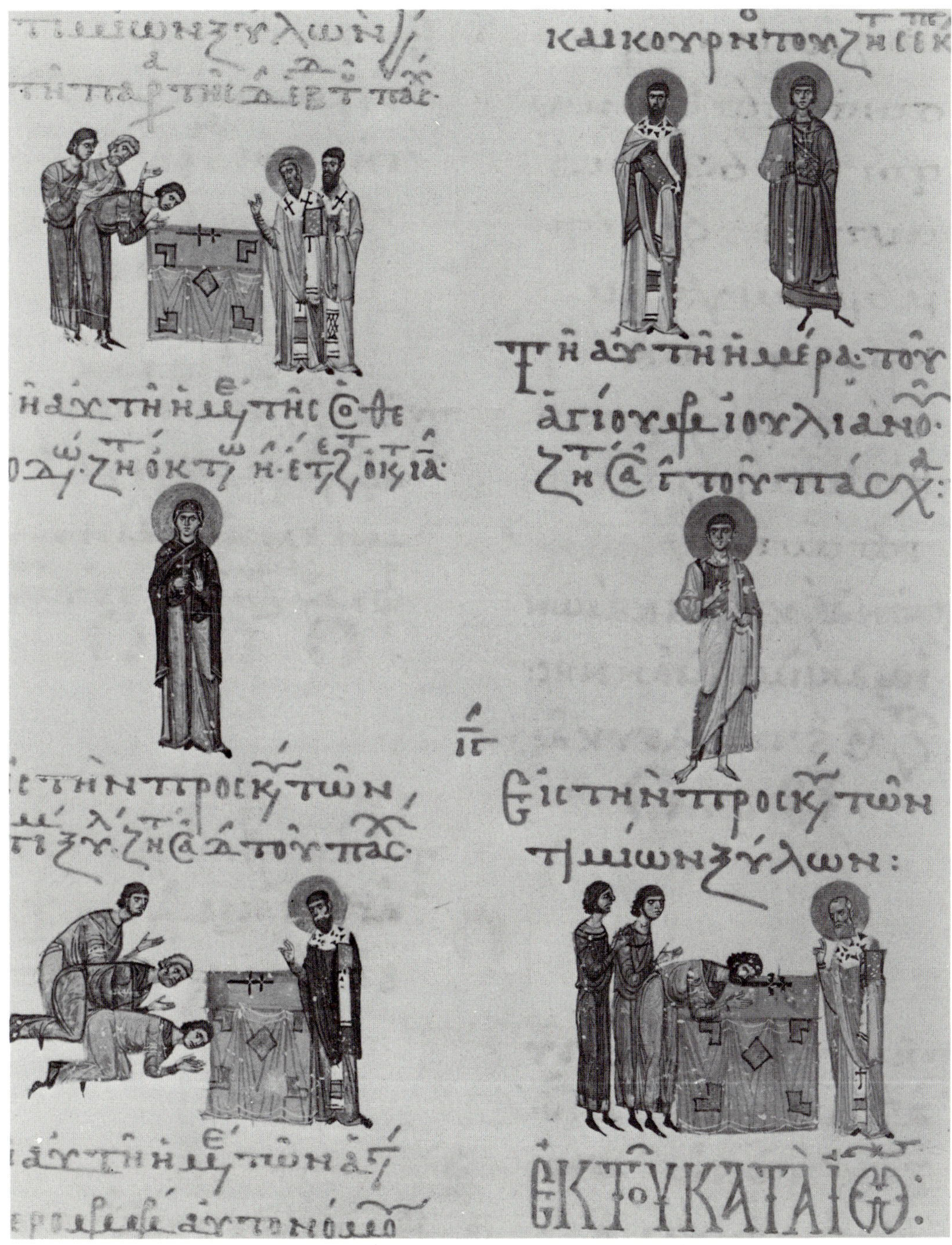

Fig. 300 *Mount Sinai, St. Catherine's. Icon.*
   Life of Christ

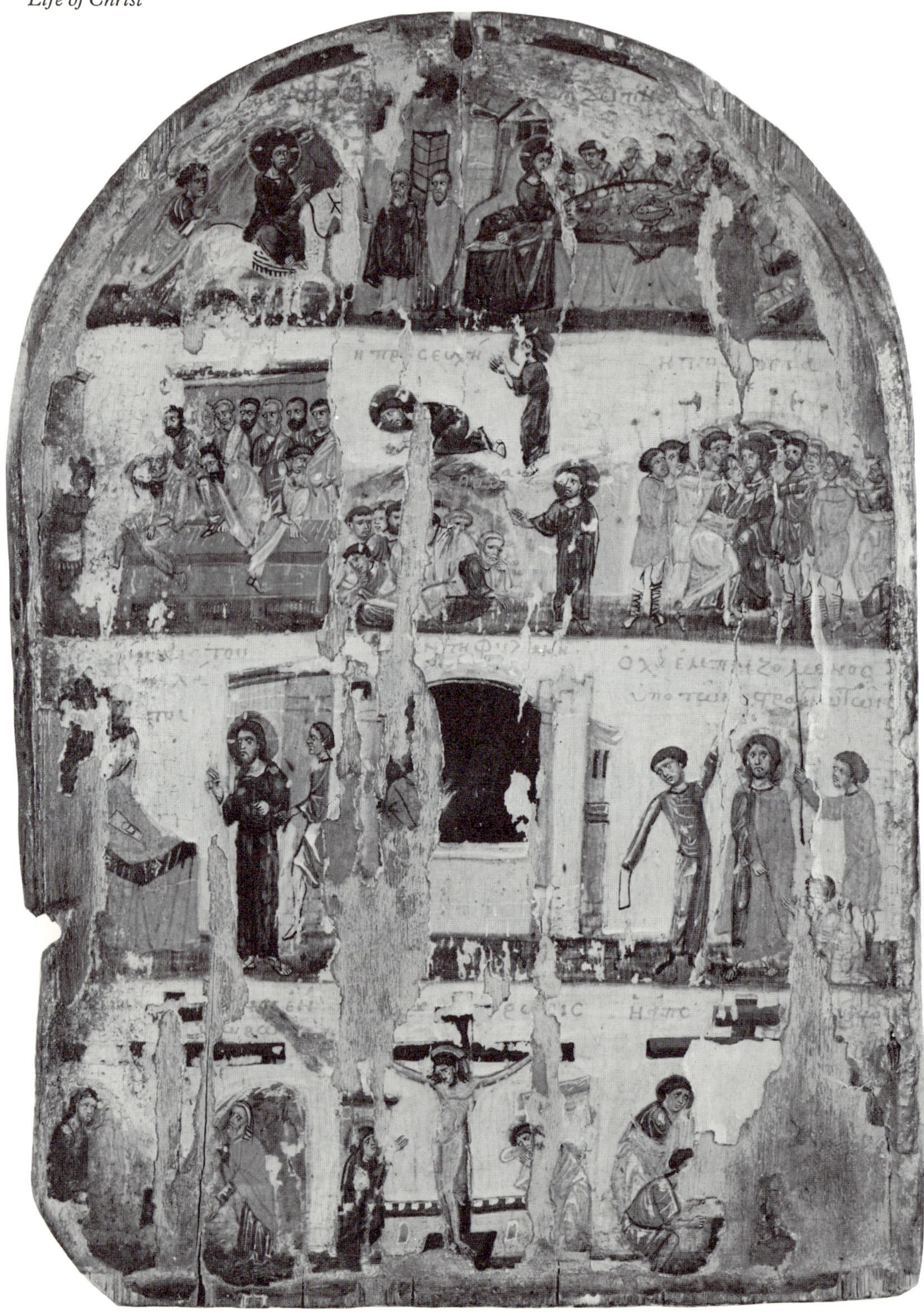

of the New Testament (Fig. 302).[66] After a depiction of the Miracle of Cana in the second row, more than half the panel is devoted to other miracles, which are followed by Passion scenes essentially based on the two lessons for Maundy Thursday, i.e., the Last Supper and the Washing of the Feet, and on some of the twelve Passion readings of Good Friday. At the very end there are the great feast pictures of the Anastasis, the Ascension, and an area now destroyed which would assuredly have depicted Pentecost. Once again we are reminded of the impact of the illustrated lectionary, whose dominating position and radiating influence became apparent also in icon painting.

The top row of the same icon is occupied by five images of the Virgin, four of which copy famous miracle icons that were venerated in churches of Constantinople. In the center is the Virgin Enthroned, who is known under the name of Platytera or Nikopoia[67] or still other names, and she is flanked on one side by the Blachernitissa and the Hodegetria and on the other by the Agiosoritissa and the little-known Cheimeutissa. In the case of the four lateral images, no doubt, various Virgin icons served as models, which the icon painter transformed into a miniature style, to which he was equally accustomed.

The panel that once occupied the extreme right of the hexaptych depicts the

Last Judgment (Fig. 303).[68] Essentially it shows the same lay-out as the two Last Judgment miniatures in the richly illustrated and almost contemporary Gospel book in Paris (grec. 74).[69] Obviously, miniatures and the icon alike derive from the same source. Because both share an extraordinary complexity, a clearly organized lay-out in horizontal rows, and a hieratic quality, achieved by symmetry and other means, the composition seems to point to an archetype in mosaic or fresco painting.[70] The place of a monumental Last Judgment in a church, as we know from the mosaic in Torcello[71] and other examples in fresco as well, was on the west wall. In the Sinai icon, the groups of the elect show a more even distribution and the zones are more sharply divided than in the miniatures, and this suggests that the icon is closer to the archetype than the Paris' miniatures. This conclusion is supported by many details, such as the fuller depiction of the choirs of the elect, or the placing of the dead rising out of the tomb at the bottom of the panel. There is no evidence, as far as we can see, for the existence of this complex Last Judgment composition in the tenth century, though some clues, of course, may have been lost. However this may be, it is not before

[66] G. and M. Sotiriou, *Icones*, pp. 125 ff. and pls. 146–9.

[67] While Sotiriou calls this Virgin Platytera, a good case for calling this type Nikopoia has been made by G. A. Wellen, *Theotokos. Eine ikonographische Abhandlung über das Gottesmutterbild in frühchristlicher Zeit* (Utrecht and Antwerp, 1961), pp. 147 ff.

[68] Ibid., pp. 128 ff. and pl. 150.

[69] Omont, *Evangiles*, pls. 41 and 81.

[70] As for the most recent writing on the subject of the Last Judgment cf. B. Brenk, "Die Anfänge der Byzantinischen Weltgerichtsdarstellung," *Byzantinische Zeitschrift*, 57 (1964), 106 ff. [B. Brenk, *Tradition und Neuerung in der christlichen Kunst des ersten Jahrtausends: Studien zur Geschichte des Weltgerichtsbilds* ("Wiener byzantinische Studien," 3 [Vienna, 1966]).]

[71] Lazarev, *Istoriya Vizantiiskoy Zhivopisi*, pl. 240.

Fig. 301 *Mount Sinai, St. Catherine's. Icon.*
Saints from September to November

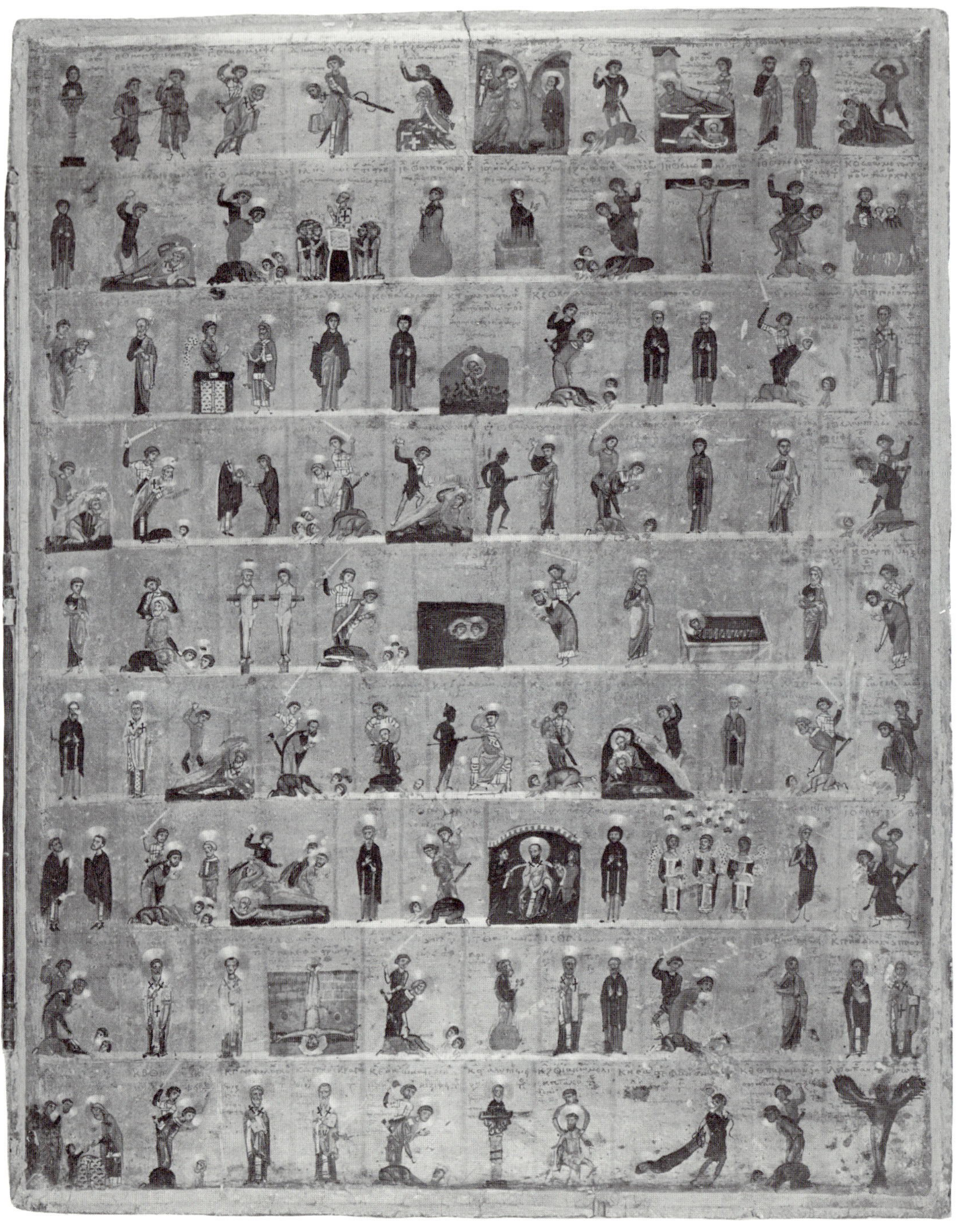

Fig. 302 *Mount Sinai, St. Catherine's. Icon.*
 Holy Images and Life of Christ

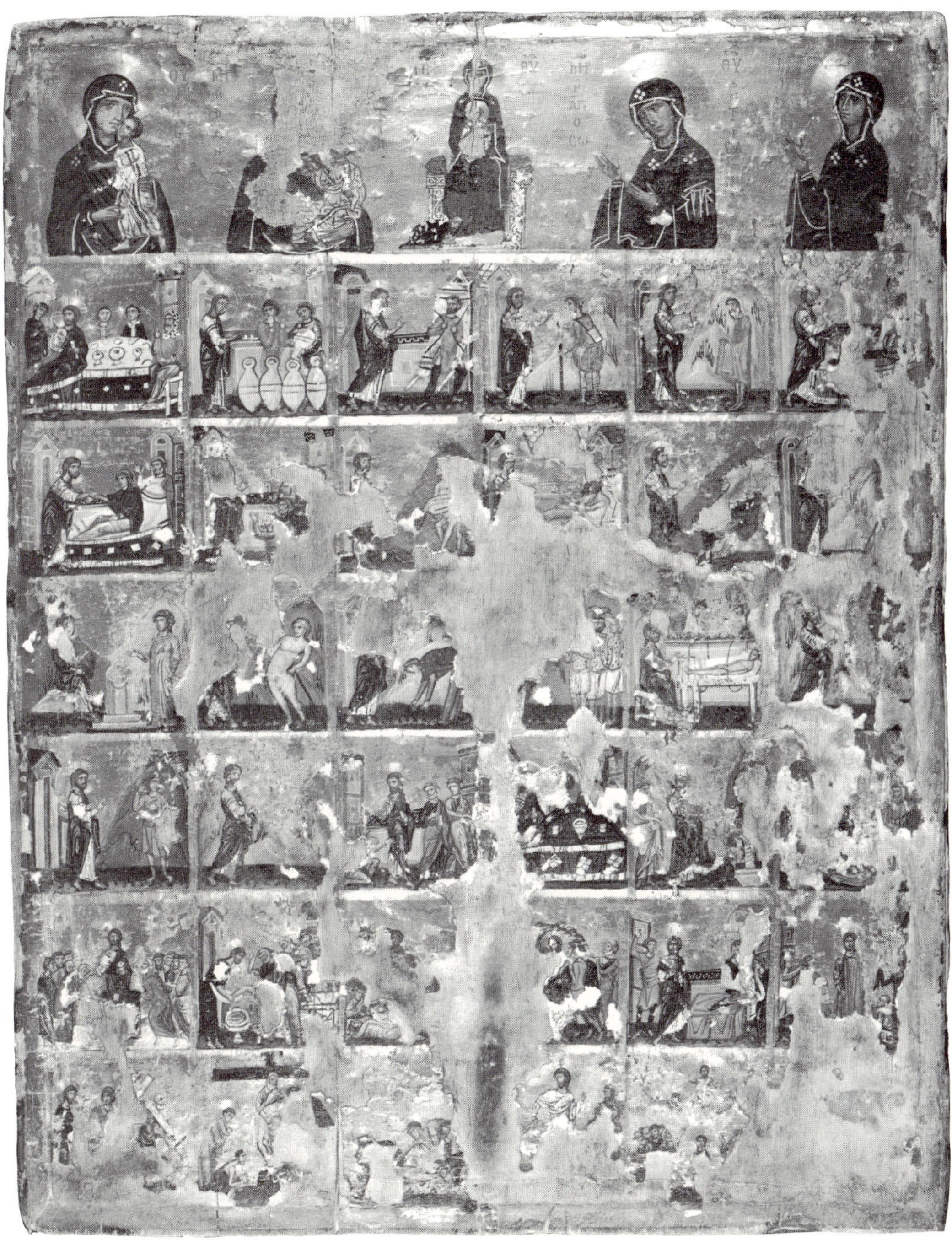

the eleventh century that this composition became firmly established and spread into miniature and icon painting, and even ivory carving.[72] All copies show the style of the capital, so there can be little doubt that the archetype was a monumental mosaic or fresco in some church of Constantinople.

As mentioned before, the location for the Last Judgment, in cases where it is included in the liturgical program, is the west wall of a church, a place usually reserved for the Death of the Virgin. Now, the first panel of our hexaptych apparently ended with Pentecost, omitting the Death of the Virgin. This suggests that the Last Judgment has taken its place, just as in a church decoration, as a substitute for a Koimesis.

Reflecting on the hexaptych as a whole, one notices basically the same range of iconographical subject matter which one finds in a Gospel lectionary, i.e., a mixture of narrative and liturgical Gospel scenes and a complete calendar. If the Last Judgment is not preserved in any lectionary, this may be accidental. Its presence in the Paris Gospel book which, as demonstrated before, possesses quite a number of feast pictures adopted from the liturgical Gospels, suggests that once it *did* exist in an eleventh-century lectionary. Even so, it is equally possible or perhaps even more likely that in our particular case the Sinai icon, because of its greater complexity, derives directly from a monumental painting. We must

reckon with repeated evidence of mutual interpenetration of the various media, an interpenetration which may have been much easier and much more frequent than is generally assumed.

Sotiriou has published a second icon of the Last Judgment (Fig. 304)[73] which I would like to discuss briefly although it dates from the early twelfth century, because it can be demonstrated that this icon also was once a part of a polyptych of which we have been able to trace the other panels among the Sinai icons. A cutting in the right side of the frame precisely matches the projection of a wing which, when joined and closed, fills the recessed area of the Last Judgment icon. On the left side, holes for hinges suggest the existence of an identical square panel which also had provisions for an outer wing. In other words, we are dealing here with a quadriptych that folds twice. The Last Judgment was not, in this case, at the extreme right, but at the right of the center. Iconographically, it is very close to the previous one without being a direct copy, and this would suggest that both were rather closely related to the lost archetype. The second panel off the center (Fig. 305), once positioned at the left of the Last Judgment, is kept in the bema of the church at the back of the iconostasis. It represents precisely the twelve feasts as they were finally accepted, and a comparison with the corresponding panel in the earlier hexaptych makes it clear that, by this stage, the concentration on the liturgical feast cycle had led to the complete elimination of narrative scenes.

---

[72] An ivory in the Victoria and Albert Museum in London (A. Goldschmidt and K. Weitzmann, *Die byzantinischen Elfenbeinskulpturen*, 2 [Berlin, 1930–34], 60 and pl. XLV, no. 123) with a Last Judgment, which is abbreviated but derived from the same archetype, likewise must be dated to the eleventh century.

[73] G. and M. Sotiriou, *Icones*, p. 130 and pl. 151.

Fig. 303 *Mount Sinai, St. Catherine's. Icon.*
   Last Judgment

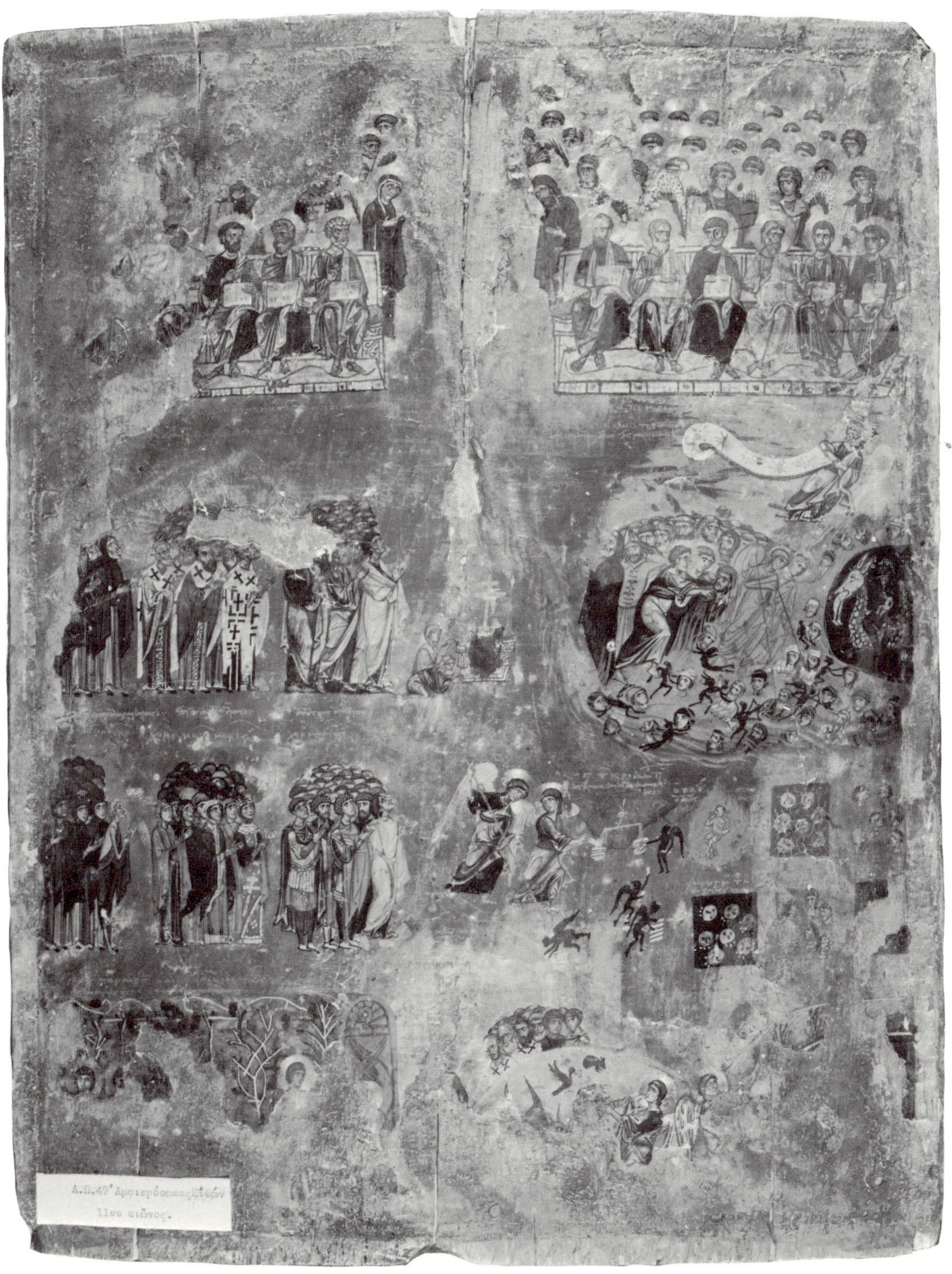

The two wings (Figs. 306–307),[74] now in the icon room of the monastery, depict at the very top the Birth of the Virgin and her Presentation in the Temple. These two scenes from Mary's infancy had become important feast pictures, and they occur twice on Sinai iconostasis beams,[75] where they precede the twelve feasts and thus serve as a kind of introduction to them. Underneath the two Virgin scenes, on the wings, are two rows of saints who, contrary to the hexaptych, are arranged not according to the calendar but to their hierarchical order. First come the great church fathers, followed by the soldier saints, the physician saints, the holy monks and nuns, and finally by Constantine and Helen. This is the liturgical order in which the saints are placed in a church decoration: the fathers of the church occupy the most honored place in the apse, then follow the soldiers and other saints, and finally, the monks and nuns take the more humble place close to the entrance of the church.

Analyzed as a whole, this tetraptych brings into focus the liturgical program more sharply than the hexaptych discussed before: (1) by giving to the Last Judgment a more central position within the polyptych; (2) by concentrating the christological cycle entirely on the twelve canonical feasts; (3) by adding the pictures of two Virgin feasts; and (4) by positioning the saints according to their hierarchical order. Thus the comparison between these two polyptychs gives us a clear insight into the trend toward an ever-increasing precision in the formulation of the liturgical program as it developed within the eleventh century. It seems appropriate to stress the point once more that liturgical programs as such were not an innovation of the eleventh century but were intensified, elaborated, and systematized at that time. One of the earlier crystallizations into a liturgical composition is the Deesis, which is based on the prayer of intercession of the liturgy. This can be demonstrated by the tenth-century ivory triptychs of the Romanus group,[76] where the theme is fully developed, with the archangels, apostles, and other saints grouped around the Deesis proper.

Yet the fact that the Deesis, together with the cycle of the twelve great feasts, forms a larger liturgical unit is compatible with the tendency toward greater complexity in the eleventh century. This may be seen in another Sinai icon, which was executed in the refined style of Constantinople in the second half of the eleventh century (Fig. 308).[77] The Deesis in the top row is flanked by the two archangels and two pairs of apostles at either side. But there was no place for all the apostles,

[74] Ibid., p. 167 and fig. 180.

[75] Ibid., pp. 107 ff. and figs. 99, 101, 125. The second beam is still unpublished. [Several scenes on this beam, though not the infancy of the Virgin, have been published in Weitzmann, "Thirteenth-Century Crusader Icons on Mount Sinai," *Art Bulletin*, 45 (1963), 181 ff. and fig. 3; idem, "Icon Painting in the Crusader Kingdom," *Dumbarton Oaks Papers*, 20 (1966), 62 ff. and figs. 22–24.]

[76] Cf. n. 36. [Now see Weitzmann, "Die byzantinischen Elfenbeine eines Bamberger Graduale und ihre ursprüngliche Verwendung," *Studien zur Buchmalerei und Goldschmiedekunst des Mittelalters. Festschrift für Karl Hermann Usener* (Marburg, 1967), pp. 11 ff.]

[77] G. and M. Sotiriou, *Icones*, pp. 75 ff. and pls. 57–61.

Fig. 304 *Mount Sinai, St. Catherine's. Icon.
Last Judgment*

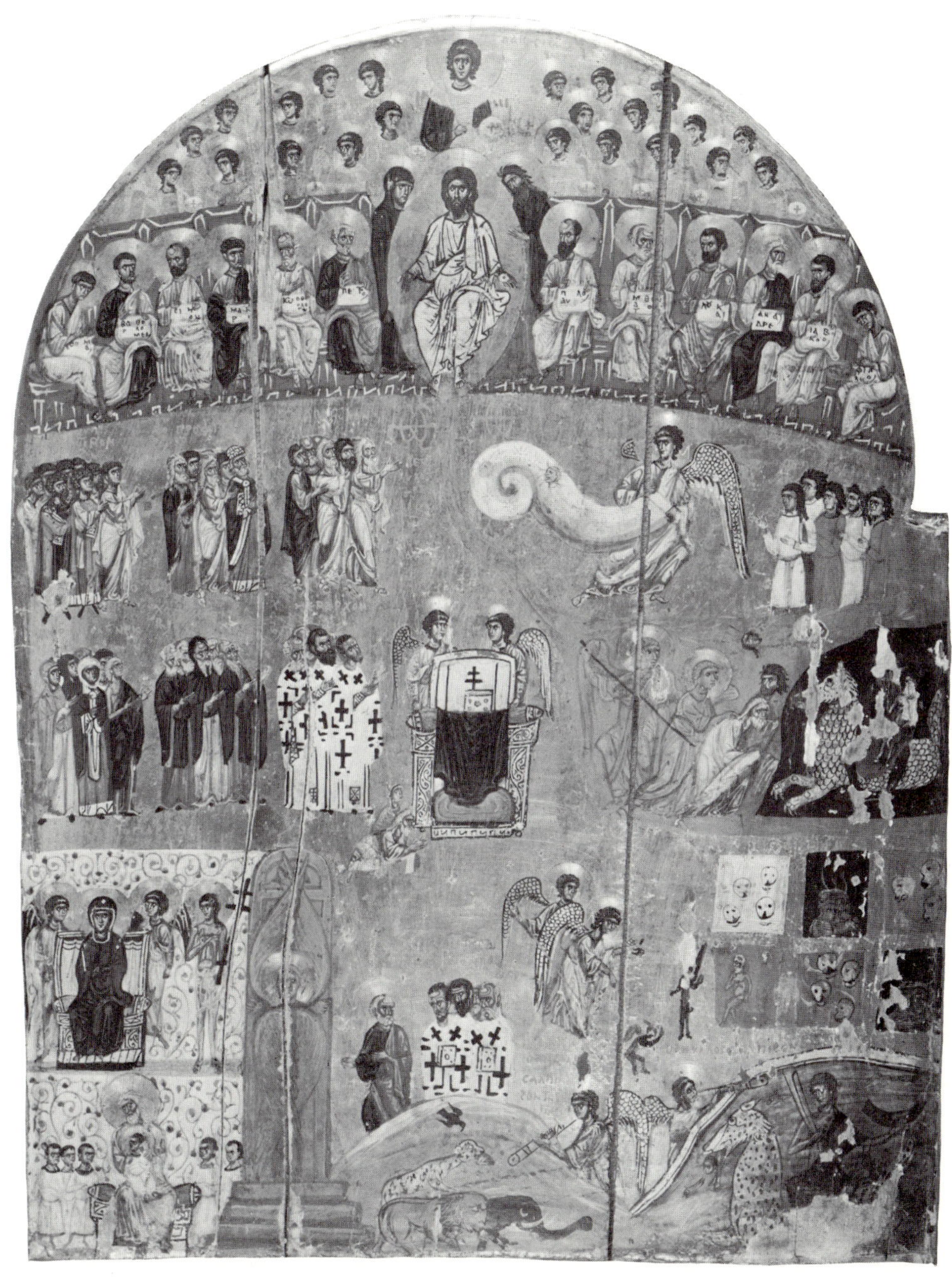

Fig. 305 *Mount Sinai, St. Catherine's. Icon.*
  Twelve Feasts

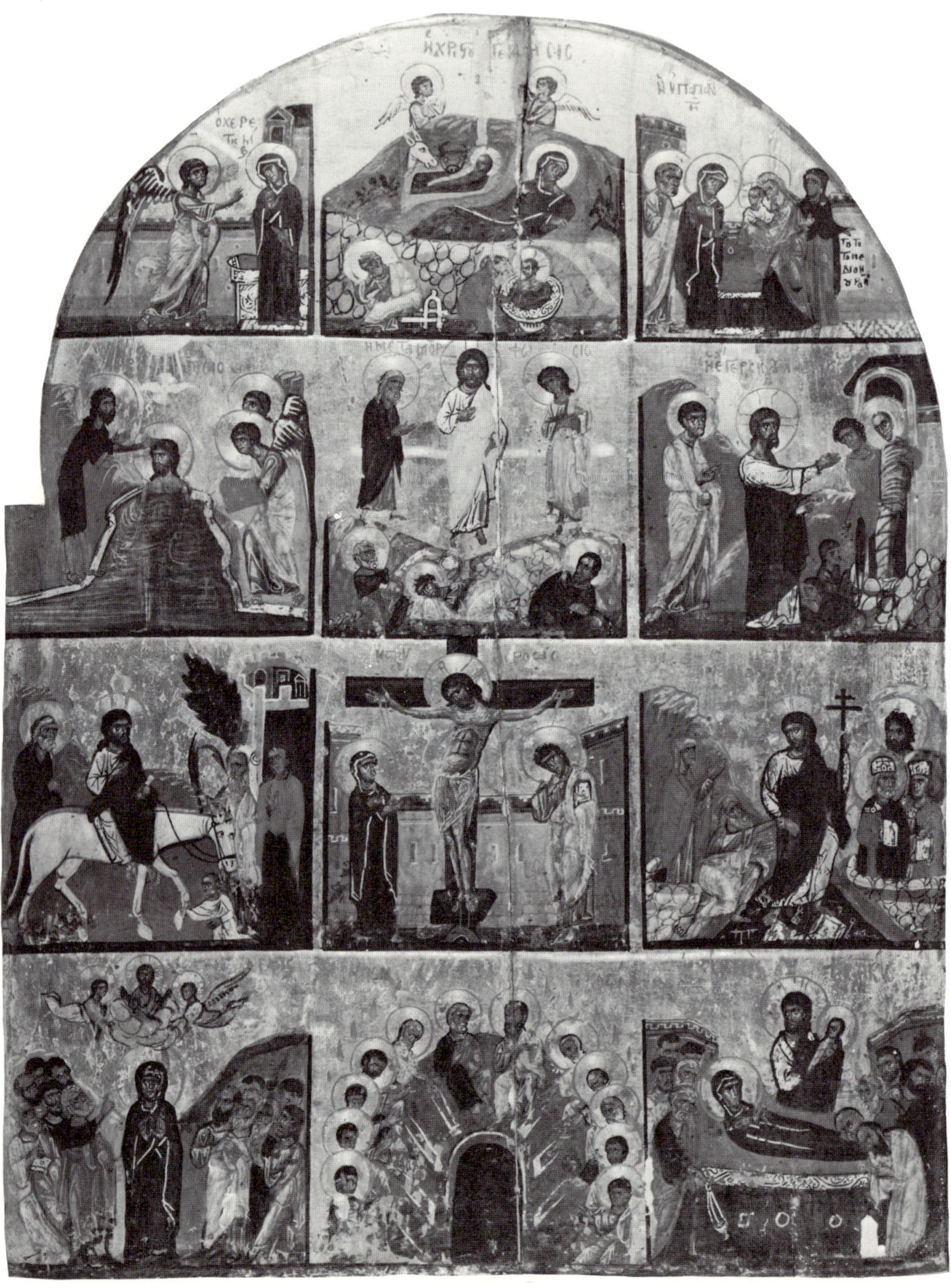

and two more pairs had to be moved to the corners of the second row. Presumably there must have been a model in which the twelve apostles were all lined up in one row, and this model assuredly was an epistyle of an iconostasis, in which, as we now know from the findings on Mount Sinai, the placing of a Deesis in the center of the beam is quite normal.[78] Moreover, as we learn from the same group of Sinai monuments, the epistyle of the iconostasis is also the place for a cycle of the twelve great feasts, sometimes with a Deesis in the center,[79] and thus we are justified in believing that the feast cycle of our Sinai icon is also derived from an iconostasis beam. The traditional arrangement on these beams is to place the individual scenes under painted arches, and the effect of such a decorative system is apparent in a few scenes from our Sinai icon.[80]

It is an open question whether the icon painter used two different iconostasis epistyles as models; it is perhaps more likely that he used as a model one epistyle which either had all the saints and feasts in one long beam or in two, the upper one being composed of the Deesis with the apostles and the lower one consisting of the twelve feasts. That the pre-iconoclastic period already had figurative representations, mainly of those saints, on the epistyle of the iconostasis we know from the description of the sixth-century iconostasis in Hagia Sophia, as described

by Paul the Silentiary.[81] Yet among the achievements of the eleventh century,[82] as we learn from the icon just analyzed, was, if we are not mistaken, the use of the twelve-feast cycle for the decoration of an epistyle of an iconostasis which dates from a period earlier than the extant instances of Sinai, which are from the latter part of the twelfth century. The icon also seems to suggest that the eleventh century already saw the introduction of the epistyle with two beams of different subject matter in separate zones, a form which so far has been known only from considerably later instances.

The program of this icon and of the previously discussed polyptychs has many features in common with the general lay-out of monumental church decoration, both in mosaic and fresco. In the eleventh-century mosaic decoration of Hosios Lukas, the Nea Moni, and Daphni, the cycle of the twelve feasts played a dominant role, at the very time that it became a central theme in icon painting. Christ, the Virgin, John the Baptist, the archangels, the apostles, and the saints are all integrated into a progam which is as systematized in monumental art as it is in polyptychs. So close indeed are the interpenetrations of all branches of painting that it becomes almost superfluous to raise the question as to which

---

[78] Cf. the thirteenth-century iconostasis beam with the Deesis and apostles: Sotiriou, *Icones*, pp. 112 ff. and pls. 117–24.

[79] Ibid., pp. 102 ff. and pls. 87–102; pp. 111 ff. and pls. 112–16.

[80] Cf. n. 76.

[81] St. G. Xydis, "The Chancel Barrier, Solea and Ambo of Hagia Sophia," *Art Bulletin*, 29 (1947), 7 ff.

[82] For the importance of the eleventh and twelfth centuries in developing a richer iconostasis cf. V. Lasarev, "Trois fragments d'Epistyles peintes et le Templon Byzantin," *Timētikos G. Sotiriou. Deltion Archaiologikēs Hetaireios*, 4th ser., 4, 1964–65 (Athens, 1966), 117 ff. [This same article appeared in *Vizantiiskii Vremmenik*, 27 (1967), 162 ff.]

Fig. 306 *Mount Sinai, St. Catherine's. Icon. Birth of Virgin and Saints*

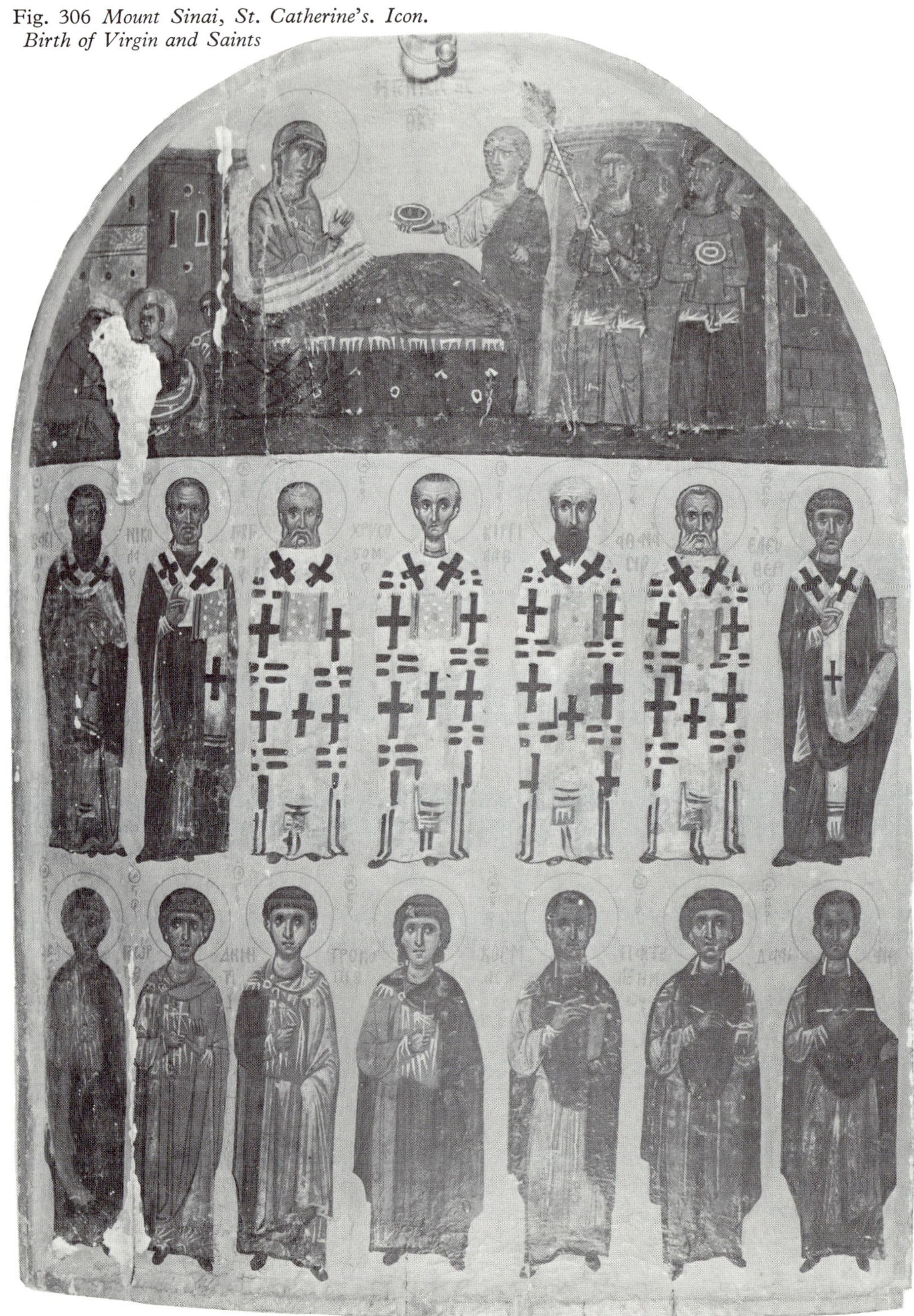

Fig. 307 *Mount Sinai, St. Catherine's. Icon. Presentation in Temple and Saints*

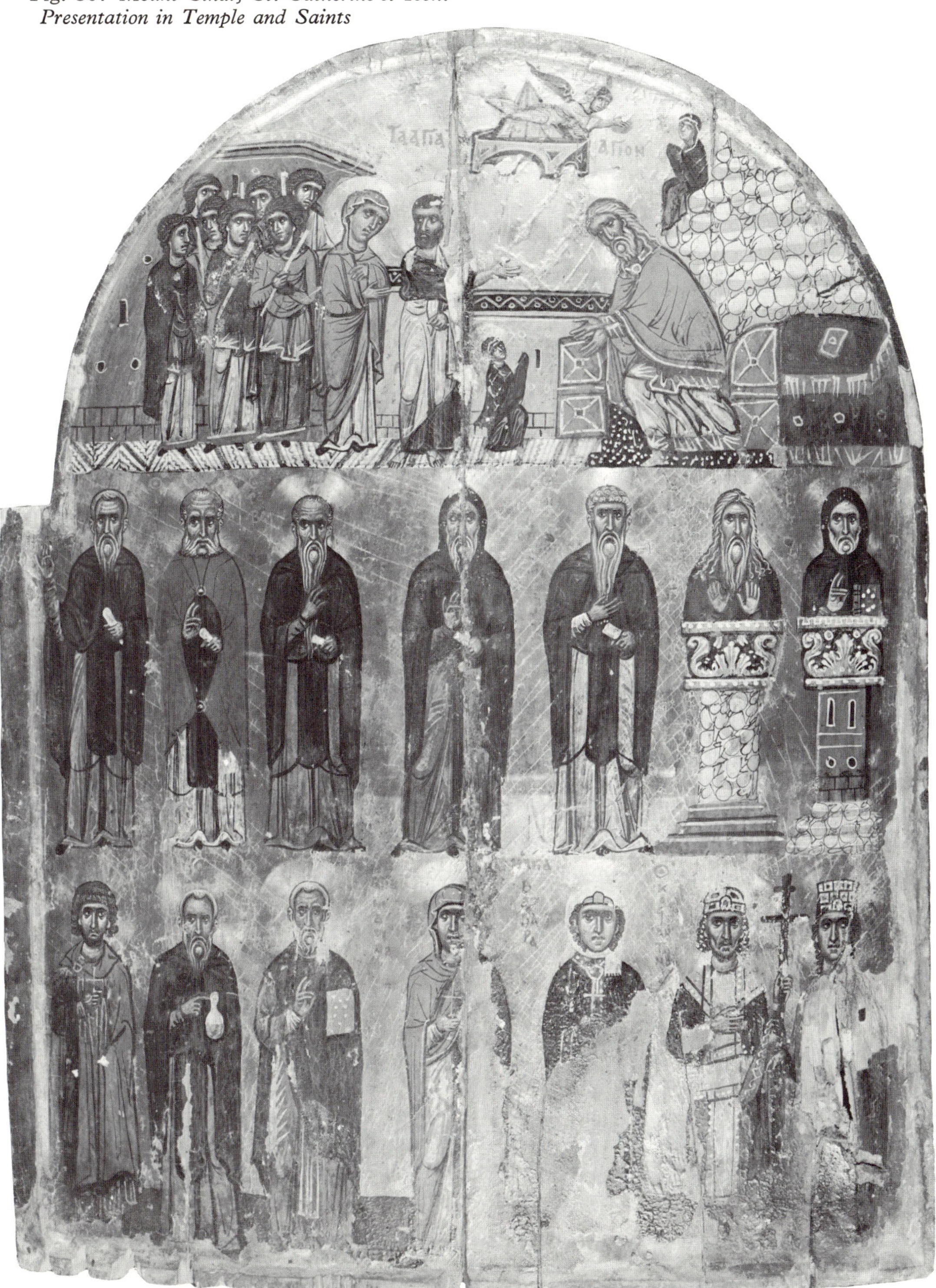

Fig. 308 *Mount Sinai, St. Catherine's. Icon. Deesis and Twelve Feasts*

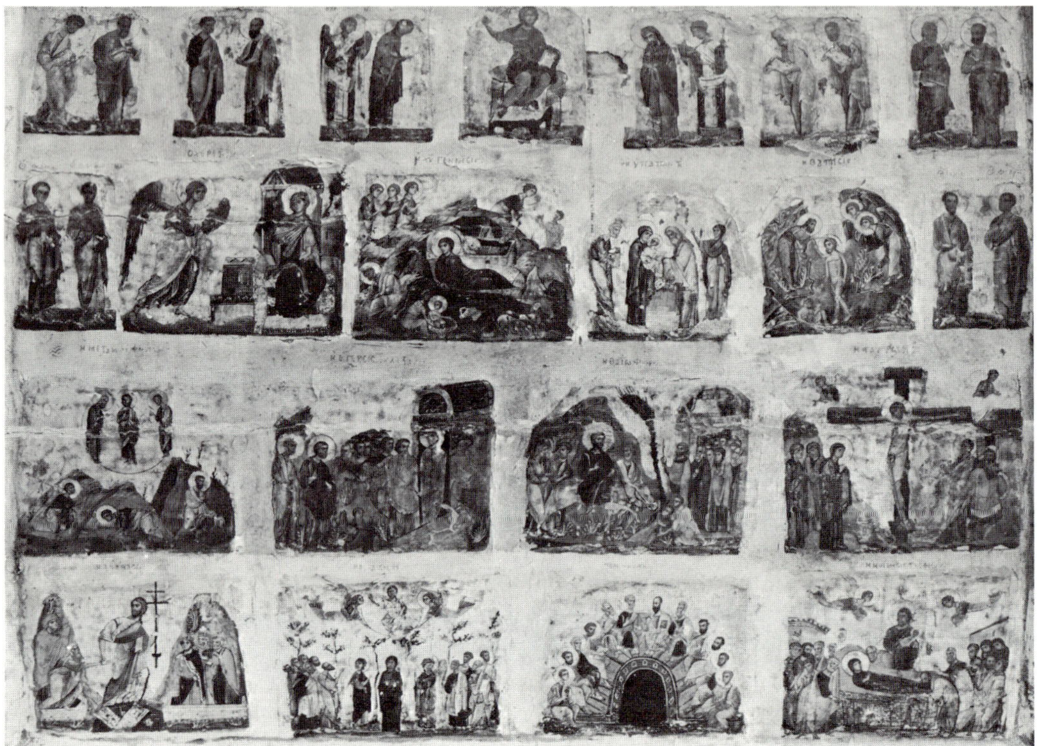

medium has the priority of invention. Liturgical programs apparently were laid out by learned clerics without regard for a special medium of the representational arts. They were, if such a comparison may be permitted, like some of Bach's music composed without a specific instrument in mind.

SUMMARY

If some generalizations about the artistic achievements of eleventh-century painting may be permitted, one would have to say this. The achievements of the Macedonian Renaissance were never to be abandoned, and a classicizing quality in the rendering of the human figure as an organic and corporeal unity

remained a stable factor as long as Byzantine art lasted, although the physical reality of the individual figure was diminished somewhat in the eleventh century in order to achieve the effect of greater spiritualization. An ascetic body depicted in billowing classical drapery became the ideal in this period, when a conciliation between monastic precepts and a continued study of the classics, which had been mutually antagonistic in the early days of Christianity, finally achieved a perfect balance. It is in the eleventh century that these two forces were molded into an indissoluble and harmonious entity of such strength that the eleventh-century style became the normalized—one may even say the "canonical"—style for centuries to come, surviving in its essence, though altered in detail, even after the fall of Constantinople.

In the iconographic realm one may note, notwithstanding the continuation of a rich tradition ever-present in Byzantine art, the development of new subject matter such as the illustrations of monastic treatises, which achieve the same richness and expressiveness as the more traditional biblical and patristic illustrations. The new ascetic and spiritualizing trend affects in this period even the miniatures of classical subject matter.

The most fundamental change in eleventh-century iconography was the transformation of a comparatively more descriptive painting into a more complex one in which the liturgical element increased steadily. Certainly liturgical art had existed before the eleventh century, but it now became by far the predominant factor in all ramifications of religious painting. It found its newly strengthened position in the concentration on and lavish illustration of the leading liturgical books: the Psalter, the menologion and, most important of all, the Gospel lectionary. In these manuscripts changes and innovations occurred which were paralleled by similar ones in icon and monumental painting, art forms which also became thoroughly impregnated with a sense of liturgical order. The culminating point in eleventh-century iconography was reached when the liturgical art crystallized into larger programs which were so thoroughly adjusted to the orthodox rite that the Church never felt the need to change them in their essence, though in detail alterations and accretions occurred from time to time. To the advantage of Byzantine civilization, the harmonious art of the eleventh century fulfilled for subsequent centuries the need of an all-pervading liturgical art.

N his fundamental treatment of Byzantine book illumination, Kondakov[1] conceived of the development of this branch of art on the basis of political history. Byzantine book illumination, he stated, emerged in the early Byzantine period, the first Golden Age, and fell back into obscurity after the conquest of Constantinople in 1204, i.e., after the end of the second Golden Age. It is true that in a final chapter he dealt briefly with selected manuscripts of a later date, but he considered them to be degenerate, assuming that the artistic production had more or less stopped after the conquest of the capital and never recuperated from its breakdown even after the return of the Palaeologan emperors in 1261. This concept was adopted by most Byzantine scholars after the appearance of Kondakov's epoch-making work. Brockhaus, in dealing with the illustrated manuscripts on Mount Athos,[2] was one of the first to follow Kondakov's judgment about the decline after 1200; but at the same time, when he came to describe certain of the Late Byzantine manuscripts like the Gospel book in Pantokratoros (cod. 47) from the year 1301 or the one in Vatopedi (cod. 938) from the year 1304 (Figs. 319–320), he could not suppress some appreciation of the artistic quality of the miniatures, describing them as "excelling by the carefulness of their decoration."[3] If one compares the evan-

gelists of these Gospels with those miniatures which Kondakov ascribes to the same period, one gets the impression that the great Russian scholar unfortunately had selected a series of provincial manuscripts for the characterization of the Late Byzantine period while those of higher quality were either not yet known in his time or were wrongly dated. Dalton's handbook[4] does not even touch the question of book illumination after the twelfth century, and Wulff[5] passes lightly over the thirteenth and fourteenth centuries, considering manuscripts of this period as disintegrated products.

Only in the last twenty years has the book illumination of the Late Byzantine period attracted more attention, but this interest, as shown by Diehl, Ebersolt, and Gerstinger,[6] concerns the iconographical rather than the stylistic aspect. The comparatively numerous classical texts with illustrations in this later period, the considerable number of historical portraits, and the huge miniature cycle

Reprinted with permission from *Gazette des Beaux-Arts*, 86 (1944), pp. 193–214.

[1] N. P. Kondakov, *Histoire de l'art Byzantin considéré principalement dans les miniatures* (Paris, 1886–91).

[2] H. Brockhaus, *Die Kunst in den Athos-Klöstern* (Leipzig, 1891).

[3] Ibid., p. 235.

[4] O. M. Dalton, *Byzantine Art and Archaeology* (Oxford, 1911), chap. vii.

[5] O. Wulff, *Altchristliche und byzantinische Kunst*, 2 (Berlin, 1924), 540.

[6] Ch. Diehl, *Manuel d'art Byzantin*, 2 (Paris, 1926), 872 ff.; J. Ebersolt, *La miniature Byzantine* (Paris, 1926), pp. 54 ff.; H. Gerstinger, *Die griechische Buchmalerei* (Vienna, 1926), pp. 37 ff. [Recent scholarship has greatly rectified this imbalance as is evidenced by the fact that V. Lazarev devoted more than a fourth of his *Storia della pittura Bizantina* (Turin, 1967) to art after 1204. For a review of this period in light of current scholarship cf. K. M. Swoboda, "In den Jahren 1950 bis 1961 erschienene Werke zur byzantinischen und weiteren östchristlichen Kunst," *Kunstgeschichtliche Anzeigen*, V (1961/62), 132 ff.; here extensive bibliography.]

of the only preserved illustrated historical chronicle of Johannes Scylitzes in Madrid[7] are chiefly responsible for this growing interest. The same scholars treated this period as a whole as decadent from the stylistic viewpoint, although in exceptional cases they find words of high praise for miniatures like those of the Johannes Cantacuzenus manuscript in Paris (Bibliothèque Nationale, cod. gr. 1242) which dates between 1370 and 1375.[8]

Alpatov was the first to recognize the peculiar artistic values of good Palaeologan book illumination. Aided by his familiarity with Russian icon painting, which owes so much to Palaeologan art, he saw more clearly than any Western scholar at that time the formative elements of Late Byzantine art. He analyzed its expressive and picturesque qualities in connection with a cycle of full-page miniatures of a New Testament and Psalter manuscript in Moscow (Historical Museum, cod. 25), a manuscript which he attributed rightly to the fourteenth century,[9] whereas Kondakov had classified it among the manuscripts of the second Golden Age.[10] No wonder Alpatov became suspicious, whether or not there might be other manuscripts, hitherto wrongly dated, among those

generally ascribed to the Middle Byzantine period.[11] Stimulated by this new trend of Byzantine scholarship, Buberl and Gerstinger in their catalogue grouped quite a number of other Greek manuscripts of high artistic quality around the Vienna Gospel Book (Nationalbibliothek, gr. 300), which contains a set of splendid Palaeologan miniatures.[12]

Even these scholars who started out to establish the existence of a highly developed Palaeologan school still maintained another of Kondakov's notions, namely, that the intervening decades of the Latin Conquest did not produce works of art of any standard. The judgment of Gerstinger that "the artistic activities of the capital were nearly completely shut off for more than half a century"[13] is typical, as is the statement of Tikkanen that "the Byzantine book illumination during the foreign rule of the Latins shows the lamentable picture of a complete disintegration of an artistic system once so firmly formulated, and of a falling back into a primitivity of artistic incapacity."[14] It must be made clear, however, that these opinions were not based upon any documentary evidence of disintegrated works of art of this

[7] [S. Cirac Estopañan, *Skyllitzes Matritensis* (Barcelona and Madrid, 1965).]

[8] H. Omont, *Miniatures des plus anciens manuscrits grecs de la Bibliothèque Nationale* (2d ed.; Paris, 1929), pls. CXXVI–CXXVII.

[9] M. V. Alpatov, "A Byzantine Illuminated Manuscript of the Palaeologue Epoch in Moscow," *Art Bulletin*, 12 (1930), 207 ff.

[10] Kondakov, *L'art Byzantin*, II, 160. A twelfth-century date was also accepted by Gerstinger, *Buchmalerei*, p. 47.

[11] Alpatov, "Illuminated Manuscript," p. 218.

[12] P. Buberl and H. Gerstinger, *Die byzantinischen Handschriften der Nationalbibliothek in Wien* ("Beschreibendes Verzeichnis der illuminierten Handschriften in Österreich," N.F., 4 [Leipzig, 1938]), Part II, 64 and pls. XXXI–XXXIIa. [For a more recent list of manuscripts attributed to the thirteenth century consult Lazarev, *Pittura Bizantina*, pp. 276 ff. and pp. 335 ff., n. 57.]

[13] Gerstinger, *Buchmalerei*, p. 37.

[14] J. J. Tikkanen, *Studien über die Farbengebung in der mittelalterlichen Buchmalerei* (Helsinki, 1933), p. 183.

critical period, but upon the preconceived idea that, because of political disturbance in Constantinople during the Latin Conquest, the social and economic conditions prevented any production of art, a theory which more than once has misled art historians.

On the other hand, looking at Byzantine painting from the viewpoint of the West, it can be observed that, after strong but not lasting receptions of Byzantine influence in the Carolingian and Ottonian periods, the most profound and the most continuous infiltration of Byzantine style that ever took place occurred at the end of the twelfth and through most of the thirteenth century. The book illumination of Saxonia and Thuringia, as Haseloff successfully demonstrated,[15] is completely dominated by the Byzantine style, and this influence is hardly less penetrating in other provinces of Germany.[16] Since the history of Byzantine book illumination had not been sufficiently developed from the stylistic point of view at the time Haseloff proved its influence upon the West, he and others after him dealt with the Eastern parallels without embarking on their dating, so that one cannot get a clear idea of which of the Byzantine documents they quote could actually have served as models. The most natural conclusion, of course, would be to assume the existence of a highly developed thirteenth-century book illumination which was capable of influencing the West throughout nearly a century. But here the Western art historians were confronted with the verdict of the Byzantinists, according to whom, as already mentioned, nothing much worthwhile had been produced in Constantinople during this critical period. One way out of this difficulty was the assumption that the great amount of spoils taken in 1204 in Constantinople was the main source for the acquaintance of the Occident with Byzantine art. One becomes suspicious, however, whether the spoils of the capital are a sufficient explanation for the powerful influence which Byzantine art exerted on the West for nearly three generations after the fall of the Eastern capital. But do we really have to assume that in the period of the Latin Conquest Constantinople did not produce anything? Why could it not have been that the Eastern capital, even in the time of foreign domination, produced those manuscripts which gave so decisive a turn to the development of Western, notably German, book illumination? But where are these Byzantine models? Are they all lost or hidden among the unpublished material, or are some of them perhaps already known and only wrongly dated?

Athens Codex 118 and the Wolfenbüttel Sketchbook

One of those German manuscripts so closely dependent on a Byzantine model, as Goldschmidt has made clear, is the Saxonian Gospel book in the Rathaus of Goslar,[17] a manuscript which can be

---

[15] A. Haseloff, *Eine Thüringisch-sächsische Malerschule des XIII. Jahrhunderts* (Strasbourg, 1897).

[16] H. Swarzenski, *Die lateinischen illuminierten Handschriften des XIII. Jahrhunderts in den Ländern an Rhein, Main, und Donau* (Berlin, 1936).

[17] A. Goldschmidt, *Das Evangeliar im Rathaus zu Goslar* (Berlin, 1910). [Byzantine influence in the Latin West during the thirteenth century is treated in the fundamental study by

dated between the years 1230 and 1240. Yet, there is another manuscript in which the Byzantine style seems to have been copied with even greater purity; this is a sketchbook in the Herzog August Bibliothek at Wolfenbüttel (cod. 61/62 Aug. oct.) which contains on twelve leaves sketches of author figures and scenes from the New Testament.[18] Rücker and Hahnloser, the editors of the sketchbook, realized that its closest connection was with the Goslar Gospels and therefore ascribed it likewise to Saxonia and dated it also between 1230 and 1240. Though rightly claiming Byzantine miniatures as its immediate source, the editors apparently knew no

parallels exact enough to be considered as possible models and consequently referred instead to monumental paintings, quoting the frescoes of the Protaton Church on Mount Athos and the mosaics of Monreale and of San Marco in Venice as the comparatively closest parallels.

Yet, for at least some of the sketches, very precise Byzantine parallels can be adduced, for instance, for two seated evangelists on folio 91 (Fig. 206), one of whom reads in an open scroll while the second holds one hand over his left knee and raises the other as if he were touching a lectern in front of him. Even in smallest details, both figures resemble two evangelists of the Greek Gospel book (cod. 118) of the National Library at Athens.[19] The evangelist reading in the scroll corresponds to the Matthew of the Athens

---

H. Buchthal, *Miniature Painting in the Latin Kingdom of Jerusalem* (Oxford, 1957). A symposium, "The Byzantine Contribution to Western Art of the Twelfth and Thirteenth Centuries," was conducted under the direction of E. Kitzinger and K. Weitzmann at the Dumbarton Oaks Center for Byzantine Studies in the Spring of 1965. Several of the papers delivered at this symposium have been published in *Dumbarton Oaks Papers*, 20 (1966): K. Weitzmann, "Various Aspects of Byzantine Influence on the Latin Countries from the Sixth to the Twelfth Century" and "Icon Painting in the Crusader Kingdom"; E. Kitzinger, "The Byzantine Contribution to Western Art in the Twelfth and Thirteenth Centuries"; J. Stubblebine, "Byzantine Influence in Thirteenth-Century Italian Panel Painting"; and H. Buchthal, "Early Fourteenth-Century Illuminations from Palermo."]

[18] F. Rücker and H. R. Hahnloser, *Das Musterbuch von Wolfenbüttel* ("Mitteilungen der Gesellschaft für Vervielfältigende Kunst," [Vienna, 1929]). [Cf. R. W. Scheller, *A Survey of Medieval Model Books* (Haarlem, 1963), pp. 78 ff.; Weitzmann, "Icon Painting," pp. 75 ff.; and idem, "Zur byzantinischen Quelle des Wolfenbüttler Musterbuches," *Festschrift Hans R. Hahnloser zum 60. Geburtstag 1959* (Basel and Stuttgart, 1961), pp. 223 ff.]

[19] P. Buberl, *Die Miniaturhandschriften der Nationalbibliothek in Athen* ("Denkschriften der Akademie der Wissenschaften in Wien," 60 [Vienna, 1917]), Part II, 23, no. 24 and pl. XXX.; A. Delatte, *Les manuscrits à miniatures et à ornements des bibliothèques à Athènes* (Liège, 1926), p. 2, no. 2 and pl. I. [For more recent literature on the Athens Gospels as well as on the other manuscripts discussed in this article cf. Lazarev, *Pittura Bizantina*; Swoboda, "Werke zur byzantinischen Kunst,"; O. Demus, "Die Entstehung des Paläologenstils in der Malerei," *Berichte zum XI. Internationalen Byzantinisten-Kongress. München, 1958* (Munich, 1958), pp. 16 ff.; idem, "Studien zur byzantinischen Buchmalerei des 13. Jahrhunderts," *Jahrbuch der österreichischen byzantinischen Gesellschaft*, 9 (1960), 77 ff.; and R. Hamann-MacLean and O. Rösser, "Der Berliner Codex Graecus 66 und seine nächsten Verwandten als Beispiele des Stilwandels im frühen 13. Jahrhundert," *Studien zur Buchmalerei und Goldschmiedekunst des Mittelalters. Festschrift für Karl Hermann Usener zum 60. Geburtstag am 19 August 1965* (Marburg an der Lahn, 1967), pp. 225 ff.]

Gospels (Fig. 204). One may follow the turns and overlappings of the folds over the right shoulder and arm or those of the end of the mantle which falls down from the left arm, partly ending in a zigzag line between the legs, partly crossing the lap and forming two outward loops. Or one may compare every turn of the zigzag of the lower edges of the tunic and the mantle in order to see how very close the Saxonian drawing is to the Byzantine miniature. The same detailed comparison can be made between the second evangelist of the sketchbook and the Mark of the Athens Gospels (Fig. 309). It is sufficient to point at details such as the system of folds on the sleeve or the tripartite arrangement of the mantle, which is draped around the waist like a sash. Even the cushion is copied faithfully, but, whereas in the Greek example it is distinguished from the mantle mainly by its colors, in the sketch it looks like a part of the mantle itself since the texture of the material is the same.

Furthermore, the figure of Luke of the Athens Gospels, who holds an open scroll in both hands and at the same time an open codex in his lap,[20] also occurs in the sketchbook on folio 78,[21] and again each single fold of the tunic and the mantle which appears in the miniature is repeated in the sketch with an amazing exactitude. Only John, who, like Luke, holds an open scroll,[22] is not found among the sketches in Wolfenbüttel.

This omission can have several causes. Either John was on one of the lost pages of the sketchbook,[23] or the model used by the draftsman may already have been fragmentary.

From this comparison between Byzantine miniatures and Saxonian drawings, we learn two facts which are of far-reaching importance for the general understanding of Western painting of this period as well as for the history of Byzantine book illumination. First, we realize that the connection between the two distant provinces of art is much closer than has been assumed hitherto. Although Hahnloser in his analysis of the sketchbook goes quite far in emphasizing the close relationship between the East and the West—a position which resulted in some unjustified criticism from German scholars who tried to limit the Byzantine influence as far as possible[24]—in our opinion he does not go far enough. In the light of the comparisons made above, it is difficult to maintain Hahnloser's conclusion that the *ductus* of the lines in the sketches deviates somewhat from the model because of the copyist's individuality and because of his German background and training. There is hardly a single line in the rather complex system of folds which cannot be traced to the evangelists of the Athens Gospels; but rather, the notion that the Western copyist had accumulated the lines of folds in a more dense system must be reversed. The drapery of the evangelists of the Athens Gospels actually possesses more

[20] Buberl, *Miniaturhandschriften*, pl. XXX, no. 84.
[21] Rücker and Hahnloser, *Musterbuch*, p. 3 and fig. II.
[22] Buberl, *Miniaturhandschriften*, pl. XXX, no. 85.

[23] Rücker and Hahnloser, *Musterbuch*, p. 4.
[24] A. Stange, "Beiträge zur sächsischen Buchmalerei des XIII. Jahrhunderts," *Münchener Jahrbuch der bildenden Kunst*, N.F., 6 (1929), 305, n. 11a.

turns and overlappings of folds than the Saxonian draftsman has copied. Nevertheless, the peculiar artistic skill of the Western artist may be seen in his capacity to transform into a pen-drawing style what the Greek miniaturist so capably expressed in a picturesque manner with colors and with an additional net of highlights. Placing the Wolfenbüttel sketches alongside the miniatures of the Athens Gospels, one may even question for a moment whether they are tracings or freehand drawings. That they are free renderings seems more probable and is supported by the fact that the Saxonian artist placed different heads upon the bodies of the evangelists, heads which also reveal a Byzantine character but do not belong to the same set of evangelist portraits as those of the Athens Gospels.

There is good reason to believe that the other figures of the Wolfenbüttel sketchbook, author portraits as well as figures from New Testament scenes, were as closely copied from Byzantine models as were the three evangelists just discussed. For some of them exact models may perhaps be found in the existing material of Byzantine book illumination, but for others the models have very likely perished.

The implications of the close connection between the Wolfenbüttel sketchbook and the Athens Gospels are even more important for the history of Byzantine art than for Western art. It can now be taken for granted that the peculiar style represented in the miniatures of Athens 118 must have existed around the years 1230–40, that is, at the time the sketches were made. Since it cannot be proved that Athens 118 itself was used by the Saxonian draftsman, one cannot rely on the date around 1240 as an absolute *terminus ante quem* for the evangelists of the Athens manuscript, but nevertheless the model of the sketchbook must have been a product of the same scriptorium and of the same period. Thus, one can hardly go astray in ascribing the Athens manuscript to the first half of the thirteenth century. Such a date may seem rather vague to a historian of Western art, who can often be accurate within a decade in a period like the thirteenth century where the development of style underwent quick changes. But in Byzantine art, where the material is scarcer, more dispersed, and less accessible, the situation is quite different, at least in the present state of scholarship in this field. The Athens Gospels itself is a good case with which to demonstrate the insecurity of dating. Sakkelion,[25] Gregory,[26] and Delatte date it in the eleventh century, while Buberl, who first recognized the late Byzantine elements in its style, dates it as late as the fourteenth century— and it is by no means exceptional for Byzantine miniatures of this style to be shifted around within the limits of four centuries.

The dating of the miniatures of Athens 118 in the first half of the thirteenth century requires a revision of the hitherto prevailing opinion that during the Latin Conquest Byzantine book illumination had entirely stopped. Judging from this one document alone, one would have to concede that miniature painting not only continued during this crucial period

---

[25] J. Sakkeliōn, Κατάλογος τῶν χειρογράφων τῆς Ἐθνικῆς Βιβλιοθήκης τῆς Ἑλλάδος (Athens, 1892), p. 21.

[26] C. R. Gregory, *Textkritik des Neuen Testamentes* (Leipzig, 1909), p. 222, no. 785.

but that it even maintained a very high artistic level, showing no signs of disintegration or decadence.

Now, a small but significant detail in the Athens miniatures is easily explained. It has been noticed that the texts on the scrolls held by Matthew, Luke, and John are written in Latin. Sakkelion and Gregory concluded from this evidence that the manuscript was made in Italy, an assumption which Buberl rightly opposed on the basis of style. By dating the Athens miniatures in the first half of the thirteenth century, the Latin inscriptions can be explained most naturally by the assumption that the manuscript was either commissioned by one of the Latin conquerors, or at least adjusted for a Latin customer.

OTHER MANUSCRIPTS FROM THE PERIOD OF THE LATIN EMPIRE

The Gospel book Athens 118 is not an isolated document. There exists quite a number of Greek manuscripts which are stylistically related to it and thus can be dated in the same period and with all probability can be ascribed to the same school. Those manuscripts which we can group around the Athens Gospels may be considered only as the nucleus of a thirteenth-century school of book illumination, yet they are already sufficient in number to show a considerable variety of figural types as well as of subject matter and a remarkable artistic quality throughout, compelling us to locate this school in Constantinople.

Most closely connected to this school is a Gospel book with the pictures of the four evangelists which formerly was in the Athos Library of Andreaskiti (cod. 753) and which was given to the

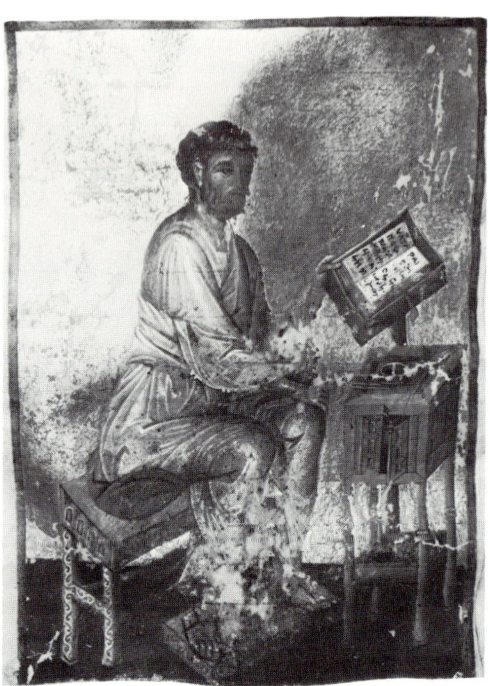

Fig. 309 *Athens, National Library. Cod. 118, fol. 69ᵛ. Mark*

University Library of Princeton (now cod. Garrett 2), along with other valuable Greek, Latin, and Oriental manuscripts,[27] by Robert Garrett of Baltimore. The picture of Luke (Fig. 310) is a precise replica of the Mark of the Athens Gospels (Fig. 309). All folds and highlights are practically identical. If it were not a general phenomenon that Byzantine illuminators of the same scriptorium work in such harmony with each other that often their individual style merges with that of the workshop, one might even be inclined to ascribe both manuscripts to the same painter. Of the remaining three evangelists, Matthew reads intently in a

[27] S. de Ricci and J. Wilson, *Census of Medieval and Renaissance Manuscripts in the United States and Canada*, 1 (New York, 1935–37), 865, no. 2.

Fig. 310 *Princeton, University Library. Ms. Garrett 2, fol. 182ᵛ. Luke*

Fig. 311 *Princeton, University Library. Ms. Garrett 2, fol. 128ᵛ. Mark*

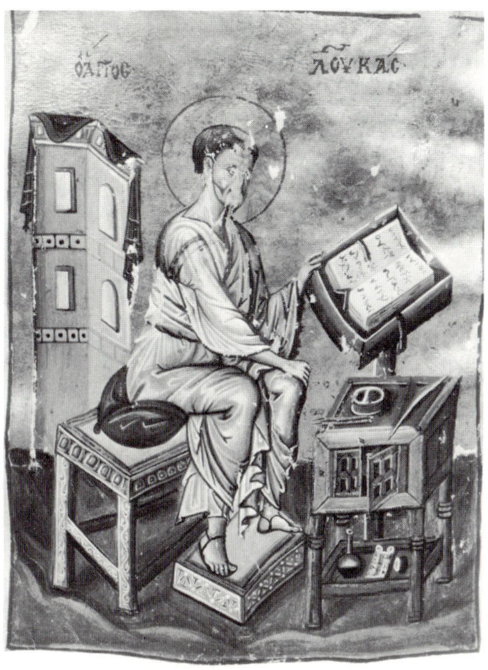

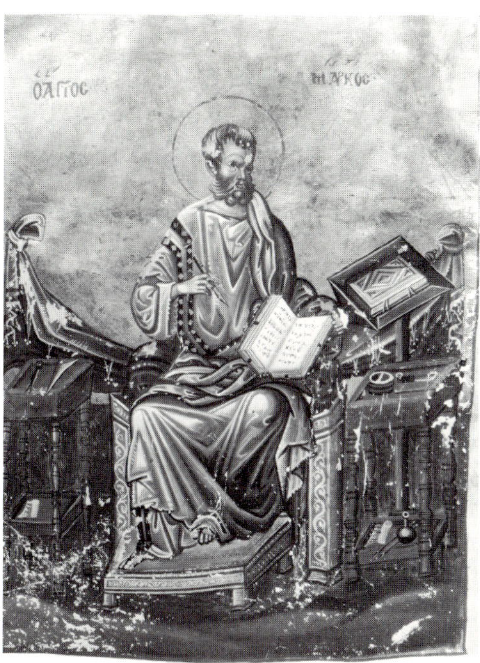

codex which he holds close to his eyes, John writes in a codex which rests on his left knee, and Mark—by far the most impressive figure of the codex (Fig. 311)— is represented in frontal position holding a pen and showing the open codex to the beholder. A lectern on each side and a drapery extending behind the figure from one side to the other give to this picture a strong symmetry and produce a hieratic impression. The date attributed to the Princeton Gospels has varied between the tenth and eleventh centuries on the one side[28] and the fourteenth on the other,[29]

until more recently Friend proposed the thirteenth century,[30] a date which now is strongly supported by the close connection of the miniatures with those of the datable Gospel book in Athens.

Two of the evangelists in the Princeton Gospels are copied exactly in a Gospel book of the Athos monastery (Iviron, cod. 5).[31] John, who reads in a codex

[28] Gregory, *Textkritik*, p. 1155, no. 1530. Kicci and Wilson, *Census*.
[29] B. W. Clark, *A Descriptive Catalogue of Greek New Testament Manuscripts in America* (Chicago, 1937), p. 63. Clark assumed the miniatures to be later insertions in a twelfth/

thirteenth century manuscript, but in our opinion there is no reason to doubt the homogeneity and contemporaneousness of picture and text.
[30] A. M. Friend, Jr., "The Greek Manuscripts [of the Garrett Collection]," *Princeton University Library Chronicle*, 3 (1942), 133 and plate.
[31] S. P. Lambros, *Catalogue of the Greek Manuscripts on Mount Athos*, 2 (Cambridge, 1895– 1900), 1; A. Xyngopoulos, *L'evangiles avec miniatures du monastère d'Iviron au Mont*

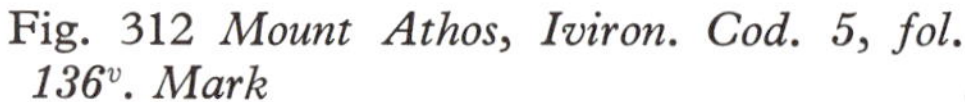

Fig. 312 *Mount Athos, Iviron. Cod. 5, fol. 136ᵛ. Mark*

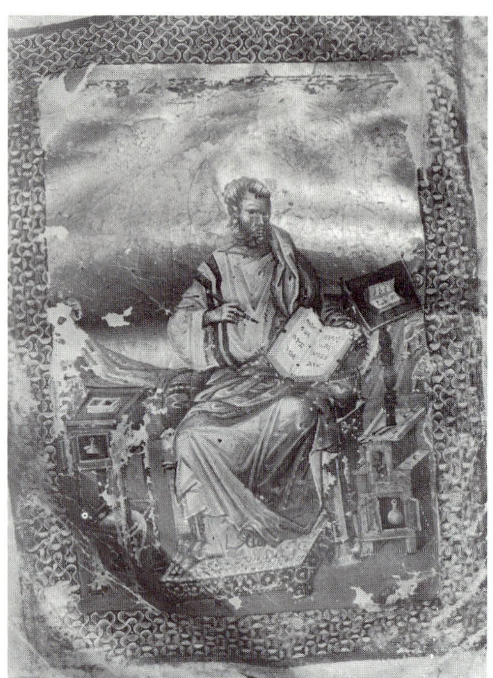

the one around Mark is composed by the crossing of twisted ribbons turned into an all-over pattern.[33] But, otherwise, if one compares the two human figures, every turn or overlapping of the folds (particularly those over the lap), or the highlights and their modeling quality, the differences are more insignificant than is usual between two manuscripts in Western art. Equally close is the comparison of the brush technique in the rendering of the hair and whiskers and the facial expression.

Of the remaining two evangelists of the Iviron Gospels, the Matthew who reads in a wide open scroll[34] is a replica of the John of the Athens Gospels;[35] and thus these two manuscripts are linked together in as direct a manner as the manuscripts of Iviron and Princeton. Only the type of Luke holding a codex in his lap with one hand and touching the lectern with the other[36] does not occur either in the Athens or the Princeton Gospels, although he is a type familiar in tenth-century and later manuscripts, particularly for Luke.[37]

which he holds very close to his eyes,[32] is identical to the Matthew of the Princeton manuscript, and the frontally seated Mark is the same in both (cf. Fig. 312 with Fig. 311). These two figures of Mark correspond to such an extent that not only their contemporaneousness is unquestionable, but once more one is tempted to attribute both manuscripts to the same hand. There are only small differences: the shape of the lectern and the fact that in the one instance it supports a closed and in the other an open codex. Furthermore, in contrast to the Princeton miniatures, all evangelist pictures in Iviron have broad ornamental frames;

Athos (Athens, 1932), p. 7 and pls. 12–57. [Numerous illustrations in Lazarev, *Pittura Bizantina*, pls. 375–82.]

[32] Xyngopoulos, *L'evangiles*, pl. 43.

[33] This ribbon ornament, late antique in origin, had already been stylized in the West into a pattern, generally called the double-ax motif, several centuries before the Iviron manuscript was made. Cf. R. B. O'Connor, "The Double-Axe Motif," *American Journal of Archaeology*, 24 (1920), 151 ff. We leave the question open whether earlier examples in Byzantine art are lost or whether the ornament in the Iviron picture came to the East under Western influence during the thirteenth century.

[34] Xyngopoulos, *L'evangiles*, pl. 15.

[35] Buberl, *Miniaturhandschriften*, pl. XXX, no. 85.

[36] Xyngopoulos, *L'evangiles*, pl. 35.

[37] For an example consult Weitzmann, *Die byzantinische Buchmalerei des IX. und X. Jahrhunderts* (Berlin, 1935), pl. XXXV, no. 196.

Fig. 313 *Mount Athos, Iviron. Cod. 5, fol. 360ʳ. Anastasis*

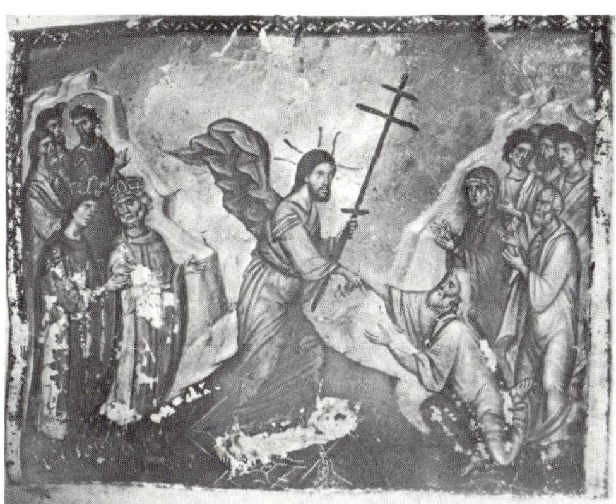

The importance of the Iviron manuscript lies in the fact that, in addition to the pictures of the four evangelists, it contains approximately thirty illustrations from the life of Christ. These scenes, as can be seen in the example of the Anastasis (Fig. 313), are represented in the same style as the evangelists and are contemporary with them, thus proving the existence of large narrative cycles of the New Testament in the thirteenth century. At the same time, they are of such quality that Brockhaus considered this Gospel book one of the most beautiful manuscripts on Athos and the "pearl" of the library of Iviron.[38]

As in the Athens Gospels, we find also in the Iviron manuscript some Latin inscriptions. The book which John reads begins, as is usual in a passage from a lectionary, with "In illo tempore"; in the book upon the lectern one can read the beginning of the Gospel, "In principio erat verbum"; and on the greatly flaked little scroll lying on the desk the word "discipulus" is discernible. However, in contradistinction to the Athens Gospels,

where all four evangelists read Latin in their books or scrolls, John is the only one in the Iviron Gospels who does so. Xyngopoulos has already pointed out[39] that the Latin inscriptions in the picture of John are over an erased Greek inscription. This seems to indicate that the Gospel book was not made for, but was adjusted to, a Latin customer.

Most scholars like Brockhaus,[40] Wulff,[41] and Xyngopoulos have dated the Iviron codex in the twelfth century; whereas two of the best connoisseurs of Byzantine manuscripts, Pokrovsky[42] and Millet,[43] were inclined to take a thirteenth-century origin into consideration. Only Gregory[44] went on record with a date as late as the fourteenth century.

Still closer than all the comparisons we have made thus far between miniatures of two different manuscripts is that between Iviron 5 and a Gospel book in the Bibliothèque Nationale in Paris (cod. gr. 54).[45] In this instance not only are all four evangelists identical types and correspond exactly in their draperies and facial features, but even minor details such as the shape of the furniture, which in the Princeton manuscript presented some slight variations, are practically the same.

---

[38] Brockhaus, *Kunst in den Athos-Klöstern*, pp. 186 and 217.

[39] Xyngopoulos, *L'evangiles*, p. 7.

[40] Brockhaus, *Kunst in den Athos-Klöstern*, p. 217.

[41] Wulff, *Altchristliche und byzantinische Kunst*, II, 535.

[42] N. Pokrovsky, *The Evangile in the Monuments of Iconography* (Saint Petersburg, 1892), p. XVIII and *passim*.

[43] G. Millet, *Recherches sur l'iconographie de l'Evangile* (Paris, 1916), p. 9 and *passim*.

[44] Gregory, *Textkritik*, p. 235, no. 990.

[45] Omont, *Manuscrits grecs*, pls. XC–XCVI. [Lazarev, *Pittura Bizantina*, pls. 384–94.]

Fig. 314 *Paris, Bibliothèque Nationale. Cod. gr. 54, fol. 111ʳ. Mark*

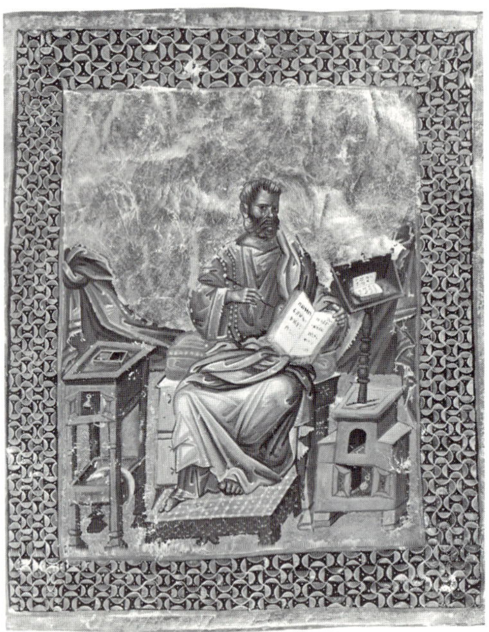

This may again be demonstrated with the figure of Mark (Fig. 314). Small details such as the placing of the ink bottles in the open compartment of both desks, or the ornament of the footstool, or the pattern of the frame—and comparison of this kind could also be made between the remaining three evangelists—make it quite obvious that in this case one set of evangelists is a direct copy of the other; and so there is no need to assume a third manuscript as a common source or intermediary link. If this is true, we would hold that Iviron 5 is the model and Paris gr. 54 the copy. Minute as the differences are, nevertheless it can be observed that the copyist of the Paris manuscript draws the lines and folds in a slightly sharper and more rigid manner and that his sense of the organic structure of the body is somewhat weaker. These small but noticeable differences exclude, in our opinion, the

possibility that the Paris manuscript may be a later replica by the same painter who executed the Iviron codex. Also, like Iviron 5, the Paris manuscript has an extensive cycle of New Testament scenes, some of which are unfinished while others were not even begun in the spaces provided for them. In this narrative cycle the inferiority of the illustrator of the Paris Gospels is even more apparent.

In the Paris manuscript, however, the Latin language is not confined to a few inscriptions on the rolls and codices in the hands of the evangelists; the whole Gospel text is bilingual, with the Greek column at the left and the Latin at the right.[46] Labarte, the first scholar to write about the manuscript,[47] drew from this fact the most natural conclusion that the manuscript was executed "a l'èpoque de la domination des empereurs français (1204–1261)." The Russian scholar Pokrovsky, by the same linguistic reason, proposed a southern Italian origin,[48] and found followers in Gerstinger,[49] Omont,[50] and Tikkanen,[51] although none of them were able to point to any existing Italian parallel. Only Millet, taking a stand against the Italian theory,[52] realized the Constantinopolitan character of the New Testament cycle, and he too, like Labarte, sought the origin of the Paris Gospels "dans l'entourage de quelque prince

---

[46] The Latin text, however, is not complete: the second half of the Gospel of Mark and the whole of Luke are missing.
[47] J. Labarte, *Histoire des arts industriels*, 3 (Paris, 1864–66), 76.
[48] Pokrovsky, *The Evangile*, p. xx and *passim*.
[49] Gerstinger, *Buchmalerei*, p. 38.
[50] Omont, *Manuscrits grecs*, p. 47.
[51] Tikkanen, *Farbengebung*, p. 163.
[52] Millet, *Recherches*, p. 646.

croisé ou de quelque prélat latin." The advocates of an Italian origin dated the manuscript in the fourteenth century, going rather to the other extreme as compared with those scholars who had dated the contemporary Iviron manuscript in the twelfth century. Moreover, Bordier's[53] date in the end of the thirteenth century is quite obviously based on the notion of a vacuum during the period of the Latin occupation. Of all the manuscripts discussed above, the Paris Gospel book indeed seems to be the latest, but at the same time its bilingual text provides a good argument for the seeking of its date within the period of the Latin empire.

The Early Phase of the Style

All evangelist pictures described so far are homogeneous in style and apparently represent a restricted phase within the development of a larger artistic movement. It is a mature phase in which the artists work easily with well-established formulae in a slightly routine manner. Phases of this kind are usually preceded by a preliminary stage in which the actual characteristics of the period are on the verge of being formulated. A manuscript which, in our opinion, represents this postulated early phase is a Gospel book in the Philotheu monastery on Mount Athos (cod. 5) the decoration of which consists of three evangelists, the picture of John being lost.[54] Matthew, reading at close range in a codex, is the same type as Matthew in the Princeton Gospels and as John in the Iviron and Paris Gospels. Mark, the most

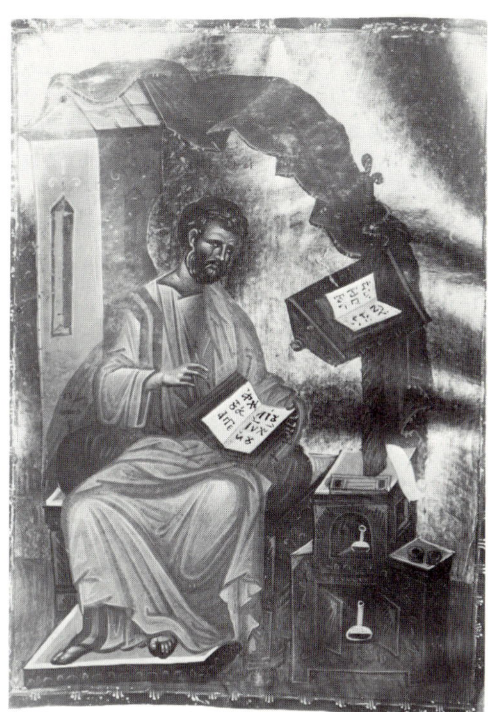

Fig. 315 *Mount Athos, Philotheu. Cod. 5. Mark*

impressive figure among them (Fig. 315), can be identified with the same evangelist of the three discussed manuscripts (Fig. 311 and 312), while Luke, writing in a scroll on his lap, is a type which does not occur among the miniatures thus far mentioned. Although the system of folds in the Mark of the Philotheu manuscript is in principle the same as in the preceding manuscripts, the drapery as a whole is softer. Harsh breaks are avoided and, particularly over the lap, the folds are less crowded and intertwined, achieving a greater plasticity in the modeling of the figure. These features go together with a more organic understanding of a well-proportioned body, in comparison to which the evangelists of all the other Gospels are stiffer and more elongated. It

[53] H. Bordier, *Description des peintures et autres ornements contenues dans les manuscripts grecs de la Bibliothèque Nationale* (Paris, 1885), p. 227.
[54] Lambros, *Catalogue*, I, 151.

should not be overlooked that the other two evangelists of the same manuscript[55] are slightly more developed in the treatment of their folds, so that the difference in the actual date between the Philotheu Gospels on the one hand and those of Princeton, Iviron, and Paris on the other cannot be very great.

It may be recalled that in Latin book illumination, as well, the style of the harsh and broken folds, as represented by the Wolfenbüttel sketchbook and the Goslar Gospels, was preceded by a short phase in which the painter tried to create the greatest possible plasticity of the body by means of a system of soft folds fitting closely to the body. The Queen Ingeborg Psalter in Chantilly (cod. lat. 1695), from the beginning of the thirteenth century,[56] is the best-known example of this phase. This raises the problem of whether the style of the Chantilly Psalter and of other French and English manuscripts of the end of the twelfth and the first two decades of the thirteenth century is already dependent upon Byzantine models in the style of the Mark of Philotheu.

Another manuscript which represents what we consider to be the early phase of our school is the codex Vaticanus gr. 1208 which contains the Acts and Epistles.[57] It is of the highest quality and is decorated with standing author portraits. Particularly the figure of Luke, who writes the beginning of the Acts upon a waving scroll (Fig. 316), shows the same kind of soft

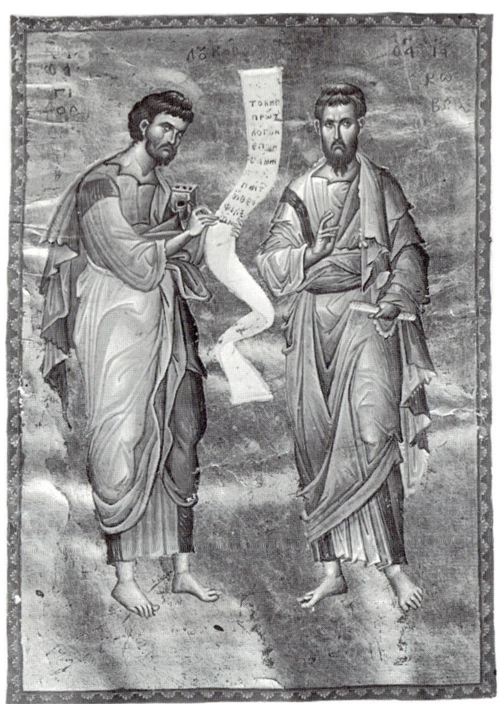

Fig. 316 *Vatican, Biblioteca. Cod. gr. 1208, fol. 4ᵛ. Luke and James*

and flowing folds over the hip and legs as the Mark in Philotheu, whereas in the figure of James, who stands beside Luke, and in the remaining four Epistle writers[58] the illustrator already employs a slightly harder style of folds together with an accumulation of zigzags at the edges of the garments. Furthermore, a close connection between the Philotheu and the Vatican miniatures may also be observed in the facial features, particularly the sharp line which crosses the cheek, and in the brush-technique of the hair.

The model of the Vatican manuscript was in all probability a tenth-century manuscript of the Macedonian Renais-

[55] Still unpublished.

[56] J. Meurgy, *Principaux manuscrits à peintures du Musée Condé à Chantilly* (Paris, 1930), p. 15 and pls. X–XIII.

[57] The Palaeographical Society, *Facsimiles of Manuscripts*. Parts IX–XIII (London, 1879–83), pl. 131.

[58] A. M. Friend, Jr., "The Portraits of the Evangelists in Greek and Latin Manuscripts," *Art Studies*, 5 (1927), 129 and figs. 92–94. [Lazarev, *Pittura Bizantina*, pl. 408.]

sance, similar in style to the Prophet book in the Vatican (cod. Chis. gr. R. VIII. 54. Fig. 42);[59] to such a model can be traced the high degree of plasticity and the well-understood organism of the body. Thus it becomes quite understandable that, at a time when a stylistic grouping of Greek manuscripts had hardly begun, Beissel[60] dated the Vatican New Testament in the tenth/eleventh century and that most scholars followed him with a date in the Middle Byzantine period. Again, Alpatov[61] was the first to recognize in the style of the Epistle writers those peculiar elements which are met in the Palaeologan period, although in our opinion he goes too far in the other direction by trying to date the manuscript in the fourteenth century.

Although we have dealt only with New Testament illustrations, other cycles of miniatures in the same style are by no means lacking. One of the most extensive miniature cycles in all Byzantine book illumination is contained in the Octateuch. On the basis of stylistic criticism, one of the five existing illuminated Octateuch manuscripts can be ascribed to the same period and school as the preceding Gospel books, namely, the Octateuch in the Athos monastery Vatopedi (cod. 602), of which today only Books Leviticus to Ruth are preserved.[62] By comparing such a scene

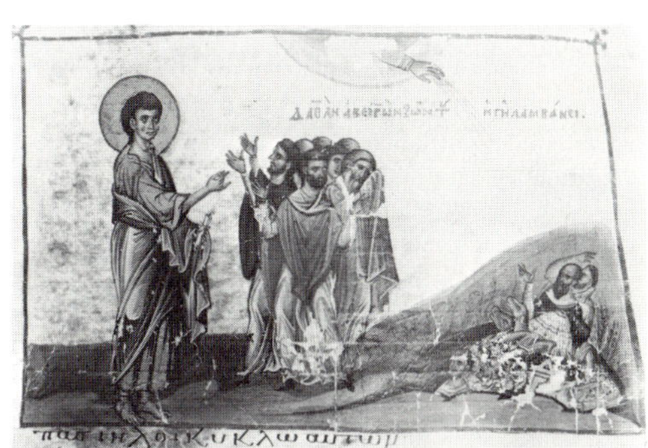

Fig. 317 *Mount Athos. Vatopedi. Cod. gr. 602, fol. 150[r]. Destruction of Korah*

as the Destruction of Korah and his Followers (Fig. 317) with the corresponding scene in the Octateuchs of Smyrna and Istanbul[63]—which represent the Constantinopolitan style of the twelfth century—the later date of the Vatopedi manuscript becomes quite apparent. In the increasing emphasis on the prolonged zigzag folds of the end of his mantle, Moses in Vatopedi 602 is typical as is the flowing quality of the drapery which adds to the restlessness of the figures of the Israelites before him. Both features were met similarly in the Mark of Athens and the Luke of Princeton (Figs. 309–310) and also in the standing authors of Vat. gr. 1208 (Fig. 316). The shape of Moses' head with the characteristic high tuft of hair on the top agrees in particular with the latter. In other miniatures of the Vatopedi manuscript the drapery becomes

[59] A. Muñoz, *I codici greci miniati delle minori biblioteche di Roma* (Florence, 1905), p. 13 and pls. 1–5; Friend, "Portraits of Evangelists," figs. 41–44; Weitzmann, *Byzantinische Buchmalerei*, p. 12 and pl. XII, no. 61.
[60] St. Beissel, *Vaticanische Miniaturen* (Freiburg i. B., 1893), p. 19 and pl. 12.
[61] Alpatov, "Illuminated Manuscript," p. 218.
[62] Kondakov, *L'art Byzantin*, II, 83; Brockhaus, *Kunst in den Athos-Klöstern*, pp. 172 and 212; S. Eustratiades and Arcadios, *Cata-*

logue of the Greek Manuscripts in the Library of the Monastery of Vatopedi on Mount Athos (Cambridge, Mass., 1924), p. 118. [Lazarev, *Pittura Bizantina*, pls. 411–13; Weitzmann, *Aus den Bibliotheken des Athos* (Hamburg, 1963), pp. 21 ff.]
[63] D. C. Hesseling, *Miniatures de l'octateuque grec de Smyrne* (Leiden, 1909), pl. 70, no. 231; Th. Ouspensky, *L'octateuque de la Bibliothèque du Sérail à Constantinople* (Sofia, 1907), pl. XXVII, no. 168.

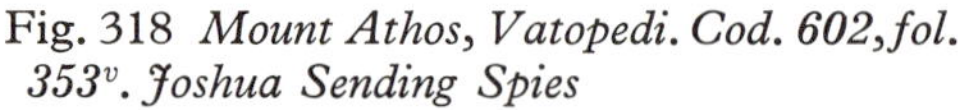

Fig. 318 *Mount Athos, Vatopedi. Cod. 602, fol. 353^v. Joshua Sending Spies*

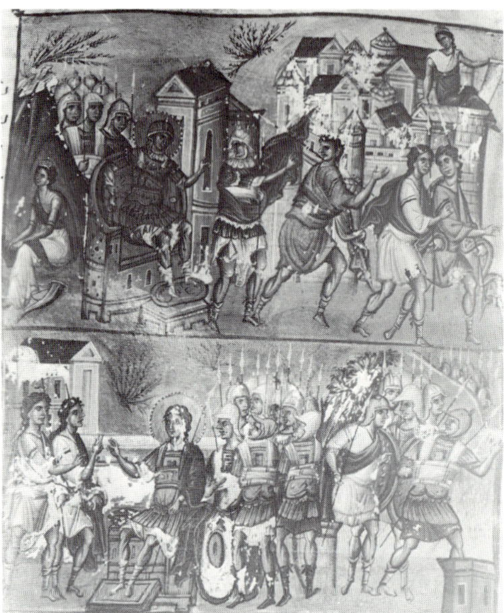

very stiff and geometrical. This is apparent in some illustrations of the Book of Joshua, for instance in the sending out of spies to the city of Ai (Fig. 318), where the mantle of the spy next to Joshua is billowed up in a strikingly manneristic way. Other late features of this miniature are the affected manner in which Joshua's right hand plays with the knob of the armchair and the type of the chair itself with its high semicircular back. On the basis of a miniature like this, one might be inclined to ascribe the Vatopedi Octateuch to the advanced and mature phase of the group.

To assume a thirteenth-century date for the Vatopedi Octateuch means once more a deviation from the opinions of most scholars, who considered this manuscript to be earlier than the Octateuchs in Smyrna, Istanbul, and the cod. gr. 746 in the Vatican which all are traditionally dated in the eleventh or the early twelfth

centuries. A noticeable exception, however, is Ouspensky,[64] the only art historian who has dated the Vatopedi codex, which he had seen and carefully studied, and which he placed in the middle of the thirteenth century. A comparatively early date as assumed by most scholars was founded, however, not on the basis of stylistic considerations alone, but on another fact which at a first glance seems to favor an earlier origin. It had rightly been observed that the scenes from the book of Joshua are much closer to the famous Rotulus in the Vatican[65] than are the corresponding scenes of the other Octateuchs. For example, the spy scene has two personifications of cities, which appear in no other Octateuch, the city of Jericho on the ground in the lower left corner, and the city of Ai placed on top of the city wall instead of a hill alongside it as in the Rotulus. How can this close dependence of the Vatopedi Octateuch upon the Rotulus on the one hand and its late stylistic features on the other be reconciled with each other ? The only possible solution lies, in the opinion of the writer, in the assumption that the actual Vatican roll had been directly available to the illustrator of the Vatopedi codex, enabling him to revitalize his style under its influence and to take over quite a number of details which do not appear in other copies. This would mean that in the thirteenth century the Vatican Rotulus was still in the imperial library of Constantinople as one of its most highly prized treasures.

Another Old Testament manuscript

[64] Ibid., p. 99.
[65] *Il Rotulo di Giosuè. Codice Vaticano Palatino Greco 431* ("Codices e Vaticanis Selecti," Vol. 5 [Milan, 1905]), [Weitzmann, *The Joshua Roll* (Princeton, 1948)].

which we would like to connect with our group is a tiny Psalter manuscript in the Vatican Library (cod. Barb. gr. 285 Fig. 200) which DeWald recently introduced into the literature of art history.[66] It contains an inserted miniature with the fight of David and Goliath, of unique importance because of its aedicula-like frame in Pompeian style which makes it one of the most classical pictures in all Byzantine book illumination. DeWald rightly pointed out that Goliath's armor has its closest parallel in miniatures of the Vatopedi Octateuch. To this observation another may be added. The peculiar treatment of Goliath's mantle with its symmetrical zigzag edges has its parallel in the similarly stylized mantle of the spy next to Joshua in the Octateuch miniature described above (Fig. 318), save that in the latter the mantle flutters in the opposite direction. DeWald assumed for the Vatopedi Octateuch the hitherto traditional date of the eleventh century and—regarding the stringier style of the Octateuch as more advanced—placed the Psalter miniature near to it in the second half of the tenth century. Now, if the Octateuch must be attributed to the thirteenth instead of the eleventh century, the Psalter miniature also has to be dated in the thirteenth century, even if one accepts DeWald's observation that it is slightly earlier than the Octateuch.

The Place of the Latin Conquest Manuscripts in Byzantine Art

In ascribing a group of manuscripts of high artistic quality to the period of the Latin conquest and in trying to fill what hitherto had been considered a gap in the development of Constantinopolitan book illumination, the author merely follows in the footsteps of those scholars who have successfully filled a similar gap in the history of monumental painting. Although the thirteenth-century frescoes and some from the end of the twelfth, which have been made known fairly recently, were not found in Constantinople itself but in various countries of the Balkans, primarily Serbia and Bulgaria, their style is generally and with good reason considered to be a radiation of that of the capital. The milestones are the frescoes of the Panteleïmon church in Nerez[67] from the year 1164, those of the Ascension church in Mileševo[68] executed between the years 1234 and 1237, and those of the Panteleïmon church in Sopoćani,[69] datable around 1265.

[66] E. T. DeWald, "A Fragment of a Tenth-Century Byzantine Psalter in the Vatican Library," *Medieval Studies in Memory of A. Kingsley Porter*, 1 (Cambridge, Mass., 1939), 139 ff. and fig. 2. [Weitzmann, *Geistige Grundlagen und Wesen der Makedonischen Renaissance* (Cologne and Opladen, 1963), pp. 44 ff., translated and reprinted herewith, pp. 215 ff.]

[67] N. Okunev, "La découverte des anciennes fresques du monastère de Nérèz," *Slavia*, 6 (1927–28), 603 ff.; Muratov, *La peinture byzantine* (Paris, 1928), pls. CLIII–CLVI.

[68] V. R. Petković, *La peinture serbe du moyen-age* (Belgrade, 1930–34), I, pls. 8b–12; II, 12 and pls. VI–XXI; N. Okunev, "Mileševo, un monument de l'art serbe au XIIIe siècle," *Byzantinoslavica*, 7 (1937–38), 33–107; Muratov, *Peinture byzantine*, pl. CLXI.

[69] N. Okunev, "Les peintures murales à l'eglise de Sopoćani," *Byzantinoslavica*, 1 (1929), 119 ff.; Petković, *Peinture serbe*, I, pls. 13–23; II, 14 and pl. CL; Muratov, *Peinture byzantine*, pls. CLXII–CLXV. [For the vast and ever-increasing literature on the Balkan frescoes see Demus, "Entstehung," pp. 20 ff. and *passim*; Swoboda, "Werke zur byzantinischen Kunst," and R. Hamann-McLean and H. Hallensleben, *Die Monumen-*

It has been observed by Okunev, the discoverer of the important frescoes of Nerez, that as early as the end of the twelfth century the Byzantine fresco style was revitalized in a classical manner. The three-dimensionality of the figures increased, their postures became more agile, their faces in particular showed a greater individualization, often a pathetic expression, and the artist exhibited a greater interest in psychological affects than had been known at any previous period of Byzantine art. Thus, features which hitherto had been considered typical of the so-called Palaeologan Renaissance can now be traced back to the period of the last Comnenes. Muratov in his *Byzantine Painting*[70] called this new movement neo-Hellenistic. This term seems, at least to some extent, to have originated from the realization that the older term Palaeologan Renaissance is too limited, since it leaves out nearly a whole century of the movement prior to the accession to the throne of the Palaeologan Dynasty. On the other hand, the term neo-Hellenistic is, in the opinion of the writer, not distinct enough, since it does not differentiate this classical movement from the one which took place in the tenth century under the Macedonians and which with equally good reason might have been called neo-Hellenistic. Until a better term is proposed, one might call this movement more generally the Late Byzantine Renaissance, although the year 1204, which is usually considered as the beginning of the Late Byzantine epoch, is too late a date for the birth of the new

movement.[71] But this term includes at least the whole thirteenth century which, to judge from frescoes and manuscripts alike, was the climactic phase of this late renaissance.

The manuscripts grouped together in the present sketch belong to the same artistic movement as the Serbian wall-paintings described above, and the terminology used for the description of the miniatures is essentially the same as that used by Byzantine scholars for the description of those frescoes. But, compared with the many dated frescoes, the chronology of the manuscripts is based solely on the date of the Wolfenbüttel sketchbook which, as already mentioned, was produced between 1230 and 1240. This, for the time being, is the only focal point around which the Gospel books of Athens, Princeton, Iviron, and Paris can be grouped. Not that dated Greek manuscripts were entirely lacking in this period but, unfortunately, those known to the writer show a style which differs greatly from that of the manuscripts treated in the present study and indicates a localization outside of the capital.[72] At first glance the

---

talmalerei in Serbien und Makedonien* (Geissen, 1963).]

[70] *Peinture byzantine,* pp. 127 ff.

[71] [Weitzmann returned to a discussion of the origins of the so-called Palaeologan style in "Eine spätkomnenische Verkündigungsikone des Sinai und die zweite byzantinische Welle des 12. Jahrhunderts," *Festschrift für Herbert von Einem zum 16 Februar 1965* (Berlin, 1965), pp. 299 ff.]

[72] The Benaki Museum in Athens possesses a Gospel book from the year 1244 (Vitr. 34, no. 4; unpublished) with the miniatures of Christ standing between the four evangelists and John and Prochoros. Although of considerable quality, nevertheless they represent a local style. A Gospel book in Brescia (cod. A. III. 12) with the portrait of Luke from the year 1257 belongs to southern Italy according to A. Muñoz, *Miniature bizantini*

situation looks more favorable for the end of the twelfth century since dated manuscripts with illustrations from that time survive in greater numbers than they do from the period of the Latin conquest. But again our hopes are frustrated, however, since among those manuscripts known to the writer not a single one can be claimed as a Constantinopolitan product,[73]

perhaps with the exceptions of a Psalter in the Vatican (cod. Barb. gr. 320 Fig. 198) which bears the date A.D. 1177[74] and contains seven miniatures of the so-called aristocratic recension which might very well have been executed in the capital. Unfortunately, its date is not above suspicion since it is written by a sixteenth-century hand. In the miniatures of this Psalter, for instance the frontally standing David[75] or the Anointment of David, not the slightest trace is recognizable of an imminent classical revival. In spite of a high technical perfection, the figures are comparatively two-dimensional, somewhat rigid, and without the inner excitement which is so typical of all figures of our group. Rather, they represent the stage of slight stagnation characteristic of the twelfth century in general, a period which seems to have lived mainly from the heritage of the tenth and eleventh cen-

---

nella biblioteca Queriniana di Brescia ("Miscellanea Ceriani" [Milan, 1910]), p. 172. The so-called Bixby Gospels in the Huntington Library in San Marino, California, with the pictures of all four evangelists, bears a date from the year 1251 but as shown by E. Goodspeed ("The Bixby Gospels," *Historical and Linguistic Studies in Literature Related to the New Testament*, Ser. I, 2, Part IV [1915]), this date is unreliable since it appears on later inserted pages.

[73] Of two Gospel books with portraits of the evangelists in Paris (Bibliothèque Nationale, cod. suppl. gr. 612 and gr. 83), the former dated A.D. 1164 (K. and S. Lake, *Dated Greek Minuscule Manuscripts to the Year 1200* [Boston, 1934–39], V, pls. 320–21) is made in a province which stylistically is not yet determined, and the other, dated A.D. 1167 and containing two extremely crude miniatures (Bordier, *Description des peintures*, p. 179; K. and S. Lake, *Minuscule Manuscripts*, 5, pls. 322–25, 330), is executed by a certain Solomon from Noto near Syracuse. A Gospel book in the Vatican (cod. gr. 758) with pictures of John and Luke, has a date from the year A.D. 1173 which, however, is uncertain (Lake, *Minuscule Manuscripts*, 8, pls. 588 and 590). A Gospel book in London (British Museum, cod. Add. 22736) with an uncontestable date of the year 1179 (Lake, *Minuscule Manuscripts*, II, pls. 144–46) possesses four evangelists in a style not unlike that of products from southern Italian schools. Another Gospel book in London (British Museum cod. Add. 5111–5112, Tikkanen, *Farbengebung*, p. 184, n.) possesses evangelist pictures of a remarkable quality which may be products of a Constantinopolitan scrip-

---

torium itself or a center nearby, but, unfortunately, they do not belong to the text which is dated A.D. 1189. Of three dated Gospel books of the last decade of the twelfth century, the cod. Vindob. suppl. gr. 102, now in Naples, from the year A.D. 1192 (Lake, *Minuscule Manuscripts*, IX, pl. 668) and the cod. Vaticanus Barb. gr. 520 from the year 1193 (Lake, *Minuscule Manuscripts*, VIII, pls. 596–99) are both undoubtedly of southern Italian origin, and the third in Moscow (cod. gr. 16) from the year 1199 (Lake, *Minuscule Manuscripts*, VI, pl. 419) shows two pen drawings of the half figure of the Virgin with Child which may have been made at any time after the finishing of the manuscript.

[74] Kondakov, *L'art Byzantin*, II, 53; J. J. Tikkanen, "Die Psalterillustration im Mittelalter," *Acta Societatis Scientiarum Fennicae*, XXXI (1903), 128 and figs. 109 and 128; K. and S. Lake, *Minuscule Manuscripts*, VIII, pl. 593.

[75] A. Venturi, *Storia dell'arte*, 2 (Milan, 1901–48), 442 and fig. 314.

turies. But although no dated manuscript from the end of the twelfth century seems to be preserved which could be connected with the classical revival, it is at least probable that the miniatures of the early phase within our group, particularly the author portraits of the cod. Vat. gr. 1208 (Fig. 316), go back as far as the end of the twelfth century. In this connection, it may be noticed that the style of the Vatican miniatures is very close indeed to the impressive icon with the twelve apostles in the Historical Museum of Moscow[76] for which Muratov proposed a date as early as the end of the twelfth century.

A much clearer contradistinction can be made between the miniatures of our group and those which were made after the coming of the Palaeologan Dynasty to Constantinople. Dated manuscripts from the end of the thirteenth and throughout the fourteenth century which represent the style of Constantinople or affiliated centers are fairly numerous, and their miniatures show, as may be judged from two dated examples from the turn of the fourteenth century, a much more advanced stage of development compared with any miniature seen so far. One is a Gospel book with the portraits of the four evangelists in the Athos monastery Pantokratoros (cod. 47) which was written in the year 1301 by a Theodoros Hagiopetrites.[77] In the figure of Mark,

---

[76] Muratov, *Peinture byzantine*, pl. CLXXII. O. Wulff and M. Alpatov, *Denkmäler der Ikonenmalerei* (Hellerau bei Dresden, 1925), pp. 114 and 270 and fig. 43.
[77] Brockhaus, *Kunst in den Athos-Klöstern*, p. 235; Lambros, *Catalogue*, I, 97; M. Vogel and V. Gardthausen, *Die griechischen Schreiber des Mittelalters und der Renaissance* (Leipzig, 1909), pp. 135–36. According to Lambros and others, the name Hagiopetrites points to the Athos monastery τῆς Πέτρας.

Fig. 319 *Mount Athos, Pantocrator. Cod. 47, fol. 114ᵛ. Mark*

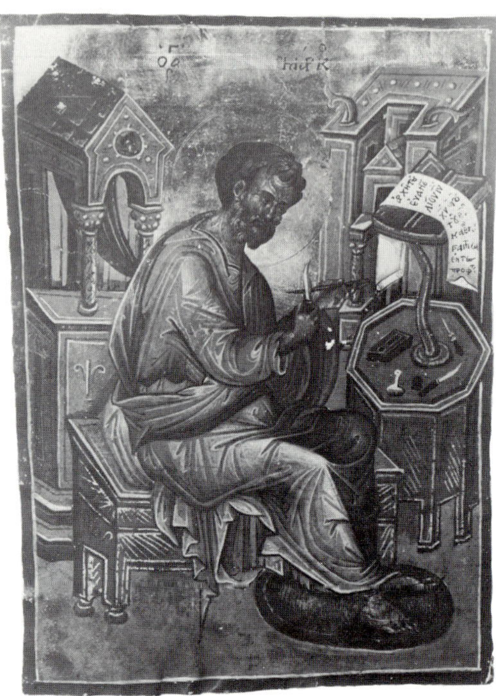

who is sharpening his pen (Fig. 319), the feeling for organic structure of the body is considerably weakened. The sloping shoulders are typical, as is the increase in the width around the waist, which gives to most figures of the Palaeologan period a curious oval-shaped outline. The drapery is no longer as closely attached to the body but tends to obscure the clarity of the bodily structure by means of a decorative system of accumulated, crumpled folds and a dense pattern of diffused highlights. At the same time, this treatment of the drapery increases the feeling of restlessness which is also reflected in the tense and nervous faces. The highlights on the flesh have a function similar to those on the drapery, namely, to dissolve plastic values by a more picturesque technique; the same is true of the treatment of the hair and the beard. Moreover, the low bench, which does its share to make the figures disproportionate by prolonging the upper part of the body, is typical of the Palaeologan period. The furniture is highlighted by golden, comb-like patterns, and likewise the architecture becomes more decorative and less structural. The rectangular niches and the houses turned into aediculae are characteristic. It is true that the picturesque elements which contribute to the dissolution of organism and structure are not always so pronounced as in the evangelist portraits of the Pantokratoros Gospels. In the second, another Gospel book from Mount Athos (Vatopedi cod. 938), which was written in the year 1304 and possesses pictures of all four evangelists,[78] the brush technique is smoother and more in the tradition of the thirteenth century. But at the same time other characteristics of the Palaeologan style are even more exaggerated. Mark (Fig. 320), who holds a codex in his lap while writing in another book on the lectern, sits on an even lower bench than in the Pantokratoros miniature, and thus the unnatural prolongation of the upper part of the body becomes far more apparent.

Judging from these two examples—which could easily be multiplied not only by more dated manuscripts but also by frescoes and mosaics like those of Kariye Djami[79]—it becomes clear that by the beginning of the fourteenth century the phase of the closest contact with the models which had stimulated the new

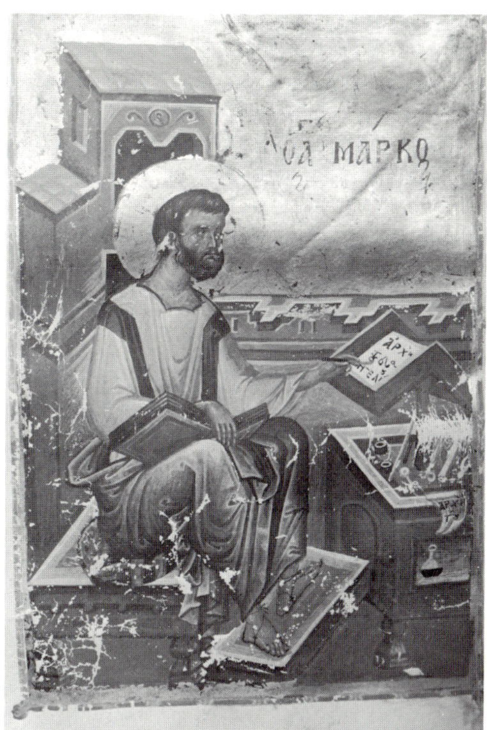

Fig. 320 *Mount Athos, Vatopedi. Cod. 938, fol. 76ᵛ. Mark*

classical movement had already passed.

It must be left to future studies to determine the sources of the Late Byzantine Renaissance.[80] At the present, it may suffice to mention that the stylistic revival goes hand in hand with the reappearance of older iconographical types. This can clearly be shown in the realm of the pictures of the evangelists, which constitute by far the largest contingent in all phases of Byzantine book illumination of which monuments are preserved. For the Matthew of the Athens Gospels, for example, who reads in an open scroll in

---

[78] Brockhaus, *Kunst in den Athos-Klöstern*, p. 235 (here quoted with the old number 714). Eustratiades and Arcadios, *Catalogue*, p. 173.
[79] [See now: P. Underwood, *The Kariye Djami* (New York, 1966).]

[80] Weitzmann, *Byzantinische Buchmalerei*, p. 23 and pls. XXX–XXXI; p. II and pl. XI, no. 57–58; pl. XII, no. 59–60; p. 12 and pl. XII, no. 61; p. 28 and pl. XXXVII, no. 208; pl. XXXVIII, no. 210.

the fashion of the ancients, instead of
writing his Gospels (Fig. 204), no parallel is known to the writer from the immediately preceding centuries. It does not
seem very probable that the Late Byzantine period, except in special cases, had
immediate access to Early Byzantine
miniatures. The main direct source seems
to have been products of the Macedonian
Renaissance. Gospel books like Stauronikita 43 (Figs. 92, 180, 203), or Paris Coislin
195, or Prophet books like Vatican Chis.
gr. R. VIII, 54 (Fig. 42), and Turin B.I.
2[81]—to enumerate only those manuscripts
of the tenth century whose date seems
uncontested—contain all those stylistic
elements which stimulated the new classical movement at the end of the twelfth
century. The general cultural situation in
Constantinople at the end of the twelfth
century, a time when classical studies had
risen to new heights with scholars like
Johannes Tzetzes and Eustathios, provided a fertile ground on which an artistic
renaissance could develop.

The influence of the renaissance was
felt throughout the fourteenth century
and even the fifteenth century until the
fall of Constantinople. It was the last of
the several classical movements which at
certain intervals from the fourth century
on had revitalized the art of the Eastern
capital.

[81] [For a more detailed discussion of the re-
liance of the thirteenth century on good
tenth-century models cf. Weitzmann, "Eine
Pariser-Psalter-Kopie des 13. Jahrhunderts
auf dem Sinai," *Jahrbuch der österreichischen
byzantinischen Gesellschaft*, 6 (1957), 125 ff.;
idem, "A Fourteenth Century Greek Gospel
Book with Wash-drawings," *Gazette des
Beaux-Arts*, LXII (1963), 92 ff.; and idem,
Geistige Grundlagen, pp. 42 ff.; herewith,
pp. 212 ff.]

"Der Pariser Psalter MS. Grec. 139 und die mittelbyzantinische Renaissance," *Jahrbuch für Kunstwissenschaft*, 6 (1929), 178–94.

(with Adolph Goldschmidt) *Die byzantinischen Elfenbeinskulpturen des X.–XIII. Jahrhunderts*, 1: *Kästen*. Berlin: Bruno Cassirer, 1930.

Die armenishe Buchmalerei des 10. und beginnenden 11. Jahrhunderts ("Istanbuler Forschungen," 4). Bamberg: Reindl, 1933.

"Probleme der mittelbyzantinischen Renaissance," *Archäologischer Anzeiger*, 1933, cols. 336–60.

Review of Fritz Fichtner, *Wandmalerei der Athos-Klöster* in *Deutsche Literaturzeitung* 32 (August 6, 1933), cols. 1514–19.

(with Adolph Goldschmidt) *Die byzantinischen Elfenbeinskulpturen des X.–XIII. Jahrhunderts*. 2: *Reliefs*. Berlin: Bruno Cassirer, 1934.

(with St. Schultz) "Zur Bestimmung des Dichters auf dem Musendiptychon von Monza," *Jahrbuch des deutschen archäologischen Instituts*, 49 (1934), 128–38.

"Abendländische Kopien byzantinischer Rosettenkästen," *Zeitschrift für Kunstgeschichte*, 3 (1934), 89–103.

"Spätantike Kaiserporträts," *Geistige Arbeit, Zeitung aus der Wissenschaftlichen Welt*, 1, No. 11 (June 5, 1934), 2.

Die byzantinische Buchmalerei des 9. und 10. Jahrhunderts. Berlin: Verlag Gebr. Mann, 1935.

"Eine fuldaer Elfenbeingruppe," *Festschrift zum 70. Geburtstag von Adolph Goldschmidt*. Berlin: Würfel Verlag, 1935, pp. 14–18.

"Zwei fuldaer Handschriften des 12. Jahrhunderts," *Marburger Jahrbuch für Kunstwissenschaft*, 8/9 (1936), 172–81.

Review of Ch. Diehl, *La peinture byzantine* and J. Ebersolt, *Monuments d'architecture byzantine* in *Geistige Arbeit*, 3 (1936), no. 14, 11.

"Das Evangelion im Skevophylakion zu Lawra," *Seminarium Kondakovianum*, 8 (1938), 83–98.

"A Tabula Odysseaca," *American Journal of Archaeology*, 45 (1941), 166–81.

"The Iconography of the Reliefs from the Martyrion," and "Illustrations of Euripides and Homer in the Mosaics of Antioch," *Antioch-on-the-Orontes*. 3, *The Excavations 1937–39*. Princeton: Princeton University Press, 1941, 135–49, 233–47.

"A Codex with the Homilies of Gregory of Nazianzus," *Record of the Museum of Historic Art, Princeton University*, 1 (1942), 14–17.

"Illustration for the Chronicles of Sozomenos, Theodoret and Malalas," *Byzantion*, 16 (1942–43), 87–134.

Review of Hayford Peirce and R. Tyler, *Three Byzantine Works of Art* in *Art Bulletin*, 25 (1943), 163–64.

"Three 'Bactrian' Silver Vessels with Illustrations from Euripides," *Art Bulletin*, 25 (1943), 289–324.

"An Early Copto-Arabic Miniature in Leningrad," *Ars Islamica*, 10 (1943), 119–34.

"Constantinopolitan Book Illumination in the Period of the Latin Conquest," *Gazette des Beaux-Arts*, 86 (1944), 193–214.

"Adolph Goldschmidt," *College Art Journal*, 4 (1944), 47–50.

"An East Christian Censer," *Record of the Museum of Historic Art, Princeton University*, 3 (1944), 2–4.

Review of Hugo Buchthal and Otto Kurz, *A Handlist of Illuminated Oriental Christian Manuscripts* in *American Journal of Archaeology*, 48 (1944), 401–5.

Illustrations in Roll and Codex: A Study of the Origin and Method of Text Illustration ("Studies in Manuscript Illumination," 2). Princeton: Princeton University Press, 1947 (rev. ed., 1970).

"The Psalter Vatopedi 761—Its Place in the Aristocratic Psalter Recension," *The Journal of the Walters Art Gallery*, 10 (1947), 21–51.

"Byzantine Art and Scholarship in America," *American Journal of Archaeology*, 51 (1947), 394–418.

The Joshua Roll: A Work of the Macedonian Renaissance ("Studies in Manuscript Illumination," 3). Princeton; Princeton University Press, 1948.

"Samson and Delilah on a Draughtsman," *Record of the Art Museum, Princeton University*, 7 (1948), 5–9.

"Euripides Scenes in Byzantine Art," *Hesperia*, 18 (1949), 159–210.

"The Narrative and Liturgical Gospel Illustrations," *New Testament Manuscript Studies*, ed. Merrill M. Parvis and Allen P. Wikgren. Chicago: University of Chicago Press, 1950, pp. 151–74, notes pp. 215–20.

Greek Mythology in Byzantine Art ("Studies in Manuscript Illumination," 4). Princeton: Princeton University Press, 1951.

The Fresco Cycle of S. Maria di Castelseprio ("Princeton Monographs in Art and Archaeology," 26). Princeton: Princeton University Press, 1951.

"Gli affreschi di S. Maria di Castelseprio," *Rassegna Storica del Seprio*, 9/10 (1949/50), 12–27.

"A Late Romanesque Ivory Virgin," *Record of the Art Museum, Princeton University*, 10 (1951), 2–6.

"A Bone Carving of the Lyre-Playing Apollo," *Record of the Art Museum, Princeton University*, 10 (1951), 6–9.

"The Greek Sources of Islamic Scientific Illustrations," *Archaeologica Orientalia in Memoriam Ernst Herzfeld*, ed. George C. Miles. Locust Valley, New York: J. J. Augustin, 1952, pp. 244–66.

"Die Illustration der Septuaginta," *Münchner Jahrbuch der bildenden Kunst*, 3/4 (1952–1953), 96–120.

"The Constantinopolitan Lectionary, Morgan 639," *Studies in Art and Literature for Belle da Costa Greene*, ed. Dorothy Miner. Princeton: Princeton University Press, 1954, pp. 358–73.

"Observations on the Milan Iliad," *Nederlands Kunsthistorisch Jaarboek*, 5 (1954), 241–64.

"Das klassische Erbe in der Kunst Konstantinopels," *Alte und Neue Kunst*, 3 (1954), 41–59.

"Heracles-Papyrus Oxyrh. 2331," *The Oxyrhynchus Papyri*, ed. E. Lobel and C. H. Roberts. London: Egypt Exploration Society, 1954, part XXII, pp. 85–87.

(with the assistance of S. Der Nersessian, G. Forsyth, Jr., E. Kantorowicz, and T. Mommsen) editor of *Late Classical and Mediaeval Studies in Honor of Albert Mathias Friend, Jr.* Princeton: Princeton University Press, 1955.

"Observatons on the Cotton Genesis Fragments," *Late Classical and Mediaeval Studies in Honor of Albert Mathias Friend, Jr.*, ed. Kurt Weitzmann *et al.* Princeton: Princeton University Press, 1955, pp. 112–131.

"The Mosaics of San Marco and the Cotton Genesis," *Venezia e l'Europa. Atti del XVIII Congresso Internazionale di Storia dell'Arte: Venezia: 12–18 Settembre 1955*. Venice: Casa Editrice Arte Veneta, 1956, pp. 152–53.

"Narration in Early Christendom," *American Journal of Archaeology*, 61 (1957), pp. 83–91.

"The Octateuch of the Seraglio and the History of Its Picture Recension," *Actes du X. Congrés d'Etudes Byzantines—Istanbul: 15–21 Septembre 1955*. Istanbul, 1957, pp. 183–86.

Review of Ranuccio Bianchi Bandinelli, *Hellenistic-Byzantine Miniatures of the Iliad* in *Gnomon*, 29 (1957), 606–16.

"Eine Pariser-Psalter-Kopie des 13. Jahrhunderts auf dem Sinai," *Jahrbuch der österreichischen byzantinischen Gesellschaft*, 6 (1957), 125–43.

Review of A. Boeckler, *Formgeschichtliche Studien zur Adagruppe* in *Byzantinische Zeitschrift*, 51 (1958), 410–13.

Ancient Book Illumination ("Martin Classical Lectures," 16). Cambridge, Mass.: Harvard University Press, 1959.

"Vorikonoklastische Ikonen auf dem Sinai," *Akten des Vierundzwanzigsten*

Internationalen Orientalisten-Kongresses München: 28. August bis 4. September, 1957, ed. Herbert Franke. Wiesbaden: Deutsche Morgenländische Gesellschaft E. V., 1959, p. 237.

"Islamische und koptische Einflüsse in einer Sinai-Handschrift des Johannes Klimakus," *Aus der Welt der islamischen Kunst. Festschrift für Ernst Kühnel.* Berlin: Gebr. Mann, 1959, pp. 297–316.

"Ein kaiserliches Lektionar einer byzantinischen Hofschule," *Festschrift Karl M. Swoboda zum 28. Januar 1959,* ed. Otto Benesch *et al.* Vienna and Wiesbaden: Rudolf M. Rohrer Verlag, 1959, pp. 309–20.

"Aristocratic Psalter and Lectionary," *Record of the Art Museum, Princeton University,* 19 (1960), 98–107.

"The Mandylion and Constantine Porphyrogennetos," *Cahiers Archéologiques,* 11 (1960), 163–84.

"The Survival of Mythological Representations in Early Christian and Byzantine Art and their Impact on Christian Iconography," *Dumbarton Oaks Papers,* 14 (1960), 43–68.

(with the assistance of E. A. Lowe and E. T. DeWald) "Wilhelm R. W. Koehler," *Speculum,* 35 (1960), 519–20.

"The Origin of the Threnos," *De Artibus Opuscula XL. Essays in Honor of Erwin Panofsky,* ed. Millard Meiss. New York: New York University Press, 1961, pp. 476–90.

"Zur byzantinischen Quelle des Wolfenbüttler Musterbuches," *Festschrift Hans R. Hahnloser zum 60. Geburtstag 1959.* ed. Ellen J. Beer, Paul Hofer, and Luc Mojon. Basel and Stuttgart: Birkhäuser Verlag, 1961, pp. 223–50.

"Die Wiener Genesis: Resumé der Diskussion," reported by Hermann Fillitz in *Beiträge zur Kunstgeschichte und Archäologie des Frühmittelalters* ("Akten zum VII. Internationalen Kongress für Frühmittelalterforschung: September 1958"). Graz

and Cologne: Hermann Böhlaus, 1962.

Geistige Grundlagen und Wesen der Makedonischen Renaissance ("Arbeitsgemeinschaft für Forschung des Landes Nordrhein-Westfalen," 107, 90. Sitzung, 18 July 1962, Düsseldorf). Cologne and Opladen: Westdeutscher Verlag, 1963.

"A Fourteenth-century Greek Gospel Book with Washdrawings," *Gazette des Beaux-Arts,* 62 (1963), 91–108.

"Thirteenth Century Crusader Icons on Mount Sinai," *Art Bulletin,* 45 (1963), 179–203.

Aus den Bibliotheken des Athos. Illustrierte Handschriften aus mittel- und spätbyzantinischer Zeit. Hamburg: Friedrich Wittig Verlag, 1963.

Review of Ernst Kitzinger, *The Mosaics of Monreale* in *Archaeology,* 16 (1963), 292–93.

"Mount Sinai's Holy Treasures," *National Geographic,* 125 (January, 1964), 109–27.

"Eine Darstellung der Euripideischen Iphigenie auf einem koptischen Stoff," *Antike Kunst,* 7 (1964), 42–47.

"Zur Frage des Einflusses jüdischer Bilderquellen auf die Illustration des Alten Testamentes," *Mullus. Festschrift Theodor Klauser.* (*"Jahrbuch für Antike und Christentum."* Ergänzungsband I, (1964), pp. 401–15.

"Ivories," and "Manuscripts," *Byzantine Art—An European Art. Ninth Exhibition held under the auspices of the Council of Europe.* Athens: Office of the Minister to the Prime Minister of the Greek Government, Department of Antiquities and Archaeological Restoration, 1964, pp. 141–45, pp. 291–95.

"The Moses Cross at Sinai," *Dumbarton Oaks Papers,* 17 (1963), 385–90.

"Crusader Icons on Mount Sinai," *Actes du XIIᵉ Congrés International des Études Byzantines: Ochride 10–16 Septembre 1961.* Belgrade: Comité Yougoslave des études byzantines, 1964, 3:409–13.

"Byzantium Gloriously Re-emerges in Athens," *Art News*, 63 (1964), 28–31, 49–52.

"Fragments of an Early St. Nicholas Triptych on Mount Sinai," Ἀνάτυπον ἐκ τοῦ « Δελτίου τῆς Χριστιανικῆς Ἀρχαιολογικῆς Ἑταιρείας » (1964–65) Τιμητικὸς Γ. Σωτηρίου. Ser. IV., 4 (1964–65), 1–23. Timëtikos G. Sotiriou. *Deltion Archaiologikēs Hetaireias*, 4th ser., 4 (Athens, 1966).

"Eine spätkomnenische Verkündigungsikone des Sinai und die zweite byzantinische Welle des 12. Jahrhunderts," *Festschrift für Herbert von Einem zum 16. Februar 1965*, ed. Gert von der Osten and Georg Kauffmann. Berlin: Verlag Gebr. Mann, 1965, pp. 299–312.

"The Jephthah Panel in the Bema of the Church of St. Catherine's Monastery on Mount Sinai," *Dumbarton Oaks Papers*, 18 (1964), 341–52.

Kurt Weitzmann, Manolis Chatzidakis, Krsto Miatev, and Svetozar Radojčić. *Frühe Ikonen*. Vienna and Munich: Anton Schroll, 1965. *Ikone sa Balkana* (Belgrade and Sofia); *A Treasury of Icons* (New York); *Vroege Ikonen* (Den Haag); *Icones* (Paris); *Icons* (London); *Icone* (Milan); *Iconos* (Madrid).

"Buchmalerei des 4. Jahrhunderts—— Tradition und Neuerung," *Neue Zürcher Zeitung*, October 3, 1965, p. 4.

"The Alexandria-Michigan-Princeton Expedition to St. Catherine's Monastery, Pictorial Art in the Monastery," *Newsletter of the American Research Center in Egypt*, 58 (June, 1966), 5–9.

"The Icons of S. Catherine's Monastery at Mount Sinai," *Eastern Churches Review*, 1 (1966), 27–30.

"The Classical in Byzantine Art as a Mode of Individual Expression," *Byzantine Art— An European Art, Ninth Exhibition held under the auspices of the Council of Europe. Lectures*. Athens: Office of the Minister to the Prime Minister of the Greek Government, Department of Antiquities and Archaeological Restoration, 1966, pp. 149–177.

"The Mosaic in St. Catherine's Monastery on Mount Sinai," *Proceedings of the American Philosophical Society*, 110 (1966), 392–405.

"Eine vorikonoklastische Ikone des Sinai mit der Darstellung des Chairete," *Tortulae. Studien zu altchristlichen und byzantinischen Monumenten*, ("Römische Quartalschrift für Altertumskunde und Kirchengeschichte" 30. Supplementheft. [Rome, 1966]), 317–25.

"An Encaustic Icon with the Prophet Elijah at Mount Sinai," *Mélanges offerts à K. Michalowski*. Warsaw: Panstwowe Wydawnictwo Naukowe, 1966, pp. 713–23.

"Various Aspects of Byzantine Influence on the Latin Countries from the Sixth to the Twelfth Century," *Dumbarton Oaks Papers*, 20 (1966), 1–24.

"Icon Painting in the Crusader Kingdom," *Dumbarton Oaks Papers*, 20 (1966), 49–83.

"Byzantine Miniature and Icon Painting in the Eleventh Century," *Proceedings of the XIIIth International Congress of Byzantine Studies: Oxford. 5–10 September 1966*. ed. J. M. Hussey, D. Obolensky, and S. Runciman. London: Oxford University Press, 1967, pp. 207–24.

"Die byzantinischen Elfenbeine eines Bamberger Graduale und ihre ursprüngliche Verwendung," *Studien zur Buchmalerei und Goldschmiedekunst des Mittelalters. Festschrift für Karl Hermann Usener zum 60. Geburtstag am 19. August 1965*. ed. Frieda Dettweiler, Herbert Köllner, and Peter Anselm Riedl. Marburg an der Lahn: Verlag des Kunstgeschichtlichen Seminars der Universität Marburg an der Lahn, 1967, pp. 11–20.

"Book Illustration of the Fourth Century: Tradition and Innovation," *Akten des VII. Internationalen Kongresses für Christliche Archäologie: Trier 5–11 September, 1965* ("Studi di Antichita Cristiana" Vol. 27 [Rome and Berlin, 1969]), 257–81.

"An Imperial Lectionary in the Monastery
of Dionysiu on Mount Athos: Its Origin
and its Wanderings," *Revue des Études
Sud-Est Européenes*, 7 (1969), 339–53.